NEW ZEALAND'S
GREAT WAR

NEW ZEALAND'S
GREAT WAR

NEW ZEALAND, THE ALLIES AND
THE FIRST WORLD WAR

EDITED BY JOHN CRAWFORD AND IAN McGIBBON

EXISLE
PUBLISHING

First published 2007

Exisle Publishing Limited,
P.O. Box 60-490, Titirangi, Auckland 1230.
www.exislepublishing.com

National Library of New Zealand Cataloguing-in-Publication Data
New Zealand's great war : New Zealand, the Allies and the First
World War / edited by John Crawford and Ian McGibbon.
Includes index.
ISBN-13: 978-0-908988-85-3
ISBN-10: 0-908988-85-0
1. World War, 1914–1918—New Zealand. 2. World War,
1914–1918. I. Crawford, John (John A. B.) II. McGibbon, I. C.
(Ian C.), 1947-
940.41293—dc 22

Text design and production by BookNZ (www.booknz.co.nz)
Cover design by Nick Turzynski
Printed in China through Colorcraft Limited, Hong Kong

Contents

Acknowledgements   7
Abbreviations   8
Contributors   10
Introduction   16

Part 1   Political, Social and International Perspectives

1   Britain and the Empire at War 1914–1918: Reflections on
    a Forgotten Victory   *Gary Sheffield*   30
2   The Shaping of New Zealand's War Effort,
    August–October 1914   *Ian McGibbon*   49
3   The Reception of Belgian Refugees in Europe: A Litmus Test
    of Wartime Social Mobilisation   *Pierre Purseigle*   69
4   The Moloch of War: New Zealand Women who
    Opposed the War   *Megan Hutching*   85
5   Te Hokowhitu-a-Tu: A Coming of Age?   *Monty Soutar*   96
6   Americans at War: Assessing the Significance of
    American Participation in the Great War   *Jennifer D. Keene*   106
7   Caging the Prussian Dragon: New Zealand and the
    Paris Peace Conference 1919   *Richard Kay*   123
8   Beckham, Waugh and the Memory of Gallipoli   *Jenny Macleod*   142
9   Return, Repatriation, Remembrance and the
    Returned Soldiers' Association 1916–22   *Stephen Clarke*   157

Part 2   The Operational Context

10 'Whom at first we did not like …': Australians and New Zealanders
    at Quinn's Post, Gallipoli   *Peter Stanley*   182
11 Bowler of Gallipoli: Witness to the Anzac Legend   *Frank Glen*   194
12 Devils on Horses: The New Zealand Mounted Rifles Brigade
    Terry Kinloch   212
13 An Awkward Salient: New Zealand Infantry on the Somme,
    15 September 1916   *Andrew Macdonald*   227
14 'New Zealand is Being Bled to Death': The Formation,
    Operations and Disbandment of the Fourth Brigade   *John Crawford*   250
15 Stopping the Storm: The New Zealand Division and the
    Kaiser's Battle (*Kaiserschlacht*) March–April 1918   *Glyn Harper* 266

16 Haig and his Dominion Commanders: The Evolution of Professional
    Citizen Armies on the Western Front   *Christopher Pugsley*   287
17 New Zealand and the Naval War   *Peter Dennerly*   308
18 From Burn to Bannerman: New Zealand Airmen
    Come of Age   *Vincent Orange*   333

Part 3   Aspects of Service Overseas and at Home
19 A Different Sort of War: The Experience of NZEF
    Transport Drivers   *Graham Langton*   344
20 On the Triangle Trail: The New Zealand YMCA
    and the Great War   *Ria Keenan*   354
21 'Come back with honour': Prostitution and the
    New Zealand Soldier, at Home and Abroad   *Bronwyn Dalley*   364
22 Preparation for a Rural Future: Agricultural Training of
    New Zealand's First World War Soldiers   *Ashley Gould*   378
23 New Zealanders in the AIF: An Introduction to the
    AIF Database Project   *Peter Dennis and Jeffrey Grey*   394
24 The Fourth Service: The Merchant Marine's War   *Gavin McLean*   406

Part 4   Home Front Perspectives
25 The Poor Cousin: New Zealand's Home Defence   *Peter Cooke*   426
26 New Zealand Churches and Death in the
    First World War   *Allan Davidson*   447
27 First World War Religion   *Peter Lineham*   467
28 'Keeping New Zealand Home Fires Burning':
    Gender, Welfare and the First World War   *Melanie Nolan*   493
29 Blueprint for the Future? 'National Efficiency'
    and the First World War   *John E. Martin*   516
30 Patriotism, Profits and Problems: New Zealand Farming
    during the Great War   *James Watson*   534
31 Debating the War: The Discourses of War
    in the Christchurch Community   *Gwen Parsons*   550
32 The Armistice: Responses, Understandings and Meanings
    for a Rural Region   *Graham Hucker*   569

    Notes   583
    Index   656

ACKNOWLEDGEMENTS

This book is based on the proceedings of the 'Zealandia's Great War' conference organised by the New Zealand Military History Committee in November 2003. This event could not have taken place without a wide variety of support.

We are indebted to the following institutions for providing assistance in bringing speakers to Wellington for the conference: the New Zealand Defence Force, the Ministry of Defence, the New Zealand–France Friendship Fund, the Australian High Commission, the Embassy of the United States of America, the Ministry for Arts and Culture and the New Zealand Lottery Grants Board. Thanks too to Margaret Calder, Chief Librarian of the Alexander Turnbull Library, and the National Library for their help in providing a venue for the conference. The New Zealand Film Archive also made a valuable contribution to the proceedings.

We acknowledge also the efforts and support of our fellow members of the New Zealand Military History Committee, Dr Stephen Clarke and Peter Cooke, who prepared the index, and all those who participated in the conference over the three days. The New Zealand Defence Force kindly provided assistance in the publication of the proceedings. Finally, we much appreciate the efforts of Ian Watt and his team at Exisle in publishing this book.

ABBREVIATIONS

AA & QMG	Assistant Adjutant and Quartermaster General	DEC	Dominion Executive Committee
AIF	Australian Imperial Force	*DNZB*	*Dictionary of New Zealand Biography*
AJHR	*Appendix to the Journals of the House of Representatives*	*EP*	*Evening Post*
ANZ	Archives New Zealand, Wellington	GOC	General Officer Commanding
ANZAC	Australian and New Zealand Army Corps	G[G]NZ	Governor[-General] of New Zealand
ATL	Alexander Turnbull Library	*HNS*	*Hawera and Normanby Star*
AUP	Auckland University Press	ICWPP	International Committee of Women for Permanent Peace
AWM	Australian War Memorial		
AWN	*Auckland Weekly News*	KMARL	Kippenberger Military Archive and Research Library, Waiouru
BED	British Empire Delegation		
CG	*Church Gazette*		
CGS	Chief of the General Staff	LHCMA	Liddell Hart Centre for Military Archives, King's College, London
CNDC	*Church News for the Diocese of Christchurch*		
CUP	Cambridge University Press	*LT*	*Lyttelton Times*
CWI	Canterbury Women's Institute	MD	Military District
		MP	Member of Parliament
		MU	Massey University

MUP	Manchester University Press	[RNZ]RSA	[Royal New Zealand] Returned Soldiers' (Services') Association
MW	*Maoriland Worker*		
NAC	National Archives of Canada, Ottawa	*SEP*	*Stratford Evening Post*
NEB	National Efficiency Board	SNO	Senior Naval Officer
NIO	Naval Intelligence Officer	SPWC	Society for the Protection of Women and Children
NZEF	New Zealand Expeditionary Force	SS Cols	Secretary of State for the Colonies
NZG	*New Zealand Gazette*	*ST*	*Southland Times*
NZH	*New Zealand Herald*	*TH*	*Taranaki Herald*
NZHC	New Zealand High Commissioner	UA	University of Auckland
NZJH	*New Zealand Journal of History*	UC	University of Canterbury
NZMR	New Zealand Mounted Rifles Brigade	UKNA	National Archives of Britain, London
NZMT	*New Zealand Methodist Times*	UO	University of Otago
NZOYB	*New Zealand Official Year Book*	UP	University Press
		USNA	United States National Archives
NZPD	*New Zealand Parliamentary Debates*	VUW	Victoria University of Wellington
NZT	*New Zealand Tablet*	WACL	Women's Anti-Conscription League
ODT	*Otago Daily Times*		
OSDWC	Otago Soldiers' and Dependants' Welfare Committee	*WC*	*War Cry*
		WCTU	Women's Christian Temperance Union
OT	*Opunake Times*	WFB	Women's Employment Bureaux
OUP	Oxford University Press		
PGD	Post-graduate diploma	WIL	Women's International League
PGDA	Post-graduate diploma in arts	WNR	Women's National Reserve
PM	Prime Minister	WPA	Women's Peace Army
PPA	Protestant Political Association	*WR*	*The White Ribbon*
PUP	Princeton University Press	YMCA	Young Men's Christian Association
QM	*Quick March*	YUP	Yale University Press

Contributors

Stephen Clarke is a graduate of the University of Otago and the University of New South Wales at the Australian Defence Force Academy. He is the Official Historian of the Royal New Zealand Returned Services' Association and is writing the RNZRSA's official history.

Peter Cooke is a graduate of Massey University. In 1996 he formed the Defence of New Zealand Study Group and edits its journal *Forts & Works*. He is the author of *Defending New Zealand: Ramparts on the Sea 1840–1950s*.

John Crawford, a graduate of the University of Canterbury, is the New Zealand Defence Force Historian. He has published and edited several works of military history. His major publications include *To Fight for the Empire: An Illustrated History of New Zealand and the South African War* (1999) and with Ian McGibbon he edited *One Flag One Queen One Tongue: New Zealand, the British Empire and the South African War* (2003).

Bronwyn Dalley is the Chief Historian, History Group, Ministry for Culture and Heritage. She has published widely on aspects of New Zealand social history. She is one of the general editors of *Frontier of Dreams: The Story of New Zealand* (2005).

Allan Davidson has written extensively on New Zealand religious history. He is a lecturer in church history at St John's College, Auckland. He teaches church history in the School of Theology at the University of Auckland where he is also Director of Postgraduate Studies.

Peter Dennerly recently retired as the Royal New Zealand Navy's Historian, having been a career officer in the Royal New Zealand Navy. His primary research area is New Zealand naval history with an emphasis on the First World War.

Peter Dennis is Professor of History at the University of New South Wales at the Australian Defence Force Academy. He is a graduate of the University of Adelaide and Duke University, North Carolina, and has taught at the Royal Military College of Canada, the University of Western Ontario, the Faculty of Military Studies, Duntroon, and the National University of Singapore. His major publications include, as joint author, *The Oxford Companion to Australian Military History* (1995) and *Emergency and Confrontation: Australian Military Operations in Malaya and Borneo 1950–1966* (1996). He was joint editor, with John Coates, of the seven-volume *Australian Centenary History of Defence* (2001).

Frank Glen is a retired military chaplain who has served in the New Zealand Police and the Australian and New Zealand defence forces. His PhD (Waikato University) traversed the work of the 2NZEF chaplains 1939–45. His most recent book is *Bowler of Gallipoli, Witness to the Anzac Legend* (2004).

Ashley Gould, a historical researcher based in Wellington, is a graduate of Massey University. He is an authority on the repatriation of New Zealand soldiers following the First World War.

Jeffrey Grey is Professor of History at the University of New South Wales at the Australian Defence Force Academy, Canberra. Among numerous books, he is the author of *A Military History of Australia* and co-editor of the *Oxford Companion to Australian Military History* (1995).

Glyn Harper is an associate professor at Massey University's Centre for Defence Studies in Palmerston North. A former army officer, Dr Harper is the author of three books on New Zealand's efforts in the First World War, including the best-selling *Massacre at Passchendaele* (2000).

Graham Hucker is a senior lecturer in education at Massey University in Palmerston North. His PhD research in history is on mobilisation, endurance and remembrance of the Great War in the Taranaki region of New Zealand.

Megan Hutching is the Oral Historian at the History Group, Ministry for Culture and Heritage in Wellington and has published widely on different aspects of New Zealand social and military history. She has a particular interest in women who opposed war in the 20th century.

Richard Kay completed his PhD in history at the University of Otago in 2001. His thesis considered the impact of the First World War on British–New Zealand relations. He is currently on his first diplomatic posting for New Zealand's Ministry of Foreign Affairs and Trade in Fiji.

Ria Keenan is a part-time student at Massey University who lives and works in Wellington. She is writing her MA (history) thesis on the activities of the New Zealand YMCA in the Great War.

Jennifer Keene is an associate professor of history and chair of the History Department, Chapman University, California. She received her PhD in history from Carnegie-Mellon University and is a specialist in American military history. She has published two books on the American involvement in the First World War, *Doughboys, the Great War and the Remaking of America* (2001) and *The United States and the First World War* (2000).

Lieutenant Colonel Terry Kinloch has served in a range of appointments in Queen Alexandra's Mounted Rifles, the last of New Zealand's mounted rifles regiments. He has been researching the First World War for several years, and is the author of *Echoes of Gallipoli: in the words of New Zealand's Mounted Riflemen* (2005).

Graham Langton has a PhD in history from the University of Canterbury. He is an archivist at Archives New Zealand in Wellington and has a long-standing interest in the First World War and has also researched and published on the history of mountaineering in New Zealand.

Peter Lineham is an associate professor of history at Massey University's Albany campus. He has written extensively on the religious history of New Zealand, and also on the religious history of Britain in the 18th and 19th centuries.

Andrew MacDonald is a journalist in Wellington and has a strong interest in defence issues. He is the author of *On My Way to the Somme: New Zealanders at the Somme 1916* (2005).

Ian McGibbon is General Editor (War History) at the Ministry for Culture and Heritage, Wellington. He has published widely on New Zealand's international affairs and military history, including guidebooks to the Western Front (2001) and Gallipoli (2005). He edited the *Oxford Companion to New Zealand Military History* (2000), and chairs the New Zealand Military History Committee, which organised 'Zealandia's Great War'.

Gavin McLean, a senior historian at the Ministry for Culture and Heritage in Wellington, has published widely on New Zealand maritime, business and heritage history. His recent titles include *Captain's Log*, *100 New Zealand Historic Places* and *Rocking the Boat? A History of Scales Corporation*. He is currently completing histories of the Tasman Express Line and of the New Zealand Governor-General.

Jenny Macleod completed her doctorate at Cambridge University in 2000 and is currently a lecturer in history at the University of Hull. Her major publications include *Reconsidering Gallipoli* (2004) and she edited, with Pierre Purseigle, *Uncovered Fields: Perspectives on First World War Studies* (2004).

John E. Martin is Parliamentary Historian in the Parliamentary Library, Wellington. He is currently researching the history of the Library, having written

The House: New Zealand's House of Representatives 1854–2004 (2004). His broader research interests include political and economic history, and in particular the relationship between labour and state policy.

Melanie Nolan is an associate professor in history at Victoria University of Wellington. She has published many articles about work on both sides of the Tasman Sea, particularly about 20th-century gender and labour relations, and her major publications include *Breadwinning: New Zealand Women and the State* (2000).

Vincent Orange retired from the History Department at the University of Canterbury in 2002. He has contributed nine articles on aviation personalities for the new British 50-volume *Dictionary of National Biography* (2004). His eighth book, *Slessor: Bomber Champion*, was published in 2006.

Gwen Parsons has recently begun a PhD at the University of Otago investigating New Zealand society in the 10 years after the First World War. Her conference paper is derived from her MA thesis completed at the University of Canterbury in 2003.

Christopher Pugsley is a senior lecturer in the Department of War Studies, Royal Military Academy, Sandhurst. Author of the seminal *Gallipoli: The New Zealand Story* (1984), he has written extensively on New Zealand's involvement in the First World War. His examination of comparative combat effectiveness between dominion forces, *The ANZAC Experience: New Zealand, Australia and Empire in the First World War*, was published in 2004.

Pierre Purseigle is a member of Pembroke College and a Visiting Research Scholar at the Modern History Faculty, University of Oxford. He graduated from the Institut d'Etudes Politiques, Lyon and studied History at the University of California, Berkeley and at the University of Toulouse, where he is completing his PhD on social mobilisation in First World War England and France. He edited, with Jenny Macleod, *Uncovered Fields: Perspectives on First World War Studies*.

Gary Sheffield is Professor of War Studies in the History Department, University of Birmingham. He has published widely on 20th-century military history, including *Forgotten Victory: The First World War: Myths and Realities* (2001).

Monty Soutar is the director of the Tairawhiti Museum in Gisborne, and was the 2004–6 Fellow in Maori History at the History Group, Ministry for Culture and Heritage. Before his fellowship, Dr Soutar was a senior lecturer at the School of Maori Studies, Massey University, Palmerston North. Dr Soutar is of Ngati Awa, Ngati Porou, Ngati Tai (Waikato) and Ngati Kahungunu descent.

Peter Stanley is the Principal Historian at the Australian War Memorial. He has published 18 books, including *The Remote Garrison: the British Army in Australia 1788–1870*, *For Fear of Pain: British Surgery 1790–1850*, *Whyalla at War 1939–45* and, most recently, *Quinn's Post, Anzac Gallipoli* (2005). He is a visiting associate professor at the Australian Defence Force Academy and an adjunct professor at the University of Canberra.

James Watson is a senior lecturer at the School of History, Philosophy and Politics at Massey University's Palmerston North campus. He has a particular interest in New Zealand political and rural history and has published widely in these areas. His major publications include *Links – A History of Transport and New Zealand* (1996).

INTRODUCTION

On 11 November 2004 an unknown New Zealand soldier from the Caterpillar Valley Cemetery, located near the French village of Longueval, was interred in the Tomb of the Unknown Warrior at the National War Memorial in Wellington. In the days preceding this event a RNZAF aircraft had carried a contingent led by the Chief of Defence Force, Air Marshal Bruce Ferguson, to France to receive the soldier's remains at a ceremony at the New Zealand battlefield memorial on the Somme. Although the Unknown Warrior represents all New Zealand's war dead, the interment focused attention on New Zealand's part in the 'war to end all wars', the Great War of 1914–18, and in particular on the Western Front. This campaign was the most costly ever undertaken by New Zealand: more of its servicemen died in France and Flanders between April 1916 and November 1918 than in the whole of the Second World War.

The Great War was undoubtedly the most traumatic event in New Zealand's history. From a population of a little more than one million in 1914, the dominion sent just over 100,000 soldiers overseas as members of the New Zealand Expeditionary Force (NZEF) during the war. In addition many New Zealanders served with the British and Australian armed forces. The loss of 16,697 members of the NZEF overseas meant that approximately 15 in every 1000 New Zealanders became victims (in Britain the comparable figure was 16, in Australia 12 and in Canada eight).[1] When deaths among NZEF personnel in

New Zealand and those who died after discharge from war-related conditions up to the end of 1923 are included, New Zealand's death toll rises to 18,166.[2] Hardly a family was unaffected in some way by this great bloodletting, which continued to have a major impact on New Zealand society long after the end of hostilities.[3]

For all its importance to their country, New Zealand historians have not given this great national effort the attention it deserves. Overshadowed by the conflict that followed a generation later, it is often depicted in misleading fashion by commentators with little knowledge of the events, and regarded with some unease as a conflict that was somehow unnecessary. New Zealand soldiers certainly seem to have had a good idea of what they were fighting for – Percival Fenwick, a medical officer, spoke for many when he wrote in his diary during the Gallipoli campaign that it 'is really rotten seeing healthy lads bowled over because Kaiser Bill wants to rule the world'[4] – but there is a tendency today to dismiss the conflict as the outcome of the dynastic squabbles of avaricious empires. New Zealand's historiography of the First World War is very limited, especially compared with that of the Second World War. A carefully planned, well-resourced and comprehensive official war history programme for the latter resulted in a series of 48 volumes that cover campaigns, unit activities and the home front. These official works are supplemented by a vast range of writings by participants and historians on aspects of the 1939–45 war.

By comparison, those seeking to understand New Zealand's effort in the First World War have only four inadequate official histories covering the main campaigns, a medical history and a range of unit histories. Relatively few analytical studies of aspects of New Zealand's war effort at home or overseas have appeared. It is telling that the official histories of the Western Front and the Sinai–Palestine campaigns, produced in the 1920s, remain the standard works on their respective subjects.

The New Zealand Military History Committee felt that the interment of the Unknown Warrior planned for November 2003 provided a good opportunity to focus public attention on the First World War, and to begin the long overdue reassessment of New Zealand's part in that conflict. The committee had convened successful conferences on the Second World War in 1995 and the South African War in 1999; it now seemed timely to turn its attention to the First World War.

The committee intended the conference to be held in the days before the interment, but a late legal challenge by a group concerned about proposals to alter the front of the National War Memorial to accommodate the planned Tomb of the Unknown Warrior meant that the interment was postponed, so the two events occurred a year apart.

'Zealandia's Great War' was held at the National Library, Wellington, from 7 to 10 November 2003. There were more than 30 sessions and a panel discussion, covering the political and social dimensions of the war, the battlefield and the home front. A screening of New Zealand First World War films was held immediately after the opening of the conference on 7 November. More than 160 people attended the sessions over the three days, including a number from Australia. The speakers included nine from outside New Zealand. These were brought to New Zealand with sponsorship from the New Zealand Defence Force, the Ministry of Defence, the Minister of Internal Affairs' Lottery Discretionary Fund, the United States Embassy, the Australian High Commission, the New Zealand–France Friendship Fund and the Ministry for Culture and Heritage.

This collection contains 32 of the papers delivered at the conference, which have been revised for publication. They fall into four broad groups, covering wider political and social aspects of the war and of New Zealand's involvement in it, operations carried out by the New Zealanders both in the NZEF and in the British services, especially the Royal Navy and the Royal Flying Corps/Royal Air Force, social aspects of the war effort overseas, and the experiences and attitudes of New Zealanders at home.

The first part addresses the origins of the war and some of its consequences, along with New Zealand reactions to its outbreak and diplomacy in its aftermath. In Western societies the First World War has long been characterised as futile, wasteful and unpopular, a conflict that began almost accidentally and was fought by incompetent generals who could not adjust to the predicament they found themselves in – a struggle that contrasted with the more justified and more competently fought Second World War. In a wide-ranging overview, Gary Sheffield takes issue with this characterisation, arguing that the Great War was neither futile nor unpopular at the time. It was a war that the British people believed had to be fought and won to halt the march of German militarism.

Sheffield also maintains that, far from proving incompetent, the British army had demonstrated its ability to adapt to Western Front conditions. A steep learning curve led to its emerging victorious in 1918.

When war erupted in August 1914 between the French and Russian empires and the Central Powers (the German and Austria-Hungarian empires), New Zealanders were gripped by a 'state of tension and uncertainty'. Would the British Empire join its entente partners? The Governor, Lord Liverpool, supplied the answer when in the early afternoon of 5 August on the steps of Parliament he read a telegram advising that a state of war existed between the British and German empires. The large crowd greeted this news 'with a tremendous outburst of cheering' and later sang the national anthem and 'Rule Britannia'. Prime Minister William Massey declared that 'New Zealand has done its duty on every occasion that the Empire required assistance, and will do its duty on the present occasion, and will do its duty in a whole-hearted manner. That we shall be called upon to make sacrifices goes without saying, but I am confident that those sacrifices will be made.... in a manner worthy of the occasion, and the highest traditions of the great race and Empire to which we belong.'[5] The enthusiastic response to the news of the outbreak of war, which was repeated at similar demonstrations of patriotic fervour throughout the country, matched that of crowds in London and other cities.[6]

Ian McGibbon examines the country's entry to the war and the dispatch of expeditionary forces to Samoa and Europe, focusing on the reasons why New Zealand felt the need to participate in the imperial effort and why it concentrated upon providing a military force. Among the issues that motivated New Zealanders, as others in the British Empire, was the treatment by Germany of Belgium. The German invasion of that small country had been the catalyst for British intervention in the conflict, and German atrocities against the Belgian people were a source of outrage. In focusing on the treatment of Belgian refugees in France and Britain, French historian Pierre Purseigle provides a perspective on the impact of the war on civilians in the main theatre of hostilities. Not all New Zealanders supported their country's involvement in the war. Megan Hutching looks at women who dissented from the majority position on New Zealand's involvement in the war, and later opposed the introduction of conscription. She concentrates on the arguments of the women's groups to which they belonged rather on their activities, and demonstrates that, despite their isolation, New Zealand women opposed to the war saw themselves as part of a global community of like-minded women.

Maori were determined not to be excluded from the New Zealand effort, as they had been during the South African War. Once it became known that Indian troops were being deployed to the Western Front, the government quickly agreed that a Maori contingent would be formed for non-combatant service. As Monty Soutar outlines, sufficient volunteers were found for the 500-man unit, which left New Zealand early in 1915. Stationed initially at Malta, it eventually went to Gallipoli, where it served with distinction. Later, on the Western Front, a new contingent formed part of the New Zealand Maori (Pioneer) Battalion, which provided effective support to the troops in the front line but left Maori dissatisfied with the second-class status that such service implied.

The United States' entry into the war in 1917 was a strategic development whose significance was lessened only by the initial inability to assert American power on the Western Front. In tracing how the United States rapidly created a mass army of four million men, Jennifer Keene provides a comparative perspective. Like the New Zealanders they joined on the Western Front, and in some cases served closely alongside, the Americans were citizen-soldiers, and their experience and attitudes throw light on the response of men to the extraordinary situation they found themselves in late in the war.

During the conflict New Zealand, with the other dominions, was drawn into the councils of the empire. From 1917 its leaders William Massey and Sir Joseph Ward attended meetings of the Imperial War Conference in London. This new status was further reflected in their participation in the Paris Peace Conference in 1919. Massey signed the Treaty of Versailles on behalf of New Zealand, and New Zealand joined the new League of Nations in its own right. In assessing the performance of Massey and Ward in Paris, Richard Kay demonstrates that they were prepared vigorously to pursue New Zealand's interests in its first venture onto the world diplomatic stage.

The impact of the war on the communities that took part in it was profound. For Australia and New Zealand the experience was important to the developing sense of national identity. The Anzac legend, born on the rough slopes of the Gallipoli Peninsula, has resonance on both sides of the Tasman. Jenny Macleod notes that though memory of the Gallipoli campaign has little national significance in Britain it is a very different matter in Australia. In both South Pacific nations the day of the landing, 25 April, has become a powerful unifying element, and an opportunity to express a sense of national pride and identity. Stephen Clarke examines the development of Anzac Day in New Zealand's national consciousness.

The second part of this collection is devoted to the military and naval dimension of New Zealand's involvement in the war, both at home and overseas. Apart from the unopposed occupation of German Samoa, New Zealand's first major effort was made, not in France as expected when the NZEF departed, but on a narrow finger of land jutting into the Aegean Sea, the Gallipoli Peninsula in modern-day Turkey. The NZEF, grouped with the Australian Imperial Force (AIF) in the Australian and New Zealand Army Corps (ANZAC), landed there on 25 April 1915 as part of a major amphibious operation involving both British and French forces. But at neither of the main landing sites did the Allies gain more than a foothold. For the rest of 1915 they would struggle to defeat a determined enemy and would eventually abandon the effort.

Peter Stanley examines the defence of Quinn's Post, one of the keys to the security of the Anzac enclave at Gallipoli. He places the operations there in the context of relations between Australian and New Zealand troops that were sometimes tense, even hostile, before the campaign but became much closer on the peninsula. Lieutenant-Colonel William Malone's major contribution to the defence of the vital post is also noted. Another New Zealand officer who served at Anzac was Southland-born Lieutenant-Colonel Edmund Bowler. Unusually, he held a staff position in the ANZAC headquarters, and his observations provide an antipodean perspective on the conduct of operations at this level. Frank Glen describes the hitherto largely ignored activities of this officer.

One of the main components of New Zealand's Gallipoli effort was the New Zealand Mounted Rifles Brigade, which was deployed to the peninsula belatedly on 12 May 1915 and suffered heavy casualties in the next three months. Its troops were prominent in the failed August offensive, and helped defend Chunuk Bair on 8–9 August. After the evacuation, the brigade remained in Egypt when the rest of the NZEF proceeded to France. As part of the Anzac Mounted Division, it took part in the Egyptian Expeditionary Force's campaign in Sinai and Palestine, performing with notable efficiency. Terry Kinloch outlines the part played by the brigade in both campaigns.

From April 1916 until the Armistice in November 1918 the New Zealand Division and various other units of the NZEF served as part of the British Expeditionary Force in France and Belgium. By the time the New Zealanders arrived at the front line, which stretched 435 miles from the Swiss border to the coast, it had long since settled into stalemate. Later in the year they took part in the Allied attempt to break the deadlock on the Somme, an offensive that opened with the tragic attack of 1 July 1916 that took the lives of 20,000 British soldiers. The New Zealand Division performed creditably when committed to the fray on 15 September. As in all Western Front battles casualty figures were high, the extent of artillery and machine guns confronting the New Zealanders with dangers that surpassed those they had faced at Gallipoli. In 1917 the routine trials of trench warfare were punctuated with several occasions when the New Zealanders again 'went over the top' – at Messines and Passchendaele. At the latter, on 12 October 1917, more than 800 men would fall in just a few hours, the greatest tragedy to befall New Zealand troops in any conflict. During 1918, the division helped to foil a major German offensive and then took part in the Allied offensive that at last drove the Germans back in disarray, inducing them to agree to an armistice.

Aspects of the NZEF's role on the Western Front are covered in five chapters. Two, by Andrew Macdonald and Glyn Harper, focus on the performance of the New Zealanders in fighting on the Somme, in 1916 and 1918 respectively. Both Macdonald and Harper attribute the New Zealanders' impressive performances in these two widely differing battles, one offensive and the other defensive, to the initiative shown by junior officers and NCOs. Other chapters look at organisational or command aspects within which the New Zealanders served on the Western Front. John Crawford analyses the decision to create a fourth brigade in the New Zealand Division. He traces its formation, training and participation in the division's relatively successful attack at Passchendaele on 4 October 1917. Despite its fine performance, 4 Brigade could not avoid the axe when manpower and practical considerations led to the decision in 1918 to return the division to a three-brigade format. Its brief history had demonstrated not only the New Zealand government's efforts to reconcile imperial requirements with the country's interests but also the proficiency with which New Zealanders approached the task of preparing a unit for battle in the latter stages of the First World War. Christopher Pugsley examines the relationship between the British Expeditionary Force (BEF) Commander-in-Chief Sir Douglas Haig and the commanders of the dominion troops serving in the BEF, including New Zealand's General Sir Alexander Godley and Major-General Sir Andrew Russell.

New Zealanders did not fight on land alone. New Zealand had long conceived its defence in terms of imperial defence, which was founded on British seapower. Before the war a New Zealand-funded battlecruiser, HMS *New Zealand*, had joined the main British fleet confronting the German High Seas Fleet in the North Sea, and New Zealand had taken the first steps to establish its own navy with the acquisition of the training cruiser HMS *Philomel*. Peter Dennerly outlines the part played by *Philomel* both in helping to escort New Zealand troops to Samoa and Egypt and in patrolling the Red Sea. In 1917 the armed merchant cruiser *Wolf* brought the war to New Zealand, the only time its waters were penetrated during the conflict. Mines laid by her off Cape Farewell and North Cape accounted for two ships, and killed 26 people. New Zealand had not made adequate preparation to meet such a threat, and the naval authorities scrambled to organise a minesweeping force once it became known, belatedly, that there were mines in local waters. As Peter Dennerly explains, New Zealand's naval war effort also included more mundane aspects, such as the supply of coal to warships and the establishment of a naval intelligence organisation that formed part of a worldwide network.

Several hundred New Zealanders served in the Royal Flying Corps (and after 1 April 1918 the Royal Air Force). Vincent Orange examines the very different careers of two New Zealand airmen – William Burn, the first to lose his life on operations, in Mesopotamia, and fighter ace Ronald Bannerman, who had the advantage of serving later in the war with far more sophisticated equipment.

The papers represent first steps towards a reassessment of New Zealand's performance on the Great War battlefields. The social history of the country's overseas effort is another field that demands attention. Much needs to be done in elucidating the experiences and attitudes of the 104,000 men (and a small number of women) transported to the other side of the globe and established in unfamiliar surroundings between 1914 and 1919.

Not all New Zealand troops faced the enemy directly. Many filled positions at base camps or served in line of communication units. Two such personnel were Les Collis and Andy Jamieson, both from the Manawatu. They were drivers of the horse transport that supported the New Zealand Division. Graham Langton uses their personal diaries to illuminate their war, which differed greatly from that of the troops in the front line and was, in many ways, similar to their peacetime experience.

The day-to-day experience of New Zealand soldiers out of the trenches is another little explored area. In the provision of home comforts to the men the Young Men's Christian Association (YMCA) was very much to the fore, among a number of organisations that sought to alleviate the conditions at the front. In activities ranging from offering refreshments and quiet reading rooms to the mounting of night patrols to help safeguard inebriated soldiers on leave, the YMCA carried out a variety of functions that contributed to the morale and discipline of the troops. As Ria Keenan notes, its motive was not entirely altruistic, but it was to be disappointed in its hopes of drawing men into the YMCA fold after the war.

For men cut off from their families and facing the prospect of death at the front, normal moral restraints were often loosened. Many succumbed to the temptations offered by prostitutes, and many paid the penalty by contracting venereal diseases. Bronwyn Dalley explores attitudes to sexuality among the troops and the efforts by both military authorities and individuals such as Ettie Rout to deal with the problem in the face of unsympathetic attitudes at home.

For all the troops the prospect of peace was a beacon of hope. Preparation for their eventual repatriation to their homeland began long before the troops embarked on the long journey home in 1918–19. Ashley Gould examines one aspect of the rehabilitation effort, the NZEF's provision of agricultural training in anticipation of soldiers taking up farming on their return. He notes the difficulties experienced in developing a viable programme, and the general reluctance of the war-weary soldiers to take advantage of the scheme.

The personnel files of the men and women who served in the forces during the First World War represent a major historical resource. The potential for using them for quantitative analysis of the NZEF is enormous, but realising it depends on transposing the information they contain to appropriate databases.

In Australia a start has been made in creating such a database for the Australian Imperial Force. Peter Dennis and Jeffrey Grey, who have been instrumental in getting this mammoth project under way, indicate some of the problems and pitfalls confronting them. Hopeful that the database can eventually be extended to the NZEF as well, they point out that a substantial number of New Zealanders served with the AIF and indicate how their data can be accessed.

Not all New Zealanders involved in the war served in uniform. A significant group of civilian participants were the men who manned the merchant ships that plied between New Zealand and Europe. The important shipping resources available in the dominion in 1914 and New Zealand's dependence on secure sea lanes ensured that the efforts of the 'fourth service', the merchant navy, would be substantial. The pre-war task of conveying produce took on added significance as the enemy sought to blockade the British Isles. But merchant ships were used for many other wartime tasks as well: carrying troops, performing as hospital ships and even as auxiliary warships. Gavin McLean not only outlines the achievements of New Zealand merchant seafarers during the war but also discusses the impact of the war on the composition and ownership of a key strategic asset.

Although the main focus of this war was on the other side of the globe, defensive preparations were also made to repel attack on the homeland, including the manning of coastal defences early in the war. Men unable to serve in the NZEF also sought a role, and many found it in the Defence rifle clubs that were proclaimed the dominion's second line of defence but which had a somewhat troubled existence, as Peter Cooke recounts. He describes the efforts to sustain the armed forces at home during the war, made difficult by the disappearance of personnel into the NZEF and a lack of resources.

The home front in the First World War is a black hole of New Zealand historiography. There was no home front volume in the series of popular histories produced after the war, akin to the substantial volumes in 'The People at War' series of the Official History of New Zealand in the Second World War, including *War Economy* (J.V.T. Baker) and *The Home Front* (Nancy Taylor). The series of official histories produced after the First World War did include a collection of essays edited by Lieutenant H.T.B. Drew, *The War Effort of New Zealand*, which covers some aspects of the war effort at home, such as training efforts, and makes some reference to the war economy. In recent years, there has been very little published work on the home front experience, with the shining exception of Paul Baker's study of wartime conscription in New Zealand. Although valuable work has been done by graduate students – some of it reflected in this collection – almost every aspect of the New Zealand experience awaits further assessment.

The chapters in the fourth section represent first steps in this reassessment. A war so all-consuming and costly had innumerable impacts on the community. Many felt a need to make sense of the conflict in order to give some meaning to the sacrifice. Allan Davidson and Peter Lineham examine the role of the churches, and religion generally, in this process. For the faithful, the war introduced many moral and theological dilemmas. The main churches allowed themselves to be co-opted to the cause of patriotism, duty, sacrifice and imperial loyalty. In doing so, they compromised their theology and emerged from the war with a tarnished reputation.

The impact of the war on women was considerable. Their loved ones went off to fight on the other side of the world, and they were left in a state of limbo, ever fearful of the arrival of the telegraph boy with shattering news of death or maiming. Although the role and experience of women in the Second World War has in recent times been much studied, the same cannot be said of the First World War. Many aspects of the political, social and economic impact of the war on women remain obscure. In terms of paid employment and political rights, Melanie Nolan argues that the war had less effect in New Zealand than in countries closer to the scene of action, such as Britain and the United States. In a male breadwinner society, making adequate provision for the dependants of soldiers serving with the NZEF became imperative. Important steps on the path towards the welfare state were taken in 1914–18, she argues, as both the state and private institutions helped to ensure that dependants received sufficient income. The records of the patriotic associations, which assisted needy dependants, offer a fascinating glimpse into the social conditions of the time.

Part of New Zealand's war effort was to continue its role as supplier of primary produce to Britain – a task that depended not only on the efforts of New Zealand's farmers but also on workers in key points in the chain of supply, such as freezing workers and watersiders. The problems of keeping these enterprises going multiplied as the demands for manpower for the NZEF increased. One solution seemed to be to increase national efficiency to make better use of the manpower that was available. A National Efficiency Board was appointed to make recommendations to the government. John Martin outlines the activities of the board and, in assessing its achievements, suggests that it had some significance for the long-term development of the New Zealand economy.

It is a common supposition that New Zealand farmers did well out of the war, helped by a guaranteed and high price in bulk purchase arrangements with Britain known as the commandeer. As James Watson notes, it is difficult to differentiate between patriotic duty and economic greed in considering farmers' motivation during the Great War. Contrary to the received wisdom, he suggests that the commandeer in fact held down returns to farmers. He points to the problems faced by farmers in maintaining production, especially because of labour and shipping shortages.

Attitudes to the war varied between communities, and depended to a large extent on economic status. Nowhere is this latter aspect more apparent then in Christchurch, which had been a centre of opposition to compulsory military training before the war. Although support for the war was substantial, it was also somewhat misleading, because the city's élite dominated the media. Gwen Parsons demonstrates a strong anti-war element within the community, focused on the working class. She outlines the various discourses promoted by the two sides of the class divide, and argues that opposition to the war did not prove any hindrance to political careers both during and after the war.

The Great War ended at 11 a.m. on 11 November 1918, when an armistice came into effect on the Western Front. It was not entirely unexpected, as the tide had clearly turned the Allies' way. In the preceding weeks, all the German Empire's allies had thrown in the towel – successively Bulgaria, the Ottoman Empire, and the Austro-Hungarian Empire. New Zealand soldiers in the field on the day reacted in a low-key way. 'So it is all over at last. Thank God for that. There is no jubilation and no excitement,' wrote Brigadier-General Herbert Hart, who had left New Zealand as a major with the main body of the NZEF in 1914.[7] In New Zealand, there was an outpouring of relief and delight,[8] tarnished only by the casualty lists that continued to appear for months afterwards and the onset of a killer at home, the influenza pandemic.[9] As Graham Hucker finds, the citizens of rural Taranaki were determined to celebrate the coming of peace despite the risks of congregating. Relief at the end of the bloodletting, thankfulness for the deliverance of victory and pride in a job well done – all helped shape opinion in this trying, though exhilarating transition from war to peace not only in Taranaki but also throughout the country. Auckland public servant Harold Ennor probably expressed the feelings of most New Zealanders when, on 12 November 1918, he noted in his diary that 'The long looked for peace has come. May it be for all time.'[10]

PART 1

POLITICAL, SOCIAL AND INTERNATIONAL PERSPECTIVES

1

Britain and the Empire at War 1914–18:
Reflections on a Forgotten Victory

Gary Sheffield

To this day the First World War remains contested territory; people still care passionately about it and hotly dispute its causes, its character, and its legacies.[1]
(Jay Winter, Geoffrey Parker, Mary R. Habeck, 2000)

Perceptions of the First World War

As the 20th century drew to a close, the debates over the role of Britain and the British Empire in the First World War showed no signs of ceasing. In Britain the conduct of the war on the Western Front lies at the heart of the controversies, while in Australia and New Zealand, the Gallipoli campaign of 1915 dominates the debate.[2] The issue of whether Britain and the empire should have become involved at all has been a source of dispute in recent years. The nature of the wartime relationship between the 'Mother Country' and the dominions and how the Great War changed that relationship have of course been a fruitful ground not only for historians but also for journalists and politicians.[3] In 1998, on the 80th anniversary of the Armistice, two influential books appeared: John Keegan's *The First World War* and Niall Ferguson's *The Pity of War*.[4] There is much to admire in both books. Keegan's is, as ever, beautifully written, while

Ferguson has some very interesting things to say about economics, and the nature of combat. On two key issues, however, the origins of the war and the combat performance of the British Expeditionary Force (BEF), I found myself in profound disagreement with both Keegan and Ferguson. My 2001 book *Forgotten Victory: The First World War — Myths and Realities* was, in part, a response to their books.[5]

Forgotten Victory reflected, and is in large part a synthesis of, the research of the last two decades. Here I will reconsider two of my major themes. First, that far from being futile, the war was fought for the very highest of stakes. It was forced upon Britain, which was compelled to fight a defensive war that it could not afford to lose. Moreover, the war was popular in the sense that it was a total 'people's war'; there was a broad national consensus that the war had to be fought and won. Second, that the British army was not the incompetent set of 'lions led by donkeys' beloved of popular myth; rather, it embarked on a steep learning curve and emerged as a formidable force which took a leading role in defeating the German army on the battlefield in 1918.

To some, these 'revisionist' views would appear to be heretical. For the New Zealand writer Maurice Shadbolt, 'Gallipoli had no more significance than a lethal bar-room brawl.'[6] This view is representative of a school of thought that sees the war as pointless. Some view it as somehow 'outside' history, disconnected from the normal course of events, and accessible only through literature and art produced by veterans of the conflict. My approach, as part of an informal global historical school of English-speaking historians that has for the last 20 years been using archival research to reassess the war, is rather different. I locate the First World War firmly within the context of political and military history. This war was, like any other, fought over political issues, and can be treated by historians like any other conflict.

The truth is that it is difficult to treat the Great War like any other: the scars on the psyche run too deep. Even to attempt to distance oneself from the emotional baggage of the last 90 years by viewing the Great War in Clausewitzian terms puts you at risk of being accused of being callous, although, gratifyingly, one reviewer described my book as 'compassionate'.[7] One can turn the callousness argument on its head. It is tragic that bereaved families have for so long been told, quite wrongly, that their loved ones died in vain. The 'One

Million Dead' of the British Empire, their widows and orphans, and descendants, deserve at the very least a sober reconsideration of *why* and *how* the war was fought.

In New Zealand, Australia, and Canada, the First World War is seen as being an important step on the road of nation-building.[8] Glyn Harper has argued that the war led to the recognition 'that New Zealand and New Zealanders were different and this difference did not imply inferiority. New Zealand nationalism and a sense of identity had been born.'[9] Tom Frame has commented that '25 April 1915 gave birth to several powerful and abiding myths which said more about Australian identity and hopes for nationhood than about a short military expedition concentrated in a place few Australians knew anything about'.[10] Perhaps much the same could be said about New Zealand and, with appropriate adjustments and Vimy Ridge substituted for Gallipoli, Canada too. In these countries, the memory of the First World War has a positive aspect that sits alongside perceptions of waste, incompetence and futility.

This positive view is missing from the British national perception of the conflict. The dominant images are, in the words of one of the most influential writers on the First World War, A. J. P. Taylor, 'brave helpless soldiers; blundering obstinate generals; nothing achieved'.[11] Moreover, the war is viewed as being fought over trivial issues. This perception is brilliantly parodied in the influential BBC TV comedy series *Blackadder Goes Forth,* when the origins of the war were reduced to: 'Some chap called Archie Duke shot an ostrich because he was hungry.'[12]

Historians, especially since 1980, have explored the riches of private and public archives to produce a composite and multi-faceted picture of Britain during the Great War that is at odds with received wisdom. But as the reception of *Forgotten Victory* indicated, little of this research has entered public consciousness. Even some historians seem to find it difficult to let go of the 'lions led by donkeys' version. I was fortunate in that this book was widely reviewed, and the positive responses greatly outnumbered the bad.[13] As Brian Bond commented, 'Most military historians who have seriously studied this subject will be in general agreement with Gary Sheffield's standpoint.'[14] By contrast, the reaction of one or two critics reminded me of Alfred Duff Cooper's comments about Liddell Hart's criticism of his biography of Haig: 'His article was a polemic rather than a review.... He set out to prove that Haig had always been wrong and it therefore followed that anyone who sought to defend him must have written a book that was misleading and worthless.'[15] Certainly, some reactions to *Forgotten Victory* seemed to be the product of emotion rather than cool analysis and knowledge of the subject.

Given the role the First World War is perceived to have played in nation-building, it is perhaps to be expected that the conflict remains politically contentious in Australia and New Zealand. The fact that it remains so in Britain is rather more surprising. For some writers on the left, there is an assumption that revisionist historians must be pursuing a reactionary agenda. In his review of *Forgotten Victory*, Frank McLynn described me as 'a simple-minded right wing ideologist'. As I pointed out in a letter to the newspaper in which this review was published, my political sympathies happen to lie on the left, not the right, as do those, incidentally, of a number of other revisionists, while still others are conservative in their politics or apolitical. Other critics further to the left of the political spectrum continue to see the First World War in starkly ideological terms. One reviewer argued that the war was 'a battle for the right of British and French capitalists to continue to exploit the workers and peasants of Africa and Asia. The revisionists are as wrong now as Douglas Haig and his gang were then. The popular view of the war is the right one, Blackadder and all.'[16] Under the interesting title of 'Misled [*sic*] attempt to justify bloody war', another review explicitly linked 1914–18 to the 2003 war in Iraq: 'The First World War raises the question – how can ... wars be stopped? Not by voting Labour! The Labour Party opposed the war, until it started and then backed it when it began – just as now.'[17]

On the right, a maverick Conservative MP, the late Alan Clark, was one of Haig's fiercest critics. His 1963 book *The Donkeys*, although panned at the time and ever since – Michael Howard condemned it as 'worthless as history' – remains in print. Clark believed that Britain was wrong to have entered the war, as its national interests were not at risk. The war destroyed an idyllic society (which existed largely, in fact, in Clark's imagination) in which inter-class harmony prevailed. Once Britain joined the war, it was a monumental error to fight on land as opposed to imposing a naval blockade: 'The sacrifice of a whole generation in Flanders was little more than a placebo to the mulish vanity of the general staff.' It is not surprising to find Clark in 1999 arguing against intervention in another Balkan war in which, he said, Britain had no interest; nor is it surprising that he entered politics out of a sense of duty, believing he had to make amends for the way that the élite had betrayed the masses in 1914–18.[18]

In the 1990s, the First World War became a vehicle for debate on Britain's role in the European Union. A Thatcherite historian, Niall Ferguson, argued that the British decision to go to war in 1914 was 'the greatest error of modern history'. Through the medium of the European Union, he argued, Germany has achieved the economic leadership of Europe that it sought in 1914, despite Britain fighting a war to prevent it happening.[19] Similarly, John Charmley's 1999 work arguing that British intervention in 1914 was neither inevitable nor desirable is implicitly, and in one place explicitly, linked to current debates about Britain's place in Europe.[20] On the left and right, there is a consensus that Britain's involvement in the First World War was a disastrous mistake.

The origins of the war

Britain fought the First World War essentially to uphold the balance of power,[21] and to keep Belgium, long regarded as the outer fortification of Fortress Britannia, from German occupation. Any assessment of Britain's decision to go to war must begin with a survey of the state of the debate on the origins of the conflict. In *Forgotten Victory* I argued that the notorious 'War Guilt' clause (Article 231 of the 1919 Treaty of Versailles) was essentially correct in blaming the war on 'the aggression of Germany and her allies'.[22] Nothing that I have read since has caused me to change that view. There is a consensus among historians that the primary responsibility for bringing about war rests with Germany and Austria-Hungary. The work of the distinguished German historian Stig Förster 'stresses that no serious historian today could be an apologist for German policy prior to August 1914'.[23] However, as Annika Mombauer has recently commented, 'there are still commentators who refuse to acknowledge Germany's large share of responsibility for the events that led to war'.[24]

It is clear that Austria-Hungary's aggression against Serbia 'plunged Europe into war'. Following the assassination of Archduke Franz Ferdinand, Vienna wanted a limited war in the Balkans, but was prepared to run the risk of a general war; the Austrian élite was astoundingly myopic as to the possible reaction of Russia. Germany's culpability is equally clear. On 5–6 July 1914, the Kaiser, in consultation with Bethmann Hollweg, his Chancellor, issued what became known as the 'blank cheque' of support for Austria-Hungary's military actions. Now, with German support, the Austrians could initiate military action. Without it, Vienna would have had to try another tack, 'something less punitive'. The German decision was taken in full knowledge of the possible consequences. In short, the German élite was prepared to risk war. Some, like General Moltke the Younger, had been urging war for some time.[25]

Why was this decision arrived at? Some apologists for German actions in 1914 point to the emerging threat of Russia. After the defeat at the hands of Japan in 1904–05, the Russian armed forces were in a state of disarray. The Great Programme of October 1913 was intended to rebuild Russian forces, possibly to deter German action against Russia's ally, France. In August 1914 completion of the programme was some years off, and even when finished would not have placed Russia in a position of military superiority.[26] There is little doubt that the implications of Russian rearmament alarmed Berlin and Vienna, and led to the view that war might be better 'sooner rather than later'.[27] This is not much of a defence for German policy in July–August 1914. How Russia would have behaved if the Great Programme had been completed in peacetime is, of course, unknowable, while the moral and political dilemmas involved in a pre-emptive conflict have been thrown into sharp focus in our own time.

During the July crisis, memory of German and Austrian 'coercion' during the Bosnian crisis of 1908 influenced Russian policy. Militarily weak, the Russian élite believed that if they stood by and allowed Austria a free hand over Serbia, Russia 'would no longer be seen as a great power'. Russia's policy in 1914 was essentially defensive in the face of Austro-German aggression. Although the fact that Russia mobilised first allowed the Germans to portray the war as a defensive one, that mobilisation did not equate to a declaration of war, as Sazonov, the Russian Foreign Minister, repeatedly informed the German ambassador. The Russians needed up to 16 weeks to put their forces in a position to fight, and this period, they believed, could be used for diplomacy. As far as culpability for the outbreak of the war goes, one inescapable fact is that 'Russia mobilized; Germany declared war'.[28]

Famously, Fritz Fischer claimed that Germany went to war in 1914 to achieve world power. In particular, he argued that at a 'War Council' on 8 December 1912 the Kaiser and senior advisers decided to go to war about 18 months hence. Historians still debate the meaning of this meeting, but at the very least the War Council provides powerful evidence of the willingness of the German élite to contemplate aggressive war. Some argue that Berlin seized on the Serbian crisis to create conditions for a war of conquest. In contrast, it has been argued that German decision-making during the July 1914 crisis was characterised by 'chaos and confusion rather than direction and design', and was concerned with the immediate crisis, rather than a Fischerite deliberate bid for world power.[29] Even so Bethmann Hollweg, supported, as we have seen, by the Kaiser, took the 'calculated risk' of seeking to split the Russian-French-British entente, without war if possible, but with war if necessary. Whether one sees Germany as deliberately starting (or risking) war in a bid for European hegemony and world power, or for some lesser stake, the finger of guilt points firmly at Berlin.

Jeremy Black has stressed that 'chance played a central role' in Britain entering the war in 1914. Britain no longer regarded France and Russia as threatening, in part because of Russian defeat at the hands of Japan in 1905, thus leaving its ally, France, open to German diplomatic pressure. A few years earlier Germany had seemed a natural ally of the British.[30] This view has much to commend it, but one should not underestimate the extent to which the Germans made the weather. German behaviour helped to create the conditions in which the three colonial powers formed an entente. In 1870–1 Prussia/Germany had defeated France, and Britain had been able to live with the consequences. Germany's aims were essentially limited and German troops stayed out of Belgium. The old balance of power was destroyed, but a new one was created and while Bismarck remained Chancellor Germany lived within it. In 1914, *pace* John Charmley,[31] things were very different, thanks to a decade and a half of German sabre-rattling, an unlimited approach to war and an attack on Belgium.

One historian has recently described the notion as 'very optimistic' that a victorious Germany would have proved to be a benign influence. Rather, 'A continental hegemony exercised by a Hohenzollern supreme warlord flush with easy victory would probably have had little room for liberalism, democracy, or British trade.' Moreover, if he had chosen to expand German power beyond Europe, 'who could then have checked him?'[32]

Robin Prior and Trevor Wilson also locate Britain's entry into the war in terms of the most simple national interest: 'survival as an independent, self-respecting state'. It had to prevent an enemy from controlling continental Europe, seizing the Channel ports and mounting a serious challenge to the Royal Navy's domination of the seas. By 1914, the importance of overseas trade to the British economy, and the problems of feeding Britain's population from domestic produce meant that the German threat 'came to surpass any menace it had confronted in the times of Philip II, Louis XIV or Napoleon'.[33]

Still, Ferguson's argument remains attractive. We know, of course, that the war that broke out in August 1914 lasted until November 1918, cost millions of lives and jerked world history into a groove that led to Stalin, Hitler and the threat of nuclear annihilation. Anything, some say, would have been better than that. That seems to be the thinking behind Richard Schweitzer's argument in his recent book *The Cross and the Trenches*. He accepts the 'compelling case' made in *Forgotten Victory* that 'Britain's vital national security interests were at stake in August 1914' in the Low Countries. Nevertheless, he goes on partially to espouse Niall Ferguson's argument 'that Germany may have evolved into a benign hegemon... the subsequent humanitarian disasters in Russia and Germany, suggest that an early German victory in the war, may, depending on one's vantage point, have been preferable'.[34]

All of this seems to turn on the ability of the Hohenzollern leopard to change his spots. The historical record – of the German army's atrocities against civilians in 1914, a consequence of a 'Clausewitzian commitment to using the most ruthless means necessary to win victory';[35] the harsh treatment meted out to occupied territories in France, Belgium and Poland; the ruthless exploitation of captured resources, including the use of forced labour; the emergence of the Hindenburg/Ludendorff military dictatorship – none of this inspires confidence in the evolution of imperial Germany into a 'benign hegemon'. The British decision-makers in August 1914 were not dealing with fantasies. They had to deal with *Realpolitik,* in the form of the gravest of threats to national survival. To imagine that Britain could stay out of the war in the face of Germany's drive to the west in 1914 is wishful thinking. As Colin S. Gray has written in a direct rebuttal of Ferguson's thesis:

> Britain had no prudent choice other than to join the anti-German coalition in 1914. Had Britain stood aside, Germany would have defeated France and Russia. Britain would then have been deservedly friendless, facing a hegemonic Germany with an undamaged – indeed probably augmented – High Seas Fleet.[36]

This situation would have been similar to the bleak prospect Britain had to face after Dunkirk, except that in 1940 the saving grace was the severe damage to the *Kriegsmarine* in the Norway campaign. In Gray's all too plausible scenario, Britain would have faced a Germany dominant on land and powerful at sea, and in the certain Anglo-German conflict that would have followed Britain's worst strategic nightmare would have come true. The reputation of imperial Germany has benefited from what came after. Hitler's regime was certainly worse than the Kaiser's, but the latter regime was decidedly unpleasant and dangerous. The First World War took on the character of a struggle between liberal democracies (for all their faults, and notwithstanding an alliance with Czarist Russia) and an anti-democratic, illiberal, militarist autocracy. This was the first of three such challenges in the 20th century, the others being Nazi Germany and Marxist-Leninism during the Cold War. In choosing to go to war in August 1914 Britain made a decision that, even in full knowledge of the ensuing carnage and suffering, remains the correct one.

'Someone else's war'?

Even if it is accepted as correct for Britain to have gone to war in 1914, does it follow that the rest of the empire should have followed suit? Dame Silvia Cartwright, New Zealand's Governor-General, in a speech delivered at Chunuk Bair on Anzac Day 2003, argued against this notion: 'New Zealanders had nothing to gain from the fight at Gallipoli. It was someone else's war. Turkey was not our enemy.'[37]

Cartwright's views do not, however, reflect the views held by New Zealanders of the Great War generation. Not only was Turkey allied to the empire's principal enemy but also it posed a threat to imperial security. Cecil Malthus, a New Zealand veteran of Gallipoli and the Western Front, believed to the end of his life that the war was justified by the need to halt German aggression.[38] Those New Zealanders who did oppose the conflict did so on grounds other than 'it was someone else's war'.[39] In 1914 the overwhelming majority of New Zealanders, Australians and Anglophone Canadians and South Africans regarded themselves as in some sense 'British', as loyal subjects of King George V and citizens of the empire. Late in life, Stan Stansfield, a New Zealand veteran, speaking of his motives for enlisting, commented on 'the British Empire business [which] was at the zenith, the peak of its power and popularity'.[40] In order to envisage an Australia that stayed out of the war, historian Geoffrey Blainey had to postulate a counter-factual country of 1914 in which a sizeable proportion of the population were of German, Austrian and Turkish origin.[41]

Even if imperial sentiment is set aside, there were compelling strategic reasons for Australia and New Zealand to become involved in the war. Australasian defence rested ultimately on British naval supremacy. If Britain had been defeated, and the Royal Navy's shield removed, Australia and New Zealand would have been effectively defenceless, and obliged to turn elsewhere, as in 1942. Dominion participation in Britain's imperial wars before 1914 contained a measure of self-interest. By proving themselves loyal, they increased the chance of Britain coming to their aid if should they be menaced by another power – either Germany or Britain's ally, Japan. Similarly, participation in the war against Germany was squarely in the national interest of Australia and New Zealand.[42] After the enormous sacrifices made by the Anzacs between 1914 and 1918, it is a sad irony that in 1941–42, when the Pacific dominions desperately needed support, Britain had almost none to offer.

The argument about whether the 1914–18 was 'someone else's war' is a prime example of the continued politicisation of the subject. The British Empire is also deeply controversial in Britain. In 2003, a Rastafarian poet rejected the offer of appointment as an officer of the Order of the British Empire (OBE) 'as a legacy of colonialism'. A few months later a parliamentary committee recommended a change of name to 'Order of British Excellence' as the former title was 'was now considered to be unacceptable, being thought to embody values that are no longer shared by many of the country's population'. This prompted one correspondent to the BBC to ask, 'Why are we always ashamed and apologetic of the British Empire?'[43] With failed states pricking the world's conscience, a modified form of imperialism appears to be creeping back onto the international agenda, reinforced by debates about the 'imperial' nature of the United States. Niall Ferguson's recent book and TV series, which emphasised the positive aspects of the British Empire, have provoked fury in some quarters.[44]

Total war

Why, given the military stalemate and appalling casualties on the Western Front, was there no compromise peace?[45] Domestic support for the war in all the belligerent states remained remarkably high in the first years of the war. Not until 1917 was there substantial wavering of resolve, and even then only Russia was forced out of the war. Until 1917, there was little pressure from below for a compromise peace. This fact allowed governments on both sides to pursue far-reaching war aims that made a compromise peace impossible. This was a consequence of total war, and the mentalities it breeds. Moreover, fundamental war aims were utterly irreconcilable. Germany sought to achieve hegemony over Europe, eventually evolving geopolitical objectives that resembled those pursued by the Third Reich a generation later, while Britain, France, Russia and later the United States sought to prevent this from occurring. The campaigns of 1914 brought the Germans important gains in Belgium and eastern France, and allowed the German army to remain on the defensive in the west while concentrating on defeating Russia. As long as the Allied armies were unable to dislodge German forces from the Western Front, Berlin saw no reason to compromise. The Allies' consent to a peace that allowed Germany to retain her gains in the west would have left both French and British security gravely weakened. Only when one side inflicted a decisive series of defeats on the other, which happened between July and November 1918, did serious diplomacy come back into play. Although the Germans tried to divide the entente by appealing over the head of the British and French to President Woodrow Wilson in Washington, this ploy was in vain. The war ended on the terms dictated by the Allies. Although much vilified, they were, in truth, not unduly severe considering that Germany had initiated, fought and lost a total world war. In comparison with the treatment that Germany meted out to defeated Russia in 1918 at the Peace of Brest-Litovsk the terms seem almost moderate. The severity of the settlement at the end of the First World War bears no comparison with that imposed on Germany in 1945.[46]

Between 1914 and 1918 Britain and the empire mobilised for total war.

Democracies cannot fight and win such conflicts without the consent and active involvement of the masses, and the creation of 'nations-in-arms' was a remarkable achievement. The onset of war weariness in Britain was countered to a large extent by a 'remobilisation' in 1917–18, involving the announcement of 'democratic' war aims and the implementation of social and political reforms. In all, 5,704,000 men served in the British army during the First World War, split roughly equally between volunteers and conscripts.[47] The army of the First World War was larger by far than any other force raised by Britain, before or since. The birth of this huge army was paralleled by the creation of a war economy to support it. In December 1916 David Lloyd George became Prime Minister. The emergence of Lloyd George, a populist politician of humble origins who won a reputation as a 'man of push and go' at the Ministry of Munitions, is a striking symbol of Britain's transformation into a state geared for total war. The creation of a centrally directed war economy capable of supplying its huge armies with sufficient quantities of weapons, ammunition and all the other equipment it needed to fight a modern, high-intensity attritional war was a considerable achievement of the British nation in arms. Without it, the victories of the BEF on the battlefields of France and Belgium would have been impossible.

There was a similar pattern in the empire. Out of a population of 8 million Canada sent 458,000 men overseas, of whom 57,000 became casualties. The 5 million Australians sent 332,000, resulting in 59,000 casualties; for New Zealand the figures were 1.1 million, 112,000 and 17,000. India found 1.5 million volunteers. Moreover, in the last two years of the war, about one-third of the BEF's munitions were produced in Canada.[48] Black Africa also made a substantial contribution. Some 40,000 carriers and porters died in the East African campaign, for example.[49]

The war put the social and political fabric of the belligerents under tremendous strain. Total war made less of an impact on the dominions than on Russia or Germany, but the stresses were still significant. In July 1916 New Zealand followed Britain in introducing conscription, the first dominion to do so. Some 10 per cent of the total population of New Zealand served overseas.[50] Across the empire, the question of conscription became entangled with war weariness. Even in loyal New Zealand, conscription proved divisive. In Canada, these problems were hugely magnified. About 35 per cent of the population were French-Canadians, but this community provided only 5 per cent of the Canadian Expeditionary Force. By comparison, in Toronto, over two-thirds of the men who were eligible volunteered.[51] In 1917 a prolonged conscription crisis, culminating in a bitterly fought election, widened the rift between Canada's Anglophone and Francophone peoples. Similarly, as the October 1915 election revealed, the whole question of South Africa's participation in the war divided the Afrikaner community down the middle. In Australia, attempts to introduce conscription were twice rejected in referenda that also proved deeply divisive.

One of the paradoxes of total war in the 20th century is that liberal democratic states have had to adopt many of the trappings and methods of authoritarian states in order to defend their values against ideological enemies.[52] For Britain and the dominions to emerge from the war with democracy not merely intact, but in many ways enhanced, was a substantial achievement.

Strategy, operations and tactics

In 1932 Basil Liddell Hart argued that between 1914 and 1918 Britain had abandoned her traditional 'way in warfare' of using naval power, and financial muscle to subsidise allies, with disastrous results.[53] Many critics have echoed his condemnation of British strategy, Alan Clark among them. In reality, British strategy in 1914–18 had strong continuities with previous practice, not least that it was a war fought in coalition with France and Russia. This simple fact severely limited Britain's strategic room for manoeuvre. As Lord Kitchener commented in August 1915, 'unfortunately we had to make war as we must, and not as we should like to'.[54] France and Russia needed far more than economic and naval contributions from Britain, vital as they were. They needed troops on the ground on the Western Front. That was where the war was won and lost.

In recent years the old idea of a crude division between 'Easterners' and 'Westerners' in the British decision-making élite has largely been discarded. Apparent 'Westerners' like Sir William Robertson were well aware of the necessity for campaigns away from France. These fell into various categories, including campaigns undertaken to ensure harmony within the coalition (Salonika, Italy), to uphold local imperial interests (the capture of Germany's

Pacific colonies) or to gain strategically significant territory (Palestine, Mesopotamia). The latter was seen as vital for the empire's place in the post-war world and even, it has been argued, to acquire bargaining chips for use should the war end in a peace of exhaustion.[55]

Such operations were undoubtedly important, but they contributed little to the defeat of Germany. The contribution of the Royal Navy, including economic blockade, was an essential component in the Allied victory, but by itself it was not enough to bring about even the minimum war aim of the withdrawal of German forces from Belgium and France. That was accomplished only by the defeat of the German army in battle, and that mighty undertaking could not have been achieved without the decisive contribution of the BEF, in which the 10 Dominion divisions played a prominent role. British and Allied strategy in the First World War was on occasion wasteful and even incompetent, but ultimately proved less wasteful and incompetent than that of Germany and the Central Powers. In the end, this was what mattered.

The change in warfare between 1914 and 1918 is graphically illustrated by examining the fate of the cavalry. In the initial, mobile stages of the 1914 campaign, British cavalry was highly effective in the roles of reconnaissance and screening the main body of the BEF, employing a mixture of mounted and dismounted action. When the front began to congeal into trench warfare, the limitations of mounted troops became clear. Major Lord Tweedmouth of the Royal Horse Guards (The Blues) recorded in his diary for 26 October 1914:

> Supposed to be a rest day. Turned out at 2 pm to support an advance by General Vaughan. Were stopped on the way and told to cover the retreat of the 20th Bde and lined the woods on each side of the road. Situation changed again and we went off at a gallop to make a demonstration. C Sqn in advance. My sword carried away just as we got to the crest between Hugh Grovenor's trench and Gerry Ward's. We got the shrapnel pretty hot then and my horse was hit in the leg and I had to stop and get into Hugh's trench. Got out presently and shot my horse with my revolver and saved all my kit. Found the led horses of D Sqn and went back with them to Zillebeke. We were very lucky considering the fire we came in for and had men wounded, and lost over 20 horses killed and wounded, mostly in C Sqn.[56]

Horsed cavalry were occasionally effective on the Western Front during trench warfare but the general experience of cavalry is neatly summarised by the historian of the 3rd Dragoon Guards:

> When the regiment left Egypt in 1914, nobody had any conception of the work which awaited the cavalry on the Western Front. By training and tradition all ranks expected to be used as mounted troops. Four years later they looked back on their campaigns, and found that only on rare occasions had they used their horses.

Instead, the regiment had performed a variety of tasks, many 'strange and distasteful', ranging from infantry work in the trenches to burying corpses, although they had carried out a very successful mounted charge almost at the end of the war.[57]

The 3rd Dragoon Guards were caught up in static trench warfare. Although this form of warfare was far from new,[58] from October–November 1914 until the end of 1917 the peculiar circumstances of the Western Front dictated that the defensive had a temporary advantage. This situation gradually changed, as new weapons (notably the tank, artillery, aircraft and light machine gun) were introduced or improved and, just as importantly, tactics were evolved to make best use of the new equipment.

A key development was the evolution of an all-arms weapons system, in which various pieces of technology, lethal and non-lethal, different troop types and effective command and control systems operated in a synergistic fashion. Striking visual evidence of the importance of this development is to be seen in central London to this day. The Foot Guards were a notoriously 'tribal' organisation, yet their Great War memorial includes a *bas relief* of an 18-pounder field gun in action, and a signaller using a field telephone. The message is clear, and echoed a theme that ran throughout the divisional history: the Guards Division was an all-arms team that consisted of far more than socially élite infantry regiments.[59]

A parallel development of the utmost importance was the emergence of three-dimensional, indirect artillery fire, an advance that was made possible by the use of aircraft for artillery spotting. These two developments transformed the conduct of warfare in a Revolution in Military Affairs (RMA), the product of 'technological development', 'doctrinal and operational innovation', and 'organisational adaptation'.[60] The German breakthrough of March 1918 demonstrated that the pendulum had swung in favour of the attacker. However, the Hundred Days offensives of August–November 1918 demonstrated that it was the Allies, and specifically the forces of the British Empire, rather than the Germans, that had learnt from the bloody battles of 1915–17 most effectively.

During the Hundred Days the Allied higher command demonstrated a grasp of what would today be called 'operational art', co-ordinating army-level offensives across a wide front. Moreover, they chose to make shallow but logistically sustainable advances, covered by artillery fire, before switching the point of attack to a different sector to keep the enemy off balance. This contrasted strongly with the German methods of the spring, when attacking forces made spectacular advances that outran their artillery and supply lines, leaving them vulnerable to counter-strokes. By this stage, the Germans were rapidly exhausting their resources of men, horses and many other essentials. The BEF, too, was running short of men, but the British had the priceless advantage of being able to fight a 'rich man's war' with apparently unlimited supplies of guns and munitions, and excellent logistic support. During the attack on the Canal du Nord in late September, 62,813 tons of ammunition were fired in only three days. Whatever criticisms can be made of the BEF's operations in previous campaigns, during the Hundred Days it was playing to its strengths.[61]

The experience of the New Zealand Division offers some 'snapshots' of the BEF's tactical learning curve. The division's action on the battle of the Somme on 15–17 September 1916 demonstrates the immaturity of the BEF's style of warfare at that stage of the war. Generally, too much was expected of the tank on its debut; tactical co-ordination between the tanks and the infantry was rudimentary; the artillery fire-plan was flawed, and gunnery techniques left a lot to be desired. The New Zealand infantry followed a creeping barrage, but some betrayed their inexperience by advancing into the British barrage. Some troops were faced by intact barbed wire, and on occasions the barrage failed to materialise. Logistic problems were compounded by bad weather and, in the words of the divisional historian, 'robbed the British of the fruit of their efforts'.

Although the New Zealanders, who displayed considerable élan and were well served by excellent battlefield leadership, did well, overall the attack of 15 September 1916 fell short of Haig's expectations.[62]

A year later, much had changed. The New Zealand Division, like the rest of the BEF, had absorbed the lessons of the Somme, retraining in the new platoon tactics.[63] It had benefited from improved gunnery, and staff work and planning at all levels, in the battles of Messines on 7 June 1917 and Broodseinde on 4 October 1917. These battles were models of 'bite and hold', in which infantry advanced on limited objectives, supported by heavy fire power.[64] The division's attack on 12 October during First Passchendaele was, by contrast, a bloody failure. Brigadier-General Herbert Hart of 4th New Zealand Brigade suggested reasons for the failure in his diary. He noted the difficulty of getting the guns forward over the ground 'absolutely shattered, ploughed up & pockmarked by shellfire', a problem exacerbated by wet weather:

> Consequently the artillery preparation was incomplete. Uncut wire was met & was insurmountable under such conditions. Mud & wire prevented our men keeping up to the barrage. Hun machine gunners, protected in concrete pillboxes during the bombardment, came out with their machine guns after the barrage passed on, & shot down our men while still struggling to get through & over the mud & wire.[65]

Plumer's Second Army had delivered three bite and hold operations in rapid succession, on 20 and 26 September and 4 October 1917. But the very success of the British artillery cratered the ground and made it increasingly difficult to get the guns forward for the next attack. In the wet and muddy conditions of Passchendaele, it proved impossible to sustain operational tempo. As the subsequent success of the Canadian Corps demonstrated, even under these conditions bite and hold could be made to work, if time and substantial engineering resources were made available to prepare the battlefield.[66] However, this methodical approach ran the risk of losing the impetus of the initial advance.

By the time of Hundred Days, matters had moved on again. Hart, by now commanding 3rd New Zealand (Rifle) Brigade, recorded that:

> The battle [of Bapaume, August 1918] is entirely different to all earlier battles in France. Troops are not so densely packed, there is greater scope for initiative & leadership. Advances are deeper & on much wider frontages …
>
> There are many tanks, whippets & armoured cars about, some going up for more work, some returning weary & battle scarred, & many derelict by the roadside … Artillery was moving forward everywhere, lorry water tanks were particularly busy & overhead there was a constant buzz from aeroplanes. The whole scene was very stirring & much less gruesome than the Somme, Messines or Passchendaele.[67]

The complexity of some operations in the Hundred Days is demonstrated by 3rd Brigade's capture of Le Quesnoy on 4 November 1918. This involved barrages by field artillery and machine gun, trench mortar and Lewis gun fire, the projection of burning oil and smoke by special companies of the Royal Engineers, a sophisticated scheme of manoeuvre for the infantry and, of course, the use of scaling ladders.[68]

The New Zealand Division was an unusually effective formation, certainly one of the best in the BEF, and under the command of the formidable Major-General Sir Andrew Russell it developed a distinctive style. However the division needs to be placed into the context of a BEF-wide process of learning and adaptation that, by the Hundred Days, resulted in the overall quality of Haig's army being very high. The term 'learning curve' should not be taken to mean that the process was a smooth upward course, and it encompassed logistics, command and staff work, and a host of other factors, as well as tactics. But the learning curve was real enough, and it helped to deliver victory on the battlefield.

Conclusion

The Allied victory of 1918 was a vital element in the relative peace and prosperity enjoyed by the West at the end of the 20th century. The defeat of Germany preserved liberalism and democracy in Europe and delivered a check to a militarist, aggressive autocracy. The fact that Britain, the dominions and their allies would find it necessary to engage in a further two global conflicts against ideological enemies – one hot, one cold – does not detract from the importance of the war of 1914–18. The argument that the world in 1919 would have been a better place if the Great War had not taken place or, more parochially, if Britain and the empire had not become involved is a red herring. A German victory in the First World War would have produced a situation significantly worse than the imperfect 'real' world of 1919. The war waged by Britain and the empire was tragic, destructive and wasteful, but it was not futile.

2

The Shaping of New Zealand's War Effort, August–October 1914

Ian McGibbon

Speaking at Gallipoli on Anzac Day 2003, the Governor-General, Dame Silvia Cartwright, referred to the sacrifice made by New Zealanders during the ill-fated campaign on the peninsula in 1915. 'For New Zealand the suffering and death had added poignancy,' she said, because 'New Zealanders had nothing to gain from the fight at Gallipoli. It was someone else's war. Turkey was not our enemy.'[1]

Cartwright's comments, which drew a measure of criticism in the following days that must have agitated her speechwriter, are yet another reflection of the ambivalence with which many New Zealanders view their country's participation in the war to end all wars, the Great War of 1914 to 1918. Eight decades on, a rising sense of nationalism, coupled with a steady diet of Western Front horror stories, have left many looking askance at New Zealand's involvement in British imperial ventures. The idea that New Zealanders were cannon fodder of the empire, led to their death by scheming and perfidious British politicians and dunderhead generals who spent the war safely ensconced in comfortable chateaux well behind the front line, permeates the popular media – and even some writing on the topic by academics. Such negative attitudes are reinforced by unhistorical, politically motivated reassessments, for example in the process that led to the legislation 'pardoning' five New Zealand soldiers executed for military crimes during the war.[2]

In this chapter I will focus on the three months August–October 1914 when the nature of New Zealand's war effort was effectively determined. I will look at the reasons why New Zealand entered the war and why its initial contribution took the form it did. I will also discuss some aspects of the dispatch of New Zealand troops overseas in that period. My aim will be to demonstrate that the First World War was very much New Zealand's war, that New Zealand's war effort was the product of its resources and pre-war planning attuned to those resources, and that New Zealand was very early brought face to face with the need to defend its interests within the imperial system.

In one sense the Great War was New Zealand's war whether it liked it or not. As part of the British Empire it was involved, like all territories and dominions, immediately King George V declared war on the German Empire (on the advice of his British ministers) on 4 August 1914. Under international law the King's enemy was entitled to attack New Zealand, and distance was not necessarily a guarantee of inviolability. Formal neutrality was not an option for New Zealand, and informal neutrality would have been dependent on an enemy's restraint.

Although it had no control over its involvement in the conflict that erupted at the beginning of August, New Zealand did have a choice about its degree of participation in the war. As a self-governing dominion, it was under no formal or constitutional compulsion to help the empire in the looming struggle, but the possibility of standing aside never entered the heads of those who determined the country's stance. New Zealand's response was characterised by ready support for the British government and offers of assistance to the imperial effort even before the war began. The strong bipartisan public support for this approach was reflected in Parliament, where the Reform and Liberal parties, which between them held 87 per cent of the seats, vied with each other to make the fullest expression of support for the imperial cause. But it was also evident in the street.

When at 1 p.m. on 5 August the Governor, Lord Liverpool, read from Parliament steps the telegram advising the outbreak of war with the German Empire, some 15,000 were there to hear him. A state of euphoria was apparent after the announcement.[3] In what was described as a 'remarkable display of enthusiasm' thousands that evening marched through the streets of the capital 'in rows 4,5 and 6 deep, upon military lines'.[4] There were similar scenes of patriotic enthusiasm in other centres.

On a small scale, then, New Zealanders replicated the evident enthusiasm with which many Europeans went to war in 1914, though such displays may not have reflected the feelings of the general population. Hew Strachan has pointed to 'passive acceptance, a willingness to do one's duty' as characteristic of the response in Europe, with 'enthusiasm … the conspicuous froth, the surface element only'.[5] Something similar probably existed in New Zealand.

New Zealand's response to the crisis owed much to the attitudes of the people both to the empire and to war and to their perception of the issues that seemed to be at stake in the clash of empires taking place on the other side of the world. But beneath such attitudes lay a bedrock of self-interest. New Zealanders recognised immediately that this war was not a contest that could be viewed with detachment. Its outcome would have global implications, which could not fail to affect a small dominion so closely bound to Britain emotionally, economically and politically.

It is difficult to judge how many New Zealanders were ambivalent about or even hostile to supporting the empire, for their voice was virtually submerged in the early months of the war. There can be little doubt, though, that a substantial majority supported New Zealand taking a full and active part in the war. This had its roots in the composition of the country – the 'kith and kin' factor. Most Pakeha New Zealanders had been in the country 40 years or less. Only in the 1890s had the number of local-born New Zealanders outstripped those born in the British Isles. In 1914, British-born still amounted to one in five in the population.[6] Even for New Zealand-born citizens ties to relatives in the 'Old Country' remained strong. Although the indigenous population did not, of course, have the same links with Britain, their numbers were low. Most Maori were, in any case, outside the mainstream of New Zealand public life in 1914.

Far from regarding the empire as a constraint upon their freedom, most New Zealanders saw it as a positive benefit and were proud to be part of it. To a degree this reflected their recognition of the value to them of imperial power, especially the Royal Navy. The worldwide network of bases that sustained this navy provided an assurance of assistance should there be any threat to New Zealand. But many also perceived a civilising mission in the empire's activities, not least in benighted Africa. To be sure, the empire gained economic benefits from its possession of colonies. For most such domination equated with progress: only a few on the left of the political spectrum decried the exploitative nature of the relationship between Britain and its colonies. Nor did most New Zealanders see any incompatibility between their strongly expressed imperial patriotism and an emerging sense of a distinctive national character.

Public attitudes to war also played a part in shaping New Zealand's response in August 1914. The long spell since a major European conflagration had left many with a romantic concept of war. War was about glory and sacrifice. New Zealanders were influenced by propaganda proclaiming the virtues of sacrifice and the duty of youth to defend the empire against its enemies. War was also lauded by some as a means of cleansing and hardening society, sweeping away the apparent 'decadence' of modern life.[7]

In part this predilection towards war was based on a profound ignorance of what might be involved in a conflict between great powers in the 20th century. The last occasion for such conflict had been the Crimean War, which was confined to a limited and peripheral area. In the ensuing half-century wars involving the British Empire had been relatively small. The South African War of 1899–1902 had certainly involved a prolonged effort, but it had not provided a clear lesson of the likely consequences of war on a much greater scale. The pointers offered by the American Civil War and the Russo-Japanese War had not had major impact. Few in August 1914 clearly conceived the nature of modern war between industrialised states.

Public opinion confirmed the government in its preference to offer substantial assistance to the imperial war effort. Such pressure might well have been sufficient in itself to ensure full-scale participation, but behind the imperial rhetoric lay the recognition that New Zealand interests were threatened by the conflict. Few doubted that New Zealand's status as a self-governing entity was at stake. A British defeat would portend all sorts of dangerous consequences. As a worst case New Zealand might become a bargaining chip in some post-war settlement, perhaps transferred to German sovereignty as the Philippines had been to United States after the American victory in its war with Spain just 14 years earlier. Much of the British Empire had been acquired in such settlements over the centuries.

Even if such a situation were avoided, any collapse of British power would leave the South Pacific dominions exposed to the depredations of some other power, perhaps Japan. Winston Churchill, the First Lord of the Admiralty, had put it bluntly at a meeting of the Committee of Imperial Defence at which New Zealand Defence Minister James Allen was present in 1913: 'If the power of Great Britain were shattered upon the sea, the only course open to the five millions of white men in the Pacific would be to seek the protection of the United States.'[8] New Zealand's fate was bound up with that of the empire, whether it took part in the war or not.

There were also more direct interests at stake. Most New Zealanders understood the economic importance of the continued availability of the British market. This had increased with the introduction of refrigeration in the 1880s, a development that had led to a narrowing of New Zealand's trade focus. By 1914 roughly 80 per cent of New Zealand's exports went to Britain. Anything that threatened that market, or New Zealand's access to it, could not fail to threaten New Zealand's prosperity because alternative markets were not readily available.

Keeping the sea routes between New Zealand and Britain open was essential. Whether heading eastwards around Cape Horn, north-eastwards to the newly opened Panama Canal or westwards to the Cape of Good Hope or the Suez Canal, New Zealand's trade on the high seas was vulnerable to enemy commerce raiders. But the danger greatly increased as ships neared the British Isles. The congested sea lanes there provided a lure to the enemy. Britain's dependence on imported food made an attempt to sever its seaborne lifeline very probable.

With its minimal resources New Zealand had no hope of protecting its trade on its own. But trade is two way. Britain had an equally strong interest in ensuring that New Zealand's cargo ships, laden with meat, dairy products or wool, reached its ports. This was not only because of its food supply problem: the fate of much British capital investment in New Zealand depended on the continued viability of New Zealand's economy.

Trade protection was a matter of seapower, of commanding the oceans across which the merchant ships moved. In any naval contest, the more powerful fleet would be in a position to sweep its rival's commerce from the seas. Naval thinking in 1914 was heavily influenced by the writings of the

American Admiral Alfred Thayer Mahan, which emphasised the importance of the decisive battle that would settle the issue of sea command. This seemed to be the lesson of Trafalgar, and it was reinforced by the annihilation of the Russian fleet at Tsushima in 1905. In these terms, then, the key to the protection of New Zealand's trade lay in the main concentration of British naval power, the British battlefleet prepared to take part in this decisive encounter. This was the Grand Fleet commanded by a later Governor-General of New Zealand, Admiral Sir John Jellicoe, a man Churchill would describe as the only one on either side who could have lost the war in an afternoon. (Of course the First World War would demonstrate that command of the seas, for trade protection purposes, could not be assured by the battlefleet alone, but this was not recognised in 1914.)

Underlying New Zealanders' approach to security in the two decades before the outbreak of war in 1914 was awareness of the imperial naval position. The shield provided by the Royal Navy seemed to grow less sure as other navies expanded. As early as 1889 the waning of British predominance had been reflected in the decision to maintain a fleet equal to the two next most powerful fleets – the so-called Two Power Standard. Above all, the Kaiser's decision in the late 1890s to challenge British naval predominance by building a German battlefleet to rival Britain's had introduced an unsettling element of uncertainty. Anxiety grew as technological changes, especially the introduction of dreadnoughts, seemed to narrow the gap between British and German fleet strengths. The possibility of a decisive defeat in the North Sea was no less a nightmare to New Zealanders than it was to Britons, so great would be the consequences for imperial security.

But New Zealand was also on the periphery of empire, far from the main British naval concentration. Questions about future imperial security in the east were raised by growing European squadrons in the region, and answered only by the British Empire allying with Japan in 1902. New Zealand welcomed this measure at the time, but the Japanese victory at Tsushima three years later awakened unease in New Zealand about relying on Japan for strategic security in the Pacific. The increasing reliance by London on the alliance, as British warships were withdrawn from the Pacific to meet the threat in the North Sea, was troubling.

These concerns were enhanced by evidence that New Zealand's strategic isolation was lessening. The German Empire had moved into the South Pacific, acquiring territory in New Guinea and Samoa, as well as islands north of the equator. The German presence seemed to increase the danger of attack by German forces on Australia and New Zealand trade and ports – and such concerns were not unjustified, as examination of German naval plans for the region from 1901 makes clear.[9]

These developments help to explain the increasing imperial fervour of New Zealanders in the period leading up to the First World War – a process that James Belich has misleadingly dubbed 'recolonisation', as if New Zealand had somehow previously been decolonised. It is not surprising that a peripheral part of the empire, worried by the future and increasingly conscious of the limitations on imperial resources, should cling more closely to the centre, to seek to emphasise dependence, to bolster the moral commitment that already existed because of its dominion status. The imperial security system – imperial defence, as it was known at the time – was under threat, and it behoved New Zealand, and the other parts of the empire dependent on it, to do all in their power to ensure its continued viability.

The idea of New Zealand supporting the empire in conflict had deep roots, having first been raised as early as 1852.[10] Offers had nearly been made in 1885 over Afghanistan,[11] but it was not until 1899 that New Zealand troops set out for an imperial battlefield, in southern Africa.[12] This effort against the Boers – more than 6000 men were ultimately involved – increased the focus on the contribution that the self-governing parts of the empire could make to imperial strength, a contribution that grew in importance as the empire's security became more problematical. In New Zealand it would lead to steps that ensured the means of helping was available in August 1914.

So the New Zealand response to the outbreak of the First World War was fully in line with the approach to defence that had evolved in the preceding 30 years and was based firmly on a perception of New Zealand's interests. The country's leaders at least, and no doubt many of those among the population at large who gave thought to the issue, were convinced that New Zealand's economic and physical well-being was bound up with the fate of Britain.

Finally, it is a mistake to assume that New Zealanders were oblivious to the issues at stake in 1914, that they 'did not investigate the causes of conflict'.[13] To be sure, there was a lack of information about the diplomacy of the crisis that arose following the assassination of the Archduke Franz Ferdinand. But New Zealanders recognised the fundamental challenge to the British Empire presented by the German Empire, and the threat to Britain's security that would be posed by German domination of the Low Countries. There was awareness, too, of the implications of Germany's naval building programme, and of its drive for colonies. Many New Zealanders believed that Germany had set out to achieve world domination and that this challenge had to be met.

New Zealand opinion was influenced by perceptions of the German Empire, the autocratic nature of its government, the militarism – 'Prussianism' – that pervaded its society. Such negative perceptions were enhanced by German violation of Belgium's neutrality. A small power, whose sovereignty had been guaranteed by treaty, was being crushed by a juggernaut. German atrocities against the Belgian people were abhorred. Many New Zealanders believed that this struggle was a contest between autocracy and democracy, that the British Empire was making a principled stand. Their belief that they were fighting for a better world would underpin their willingness to sustain their war effort over the next four years.

Every aspect of the imperial war effort became New Zealand's war, not least the conflict with the Ottoman Empire that began on 5 November 1914 when Constantinople declared war on the British Empire. Defeating the Ottomans was therefore a key imperial interest, and, as Churchill and some others perceived, seemed to offer a road to victory that did not require battering the German armies in France and Flanders and that took advantage of Allied command of the Mediterranean.

To suggest that the attack on the Gallipoli Peninsula was not New Zealand's war, as Silvia Cartwright did in April 2003, is to misunderstand the nature of the conflict and the imperial war effort. The Ottoman Empire was not some peaceable state suddenly and unjustly subjected to attack by Allied forces. Following its declaration of war it had, after all, invaded Egypt, and in February 1915 threatened the Suez Canal. It had also sided with the empire's enemies in Europe. Under international law, the British and French empires were permitted to invade Ottoman territory and to seek to resolve the conflict by force of arms.

A New Zealand contribution

New Zealand's strategy in the First World War was relatively straightforward: to do all in its power to help the empire to win the war or at least not to lose it. It did this by providing an 8000-strong expeditionary force, formed as two brigades: one infantry, the other mounted rifles. At the time of its departure it was intended that this force would join the BEF, which had been rapidly deployed in France and Belgium. But in fact it disembarked in Egypt, and served with the Mediterranean Expeditionary Force in the Gallipoli campaign as part of the New Zealand and Australian Division. Later, after the evacuation from Gallipoli, two further brigades augmented the infantry brigade to form an infantry division, the New Zealand Division, which was sent to France to join the British Expeditionary Force. Most of the mounted brigade remained in Egypt where it formed part of the Anzac Mounted Division.

The nature of New Zealand's wartime contribution was dominated by its pre-war preparations. These had focused on the army, a force that could be provided without huge capital outlays. A citizen army based on part-time service, with only a limited number of regulars for key positions, offered a relatively inexpensive form of defence provision.

In the five years before 1914 the government had addressed the possibility of dispatching an expeditionary force to assist the empire, and there had been a substantial reorganisation of the military forces to better ensure that this task could be carried out quickly and efficiently. These changes had been prompted in large measure by talks in London in 1907 and 1909 that had stressed the importance of military co-operation and the need for standardisation of forces. The establishment of an Imperial General Staff had been a step in this direction, and in 1909 imperial and dominion leaders agreed on the need for a 'plan for so organizing the forces of the Crown wherever they are that, while preserving the complete autonomy of each Dominion, should the Dominions desire to assist in the defence of the Empire in a real emergency, their forces could be rapidly combined into one homogeneous Imperial Army'.[14]

Strongly influenced by these discussions, Prime Minister Joseph Ward asked the Chief of the Imperial General Staff, General Sir William Nicholson, for advice on New Zealand military preparations, including 'the organization of the Expeditionary Force'.[15] In his report, Nicholson advocated the development of a 30,000-strong army, organised on a territorial basis, 'well trained, complete in all arms, and provided with a due proportion of administrative services'.[16] Under his scheme, each of the four military districts would have an infantry brigade, a mounted rifles brigade and an artillery brigade. This would provide a balanced force that New Zealand could provide, given the number of young men available. Nicholson suggested that an expeditionary force of 10,000 could be drawn without difficulty from such an organisation. The force might comprise an infantry brigade, an artillery brigade and a mounted rifles brigade, along with sundry other units.[17]

The upshot of these deliberations was the decision by Ward's government to replace the existing amateurish Volunteer Force with a Territorial Force, and to introduce a system of compulsory military training for all 18- to 25-year-olds to ensure sufficient men to fill out the ranks of the 30,000-strong army. The government never gave serious thought to creating an entirely mounted Territorial Force, despite what has been described as the 'alleged genius' of the 'archetypal New Zealand soldier… for mobile, open and irregular warfare',[18] as recently demonstrated in the South African War. Many men from rural districts could have provided their own mounts, but not so most city and town men. A fully mounted Territorial Force would have required the army acquiring sufficient horses for the purpose, and making arrangements for their sustenance. This would have been a hugely expensive exercise for a force that trained on a part-time basis, including only a short annual camp. Infantrymen were also required, and were most easily trained under the compulsory training and Territorial system put in place in 1910–11.

The new arrangements were instituted in 1911, under the guidance of a number of imperial officers brought out to New Zealand for the purpose, led by the austere but competent Major-General Alexander Godley. Although the new system was developed partly with an expeditionary force in mind, it was not until October 1912 that specific preparations for such a contribution began; by this time the Reform Party led by William Massey controlled the Treasury benches. Pointing to the need for rapid action on the outbreak of war, Godley secured Minister of Defence James Allen's approval for planning to start. Discussions with Australia followed, centring on New Zealand making available an infantry brigade to form a joint division. It was Allen, following Nicholson's earlier recommendation, who suggested the idea of a mounted brigade in addition to an infantry brigade.[19] His discussions with British military authorities in London in early 1913 reinforced the idea of providing the two brigades. On 21 June 1913, the Cabinet agreed that a 7500-strong expeditionary force based on an infantry brigade and a mounted rifles brigade would be raised at the time of an emergency by calling for volunteers from the Territorial Force.[20]

These plans underlay New Zealand's initial response to the crisis just over 13 months later. When, on 31 July 1914, Massey warned Parliament that if war began it would be asked to send an expeditionary force, he indicated that 'an understanding has been arrived at with regard to the numbers and constitution of a Force which will fit in with Imperial requirements'.[21] There was no incentive to change the prescription when, on 7 August, the British government accepted New Zealand's offer of an expeditionary force. Speed was considered of the essence, because of the prevailing view that the war would be short. Godley had made clear his belief that the powers could not afford to fight for long because modern industrial society could not stand for long the withdrawal of huge amounts of capital and labour. In his opinion, this, and the likely consequences of defeat, ensured that the initial clash would be very violent as both sides sought to settle the issue rapidly.[22] Massey's desire that New Zealand be first in the field with its contribution made any reconsideration of the planned contribution even less likely. He assured London that, if necessary, the force would be ready to leave within four weeks of the declaration of war. On 8 August he proudly proclaimed the likelihood 'that the first contingent to be dispatched to the assistance of the Empire from any part of the world will be dispatched from New Zealand'.[23]

There was no criticism either then or later about the decision to send a mixed infantry-mounted rifle force. Only recently has the suggestion been made that New Zealand should have concentrated on mounted riflemen. In his recent general history of New Zealand, James Belich indicts the New Zealand government of the time for not considering such an approach, which, he suggests, would have been more in keeping with the skills and aptitude of New Zealand's men and, above all, would have allowed them to avoid operating in the trenches of the Western Front. The siege-like nature of the fighting on that front was not, of course, envisaged by anyone in August 1914, but it certainly was by early 1916 when the decision was taken to create a New Zealand infantry division for service in France, leaving the mounted rifles brigade to serve in Egypt as part of an ANZAC division.

But could New Zealand have provided a full mounted division, even if it had wanted to? The experience of August 1914 suggests that it would have faced many practical difficulties. Massey's government feared that finding enough horses for the expeditionary force's mounted brigade would prove difficult. This did not prove to be the case – 3818 horses would eventually leave New Zealand with the NZEF's Main Body – but clearly a larger mounted force would have presented problems. 'There was not the number of suitable horses in the country there was before the Boer War', Massey lamented in Parliament on 9 September.[24]

Finding more than double the 3818 in August 1914, not only to mount the other brigade but also to train reinforcement drafts, would have been impossible. Acquiring horses from overseas sources when demand was high would have added immensely to the cost of New Zealand's war effort. The same practical obstacles stood in the way of forming a mounted division after the evacuation from Gallipoli in early 1916, a step that would have required two further mounted brigades. Given these practical considerations, it is not surprising that such a course was not seriously considered.

The other strand of New Zealand's war preparations was naval. Here again New Zealand's action has come under fire from James Belich. He criticises the government for scarcely even considering making a naval contribution the centrepiece of its war effort, another way in which, he suggests, it might have avoided the agony of the Western Front. Such action, he claims, 'would have stimulated industry more than an army', ensured 'more New Zealand say in strategy' and 'might have been just as useful to Britain as a military contribution'. He insists that the government, in failing to make a larger naval effort, disregarded 'its own direct interests', which demanded attention to the protection of New Zealand's cargo and troopships at sea.[25]

As with the composition of the NZEF, New Zealand's wartime response was determined by pre-war preparations, which were influenced by the resources available. To suggest that New Zealand should have concentrated on making a naval contribution in the First World War is really to suggest that New Zealand should have begun developing a navy at least four years before the war – the time taken by Australia to create the Royal Australian Navy. But what sort of navy could New Zealand have supported? Navies are expensive. They require not only expensive capital items but also full-time seamen to man them. Australia had just sufficient resources for a viable navy. New Zealand would have struggled. Even 90 years later, it faces difficulties in sustaining a minimal navy because of the capital cost of warships and the infrastructure needed to maintain them.

That New Zealand had not followed Australia's course was not an indication of lack of concern for naval defence. In the three decades leading up to the First World War it had in fact given considerable attention to its naval requirements. The primary method adopted was to subsidise the Royal Navy, initially to help ensure that sufficient warships were stationed in the South Pacific generally and New Zealand waters in particular to meet local defence needs but later to help ensure that the Royal Navy maintained its strategic edge over its main rival, the Imperial German Navy. New Zealand adhered to this system even after Australia moved in the direction of forming its own navy.

James Allen and the Reform Party pressed for New Zealand to follow Australia by creating a local New Zealand navy, but Ward and the ruling Liberals resisted such an approach. Building a navy seemed likely to leave New Zealand a junior partner in an Australasian naval effort, went against the concentrating trend of imperial naval policy and did not seem a sensible course in light of New Zealand's meagre resources and many domestic development needs. Nor would it meet New Zealand's naval requirements in terms of protecting the long sea routes between New Zealand and Britain. The Liberal government regarded subsidies to the Royal Navy as a more appropriate form of naval contribution than setting up a local force. The system developed after 1887 had allowed the training of New Zealanders in an Australian Auxiliary Squadron financed by the colonies.

But when Reform came to power in 1912, the way was opened for Allen, now as Minister of Defence, to pursue his goal. He managed to persuade the British authorities to help New Zealand make a start on its own naval training scheme. He looked to a time when New Zealand could maintain a small force that might co-operate with the newly formed Royal Australian Navy. The upshot was the assumption of control by New Zealand of the aging cruiser HMS *Philomel* as a training ship on 15 July 1914, even as the crisis in Europe was mounting.

Although New Zealand handed the ship over to the Admiralty once war began, it represented no great addition to imperial naval strength. Its condition was so decrepit – a product of its age and prolonged neglect during its previous service in the Persian Gulf area – that it had little combat value. It would spend most of the war in a gunboat role in the peripheral Red Sea area.

Given the state of New Zealand naval resources in August 1914, there was little more that New Zealand could have done in this field after handing over *Philomel* and sending off naval reservists in New Zealand. It had no chance of acquiring more vessels from Britain after war began: the Royal Navy needed all available ships. New Zealand did not have the industrial capacity to embark on a major shipbuilding programme. It could perhaps have sought to purchase more ships from neutrals, but how would it have manned them? Most of *Philomel*'s crew, after all, were British personnel on loan. Even those New Zealanders trained under the pre-war naval scheme and serving in the Australian Squadron – this group had refused invitations to transfer to the New Zealand naval forces earlier in 1914[26] – would not have sufficed. In any case, the legislation setting up the New Zealand naval forces provided for Admiralty control of any New Zealand warships in wartime – or even if war became imminent.

New Zealand could, however, have provided men over and above the reservists to the Royal Navy, as it would do on a considerable scale in the Second World War. But in August 1914 the Royal Navy had more men than it could accommodate on the ships it then had available. So many men were surplus that First Lord of the Admiralty Churchill set about forming them into an infantry division – the Royal Naval Division. It was in this unit that Bernard Freyberg, arriving from North America, secured a commission. Had New Zealand insisted on providing men for the Royal Navy they would most probably have ended up serving as infantry in this or a similar naval division and probably on the same fronts that the NZEF would serve on (the Royal Naval Division served both at Gallipoli and on the Western Front). In such a unit they would have had even less national identification than a New Zealand infantry division.

Although *Philomel* added little to imperial naval strength, New Zealand had made a more direct contribution: the battlecruiser HMS *New Zealand*. Built as a result of a dramatic offer made by Sir Joseph Ward in 1909 at a time of a scare about the state of the Anglo-German naval arms building race, she formed part of the Grand Fleet, the main British naval concentration facing the German fleet on the other side of the North Sea. Some consideration had been given to stationing her in the Pacific region before the war, as part of an ill-considered 1909 plan to build a Pacific battlefleet, but New Zealand had readily agreed to her being stationed in the North Sea. It was not just that the ship had been given to Britain without strings attached; the New Zealand authorities recognised that a defeat by the German fleet would rip away the foundations upon which New Zealand's security rested.

The protection of New Zealand's trade was left to the Royal Navy, which had the necessary ships and bases to provide it in the area of most danger, the Atlantic approaches to the British Isles. Given the nature of New Zealand's defence strategy – adherence to imperial defence in which trade protection was approached as a co-ordinated worldwide system controlled by the Admiralty – and the mutual interest of both British and New Zealand governments in the safe passage of the trade, this was a sensible arrangement. Nothing New Zealand could have done on its own initiative would have reduced significantly the losses suffered among 'New Zealand' ships on the trade routes to Britain. Accusations that it neglected this aspect of its defence requirements are misplaced.[27] The losses were, in any case, largely attributable to faulty tactics, not a shortage of material. Once the Admiralty, reluctantly, resorted to the age-old tactic of moving merchant shipping in protected convoys late in 1917, the U-boat menace was contained.

The occupation of German Samoa

The first naval task undertaken by the New Zealand naval forces was the protection of the Samoa Expeditionary Force, which left Wellington on 15 August 1914. This operation arose from a British request, on 7 August 1914, that New Zealand send an expeditionary force to seize the wireless station near Apia as 'a great and urgent Imperial service'.[28] For a country that had long aspired to control Samoa, such a request was most welcome, and not unexpected. Exchanges between Godley and British military authorities in 1913 had indicated that New Zealand might have the task of seizing German Samoa in the event of war.[29] Not surprisingly New Zealand responded to the invitation with alacrity, quickly raising a 1370-man force.

The departure of what was initially termed the 'advance guard' of the NZEF focused attention not only on the strength of the enemy forces available to intercept it at sea but also on those likely to oppose it at Samoa. The former comprised the ships of the German East Asiatic Squadron commanded by Vice-Admiral Graf (Count) Maximilian von Spee. Their operating base was at Tsingtao in China, but at the outset of the war they were in the Caroline Islands. The main units were the armoured cruisers *Scharnhorst* and *Gneisenau*, both mounting 8.2-inch guns.

The government is reputed to have asked London what defences there were in Samoa, and to have been enjoined by the British Colonial Secretary to 'See *Whitaker's Almanac*'.[30] This at least was the recollection of Minister of Marine F.M.B. Fisher, as published by Downie Stewart in 1937.[31] But a careful search at Archives New Zealand could find no evidence of such an exchange. Despite the continuing credence given to it by New Zealand historians,[32] the story is almost certainly apocryphal. In reality New Zealand looked to Australia for advice about likely forces in Samoa. The authorities in Melbourne duly advised that there was in Samoa a German-officered constabulary of about 80 men and a gunboat. The possibility of this force being augmented by reservists from merchant ships or men from warships was not overlooked.[33]

When the force left on 15 August, *Philomel* and two imperial cruisers of not much greater capacity, HMS *Pyramus* and *Psyche*, escorted it. Nobody had any illusions that these aged warships could have lasted 'five minutes' against von Spee's squadron.[34] For this reason the Admiralty had arranged for the force to rendezvous at Fiji with the Australian battlecruiser *Australia*, more than a match for *Scharnhorst* and *Gneisenau* with her 12-inch guns, and a French cruiser. But there was a misunderstanding about this plan, and when the Samoa Expeditionary Force was a day out of New Zealand it was diverted to Noumea. No advice of this change was sent to Wellington. Apart from the need for radio silence, the troops were regarded as an imperial responsibility once they sailed. So the change did not prove a problem for Massey when he eventually learned of it, though later commentators have, with some justification, tended to regard it as evidence of New Zealand's loss of control over its troops. Certainly, the British government was remiss in not advising Wellington of the change. The change increased misgivings in the Cabinet about the wisdom of sending the force north with such an inadequate escort. Allen, five years later, would recall that the government had been 'very, very anxious' for days after the force left Wellington.[35] There is no truth, however, in the assertion, first made in the account of the expedition published in 1923, that the force 'narrowly escaped disaster' on the night of 19–20 August when the 'Scharnhorst and Gneisenau... had passed south'.[36] Fisher claimed that the German cruiser missed the troopships 'by less than fifteen miles'.[37] This no doubt forms the basis for Michael King's assertion in his history of New Zealand that the German cruisers passed within 25 kilometres of the troopships in the night as they made for Noumea.[38] In fact von Spee's squadron was well to the north at this time, and at no stage operated near New Caledonia. Two days before the Samoa Expeditionary Force set sail, von Spee had decided to head for the west coast of South America.[39]

When the New Zealand troops landed at Apia on 29 August, they met no opposition. Much was made of the fact, both then and since, that this was the first enemy territory to fall to imperial forces,[40] but in fact this is yet another myth. The honour of securing the first German colonial prize went to British forces that had ended German resistance in the West African territory of Togoland four days before the landing at Apia.[41] The occupation of Samoa did, however, lead to the first New Zealand–German armed confrontation of the war, when Scharnhorst and Gneisenau appeared off Apia on 14 September. The gunners of D Battery, deployed with their 15-pounders and 6-pounders on the beach, found themselves looking down the barrels of the German cruisers, but no shots were exchanged. The risk of destroying German property was thought to be the reason for von Spee's restraint, especially as he had no qualms about destroying French property at Papeete eight days later.

The dispatch of the NZEF

The Main Body of the NZEF had, in the meantime, been readied for departure. Volunteers had come forward in droves – some 14,000 in the first week of the war alone[42] – and the pre-war preparations now paid dividends. Massey was able to tell London that the force could if necessary leave before the end of August, though he indicated that a few weeks' delay would be helpful. In the event, the departure date was set as 25 September, despite the fact that the location of von Spee's squadron was not known for certain. A 'very uneasy' government decided to take the risk because the alternative appeared to be a delay of six weeks, while a stronger escort was arranged.[43] Such a delay would mean that the Australian expeditionary force would be in the field well before New Zealand's: the Admiralty had indicated that it would not postpone the AIF's departure to await the New Zealanders. Two ships from Auckland put to sea on the 24th with the intention of linking up with the eight other troopships that would leave Wellington next day. But during the night Massey received a cable from the Australian Governor-General suggesting, incorrectly as it later transpired, that ships crossing the Tasman might be in serious jeopardy. The two Auckland ships were hastily recalled. Fisher later recalled seeing Massey during the night 'sitting at the head of the Cabinet table, his head on his hands, and great beads of perspiration standing out on his large head' as he awaited news that the ships had returned safely.[44] The troops in Wellington, already on their ships, were disembarked next morning.

After this scare Massey resolved not to let the NZEF depart without an adequate escort. He would have faced serious political problems in taking any other course: several ministers, including especially Minister of Internal Affairs and leader of the Legislative Council Francis Dillon Bell, threatened to resign unless adequate provision was made. Even when evidence mounted that von Spee's squadron was heading for the eastern Pacific, Massey's approach remained unchanged. News of the raid on Papeete prompted the naval authorities to again raise the possibility of the NZEF moving across the Tasman to join the AIF. When the Governor, Lord Liverpool, represented these views to Massey, the Prime Minister jibbed. Liverpool appears to have suggested that he could take responsibility, as Commander-in-Chief of the New Zealand forces, for dispatching the force. Almost certainly he was trying to find a way around Massey's political problem – his unwillingness to take responsibility for sending the force with any shadow of risk. When Massey said that any attempt to follow such a course would be followed by his immediate resignation, Liverpool desisted, thereby avoiding a constitutional crisis that would no doubt have had important implications for New Zealand's war effort. As it was Massey remained bitter about the Admiralty's attitude: three years later in London he insisted that 'it was a risk which we should not have been asked to take'.[45]

Even advice that radio intercepts placed the German squadron in the vicinity of Easter Island received on 4 October left Massey unmoved. When the NZEF eventually left Wellington 12 days later, the heavy cruiser HMS *Minotaur* and the

Japanese semi-battlecruiser *Ibuki* accompanied it. Crossing the Tasman, it rendezvoused with the AIF at King George's Sound in Western Australia, and set off with it across the Indian Ocean with the intention of passing through the Suez Canal. The crossing was marked by HMAS *Sydney*'s sinking of the detached German cruiser *Emden* at the Cocos Islands, an incident that merely confirmed the New Zealand government's earlier concern about the adequacy of the escort. Commander of the NZEF Godley believed that the convoy had had a narrow escape: had *Emden* learned of its passing, he later wrote to Colonel A. W. Robin in Wellington, 'she would have steamed into the middle of us, and started firing torpedoes right and left until she had sunk half a dozen of us, and the ships of our escort could not have replied without hitting some of us'.[46]

In Massey's and Allen's eyes the escort problems seemed to have justified the government's pre-war approach to naval policy. Allen acclaimed *Sydney*'s victory over *Emden* as the 'complete answer' to those who had objected to this policy.[47] On the face of it, New Zealand's pre-war naval policy had not proved capable of meeting the country's local naval needs, but of course these were only part of the national naval requirements. Although Massey and Allen accepted that nothing could be done for the duration of the war, they were determined to press on with the policy of creating a local New Zealand navy when peace returned.

The troops of the NZEF expected that they would shortly be in action with the Germans on the Western Front, but such expectations were soon dashed. While the Australasian convoy was crossing the Indian Ocean, the Ottoman Empire entered the war on the side of the Central Powers, Germany and Austria-Hungary. Worried about the security of the Suez Canal, the vital imperial link, the British authorities decided to disembark the two expeditionary forces in Egypt as a precautionary measure. This was a wise move, for, as noted above, the Ottomans advanced towards the Suez Canal in early 1915. Some New Zealand units were deployed, and in the relatively limited fighting that developed the NZEF suffered its first combat death.

Conclusion

New Zealand had acted with much speed to hoist its colours with those of the empire. In less than two months after the King's declaration of war it had raised two expeditionary forces, the equivalent, on a per head of population basis, to the raising of a 400,000-strong British force.[48] Its capacity to do so reflected not only the preparatory work of the preceding four years but also the mood of the population, determined to make a contribution as quickly as possible, and hopefully earlier than any other dominion, to the collective effort. New Zealanders believed that this was their war, and that they should share the burden – and the glory. Massey and his ministers had made mistakes: their determination to send the force as soon as possible even led them, briefly, to accept some risks to the safety of both expeditionary forces. But in the case of the NZEF they had resisted pressure from London to act before suitably powerful warships arrived to ensure the safety of the force. The escort problems with both expeditionary forces had been a rude awakening to the implications, and dangers, of relying on the Admiralty. They made a deep impression on the senior New Zealand ministers. Coming on top of difficult negotiations with the Admiralty immediately before the war, they reminded Massey and Allen of the need vigorously to defend the dominion's interests within the imperial framework. The events of August– October 1914 provided a microcosm of the problems New Zealand would face in other spheres of the war effort over the next four years.

3

THE RECEPTION OF BELGIAN REFUGEES IN EUROPE: A LITMUS TEST OF WARTIME SOCIAL MOBILISATION

Pierre Purseigle

In October 1914, in the district of Waipu, local Maori gathered around a flagstaff especially erected to hoist the Belgian flag under the national ensign. This symbolic gesture was meant to convey the admiration aroused by the Belgian nation, which since 1 August had been suffering invasion by Germany. Through a revealing process of identification, one chief equated Britain's former dominance over the Maori with the sort of 'paternal care' that was now being extended to Belgium in its battle against the Kaiser's armies. Maori, he said, had met to honour the flag of the Belgians, 'a people who had raised … the hurdles over which the enemy would have to jump before New Zealand could be reached.'[1]

The chiefs' speeches provide an insight into New Zealand perceptions of the events taking place in north-west Europe, and of Belgium's place in them. On 25 November, the headmaster of Roseneath School in Wellington wrote to the Belgian Consul to tell him that the school children had 'spontaneously decided to forego [sic] their picnic and prizes and donate the whole of the net proceeds [of their annual garden fête] to the Belgian Relief Fund'.[2] That the fate of Belgium could prompt such a response from its remotest ally indicated that the New Zealand population was aroused to action in a similar fashion to other Allied participants. The image of Gallant Little Belgium has always received the critical attention of historians, if only because of a desire to deconstruct Allied propaganda. But the same cannot be said of the Belgian refugees. Their fate has been consigned to the margins of both the historiography and the collective memory of the First World War.[3]

The invasion of Belgium in August 1914 is notable not merely for the military operations involved. In the first weeks of the war, the German army's advance also highlighted the civilian dimensions of the conflict and its characteristic 'totalising logic'.[4] More than a million Belgian men, women and children fled from their homes before the German tide and went into an exile that would last for the duration of the war.

This exodus of people led to an unprecedented encounter between Belgian civilians and the communities of the Allied nations in which they sought refuge, mainly in France and Great Britain. A cultural history of this encounter may shed some light on the nature of home front responses to the war in these countries. In fact, the contact of Belgian refugees with the Allies' home fronts brought into sharpened focus the issues at stake and helped to establish the ethos of home front involvement in the war. The reception of Belgian refugees reveals the strengths and tensions of the process of social mobilisation at work within the belligerent societies.

Obviously, full justice cannot be done here to the scope and complexities of such a topic. Treatment will be confined to Britain and France, with only passing references to the Netherlands and Switzerland. Locating the 'Belgian refugee' within the war culture will underline the significance that their experiences ought to have in the historiography of the Great War. Furthermore, analysis of the humanitarian response to their situation will throw light on the social mobilisation of the Allied societies concerned. Ultimately, there was a shift in perception of the refugees that helped ensure that their wartime ordeal would fade from public memory.

The Belgian refugee in the war culture
The historiography of the Great War has stressed the importance of the 1914–18 'war culture'. This wartime system of representation both enlisted and translated the cultural, moral, and ideological commitment of each nation to

fight an uncivilised enemy to the bitter end, since not to do so might lead to the destruction of its own culture, identity and way of life. Industrialised warfare was thus construed as a life-and-death struggle and in some cases as a crusade.[5] Even so, the war experience led to a constant reconfiguration of that conception. A cultural history of refugeedom in the First World War indeed reveals a many-faceted experience.

A point of crystallisation

The 'refugees' helped create and also embodied the war culture. Their prominence in the war narratives encouraged a vision of the conflagration as a war for civilisation against barbarity, one waged in confident expectation of retribution in the form of reparations. The singularity of refugees' experience conferred upon them a distinctive place in communities that had been spared the horrors of actual military operations. Rallying under the common flag of a sacred cause, the victims of invasion found refuge with their outraged 'brothers-in-arms', indignant over the treatment that had been meted out to them. Refugees thus appeared to be the overwhelmed victims of a cruel conflict.[6] The French and British civil societies fully recognised the disproportionate ordeal they were going through, and of the unequal distribution of the burden of war.[7]

Refugees were considered as heroes. Their very presence at the rear was testimony to the courageous resistance that their nations had put up to the invader. In wartime Paris, tributes to Belgium and other invaded countries loomed large in the work of patriotic songwriters, thus attesting to the significance of the refugee in the popular culture.[8]

Accordingly, the assistance provided to the Belgian refugees became 'a striking tribute to the country which commanded the world's admiration'.[9] As a New Zealander put it then: 'This is not charity: it is justice. But for these fellows we should be eating sauerkraut and drinking lager already'.[10]

Perceptions of refugees were shaped by the manner in which they left the battle zones. They embodied the sufferings and distress brought about by the invasion, and their arrival in French and British towns had a big impact on local populations. As one English observer wrote, 'No one could describe that occur[rence], you should live in it to realize it – the sad, weary faces of those poor homeless, penniless people some having lost their children & relations in the [illegible].'[11] And a French paper reported:

> *A la gare de l'Est.*
>
> *L'animation est toujours aussi grande aux abords de la Gare de l'Est, où une foule, anxieuse ne cesse d'attendre jusqu'à une heure avancée de la nuit les réfugiés autour desquels chacun s'empresse.... L'exode des départements envahis continue toujours. C'est un défilé lamentable de pauvres hères qui emportent avec eux tout ce qui leur reste. Il est difficile de voir plus triste spectacle.*[12]

The Times put it like this:

> This invasion has turned London into a city where allied tongues may be heard everywhere. In omnibuses and trains, in the shops and theatres one sees foreigners and one listens to foreign speech.... The bulk of London's French and Belgian guests are women and children, whose men are under arms but have sent their families to the safety of a sea-girt home. Yesterday, the Government gave an official welcome to the homeless victims of the barbarian, but the people, as we know, had not waited for an official pronouncement.[13]

The refugees' experience and their contact with the enemy fostered the hatred of the enemy that soon lay at the heart of war culture. It was strengthened by recourse to sacred images and words.[14] Besides the ideological vindication of the conflict, from August 1914 the war culture focused on the person of the enemy, the 'Boche', the 'Hun', illustrating, as Jeismann put it, a process of 'ethnicisation of the historical and political consciousness'.[15]

Assisting the refugees: a wartime duty

The refugees were gratified by their reception. It constituted, according to *The Times* in London, the 'country's obligation of honour',[16] a duty, which the authorities conjured up to underline the demands of wartime solidarity.[17] Home front generosity provided the basis for the assistance to the first civilian victims of the invasion, who were obviously in dire need of both material and moral support.[18]

Furthermore, the reception of refugees linked morality and law, since there was a need to institute legal measures to reflect the moral demand of reparation for the harm suffered by the refugees.[19] In France, parliamentary debates as well as prefectorial archives disclose the extent to which this moral dimension underpinned both the legal protection of the refugee and public policies.

> *En toute circonstance, tant au parlement qu'au cours des instructions renouvelées de mon administration, il a été proclamée que l'assistance aux réfugiés correspond à une véritable dette contractée par la nation à l'égard d'une catégorie de citoyens qui a eu à supporter la plus lourde part des misères provoquées par la guerre ou des sacrifices exigés par la défense nationale. Il en est résulté que cette assistance ne constitue pas une faveur qu'il est loisible d'accorder ou de refuser aux intéressés dans des conditions qui laissent place à l'arbitraire, mais un droit réel....* [20]

The reception of First World War refugees also derived great importance from its patriotic character.[21] In repeatedly invoking this aspect, the authorities were above all concerned with bolstering their own population's confidence and countering the adverse effects on morale of the refugees' fate. The preservation of morale in this respect was an aspect of the wider national defence actions that the *Union Sacrée* – or its British equivalent, the Party Truce – had imposed upon the people of France and Britain.

Figures and functions of the refugee

The experience of 'Belgium in exile' must not be reduced to a limited set of discourses and symbolic productions. Reconstructing the actual situation of the refugees, both as individuals and collectively, is the critical task of the historian.[22] It is one made all the more difficult by the symbolic and emotional response to the fate of the invasion's victims. Hence, in the same way as historians now distinguish the cultural perception of the 1914 German atrocities from what actually happened, it is important to distinguish between perception and reality in relation to refugees.[23] The history of the 'refugee' is inseparable from that of the 1914 atrocities. These indeed provide the backdrop to the refugees' experience, and it is important to bear in mind the ways in which they were produced, disseminated and used.[24] On their arrival as well as in the course of their settlement, Belgian refugees functioned as vehicles for depictions of the enemy. Belgian and French refugees arriving at the Gare du Nord in Paris told of 'dreadful things'.[25] According to *The Times*:

> as they sit there they are talking about one thing – of what the 'Bosches' [*sic*] have done to the villages they have passed through already. 'They cut the hands off the little boys, so that there shall be no more soldiers for France. They kill the women, and the things they do to the young girls, monsieur, are too terrible to be told. They burn everything and steal and destroy. Back there is nothing but wilderness.'[26]

Among people who had been spared the horrors of the invasion, the refugees' descriptions of the invasion seemed all the more authoritative for their direct personal experience. Thus, in the French primary schools, as a deputy-prefect put it:

> The little refugees quickly become important. They tell what they saw. We gather around them. The teacher shows a bit more of tenderness towards them. They are back from the front. Sometimes, one even calls them *les poilus*.[27]

The importance of the role played by the 'refugees' in the process of mobilisation is revealed in the social functions they performed among the British and French populations. The refugees' distress helped to mobilise these communities because it fitted current objectives. The idea was then to 'create around the war victims a brotherly and affectionate atmosphere',[28] which would testify to that 'magnificent national unity, which, out of all French souls makes one single enthusiastic and vibrating soul: the very soul of France'.[29] Despite its uniqueness, refugees' experience played a part in creating the all-important national unity with the very existence of the nation at stake. The solidarity revealed by the reception of refugees also illustrated an important negative dimension to the integration and engagement of nations bracing themselves for the onslaught of a hated enemy. Not merely war victims, the refugees had fallen prey to a 'barbaric' enemy. In fact, when a French local newspaper set out to compare 'their practices and ours' and to castigate 'the breaches of the rule of war', it felt the need to do no more than describe 'how they [were] treating the Belgians'.[30]

The refugees' situation, as innocent victims of military operations that went beyond the bounds of traditional laws of war, reinforced the notion that the war must be fought to the bitter end. The war was seen in social-Darwinist and ethnic terms as a life-and-death struggle.[31] The image of the Belgians was bound up in a perception of the war in which the 'refugee' figured prominently. In a nutshell, the term 'refugees' was a code word for the stakes involved in the war. It provided a basis for mobilising the home front.

A litmus test of social mobilisation

Surprised by the flood of refugees, British, Belgian and French commentators constantly resorted to maritime metaphors to describe it, conjuring up the 'Teutonic tide' and its 'formidable waves'.[32]

> Since the devastation of that heroic little land began, its inhabitants have turned to England, their only available shelter, and a stream of fugitives, largely destitutes, has set in to our shores. At first, it trickled, it now flows strongly, and it may yet become a cataract. Whatever the magnitude, it must not only be received, but welcomed and instantly provided for, until this tempest be overpast.[33]

The waves of refugees caught Allied authorities by surprise, but they strove to respond to the situation amidst the confusion of mobilisation for war. National organisations such as the War Refugees Committee (WRC) or the *Secours National*, supported by the British and French governments respectively, laid the institutional and legal foundations of the reception, while local refugee committees provided the personnel that dealt with the arriving refugees. The number of such local committees created in England eventually stabilised at around 1500 in 1915. Most of these committees, which represented the compassionate face of the welcome to refugees, had been formed spontaneously on the initiative of local worthies, notable individuals, or existing institutions or communities.[34] The Newport refugees committee perfectly illustrates the process. On 16 September 1914, the mayor convened a meeting at which volunteers concerned about the welfare of Belgian refugees formed a committee.

Following a public appeal, offers of hospitality were forwarded to the WRC. In the meantime, the committee was enlarged to include various personalities and organisations representative of the community. Anxious to retain official endorsement, the committee kept the mayor as its chairman. The free and regular collaboration of the local newspapers, the *South Wales Argus* and the *Monmouthshire Evening Post*, proved beneficial.[35]

Beyond these organisational aspects though, the appearance of Belgian refugees in the rear areas constituted a decisive and significant moment for the belligerent societies – one in which they were brought face to face with the realities and disasters of modern warfare. Parisian newspapers recounted the dramatic impact which the 'painful sight' of the arriving refugees had on civilians.[36] Similar scenes were also taking place at Folkestone, the refugees' gateway to Britain, where 'each boat was carrying a contingent always worthier of help and pity'.[37] In London, the reception and distribution of refugees was organised at Victoria, Charing Cross and Liverpool Street stations. In Northampton, where about 200 refugees reached their final destination, they had brought along the distress of war.

> The arrival of the first batches of Belgians here, and train loads on their way north brought home to us the tragedy of their martyred country.... Kind hearted ladies were ready at the station with steaming coffee, buns, sweets, which they eagerly devoured, smiling wondrously the while at the contrast between their reception here and the horrors from which they had fled.[38]

During the first weeks of the conflict, when the restriction of information prevented civilians from knowing what was going on at the front, the arrival of Belgian refugees constituted one of their first exposures to the consequences of the conflict. In those same stations where the tragedy of separation had been played out as sons, husbands, brothers and fathers left for the front, the tragedy of the refugees was now unfolding.

> One evening another and myself were sent to Charing Cross to meet a late train, after waiting, an hour in the very dimly lighted station we went to the trains, [which] at the last moment, were all being sent into Victoria & we were hurrying

out when a young man came up to us seeing our sashes and asked if we spoke French & then told us his pathetic story – he was trying to meet all the refugee trains to find his mother & sisters – refugees from Brussels – & apparently had been doing this for nights....[39]

Intermediary communities and reception of refugees

At the outbreak of the hostilities, communities of all sizes attempted to cope with the catastrophe. Knowing of Belgium's Catholic heritage, private or official organisations were anxious to involve local Catholics and their charitable associations in the relief efforts. In Northampton, the latter had in fact taken the initiative before realising that they had insufficient resources and calling upon other denominational or social groups to help. Likewise, at the suggestion of the WRC, the Catholic Women's League (CWL) took charge of welcoming refugees at the stations. Refugees recognised the league's volunteers by the white sashes they wore with '*Ligue des Femmes Catholiques*' written across them in black letters.[40] CWL volunteer Miss Essington-Nelson described meeting trains at Victoria and Charing Cross:

> When the trains arrived we helped in the sorting, ourselves trying to find the Belgians from French, Russians, American & even Armenians. Girl guides were there with coffee, soup, etc. & the women's emergency corps was doing excellent work. At one end of the station a man, appointed for the task, sat on a raised platform with lists of hotels, boarding houses & lodgings with the prices, for those who could pay for themselves ... After helping them into the motor busses we left them to pass out, amid the cheers of the crowds outside, to the different depôt[s] where the first nights were always spent in order to register them.[41]

Though mainly Roman Catholic, Belgium, like other European nations, had a diversified religious composition, as illustrated by the charitable work carried out along denominational lines by the Jewish War Refugees Committee.[42]

The reception of refugees highlights the mechanisms underlying the collective response to the war. Its emphasis on unity must be re-evaluated in the light of discriminatory processes that both propped up the war effort of local communities and reinforced national mobilisations. The support provided to refugees demonstrates the importance of specific group solidarities for the general war effort. The *Amicale des instituteurs et institutrices de l'Hérault* (Friendly Association of Primary Teachers) provides an example of professional solidarity redirected in favour of the Belgian refugees. Among its various initiatives, the association set up a special relief fund, the *Franc des Camarades Belges*, by which French primary teachers supported their Belgian counterparts.[43] Likewise, the Railway Executive Committee, on behalf of the British Railways, decided to offer hospitality to Belgian railwaymen, while the National Fire Union held its hand out to Belgian fire-fighters.[44]

Civil societies thus consented to a formidable effort, particularly in favour of the Belgian refugees. However, this massive involvement appeared somewhat paradoxical. Civil society's spontaneous mobilisation helped the state to cope with the crisis of war, but the conflict led, in due course, to a strengthening of the state's control over civil society.[45]

Before long, as charitable energy faltered, the state was forced to bolster and in places supplant private philanthropy in order to sustain the refugees.[46] Two chronologies – material support to refugees and attitudes to refugees – converged but did not perfectly coincide with each other.

As early as 1915, local and national organisations noticed a worrying drying up of the financial resources they had previously tapped.[47] In response, the WRC and the Local Government Board launched a remobilisation campaign that ceased only with the repatriations following the war. Herbert Samuel, the chairman of the board, forwarded to the British press on 7 January 1915 a letter outlining the principles that governed refugee relief. It contrasted the British effort with that of neutral Holland:

> The sympathy of the British people for the Belgians had shown itself, among other ways, by the widespread offer of hospitality to the refugees. Committees in many of the towns and counties, and individuals throughout the country, have gladly given shelter and maintenance to some scores of thousands of those who have been obliged to abandon homes laid desolate by the German invaders. But the small country of Holland is generously giving refuge to twice as many Belgians as Britain.... In view of all that these refugees have suffered and of all

that Belgium has done for the cause of the Allies, I trust that it is only necessary
for the present urgent need to be made known to the country in order to evoke
a response adequate to meet the situation.[48]

Admittedly, shortages and economic disturbances weighed heavily on private
initiative, of which the middle and upper classes were the backbone. But the
discrepancy between this chronology and that of the national mobilisations,
whose crisis began in 1916,[49] helped turn the refugees' reception into a
paradoxical confrontation.

From solidarity to oblivion

Up to the beginning of 1915, the refugees' fate symbolised the barbaric nature
of German warfare: they were regarded as heroic victims of German militarism
and treated as such. Yet from 1915 onwards tensions surfaced and relations
between the Belgians and their hosts deteriorated. 'Boches du Nord', 'Dirty
Belgians', 'German' and other terms of abuse were hurled at the exiles, who
unsurprisingly resented them. Their representatives were prompted to call for
due respect to be shown to refugees.[50] Even though physical confrontations and
clashes were rare, an anti-Belgian riot broke out in May 1916 in London. The
crowd subjected Belgian citizens and property to the type of treatment it had
inflicted on identified or suspected Germans after the outbreak of the war.
Allied refugees and enemy were lumped together, as a letter by a Fulham
inhabitant reveals:

> The Belgians here are causing a lot of trouble. On Sunday, they nearly murdered
> a policeman and a soldier and yesterday the English people and kids collected in
> hundreds in Liller [illegible] Rd where a lot of Belgians have opened shops & last
> night the scene was beyond description. They have served them like they served
> Landsowne and the other Germans. Windows & shops smashed up everywhere.
> With the Irish Germans etc. now the Belgians we have our share of the
> troubles.[51]

Little by little, such prejudices, frustrations and sufferings soured relations
between the Belgian refugees and their hosts.

The diary of Miss Coules, written in London between June 1914 and November 1915, describes the successive changes of perspective among the British population:

> Everyone was Belgian mad for a time. Mother helped furnish a home for Belgians & gave a monthly subscription & Mercedes got up a choir of 20 girls – we called ourselves the Black Dominoes, as we wore long black cloaks and masks – to sing the national anthems of the allies in the streets, in aid of the Belgians. We made quite a considerable sum, & it was great fun. But the Belgians are not grateful. They won't do a stroke of work & grumble at everything & their morals…! It may be true enough that Belgium saved Europe, but… save us from the Belgians! As far as I am concerned, Belgianitis has quite abated.[52]

An interesting testimony to the fickleness of some sections of the British upper class, Coules's comments state the main criticisms of Belgian refugees: their lack of enthusiasm for work and alienating mores and lifestyles. Obviously, there were dubious and shady individuals among the refugees. Nevertheless, Belgians, Britons or French concurred in admitting the small proportion of problematic characters and agreed that this ought not to have led to systematic generalisations and condemnations. From London to Wales, from Paris to the French provinces, the mundane and commonplace qualities and flaws displayed by the refugees were acknowledged.

To a certain extent, the home front ambivalence towards participation in the war effort underlay attitudes towards Belgian exiles. Barred from the 'Myth of the War Experience',[53] civilians were fully aware of being ancillaries to the conduct of a war that was embodied in the figures of the Tommy and the *poilu*. Social practices as well as language and symbolism were moulded by a wartime morality – an 'ethics of mobilisation' – that undeniably relied on traditional social codes and visions of social order.[54] The frontline soldier stood out as the principal character and role model in this narrative, which highlighted the need for duty, sacrifice and solidarity among the civilian population.[55] However, as the war dragged on, owing to the military stalemate, the home front came to formulate its part in the national script in a different way. Although the soldier still retained his prominent character, civilian populations became involved in a process of victimisation caused by restrictions and hardships and, above all, the grief stemming from soaring casualties.

With attitudes reinforced by deep and reciprocal ignorance,[56] and the alien quality of the refugees evident from their language and classification, public perception of them changed. Refugees were no longer viewed with the same sympathy that had greeted them on arrival. With every family in France and Britain now facing grief and mourning, refugees found themselves being accused of enjoying a safe and idle stay and of grim opportunism:

> How fast do the deaths go; and how many of our Belgian friends seem to have confused and vague memories of what they suffered. Let's not incriminate these friends. Moreover, they suffer as well, in their flesh, in their heart, in their interests; today, everyone attends to one's own pain.[57]

The growing disappointment of the host communities matched the initially sympathetic perception of the 'refugee', which eventually turned against the exiles themselves, who became the victims of their hosts' self-delusion, as a French deputy-prefect conceded in 1915:

> We tended to make ascetics and martyrs of the refugees. They are men like the others, but they suffered more than the others: this should make us admire their qualities more than we do, and make us more lenient towards their flaws.[58]

Local populations no longer ascribed any dignifying quality to the refugees and increasingly demanded from them a total participation in the war effort.[59] To counter this trend, Madame Vandervelde, a notable Belgian, toured Britain denouncing growing misunderstandings and abuses. As the *Glasgow Herald* reported:

> On one occasion, when 300 brave Belgian soldiers had arrived at Liverpool Street Station, after making their way out of their own country occupied by the enemy by hairbreadth escapes on their way to join the fighting forces, a comment was made in the press as to why these men were making a hiding place of England. The rumour once started gained currency at the expense of a country

always willing to give to the uttermost of its manpower. Several times young Belgians had come to her in her office in the most absolute despair because they had been insulted in the streets by people who said they ought to be fighting.[60]

Chronology here proves particularly meaningful since the negative attitude towards refugees was not affected by either the morale dip of 1917 or the military successes of 1918.

A comparison of the situation in other countries, such as neutral Switzerland or Holland, would be illuminating. In the very different geopolitical context of Switzerland especially, there were striking similarities in the mechanisms of mobilisation and the solidarities displayed in favour of the Belgian refugees.[61] A strong case can be made for a comprehensive study of the reception of French refugees, for it reflected the inner strains of imperial societies at war. Significantly, the prominence given to French victims of the military operations in France did not prove sufficiently resilient to overcome regional tensions and linguistic otherness within the national community.[62] Refugees from Alsace-Lorraine and the northern regions actually suffered slanders from their southern fellow citizens, who, mistaking them for German speakers, hurled at them the abusive term 'Boche' ('Hun'). Evidence garnered from official scrutiny of mail bore out the recurrence of these feuds, suggesting that the 'gap between the North and the South (*Midi*) seemed to grow wider'.[63] In fact, social mobilisations rested on discriminatory processes that may have turned out to be successively inclusive and exclusive. They were at any rate rooted in the social fabric of the belligerent societies and strongly correlated to the pre-war national unification of France and Britain.

I am nonetheless wary of concluding that bitterness and tensions obliterated the refugees' gratitude. Undeniably, the British and French communities that welcomed them derived a legitimate and well-founded pride from the help they provided. In fact, this inter-Allied solidarity was celebrated on several occasions even before the refugees' repatriation, as occurred, for example, in 1916 in Cardiff, where the refugees planted a tree in tribute to the city's hospitality.[64] Yet, the singular experience of the refugees soon slipped from the collective memory. They would be counted among '*les oubliés de la Grande Guerre*', those we forgot. I would indeed suggest, as Annette Becker has pointed out with regard to the occupied populations, civil deportees and prisoners of war, that this relative obscurity derived from a long-lasting disregard for the complex processes of victimisation within the belligerent societies.[65] The experience of Belgian refugees is typical of the problems of memory that confront historians:

> Soldiers had a chance to become heroes; but no refugee was lionized. Even in death, military and civilian casualties were accorded different treatment. There are no war graves for the thousands of refugees who died en route to a 'place of safety'. The literature of war scarcely paid them any attention. No Owen or Remarque dwelt on their plight; no 'passing-bells' tolled for the refugees who moved – and sometimes died – like cattle. The contrast deserves to be included in the ironies of the First World War.[66]

Although Peter Gatrell does not here take into account changes over time in the characterisation of 'refugees', he certainly underlines a common feature of the predicament of the First World War's exiles. In Belgium itself, the refugees were conspicuous by their absence from the commemorations and the memorials erected following the war.[67] Ultimately, the neglect of the refugee experience, in both collective memory and academic circles, can be attributed to its transitional nature.[68]

A comparative and trans-national study of refugee experience in the First World War along the lines sketched above would be valuable. My perspective obviously owes a massive debt to the growing interest in the cultural history of the Great War. However, the history of Belgian refugees above all demonstrates the irrelevance of the division that is traditionally drawn in the historiography of war between the military, cultural and social dimensions. The very displacement of those populations bore witness to the coming in Western Europe of the age of 'total war'.[69] Although military operations on the Western Front directly affected only a minority of civilians, they were characterised by 'the growing, deliberate implication of civilians' and 'the erosion of the distinction between the military and civilian society'. The 1914–18 refugee experience, therefore, represents a defining moment in the history of warfare, which thenceforth implied not merely the defeat of the enemy army but also the submission of the enemy population.[70] Moreover, the reception of refugees in host nations across

Europe highlights another critical change in the character of war: the extensive mobilisation of the home fronts. Their commitment to the war effort provided the material and ideological support essential to an industrial conflict waged on a global scale. The reception of refugees indeed proved a litmus test of the type of social mobilisation inseparable from 'total war'. Ultimately, this research would not only contribute to a better understanding of the changing character of war but would also attempt to recover a group of people who, on the road to 'total war', 'have fallen into the cracks of history'.[71]

4

THE MOLOCH* OF WAR:
NEW ZEALAND WOMEN WHO OPPOSED THE WAR

Megan Hutching

On 5 August 1914, at 1 p.m., the Governor of New Zealand, Lord Liverpool, stood on Parliament steps in Wellington and read the message from London announcing the state of war with Germany. The New Zealand government, he added, had sent a message of support to Britain pledging that the dominion would be prepared to make any sacrifice to maintain her heritage and her birthright.[1] The Prime Minister, William Massey, and the Leader of the Opposition, Sir Joseph Ward, echoed these sentiments when they spoke.

The news was greeted with public displays of excitement throughout the country. *New Zealand Truth* reported that the

> announcement was received with a cheer that displayed the tense emotions of
> the crowd. All as one man bared their heads and sang the National Anthem....
> Old men on the outskirts of the crowd were seen with tears tracing their cheeks
> and women with handkerchiefs to their eyes.[2]

In Christchurch, where the pre-war anti-militarism movement that had opposed the compulsory military training introduced under the Defence Act 1909 had

---

* Moloch: a system or principle to which terrible sacrifices are made.

been strongest, the news was greeted with much the same emotion. In the shops there was a run on Union Jacks, and audiences at the cinema stood and cheered when a portrait of the King was flashed on the screen as a band played the National Anthem. In the evening the Cadet Bugle Band marching through the streets played the martial airs that had been popular during the South African War. Crowds gathered to accompany them with cheers and songs, waving Union Jacks.[3]

There were similar scenes in Auckland. Several hundred people were present when the news was posted on the *New Zealand Herald*'s noticeboard in Queen Street. It was greeted with the singing of the National Anthem and cheers for the King, France and Russia. A large crowd gathered in Queen Street in the evening.

> For several hours the crowd in front of the Herald office was the centre of enthusiastic demonstration. Patriotic cheers and songs were continually given. A group of young men carrying Union Jacks led a procession up and down Queen Street.[4]

In the light of such popular acceptance of the war, it is unsurprising that the existing anti-militarist organisations felt it best to keep a low profile. The National Peace Council suspended all its public work in 1914, 'as the war fever is too acute to allow of any meetings being held', but held private 'study circles' for the 'education of the people in the deeper principles of the great Peace Question'.[5] That does not mean that there was no opposition to the war, merely that it took some time for it to be voiced. It was those organisations that had opposed compulsory military training because of a moral objection to war that formed the nucleus of the anti-war movement in New Zealand. The Society of Friends, the Canterbury Women's Institute, the New Zealand Freedom League and the National Peace Council all publicly declared their opposition to the war once the initial fervour had abated. Women who did not support the war tended to be those who had also been against the introduction of compulsory military training. They remained members of the old anti-compulsory military training groups and joined the new organisations such as the Women's Anti-Conscription League and the Women's International League when they were established, changing their arguments slightly to deal with the new menace, but reaffirming their opposition to war in general and this one in particular.

Their argument was generally couched in terms of women's inborn opposition to war because, as bearers of children, they had a natural interest in protecting life. It is what I call the biological argument.

I shall begin by considering the international context within which these women were thinking and acting. Brief mention will be made of some of the women's groups overseas with which women in New Zealand had contact.

The members of the Canterbury Women's Institute kept their fingers on the pulse of the peace initiatives overseas. At the end of 1915 Sarah Saunders Page and Ada Wells wrote to Jane Addams in Chicago expressing 'satisfaction and joy at the mission undertaken by Henry Ford and friends on behalf of peace'.[6] The letter was written to Addams in her capacity as President of the Woman's Peace Party, which had grown out of American women's struggle to be granted suffrage. Organised in 1915, this party had as its principal demand that war be abolished. As women, its members felt 'a peculiar moral passion of revolt against both the cruelty and the waste of war'.[7]

In Britain there were female opponents of the war and they were to some extent organised, but the number of women involved was very small, as was the case in all countries. The Women's Peace Crusade, established in 1916, included among its members some well-known suffragists, such as Charlotte Despard and Ethel Snowden, and had links to the Independent Labour Party. The crusade wanted a negotiated peace as soon as possible.

The Australian Freedom League, which had been founded to oppose compulsory military training, was 'actively pacifist' before the war and had included a number of 'radical and progressive' women, but it 'declared a truce once Australia became embroiled in the imperialist conflict'.[8] Vida Goldstein, suffrage fighter, feminist and the first Australian woman to stand for the federal Parliament, was an important member of the Women's Political Association, a feminist organisation based in Melbourne. The association was 'strongly pacifist'[9] from the beginning of the war. After war was declared Goldstein, along with Adela Pankhurst and Cecilia John, founded the Women's Peace Army (WPA). The organisation was militantly anti-war, and while it confined its activities to the dissemination of peace propaganda, it did so in such a way as to make itself noticeable: its members 'participated frequently in the "cut and thrust" of soapbox oratory along the banks of the Yarra River on Sunday afternoons in Melbourne'.[10] Needless to say, there were many who did not support the women's stand and the meetings were often broken up by soldiers, unsurprisingly, considering that the high point of the meetings was the singing of the song 'I didn't raise my son to be a soldier'.[11] Goldstein assumed the existence of a universal female temperament that was 'governed by the biological function of nurturing life,'[12] and stated that the time had come when 'the mothers of the world shall refuse to give their sons as material for shot and shell'.[13] Adela Pankhurst visited New Zealand in 1916 at the invitation of several women's groups and spoke out against the war at public meetings around the country.

Probably the most significant event for anti-war women in New Zealand, however, was the International Congress of Women that met at The Hague in April 1915. The congress was held as a result of the perseverance of Dr Aletta Jacobs, a Dutch doctor and suffragist. At its 1913 meeting in Budapest the International Woman Suffrage Alliance had agreed that the next biennial gathering would be in Berlin in 1915. With the advent of war, German suffragists felt that it would be impossible to have the meeting there and recommended to Jacobs that the convention be abandoned. But, Jacobs thought,

> because there is this terrible war the women *must* come together somewhere, some way, just to show that women of all countries can work together even in the face of the greatest war in the world. Women must show that when all Europe seems full of hatred they can remain united. I felt that the alliance should do that and we should invite the alliance to meet in Amsterdam.[14]

Jacobs met with opposition, however, as some of the alliance's representatives in the Allied countries voted against holding an international meeting during the war.

Among the letters of support she received was one from Scottish lawyer and suffragist Chrystal Macmillan suggesting that the meeting be one of individuals rather than representatives from the member countries. Jacobs found this an excellent suggestion and 'therefore invited as many women as I could reach in different countries to discuss together what the congress should be and to make up the preliminary program'.[15]

Over 1000 women from 12 nations attended in an atmosphere that was remarkably free from tension despite the presence of representatives from both Allied and Central Powers countries. It had been agreed that there would be no discussion of the causes or conduct of the war; instead the meeting would concentrate on methods of bringing about peace. The congress agreed on 20 resolutions and put forward a practical solution for ending the war: a continuous conference of neutral states.

The resolutions that emerged from the congress are interesting for a variety of reasons. They were reported fairly extensively in 1916 in the *Maoriland Worker*, which commented that 'for the first time in history women have raised their voices in protest against the uselessness of sacrifice. The international congress of women at the Hague was undoubtedly due to the awakened consciousness of women to their responsibilities.'[16] New Zealand women thus had the opportunity to find out the details of the congress.

After 1915 the steering committee of the congress called itself the International Committee of Women for Permanent Peace (ICWPP), which in turn evolved into the Women's International League for Peace and Freedom (WILPF), the oldest surviving international women's peace group. The ICWPP, based in Amsterdam, proselytised actively throughout the world, using its contacts among suffrage and international women's organisations. Chrystal Macmillan worked as secretary, with Emily Hobhouse standing in when Macmillan was away. In 1915 Hobhouse wrote to Ellen Vickers Howell of the Canterbury Women's Institute, telling her of the ICWPP's desire to start a branch in New Zealand and asking if the CWI would take the lead in establishing one. Hobhouse felt that it was important that New Zealand be represented on the ICWPP because the country had 'given the world such a fine lead in regard to the position of women', a reference to women's suffrage.[17] At the annual general meeting of the CWI in March 1916, the president, Ada Wells, spoke of the letter received from the ICWPP, and the meeting resolved to affiliate to the committee if that was acceptable.[18] By December 1916 Marianne Jones of Hillsborough and Annette D'Arcy Hamilton of Mount Eden had established a New Zealand branch in Auckland, and branches in Wellington and Christchurch had been organised.

The significance of the ICWPP has now become obvious. Despite being 12,000 miles away from the war in Europe, New Zealand women knew what their sisters in Britain, the United States and Europe were thinking and doing to oppose the war. They managed to keep in contact with these women as far as was possible considering the circumstances of war and could take sustenance from the fact that, while in New Zealand they were a very small number of voices crying out to be heard amid the clamour of support for the war, there were other women in the world who thought as they did and from whom they could derive support and solidarity.

Opposition to conscription

Meanwhile, concern was growing about the possible introduction of conscription in New Zealand. By 1915 it had become obvious that the unpredictable volunteer system was too inefficient. In August that year the Liberal and Reform parties had reluctantly formed a National government, which felt it could no longer rely on the inefficiencies of the voluntary system. So, in what was seen by many as a preliminary to conscription, although the authorities strenuously denied this, the government passed the National Registration Act in October 1915. Under the terms of the legislation eligible men were required to say whether they were prepared to volunteer for overseas service, for civil service in New Zealand or for neither. Most indicated that they were prepared to serve overseas, although a sizeable minority refused to volunteer for either military or civil service.[19]

The Canterbury Women's Institute registered its protest against the passing of the National Registration Act by writing to G. W. Russell, the Minister of Internal Affairs, and to Massey. In the letter, signed by Sarah Saunders Page, the CWI said that by compelling men to undertake military service, the government was 'filching their freedom of choice'. Conscription would also deny people their 'citizen's right of free thought, free speech and public discussion on the questions of the utmost importance to the community'. The war would not be ended by supplying 'increasingly large armies for the slaughter of men and the infliction of suffering on other peoples'.[20]

The reaction from both Russell and Massey to the letter is unsurprising. Russell agreed that world democracy was the only hope for an enduring peace but felt that was an ideal and the time was not right to 'place ideals before practical effort. At present the only hope of peace lies in the defeat of Germany.'[21] The Prime Minister was less patient. 'I should like… to add my opinion that the present is hardly the time for passing abstract resolutions, but rather a time when the whole of the women of New Zealand might well be considering how they could best strengthen the hands of the Government and help it to fulfil its obligations in the defence of the Empire.'[22]

Sarah Saunders Page replied on the CWI's behalf. War, she said, 'never ends war. It is ended by conference' and to that end her organisation urged the government to ask England to initiate such a conference.[23] She continued by saying that while the Prime Minister had mentioned instances of atrocities, the CWI believed that 'war is all atrocity' and 'the supreme national and international crime' and that it was men's duty to live for their country not die for it.[24] The letter illustrates particularly well the philosophical framework from which these women drew their ideas. Page voices a strong concern for social justice and a belief in civilised methods such as arbitration for solving disputes rather than resorting to the 'atrocity' of war.

The women's section of the Social Democrat Party had sent a resolution to the government protesting against the registration legislation on the grounds that it was 'undoubtedly for the purpose of aiding militarism and is the thin end of the wedge for the introduction of conscription'.[25]

Both these groups were right to feel apprehensive, for early in 1916 the government introduced the Military Service Bill, which provided for conscription. It was an innovative system designed to please as much of the population as possible. The volunteer system was not abolished and conscription would be enforced only in areas where there were insufficient volunteers to make up the quota.[26]

As might be expected, anti-militarist groups did not view the bill favourably. A new women's organisation, the Women's Anti-Conscription League (WACL), based in Wellington, was founded in 1916 to protest against conscription, which it opposed 'because under it the sacredness of human life is ruthlessly violated'.[27] Their objection, although rooted in a dislike of the war, was to the compulsion involved: 'The question of participating in the destruction of human life in war is, and should remain, a matter of individual conscience, and no Government, whether representing a majority or minority, has any right to compel any person to kill or be killed'.[28] The women were concerned that the Military Service Bill provided no grounds for appeal because of conscience. They felt that those who refused to fight in the war for conscientious reasons were just as courageous as those who volunteered and should be allowed the 'liberty to follow the dictates of their consciences'.[29]

The league referred to its members' special interest, as mothers, in opposing conscription, tying their argument to a dislike of militarism: 'The mothers among us revolt against the idea that there is no better use for their sons than to be compulsorily sacrificed to militarism, war, and wholesale slaughter'.[30] Women, they argued, had most to lose by the adoption of conscription – although those men forced to fight against their will and those conscientious objectors sent to detention camps may have found that difficult to believe.

In June 1916 a deputation of women from the league waited upon the Prime Minister to put forward their views on conscription. Mrs J. Aitken, who was also president of the Wellington branch of the Women's International League and a member of the Housewives Union, told the Prime Minister that 'as mothers they protested against their sons being conscripted if they objected to go to the war.... No Government had the right to take their boys away from them, and for that reason they were going to fight conscription for all they were worth.'[31]

At this time the bill was in its third reading but still had to go to the Legislative Council, and when pressed about provisions for those who had religious objections to war, Massey 'with an emphatic gesture' declared that:

> 'The State comes first!' 'You'll drive him at the point of a bayonet!' interjected a
> lady whose voice could be heard above the uproar. 'If he won't do his duty he
> must be driven!' said the Prime Minister with a stronger gesture of emphasis.[32]

The Act passed in August 1916 allowed religion as a ground of appeal against conscription but made no provision for those who objected to military service on grounds of conscience.

Opposing militarism

The Canterbury Women's Institute had long been an opponent of militarism. It had made its opposition to the war in South Africa clear and its members had been forthright in denouncing the introduction of compulsory military training. The advent of war in 1914 did not alter the position of the CWI, which saw itself as having 'steadily worked for the peace of the nations and against the truculent and aggressive spirit so much in evidence in the Dominion'.[33] Members such as Sarah Saunders Page and Ada Wells opposed the war and conscription, and were very active in working to protect the rights of conscientious objectors.

Page, a Quaker and socialist, was born in 1863. She married Samuel Page in 1896 and had two sons: Robin was imprisoned as a conscientious objector in 1918, and Fred established the No More War Movement in New Zealand in the early 1920s. After Fred's death in 1926 his mother took over the organisation of the movement. Sarah Saunders Page stood in local body elections on a platform of national issues and anti-militarism, and the municipal ownership of housing, land, kitchens and laundries. She died in 1950.

Ada Wells was also born in 1863 and emigrated with her family to New Zealand when she was 10 years old. A teacher, she was actively involved in the women's suffrage campaign in the 1890s. In 1896 she became the first national secretary of the National Council of Women, and was a founder of the CWI, of which she was president for many years. She also became involved in local body politics: she served on the Ashburton and North Canterbury Charitable Aid Board and was the first woman to be elected to the Christchurch City Council in 1917. Like her close friend Page, she provided aid to conscientious objectors during the First World War. Ada Wells died in 1933.

In a series of questions and answers in the *Maoriland Worker*'s 1916 Christmas issue, the CWI asked why New Zealand was at war, why conscription was necessary and whether war protected women and children. One of the reasons used to persuade men to enlist was that they would be protecting their homes and families by fighting the enemy. The CWI was unconvinced by that argument. In the South African War, it claimed, although incorrectly, that 20,000 women and children had been killed as opposed to 4000 men, so the numbers of women and children dead in Europe during the present conflict could only be much higher as so many more men had been killed there. The message then said that women and children first was the order of the agony in countries where the war was being fought.

The CWI felt the war was being fought to maintain the balance of power in Europe. 'This means that Europe is divided into two opposing armed camps, which are continually in a state of preparedness for war.'[34] The desire to maintain a balance of power could only mean conflict would ensue. The CWI made a connection between the issue of the balance of power and the fact that no terms of peace had been published during the war. The reason was that the great powers had not been able to come to any agreement over how they would apportion the spoils of war. The implication was that if the 'balance of power' mentality stayed the same, then future wars would be inevitable because the powers would always be competing to get the balance in their favour. The solution was an organisation that would mediate in international disputes.

Although it did not explicitly argue it here, the CWI was firmly in favour of international arbitration. Ada Wells, the CWI president, reflected the opinion of the group as a whole when she said that international arbitration was not 'a chimera, but an actual fact of great and growing importance'.[35]

Another women's organisation that contributed to this Christmas issue was the Women's International League. Its objectives were to ensure that in the future national differences would be settled by means other than war and to demand that women have a 'direct voice in the affairs of the nation'.[36] The WIL had chosen to wear a silver badge showing a dove with an olive branch surrounded by a band with the league's name on it. It was felt to be very appropriate: 'Who should proclaim against war and for peace if not the suffering mothers, and even in these days of jingoistic patriotic muzzling that prevails, surely the heartbroken mothers and wives may be allowed to wear a silent protest against it, in the Dove of Peace?'[37] The CWI had referred to the suffering of women in times of war in its message, but the WIL argued somewhat differently. Through the sufferings of war, the WIL felt, 'women may find a new and real bond of unity, a unity which will be stronger than ties of race, blood, creed, or colour'.[38] The league was hoping not only for international arbitration but also for women's interests to become international. Their message was directed to the 'mothers of the world' because 'to them has fallen the task of bringing into the world those human souls which in war are but food for cannon'. It was up to the mothers to educate 'public opinion and to stir up a desire and love for universal peace'.[39] Here is a classic example of the use of the biological argument to advocate for women's inherent identification with peace.

The message continues in much the same vein by elaborating on the idea of women's solidarity: 'The mothers of the world must seek to create an international solidarity which shall stretch from sea to sea, from shore to shore. We call upon them to throw their combined strength against the forces that prevent the peaceful solution of international disputes.'[40] War, they felt was an outmoded system for which there was no longer any need. Like the CWI, they felt that the warring governments should 'declare the terms upon which Peace may be proclaimed'. Peace was not a 'negative thing', but the 'result of the most strenuous effort of mind and spirit'. If women were prepared to expend that strenuous effort and propagate the 'ideals of Love and Internationalism' then peace would be assured.[41]

The WIL differed from the CWI in calling for an international movement of women to work together for peace. The two organisations had a similar aim though in wanting international arbitration in the future. They both felt that women were equally affected by the horrors of war and that women had a special interest in working for peace because they were the bearers of children (and therefore the mothers of soldiers) and so had a natural inclination to support the conservation of life. The affinity that the arguments of the two organisations had with those used by similar groups in Europe, Australia and America suggests strong philosophical links and a close-knit global community of women and ideas to which New Zealand women belonged, despite their geographical isolation.

5

Te Hokowhitu-a-Tu: A Coming of Age?

Monty Soutar

Haere e tama ma.

Haere me te whakaaro ki te pupuri i te rongo toa a o tatou tupuna.

Kia wehi ki te Atua.

Whakahonoretia te Kingi.[1]

Farewell young men.

Go and uphold the name of our warrior ancestors.

Fear God.

And honour the King.

So spoke tribal elders on hearing, in September 1914, that a Maori contingent would be allowed to participate in the war. Their parting injunction encapsulates those qualities they regarded as important for their sons who would go to war: their proud warrior ancestry, their spirituality and a developing sense of patriotism.

This chapter will not concentrate on the history of the Maori contingent overseas, although there will be a brief overview of their service abroad. Rather I propose to examine more fully the motivation behind the Maori desire to serve as an ethnic unit in the NZEF, and to consider the effects this service had on the Maori people.

A paper written in 1943 by Sir Apirana Ngata forms much of the latter part of this chapter. No individual had a better understanding of the position of Maori in New Zealand society during the First World War. From 1914 Ngata had been a member of the Native Contingent Committee that provided advice about the recruitment and organisation of Maori servicemen. Between the wars he had been at the forefront of Maori development and knew first-hand the key issues with which iwi had been grappling.

Background

When the war began some tribes offered themselves immediately for any force that might be raised. At first there was no intention to send a separate Maori unit: it was the policy of the imperial government not to encourage the use of native troops in wars between Europeans. However, when news came that both Indian and Algerian troops were heading for the battlefields of Europe, the offer of a Maori contingent was accepted.

The contingent committee, made up essentially of the Maori members of Parliament, insisted that the force to be raised be recruited and organised as far as possible on tribal lines under tribal leaders. The Native Contingent, as it was to be called, would consist of 500 troops.

Maori officers led the troops, but Pakeha officers filled the higher commands. The contingent trained for four months at the Avondale Racecourse in Auckland before sailing for Egypt in February 1915. At first the authorities were opposed to the contingent taking part in the war at all, except as a garrison force. This reluctance was not due to any doubt about the fighting quality of the Maori soldier, but rather to the government's view that a race that had been facing extinction and was now making a brave struggle to survive should not face depletion of its numbers on the battlefront.[2] When the infamous landing at Anzac Cove took place on 25 April 1915, the contingent was stationed at Malta in a garrison role.

Ten weeks later, because of the severe New Zealand losses sustained at Gallipoli, the Maori contingent was also sent to Anzac Cove. In July, 16 officers and 461 rank and file went ashore. Like the rest of the New Zealand units at Gallipoli, the fresh contingent soon became a shadow of the force that had landed. By September, only 60 men remained on the peninsula. Returning sick and wounded increased their number to two officers and 132 men by the time the ANZAC forces were evacuated in December.[3]

During their time at Gallipoli the Maori contingent served for the most part as pioneers, clearing the soil from mine workings, dragging the water tanks up onto the spurs and digging the communication trenches.[4] This important but seemingly second-class role is often highlighted in the oral traditions passed on to the descendants of those Maori soldiers.

The Maori contingent was used in an aggressive role in the ANZAC effort to take Chunuk Bair and later Hill 60. During the August offensive against the heights of Chunuk Bair, they made a night advance on the foothills to help open the way to the top of the hill. The task before them was to advance with empty rifles against a foe entrenched in seemingly impregnable positions on the grim dark heights above. The work had to be done with the point of the bayonet. Orders were specific: not a shot was to be fired and the enemy trenches must be taken by surprise attack. The Maori soldiers were successful and Captain Peter Buck wrote:

> I knew that a Turkish trench had been captured in the darkness at the point of the bayonet [when the fire of the Turks was silenced]. But more wonderful to me was that the night air was broken vigorously by the Maori war cry of 'Ka mate, ka mate! Ka ora, ka ora!' . . . my heart thrilled at the sound of my mother tongue resounding up the slopes of Sari Bair.[5]

This proved to be one of the few successes the New Zealanders experienced in the failed offensive: for the remainder of the attack their casualties were cripplingly high.

Attached to the mounted rifles units, the weakened Maori contingent was committed again in late August to seize Hill 60. In an attempt to reach the hill, a bayonet charge across open land was ordered. Here the unit was virtually destroyed as a fighting body. The Maori losses led divisional commander Alexander Godley to split the remainder of the contingent among the four battalions of the New Zealand Infantry Brigade, all of whom had also suffered severely.

In December 1915, the surviving members of the contingent were evacuated to Egypt where the 300-strong second Native Contingent joined them. Along with the shattered Otago Mounted Rifles they were reformed into a pioneer battalion, and Maori participation in the rest of the war was in a support role as pioneers. In spite of this, they also suffered heavy casualties in France, their duties consistently carrying them into the fire zone.

Throughout the war the contingent and its reinforcements drew more than 2500 men overseas, including 470 Pacific Islanders. Casualties included 336 men killed on active service, and over 700 wounded.

Recruitment

The First World War was not the first time Maori had asked to participate as a unit in a war involving the British Empire. In 1900 a Maori contingent was offered for service in the South African War. When the proposal was declined, some Maori, most of mixed ethnicity, enlisted and served in the several contingents that went to South Africa. They went abroad under surnames like Poynter, Pitt, Walker, Joseph, Arthur, Withers, Vercoe, Ferris and Boyd.[6]

In the First World War, Maori involvement was intended to be voluntary. The initial response to the call for recruits was pleasing, considering the historical relationship of some tribes with the Crown, represented by the government in New Zealand. The 2500 Maori who served overseas were drawn from a population of 63,000. Behind those figures, however, were facts that to outsiders might appear less admirable. Indeed, the response from the tribes varied. Ngata wrote:

> Some rallied as freely as the most patriotic Pakeha communities; others hardly
> at all. It was not that the latter were not brave or not derived from warlike
> stock. The internecine warfare of pre-Pakeha days had produced from all tribes
> men trained to arms and women sworn to breed warriors to defend the tribal
> estate and honour.[7]

The unevenness of the recruiting was a reflection of how each tribe had fared at the hands of the Crown. While an inherent fighting spirit motivated the majority of those young men who did enlist, they belonged to iwi whose experiences with the Crown made them more amenable to notions of civic responsibility and service. They included Ngati Kahungunu and Ngati Porou on the East Coast, and Te Arawa in the Bay of Plenty, who not surprisingly were represented by two of the more dedicated members of the Native Contingent Committee, Sir James Carroll and Apirana Ngata. Both had underaged sons in the contingent: Ngata's son was 15 when he enlisted.

The tribal elders in these districts were motivated by ideals of patriotic service and the obligations of citizenship inherent in the commitment signed by their ancestors to the Treaty of Waitangi. In the preamble to the treaty, if one accepts the words at face value, a motivating force on the British government to annex the country was its concern for the protection of Maori, their rights and property. While it was recognised that the British had two voices – the state (as in the Colonial Office) and the Crown (as in the monarch) – it was to the monarch that all Maori chiefs paid heed. The might of the Crown was personified in the person of Queen Victoria, in much the same way as the power and authority of tribes were personalised in the chiefs, acting on behalf of their people. Regardless of the passage of time, many Maori in 1914 retained a sense of loyalty to and trust of the monarch, despite the behaviour of the settler government when it was established and to which the British Parliament transferred authority. This trust and sense of loyalty are relevant to understanding the commitment of tribes like Ngati Porou, Ngati Kahungunu and Te Arawa in the First World War.

Conscription

The iwi that were most unmoved by the empire's call to fight were those from the regions where the conflicts of the 1860s had been most bitter and who, as a result, had endured the confiscation of large tracts of their tribal estate – especially those in Waikato and Taranaki. Nursing an inherited sense of grievance against the Crown, represented as they saw it by the government and Pakeha generally, these destitute and aggrieved communities were in no mood to appreciate the obligation to serve abroad in the armed forces.

Because of the reluctance of these tribes to enlist, the government discussed the possibility of applying its conscription policy to them. They had already begun conscripting other New Zealanders into the armed forces, but had not extended the policy to include Maori. As the war drew on, however, it became obvious that the constant need for Maori reinforcements would drain the manpower of some tribes, while others with minimal enlistments would be hardly affected.

In 1917 the government, in an ill-advised move, decided to apply conscription to one electoral district, Western Maori, of which the Tainui and Taranaki tribes were a part. Ballots were drawn from eligible men of Waikato and Ngati Maniapoto, both Tainui iwi, and purposely included some members of the Maori King's family. It was hoped that their compliance would encourage would-be dissenters to follow their example.

When none of the men presented themselves at the army office the Defence Minister, Sir James Allen, visited Ngaruawahia in an attempt to persuade Waikato leaders to co-operate. With their men facing imprisonment, Tupu Taingakawa, spokesman for the King and son of Wiremu Tamehana Tarapipipi, the Maori Kingmaker, received with contempt the olive branch held out by Allen. 'Ko wai te wha?' (Who will suffer?), the old chief remarked. 'My people cannot suffer more than they have done in the loss of their lands and of their mana', meaning that nothing the law could do now would be worse, and so nothing mattered.[8]

Their refusal to serve was not readily understood and the sequel was the imprisonment of those selected in the ballot who had not presented themselves. Ngata commented on the ineffectiveness and partiality of the policy:

> As a device for securing men for the Maori contingent conscription was a dismal failure. As Government policy it was justified solely by the theoretical equality of Maori and Pakeha under the law of their common land. It took no cognizance of historical facts barely half a century old. It ignored the hurt done to a large section of Maori people whose offence was a vain attempt to stem the encroachments of an aggressive and not too scrupulous Pakeha colony. An old wound was reopened that time and the emergence of other interests might have rendered less sensitive. Suspicions and resentments, the aftermath of the Land Wars 50 years earlier, were foolishly if not wantonly stirred to renewed activity.[9]

The imposition of conscription on the Waikato and Ngati Maniapoto people had long-lasting effects and the breach it caused has probably only been restored in recent times with the Tainui settlement. Applying the policy to one electoral district was a mistake and resulted in only a handful of Tainui men ever being put into uniform. P.S. O'Connor, in his review of Maori recruitment in the First World War, noted that by 1919 only 74 Maori conscripts had gone to camp out of a total of 552 men called up. 'None had been sent overseas, 111 had been arrested, and nearly 100 warrants were still in the hands of the police.'[10] Such a poor outcome begged an examination of the reasons for the resistance. Ngata, involved in the post-war commissions set up to investigate claims and grievances, wrote:

> The position was clear enough to those who had studied it closely among the disaffected peoples. The mote in the brother's eye had to be removed before he could be expected to begin to see things as other men saw them. The duty of the Maori leaders was to convince men in authority of the existence and stubbornness of the obstruction and of the urgent need for removing it. So the long-standing grievances arising from unfulfilled promises, from the arbitrary acts of Government land-purchase officers or, most serious of all, from the punitively excessive confiscation of native lands, dominated the political activities of the period immediately following the War.[11]

A coming of age?

It is often said that New Zealand came of age as a nation in the 1914–18 war. But what of the Maori soldiers? Had their participation in the NZEF led their fellow New Zealanders to accept them as equals at home? Did race relations in this country improve significantly as a result of the Maori contingent going off to fight the common enemy? It was with these thoughts in mind that I titled this essay 'Te Hokowhitu-a-Tu: A coming of age?'. The answer to these questions is best left to Ngata:

> The Maoris were allowed to take part in the fighting in Gallipoli and later in Flanders. But they were organised as a Pioneer Contingent and emerged with that status. Every surviving member of that Contingent knows that its service stopped short of the maximum, because it was not a front line unit; and this, not withstanding that the unit suffered heavy casualties at the Dardanelles and in

Flanders, that its duties carried it into the fire zone and that it endured the hardships of the cold European winters and the constraints and monotony of static trench warfare. Nothing could compensate for the fact, that it was denied the privilege of 'going over the top' and the exhilaration of charging headlong to engage the enemy in hand-to-hand combat.

In front of the Lobby fires of Parliament Buildings, when the service of the Maori in the last war was referred to, returned soldier M.Ps. qualified their praise by saying with a mental shrug of the shoulders, 'but of course they were not in the front line'. I noted this reservation made by men in high places as a matter of outstanding importance. In the final analysis the judgment of a friend, albeit of another race, is the measure of one's standing. To him you can appeal, that his concern about your welfare brought about the very situation he appeared to deplore. The role of the Maori in the last war was defined for him against his own inclination and the call of his warrior ancestry. But that shrug of the shoulders could not be dismissed merely as fireside chatter. It was one of those comments of public men in a communicative mood, which one stored away in one's memory for a day to come. The Maori soldier through the well-meant solicitude of his friends and mentors did not come of age at the end of the last [1914–18] war. [12]

What was achieved by Maori service in the First World War? If Maori returned men had not come of age in New Zealand, what then was gained by their involvement in the 1914–18 conflict? On a personal level, they had come home with a more confident bearing and a better appreciation of their place in the world. They knew they had played a praiseworthy role in the greatest overseas activity of which their country had been part, they had seen close-up the might of the British Empire and they had learnt what it meant to serve that institution. Most of all, they had earned a respect in their communities that would last for their lifetimes.

After the war, photographs of these men in their khaki uniforms were hung in homes and on marae throughout the country. Stone monuments, dining halls and even a church were erected as memorials to those who served, while returned soldier organisations and Anzac Day commemorations helped to keep memories alive. The names and places where relatives had fought or been killed were passed on to children. Mothers and grandparents, who registered the children at the native schools, took great pride in placing the names in the school register for they understood the cause for which the men had fought and to which the children were now committed.

The Maori soldiers' participation in the war also led to the economic growth of a large section of their people, particularly among those iwi whose voluntary enlistments had been strongest. In their rural and remote communities the returned men were able to help their kinsmen understand and appreciate the opportunities presented by the world beyond the village. They felt education was the pathway to opportunity for their children and they became the staunchest supporters of their local schools. The focus on education increased employment opportunities in industry, where some skill was required, provided openings in clerical work and improved land utilisation. Some Maori even ventured into business on a small and experimental scale.

The camaraderie resulting from the shared experiences of the training camps and the battlefields allowed men of different tribes, some of whom were to become leaders among their people, to form networks that might otherwise not have occurred. Some had also made close friendships or contacts with Pakeha soldiers in the NZEF, and these relationships were extended into business and social affairs. The influence of such contacts would be further seen in the joint war effort in the Second World War. 'One may say,' wrote Ngata, 'that the Maori soldier element gave an adventurous turn to the process of acculturation and broke through the tribal cordons that threatened to keep Maori communities apart.'[13]

In 1919, race relations between Maori and Pakeha were in an embryonic stage. The country was still very young and not enough history had passed between the two races for both to claim a coming of age. It can be said, however, that the soldiers of the Maori contingent and the subsequent New Zealand Maori (Pioneer) Battalion were responsible for an expansion in the Maori outlook on the world and for an appreciation and interpretation among iwi of events abroad after the war. At the outbreak of the Second World War, these veterans would be the first to support the idea of a Maori rifle battalion, for they understood and appreciated the spirit that moved their sons to venture where they first broke the trail.[14]

A verse from the well-known war song composed by Sir Apirana Ngata for the return of the Maori Pioneer Battalion:

Te Ope Tuatahi	We greet the First Contingent
No Aotearoa	From the North Island
No te Waipounamu	From the South Island
No nga tai e wha	From the four coasts
Ko koutou ena	'Tis you
E nga rau e rima	The five hundred
Ko te Hokowhitu Toa	The warriors
A Tumatauenga	Of Tumatauenga
I hinga ki Ihipa	You fell in Egypt
Ki Karipori ra ia	In Gallipoli
E ngau nei te aroha	And I am bereft with sorrow
Me te mamae.	And pain.

6

AMERICANS AT WAR: ASSESSING THE SIGNIFICANCE OF AMERICAN PARTICIPATION IN THE GREAT WAR

Jennifer D. Keene

There are many ways to assess the American military experience during the First World War. One is to explore the impact that raising a mass army had on the American military. Another is to examine how American soldiers themselves interpreted the war and their participation in it. Finally, one can place the American effort in the overall context of the war by considering how the American experience compares with that of other combatant nations and what overall contribution the Americans made to the final victory. These various approaches all help to answer the always present question about American involvement in the war: what difference did it make? Examining how the war shaped institutions and individual lives, reasserting the primacy of combat as an essential American experience during the war, and assessing Americans' role in the final victory leave little doubt that American military involvement had far-reaching significance.

Creating a wartime army

When the United States entered the war in April 1917, the government initially hoped that the nation could limit its involvement to financial and material support of the Allies. Within a month of declaring war, however, it became clear to President Woodrow Wilson that the United States would have to send troops as quickly as possible to the Western Front. The country now faced the choice of raising this wartime force through volunteers or turning to conscription to fill the ranks. The government hedged at first, allowing men to volunteer for the army until December 1917, but then relied almost exclusively on conscription to raise the bulk of the wartime force. The decision to conscript the majority of the wartime army was a pivotal one for American society. Conscription had a long history in the United States. Until the First World War its main purpose was to spur voluntary enlistment as individuals sought to avoid the tainted label of conscript, a category of soldiers the public viewed as unpatriotic and the army considered untrustworthy on the battlefield. The government justified the decision to institute a mass draft with the argument that in total war the nation needed to allocate its manpower resources wisely. In 1917, the government renamed conscription 'selective service' and successfully convinced the American public that the draft was an equitable, efficient and honourable way to ensure that neither the civilian economy nor the army suffered from the impulsive decisions of individuals. The promise to match the right man with the right job in either the military or civilian workplace earned the draft general acceptance as a manpower management technique suitable for the modern age. Overall, 72 per cent of the four million troops raised during the war were drafted, representing a dramatic, if temporary, expansion of the federal government's power to make life or death decisions for individual citizens.[1]

In the end, however, solving the riddle of how to bring men into the military proved less significant than what happened once these civilians entered its ranks. The war forced the US Army to reinvent itself almost overnight from a relatively inconsequential force of 300,000 active service and reserve troops that fought small wars close to home and maintained peace into a modern military capable of sending millions of men thousands of miles overseas to fight in a heavily mechanised and tactically difficult war. The challenges were staggering: raising and training infantry soldiers, selecting and instructing officers, recruiting the engineering, communication and medical troops required to support combat operations, building training camps, equipping these troops and then transporting them overseas where they would finally confront the reality of fighting a war that had stymied the best military minds for three years.

How the American military chose to assign, train, officer and discipline its citizen soldiery to meet these challenges influenced more than how the United States fought the war. These decisions also affected the type of institution that the modern American military became. American citizen soldiers proved less malleable than many army officials had hoped, contesting a whole host of army policies and practices while they served. Their sheer numbers and the army's clear dependence on them largely explain officials' subsequent willingness to make concessions to their wartime force when formulating a host of manpower, leave and punishment policies. Reformers within the top echelons also played an important part in carving out an official place for soldier opinion in the policy-making process by urging the army to establish a more co-operative and less coercive relationship with its new recruits.

Perhaps the most important transformation that took place over the course of the war was the changing meaning of obedience. Army officials no longer simply commanded obedience: they negotiated it. Such negotiations took place in other Allied armies along the Western Front, as troops set limits on the amount of violence they would accept in raids, daily shelling rituals and pitched battle. Within the American army, however, much of this negotiation over the meaning of obedience occurred behind the lines. This was partly because of the changing structure of the American military, which was transformed during the war from a force in which the vast majority of soldiers fought into a large bureaucratic organisation that assigned 60 per cent of its troops to non-combatant duties.[2] Important to the war effort, yet often disappointed with their stint behind the lines, these troops proved difficult to discipline. As crucial, however, was the right that all American soldiers asserted as citizen soldiers to change or challenge offensive or unpopular policies from the very first day they stepped into a military training camp. In their quest to mould army disciplinary doctrine along more acceptable lines, citizen soldiers did not hesitate to enlist help from their families, outside agencies or their political representatives to sway army decisions in their favour.

The power of public opinion to shape disciplinary policy was evident throughout the war. The modified use of the death penalty provides just one example of how outside civilian concerns intervened to influence disciplinary policies. In May 1918 President Wilson began reviewing the death sentence convictions of two soldiers who fell asleep on sentry duty in a forward trench and two others who refused to drill after being up all night on guard duty.

Secretary of War Newton Baker urged the President to commute the sentences in these well-publicised cases after receiving hundreds of letters from concerned mothers 'whose general anxiety for the welfare of their sons is increased by apprehension lest exhaustion or thoughtlessness may lead their boys to [similar] weaknesses'.[3] American Expeditionary Force (AEF) commander General John J. Pershing, however, recommended that the sentences be carried out to 'diminish the number of like cases that may arise in the future'.[4] In the end, the President decided that the American public would accept executions only for mutiny, desertion, espionage, rape and murder and commuted the sentences. Wilson's decision dramatically curtailed the use of executions as a disciplinary tool in the wartime army, and the 11 AEF soldiers executed during the war were all convicted of murder or rape, crimes that often received the death penalty in civilian society as well.

The vast majority of wartime disciplinary struggles, however, occurred far from the eyes and ears of concerned civilians and involved much less than the death penalty. Throughout the war, American officials struggled to keep unauthorised absences, racial rioting and work slowdowns among rear area troops to a minimum. Behind the lines, the army adopted an array of persuasive and manipulative techniques intended both to convince and trick soldiers into conformity. To prevent soldiers from spending too much money on alcohol, for instance, the army set up mandatory savings accounts that effectively reduced the monthly pay given to each soldier. Giving soldiers less money preserved the façade of compliance with otherwise unenforceable orders regulating soldiers' visits to French cafés. Persuasion was another popular technique, as camp officers undertook a massive propaganda campaign to convince enlisted men that saluting their officers was simply a sign of respect and not a symbol of sub-servience. AEF officials quickly curtailed the practice of punishing disobedient non-combatants by sending them to hard labour along the front lines after officers noted a drop in morale among combatant troops who began to wonder whether it was an honour or punishment to serve at the front.

By far the most successful way for a white soldier to disobey an order was to give a racial reason for doing so. White soldiers could walk by black guards without showing a pass, assault black troops, refuse to salute black officers and even destroy army property or kill black soldiers with little fear of punishment from white authorities.[5] At first glance, the tendency of officers to look the other way when enlisted men committed these offences seems to reveal little more than shared racial prejudice. But the ramifications of letting racial prejudice serve as a legitimate reason for soldiers to disobey legally given orders or ignore an officer's rank undermined the entire basis for command authority. Letting enlisted men choose which orders they would obey set a dangerous precedent that the army increasingly tried to avoid by carefully orchestrating how white and black troops came into contact with one another. The Washington-based General Staff explicitly saw how white soldiers' racial prejudices were circumscribing the army's authority when it rejected a plan to assign black soldiers primarily as cooks for white units. Advocates of this plan pointed out the importance of freeing up white men for infantry training, and claimed that having black men perform these menial duties within white units would both maintain the racial status quo and quicken the pace of readying white infantry troops for deployment overseas. The General Staff immediately recognised, however, that if the army embraced this plan it would subsequently be impossible to use kitchen duty as a punishment or legitimate assignment for white troops. 'There is at present widespread objection in the service to the performance of duties of a menial nature, but to admit their menial quality by assigning such duties exclusively to an inferior race would make it well nigh impossible to persuade white men to ever again resume these duties,' wrote one General Staff officer.[6] The gain in training time was not enough to counter-balance the further erosion in army authority that would result from this policy, even though it complemented the army's decision to use black troops primarily as non-combatant laborers.

Besides problems with obedience and race relations, army officials also soon realised that American soldiers did not have a strong ideological commitment to the larger national purpose for declaring war. One soldier poet put it best:

> 'Made safe for democracy seems mighty fine,
> but high-soundin' politics ain't in our line.
> 'Tain't that made us chuck up our jobs and enlist
> For givin' the Kaiser the taste of a fist,
> But this is the notion stowed under our lids:
> We're makin' it safe for the Missus and kids.'[7]

After listening to the men in his unit, one second lieutenant concluded 'that nine out of ten of our enlisted men do not know what they are fighting for, the idea is simply to kill the Boche'.[8] Throughout the war, the vague dedication that American soldiers exhibited to the goal of killing Germans and saving France troubled officials who believed that troops would need stronger ideological motivation to continue fighting into 1919, the earliest date that American officials envisioned the war ending. Pershing remained steadfast in his conviction that political education and building morale remained the responsibility of unit officers. Stateside officials, however, deemed political indoctrination to be as important as marksmanship training for the modern soldier, and introduced systematic political education into the training camps.

Officials at home and overseas disagreed over whether troops needed a sophisticated understanding of the war's causes and goals to perform well on the battlefield, but they agreed that soldiers' views mattered to those at home. Throughout the war, officials tried to resolve the logistical problems that prevented most troops from voting. In their arguments for collecting the soldier vote, high-ranking officials expressed complete faith that soldiers in the field would remain loyal and supportive of the war, even if civilians balked at the anticipated high casualties and began to clamour for a negotiated peace in 1919 or 1920. 'It is not unlikely that the time may come when our soldiers in the field, in the aggregate, may be able to see more clearly what the necessities of the situation require than do the voters at home,' argued the head of the War College Division. 'In such an event, they should not be deprived of their right of suffrage, not only because it is their right, but because their deprivation, at such a time, might seriously endanger the interests of the nation.'[9] The faith that American officials placed in their troops' commitment to fight until victory proved well founded.

The soldiers' war

For good or ill, the wartime experience established the principle within the modern American military that soldiers' preferences mattered and diluted the concept of unquestioning obedience to orders. For individual soldiers who served, these institutional legacies were less important than the personal impact of the war. For many soldiers, the war became a pivotal moment in their lives because of the memories or disabilities they brought home, the opportunity it offered to take part in an historic event or the post-war financial hardships that many in this veteran generation blamed on the government's mismanagement of the war. For the individual veteran, therefore, the war had an intensely personal meaning that sometimes, but not always, mirrored its larger political significance. In a letter home in the fall of 1918 to his local newspaper, Sergeant Judson Hanna tried to prepare his Pennsylvanian community for the changes that they would certainly notice in those who had fought on the Western Front. 'Some men who went though the big barrage still show the effects of it. Let a door slam, and a big healthy man will jump as if stung.' But, as Hanna explained, general nervousness was the least of the combat veteran's problems: often their experiences under fire had reshaped their entire personalities. To support this contention, Hanna described the changes he noted in a friend after he was covered with dirt from exploding bombs during an artillery barrage. As he hugged the ground, this friend felt a shell fall right beside him. 'The soldier waited in this makeshift grave for the bomb to explode, knowing the uselessness of trying to escape, and trying to prepare his mind for the bumping off of his body. Those seconds of agonized waiting for an expected tragedy may change a whole man's character. This bomb was also a dud, but the man today goes around with a strained face and seems always listening for something.'[10]

Other soldiers returned home with more visible scars of their time in combat. When word came that Private Joseph Maleski's unit would soon enter the line, 'I knew I felt good. This is what I had enlisted for. This is what I came for. I was going to get a crack at the Germans.' As his unit charged successfully across an open field and into the woods around Château-Thierry, he and his comrades began laughing about their good fortune. 'One would say "That fellow can't spell our names" and another would answer "Yes, his shells can't hit us unless they have our names on the cover."' This banter reflected the common superstition among soldiers that dying or surviving had more to do with fate than luck. Unfortunately, the shell with Maleski's name on it soon found him and shattered his leg. 'Are you in much pain?' asked a surgeon at the field hospital. No, Maleski replied, but then admitted that he could not feel his toes.

When I woke up the surgeon asked me how I felt. 'All right.'

'Any pain?'

'No sir.'

'Can you feel your toes now?'

'Yes sir.'

He laughed and went on to the other men. The third day I was there he asked the same questions and I gave the same answers. Then he didn't laugh any more. His face became very serious and he said: 'I guess my boy I'll have to tell you now. You haven't got any toes. We had to cut your leg off about the knee to save your life.'[11]

The story of one African American veteran, Horace Pippin, gives some additional insight into the effect of combat on an individual life. Pippin was a self-taught artist who carried a sketchbook with him throughout the war. Like other members of the 369 Infantry Regiment, a unit that served with the French, Pippin's life revolved around the routine of 20 days in the trenches followed by 10 days in the rear. Soon, he was a seasoned veteran who 'had seen men die in all forms and shapes'.[12] Pippin's war came to an end during the assault by 369 on Sechault in late September 1918. On the second day of the advance, Pippin was hit in the shoulder as he dived for cover into a shellhole. Another soldier bound his wound before leaving Pippin there to fend for himself. Pippin tried several times to climb out of the hole and head for the rear, but each time shots from a German sniper drove him back down. Finally, Pippin was too weak to do anything more than wait for help to arrive. The first sign of hope came later in the day when a passing French sniper discovered him. Before Pippin could warn him to stay down, the German sniper shot the French soldier through the head without even knocking off his helmet. 'He stood there for at least ten seconds before he slipped down and when he did, [he] slid down on top of me. I had lost so much blood by this time I couldn't even move him.' Pippin lay immobilised with the dead French soldier over him for several hours, thankful for the water and bread that the man carried.[13] Finally, a rescue party arrived and put him on a stretcher by the side of the road. Pippin waited in a steady, cold rain for another 12 hours before an ambulance transported him to a field hospital.

Returning home with a steel plate in his shoulder and a nearly useless right arm, Pippin only worked sporadically after the war. His family survived on his $22.50 a month disability allowance and his wife's work as a laundress. Pippin was not a recluse, however. He took an active interest in his community and served as commander of his local black American Legion post in West Chester, Pennsylvania for several years. Yet despite his normal outward appearance, Pippin experienced bouts of depression and was haunted by his memories of combat. He tried writing about and sketching his experiences, but was unhappy with the results. He finally decided to try painting, using his left hand to guide his right. Pippin spent three years working on *The End of the War, Starting Home* (1930–3), trying to get right the image that he had been carrying around in his head since returning home. In these early years, his friends and family were supportive of what they saw as nothing more than a harmless hobby and Pippin sometimes used his paintings to settle outstanding bills. In 1937, however, Pippin was discovered by the Philadelphia art community and soon received national recognition as a true primitive much like his better-known contemporaries Jacob Lawrence and Grandma Moses. Although this rags-to-riches tale seemingly provided a happy ending to Pippin's story, his physical pain, taste for alcohol and mounting family problems made this success bittersweet. In 1946, Pippin died of a stroke.

The war, Pippin wrote, 'brought out all of the art in me'.[14] His paintings offer an unflinching glimpse of the harsh, brutal and sometimes poetic aspects of modern warfare. Pippin painted the terrifying moment when mustard gas descended on troops scrambling for their gas masks, the desolate terrain left lifeless by constant artillery bombardments, the fearless feats of aerial pilots engaged in a dogfight, the isolation that each man felt even while surrounded by his comrades and the final moment when German soldiers came out of their holes in the ground to surrender. For Pippin, combat in the First World War was the defining moment of his life, and his paintings are among the best, if not the best, by any American artist of the conflict.

For all the pain and horror that many American soldiers witnessed, they took solace in the sense of having participated in a great historic event. 'I wouldn't have missed it for anything,' exclaimed one soldier to his wife, content that he and his comrades had passed the test of courage in their first sustained encounter with the Germans.[15] American soldiers' romanticism and enthusiasm about the war were particularly striking to Allied troops, especially the French who often remarked that the Americans reminded them of themselves in 1914.[16] Indeed, the truly disgruntled soldiers within the AEF were those assigned to labouring or specialist tasks behind the line. Whatever crisis of morale existed in the American army during the war took place, not at the front, but in the training camps and dock facilities where non-combatants laboured unloading boxes, building roads or transporting supplies. It was not so much that these troops wanted a chance to die for their country, as that they wanted the recognition and respect that naturally went to combatants. Private Paul Maxwell entitled his post-war memoir 'Diary of a Dud', a conclusion that many non-combatants reached about their military careers.[17]

It is perhaps worth pointing out, however, that the front-line combat soldier did not have a monopoly on witnessing horrific scenes during the war. On 5 July 1918, over 40,000 white troops and 3000 black troops in Camp Dodge, Iowa were marched before a scaffold to watch the execution of three African American soldiers who had been convicted of raping a white woman. Critics called these hangings a 'legal lynching', and the execution earned a prominent place in the wartime memories of these unwilling observers. 'It was a very hot day with no wind,' one officer present at the scene later recalled. 'Thus the voices of the condemned men really reached the thousands of soldiers surrounding the scaffold. It was a horrible event. Most of us were not experienced soldiers, just ordinary young guys.... I was concerned that my recruits facing the scaffold might even panic.... I saw some of them weaving in ranks trying to stand at attention.'[18] The first intentional death that these troops encountered came at the hands of their own army rather than the enemy's and remained as traumatic a memory as anything they later witnessed along the Western Front.

The American way of war

These life and death experiences provided the most tangible evidence for soldiers that control over their own destinies had largely been taken over by forces greater than themselves. Indeed, as in all wars, commanders made a host of decisions that shaped the contours of the American fighting man's experience. In retrospect, the American decision to retain the national integrity of its army and to take over its own sector of the Western Front probably increased the number of casualties in the AEF, exactly the outcome Pershing was trying to avoid when he insisted on keeping American troops under American command. American military leaders felt that by developing a unique American approach to combat, they could avoid the mistakes, as they saw them, of the Allied armies on the battlefield. If Pershing had been able to complete his initial plan of fully training 3 million men to make a decisive attack against Metz in 1919, the American commander may have fulfilled his goal of restoring a war of movement onto the battlefield that lessened the human cost of battle along the Western Front. Instead, the quick pace of events in the wake of the failed German spring offensives in 1918 forced American troops into battle much sooner than Pershing intended. As he hoped, his troops fought aggressively and, as he feared, they died copiously.

Despite Pershing's ultimate intention to go it alone, throughout 1918 the AEF depended on French and British aid to train, transport and arm their force. Pershing successfully deflected the French demand that the Americans simply provide fresh infantry troops for French divisions. Nonetheless the majority of American troops spent a substantial amount of time training with French units and until the fall of 1918 most American divisions fought as attached units to the French army. Several divisions also fought and trained with the BEF. One American regiment even served for a short time with the New Zealand Division, where they succeeded, according to a unit historian, in 'winning the hearts of the New Zealanders and making a name for ourselves'.[19]

American troops arrived in France brimming with training camp lectures about how American initiative and enthusiasm would reintroduce a war of movement onto the Western Front. 'The sole idea of the American Army,' one soldier recalled, 'was to attack, to push forward.'[20]

Feeling that the Kiwis shared this sentiment, members of the 317 Regiment were pleased to learn that they would receive their baptism of fire while serving with the New Zealand Division because 'they made it their business whenever entering a new part of the line, to start right in with their aggressive spirit letting the Germans know at the beginning that they could expect no rest,' wrote First Lieutenant Edley Craighill.[21] The Americans were duly impressed with a New Zealand chaplain who presided over the front-line burial of the first casualty from an American company despite the fact that 'shells from both sides were whizzing over head ... '[22] During his first stint alongside New Zealand troops, Joseph Morris, as instructed, studiously watched the saps along the front line for any sign of enemy infiltration and at one point through the rain became convinced that he saw the enemy approaching. Morris fired off a few rounds, then retired certain that he had successfully downed a German infiltrator. An investigation the next day uncovered two neat bullet holes in an empty black petrol can, the 'soldier' that Morris had stopped the night before. On a less humorous note, novice nervousness resulted in this company's first casualty when a corporal returning from a stint guarding a work party in no man's land did not hear a command to halt and was shot and killed by a man in his own outfit.[23] Initially, American soldiers interpreted Allied lessons about using caution in the trenches as a clear sign of the defeatism they had heard so much about from their officers. Over time, however, American soldiers learned to mimic Allied soldiers' survival strategies and to admire their staying power. One of the major annoyances that French soldiers expressed about Americans by October 1918 was their extreme eagerness for the war to end. 'They are waiting for the peace with a lot more impatience than us, which is very strange,' noted one French soldier in a letter home. 'They haven't even been fighting for that long. What would it be like if they had four years to their credit!'[24]

Although common soldiers came to respect the accomplishments of their Allied counterparts, commanders continued to make less favourable comparisons between the armies under their command and those that were not. From the American perspective, wartime comparisons between their army and the Allies tended to focus on the unique contribution that American initiative and aggressiveness could make to the final victory, while Allied commanders targeted the tremendous manpower resources going to waste owing to poor leadership within the American military. Once victory was assured, the war of words between the Americans and the Allies sharpened dramatically. '"We won the war", you don't hear anything else when you talk about the peace with them,' complained one French soldier in a letter home.[25] In January, the AEF General Staff sent the American Commission to Negotiate Peace a comprehensive analysis of the US Army's pivotal contributions. Army officials expected this information to help the commission secure a prominent role in the peace negotiations. GHQ claimed exaggeratedly that the US war effort had dwarfed those of France, Britain and Germany in size, scope, and quality. This report downplayed the US Army's dependence on Allied supplies and instead detailed the transportation infrastructure the Americans would eventually leave for the French. The authors of this report gave the American troops who had fought under French command during the German 1918 spring offensives full credit for stopping the German march to Paris at Château-Thierry in June and for the success of the Allied counterattack that summer. AEF staff officials, however, saved their most illustrious praise for the operations they had conceived and commanded themselves. They based the US Army's claim to have single-handedly saved France on its troops' success in overcoming the Germans in hilly, densely forested terrain during the St Mihiel and Meuse-Argonne offensives. 'It is notorious that while we were fighting to the limit in the Argonne, the French Army was doing little more than observing the enemy with a view to taking over positions abandoned by the enemy. The British were doing little more … But the American divisions in their ranks were given the most difficult enterprises, suffered the heaviest casualties, and by their energy and dash were in a very large measure instrumental in pushing forward the Allied lines.'[26]

Today, there are few historians who would venture to paint the American contribution in such stark and nationalistic terms. The consensus now is that although the Americans did not single-handedly win the war in 1918, they did make a valuable contribution on the battlefield that extended beyond the sheer promise of fielding a larger and more perfectly trained army in the future. At key moments in the German spring offensives in 1918, American troops helped to stop the Germans from taking Paris. Newly arrived American divisions added key strength to the French-led counter-offensives over the summer, and in the fall American-commanded assaults pinned down large numbers of German troops, helping to make possible British and French advances to the north. Yet, in the process of muting the initial over-enthusiastic appraisal from participants about their role in the final victory, First World War historians have perhaps swung a bit too far in the opposite direction, to the point that the extensive suffering and sacrifice on the Americans' part has been dropped from consideration altogether.

When one compares the American experience with that of the French or British, it is not hard to see why the significance of American participation seems to diminish rapidly. The country entered the war quite late, took more than a year to field an independent army and lost comparatively few men – nearly 53,500 from combat, as compared with 1.3 million for France and 900,000 for Great Britain. Fully engaged from the opening days of the war, France and Britain lost an average of 900 and 457 men a day, respectively, over the course of the war. For the Americans, the bulk of the fighting came in the last six months of the war, with the first year primarily given over to training and transporting troops overseas. The overall American average of 195 deaths a day reflects this lag between the American declaration of war and heavy involvement on the Western Front.

These figures are often used as evidence to dismiss the war as a quick adventure for American troops. Yet phrasing this comparative question somewhat differently suggests another conclusion. Once American troops became fully engaged along the Western Front, their losses mirrored those of their Allied counterparts. When the Americans began fighting in earnest in the summer of 1918, deaths averaged 820 a day, not too far off the French figure and almost twice as many as the British.[27] This comparison helps us to begin recovering the ferocious nature of the fighting encountered by the 1.2 million American soldiers who found themselves on the front lines in the fall of 1918.

As in other armies, American casualties were unevenly spaced among the moments when the Americans took part in maintaining the trench deadlock and when they participated in the 1918 counter-offensives and offensives that halted the German spring offensives and pushed German troops toward the Rhine. Soldiers' own words offer the best evidence of their front-line experiences, and American soldiers filled their diaries, letters and memoirs with vivid descriptions of the agony of combat. 'To be shelled is the worse thing in the world,' noted one soldier. 'It is impossible to adequately imagine it. In absolute darkness we simply lay and trembled from sheer nervous tension.'[28] Clayton Slack privately concluded, 'Those that weren't scared, weren't there.'[29] After he was wounded during a raid, James Reese Europe, a famous musician serving overseas, wrote a signature jazz composition 'On Patrol in No Man's Land' that mimicked the sounds of falling bombs and the rat-a-tat of machine-gun fire. His collaborator Noble Sissle vividly remembered walking through the gas ward of the hospital to visit a wounded soldier in France. 'As you walked down the aisle by the rows of cots,' Sissle recalled over 20 years later, 'you could see how the different ones were suffering. Some of them in places where their eyes were, were just large bleeding scabs; others, their mouths were just one mass of sores; others had their hands up, and there were terrible burns beneath their arms, where the gas had attacked the moisture there…. I had often heard of the horribleness of the torture, but… these scenes are generally kept from the soldier in order to keep from lowering his morale.'[30] In the trenches, American troops confronted the familiar challenges of rats and lice. 'We soon became tired of killing them … ,' noted one combat veteran. 'I have often wondered why there were so few rat bites. Probably the rats felt that it was not worthwhile fooling with live humans when there were so many dead ones around.'[31]

Although there was no American repeat of the 20,000 men lost on the first day of the Somme, in the autumn of 1918 the Americans began fighting in the dense and heavily fortified Argonne woods. The Meuse-Argonne campaign cost 2550 casualties a day and left 26,000 dead in a mere six weeks. In this battle, the Americans succeeded temporarily in breaking out of the trench deadlock to resume a war of movement, only to find themselves digging in once again as the army encountered problems resupplying its troops in the field and refining original battle plans in light of actual circumstances along the front lines.

The rapid pace of the Allied offensive forced Pershing to commit a significant number of undertrained troops to battle, and the combat performance of these troops varied tremendously. AEF generals complained of widespread straggling and estimated that close to 100,000 of the 1.2 million men committed to the battle either purposely or inadvertently lost contact with their units. Perhaps more surprising than the cases of undertrained troops who fled when confronted with machine-gun bursts and artillery explosions were those who, according to one inspector general, when issued rifles asked to be shown 'how to work this thing so that they could up and get a "boche"'.[32] Sending these untrained men into battle, wrote another inspector, was 'little short of murder. How we have escaped a catastrophe is a clear demonstration of the German demoralization.'[33] By early November, infantry-artillery co-ordination improved, night assaults began and aerial bombing and gas attacks supported troops' advance – all signs that the AEF was still learning in the field when the war came to an end.[34]

Even if we are satisfied that the American combat experience deserves consideration alongside that of other combatant nations, another comparative question still remains. How did American soldiers react to their serious losses within such a short time? In the Meuse-Argonne campaign, the Americans contended with poorly trained replacement troops, heavy casualties among line officers, straggling and traffic jams that prevented supplies from reaching the front. There was never, however, any large-scale demoralisation within the army even after the high cost of the offensive became apparent to most soldiers. Over the course of the war, the AEF experienced its share of discord within the ranks, but always over issues related to defining the place of a citizen soldier within the army of a democratic nation – namely struggles over the meaning of discipline, race relations, the legitimacy of non-combatant work and post-war fraternisation with the Germans. At the front, soldiers proved capable of absorbing the personal trauma of participating in combat without losing faith in their leaders or the justness of the war. As Donald Kyler recalled,

> I had seen mercy killings, both of our hopelessly wounded and those of the enemy. I had seen the murder of prisoners of war, singly and as many as several at one time. I had seen men rob the dead of money and valuables, and had seen men cut off the fingers of corpses to get rings. Those things I had seen, but they did not affect me much. I was too numb... [but nonetheless] I had the determination to go on performing as I had been trained to do – to be a good soldier.[35]

Conclusion

At the end of the war, American officials had reason to be proud of their success in turning a small professional force of 300,000 into a modern mass army of over 4 million in little more that a year and a half. At the time of the Armistice the Americans still could not match the tactical and logistical sophistication of their Allies. Yet, overall, these faults are less surprising than the speed with which the Americans fielded an army that could fight well enough to help secure victory for the Allies. Rather than single-handedly winning the war, the United States more than likely prevented Britain and France from losing it. This was a worthy enough accomplishment that allowed millions of men on both sides to survive.

Whether considered from the perspective of creating a modern American military or the lives of individual soldiers, American participation in the war also had tremendous importance for the nation and its citizenry. Conscription and combat defined the domestic significance of the war for the United States. For the first time in its history, the country raised a mass national army and its citizen soldiers used their collective influence to mould internal manpower, disciplinary and racial policies. The United States suffered severe losses during its major combat operations, experiencing the full scope of horrors associated with combat along the Western Front. Within the annals of the history of the war, the domestic history of the nation and the personal narratives of individual soldiers, therefore, American participation in the First World War was a pivotal moment after which nothing was the same.

7

CAGING THE PRUSSIAN DRAGON: NEW ZEALAND AND THE PARIS PEACE CONFERENCE 1919

Richard Kay

We are proud that our Dominion has been privileged to take part in liberating the world from the dragon of Prussianism. (*New Zealand school children to British Colonial Secretary, 19 November 1918*)

The historical literature concerning New Zealand's role at the Paris Peace Conference in 1919 is virtually non-existent. New Zealand historians have failed to fully appreciate the contribution made by New Zealand's Prime Minister William Massey and his Liberal coalition partner Sir Joseph Ward.[1] This is a remarkable oversight given the recent avalanche of academic writing on the First World War and the fact that Paris was the first time, apart from purely technical conferences, that New Zealand appeared as a separate entity at an international gathering.[2] The outcomes of the Paris Peace Conference also had significant consequences for New Zealand's external relations, particularly with the British Empire, the Pacific and the emerging power of the United States of America and Japan.

More than 80 years after Massey signed the Treaty of Versailles on 28 June 1919, it seems timely to reconsider the role he and Ward played. This chapter examines what results their actions had for New Zealand and intra-imperial relations. In doing so, it sheds light on a neglected period in New Zealand international relations when a conservative New Zealand Prime Minister went head-to-head with not only the President of the United States but also an Australian Prime Minister. It will also consider whether the significant cost of New Zealand's involvement in the First World War – over 18,000 lives and at least £60 million – was repaid in the final peace settlement reached with Germany.

Without doubt New Zealand could claim to have had the most 'chaotic end' to the First World War. Just before 11 a.m. on Monday, 11 November 1918 the following telegram from the British Colonial Office arrived on the desk of New Zealand's first Governor-General, Lord Liverpool: 'MOST URGENT Armistice signed 5 a.m. this morning. (Signed) LONG'. Under instructions from the British government, Liverpool withheld news of the Armistice from his New Zealand ministers and the general public for the next 15 hours. At 8.15 a.m. the following day Massey announced that a general armistice had been signed with Germany. A battery gun salute greeted the residents of Wellington and every postal station in New Zealand received a simple message that read: 'Armistice signed'.[4] The strange delay and the influenza epidemic sweeping New Zealand did not affect the planned festivities. Massey declared the day a national holiday and there were spontaneous scenes of wild public celebrations throughout the country.[5]

In New Zealand, the cessation of hostilities on the Western Front had been expected for some weeks. After the initial successes of their spring offensive, Germany's military situation had deteriorated in the last quarter of 1918 following sustained Allied counter-attacks. This forced the new German Chancellor, Prince Max of Baden, to request an armistice under the terms of United States President Woodrow Wilson's Fourteen Points. On 26 October 1918 General Erich Ludendorff, nominally the German Deputy Chief of Staff but the virtual dictator of German policy for the last two years of the war, admitted defeat and resigned to facilitate the peace negotiations.

Two days later the British Prime Minister, David Lloyd George, cabled Massey advising him that he 'ought to be prepared to start for Europe without any delay'. The Australian Prime Minister, William Morris Hughes, had anticipated victory by staying in London. The journey for Canada's Prime Minister, Sir Robert Borden, was just a short dash across the Atlantic Ocean.[6] The British government advised Massey 'to come prepared with all material' to present

New Zealand's case for Samoa, a German colony in the Pacific captured by New Zealand military forces in the first weeks of the war.[7]

In late November Massey revealed in Parliament that the fate of the German colonies hung in the balance. He argued that without a New Zealand presence in Paris, no guarantee could be given that Samoa would remain in New Zealand or British hands.[8] During this speech, Massey signalled his preference for a punitive peace settlement that stripped Germany of its colonies, destroyed its ability to wage war and financially compensated the Allies.[9] He deemed the tiny phosphate-rich island of Nauru vital to New Zealand's interests as a place to 'procure fertilizers cheaply'. He was not, however, prepared to accept any peace that threatened dominion autonomy, declaring that: 'We are going to retain the right to manage our own affairs'.[10] In terms of indemnities, Massey wanted to extract a share for New Zealand 'in proportion to her population and her expenditure on the war'. His final hope for a lasting peace lay in the destruction of the German navy. Massey hoped that New Zealand would be able to claim 'a handy little cruiser or two... for policing the South Pacific'.[11] Massey stated firmly that in Paris he would try 'to make it impossible, at all events for a very long time to come, for any ambitious, unscrupulous nation such as Germany... to again plunge the world into war'.[12] Ward shared Massey's hard-line views on the approaching peace talks except on one important element: the League of Nations. Ward predicted that its creation would be a 'great thing' for the future stability of the world.[13]

On 12 December the New Zealand delegation left Wellington. New Zealand's most informed external policy adviser, Minister of Defence Sir James Allen, for the third and last time became the acting Prime Minister. During the five-week voyage, Massey and Ward could do little to influence events in London and Paris. Consequently, they missed the crucial debate concerning separate dominion representation at the Peace Conference.[14] On 13 January 1919, at a meeting of the Council of Ten, Lloyd George accepted Wilson's proposal that Australia, Canada and South Africa would have two delegates and New Zealand only one.[15] When Massey and Ward first heard the news that New Zealand would only have one representative they felt betrayed. Ward talked openly of returning home and Massey described the decision as 'a sort of slap in the face' but the New Zealanders put on a brave face and refrained from criticising the British government.[16] Before their departure for Paris, Massey stated that 'the trouble is with certain of the Allies, who reckon each dominion representative as one additional vote for Britain'. Clearly the two New Zealanders blamed the United States and France for the decision.[17]

On 23 January the British Imperial War Cabinet, now designated the British Empire Delegation (BED) in Paris, considered the issue of New Zealand representation. Initially Massey and Ward pressed for the same arrangement as for the other three dominions. In view of New Zealand's enormous sacrifices, Massey argued that one representative was 'unsatisfactory'. He was annoyed 'that for the first time, and on debatable grounds, South Africa had been given precedence over New Zealand'. Massey considered that South Africa 'had done little or nothing for the Allies' cause' in the war.[18] He had a point. New Zealand's war effort had demanded a considerable investment of manpower and resources. During the First World War, New Zealand had mobilised 124,211 men, which represented about 20 per cent of the male population. This was the highest figure for any of the dominions involved in the First World War – a fact recognised by Lloyd George himself in his *War Memoirs*.[19]

Ward noted that he could not defend a decision to remain in Paris and that he would be obliged to go home. Lloyd George promised to take Ward's comments into account but the best he could offer was an occasional place on the five-member British Empire contingent.[20] After much negotiation and contemplation, Ward finally accepted the offer. The press were advised that he had been 'appointed a member of the British Empire Delegation on every possible occasion', enabling him to attend its regular meetings twice a week.[21] In reality, Ward had been neatly sidelined from the main event. This suited Massey. 'Naturally we are disappointed,' Massey wrote to Allen, but he concluded 'it really doesn't matter and I do not think that the Dominion will suffer in the slightest'.[22] Massey did learn one salutary lesson from the episode. He realised that if he wanted to achieve his twin goals of punishing Germany and rewarding New Zealand, he would have to assert a distinctive New Zealand voice on three issues: first, over the fate of German Samoa; second, over the final disposal of phosphate resources of Nauru; and third, over the severity of reparations. In the process, Massey knew such a strategy carried risks, especially in negotiations with the most powerful nations at the Peace Conference.

The fate of the German colonies in the Pacific presented the New Zealand pair with the second test of their diplomacy. The major questions concerned whether the colonies should be returned to Germany and, if not, who should get them and under what terms. Throughout the war, Massey and Ward had argued consistently for the retention of the German colonies, especially Samoa. After considerable deliberation, British policy accepted that Germany should forfeit its colonies in any peace settlement.[23] In late December, Lloyd George pledged: 'One thing was quite certain, that none of Germany's colonies would be returned to her'. He did maintain, however, that one of Wilson's Fourteen Points, the principle of self-determination, should be applied to the indigenous inhabitants of the colonies.[24]

When the matter came to be discussed at the Peace Conference, Wilson argued that the mandatory power should 'not exercise arbitrary sovereignty over any people'.[25] This was a direct challenge to the position of the three British dominions – Australia, New Zealand and South Africa – who wanted direct annexation of the German colonies in their possession. In the face of Wilson's opposition, the British position began to waver. The British Foreign Secretary, Arthur James Balfour, stated that he was 'personally in favour of attempting the Mandatory system, but it is full of difficulties'.[26] From an economic point of view, Massey opposed the very basis of the mandate system, saying that 'no country to which the mandatory principle was applied could be properly developed, owing to the difficulty of financing the necessary undertakings'.[27] Lloyd George still clung to the hope of finding a resolution that would appease American concerns without endangering imperial unity.[28]

On the morning of 28 January Massey then gave what American historian William Roger Louis has described as 'a rambling defence of New Zealand's claims to Samoa'.[29] In Massey's view, Australia and New Zealand were 'in the same boat' and 'Samoa was of vital importance to New Zealand'. He avoided mentioning the catastrophic effects of the influenza epidemic on the Samoan population. Massey even listed New Zealand's very own 'highly successful' race relations record with Maori. To underline how enlightened New Zealand colonial administration of Samoa would be, Massey noted that one of his Cabinet colleagues, Dr Maui Pomare, was a Maori.[30] Borden felt that Massey had made a 'good point (that Samoans and Maoris are of the same race) but he seemed hardly to understand the strength of his position'.[31] Massey then floated a provocative question: 'What would Washington have done had it been suggested to him that a mandatory power... should be given charge of the vast territories in North America not at that time colonised?' Massey argued that the American settlers would have 'protested' at such an offer, just as New Zealand was doing. According to Lloyd George, this was one argument which 'perceptibly nettled' Wilson.[32] Following Wilson's rebuttal of Massey's potted history, the meeting was adjourned. According to the British Cabinet Secretary, Maurice Hankey, all the major powers were now 'favourably disposed towards the mandatory principle... [and]... the Dominions were rather isolated'.[33]

Later that afternoon Lloyd George convened a meeting of the BED to work out a compromise. In order to placate Wilson and restore Anglo-American harmony and faith in the peace process, Lloyd George knew that the dominions would have to modify their stance. The meeting agreed that the three dominion prime ministers – Hughes, Massey and South Africa's General Louis Botha – should develop a resolution to express the BED's views on the mandatory system. In effect, the BED had accepted the mandatory principle. It remained, however, an amorphous concept that needed to be defined. That night a member of the Australian delegation drafted a resolution outlining the terms of the mandates. Three different classes of mandate were devised: A class, which generally applied to former territories in the Ottoman Empire, securing them a great deal of autonomy and freedom; B class, for those territories in Central Africa where the mandatory power would have a greater degree of responsibility, ensuring the prohibition of slavery, arms trafficking and the movement of liquor; C class, which accounted for territories such as South-west Africa and the South Pacific Islands, allowing them to be administered as 'integral portions' of the mandatory state.[34] After a 'rather stormy' meeting of the BED on 29 January, Massey and Hughes agreed with the proposal. The American delegation had already seen a copy of the draft resolution and Wilson thought it was the 'basis for an agreement'.[35]

The next day Lloyd George submitted the British Empire's mandatory system to the Council of Ten. The discussion that followed, according to Lloyd George, 'was the only unpleasant episode of the whole Congress'.[36] Wilson lost his temper in the morning session after the appearance of articles in Le Matin, The

Times and the Paris edition of the *Daily Mail*, which reported that the British Prime Minister was sacrificing the vital interests of the dominions and threatening the unity of the British Empire 'for the sake of *beaux yeux* of America'.[37] Hughes was portrayed as being 'at the bottom of the whole thing', but a British observer noted that Botha and Ward played a significant hand in the conspiracy.[38] The three elder dominion statesmen had demonstrated a remarkable insouciance about this threat to the harmony of British-American relations at the Peace Conference.

Following some heated remarks by Wilson, Massey provided the occasion for the most serious disagreement between the dominions and the United States during the Paris Peace Conference – a fact that has been overlooked by Australian historians in their portrayal of Hughes as the 'conquering hero'.[39] Massey told the council that he 'expected some fairly clear and definite statement from President Wilson' with regard to the C class mandate proposal as it was of the 'utmost importance' to the dominions. He would accept the compromise only because 'he did not want to waste any more time than he could possibly help, or place any more difficulties in the way of settlement'. Massey's address produced a blunt response from Wilson, who asked if New Zealand and Australia had presented an ultimatum to the conference? He also wondered if the proposed compromise was their maximum concession? If they did not get this, would they try to stop the whole agreement? Stunned by Wilson's frank accusation, Massey replied meekly, 'No.' At this stage Hughes's hearing aid apparently malfunctioned and he began to launch into a subject irrelevant to the exchange. Wilson interrupted Hughes, asking if he had heard the question. Hughes began fiddling with his hearing aid and said that he had not. Wilson repeated his statement and asked if New Zealand and Australia were prepared to take part in the agreement if the proposed compromise was not passed. Hughes then made his famous reply: 'That's about the size of it, President Wilson'. Lloyd George recalled that 'Massey grunted his assent of this abrupt defiance'.[40]

After a 'friendly and most impressive speech' by Botha, the conference moved rapidly towards agreement. Wilson agreed 'that they had arrived at a satisfactory provisional arrangement' over the fate of German and Turkish territory outside Europe.[41] With the German colonies granted unofficially to the dominions, Massey and Hughes no longer insisted on an immediate assignment. The decision gave both sides an illusion of victory.[42] While President Wilson won his prime objective with the placement of all German colonies under a League of Nations mandatory system, the dominions had secured direct control over their occupied territories in all but name. Massey and Ward were the first to appreciate the magnitude of this triumph. In Massey's estimation, 'a satisfactory arrangement' had been made respecting Samoa:[43] he had gained freedom from the leasehold restrictions he feared and had succeeded in removing the German threat from the Pacific.

The question of how to secure New Zealand and Australia from the Japanese presence in the Pacific became the next priority for Massey and Hughes. The new British Colonial Secretary, Lord Alfred Milner, had been instructed by the BED to clarify the exact nature of the mandatory rule. On 8 March Milner submitted his memorandum to the BED, explaining that Australia and New Zealand were particularly 'anxious' that no naval bases should be built on the Pacific Islands, especially those north of the equator.[44] This was hardly surprising. Allen had warned Massey of the dangers to British shipping if the Japanese occupation of the Marshall Islands went unchecked. By occupying these strategic islands, Allen believed that Japan had made its intentions 'to rule the Pacific Seas' loud and clear. Massey's options to frustrate Japanese expansionism were, however, very limited. As historian S.P. Tillman has pointed out, 'By its largely successful advocacy of its own claims in the Pacific, the British Empire almost automatically secured for Japan the islands to which it laid claim.' Massey's best hope to salvage some security for New Zealand from the Japanese threat lay in building safeguards into the mandate package.[45]

When Milner's memorandum came up for discussion at the BED meeting on 8 March, Massey again joined forces with Hughes and insisted that Japan should be granted a C class mandate for the Pacific Islands north of the equator. As far as the southern dominions were concerned, such an arrangement would serve a double purpose. Under a C class mandate, Japan would be prohibited from raising indigenous armies and erecting military and naval bases; it would also be obliged to report to the League of Nations. This would afford the dominions at least some measure of security while maintaining the right to control trade, immigration and navigation laws in their own mandates. Australia and New Zealand did not want any restrictions placed on the application of their own laws of immigration and navigation in New Guinea and Samoa. In exchange, Massey and Hughes were prepared to accept that Japan should have the same freedom of action they wanted to enjoy. According to Duncan Hall, Massey and Hughes felt 'it was better to allow the Japanese to close the door in the north in order that they should be able to exclude the Japanese from the south'.[46] As a result, when the allocation of the mandates took place on 7 May 1919, New Zealand and Australia were granted C class mandates for Samoa and New Guinea respectively and Japan for the islands north of the equator. Massey's fears that the influenza epidemic that had raged through Samoa would complicate matters never eventuated.[47] The Pacific Islands now delineated the new international frontier between the Japanese and the British Empire, representing the manifestation of the sphere of influence doctrine espoused in the Anglo-Japanese Agreement of 1917.

The interest of the dominions in the Japanese mandates was directly related to their opposition to the racial equality clause in the League of Nations Covenant. On 13 February 1919 Japan formally introduced its proposal on racial equality to the Commission on the League of Nations. In late March the dominion prime ministers met with Japanese representatives in Borden's apartment to work out a compromise. Borden felt that General Jan Smuts, the South African delegate to the peace conference, and Massey would have agreed to a draft resolution containing the principle of racial equality 'without hesitation but Hughes would not consent to anything'. Hughes remained defiant, privately threatening to walk naked into the Seine before agreeing to the resolution.[49]

Massey's attitude on the racial equality issue calls into question his xenophobic credentials. The issue also demonstrates the limits of his relationship with Hughes. Historian Sean Brawley has characterised Massey as the Australian Prime Minister's 'closest ally in the fight against racial equality'.[50] Yet Massey, with an apparent disregard for Anzac co-operation, supported Borden's compromise resolution with the Japanese. Australian historian Eric Andrews has also suggested that Massey's support for Hughes was not as unequivocal as Brawley makes out. Andrews has pointed out that Massey did not even publicly support Hughes on racial equality – unusual behaviour for a supposedly close ally.[51] We can only guess the motives behind Massey's decision to support Borden's amendment. It certainly did not equate with the provisions of New

Zealand's domestic immigration laws for 'keeping New Zealand white'.[52] Massey appears to have been impressed by Japan's trusted service to the Allied cause during the war, consistently pointing out that the Japanese had 'played the game'. In the first months of the war, the Japanese navy had come to the rescue by helping to escort the NZEF's Main Body across the Pacific and Indian Oceans, keeping the threat of German cruisers at bay.[53]

The driving force behind Massey's motivation probably lies in his long-term strategic thinking. The clue is his consistent support for the renewal of the Anglo-Japanese Alliance. In the absence of the credible British naval presence in the Pacific, Japan represented the greatest threat to New Zealand's interests in the region. Massey probably thought that supporting Borden's resolution would protect Anglo-Japanese relations and the security interests of the dominions. In other words, Massey considered it prudent to keep the Japanese as an ally rather than make them a potential foe. Consequently, he does not appear to have been motivated by a genuine desire to promote human rights. It is important to remember that his government passed the Immigration Restriction Amendment Act in 1920, a piece of legislation which, according to historian P.S. O'Connor, 'brought to a successful end the long search for an instrument of policy which would both keep New Zealand white and be acceptable to the imperial government'.[54] Whatever the outcome, New Zealand could live with the consequences of ratifying or rejecting the resolution. Massey had cleverly exploited the situation to enhance his own reputation at the Peace Conference. He seemed a reasonable and moderate peacemaker, knowing full well that Hughes's opposition would defeat the passage of the clause.

Massey's flirtation with the racial equality clause came to an end on 26 March. Confronted by an immovable Hughes, Smuts reported to the Japanese delegation that 'Massey felt bound to follow Hughes'.[55] Once the Australian Prime Minister made his position non-negotiable, Massey felt obliged, like the rest of the BED, to stand beside Hughes to maintain imperial solidarity. Massey seemed quite prepared to see the Australian Prime Minister shoulder all the blame while retaining New Zealand's right to exclude prospective immigrants on racial grounds. He appeared moderate and reasonable, even liberal, in comparison with his colleague. Massey had intelligently played both sides. On 29 March Smuts told the Japanese delegate, Baron Makino, that if his country insisted on bringing up the issue at a plenary session, 'I must warn you that… if Hughes of Australia opposes it, as he undoubtedly will, I shall have to fall in line and vote with the Dominions, like a "good Indian".'[56] In analysing the situation, the Japanese delegation had come to the same conclusion, arguing that 'Massey believed he had to support his Australian colleague [and] that the British Empire Delegation as a whole had to stand together'. On 11 April the issue of racial equality came swiftly to an end at the League of Nations Commission. Wilson, as chairman, ruled the amendment invalid because it had failed to achieve the unanimous approval of the entire commission.[57]

With the defeat of the Japanese racial equality clause, the Massey–Hughes partnership in Paris dissolved over the future of the tiny phosphate-rich island of Nauru. As early as January 1915 the New Zealand government had shown an interest in securing a cheap source of fertilisers.[58] The most serious challenge to Massey's aspirations for Nauru was Australian demands. Massey, under pressure from the New Zealand Farmers' Union, 'strongly' favoured keeping Nauru as a British possession.[59] With the acceptance of the mandatory principle by the Council of Ten, Nauru could no longer be directly annexed by Great Britain, Australia or New Zealand. The focus of the dispute now centred on which country would act as the trustee and the type of mandate it would receive.[60]

Over the next two months Hughes and Massey lobbied the British government. Massey's principal goal was to frustrate Australian designs and hold out for a phosphate settlement with the British. Massey reassured a close colleague:

> I am fighting Australia for control over Nauru and Ocean Island, the two phosphate Islands in the Pacific which are at present in dispute. As a matter of fact I do not think that either Australia or New Zealand will get the Islands but that the British Government will finally obtain control and this will ensure our getting our supplies of phosphates at a reasonable price.[61]

In early April Massey suggested to Milner that the creation of a commission representing the three countries could reconcile the requirements of British control and dominion access to the phosphate.[62] Milner seemed to take Massey's idea on board. By the end of April Milner argued that the mandate should be given to Great Britain and a joint commission should be established to distribute the resources of Nauru. Milner saw this as the 'best means of exploiting them with fairness to all parties mentioned'. At the eleventh hour, however, Hughes decided to 'jump a claim for Australia' and backed out of the agreement against the advice of his own Cabinet. This merely convinced Milner of the 'absurdity of Australian claims'. Lloyd George concurred with this assessment. Massey had outmanoeuvred Hughes.[63]

At the BED meeting on 5 May Massey and Hughes quarrelled over Nauru. Their heated exchange marked the end of the Anzac front at the Peace Conference. Hughes insisted that Nauru was Australia's by right, and threatened that 'non-recognition' of Australia's claim 'would have a most unfortunate effect in every way'.[64] When, in Hughes's words, 'Massey objected in a most offensive way to Australia having mandate, insisting that it should go to Britain',[65] Hughes reacted violently, calling New Zealand's opposition an 'intolerable insult to Australia'. He could not understand New Zealand's objection and even accused Milner of corruption in trying to protect Balfour's shareholdings in the Pacific Phosphate Company. His frustration escalated into a general condemnation of the peace process and he promised that if Australia was 'robbed' of Nauru he would not sign the Peace Treaty. Alarmed at this turn of events, the Australian Cabinet balked at this strategy of brinkmanship by Hughes and advised him to rely upon negotiation to extract some financial compensation.[66]

Despite fierce opposition from Hughes, the Peace Conference allocated the Nauru C class mandate to the British Empire pending settlement between Great Britain, Australia and New Zealand.[67] Massey and Hughes continued to 'row' in meetings and flooded Milner and Lloyd George with pertinent information to strengthen their respective positions. Finally, after six weeks of protracted negotiations, a deal seemed imminent.[68] On 27 June Milner at last succeeded in meeting both Massey and Hughes to discuss a draft agreement that placed Nauru under a British mandate with Australia, Great Britain and New Zealand sharing the phosphate resources. After a 'heated discussion' Milner's perseverance paid off. Agreement was reached that the British would hold the mandate with Australia acting as the administering authority in consultation with Great Britain and New Zealand. The distribution of Nauru's phosphate rock was split three ways, Australia and Great Britain each receiving 42 per cent and New Zealand 16 per cent. The same ratio was applied to the cost of buying the Pacific Phosphate

Company, estimated at £3 million. On 2 July Hughes, Lloyd George and Massey officially signed the Nauru Island Agreement.[69]

With the fate of Samoa and Nauru sealed, direct New Zealand interest in the Peace Conference faded, although Massey did keep himself busy as a member of the Commission on the Responsibility of the Authors of War and Enforcement of Penalties. Under the chairmanship of the American Secretary of State, Robert Lansing, the commission was established to 'study questions concerning the origins of the war and culpability for it, offences against the laws and customs of war in its conduct, and the constitution of a tribunal to try the accused'.[70] Massey's appointment signalled Lloyd George's commitment to implementing his hard-hitting election pledges on war crime punishment. Massey, a well-known hard-liner, believed that the 'Kaiser was a criminal, and should be made to answer for his crimes'. Massey became chairman of the Sub-Commission on Criminal Acts and catalogued no fewer than 32 criminal acts.[71] As he remarked to his colleague, 'Occasionally I am left for a week on my own resource as sole representative for the British Empire. When I come back to New Zealand I shall be passing as an authority in International Law!!!'[72]

In contrast to Massey's contribution, Ward played a limited role at the Peace Conference. His direct participation was restricted to attending BED meetings twice a week and a handful of plenary sessions, which he found to be of little use. Isolated from the intimate meetings of the dominion prime ministers and the Council of Ten, Ward found that he could exert little influence over Massey. He complained that he was never consulted. Inevitably, the *raison d'être* of their wartime relationship began to disappear as the conclusion of the peace settlement drew nearer. Both leaders became restless and turned their attention towards the New Zealand political scene. The major question confronting Massey and Ward related to the future of the National government: would the wartime coalition survive the coming of peace? Ward began working on a new radical Liberal manifesto and Massey instructed Reform members to start working on an election strategy. By the start of June, Liverpool informed Milner that Massey and Ward's absence had 'gravely imperilled their hold on the country and their parties'.[73]

As the post-war political landscape began to dominate New Zealand thoughts in Paris, the reparations question came to be debated as part of the general peace settlement. At the BED meeting held on 11 April Massey and Hughes were 'bludgeoned' into submission by Lloyd George to accept a compromise, which allowed an impartial Inter-Allied Reparations Commission to assess Germany's liability and capacity to pay.[74] Massey initially opposed the proposal, fearing that the postponement of the imposition of a final figure on Germany would merely extend the wrangling over reparations and Germany would escape payment of the whole costs of the war. Having committed himself so publicly to making Germany pay an indemnity in proportion to the dominion's population and war expenditure, Massey could not return to New Zealand and confront his opponents in a general election empty-handed. He was bitterly disappointed that the Reparations Commission could not reach a consensus, calling the meetings a 'fiasco'.[75] Eventually Massey dropped his objections in the face of hostile criticism from the whole BED. He concluded that there was no point in fixing a final sum if Germany could be made to pay more.[76]

On 7 May Massey and Ward witnessed the presentation of the draft treaty to the German delegation in the Trianon Palace at Versailles.[77] The Allies gave the German government delegation 15 days to submit its written observations on the draft treaty. Massey expressed his disappointment at the leniency of the reparation clauses, which did not force Germany to pay the 'full cost' of the war. He admitted that Great Britain and the dominions could only expect to recover 25 per cent of their war costs. Massey was careful to point out that extreme reparation demands would serve only to spread the Bolshevik message in Germany. He told the press that it would be very easy to find 'flaws' and 'imperfections' in the treaty, but he called for unity to counteract its weaknesses. On 29 May the Germans issued a damning criticism of the draft, refusing to sign the treaty because it violated the principles of Wilson's Fourteen Points and the pre-Armistice agreements.[78]

Over the next two days Lloyd George summoned the BED to his apartment to discuss Germany's reaction to the peace treaty. On 1 June Lloyd George asked the delegation if they favoured the draft treaty in its present format and, if not, whether they were prepared to negotiate concessions with Germany to encourage an early signing. Massey, who experienced great 'difficulty' in answering 'yes' or 'no' on the subject, suggested that the important points of the draft should be closely studied one by one. He blamed the current difficulties on the American domination of the peace talks and admitted that he did not understand the position of the Fourteen Points.[79] Given American opposition to excessive reparation demands, Massey reported to Allen that 'Wilson seems to be able to exercise a dominating influence and British interests very often appear to be compelled to take second place in consequence'.[80] Despite the 'sustained pressure' of practically the whole BED, Massey supported Lloyd George's refusal to renegotiate the reparation clauses and settle on a fixed sum. Even though he considered the clauses 'dangerously indefinite', the Inter-Allied Reparations Commission now represented Massey's best hope to recover some of New Zealand's staggering war debt under the contentious heading of pensions and disablement allowances. New Zealand had incurred a debt roughly the equivalent of £100 per capita and he doubted that Germany had suffered proportionately as much. Massey feared that any fixed sum now would be too small, as the BED had clearly swung in favour of a more moderate peace. Ironically, one of the reparation clauses' greatest opponents had now become one their greatest champions. In Massey's opinion, 'Germany caused the war, Germany lost the war, and Germany should be compelled to pay as far as possible'.[81]

Smuts mounted a comprehensive attack on those sections of the treaty that he considered too harsh and observed that Massey's version of a Carthaginian peace would end in renewed hostilities. Massey dismissed Smuts's criticism by arguing 'that immunity from punishment encouraged crime'. Massey was no apostle of a soft peace; he wanted to prevent any resurgence of German militarism. The League of Nations was no guarantee of security, in his opinion, and he refused to reimburse Germany for German property confiscated in Samoa and New Zealand. He even doubted that a treaty firmly committed to Wilsonian principles could produce a lasting peace. Logic dictated that there was nothing to be gained from granting concessions to the Germans. He did not want the BED to alter the German colonial settlement or repudiate the so-called war guilt clause. Massey feared that 'the next generation would probably see a still more terrible war' anyway. To underline his hard-line approach, Massey wanted the Kaiser charged on a 'moral offence'.[82]

At the end of the meeting Lloyd George secured a resolution outlining the concessions the BED was prepared to offer Germany. British interests were seemingly unaffected by the proposals.[83] After more horse-trading between

Lloyd George, Wilson and Clemenceau, on 16 June the Allied counter-proposals were delivered to the German delegation. The council agreed that no further concessions would be granted. On 22 June the Allies issued an ultimatum to the German government: it was given 24 hours to accept the treaty unconditionally or face the termination of the Armistice. Conscious that the shattered German army was too weak to resist an Allied invasion, the German government agreed next day to sign the treaty.[84]

On the 28 June 1919 Massey lined up with other dominion representatives in the Hall of Mirrors at Versailles. After South Africa's Smuts, Massey wrote his initials and surname to become the seventeenth signatory.[85] With this act, Massey had established New Zealand's right to accede to the treaty and had simultaneously secured membership of the League of Nations in all respects the same as that of the other members of the international community.[86] Massey did not hang around for the celebrations. Thanks to trains, planes and automobiles and a Royal Navy destroyer, he made a desperate attempt to catch Ward, who had already left Paris. Twelve hours later, at 2.15 a.m., Massey boarded the *Mauretania* near Portsmouth.

Massey may not have been a 'force' at the conference, yet his contribution was in no way 'bland' or invisible, as one historian has described it.[87] Up until this point no other New Zealand statesmen had been so aggressive in pursuing New Zealand's foreign and security policy objectives. Although some of Massey's and Ward's aims were compromised and unrealised, their core objectives were accomplished. The New Zealand delegation accepted this truth of diplomacy: Massey described the peace process as 'the effort to adjust all sorts of Allied difficulties and differences'.[88]

In Paris, Massey had demonstrated a deft hand in his partnership with Hughes. Initially, Massey and Hughes co-operated to achieve their congruent interests, which embraced the colonial settlement, reparations and the sanctity of their domestic immigration laws. They worked effectively as a team to blunt what they considered to be the main threat to their interests: Wilson's idealism. Their co-operation provided a formidable barrier to the other delegates, especially the United States and Japan. Eventually, as the issues were settled one by one, the Massey–Hughes partnership unravelled over the fate of Nauru. Massey complained of Hughes and the fact that he was 'most unreliable and [has] done nothing to assist me in anything where the interests of New Zealand have been concerned'.[89] The trans-Tasman relationship, however, remained a partnership of convenience. It could be renewed at any time when the common interests of the two dominions were threatened by the diplomacy of the British Empire. For example, at the 1921 Imperial Conference Massey and Hughes resumed their alliance to seek a continuation of the Anglo-Japanese Alliance because both considered stable Anglo-Japanese relations important for their security interests in the South Pacific. At the 1921 Imperial Conference, Massey warned that if the Anglo-Japanese Alliance was not renewed, the British Empire ran the grave risk of turning a 'loyal friend into a very dangerous antagonist'.[90]

Massey's relationship with the American delegation represented his greatest personal failure in Paris. In contrast with his good relationship with Lloyd George, Massey's intense Anglo-centrism and realist conception of diplomacy brought him into direct conflict with President Wilson. Ward's meddling hand also played a part. Massey missed a vital opportunity to establish good relations with the United States and to bring American weight to bear on Japanese expansionism in the Pacific. In co-operating with the Americans, he might have been able to enhance New Zealand's security. Instead, Massey appeared intransigent and extreme in his attempts to punish Germany and annex Samoa. He conveniently blamed the United States for frustrating his own peace aims and making the Paris Peace Conference 'unbusinesslike'. Massey felt that 'it would have been far better had the Conference begun with the discussion of the actual peace terms rather than take up so much time with such matters as the League of Nations'. He found Wilson to be a rather 'specious' politician, and resented his domination of the peace conference. Massey found the company of French Premier Clemenceau far more convivial.[91]

Personalities aside, Massey and Ward achieved significant results for New Zealand. Along with Hughes, Massey shifted temporarily the focus of British policy-makers to the Pacific region, where the interests of New Zealand and Australia predominated over imperial concerns. On Samoa and Nauru, Massey achieved the substance of what he wanted. He worked tirelessly for New Zealand's interests in this region, securing Samoa as an integral portion of the British Empire, acquiring cheap phosphates for the dominion's economic development and eliminating the German threat in the Pacific. With the establishment of the mandate system and the defeat of the racial equality clause,

Massey could also claim to have contained Japanese expansionism. According to the New Zealand diplomatic historian Anne Trotter, 'Superficially at least, New Zealand's security seemed to be enhanced by these arrangements.'[92] New Zealand would not have been quite as comfortable in 1939 had it not been for Massey's efforts in liquidating Germany's empire.

With the benefit of hindsight, some of Massey's aims were not attainable. Massey had delusions of grandeur, foreseeing a time when the entire Pacific would become a British sphere of influence. Whether this represented a manifestation of his British Israelite convictions requires further investigation. Yet we can say with some assurance that Massey saw the Peace Conference as an excellent opportunity to revisit the whole Pacific question. He wanted a complete readjustment in the government of the New Hebrides, Fiji and Tonga, advocating the exchange of territory as the basis of any negotiations.[93] In spite of his persistence, the French refused to discuss the fate of the New Hebrides. Balfour informed Massey in blunt terms that the New Hebrides 'had nothing to do with the Peace Conference. This is clearly the French view also.'[94] The British were as reluctant as the French to approach issues outside the immediate scope of the peace talks. Milner deflected Massey's suggestion that New Zealand could administer Fiji, by promising that the British government would consult the New Zealand government over any future adjustment to Fiji's governance.[95]

It could be argued that Massey's short-term objectives also undermined the viability of New Zealand's long-term security interests. The Prussian dragon had been temporarily caged. The Treaty of Versailles did not effectively crush German power. It merely provided the worst of both worlds – it was not ruthless enough to prevent a resurgence of German militarism and not reasonable enough to conciliate the German people. The so-called 'war guilt' clause of the treaty, as British historian Gary Sheffield has pointed out, developed ironically to limit German responsibility to pay reparations, and was cruelly exploited by the Nazis in the 1930s to undermine the treaty's validity.[96] New Zealand's decision to support the secret Anglo-Japanese Agreement of 1917 could also be criticised as short-sighted. The acquisition of the islands north of the equator encouraged and legitimised Japanese expansionism. Japan had increased its geographical proximity to Australia and New Zealand and the restrictions of the C class mandate were deceptively weak. The conditions of the mandates were paper tigers. In the end, Massey wanted more assurance to check the Japanese threat to New Zealand security. After the war, he began promoting the need for a powerful British naval presence in the Pacific, but in the end he had to be satisfied with a second-best solution: the development of a British naval base in Singapore to allow the British fleet, normally based in European waters, to operate against Japan if necessary.[97]

In terms of winning an indemnity for New Zealand, Massey's aspirations were severely dented by the peace process. Initially, he left Wellington promising to extract from the Germans in the peace treaty the full cost of the war to New Zealand, which he calculated to be £100 million.[98] During the peace negotiations, Massey's hopes were dashed and he gradually reduced his reparation demands as it became clear that the BED would not support hefty payments.[99] On his return to New Zealand Massey admitted defeat, claiming that 'one man's opinion does not go far in a Conference of sixty or seventy members'. He had to be satisfied with the right to confiscate all German property in New Zealand and Samoa and the reparation clauses that included reimbursement for disablement allowances and pensions for the civilian dependants of combatants.[100] Massey tried to put a brave face on the settlement. He predicted that New Zealand could reasonably expect £12 million for the pensions and disablement fund over the next 30 years.[101]

The New Zealand delegation had gone to Paris expecting to crush Germany and solidify the power of the British Empire. Of the two ministers, Massey played the more prominent role in ensuring that New Zealand's interests were not forgotten by Great Britain. He even found time to negotiate an extension of the imperial commandeer of New Zealand's primary products.[102] The conference debates concerning important issues of policy confirmed the simple fact that Great Britain could not have pursued a peace settlement entirely separate from dominion interests. For Massey, the Peace Conference demonstrated that New Zealand's interests could not be totally safeguarded within the imperial framework. Massey and Ward demonstrated in Paris that New Zealand had developed its own foreign and security policy interests well before the advent of Michael Joseph Savage and the first Labour government in 1935. An appreciation by New Zealand historians of the importance of Massey and Ward in the evolution of New Zealand's foreign policy tradition is long overdue.

8

BECKHAM, WAUGH
AND THE MEMORY OF GALLIPOLI

Jenny Macleod

In October 2003, England played Turkey in Istanbul in the crucial qualification game for the Euro 2004 football tournament. Among the banners in the crowd, one read '[David] Beckham remember Gallipoli'. It is unknown what England's captain made of the historical reference, but it is apparent that the journalist reporting this story had only a vague understanding of the campaign. He explained that the banner referred to 'the First World War battle where 22,000 British and Commonwealth soldiers died in a futile last stand against Turkish and German troops'.[1] The memory of Gallipoli was thus shaped to fit the banal circumstances of a football match – for the Turkish owners of the banner, it suggested the promise of victory; for the journalist, it was a do or die opportunity or 'last stand', tinged with the obligatory idea of its futility.

Nor is this the first time that the Gallipoli campaign has been used to inspire sportsmen: in 2001 Steve Waugh and the Australian cricket team stopped off in Turkey en route to the Ashes series in England to recreate the game played by Australian Light Horsemen at Shell Green on 17 December 1915. The excursion was intended as both homage and inspiration. One journalist reported Adam Gilchrist's comments:

His voice occasionally wavering with emotion, Gilchrist spoke of the impact the day had on him and his team mates. 'You might have got me at a bad time,' the Australian vice-captain said. 'It's just a big day. We've learned so much. If you can't take something out of this… you never will. The leadership, support and teamwork you would need to be successful in any operation [during a war] – this [Gallipoli] is the extreme, and that can filter down to any operation or any sport.[2]

But as another journalist pointed out, 'sacrifices on the battlefield and the cricket field are not the same. Let's not forget.'[3] Similarly, Steve Waugh commented, 'It puts things into perspective for us because people call us heroes but we just play sport and we're good at it.'[4]

If we compare these two sporting uses of Gallipoli, at least we can say the banner in Istanbul was based on firm historical foundations – they were remembering a great Turkish victory. In contrast, and notwithstanding their respectful intentions, the Australian cricket team were harking back to a humiliating defeat to inspire them for a match where their former brothers in arms were now their opposition and, rather than being untried newcomers, they were now the all-conquering team to beat.

In Britain, historical allusions in the reporting of sporting events are not uncommon. International fixtures often provide an opportunity for chauvinism, not least when England plays Germany at football.[5] But, tellingly, Gallipoli references are not part of the headline writers' repertoire. The campaign simply does not loom large enough for the British general public.

Further examples abound of the differing resonance and memory of Gallipoli in Australia and Britain. Every year on Anzac Day, the anniversary of the landings on the peninsula is marked by commemorative ceremonies throughout Australia and wherever Australians congregate throughout the world. It is sufficiently culturally and politically significant that in 2004 the Australian Prime Minister John Howard ignored the risks and visited Australian troops on service in Iraq on 25 April,[6] while thousands of Australian backpackers travelled to the peninsula itself, despite government warnings of a terrorist threat.[7] Such events are afforded extensive newspaper coverage each year, often including special supplements and editorials. In Britain, the anniversary is marked at locations with specific links to the campaign such as Bury or Eltham in London, or by expatriate Australians and New Zealanders. In Edinburgh, the Scottish National War Memorial holds a commemorative service each year, but in 2004 chose to schedule it for Friday, 23 April. One Australian backpacker felt so strongly about marking the correct day that she decided to organise a ceremony at the Australian-themed Walkabout pub in the city on the proper day.[8] British newspaper coverage was brief and limited to reporting Australian commemoration.[9]

The question is, then, how did this happen? Why does Australia remember Gallipoli so keenly, when Britain does not? Why does Australia *continue* to remember Gallipoli so keenly – and, bearing in mind the cricketers' investigation of a defeat as an inspiration – so flexibly?

The answer lies in the way that history is socially constructed – the way in which the remembering (or indeed the forgetting) of any given event, the writing of its history, is affected by the identity and location, both geographical and temporal, of the author. This means that historical memory is both malleable and multi-faceted. If we consider some of the early historians of the campaign, it is possible to see how their personal concerns and their societies shaped the way they wrote about Gallipoli, and how the nature of those societies and their involvement in the campaign affected the resonance of those accounts.

The key figure in the Australian history of Gallipoli is Charles Bean. He worked as the official correspondent with the AIF throughout the war, and agreed from the outset that he would write a history of the war upon his return. Although it was his flashier British counterpart, Ellis Ashmead-Bartlett, who made a splash with the scoop of the Anzac landings,[10] Bean's work is far more significant overall. His journalism, his editorship of *The Anzac Book*, his labours as official historian, and his activities as the guiding light of the Australian War Memorial profoundly shaped and propagated what has become known as the Anzac Legend.[11]

The relationship between Bean's two main jobs is instructive. His diligence as war correspondent laid the groundwork for the official histories, not only in terms of gathering evidence when few other sources were readily available, but also in setting out the priorities he would pursue: the front-line focus, the emphasis on the individual and the extrapolation from that into an interpretation of what it was to be an Australian. Where the two tasks differed, however, is that as a war correspondent Bean aimed to bear witness to the role of the Australians in the campaign, but when he came to write up the story in the official history he had an elevated view of his task: he was 'constructing the permanent memorial in writing of Australia's effort in the war'.[12] Indeed his official history captures and preserves the memory of the deeds of individual Australians in a way that is of civic and national value.

Bean's approach to his task has much to do with the time in which he lived. He had absorbed some of the intellectual ideas of his day, particularly social Darwinism, and assumed that it was possible to identify racial and moral characteristics in the Anzacs that were central to national identity. Bean's theme throughout, then, is the nature of the men produced by the young nation of Australia. He argues that the experience of working and surviving in the bush had percolated through Australian society, and that in combination with the egalitarian nature of society this produced men who were independent, resourceful, adventurous and full of initiative. Bean later wrote that among the questions he needed to answer in his history was 'How did the Australian people – and the Australian character, if there is one – come through the universally recognized test of this, their first great war?'[13] That he took this view also has much to do with the fact that he was writing in the early days of Australia as a federated country; its history, it was felt, was largely a blank canvas and here was the first significant episode to be painted.

The Anzac Legend that Bean created in interpreting the actions of the AIF proved tremendously powerful in a newly federated country that was thirsting for a sense of identity. Yet even the most evocative and influential episode in history will fade away if it is carved in stone and left untouched. History risks becoming a museum piece, appropriate to the time and space in which it is created, but out of reach and increasingly irrelevant if it is not updated. This is what had almost happened to the Anzac Legend by the 1960s, when it was widely predicted that Anzac Day would die out with the Anzacs themselves.[14] Yet, the progress of the Anzac Legend since that date illustrates not only the continuing influence of Bean but also more generally the sometimes difficult relationship between historians and the public memory of historical events.

From the mid-1960s, a new generation of historians, Ken Inglis and Bill Gammage in particular,[15] returned to the story of Gallipoli, to studying Bean's work and to Bean's way of doing things. Thus *The Broken Years* focused on the individual's experience of war, yet it did so in a way that was appropriate to the 1970s, admitting some of the darker sides of war and concluding that it was an unrelieved tragedy. Work such as this was vital to the reinvigoration of the Anzac Legend, and set in train the revival it is now undergoing. It shows the way in which history must be subtly reshaped to suit the society it is written for in order to remain relevant.

A crucial part of the Anzac revival has been the engagement of journalists, and prominent among them has been Jonathan King. Since organising a re-enactment of the First Fleet's journey to Australia for the 1988 Bicentennial,[16] he has been deeply engaged in the promotion of traditional Australian history. He is particularly interested in retelling the stories of Gallipoli. He has said, 'One of the best things I've done in my life is to interview the last 10 Gallipoli diggers. I fell in love with them – totally, madly, deeply. They were just such gentle old giants that they brought a 1915 breath of fresh air from Australia back in.'[17] In addition to his TV documentaries, and newspaper articles on Anzac Day and landmark events, he has written a book about Alec Campbell. At the age of 16, Campbell served as a water carrier at Gallipoli during the final weeks of the campaign. When he died in 2002 he was the last known surviving Anzac and was afforded a state funeral. King's book, *Gallipoli: Our Last Man Standing*,[18] demonstrates both the way in which the Anzac Legend can be reshaped and the continuing influence of Bean.

As one might expect from a journalist, the book is evocative and engaging; but there is also a good deal of padding to spin out Campbell's brief participation in the war as far as possible. King smooths out some of the non-conformist aspects of Campbell's life, and has worked hard to fit the last Anzac's story into Bean's mould. His brief service as an Anzac soldier may not have been typical, but we are told that 'the extraordinary life he led encapsulated what it means to be Australian'. Campbell may not have gone 'over the top' at Gallipoli, but he was 'a little Aussie battler'. 'A fighter from boyhood, he rolled with life's punches, always bouncing back to fight another day.' He grew up in the bush, a fair dinkum Australian, a wild and restless boy who just wanted to be out in the bush with a gun.[19]

And *Our Last Man Standing* fits the society it was written for – one that now chooses to venerate the gentle, brave and resourceful Simpson and his donkey rather than the vicious, brave and resourceful Albert Jacka VC. It is fortuitous then, perhaps, that the idolised last Anzac was a water carrier who never went over the top but nonetheless 'dodged his share of bullets', landed under enemy fire, and therefore 'earned his full credentials as an Anzac'.[20] Perhaps with the Ashes stopover fresh in his mind, but with little understanding of Scottish history, King asserts that the Campbell clan are warriors who fight the English.[21] And as he describes the evacuation, King tells us 'the question they could not stop asking themselves was, what was the point of their dying, if we are just going to abandon the campaign by sailing away?'[22] This is not a question King bothers to answer. He thereby perpetuates the modern idea that the First World War was futile.

Popular history such as this tends to exist in parallel with scholarly work, and the two rarely intersect. Indeed their concerns and approaches can be markedly different. For example, it would be surprising if an academic expressed King's infatuation with the Anzacs in the same terms, for it represents an emotional connection with the past that is largely absent from or at least unspoken in academic discourse, which is steeped in the conventions of objectivity and detachment. Yet the Anzac Legend's focus on the individual facilitates just such a close identification with historical events, and this visceral bond is at the heart of the legend's resonance. It could well be argued that the popular memory of the war, which is above all an emotional history of it, identifies the essential truth of the war – suffering, heroism, futility – in a way that detached historians, who are supposed to make sense of it all, do not.

There are various ironies here, not least the fact that the very process of questioning and subtly reshaping past events, which has fuelled the wider engagement in the subject, has in turn provoked criticism of the continuing questioning of the legend. One example occurred when a group of academics' discussions on Gallipoli were brought to public view. In October 2002, a conference organised by the Australian War Memorial and Curtin University called 'Australia in Peace and War' was held in Çannakale, Turkey. It was a friendly and fascinating conference where numerous original research papers stimulated many rewarding exchanges. The one unusual feature of the conference, however, was that among the attendees was the *Australian* newspaper's history correspondent, Jonathan King. When he returned home, he wrote up an article under the headline 'Charge of the rewrite brigade'. Despite the woeful pun, King's article could have usefully served to generate open-minded public discussions of the Anzac Legend. As Peter Stanley of the Australian War Memorial was reported to have said: 'All this criticism showed the old Anzac legend has life in it yet. We are not destroying Gallipoli but updating the interpretation and enriching our understanding of it.'

Perhaps some of these ideas may have been challenging to some readers: 'Those Anzac soldiers were not all heroes, nor were the Anzacs all country boys either. It is time to dismantle the monolithic images of the Anzacs and update the reality.' [Attributed to Martin Ball, a Melbourne-based historian.]

But the real problems flowed from the reasonable questioning of the linguistic obfuscation inherent in describing the actions of April 25 as a 'landing'. As he did elsewhere in the article, King misattributed the quote, wrongly attributing it to John Lack: 'The landing was nothing but an unjustified invasion of foreign soil like the British invasion of Aboriginal land in 1788 ... and we should put the two coves together – Sydney Cove and Anzac Cove – because both invasions were just as bad as each other and cost a lot of lives.' This was part of a broader political edge, absent at the conference, that King added in his account: 'Instead of commemorating the heroism of Australian soldiers who landed on that fatal shore in 1915, the conference in October concluded that Australians should reframe the landing as an unmitigated disaster and apologise to the Turkish Government for invading their country.'[23]

Journalists in New Zealand picked up the story. The conference delegates became the 'self-styled Rewrite Brigade', a copy editor's headline asked 'Did historians drink too much', and Foreign Minister Phil Goff was quoted as saying 'an apology had not been sought and there were no plans to offer one'.[24] Some of the historians named in the article consequently received angry letters from the public.

The incident prompts various questions for the historian. Why is there such a gap between public history and academic history? What implications are there for institutions like the Australian War Memorial that try to straddle the two? Perhaps we should revel in controversy as the opportunity to educate. Christopher Pugsley took the chance to discuss the supposed comments made to the effect that the Anzacs were cowards and not particularly good fighters. No doubt many more people will read that newspaper article than his scholarly chapter on the same theme.[25]

Another intervention by a journalist in the history of Gallipoli also reflects the popular engagement with the subject in Australia, as well as the continuing influence of Bean. Les Carlyon's 2001 book, *Gallipoli*, topped the bestseller charts in Australia.[26] His canvas is broader than King's: he seeks to contextualise the extraordinary phenomenon of Anzac Day and the nature of the peninsula today by telling the story of the campaign from the point of view of the politicians, the generals, the admirals, the Turks and the men. Above all, however, this is the story of the Australians. A typical bias therefore remains, despite Carlyon's inherent fairness exemplified by his acknowledgement that the Helles landings were far bloodier than Anzac. He is critical and enquiring, investigating the controversy over stragglers, or pointing out the deficiencies of New Zealand and Australian officers, including Alexander Godley and Francis Johnston. Yet he saves his greatest venom for the bungling British officers, Aylmer Hunter-Weston and Frederick Stopford, and the ferocity of his sarcasm marks him apart from the usual academic approach, as does his post-modern decision to insert both his own experiences of visiting the peninsula and novelistic flights of imagination.

Carlyon is trying to convey the mythic aspects of Gallipoli, arguing that 'the siren-call of this beach has little to do with facts or common sense or the dessicated footnotes of academics'. He thus evokes the romantic aura of the campaign through references to 'history's stadium', 'Samothrace, home of Poseidon', Napoleon and Alexander, the Via Dolorosa, Golgotha, Homer and Shakespeare. General Sir Ian Hamilton is cast as Don Quixote, and more Hamlet than Henry V.

Interestingly, then, Carlyon combines elements of the Australian and British traditions in portraying the campaign. He has the heroic individualism of Bean and the Anzac Legend, updated by the revisionism of more recent historical scholarship, and he has the romanticism embodied in much British writing on Gallipoli. The particular characteristics of British accounts of the campaign flow from the broader role that the imperial power played in Gallipoli, and from the different purpose of the books' authors. These accounts were not forging an identity for a new nation; rather they were engaged in the less ambitious task of rescuing the reputation of a humiliating defeat. In doing so, various themes emerge in the British portrayals of Gallipoli, which may be termed a heroic-romantic myth.[27]

The key elements of this myth are, first, a smokescreen of allusions to the romance of Gallipoli and the heroism of its participants in order to distract from the bitter pill of defeat. Second, there is an insistence on the strategic value of the campaign (both in terms of its vision and achievements) and the transfer of blame for failure to decision-makers in London.

In developing the story's heroic and romantic strands, British authors not only convey a favourable view of warfare but also allude to earlier legendary battles and warriors, and there can be few locations that offer a richer backdrop of stories, fables and classical associations. Gallipoli is separated from the battlefield of Troy by the narrow straits, the Dardanelles. This was the ancient Hellespont which Leander swam across to reach Hero, and which Xerxes crossed on a bridge of boats. Moreover, the campaign lent itself to comparison with Greek tragedy – explicitly to a cycle with three distinct parts (landing, trench warfare and evacuation) and perhaps implicitly to a proud hero humbled (the British Empire).

Just as Bean's social Darwinism was consistent with wider attitudes in society, so this propensity to romanticise war drew on common attitudes, familiar motifs in art and literature, and lessons from public school. Among these were the cult of chivalry that idealised the knight of the Middle Ages, and muscular Christianity, both of which developed in the 19th century. Thus the generation of men who fought at Gallipoli had been brought up on martial stories they were ready to compare to their own experiences: Hector and Achilles, Richard the Lionheart, the charge of the Light Brigade, Ivanhoe and so on. Crucially, such stories idealised heroic failures as often as victories. Other possible contributory sources of the heroic-romantic myth include late Victorian Britain's glorification of death, and Romanticism's obsession with death and decay. And to this list must be added the Hellenism that was central to an English public school education of this period.

It is possible to trace these attitudes and motifs through various influential British accounts of Gallipoli. It can be seen in John Masefield's work of propaganda for the United States with its allusions to *The Song of Roland*. A.P. Herbert's *The Secret Battle* shows Harry Penrose being inspired by his knowledge of the Classics as a counterpoint to his disillusionment and shellshock on the Western Front. Ernest Raymond's *Tell England*, with its title reference to Simonides' epitaph to the Spartans, presents the campaign as a crusade. Although Churchill eschews similar references in his *World Crisis*, he was quite capable of elevating the campaign in other ways, given the literary power of his prose. [28]

But perhaps the most notable example of the British tendency to romanticise the campaign is General Sir Ian Hamilton's *Gallipoli Diary*. Published in 1920, this was far from being the reproduction of nightly scribbles made by the commander-in-chief during the campaign. It was a carefully crafted memoir in diary form, designed to defend his reputation and that of the campaign. Here are just three examples to give a flavour of his prose style. The first is a description of the peninsula shortly after his arrival:

> No other panorama can touch it. There, Hero trimmed her little lamp; yonder the amorous breath of Leander changed to soft sea form.... Against this enchanted background to deeds done by immortals and mortals as they struggled for ten long years five thousand years ago, – stands forth formidably the Peninsula. Glowing with bright, springtime colours it sweeps upwards from the sea like the glacis of a giant's fortress. [29]

In the wake of his order to the Anzacs to 'dig, dig, dig' rather than evacuate, he wrote: 'Be the upshot what it may, I shall never repent that order. Better to die like heroes on the enemy's ground than be butchered like sheep on the beaches like the runaway Persians at Marathon.' [30] This is his conclusion on the landings at Helles: 'Blood, sweat, fire; with these we have forged our master key and forced it into the lock of the Hellespont, rusty and dusty with centuries of disuse. Grant us, O Lord, tenacity to turn it; determination to turn it, till through that open door *Queen Elizabeth* of England sails East for the Golden Horn!' [31]

These kinds of romantic and heroic allusions suggested that the warfare at Gallipoli was in keeping with a noble tradition, that perhaps it was not so ghastly or modern after all. In particular, it was a world away from the Western Front.

The other oft-repeated strand in British writing on Gallipoli refers to its strategy. This was the central issue for the British, for the men who instigated the campaign. They defend its strategy in two ways: in terms of its potential and in terms of its effect. Thus the idea of attacking in the East is firstly portrayed as an imaginative shortcut to victory, one that was in keeping with Britain's traditional recourse to utilising its naval power in a peripheral attack. And despite the slim chance of success at Gallipoli and the Dardanelles, the prospect of victory in the East has retained its potency as an alternative to the grim slaughter of the Western Front. The strategy is secondly defended as having had decisive results, despite not having secured its most obvious goals. Thus it is frequently claimed that Gallipoli facilitated the later victories in the East by destroying 'the flower of the Turkish Army'. And underlying these strategic claims is the carefully veiled suggestion that the politicians in London, especially the dead hero Lord Kitchener, by their ineptitude and indecision made the soldiers' task impossible.

Again, Hamilton's *Gallipoli Diary* illustrates these points. An important subtext is the demonstration of the very difficult task he was set. Hamilton wanted to show that he had been let down by the politicians in London and particularly by Kitchener, though he denied that he was trying to belittle the former Secretary of State for War. He later wrote in a letter, 'Through the Diary I am always struggling up against his Colossus who overshadows my whole horizon – and that is what has led so many reviewers to think I am attacking K. who really was looming too big in my mind.'[32]

Hamilton's difficulty, as this letter suggests, was that to make his own case he had to attack an important and revered figure, someone who he had loyally served as chief of staff in the South African War. Explicit criticism was therefore out of the question. Instead, Hamilton did two things in his diary. First, he published a very full description of his preparations for the landing – amounting to approximately one-fifth of the book's length. This demonstrated how difficult the task of landing on the peninsula was, how inadequate were the War Office preparations and how hastily he was expected to depart from London. His 'diary' entry for 12 March 1915 includes the comment that 'the Dardanelles and Bosphorous might be in the moon for all the military information I have got to go upon'.[33] He thereby establishes the idea that the campaign was ill served by the War Office and that the very achievement of landing on the peninsula was extraordinary.

The second of Hamilton's solutions to explaining failure without explicit criticism was to insert into his text many of the cables and letters that passed between himself and London, content to leave them to tell their own story. They provided copious evidence of his attempts to secure further men and armaments, thus creating the impression that he was continuously being rebuffed by a short-sighted War Office.

It is also possible to discern this heroic-romantic myth in Brigadier-General Cecil Faber Aspinall-Oglander's British official history of the Gallipoli campaign.[34] It, too, points out the errors at the grand strategic level that contributed to failure on the peninsula. This was highly unusual. Brigadier-General Sir James Edmonds, the director of the Historical Section, Military Branch, and therefore the man with overall responsibility for the British official history series, had very firm views on their nature. He aimed to produce a technical staff history rather than a popular work for the general public, favouring detailed and accurate information, eschewing overt expressions of opinion and avoiding criticism and controversy. The discussion of grand strategy, such as it was, was left to the naval histories.

To overcome Edmonds on this point, Aspinall enlisted the help of Churchill – never a disinterested party in the question of the Dardanelles strategy – and pushed for the issue to be discussed at a meeting of the Sub-Committee for the Control of the Official Histories in March 1928.[35] The problem that prompted such a move was Aspinall's reference to the government indecision that had allowed both the Second Battle of Krithia and the attack at Aubers Ridge on the Western Front to go ahead when there was a shortage of ammunition. To Aspinall, this episode was symptomatic of the failure in London to support the Gallipoli campaign and give it the backing it required to succeed.

At the meeting, Edmonds explained his approach:

> GENERAL EDMONDS said that two persons could not write in the same style. He had been inclined to hint a thing rather than to state it baldly. Taking the Battle of Loos, when Lord French and General Joffre were clamouring to have as many Divisions as possible, he put in the History what Divisions were sent to France, and at the same time said that four Divisions were sent to the Dardanelles, but he did not rub it in. We did not, he considered, want everybody to see the troubles we had had and the mistakes we made.[36]

Years later, Aspinall recounted the progress of the meeting to Liddell Hart:

> I was also amused to hear what he [Edmonds] told you about his dislike of telling
> the truth in an official history! That explains why he was so 'down' on my
> Gallipoli, and tried to persuade me to water it all down. I eventually had to go
> to Winston, who attended a special meeting of the CI Defence to discuss the
> whole matter, with Edmonds and me as witnesses, and at which, thanks to
> Winston's support, I was successful all down the line. But I remember Edmonds
> telling me that 'In ten years' time your book will carry no more weight than an
> article in the Sunday Press. It will lower the reputation of the War Histories, and
> you'll live to be ashamed of having written it!'[37]

The question of who was responsible for defeat is not relevant just to the British historiography of the campaign. It is, of course, keenly discussed in Australia, particularly in regard to controversies over landing at the wrong beach, and callous and incompetent orders at The Nek. But it plays out at a more general level as well, and provides another piece of the jigsaw in explaining Bean's approach. Australia's junior political role in the empire means that Australia did not own responsibility for the campaign: strategic decision-making for the empire's resources was made in Britain. Australia's most important contribution was manpower. It was therefore natural for the Australian official history to tell *The Story of Anzac* rather than taking a broader view. Moreover, that irresponsibility brought a kind of freedom – since, undoubtedly, the failures at the strategic level were largely responsible for the defeat at Gallipoli, a space was provided for the Australians to proclaim their local achievements in spite of the overall picture.

In a far more muted way than in Australia, the British memory of Gallipoli also declined and revived over time. Once more a journalist was involved and his work provides further evidence of the malleability of historical memory. The Australian war correspondent of the Second World War, Alan Moorehead, published his *Gallipoli* in 1956.[38] It is a compelling and entertaining tale of the campaign, with vivid pen portraits of many characters. It coincided with a new British failure in the Mediterranean, Suez, in the autumn of 1956, and updated the common evaluations of the campaign in the wake of the experience of 1939–45. The story benefited from a renewed appreciation for Dunkirk's gallant defeat and evacuation that led to later victories, the possibilities of amphibious operations with the D-Day landings in Normandy and, above all, the rehabilitation of Churchill's reputation.

Moorehead's book was highly successful: it won two prizes and was widely reviewed. Despite the fact that Moorehead's snappy prose was a world away from Hamilton's grandiloquence, it is interesting to note the romanticism the subject could still provoke:

> To many of my generation, the Second World War generation, the thought of Gallipoli, during many years of our boyhood and youth, exercised an especial and powerful fascination. It was the great, sad and stirring myth in whose shadow we grew up. The enormous, slaughterous battles of the Western Front sickened and horrified me (they still do); contemplation of them left my spirit bruised and dazed; but I thought (I still think) that I could understand Gallipoli. It blended the classical and romantic in my small but ever-to-be enlarged store of experience; Virgil and Euripides taught me something about it: Thucydides more; it ranged itself in my imagination with Thermopylae and Marathon, and the dire, doomed Athenian expedition to Sicily. The poets and the novelists whom I most admired wrote about Gallipoli. They all seemed to have fought there. More than one had died there. In my time, I suppose, I have read almost everything that has been written about Gallipoli.[39]

This illustrates both a core strength and weakness in the memory of Gallipoli. Central to its resonance is that sense of Gallipoli's difference from the quagmire of the Western Front that looms so large in the popular imagination in Britain. But these literary flights of fancy cannot be the basis of widespread inspiration – they provide comfort to the bereaved and the defeated, they attract the interest of military enthusiasts, but they do not reach out far beyond that. Thus although Moorehead inspired Robert Rhodes James, among others, to study the campaign, and he has been credited with the more widespread growth of interest in the First World War in the 1960s, his book was not the prelude to a widespread popular engagement with Gallipoli in Britain.[40]

The campaign has continued to fascinate military historians who tend to approach it from the strategic point of view. That combination of beguiling interest and hard-headed technical appraisals has its roots in the emphases of the heroic romantic myth that marked out the British participants' accounts. But Gallipoli has not taken on a wider national significance – the engagement with the campaign remains professional or local and personal, a level at which the myth has provided solace.

Yet, in contrast to the British heroic romantic myth of Gallipoli, the far more ambitious Australian Anzac Legend continues to resonate at a national level; Bean's focus on the individual and national identity remains – updated, yes, but still recognisably intact. This is due not only to his skills as an author and promoter but also to the nature of the society he was writing for – a young nation thirsting for a shared identity. As one backpacker remarked on Anzac Day 2004, 'We don't have a lot of history, but the history we do have means a lot to us.'[41]

E.H. Carr argued that history is like a mountain which takes on different shapes from different angles of vision; the power and influence of the Anzac Legend is such that Gallipoli is a mountain that is most often viewed from the southern hemisphere.

9

RETURN, REPATRIATION, REMEMBRANCE AND THE RETURNED SOLDIERS' ASSOCIATION 1916–22

Stephen Clarke

The Roll of Honour for the New Zealand Expeditionary Force in the Great War 1914–1918, published in 1924, recorded that 16,697 men and women died while on active service overseas.[1] Many of these names were immortalised in stone on the hundreds of local war memorials throughout New Zealand that became the focal point for remembrance on that day of great sorrow: Anzac Day. This memorialisation was all part of a sacred pact: 'We will remember them'. But what do we know about the more than 80,000 members of the NZEF who came home? In diaries and memoirs of returning soldiers it is difficult to find a description of the actual journey back to New Zealand, let alone the transition from soldier to civilian. Even in memoirs or oral interviews recorded years later, accounts of the immediate post-war years are absent or vague. There is a 'Great Silence' about the experience of returning from the Great War, and historians have not broken this, despite their renewed interest in the First World War. However, as French historians Stephane Audoin-Rouzeau and Annette Becker argue, 'One of the very first questions that should be explored and understood is that of the return of the soldiers.'[2] Where to start? This chapter examines the beginnings of the organisation that represented the collective voice of the returned soldier – the Returned Soldiers' Association, as the present-day Royal New Zealand Returned and Services' Association or RSA was originally known, which by 1920 had signed up nearly three-quarters of the returned soldier population – and surveys some of the themes of the New Zealand experience of return.

The rise of the RSA

Wounded soldiers from the Gallipoli campaign began to return to New Zealand from July 1915. They soon found that they faced many problems. By late 1915, they were meeting throughout the country to air their grievances and discuss the idea of forming returned soldier associations in their own localities.[3] To Christchurch belongs the honour of being the first centre to formally establish an exclusively returned soldiers' association, which came into existence during December 1915.[4] Similar associations sprang up in many other places during early 1916.[5]

In the formation of these groups and the eventual establishment of the New Zealand Returned Soldiers' Association, one figure stands out: Captain Donald Simson. In London, in 1915, the New Zealand-born veteran of the South African War joined the British Section of the NZEF, which was absorbed into the New Zealand Engineers upon arrival in Egypt. Wounded at Gallipoli, he was repatriated to New Zealand in July 1915. Against the advice of the military medical authorities, for Simson was suffering from neurasthenia (shell-shock), he toured throughout the country publicising the need for a returned soldiers' movement and overseeing the formation of several local associations, including Christchurch, Dunedin and Wellington.[6] The accounts of these early local associations also mention his public proposals to form a national association, lest returned men be isolated in local groups or, worse, divided between several national veterans' organisations.[7]

Delegates assembled in Wellington on 28 April 1916.[8] The widespread interest in the formation of a national association was revealed by the presence of more than 30 delegates from Hamilton in the north to Invercargill in the south, and even from the Chatham Islands. A large number merely represented returned soldiers in their area rather than associations *per se*, which were yet to be formed. The only major centre not to be represented was Auckland, which was in the process of organising a local association. The delegates looked to

Captain Simson for leadership and he was unanimously elected to chair the conference that he had striven to convene during the previous six months. A good deal of the delegates' time during the two-day gathering was devoted to the organisational and constitutional issues involved in establishing a New Zealand Returned Soldiers' Association, with headquarters in Wellington, and branches throughout the rest of the country. Delegates also discussed matters that would continue to be the centre of attention throughout the history of the RSA – membership, repatriation and the treatment of disabled soldiers.

After the delegates returned to their towns and cities, new associations emerged, while existing associations voted to affiliate with the NZRSA. This was an important development because it meant that, from the outset, returned soldiers would be represented by one strong body rather than divided between several weaker organisations, as was the case in Britain and Canada until the 1920s.[9]

A second conference was held in Wellington in July–August 1916. This time the Auckland RSA was represented. The most important outcome of this conference was the decision to promote the formation of local associations which would then affiliate with the NZRSA. This enabled each association to be self-governing, united only by bonds that could be broken at the discretion of either body. The requirements for affiliation were only the admittance of members under certain qualifying criteria, mainly that they had been honourably discharged from active service in the present war (extended to members of other British and dominion forces in 1918 and veterans of the South African War in 1920), and that each branch pay a levy towards the maintenance of the national headquarters. What may appear to have been a potentially weak bond would actually serve the organisation well and prove a source of strength. Because each local association was owned and run independently it was supported by its local community. In short, the RSA movement would combine the strength of parochial support with the status and power that came from being a part of a large national organisation. The conference also ratified the constitution and shortly afterwards the Dominion Executive Committee (DEC) developed a public manifesto that advocated the principles of a non-sectarian, non-political association serving the interests of returned soldiers and all war dependants, with concentration on the rehabilitation of the returned soldier into civilian society and the fostering of clubs.[10]

The greatest sensation of the conference was the defeat of Simson for the presidency by Captain William Tutepuaki Pitt, also a South African War veteran and a representative of the Gisborne RSA. Simson's outspokenness and self-serving demeanour, as well as speculation that he held political aspirations, had unsettled returned soldiers who feared he would harm the public image of the newly formed organisation.[11] Embittered by his defeat, Simson tried to block the registration of the association and to form a rival organisation. In this he was unsuccessful: the NZRSA was duly registered as an incorporated society in January 1917.[12] Because of his opposition to the RSA, Simson enjoyed a mixed reputation within its institutional memory. But even his contemporary critics credited him with playing a pivotal role in raising awareness throughout the country of the plight of returned soldiers and the need for a national association to represent them. For this Simson deserves the title of founder of the RSA.[13]

The departure of Simson was only the beginning of a succession of rapid changes in the executive of the NZRSA during its formative years. The election of Pitt, one of four Maori officers controversially sent back to New Zealand for alleged incompetence after the August 1915 offensive at Gallipoli,[14] reveals that Maori returned soldiers were welcomed in the RSA as fellow 'diggers'. Talk of separate Maori RSAs was opposed on the basis that Maori and Pakeha had fought together.[15] However, Pitt's term as national president ended in most unfortunate circumstances in late 1917 with his resignation, following allegations that he had misappropriated £150 given to him by a benefactor for RSA purposes.[16] Pitt was chosen as NZRSA president because returned soldiers placed their trust in an officer to lead them, as they had done during the war, but unfortunately in this case the officer concerned was not equal to that trust.

If the RSA was not at first fortunate in its choice of presidents, a succession of able and dedicated men certainly followed. After Pitt's resignation, James Harper acted as president until he was appointed to represent the NZRSA on the War Pensions Board in February 1918. Elected president later that year at 25 years of age, Claude Wilfred Batten was the youngest-ever national president. A clerk in his family's Wellington importing business before the war, Corporal Batten had served at Gallipoli before being repatriated sick to New Zealand in October 1915. A foundation member and inaugural general secretary, Batten demonstrated his commitment to the association when he worked unpaid for several months at a time. As general secretary and later inaugural editor of the NZRSA's publication *Quick March,* Batten was literally the face of the NZRSA during its formative years. When Batten resigned in January 1919, after being appointed as Wellington District Repatriation Officer, Dr Ernest Boxer stepped into the position, in which he was confirmed at the annual conference later that year. The English-born doctor had served with No. 1 Field Ambulance at Gallipoli before being invalided back to New Zealand in late 1915. Major Boxer had been elected inaugural president of the Hastings RSA upon its establishment in 1916; he had become vice-president of the NZRSA in 1917, and had served as acting president in early 1918. A man of intellect, sound judgment and tact, he steered the association through a difficult period of internal division and away from party political action. He was also a visionary who urged the association to aim above parochial self-interest to the greater good of the nation and empire. Upon Boxer's resignation for health reasons in 1921, Major-General Sir Andrew Russell, the former commander of the New Zealand Division, who himself had required two years to recover from the strain of the war, began his long and distinguished term as president. Russell was both respected and popular among his former soldiers, who affectionately called him 'Daddy' and 'Ariki Toa' or simply 'Chief'. His example, as well as encouragement to his former subordinate officers, also signalled the influx of the officer corps into the organisation. Russell personally championed the principle that an officer's duty of care to his men did not terminate with the end of the war. Russell's decision to take up the presidency, as well as his subsequent tenure, meant that, by the early 1920s, the RSA was well established as a respected institution in post-war society.[17]

The road to that point, however, had been a difficult one. The first annual report of the NZRSA noted that its inaugural year had been 'largely experimental', and that despite a national membership of 4000 members the original estimates of the development and financial strength of the association had been 'unduly optimistic'.[18] The financial situation of headquarters was precarious as local associations, under financial pressures themselves, were slow to forward their membership dues. The national association was kept afloat during this period only by the efforts of Gallipoli veteran and unofficial war artist, Horace Moore-Jones, who, under the RSA's sponsorship, toured the country throughout

1916–17 exhibiting his sketches of Gallipoli. This provided the RSA with not only much-needed funds but also invaluable publicity.[19]

With a view to publicising the merits of membership, the RSA launched its own paper, *Quick March*, on Anzac Day 1918. It provided both a lively and invaluable means of keeping members up to date with RSA news, information about repatriation, and land and pension schemes, and a source of entertainment with stories, skits and cartoons, most of them dealing with war nostalgia. At its height in 1919, *Quick March* was the fastest growing paper in New Zealand with a nationwide readership.

The NZRSA annual report for the year 1917–18 was more positive in tone: the membership had more than doubled to 10,000 members spread among 30 local associations.[20] The introduction of a national membership system during the year went a long way towards securing greater control over membership. The annual conference in 1918 also extended free honorary membership to returned nurses, who received their own special badge.[21] It was the beginning of a tradition of returned servicewomen as honoured members of the RSA. Together with mothers, wives and sisters organised as Auxiliary Ladies Committees (later known as Women's Sections), these women made a contribution that far exceeded their numerical strength.[22]

The first year of peace, 1919, would be a critical one for the fledging RSA movement. The return of tens of thousands of returned soldiers would provide not only a great boost but also a significant challenge, just as it would for society as a whole. In fact, peace celebrations themselves were short-lived in New Zealand as the worldwide influenza pandemic swept through the country during November 1918, killing as many as 8600 people. The unusually high mortality rate among young male adults struck the returned soldier population hard. For example, the Christchurch RSA lost its president, secretary and one other executive member, in addition to over 60 returned soldiers in the district.[23]

The great bulk of soldiers, 52,833 men, were repatriated during the 12 months following the Armistice. By Christmas 1919, only 792 remained overseas.[24] The RSA successfully attracted the returning men as they sought an organisation that would mitigate their transition from soldier to civilian. The rate of growth was indeed impressive. From 10,000 members in 1918, the membership swelled to 25,000 by mid-1919.[25] This expansion brought not only enhanced strength and financial security but also organisational problems as local associations and headquarters grappled with keeping on top of such rapid growth in a membership that was significantly mobile during the restless post-war years. The greatest problem faced by the organisation, however, was to restrain the high expectations of its members.

By 1919, growing dissent arose as sections of the RSA felt that the government was reluctant to meet their demands concerning repatriation, land settlement and pensions. During the immediate post-war period the RSA had the youngest and most outspoken membership in its entire history. The threat of direct action by recently demobilised members of a citizen army was not a trivial concern, as demonstrated when between 1000 and 2500 members of Wellington RSA and supporters marched down Lambton Quay and held a rowdy demonstration at Parliament in an effort to seek a larger gratuity payment from the government. The Dominion President, Dr Boxer, on hearing of the demonstration from his home in Hastings, sent a telegram to Prime Minister Massey expressing regret and assuring him that such actions were neither the style nor the policy of the NZRSA.[26] Boxer's reaction reveals the growing division within the RSA movement by 1919, with some associations venting their anger at headquarters out of sheer frustration. The main rift was between the largest and most radical local association, the Auckland RSA, and the national body.

Dissatisfaction over the system of headquarters control had first been expressed at the 1918 annual conferences. In 1919 a new scheme of district organisation was established, with four districts based on the main centres.[27] This seemed to satisfy the demand from local associations for decentralisation, but a dispute over who would control funds allocated to the district committees led the Auckland RSA, together with the Auckland District Committee, to threaten the NZRSA with legal action.[28] The dispute had got out of hand and a special conference was convened in Wellington for October 1919.

This was the most important gathering of the period since it debated the key issues of organisation and *modus operandi*, including whether the association should enter mainstream politics. The Auckland RSA was driving both issues. It brought forward a proposal that would have given far more power to the districts: local associations would be affiliated to the district associations rather than directly to the NZRSA and district representatives on the national executive would possess the power of veto. In short, Auckland did not intend to be a silent party to national policy with which it did not agree. Delegates warned that the scheme made no provision for an annual conference and effectively eliminated local voices at the national level. In the end, new compromise arrangements did give the districts some responsibility and power while retaining the annual conference and the DEC as the overall policy-making body.

The Auckland delegates, however, were not impressed with this watering down of their scheme. A heated debate resulted, during which the outspoken Auckland RSA secretary, E.F. Andrews, claimed that the national body was run by a 'clique' and that if the new constitution were passed the Auckland RSA would leave the NZRSA. Andrews may or may not have been bluffing, but having peered into the abyss both the Auckland RSA and the NZRSA wisely pulled back from the edge. The conference finally agreed to the establishment of a district system, although the final details would not be settled until the following year. Five districts were eventually established: Auckland, Wellington, Nelson and Marlborough, Canterbury and Otago.[29]

Closely intertwined with the campaign for greater local autonomy was the desire to have a greater public voice through the mechanism of direct political action. A non-political stance had been incorporated into the constitution of the NZRSA from the outset and vigorously adhered to throughout the war years.[30] With the collapse of the wartime coalition of the Reform and Liberal parties, the general election of late 1919 provided fertile ground for political action. Once again, the Auckland RSA led the call for change.[31]

At a series of meetings throughout early 1919 Auckland decided to send to the annual conference a remit calling for a change to national policy to enable direct political action, together with a political platform that included a demand for legislation to compel employers to reinstate returned soldiers, equal pay for equal work, a comprehensive land settlement policy, state housing for returned soldiers and a white New Zealand policy. Each parliamentary candidate would be asked to support the platform in writing, which was common practice in 'various non-political organisations', as *Quick March* noted, but Auckland wished to go one step further and campaign against those candidates who did not pledge support.[32] The prohibition of such political action was reaffirmed at the May conference,[33] but the Auckland RSA continued to fight. At a special general meeting in July 1919, Auckland members called for a returned soldiers' political party and adopted a more extreme platform, including the imposition of a penal tax on all large land holdings not being fully used, the takeover of unoccupied Maori lands for settlement and the reduction of the cost of living by a rigid control of profits.[34]

The issue of political action was fully debated at a special conference held in October 1919. The Christchurch RSA now joined forces with the Auckland RSA in declaring that political action of some kind should be taken to secure the rights of returned soldiers. The lengthy debate again revealed that though most members were opposed to party political action there was support for some form of political action. A compromise was struck with the adoption of an amendment to the constitution, by 50 to 36 votes, to replace 'non-political' with 'non-party political'. This enabled the RSA to take limited political action, in the form of submitting questions to candidates, without influencing members in regard to any candidate for public office.[35] The NZRSA itself published a statement before the 1919 general election outlining issues that were still outstanding.[36] At the annual conference the following year Boxer congratulated delegates on having 'laid [to rest] forever the Political Ghost'.[37]

The Auckland RSA, however, was slow to accept the decision. In 1921 it decided to nominate candidates for the Auckland City Council and Hospital Board. When reminded that this action contravened the NZRSA constitution, Auckland 'compromised' by issuing a notice that there were no official RSA candidates, though it still listed the names of those candidates it would have supported. These candidates subsequently appeared under the banner of the militant Protestant Political Association, angering Roman Catholic members of the Auckland RSA: it was clear how necessary it was for the RSA to refrain from direct political action.[38]

The debate over whether to enter politics was not unique to the RSA. It was common to veteran organisations throughout the empire during this period, as they sought to gain maximum benefit from their position in society. The decision to remain outside politics and to speak only on matters concerning returned soldiers, thereby not dividing its own membership along party lines and ensuring bipartisan support, was a wise one.

The NZRSA may have refrained from entering party politics but its views were certainly heard in the corridors of power. For a start, MPs J.G. Coates (later to become the first returned soldier Prime Minister), J.B. Hine, T.E.Y. Seddon and William Downie Stewart returned from the war and resumed their seats in Parliament during 1919, all but Seddon holding ministerial posts during this period. After defeating Labour candidate Robert Semple in Wellington South in the 1919 general election, Wellington RSA President George Mitchell became the RSA's spokesman in Parliament. In 1921, John A. Lee, Auckland RSA executive member standing for Labour, was defeated by fellow Auckland RSA member and Reform candidate Clutha Mackenzie in the Auckland East by-election. In the general election the following year, however, Lee got revenge on the former editor of *Chronicles of the NZEF*.[39] This Herculean contest between the one-armed Lee and the blind Mackenzie indicates not only the tenacity of these two war-ravaged warriors but also that the RSA included among its ranks the full spectrum of party politics. In this way, the problems faced by returned soldiers were represented to the government from within by returned soldier MPs and from without by the RSA. The RSA concerned itself with an array of national issues, from defence to immigration policy, but its overwhelming focus was the welfare of returned soldiers and war dependants. Returned soldiers and their organisation had a special status in post-war society, as revealed by the frequent use of the upper case 'Returned Soldier'. Their service and the sacrifice of their comrades gave them a special stake in society, and the RSA was not averse to using the 'politics of patriotism' to remind politicians that they had a duty to listen to them.[40]

There is no doubt that the divisions of 1919 had distracted the RSA from more important issues, such as repatriation, as Boxer noted in his address to the 1920 annual conference.[41] This was a young organisation finding its institutional feet. The larger local associations were frustrated by the apparent lack of government action: the national body itself became the target of criticism. During this period there was constant insinuation that headquarters was either cowering before or actually in collusion with the government. Even worse was the criticism targeted at DEC members personally, particularly the charge that they were more concerned with securing their own positions than the interests of returned soldiers. In 1919, for example, A.B. Sievwright, of the Wellington RSA, called for a return showing the salaries as well as any government positions held by DEC members. Most interesting, however, was his call for each member's war record, as if length and extent of service somehow created a measure of worthiness for holding office.[42] To question a returned soldier's war record was as serious an aspersion on his character as one could find in post-war society, akin to being called a 'shirker'. Such bitter attacks on the leadership of the RSA reveal the frustration and anger within sections of the membership and the returned soldier community in general. It reveals, moreover, how quickly the optimism of peace had been replaced with pessimism and bitterness.

For its part, the national body was in an unenviable position, caught between the high aspirations of local associations and their members and the reality of government policy. The dispute was a classic example of the periphery of an organisation becoming frustrated with its central hierarchy without fully understanding the problems it faced. The RSA had come perilously close to a split and all parties deserve praise for ensuring that this calamity was avoided. The greatest credit, however, must go to Boxer, whose tactful leadership helped the association through its most important period, when disputes over organisation and methods threatened its unity and very existence. Above all, the debate reveals the emotional involvement of members as they attempted to create an organisation that would best serve the concerns and needs of returned soldiers.

After a year of considerable drama, the RSA settled into a period of constructive consolidation from 1920. The organisational structure was now established and there was some stability of leadership. With the NZEF now fully repatriated, new associations were forming and growing at an incredible rate. In 1920 the RSA reached its post-war peak membership of some 57,000 members – more than two-thirds of the returned soldier population.[43] The RSA now spread out from the main cities and provincial centres to smaller rural towns – Kawakawa and Kaiapoi, Te Awamutu and Temuka, Whangarei and Westport – thus doubling the number of associations to 60. Furthermore, the larger local associations, such as Auckland, now had numerous sub-associations. This growth, in turn, meant that the financial side of the association was now more certain.[44] A tangible sign of this new sense of optimism and permanence was the RSA clubrooms that were going up throughout the land.

From the outset, the RSA viewed clubs as an essential element in repatriating the returned soldiers.[45] The culture of comradeship that had sustained soldiers through the ordeals of the war would now assist their repatriation into civilian society. The NZRSA was essentially a traditional male institution but with one considerable difference: the prerequisite for membership was not wealth, class, religious, or sporting allegiance but war service. This extraordinary shared experience and the bond it engendered made this a club like no other.

During the immediate post-war years RSA clubrooms were built at a faster rate than war memorials. The subscription of large amounts towards the building projects, which in the main centres were significant, signifies that the public supported the need for a place for returned soldiers to gather and relax.[46]

There was, however, some concern over whether the clubs would continue the wartime male culture and pose a threat to civil society. The Christchurch RSA secretary, W.E. (Bill) Leadley, responded to this criticism by promoting the advantages of the RSA movement:

> The war had made a difference to the men. They had learnt something of the true meaning of comradeship and brotherhood. Friendship formed in the trenches would last a lifetime. It was felt desirable to keep intact the bond of comradeship of those who were brothers in arms and who fought the battles of the Empire side by side. This would provide a new and lasting basis of good citizenship.

The clubs were to foster a new social order based on the principles of self-sacrifice and comradeship. Leadley reiterated the view of the RSA movement: 'The clubs, because they form meeting places for returned men, have proved a very valuable factor in the work of repatriation'. These were the carrots with which to win over the public, but Leadley was not averse to waving the stick: 'if returned men were not provided with an opportunity for rational social enjoyment they would seek other less desirable means of amusement'.[47]

This raises the question of how much the RSA provided a form of social control in post-war New Zealand. The RSA leadership certainly sought to channel returned soldiers into work and respectable pastimes and away from more disreputable aspects of male wartime culture; this was important not only for the men themselves but also to maintain the goodwill of the public and government. Anxious to ensure that the public and government would willingly continue to support its aims of successful repatriation, the RSA was intensely concerned with the image of returned soldiers. The one theme that permeated every aspect of the early RSA was its concern, bordering on obsession, with the idea of *respectability*.

So what was the atmosphere of the early clubs? The new décor, together with the youthfulness of the members, made the clubs modern and lively places. Sport played a large part in the early RSA and, apart from the ubiquitous billiards, RSA teams entered local competitions in rugby, soccer and hockey in the winter and cricket in summer. In 1920, for example, the Palmerston North RSA rugby team won the senior competition.[48] This sporting emphasis is a corrective to the pervasive image that all returned men were physically scarred by their war experience. The fact that returned soldiers preferred to form their own sports teams rather than play for established clubs also reveals the continuing strength of wartime bonds.

But the RSA's activities were by no means confined to traditional male sporting pursuits. There was an array of cultural activities, such as debating, but most popular was music: many associations established concert parties, brass bands and even full string orchestras but choirs were the most popular. If the New Zealand Division had been known as the 'Silent Division', soldiers certainly exercised their vocal cords on their return. For example, the Dunedin RSA Choir, formed in 1919, quickly becoming a fixture on the Dunedin social scene, where it has remained ever since.[49]

The most popular form of entertainment – 'smoke concerts' – were purely a returned male domain. With their skits, songs, some speeches, much smoking and plenty of drinking, they best recreated the wartime bond of comradeship and humour of the NZEF.

This raises the question of the place of alcohol in the life of the RSA. Contrary to later public perceptions, the early clubs were 'dry' and the strongest beverage members could purchase was a cup of tea. At the special conference of the RSA in October 1919, a motion to request Parliament to grant RSA clubs charters to sell alcohol was overwhelmingly rejected, with only two delegates in favour.[50] This aversion to the introduction of alcohol was a part of the widespread desire for respectability. The RSA rallied against what it viewed as biased press reports identifying 'Returned Soldiers' as the perpetrators of drunkenness. The returned soldier was to be identified only with honourable actions.

The RSA was itself concerned with the problem of alcoholism among returned soldiers and an early advocate of alcoholism as a disease rather than a moral failing.[51] This perhaps explains the advertisement in *Quick March* for 'Drinko', promoted as the 'drink habit cure', which appeared, ironically, on the same page as advertisements for various brands of beer and liquor.[52] RSA members themselves were far from teetotal. Recalling their experience in old age, a number of veterans indicated that heavy drinking was a part of the culture of some RSA clubs during the 1920s.[53] Such cliques of heavy drinkers were a legacy of the war and evidence that not all returned soldiers could be successfully reintegrated into society. It is to this process that we now turn.

Repatriation

Because of the numbers involved, the resettlement of the First World War soldiers required an effort unprecedented in New Zealand's history. The majority of returned soldiers found jobs themselves and navigated the transition back into civilian life under their own steam. For many returned soldiers, however, there were considerable difficulties to overcome: sick and wounded men had to recover their health; permanently disabled men had to be trained in new occupations; those who had apprenticeships or student training interrupted by the war or had not begun a trade or a profession required schemes; and for most the war had postponed marriage and the setting up of a home. All these problems were lumped together under the term 'repatriation', which, after the Second World War, would be more appropriately called rehabilitation.

The New Zealand government had moved swiftly to provide for the returned soldier, passing the War Pensions Act and the Discharged Soldiers' Settlement Act during 1915, before the RSA had even been formed. Repatriation administration also began during that year with the formation of the Discharged Soldiers' Information Department.[54]

This response did not satisfy the RSA, which agitated for the introduction of a comprehensive rehabilitation scheme for returned soldiers. Just as the government had placed the country on a war footing to win the war, so a comprehensive national plan would be required to win the peace. In late 1917, the DEC drew up a repatriation policy that encompassed the provision of employment, occupational and education training, financial assistance towards business ownership, an efficient system of land settlement, home ownership and an adequate pension scheme both for soldiers and their dependants. Reaffirming that repatriation was a state responsibility, it specifically called for the establishment of a Repatriation Department under the control of a single minister. The RSA also requested the right to express its opinion on all proposed legislation affecting returned soldiers.[55]

The philosophy of the RSA towards repatriation was two-pronged. At the level of the returned soldier, it encouraged self-sufficiency. On a national level it pressed the government to provide national direction and the opportunities for returned soldiers to take their place in society. It was a continuation of the self-help ethos of the late 19th century, combined with the New Zealand tradition of state assistance for the deserving. The soldier had fought for the state, argued the RSA, and it was now time for the state to help the soldier to resume civil life. The association's rhetoric emphasised equity and fairness for the returned soldier: 'a square deal', 'playing the game'.[56] The RSA was quick to denounce the notion that the soldier was looking for any reward or special treatment: all he wanted was assistance to allow him to resume life at a level he had been accustomed to before the war. For the fit returned soldier this meant a job; for the disabled retraining or a pension; and for the dependants of dead soldiers adequate pension provisions.

The RSA also believed that action was required during the war. As one prominent returned soldier Cabinet minister pointed out at the end of the war, the men who had returned during the conflict had been suffering from injuries and disease.[57] The government's preference for a piecemeal approach until after the war, when the full extent of the problem would be known, brought condemnation from the RSA.[58] The association did as much as it could to assist, but it was limited by its own meagre resources.

With the end of the war, the government finally announced its repatriation scheme. The Repatriation Act 1918 provided for the establishment of a Repatriation Department under the control of a board of four ministers.[59] The stated aim of the department was 'to help every discharged soldier requiring assistance to secure for himself a position in the community at least as good as that relinquished by him when he joined the colours'.[60] The form of assistance was divided into three areas: employment, training and financial assistance. The department's philosophy was one of decentralisation so that returned soldiers could have ready access to repatriation assistance. In the four main centres, district boards were established with paid staff. The membership of the boards represented employers, unions, farmers, industry, patriotic societies and returned soldiers, including a representative of the RSA. In many respects the legislation was a comprehensive and innovative approach to the problem of repatriation. The RSA took umbrage because it had not been fully consulted but vowed to support the new department.[61]

The RSA continued to maintain, however, that repatriation would succeed only as part of a greater scheme of post-war reconstruction of the New Zealand economy. In May 1919, the DEC publicised a draft scheme for 'national reconstruction', which included rational distribution of labour, state development of new industries and state ownership, a dominion hydro-electric scheme, improved infrastructure and the need for a new fiscal policy.[62] In essence the RSA was calling for a planned economy, which would not only assist repatriation for returned soldiers but also create a better country. This rather radical call for state intervention reflected the returned soldiers' war experience where the army had overseen every aspect of their lives and everyone was working towards a common end. It reveals the RSA as a visionary organisation searching for new solutions. In fact, the policy was too advanced for the *laissez-faire* Massey government and it would take the Great Depression of the 1930s before a government would adopt such a policy. In such large-scale schemes one can observe the aspirations of the RSA not only to assist the repatriation of returned soldiers but also to ensure that they returned to a land fit for heroes. The dead must not be allowed to have died in vain.

If such a policy was the dream, the RSA never lost sight of reality and continued to work to secure gains from within the repatriation system. Although the RSA, unlike its Australian counterpart, was not represented on the Central Repatriation Board, it had some positive influence on repatriation administration at the grass-roots level in towns and communities, as a result of the decentralised nature of the department. The RSA also formed its own Repatriation Committee to monitor closely the department's progress and amend anomalies and extend allowances. Its reports reveal a rapid change of attitude from criticism to open praise of the government's repatriation policy. The success of the policy was undoubtedly the close relationship that developed between the Repatriation Department and the RSA. The life of the department was also extended for a further six months as a result of RSA lobbying, but by the end of 1922 the department concluded that the task of repatriation had been completed and the RSA declared that its work had given the greatest satisfaction to all returned soldiers.[63] By the end of the decade, however, the department's closure, and the RSA's acceptance of it, would be shown to have been premature.

The government, had moved quickly to introduce comprehensive pension legislation. Upon the return of large numbers of wounded men during the war, injustices and anomalies began to appear. The RSA immediately sought to rectify these. One of its most important battles was that against the anomaly of pre-war disability being taken into account when fixing a pension. The RSA condemned this practice on the grounds that the acceptance of a man for military service was conclusive evidence of his physical fitness. The lack of success with this campaign, among others, revealed to the RSA the need for representation on the War Pensions Board, which it gained in late 1917 after a lengthy campaign.[64]

A major concern of the RSA throughout the war and post-war years was spiralling inflation, which reduced the real purchasing power of war pensions because they were not indexed to the cost of living. In December 1921, a DEC deputation presented to Cabinet a full report outlining the impact of inflation on war pensions. Massey promised a commission to review war pensions in consultation with the RSA. The most comprehensive submission to the War Pensions Commission came from the RSA. Although the commissioners praised 'the excellent manner in which the case for the soldiers was presented',[65] their recommendations, which were incorporated into the War Pensions Act of 1923, did not include raising the value of the basic pension, a long-standing RSA claim; the government preferred instead to introduce an extra economic pension for those in need. This provision was a defeat for the RSA's request for a universal increase as of right, rather than by claim, but the final result was nonetheless an increase in income for a large number of returned soldier pensioners. Furthermore, eight out of the 10 demands made by the RSA were implemented with the new legislation. The major success was the establishment of a War Pensions Appeal Board to examine all appeals against decisions of the War Pensions Board, which the RSA had been calling for since 1919. The 1923 War Pensions Act was a major victory for all returned soldiers and war dependants, and a tribute to the RSA's persistence.

By 1922, therefore, the RSA had achieved much of its repatriation policy. It had been an uphill battle, with the RSA placing immense pressure on the government. There is no doubt that without this pressure much less would have been secured. This work of the RSA on a national level benefited not just association members but all disabled returned soldiers and war dependants.

The real impact of the RSA's welfare work, however, is best revealed by focusing on the immense amount of work undertaken by local associations on behalf of both returned soldiers and dependants. Most of this work went unpublicised, known only to the grateful recipients. This advocacy role was at the very heart of the RSA spirit of comradeship embodied in its early motto: 'All for Each and Each for All'.[66]

The international fluctuations of the post-war economy and its adverse impact upon repatriation made the welfare work of the RSA even more important. The immediate post-war boom and its devaluing effect upon war pensions influenced the RSA to call for an interventionist fiscal policy.[67] This call became even louder when the inflationary bubble burst and was followed by a significant economic recession and rising unemployment. In the face of government inaction the RSA took matters into its own hands, forming an unemployment committee at headquarters in 1921 and in the following year devoting much of the inaugural Poppy Day Appeal proceeds to relief work for unemployed returned soldiers.[68]

The economic slump, and its negative impact on the land settlement scheme, pensions and repatriation in general, was a considerable blow to returned soldiers. Letters from returned soldiers and editorials published in *Quick March* spoke of a sense of betrayal, of a world which had forgotten the sacrifice of the soldier, and of lost opportunities.[69] It asked when the state's responsibility for the returned soldier ceased, a question debated at the 1921 annual conference in relation to relief schemes for the unemployed. Dominion President Sir Andrew Russell believed that 'the returned soldier should stand on his own feet and take his position with the rest of the community'. The feeling of most delegates, however, was summed up by G. W. Lloyd of Canterbury, who argued that 'the country was not keeping promises made when the men went away. The soldier did not ask to be spoon-fed, but he asked that these promises be fulfilled.'[70] The issue revealed a burgeoning gulf between the leadership and a significant section of the rank and file. However, it was the widespread impression of unfulfilled promises that persisted and made a lasting impact on the collective psyche of the RSA: a vision of 'the land fit for heroes' betrayed. It was a belief strengthened by the appearance of the widely publicised prematurely aged or 'burnt-out digger' figure and veterans' premature deaths from the late 1920s. The RSA's fervent call for a comprehensive rehabilitation system during the Second World War would also stem from this belief.

Remembrance

Although the primary objective of the RSA was the provision of material and moral support for returned soldiers and their dependants, another fundamental objective of the organisation was to safeguard the memory of those who had not returned. To fail to do so would, in its view, have amounted to the denigration of dead comrades and their grieving families. This role is most evident in the RSA's long campaign to have Anzac Day observed in a manner befitting its sacred status, but also in its role in the establishment of those focal points of Anzac Day ceremonies – the war memorials.

For the very first Anzac Day in 1916 the national body had not yet been formed and only a few local associations existed. Nonetheless, and as early as February 1916, the Christchurch RSA had formed an 'Anzac day sub-committee' to consider how best to commemorate the first anniversary of the Gallipoli campaign. The government suggested church services, together with recruiting meetings, as an appropriate means of commemoration. Returned soldiers considered a simple combined memorial service similar to those held at the front more appropriate.[71] The fact that most towns accepted this form of service testifies to a widespread public belief that the soldiers had earned the right to speak on such issues.

The RSA quickly assumed the role of guardian of Anzac Day. Considerable vigilance would be required: over the next five years the observance of Anzac Day revealed problems that would require resolution before the day would be acceptable to returned soldiers and the wider community. The RSA began by successfully lobbying the government during 1916 to protect the word 'Anzac' from being used for commercial purposes. Later it secured the withholding of totalisation licences for race meetings on Anzac Day.[72] It was the beginning of the sanctification of the word and the day.

In 1917, however, 25 April had been set aside for municipal elections in many parts of the country. With legal advice that the elections could not be changed, the government officially suggested that Anzac Day be transferred to St George's Day on 23 April. The NZRSA regretted this situation but acknowledged the position of the government and advised local RSAs to observe Anzac Day as best they could.[73] The fact that many communities observed 25 April reveals the aura of sanctity that the actual date had already gained by 1917. The RSA justifiably viewed this result and the government's agreement to prevent a similar recurrence in the future, as a victory for the influence of returned soldiers.[74]

From 1917 the RSA began actively to secure control of the public observance. In a two-pronged approach, Dominion President Boxer urged local RSAs to take over their local public commemoration while the national body lobbied to have Anzac Day legislated as a 'close' holiday (ie: a day on which shops etc. were closed), similar to Good Friday or Sunday.[75] In most centres, local RSAs preferred to co-operate with the civic authorities and, in any case, their opinions were deferred to on such matters. Despite constant RSA pressure, the government hesitated to act, initially preferring to wait until after the war, when it suggested to the British government that there be one commemorative day for the whole empire. While sympathetic to the idea, the RSA believed that the first priority was recognition of the special place of Anzac Day. 'Anzac Day is a New Zealand Day, a National Day', declared *Quick March*.[76]

The government's inaction meant that Anzac Day in both 1918 and 1919 was marked by considerable confusion, with some businesses remaining open. For returned soldiers this was another reminder of the selfish commercialism they found on returning from the war. On Anzac Day 1919, irate Auckland returned soldiers identified offending firms as they marched down Queen Street; more 'direct action was not very far away', reported *Quick March* under the heading 'ANZAC DAY – "BUSINESS AS USUAL"'.[77]

Despite this unsatisfactory situation and the government's reluctance to act, Anzac Day 1920 was widely considered the most solemn and impressive yet held.[78] The day fell on a Sunday and provided the 'close' conditions that the RSA was lobbying to achieve by legislative means when 25 April fell on other days of the week. The solemnity of the ceremony was enhanced by the adoption in many centres of the RSA's new universal form of Anzac service.

In a move intended to secure uniformity of observance throughout the country, Dr Boxer promoted a model Anzac Day service that represented a symbolic re-enactment of a burial at the front, complete with a solemn parade of returned soldiers behind a gun carriage accompanied by a uniform bearer party that later formed a catafalque guard, with bowed heads over reversed arms, around a symbolic bier consisting of wreaths and a soldier's hat. The chairman, a returned soldier, ensured that addresses were confined to mourning and remembrance. The marches and hymns were also deeply mournful. The climax came with the burial service conducted by an army padre, during which a pause symbolised the committal. The service concluded with a three-volley gun salute, followed by the sounding of the 'Last Post'.

Boxer, effectively choreographing a ritual of mourning, stressed that the essential aspect of the service was 'to get the audience in the right mood for its sacredness'. Participants, for example, were to be requested not to applaud during the service. The ceremony was run by the RSA, but the mood was appropriate for the thousands of New Zealand families who had been deprived of the solace of funerals for loved ones lost overseas. Boxer acknowledged that returned soldiers 'may not feel this [mood]' but that the relatives 'certainly will'. Returned soldiers would have ample opportunity to remember in their own way within the confines of RSA clubrooms later in the day.[79] Many centres, such as Dunedin, adopted the entire 'Boxer Service', as it was known, while others incorporated parts of it into the service they had developed over the preceding years.[80] More than the form, however, it was the sentiment that was universal throughout New Zealand and appropriate during the immediate post-war period. Although reformed in later decades, the 'Boxer Service', ritualised the solemn mood of Anzac Day observances in New Zealand, in stark contrast with the more celebratory nature of the observance in Australia.

By 1920 it was apparent that most New Zealanders wanted Anzac Day observed as a sacred day. Later that year the government finally introduced the Anzac Day Bill with the purpose of legislating the day as a 'close' holiday. A late amendment by Prime Minister Massey removed the words 'and in all respects as if Anzac Day were a Sunday' and amended the bill so that only hotels and race meetings could not operate.[81] The impact of this change, according to the RSA, was to make Anzac Day 1921 a 'muddled holiday'.[82] Most businesses closed, but some theatres and picture shows remained open. For the RSA the day had to be strictly one of sombre mourning: any form of entertainment was viewed as disrespectful to the dead and their families.

In response to renewed RSA pressure, Minister of Internal Affairs William Downie Stewart, an RSA member himself, introduced the Anzac Day Amendment Bill into Parliament in October 1921. He argued that it would answer 'a very widespread demand for the reinstatement of the original request of the returned soldiers – namely, that the day should be treated as a holy day, as a Sunday'.[83]

Anzac Day 1922 was observed throughout New Zealand as a full statutory holiday; for most people, however, it was a *holy day*. Another symbol of remembrance – the red poppy – also made its appearance for the first time that year with the RSA's successful inaugural Poppy Day appeal the day before. Unlike Britain, Canada and even Australia, the RSA had not held its inaugural poppy appeal in association with Armistice Day 1921 because the ship carrying the poppies from France arrived too late for the scheme to be properly publicised. The RSA's decision to postpone its poppy campaign until Anzac Day 1922 established an historic precedent whereby the poppy became forever associated with 25 April in New Zealand.[84]

After five years of relentless pressure, the RSA could finally herald the day as a 'worthy' tribute to the memory of the dead.[85] The sanctification of Anzac Day had been completed. In pressing this issue the RSA had been in tune with the feelings of most New Zealanders.

In fact, the solemnity and sombreness of Anzac Day 1922 was a far cry from the almost celebratory observance by soldiers in Egypt on Anzac Day back in 1916. On that first anniversary of Landing Day, as it became commonly known among Gallipoli veterans, a commemorative service had been followed by a holiday and football.[86] What had happened in the intervening years? The RSA was keeping faith with the families of the dead, who required a special day of remembrance. This was the public ritual of Anzac Day promoted by the RSA, but it also oversaw a private ritual of its own members later in the day, which centred on reunion dinners or more informal gatherings in RSA clubrooms. The soldiers' ritual was neither as sombre nor as spiritual as the public ritual but then returned soldiers did not share the public's mythology of war – only its reality. The themes of comradeship and remembrance permeated this ritual. The talk was of past mates and wartime events, and alcohol helped to lubricate reminiscences and recall wartime binges. Although very different, the public and RSA rituals shared a commitment to remember.

In the early 1920s there was one other significant development in the Anzac Day ritual, as ceremonies shifted from halls to war memorials. With so many soldiers buried overseas, each memorial became a surrogate tombstone for the community's grief. The RSA played a significant role in the construction of these permanent symbols of remembrance.

The early call by some local RSAs was for soldiers' clubs as the most appropriate – living – memorial. The Hawera RSA, for example, approved of the decision in early 1919 to erect a hall as the town's memorial with the idea that the RSA's clubrooms would be attached.[87] The process by which utilitarian memorials were thoroughly discredited by the end of 1919 in favour of ornamental memorials whose sole purpose was commemoration, as a result of a campaign initiated by Sir James Allen who had lost his son at Gallipoli, has been well documented.[88] The RSA subsequently abandoned its call for combined memorial soldiers' clubs in favour of separate campaigns for clubs and for war memorials. In fact, the RSA now actively opposed the efforts of those councils that wished to build utilitarian memorials in favour of the obelisk, the cenotaph and the arch.[89] In the context of this new atmosphere, the proposal for a combined memorial hall and RSA clubrooms in Hawera was abandoned in favour of a triumphal arch and adjacent but separate RSA clubrooms.

The long return

By the end of 1922, the RSA was firmly entrenched in New Zealand society: the badge was already a familiar symbol, the first Poppy Day Appeal had been launched and clubrooms were being erected around the country. The organisation had survived the period of division over the best means of organisation and mode of action. It had largely achieved its main objective of providing for returned soldiers and their dependants. It had also led the way in determining how best to remember the dead. In short, the RSA had helped tens of thousands of returned men along the road from soldier to civilian and had played a considerable role in the country's return to normality in the aftermath of the Great War.

But the success of the RSA undermined its very existence. The successfully repatriated soldier had less need for an association whose purpose had been to oversee that repatriation. Advertisements for engagement rings and baby formula in *Quick March* during the early 1920s provide some evidence that RSA members were successfully completing the transformation from soldier to civilian.[90] As husbands and fathers returned soldiers had little time or need for the RSA and failed to renew their membership in droves. From a peak of 57,000 members in 1920 the membership decreased by nearly 60 per cent over the next two years to just over 24,000. Many small RSAs closed. The dramatic decline of the RSA throughout the 1920s, which would see it bottom out at a mere 6000 members nationwide in 1927, had begun.[91] It was certainly a bittersweet development for the RSA: although it signalled the successful repatriation of large numbers of returned soldiers, it marked the end of a vibrant period in the association's history.

The drop in membership was naturally a matter of grave concern to the RSA hierarchy. By November 1922, the DEC was seriously considering the future and even contemplated winding-up the NZRSA.[92] The problem remained, however: who would stand up for those less fortunate returned soldiers who continued to suffer the physical and psychological impact of the war as well as the thousands of war dependants? As *Quick March* reminded all returned soldiers in 1922, 'a strong active RSA is necessarily a good insurance policy for a square deal'.[93]

How to maintain a returned soldiers' organisation during a long period of peace would be the challenge for the RSA over the next two decades. The war cast a long shadow. For considerable numbers of veterans a return to normality would be a long process and, for some, it would never be complete.

PART 2

THE OPERATIONAL CONTEXT

10

'WHOM AT FIRST WE DID NOT LIKE ... ': AUSTRALIANS AND NEW ZEALANDERS AT QUINN'S POST, GALLIPOLI

Peter Stanley

The place to begin is the first fighting shared by Australians and New Zealanders: the Battle of the Wazza. In what was perhaps the largest single episode of misogynist violence in the two countries' history, on Good Friday 1915 hundreds of soldiers rioted in one of Cairo's brothel quarters. As has been well documented, they broke into brothels and prostitutes' apartments, destroying furniture and property, burning possessions in the streets. When the local fire brigade arrived soldiers cut their hoses and drove the firemen off. Only when British mounted police and picquets arrived did the rioters disperse. In the aftermath of the disturbance there were many contradictory explanations for who had started it and why. Australians blamed New Zealanders; New Zealanders blamed Australians. 'Some Australians started to wreck a house...', explained a Wellington machine-gunner.[1] A company commander in the same battalion described the rioters as 'mostly Australians with a few Tommies'.[2] Charles Bean spoke to Australians and decided that 'there is no question that in this scrap a leading part was played by the New Zealanders'. Witnesses before the court of inquiry convened the next day unanimously testified that, for instance, 'A few New Zealanders seemed to be the cause of the trouble'.[3] They all blamed the wretched Egyptian prostitutes and took out their hostility on the hapless Egyptian firemen and the British territorials summoned to suppress the riot.

Three weeks later some of the men who had been in the Sharia Waag el Birka that Good Friday evening found themselves part of a rough firing line on a steep, scrubby ridge on the Gallipoli peninsula. They included Australians, members of half a dozen battalions, and New Zealanders, mainly members of the Auckland Battalion. The Australians had come ashore earlier on 25 April. The New Zealanders had landed later in the day and been led up over Plugge's Plateau and towards the head of what would be called Monash Valley to reinforce the straggling firing line the Australians were forming on what they knew as the second ridge. Turkish bullets were singing through the scrub from the east and Turkish shrapnel was bursting in what became known as Shrapnel Gully, to their west. An Auckland man, Private Frederick Scarborough, evoked the scene in an account based on his diary: 'we don't know quite where we are. Firing is fierce & heavy: some places we are further ahead than others & troops are all mixed up.'[4]

Private Alfred Smith was a member of a small, leaderless group of Canterbury and Auckland men who found themselves about the same spot among a group of Australians, also without an officer.[5] Unsure of where they were or what they should do, the two groups drew apart and conferred separately. Sixty-three years later he remembered, 'the Aussies had a talk and we had a talk' and a corporal suggested that it was better to stay where they were rather than try to retreat through the shelling. Before joining them in scratching rifles pits an Australian said sternly, 'You will forget about the Battle of Waza! [sic].' 'We all shook hands,' Smith remembered, 'and said that we would forget bygones and we settled down.' Soon after, Major Tom Dawson of the Auckland Battalion arrived and took charge. The shallow scrapes that Dawson's men were digging with their entrenching tools were the beginning of what became known as Quinn's Post.

Here, at the crucial point of the Anzac line, at the moment at which it solidified – where it would remain until the evacuation – with Australian and New Zealand troops intermingled, the fact of the Wazza riot was sufficiently important for them to shake on putting it behind them. Clearly, though they were all to become Anzacs, they were both divided by existing attitudes and animosities and united by shared endeavour and, soon enough, loss. How did Australians and New Zealanders think and act toward each other in the first year of the Great War?

* * *

With notable exceptions, Gallipoli still tends to be viewed in a national perspective: sometimes, as with, say, Bill Gammage's *The Broken Years* or Chris Pugsley's *Gallipoli: the New Zealand Story*, legitimately and productively, but even supposedly general studies often betray a preference for one national experience. Even the late John Robertson, though producing a penetrating and undervalued interpretation of the campaign, managed to write a book entitled *Anzac and Empire* without using New Zealand sources. For every Tim Travers's *Gallipoli* there is a Les Carlyon's *Gallipoli*, books in which the campaign is represented unduly as, in this case, an Australian experience, which largely excludes or ignores other national experiences and perceptions. It is particularly important to consider service on Gallipoli from a comparative perspective. Commonalities and contrasts enable us to view both national and multi-national experience in a new way.

A study of Quinn's Post is well suited to provide a comparison. Quinn's, located at the inland extremity of the main Anzac line, was the critical point for both Anzacs and Turks. Had it been lost by the Anzacs or seized by the Turks the defence of the entire Anzac position would have been compromised. Australians largely held Quinn's from 26 April to the end of May; New Zealanders garrisoned it in June and July and Australians again from early August to the evacuation. Quinn's is justifiably celebrated in the memory of both Australia and New Zealand (and as 'Bomba Sirt' in Turkey, though a dearth of accessible records makes the comparison unfeasible). But the shared Australian and New Zealand experiences of Quinn's have not been explicitly compared. This chapter, derived from a broader study of Quinn's and its place in Anzac and in the Gallipoli campaign, examines how Australians and New Zealanders viewed, recorded, judged and responded to each other in that place. Through that narrow loophole I hope to be able to reflect on their broader relationship, at least in the first year of the Great War.

This is a subject which Australians and New Zealanders periodically canvass, usually, though not invariably, from their national standpoints. The most recent treatment of the question has been James Bennett's article in *War and Society* in

October 2003.[6] In a long and somewhat unfocused piece, Bennett discusses the 'chameleon-like New Zealand identity' during the Great War. Although insufficiently grounded in the experience of military service and the resultant evidence – for example, Bennett presents William Malone and Alexander Godley as similar in command style, whereas the evidence strongly suggests a profound contrast – his article revived the subject and suggested several axes on which the Australian and New Zealand relationship can be explored. After traversing disciplinary policies, venereal disease, war memoirs and histories and the iconography of war memorials, Bennett's unadventurous conclusion is that 'the Kiwi… did not see himself as an honorary Australian'. And why should he have?

* * *

I would argue that few at the time did. The Australian and New Zealand perspectives differed from the start. Even on the voyage to Egypt the 10 freshly painted grey New Zealand transports presented a different, more uniform appearance from the Australian ships. New Zealanders noted with pride and a corresponding disdain that their ships kept a more complete blackout than the Australians. A brief stay in Hobart gave New Zealanders a rare opportunity to patronise their trans-Tasman counterparts. Hobart looked like 'a very old fashioned place' to James Bayne of the Wellington Battalion. In Albany Godley's ADC, Lieutenant Arthur Rhodes, found the AIF 'very untidy and slovenly… we are superior to them in every way'. Some New Zealand officers evidently encouraged this attitude.[7] In return, John Treloar, a young staff sergeant in William Bridges's Australian Division head-quarters, saw some New Zealanders while ashore at Albany the following day. He thought that 'our men are better' physically and decried the New Zealanders' colourful piping and puggarees as 'a puny effort'.[8]

Whether Rhodes's and Treloar's disdain was widely shared is hard to say. It is always difficult to comment authoritatively on such attitudes, not least because of the difficulties of locating evidence on which reliable generalisations can be based. I have attempted to read enough individual diaries, letters and memoirs to make confident inferences, but we need to be wary both of inferring from isolated examples and of using incidents to buttress received views. New Zealanders, for example, were not always the 'well behaved gentlemen' they have been portrayed as: their diaries disclose many examples of larrikinism.[9] Nor were relations generally anything but cordial. Both New Zealanders and Australians, united in a great imperial cause, cheered the other when troopships passed. New Zealand diaries often refer to friends in the AIF, and the force's nominal roll discloses that about 800 New Zealanders served in AIF units on Gallipoli.[10] Both damned the 'No Colonial need apply' mentality they struck among some British officers.[11] It is notable, however, that New Zealanders were far more ready to accept and use the term 'colonial' than were Australians: James Bennett concluded that New Zealand 'remained a colony in sentiment and in real terms'.[12]

Idleness and leave in Egypt provided ample opportunities for men of both forces to form negative impressions. An Auckland officer complained that his roller-skating at Luna Park was spoilt by a party of drunken Australians. Alluding to the bad name Australians had earnt in South Africa, he noted that 'our own boys are doing remarkably well'.[13] A Canterbury medical student explained that the AIF had 'a bigger proportion of roughs'. Australians, he complained, 'walk past in the streets without even a "good day"'.[14] A Wairarapa man agreed, acknowledging in a letter home that before the landing 'a sort of coolness' had prevailed between the two.[15] When a music hall song mentioned New Zealanders but not Australians a Wellington Mounted Rifleman crowed that 'I suppose the Australians there said, "Those damned Pig Islanders have scored again!"'[16] The rivalry was played out in desert training around Cairo. Sham fights between the two forces became, as a Canterbury officer recalled, 'especially keen against the Australians, whom at first we did not like', he explained, ambiguously, 'being very parochial'.[17]

Some units of the two forces were brought into a close association. While Australia's first three infantry brigades formed its own 1 Division, 4 Australian Infantry Brigade, the New Zealand Infantry Brigade, the New Zealand Mounted Rifles Brigade and 1 Australian Light Horse Brigade were brought together to form what was called the 'New Zealand and Australian Division' under the British commander of the NZEF, Major-General Sir Alexander Godley. 'Abnormal' in composition, the division's very title reflected the ambivalence of its members.[18] Australians talked of the 'Australian and New Zealand Division', New Zealanders described the 'N.Z. Division… including

5000 Australians attached'.[19] Allocated the vital Section 3 of the Anzac line, on Gallipoli the New Zealanders and Australians of Godley's division would meet, among other places, at Quinn's.

The fighting on Gallipoli in some cases entrenched the critical view formed in training. A Wellington sergeant-major recorded in Maori his view of the disordered Australians he met on Walker's Ridge on 26 April: 'Re Australian troops – pakaru'; that is, broken; in disarray.[20] His legendary commanding officer, William Malone, was livid about the way he had 'got messed up by the Australians' in the defence of Walker's Ridge, and he and George Braund had a stand-up fight over Braund's plans for attacks that Malone regarded as unjustifiable.[21] However, the shared experience of combat tended to erase the petty differences they had noticed in Egypt. A particularly observant New Zealand sapper, Ernest Clifton, detected signs of a change early in May: 'One would hardly know these Australians, Officers & men as the same who were in Egypt haggling at one another'.[22] As the campaign developed both asserted that they preferred to serve alongside each other rather than with some of the British troops they had encountered – all the time professing an admiration for the regulars of 29 Division. A bond developed between members of the two Australasian forces, one stronger than the relationship with their British counterparts. Indeed, we might generalise that through the war the Australian–New Zealand relationship grew more definite, while their relationship with Britain, though overwhelmingly positive, became increasingly ambivalent when measured against the shortcomings of the British forces and their members.

This process helps to place in context an incident described in the revised diary of Private Raymond Baker of the Canterbury Battalion. Two Australian stretcher-bearers saved Baker's leg, and perhaps his life, by selecting him from among a line of mostly British wounded after he had lain for three days without attention in the August heat. An Australian stretcher-bearer noticed a fernleaf charm that Baker wore around his neck – by this time he had lost his tunic and anything that distinguished him from other wounded.

> 'Hullo mate, Pig Islander?... How long have you been here?'
>
> 'This is my third day...'
>
> 'Oh hell. Catch hold, Harry.'

The two men carried Baker onto a waiting lighter despite the protests of 'some very Englishy Officers' of a Kitchener battalion, winking at him in a trans-Tasman conspiracy. He was taken aboard a hospital ship and was home for Christmas.[23] Despite resentments and tensions, then, the relationship between the two forces' members was essentially positive.

* * *

Quinn's Post provides an opportunity to test perceptions and reactions for both Australasian forces. Within days of the landing Quinn's became a warren of trenches and tunnels clinging to the very edge of the cliff. Turkish trenches lay between 10 and 30 yards away, so close that a bomb fight, beginning on 1 May, continued throughout the campaign, without cease. Because its situation was so vital Quinn's became the subject of repeated Turkish attacks up to the end of May, and of a succession of Anzac sorties in May and June. All failed, but the bodies of Turkish and British empire dead lay rotting in the narrow no man's land, tainting the air. Quinn's was a place of horror for all who served there, as units were moved in and out for brief but intense and costly tours of duty. For the first month the main units were Australian, of John Monash's 4 Brigade and Harry Chauvel's 1 Light Horse Brigade.

Quinn's was horrific and dangerous, and the men who held it guaranteed the security of the Anzac line. But it is apparent that their precarious hold derived partly at least from what the Australians did and how, rather than just the inherent characteristics of the position. For example, the first Australian tenure in Quinn's was deficient. The trenches were shallow and exposed to sniper fire partly because there were too few sappers: though three field companies worked in the Australian Division's sector, Godley's New Zealand and Australian Division had only one hard-pressed New Zealand field company. It suffered heavy casualties, leaving even vital spots like Quinn's without adequate engineering support. Neither Monash's infantry nor Chauvel's light horsemen could be induced to dig as much as was needed. Nor did they gain superiority over Turkish snipers, who could fire into the back of Quinn's from Baby 700, or over Turkish bombing, which forced the evacuation of parts of the front line. As Ian Hamilton explained to Birdwood, Chauvel had 'made me feel downhearted… when he told me how his men had lost all initiative, and had permitted the enemy's fire entirely to dominate them … '[24] Both Chauvel and Monash went on to become Australia's most prominent and successful commanders in the war, but as brigadiers on Gallipoli neither was able to master the challenge of commanding at Quinn's. Indeed, under its Australian garrison Quinn's came as close as it ever was to being lost.

In the early hours of 29 May the Turks exploded a mine under Quinn's and in the resultant chaos seized a portion of the front. Desperate counter-attacks, in which Hugh Quinn, the post commander was killed, at last ejected them. The 29 May attack seems finally to have persuaded Godley and Birdwood that this vital position could no longer be entrusted to the exhausted Australians, and their relief was almost immediately arranged. From 30 May New Zealand infantry took over, and between then and 5 August Quinn's was held almost entirely by New Zealanders, and the New Zealand records of that tenure are abundant and clearly different from those of the Australian periods. In New Zealand hands Quinns became a very different place with a distinctive texture. It was natural for New Zealanders to want to distinguish themselves from the more numerous Australian counterparts. On the very day that Godley decided on the relief of Quinn's by New Zealanders he told the Defence Minister, James Allen, how he was looking forward to the arrival of correspondent Malcolm Ross because he 'did not like being dependent for a report on our doings on the Australian war correspondent Captain Bean… though he is a very good fellow'.[25]

As they arrived at Quinn's, New Zealanders generally expressed dissatisfaction with the Australian tenure of the post. William Malone, who visited it a week before the Turkish attack of 29 May, thought its Australian garrison did 'not seem anything like as keen as our men'. He found that they had few soldiers observing the Turks and 'no sort of plan' for the post's defence.[26] When Cecil Malthus entered the trenches with the Canterbury Battalion he charitably decided that 'the desperate nature of the fighting must have prevented the Australians from making any elaborate system of fortifications'.[27] Other New Zealanders were less forgiving, declaring that 'they can't get the Australian infantry to work'.[28] It is easy to criticise men obliged to remain for a day in what was arguably one of the worst combat experiences in a war full of horror, and the New Zealanders generally refrained from criticism. They were entering a position which had been the location of continuous and heavy fighting for over six weeks, and the evidence of it was all around them. As they emerged from the saps leading to the firing line they saw 'in every bay... these old Australian coats covered in blood and shattered where they had withstood the bombing'.[29] Men described how maggots wriggled in every fly-infested trench, how the bodies of their mates lay bloated and stinking within a few feet, and how at any moment a bomb might lob into a trench to mutilate or kill. The wonder was that Quinn's had held in such disgusting and stressful conditions.

Though the departing Australians gratefully left, without regret, Captain Terence McSharry, a Queenslander, was asked to stay on as the post's adjutant. Though tired – he had gone for days without a wash, without taking his boots off and without having more than a few hours' rest – he felt 'rather flattered'. He knew Quinn's to be 'the weakest in the position and we get all the Turkish attacks here'. Anxious that it should not be endangered again, he remained to nurse the New Zealanders into becoming Quinn's new garrison. McSharry's initial impression of the New Zealanders was poor. After several days he loyally confided to his diary that they 'don't work the post as well as the 15th'.

McSharry's misgivings about the New Zealanders' fitness seemed to be confirmed on 5 June when a Turk 'sneaked up to our parapet' – something that had not been achieved before – 'then threw bombs right over'. They rolled down the hill and wounded Colonel Charles Brown of the Canterbury Battalion. McSharry raced to the spot and himself 'got this Turk with percussion bombs'. By this and other actions McSharry endeared himself to the new tenants. Canterbury Private Ernest Williams described in his diary how an anonymous Australian captain moved about 'like an inspiring god': this can only have been McSharry.[30] If the Canterburys were abashed by this lapse during their tenure the post was about to be transformed.

The men of Charles Brown's Canterbury Battalion found Quinn's as tough a proposition as their Australian predecessors. In the first week of June the Canterbury and Auckland Battalions made two further sorties which showed the folly of attempting even raids against 'Turkish Quinn's', costly failures which demoralised many who participated in or heard about them. The repulse of the two New Zealand sorties prompted Australian condescension. Charles Bean recorded, with evident distaste, Colonel James McCay's sneering 'Oh, is that the job that the New Zealanders are held up by?'[31] The Anzac commanders moved to solve their most pressing tactical problem. On 9 June Malone's Wellington Battalion was switched from Courtney's Post, the next position to the south, to Quinn's. Malone had spent the first week transforming Courtney's from a dirty, untidy and dangerous post into one in which the New Zealanders gained the upper hand. Godley evidently wanted Malone to do the same for his most critical position.

As is well known, Malone's men spent June achieving two transformations at Quinn's. Physically they dug and sandbagged and wired and cleaned up, turning what had been a wretched and filthy warren of shallow, crumbling saps into a veritable fortress. They also contested and overcame the Turkish superiority of fire, locating and killing snipers and throwing several bombs for every one thrown at them. By the end of June the initiative had shifted. It was now the Turks who felt their trenches to be a death trap.

Terence McSharry's diary provides a commentary on Malone's transformation of Quinn's. McSharry gradually warmed to the men who had displaced his fellow Queenslanders, and they to him: 'I'll soon be a New Zealander,' he jotted in his diary. But despite the growing rapport between McSharry and the new garrison, he never quite became reconciled to Malone. At first McSharry found Malone's strictness hard to take, particularly as much of what Malone found unsatisfactory had been created by McSharry. 'Malone is an old woman,' he scribbled in his diary, 'I am fed up.' McSharry asked to be transferred back to 15 Battalion, now resting in readiness for the August attacks. Malone's devotion to order bemused a man intolerant of 'red tape in the presence of the enemy'. Malone played up his eccentricity, joking that he planned to plant roses on the terrace outside his dugout and entertain visitors to tea. McSharry never quite got the joke. 'He has wonderful ideas about turning Quinn's Post into an ornamental garden,' McSharry complained in bemusement. Malone's vision was incongruous when the entire post, and particularly no man's land, remained foul-smelling and fly-ridden. Though the two remained 'civil', Malone's eccentricities left McSharry cold. He thought that Malone was more interested in organisation than defence: 'I hope the Turks don't attack while he is here'.[32] In fact, Malone's devotion to strengthening the physical defences of Quinn's and his training of its defenders made the post stronger and more secure than it had ever been, ensuring that, from June, the Turks made no serious attempt to storm Anzac's most vulnerable position.

Despite McSharry's scepticism, Malone had made a difference at Quinn's. When senior Australian medical officer Lieutenant-Colonel Joseph Beeston visited the post early in July he was surprised to find it 'very clean', with 'not a speck of dirt about', and even 'little tins for "fags" and matches burnt'.[33] The contrast with the slovenly state that the New Zealanders had inherited was striking. If Quinn's was now clean, it was also safe – and as a result from August it practically disappears from both Charles Bean's diary and from his official history. It was made impregnable by the New Zealanders who held it. This has not been acknowledged in Australia, and there has never been any admission that the more casual Australian approach to the position's defence arguably made it more precarious than it need have been.

This transformation derived largely from Malone's characteristic determination to impose order on the inherently chaotic business of war. He was the driving force behind the building work, though the detail was often left to a New Zealand sapper, Sergeant (later Lieutenant) Wallace Saunders, whose diary frankly chronicles the work and documents who thought of and did what. Malone and his battalion were proud of their achievement at Quinn's, but the cost of it was arguably to contribute significantly to the tragedy that consumed him and the post in August. The exertion of the fatigues they performed, the effects of bad food and water in the summer heat in the fly-blown trenches, added to the strain of holding trenches in which bomb-fights literally never ended, sapped the strength and resilience of Malone's battalion. Every infantry unit in the New Zealand and Australian Division committed to the August offensive was weakened by diarrhoea and exhaustion, but arguably none so much as the Wellingtons, who were kept at the punishing regime by Malone. The battalion was destroyed on Chunuk Bair: 310 of its members, including Malone, have no known grave. How much the rigours of holding and building Quinn's contributed to their failure on Chunuk Bair is open to speculation.

* * *

It is important to note that Quinn's garrison remained almost exclusively New Zealand through June and July. Not until the eve of the August offensive did the men of 2 Australian Light Horse Regiment return to Quinn's. They could do little about the all-pervading reek of decomposing corpses lying in dozens beyond the parapet, but they moved into a post that bore little resemblance to the dirty, bloodstained, jerry-built maze they had last seen in May. When they returned, however, Quinn's reverted to an all-Australian position. It seems that Godley and his staff consciously tried to keep Australians and New Zealanders distinct, and it is likely that both were more comfortable working independently. When in June ANZAC staff pondered forming a mining company to replace the improvised infantry work gangs, Lord Charles Bentinck, the division's AA & QMG, minuted that 'mixing of Aust & NZ personnel is not a success and had better not be tried again'.[34] It might be interesting to examine the comparable relationship between the Australian Light Horse and the New Zealand Mounted Rifles units which shared the defence of Walker's Ridge and Russell's Top.

Though New Zealanders and Australians shared an experience of Gallipoli and continue to share a memory of Anzac, it has not always been based on either a close association, or a relationship that was necessarily harmonious. For all that the two nations are closest to each other, they also have a history of difference, which derives partly from the traumatic circumstances of Quinn's Post in the summer of 1915. Although we need to explore and remember the strength of a military history that has much in common, we should also not ignore or diminish the tension within the relationship.

New Zealanders understandably feel aggrieved that Anzac has been appropriated by Australia. This is not a recent phenomenon. In 1917 a correspondent to a New Zealand paper was demanding to know: 'ANZACS: Why are New Zealanders excluded?' Anzac could divide and unite the two neighbours.[35] At Quinn's, as at the Wazza, Australians and New Zealanders could express differences about each other's character, conduct and competence. This deepens our understanding of what we might nevertheless regard as an Anzac experience.[36]

BOWLER OF GALLIPOLI:
WITNESS TO THE ANZAC LEGEND

Frank Glen

Edmund Robert Bowler was born at Inchclutha, 40 minutes' drive south of Dunedin, in 1866. He married Mary Ethel Hepburn and in 1892 they settled in Gore (population 1800), where he opened a legal practice. Bowler invested in local industry and became a director of several companies. He built a sizable home, Athelstane, where he and Ethel entertained, and sent his two eldest daughters to a finishing school in Switzerland. His quiet, gentlemanly manner endeared him to the wiry southern pioneering stock, which helped his practice to thrive.

Although he was elected a borough councillor, pressure of work in his practice forced him to resign. He remained an active Freemason and member of the Otago and Invercargill clubs, institutions which, in that era, had a degree of social élitism beyond the average citizen.

Military career

Commissioned as lieutenant in the Gore Volunteer Rifles in 1894, during the fortress New Zealand period, Bowler was promoted to the rank of captain in 1900 and commanded the Mataura Mounted Rifle Company. 'The Company under his guidance became a strong and efficient body and was well handled. He was a good officer, strict in having duties carried out, and well liked by all under his command.'[1] In 1907, then a lieutenant-colonel, he commanded 7 Southland Mounted Rifles. Unlike the Territorial Army in Great Britain, the New Zealand Territorial Force of 1914 was the primary element of the New Zealand armed forces. As such, it had to 'be able to take the field at once on the outbreak of war. It is the New Zealand Army.'[2] This force was 99 per cent non-regular in composition.

On the outbreak of the First World War Bowler was appointed to command the NZEF's 2nd Reinforcements. He arrived in Egypt early in February 1915 to assume the task of divisional provost marshal and senior exercise umpire to Major-General Godley's New Zealand and Australian Division. Godley recommended to Lieutenant-General Sir William Birdwood, commander of the ANZAC at Gallipoli,[3] that Bowler would competently fill the role of assistant provost marshal in the ANZAC Headquarters. A flattered Bowler accepted the appointment, and was made a beach landing officer for the Dardanelles campaign. On 25 April 1915, he directed ashore 1 Australian Brigade, and three weeks later commanded the inner beach defences at Anzac Cove.

Later in London, after being medically evacuated from the peninsula on 9 September, Bowler became an outspoken advocate in favour of evacuating the Anzacs from Gallipoli. He was convinced that the mounting casualties suffered by New Zealand would result in unknown ethnic and socially undesirable consequences. His friendship with Thomas Mackenzie, the New Zealand High Commissioner in London, gave him an opportunity to press his case. Although the Gallipoli experience affected Bowler's health, it did not impair his energy when back in New Zealand; he founded the Gore Returned Soldiers' Association in 1917.

Bowler's philosophy of life following his Gallipoli experience can be gauged by his speech at his public farewell in Gore after he retired from his legal practice to move to Timaru.

> Departing from Gore was not without its sorrows.... A correspondent in the
> local press had thanked God that the Victorian age...[had] passed, but... they
> should thank God for that age, as then Britain was at the zenith of her glory; then
> she produced greater statesmen and the greatest literary men.... In those days,

> they had been satisfied with simpler things and they... worked harder than did the younger element today.[4]

In December 1927 Edmund Bowler died of illness that his medical records attributed to his service at Gallipoli.

The Bowler letters and papers

In accordance with a pre-arranged understanding Bowler wrote frankly and confidentially on military matters to his wife Ethel and gave no thought to censorship. He justified his indiscretion with the thought that by the time his letters arrived in Gore the contents would be public knowledge. His criticisms were directed at two individuals, General Sir Ian Hamilton and Lieutenant-General Sir Frederick Stopford,[5] and the overall planning of the Gallipoli campaign, including the Royal Navy's lack of support for the operation. His views were probably more fully expressed in his daily diary, now lost, which he used to write his weekly letters. He used the phrase 'the dust of poor generalship' frequently.

The letters provide confirmation, by the only New Zealander to serve on the ANZAC HQ staff, of the rise of the Anzac legend. They note the personal relationships between some senior officers, provide insights into the staff corps culture and focus on the soldierly characteristics now acknowledged as the legend's foundation. Early in the landing, Bowler recognised the initial Anzac innocence of war, which was transformed from civilian mateship into its military equivalent in the face of wounding, suffering and death. He was a witness to the willingness of the Anzacs to accept death for the preservation of the empire. He considered, as did Charles Bean, the long-term political consequences for Australia and New Zealand should they be defeated: such an outcome would undermine the sense of God-ordained superiority of the white Caucasian.

Before the First World War Bowler believed Great Britain enjoyed a special social and political relationship with New Zealand, but Gallipoli led him to the conviction that Great Britain, if it wanted empire support, should ensure that the dominions were represented in the making of imperial foreign policy. He describes the Anzacs as the finest soldiers in the world. Unlike Bean, he makes no distinction between the cultural characteristics of the Anzac partners: they were one Caucasian antipodean family. Maori had their place within this demography. Where Bowler's criticisms of the campaign are strident, he exposes a growing insight about himself. He may well be a 'British' officer, but he is distinctively a New Zealander, who has learnt to think, especially in relation to the economic use of men in battle.

For God, King and Empire

For many, the war was a religious crusade. The Methodist Church in New Zealand mirrored the opinion of most of the country's 85 per cent Protestant population and not a few Roman Catholics.

> We join earnestly in prayer that God will defend the right, and cause the grinding militarism of Germany to cease. We regard the British Empire with all its defects as being, in practical righteousness, the largest installment of the Kingdom of God that has yet arisen among men.... We Earnestly pray that God Almighty might avert calamity from that dispensation of righteousness and liberty which it has been the glory of our Empire to spread over the world.[6]

After a shipboard church parade on 11 April, Bowler wrote to Ethel, 'I shall be able to do my duty manfully and if I fall you must not grieve but rather be proud that I have been able to do something for a great cause.'[7] The great cause was the defence of the empire from a predator nation and, above all, maintaining the status quo.

The beach landing officer's equipment, so essential to success, was planned to consist of 150 wine casks, on which the engineers would build floating piers, 60 signposts, 40 pounds of white paint and the requisite number of paintbrushes for sign-writing. There were also 50 casks of water for the beach party, a dozen each of green, red and white signalling lamps, 140 oil and tar flares, 100,000 sandbags, five telephone nets with the required posts and wire,[8] 20 shovels, 34 latrine flags and five tents.[9] At a convenient stage during the landing, pre-built piers and structures engineered from the wine casks were to be delivered to the beach by the navy, where Bowler and his team were expected to complete piers in his sector during the landing.[10]

Lieutenant-Commander Charles Dix RN was the principal naval beach landing officer.[11] He had 'An elaborate chart… with green lines for telephones, red for visual, black for messengers, blue for megaphones, and so on. It was pretty,' Dix recalled, 'but in the event quite useless – we were expecting and planning for a beach, not a second rate goat track.'[12] It was a sentiment affirmed by Bowler several days after the landing. When the equipment arrived from Alexandria the items had been reduced by 50 per cent: the most serious omissions were the casks needed for the piers. Only a single telephone net of the original five was sent with two shovels and 17 latrine flags, less than half the items needed for the most basic of hygiene precautions ashore.[13] This was an early warning of the chronic shortage of equipment and ammunition that was to plague the entire campaign.

Dix predicted 'we are in for a devil of a doing',[14] but he was flattered by an invitation from Birdwood to 'accompany him when he lands as a sort of naval staff officer. Isn't that topping!!'[15] Bowler, on the other hand, was distinctly apprehensive: 'the chances of my coming out of it safe and sound are probably very small as landing… at dawn or early morning we may expect to meet very heavy fire from the enemy'.[16] On the morning of 25 April, in company with Colonels MacLaurin and Thompson and Major Irvine, Bowler sat quietly smoking and discussed their chances of surviving.[17] 'Approaching the enemies [*sic*] coast – we look assiduously out for any indication of our covering party landing but cannot see it – dawn approaches,' he wrote. 'The landing commences but we do not see covering party land – they must be ahead of us. Piquet boat comes close up and we get into boats, Hancock and I, and Beach Party in leading boat.'[18]

The beach had been divided into four sections and Bowler was responsible for the southernmost No. 1. 'Memory of the day is a blur or blank. Shells are continually bursting around us and it is wonderful how few are hit.'[19] He was anxious for the safety of the wounded as Turkish artillery had 'enfiladed us and swept the beach with shrapnel… I was… standing with General Birdwood and it burst all around us but fortunately did not hit us.'[20] The events of the first day were marked by the stoic behavior of the wounded: the honour of being the first New Zealander ashore was overshadowed by 'the heroism displayed by the men – mostly Australians'.[21] Bowler doubted whether the Australians, whom he directed towards what he described as a 'heavy fight', could hold their beachhead.

'If we are beaten back we are scuppered as we could never reembark and would have to fight it out with the Turk on the beach.'[22] He ignored Hamilton's order to leave the wounded ashore and instructed that they be ferried from the beach to hospital ships by any and all possible means. He saw to it that not one pinnace or lighter left the beach without a quota of wounded.[23]

After 13 days Bowler wrote, 'It is hard to convey on paper... a description of our position – at present we are hanging on to a sort of eagles nest backed by our ships guns without any material advance.'[24] Those Anzacs who landed on 25 April had never encountered fighting of such intensity – the New Zealanders were only marginally more familiar with military life and active soldiering than the Australians – so they went ashore with dash and vigour but also a woeful innocence. 'I stood on a wharf for three days with shrapnel flying around,' he wrote, and saw 'about 3000 wounded taken off to the ships and heard not a cry or a moan from them. It was a dreadful experience'.[25] Bowler was shaken by the numbers of lives that war demanded: 'Col MacLaurin, Col Onslow Thompson and Major Irvine – all very fine fellows – are all killed'. He doubted if there 'was ... ever such an operation as ours.... It is not contemplated at all in Field Service Regulations'. He had already learnt that the rifle was 'no good... without the spade and pick as our casualties on the first three days showed too plainly'.[26]

Bowler hoped the stalled operation could be got moving again by the attack of the Otago Infantry Battalion on 2 May in support of the Australians to secure the The Nek But the Otagos arrived late. The resulting disaster reduced the battalion to 365 men from the original 800.[27] 'Our Otago Infantry Battalion... lost a lot of men,' Bowler lamented. 'We cannot bury them as they are in a fire swept area and in some parts of the trenches their proximity is very evident.'[28]

He was angry that the New Zealand Brigade and an Australian brigade were sent to Helles on 4 May. 'Why not push in here – this seems to be the right place.'[29] Convinced of the correctness of the original staff plan to take the Sari Bair heights from Anzac, he saw this redeployment as a desperate measure that would not help the Anzac sector.

Within a fortnight of the landing newspapers arrived: 'I have seen a Cairo paper published about 1 May which is crammed with lies as to our successes and prisoners taken etc. I am convinced now that in war all reports we read are not to be accepted at all when one finds ones own show misrepresented.' News that there was rejoicing in New Zealand over the achievements of the troops saddened him: 'I'm afraid they do not know of our casualties or they would not rejoice much.'[30] Noting that the 'paper contains awful lies about our successes', he queried whether all men were liars in war.[31]

On 7 July, Bowler issued instructions to the divisional provost marshals outlining procedures for interrogation and treatment of Turkish prisoners. Prisoners were 'Not to be interned in unhealthy localities', were to be properly clothed and fed, and were to be 'treated humanely; suffering whether physical or mental, must not be inflicted upon them'.[32] He built at the southern section of the beach a compound that was merely a holding pen for Turkish prisoners, who were later taken off to Mudros.

Bowler was impatient for news from Helles: 'our two infantry Brigades are still being retained by GHQ… another breach of agreement. We are being treated in a sorry manner… but it does not do here and in war to be pessimistic.'[33] He was appalled by the physical appearance of the Marine Light Infantry of the Royal Naval Division: 'Poor boys – they are a cheap looking lot… What can you expect from men drawn from cotton mills etc.' Nor was the transitory nature of the war lost upon him. 'In the future there may be many mourning ones [coming] from Australia and NZ to find the graves of their lost ones, but I am afraid it will be little use as it is almost impossible here to retain identity of the graves.'[34]

Bowler constantly deplored the shortage of howitzer ammunition: 'a plentiful supply would have saved many lives as they are the only guns that can do any real searching fire in this horribly broken country'.[35] This deficiency, he considered, lay at the root of the stalemate, despite the fact that Lord Kitchener warned Hamilton there would be a limit to the equipment, munitions and men. 'We all feel we are being badly treated by Gen. Headquarters and not given a fair show here – being only treated as a side show.' Bowler's use of the word 'all' indicates he may well have been expressing the mind of his peers in the ANZAC HQ. On the return of the Australian brigade from Helles on 17 May, 'or what is left of them,' he reported the casualties at 1100 and the brigade staff 'wiped out'.[36]

One month into the campaign, Bowler wrote that 'our men showed themselves to be of real grit – in fact I am satisfied now that they are the best fighting material in the Empire and none of the English troops can hold a candle to them.

Above: The announcement of the declaration of war with Germany, 5 August 1914. The Governor, the Earl of Liverpool, is in the centre of the photograph and is holding the telegram containing the fateful news. To his right is Prime Minister William Massey and on his immediate left is Sir Joseph Ward, the Leader of the Opposition. Other dignitaries can also be seen on the steps leading into Parliament. [Alexander Turnbull Library, S.C. Smith Collection, G-45239-1/2.]

Below: Canterbury troops of the New Zealand Expeditionary Force's Main Body march through Christchurch in September 1914, before sailing for Wellington. [Alexander Turnbull Library, *Press* (Christchurch) Collection, G-8307-1/1.]

Above: A poster produced in 1915 by the British Empire Union, which focuses on German atrocities. [Alexander Turnbull Library, Eph-D-WAR-WI-Gr.]

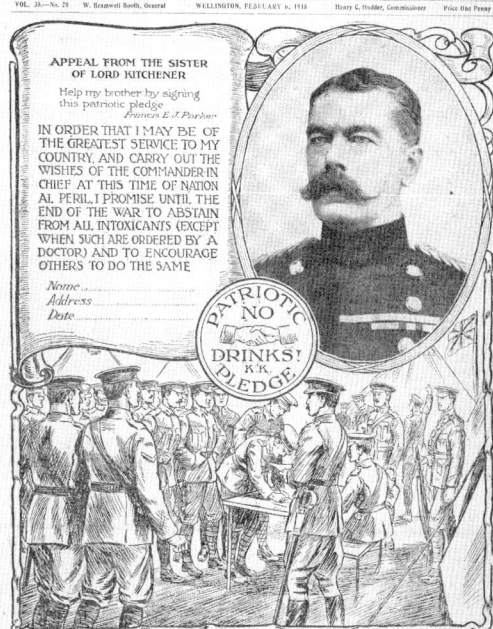

Right: The front page of the *War Cry* of 6 February 1915, which promoted the popular pledge to abstain from alcohol during the war. [Alexander Turnbull Library, S-L 636-front.]

Below: [From left] Lieutenant-Colonel W.B. Lesslie, Private John Simpson [Kirkpatrick] and his donkey, Lieutenant-Colonel Edmund Bowler and Major C.H. Villiers Stuart outside Bowler's dugout, May 1915. [KMARL.]

THE

WAR CRY

AND

OFFICIAL GAZETTE OF THE SALVATION ARMY IN NEW ZEALAND

International Headquarters: 101 Queen Victoria St. London. E.C. Territorial Headquarters: Corner Taranaki St. and Courtenay Place, Wellington

VOL. 35.—No. 20 W. Bramwell Booth, General WELLINGTON, FEBRUARY 6, 1915 Henry C. Hodder, Commissioner Price One Penny

APPEAL FROM THE SISTER OF LORD KITCHENER

Help my brother by signing this patriotic pledge
Frances E.J. Parker

IN ORDER THAT I MAY BE OF THE GREATEST SERVICE TO MY COUNTRY, AND CARRY OUT THE WISHES OF THE COMMANDER-IN CHIEF AT THIS TIME OF NATION AL PERIL, I PROMISE UNTIL THE END OF THE WAR TO ABSTAIN FROM ALL INTOXICANTS (EXCEPT WHEN SUCH ARE ORDERED BY A DOCTOR) AND TO ENCOURAGE OTHERS TO DO THE SAME

Name..........
Address..........
Date..........

PATRIOTIC NO DRINKS! K.K. PLEDGE

AN APPEAL THAT HAS THE WHOLE-HEARTED SUPPORT OF EVERY SALVATIONIST.

Mrs. Parker also asks that the Parents, Wives and Families of Soldiers should abstain from intoxicating drinks.—(*See Leader, page 4.*)
Our pictures show (1) The Pledge. (2) Lord Kitchener. (3) The Badge, much enlarged—its actual size is that of a sixpenny piece. (4) A Camp Scene that we hope will be often repeated.

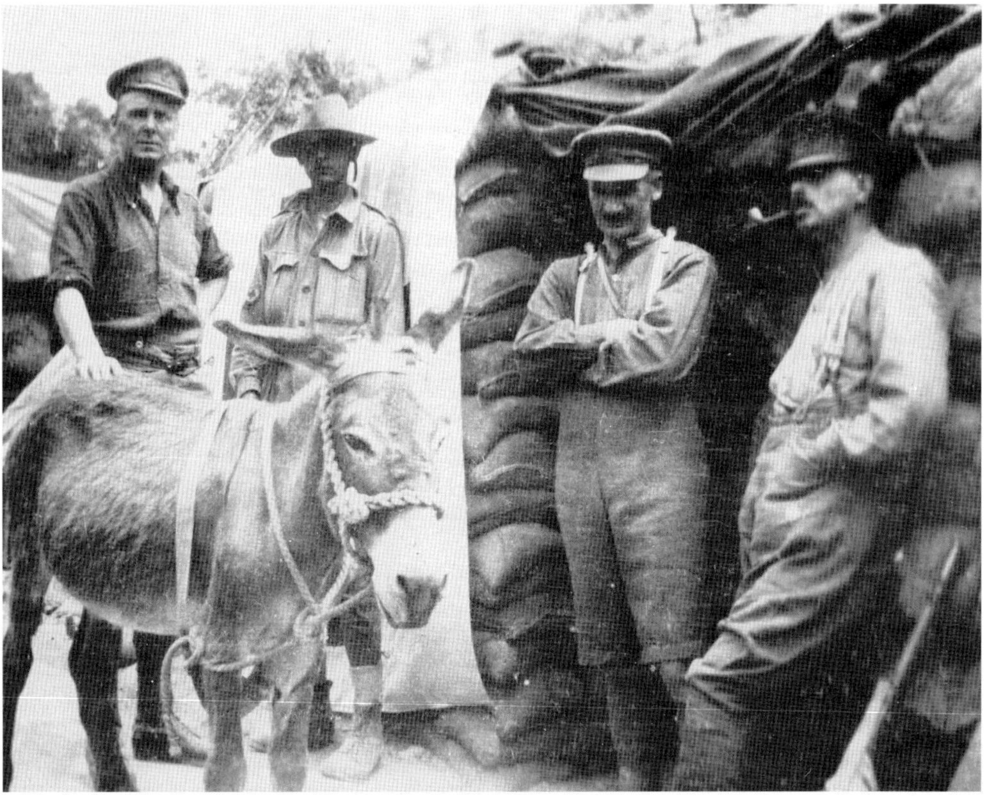

Above: The terraces of Quinn's Post looking towards Pope's Hill. This photograph was taken by Charles Bean in July 1915, after the reconstruction of the position under Malone's command. [Australian War Memorial, G01026.]

Left: New Zealand soldiers in the front line at Quinn's Post, less than 15 metres from the nearest Turkish position. [Alexander Turnbull Library, Susan Duncan Collection, PA1-0-1019-47-2.]

Above: Les Collis in 1916. [Collis family.]

Left: Andy Jamieson soon after he enlisted in the NZEF. [Jamieson family.]

Below: New Zealand Army Service Corps wagons at a ration dump at Steenbecque, France, 1916. [Alexander Turnbull Library, RSA Collection, G-12903-1/2.]

Above: The first wounded soldiers back from the Gallipoli campaign disembark from the *Willochra*, Wellington, 15 July 1915. On board was Captain Donald Simson who went on to found the New Zealand Returned Soldiers' Association. [Alexander Turnbull Library, RSA Collection, G-8354-1/1.]

Below: A knocked-out tank near the Brown Line on 15 September 1916. [KMARL, Huse Collection.]

Above: New Zealanders enjoying a quick meal in a reserve trench, on 15 or 16 September 1916. [KMARL, Huse Collection.]

Above: A Caudron of the type operated by George Merz and William Burn. [Royal New Zealand Air Force Museum.]

Below: A Sopwith Dolphin like that flown by Ronald Bannerman. [Royal New Zealand Air Force Museum.]

When I say our men I mean Australians and New Zealanders ...'[37] The continual recurrence of the 'paucity' of howitzer ammunition led him to remonstrate about this 'burning question', an irritation that did not silence his praise of the Anzacs.

> What wonderful fellows our Australians and New Zealanders are. There are no soldiers or fighters like them.... Nothing daunts them. Tales are told of men being smothered with rubble caused by 11 inch shells... and after being saved rushing for the pieces and quarrelling as to who is to have them or to shoot thro' the remaining loopholes. They have absolute confidence in themselves and in their ability to beat the Turk.[38]

Commandant of Anzac Cove's inner defences

One of the most recorded events by those present at Anzac Cove was the sinking of HMS *Triumph* on 26 May 1915.

> To put it crudely one couldn't see them for smoke – they were making off as fast as steam could carry them... so that now we are left with only the destroyer and trawlers to support us... this is a distinct score for the enemy and, I am afraid it opens our eyes... our boasted dominion of the seas for the time being is shattered.[39]

On the same day Bowler was again angered when three destroyers approached his beach, preparing to disembark troops in broad daylight. With no prior warning, he watched helplessly as Turkish artillery hit the leading destroyer. There were 40 casualties among the 1700 mainly Australian troops who landed. 'A deplorable incident,' he wrote, 'and quite unnecessary and ... the result of the bungling of the Navy who in the first place should have bought the men ashore at night ... and secondly failure to instruct the destroyers... to the method of disembarkation ... The General and all of us are... incensed at the useless waste of good men.'[40] This is a typical example of Bowler's complaints about poor staff work.

At the end of May, he noted that it was '5 weeks since we landed and what do we show'.[41] Nonetheless, he was not all criticism; he had some firm ideas of his own on how to break out from the eagle's nest. 'They should push in here and give us reinforcements for that purpose',[42] and he correctly appreciated that 'at present we are only containing a certain force of Turks and gradually frittering away our forces'.[43] By then, too, Birdwood and his staff were beginning to develop a left flanking attack for an assault on Hill 971. Bowler was ambivalent and wavering: 'We ought to be in France[;] we are doing no good for the main end here and the fate of the Dardanelles will yet probably be sealed on the fields of France and Belgium'.[44]

The August offensive

'We want stacks of it [howitzer ammunition] to use and sow the ground with.'[45] Bowler wrote that he, General Cunliffe Owen and Colonel Cameron had 'an interesting discussion on artillery and its use in war, the General discoursing on cooperation and coordination. He promises to make notes on the experience gained by our gunners here. They have learnt by experience in war 'what they should have learned in training.'[46] His hint that the gunners ought to have learnt more in training was well attested to by the commander of the Australian Divisional Artillery, Colonel J.J.T. Hobbs.[47]

> I had a great deal of... trouble trying to get the New Zealand artillery on the triangles within their zones, especially Lonesome Pine and Johnson's Jolly. Even now they are doing no good and appear to be dropping shells into our own trenches.[48]

Moreover, Godley wrote to Hamilton regarding 4.5-inch howitzer ammunition only to have one of his staff officers respond that it was not possible to increase the daily allowance. Braithwaite directed Godley to note 'in your daily "Report on the Situation"... amounts fired in excess of the normal allowance'.[49] Hamilton's early request to the War Office for additional munitions received a blunt reply: 'The ammunition supply for your force was never calculated on the basis of a prolonged occupation of the peninsula. It is important to push on.'[50] After seven weeks ashore, the heat, flies and sickness had taken a toll on all ranks. 'I'm afraid if we stay here much longer,' Bowler wrote, 'disease will break out among the men more deadly than bullets.'[51]

The New Zealand force at Anzac Cove was an extended family linked by civil trades, kinship relationships, sports activities, common religious denominations, politics and cultural achievements. In all these attributes, it was clear New Zealanders, including Maori, shared much with their Australian cousins. Despite their differences, Australians and New Zealanders were all ordinary citizens and volunteers in a combined army dedicated to the restoration of the peace. The egalitarianism of their soldiering was obvious.

> I meet Major O'Neill (Doctor of Dunedin) who has a clearing station… under Popes Hill – have a morning cup of tea with him and… learn… the sad news of the death of young Hugh Paterson, son of Mr. & Mrs. J.B.P. – Hugh was a dresser in his station and… had been killed on the 7th two days before…. He had just got his mail from home and was discussing the news with his comrades when it happened. They were occupied while I was there in carving a wooden cross for his grave and were very sad about it. [52]

Bowler's bitterness at the inept leadership within the 'eagles nest' could not be disguised. There was 'No aeroplane… to discover the guns on our left flank or… position of the enemy although there are seventeen or eighteen aeroplanes down south. We are left here to stew in our own juice – the name of Ian Hamilton will be "mud" in New Zealand and Australia after this show is over.' [53]

Bowler's fears that diarrhoea and unburied bodies would undermine the health and morale of the Anzacs had become a reality, yet their reason for fighting was unchanged: 'The job we have here seems such a hopeless one under present conditions. The Turk's positions in front… and, to get them out… some turning movement must be made… any attack can only mean great loss of life and probable failure.' [54]

After dining with Birdwood on 17 June, Bowler was elated: 'an attack will be pushed in here assisted by some other divisions to be landed… or here abouts. It should have been done long ago as Turks have now heavily entrenched our left.' Soberly he reflected that 'Whatever way it is done there will be heavy casualties and New Zealand and Australians will have to face another heavy list.' [55]

Bowler went to Helles with Lieutenant-Colonel Arthur Bauchop aboard a

Royal Navy trawler. He did not feel hopeful about the prospects at Helles and would have agreed with Bauchop's conclusion: 'I really don't think they can go in on this place'.[56] Back at Anzac Bowler pondered the British predicament: 'Our scientific men are being left behind by them or some method would have been devised… of combating or neutralizing the submarine'. He had no faith at all in the Royal Navy. 'When will the eyes of England and its dependencies… be opened to the fact that this is a war in which we are right up against it… the whole energies of the Empire have to be devoted to one end… the smashing of the German.'[57]

Bowler was adhering to his Presbyterian and legal code: the truth was truth, and equality of personal and material sacrifice from all was necessary if victory was to be certain. 'It sickens me to read… of the prosperity of the farmer. No man at the present time should be able to exploit the nation by making extraordinary profits and if it were properly organized… such could not happen.'[58] This was an opinion similar to the socialist philosophy of Peter Fraser, a labour activist and future New Zealand prime minister who would be imprisoned in December 1916 for publicly advocating thoughts similar to Bowler's. Fraser shared Bowler's belief in the need to legislate against war profiteers, monopolists and the exploitation of working people. Both wanted to check capitalistic opportunity occasioned by the war. If lives were to be sacrificed or conscripted, so too should be the national wealth.

Disillusionment

Physically exhausted, Bowler was invalided off Anzac with severe dysentery on 8 July. He was sent to Malta, where he wrote that he hoped General Stopford, who was to command the attack on the left flank, would 'be set with combined success'. On returning to Gallipoli, he learned of the disastrous failure at Suvla, which left him depressed about the state of Britain:

> Want of ammunition – want of foresight – lack of generalship, it seems as if it is
> all a judgment upon the country – and… what is one to say of… 200,000 men,
> Welsh coalminers, who will go out on strike, refuse to supply what is the life
> and essence of the country's needs (coal) at the present time while our
> countrymen who are trying to do their duty at the front are dying like flies for

need of the very things which are supplied by means of such coal. Can a country which permits such a thing be right at heart – I almost doubt it – … I believe the trouble has arisen through the cursed system which allows classes such as coal owners, armament makers etc, to make a profit out of the supreme needs of the nation in this its hour of peril. Oh, the English people sicken me – I almost wish I were some other race – a Jap or a heathen Chinese.[59]

Here Bowler echoes the common contemporary view of Asians as the 'Yellow Peril', threatening Australasia.[60] Both he and Bean believed that the Anzacs alone possessed the once universal British characteristics of patriotism, moral courage and pride of race.

On his return to Anzac in the second week of August Bowler could not subdue his pessimism: 'This war is crushing our young manhood but we must rise triumphant yet from the chastening process thro which we are passing… Still it is a long and grievous process and would that it were all over and done with.'[61] At Mudros bad news awaited him. The New Zealanders had taken Chunuk Bair, with heavy casualties, but the British troops that replaced them had been driven off.

It appears to be another hold up and the casualties we hear are awful. 23 000 of which NZ and Australia contribute 10 000 surely it cannot be true – poor NZ and Australia – my heart is stunned for the people at home and what friends shall I find are gone when I get back to Anzac.[62]

The Anzac failure on Chunuk Bair led him to give vent to all of his doubts:

In detail our Army Corps were unable to stay on Hill 971 [*sic*, Chunuk Bair] and were driven off it and afterwards the other divisions were driven back 2 miles after making 6 miles in…. It is a defeat; view it how they will althou' I expect the British public will be led to believe it is a success.[63]

'Poor New Zealand and Australia – my heart is sore for their people. What sacrifices to make and so little to show for it all.' Bowler drew no comfort from the Anzacs' splendid work: 'going further up [the rank structure] one is struck by the horrible incompetence'. Intuitively, Bowler felt the British were 'played out … everything seems to be so mismanaged and one wonders will we ever blunder through this great war to final victory – I am about inclined to doubt it.'[64]

Bowler was the victim of cross-cultural conflict: was he British or was he a New Zealander? Since the landing a conflict had developed within him between his colonial origins, education and independence and his inherited British cultural and social conventions. He was at that time the only surviving antipodean on the ANZAC staff, apart from Birdwood's Australian aide. In the face of such Anzac death and suffering, the independence of mind that had won Bowler his staff position was leading him to question his sense of nationhood. Was the decimation of his country's manhood worth the cost of belonging to the empire? How much were their deaths due to incompetence?

Almost all his friends in the AIF and countrymen such as Colonels Bauchop and Malone had been killed, and he was weary. 'Now my duty is plain – namely I ask General Birdwood to relieve me of my present appointment and offer myself to General Godley to take up a command.' He left the matter in Birdwood's hands. His confidence in the Anzacs never faltered: 'Our men did their part and have shown themselves to be the best troops in the world. None at any rate here can equal them and all hands generally recognize that. But thru the delay of a silly old general [Stopford] on our left all they did was rendered of no value.'[65] Depressed and overcome by the human sacrifice that resulted from the failed offensive, he wrote, 'The fact is our force – the whole Army Corps – is done up completely and needs to be withdrawn…. They have played their part and are sick of the futility of it all and of seeing their efforts nullified by the mistakes of others.'[66]

As Assistant Provost Marshal, Bowler visited his surviving few old friends within the boundaries of the expanded Anzac enclave. 'In spite of our expenditure of life there is another complete holdup here and there is only the old trench work going on with its accompanying artillery and sniping. The sound of it sickens me.' Winter was on the horizon: 'So far no rain to speak of – we rather long for a little to lay the dust only I suppose when it does come it will come in torrents and wash us all out'.[67] He shifted his quarters into a dugout that smelt of death: 'Yesterday marked the completion of the fourth calendar month that we have been in this stinking place. How the months slip by.'[68]

Bowler may well have felt aggrieved at being overlooked for a field command and was likely smarting at being relieved of his beach command, but he drew some comfort from being a survivor.

> The place is really nothing but a butchers shop... or having 25 000 rabbits rounded up on 600 to 1000 acres paddock with sportsmen outside potting them when they come out of their holes.... The losses of all those men prey on my mind and keep me from sleep and it seems so all unavailing with no glimmer of hope ahead.[69]

Evacuation

When the *Aquitania* left Anzac Cove in mid-September and set course for England, Bowler was aboard, having been invalided off the peninsula for the final time. His fear was the approaching winter:

> I am one who thinks... objections should not be allowed to bar the way [for evacuation]. The objections are... the terrible loss of prestige to Britain and its effect in India and Egypt and the second the great loss of men and material... sustained to carry out any such retirement. It would be a staggering loss but... considerably less than what will be incurred by carrying on.[70]

By the time he arrived at Southampton Docks on 25 September, Bowler was resolved to speak with Thomas Mackenzie, the New Zealand High Commissioner.[71] He wanted to do something positive to recover the living from Anzac.

While he was in London, Bowler suggested to Claris, his daughter, that she should consult *Whitakers Peerage, Baronetage, Knightage and Companionage* for the family backgrounds of those with whom he was associating. In the space of a few days he had had a long talk with former New Zealand Governor Lord Plunket at the New Zealand High Commission. 'Mrs. Parker sister of K[itchener] of K[hartoum], the Dowager Catherine, Lady Decies and other ladies of high breeding whose names I did not catch. The Lady Decies invited us to her house for afternoon tea on Monday so there we must go.'[72]

He took Sir James Mills, a prominent shipping and industrial director with

family and business interests in Bowler's home territory, to the Naval and
Military Club. [73] 'But I am always thinking of the boys left at Anzac and feeling
one should not be tasting the joys of London while others are hanging on
there.' [74]

Critical of those in authority, Bowler described them as 'effete and worthless'
and reiterated that the dominions ought to have more to say in the councils of
the Empire. If the blood of the empire's youth was to be spilled then it was time
for the dominions to challenge 'such a crowd that now guide the affairs of our
nation'. His irritation mounted. Public comments by Lord Milner of the War
Cabinet about the evacuation of the troops from Anzac, likely to alert the Turks
to the possibility, were the limit: 'It is enough to make Colonials sick of them
and their blessed politicians and ministers'. [75]

At a private lunch arranged by Mackenzie on 15 October 1915, Bowler gave
'some idea of the casualties and evacuations up to the end of August – he is very
pessimistic and disgusted and enraged at the mismanagement and spinelessness
of the authorities – considers that [Prime Minister William] Massey should come
out.' [76] He also listed the numbers of New Zealanders evacuated sick and
wounded, as well as the casualties sustained at Chunuk Bair.

Bowler's remarks ought to be considered beside the attitudes of Massey, who
'frequently protested… the methods adopted by the [British] both in the
operations and the economic arrangement' of the war where New Zealand
troops were involved. [77] This was so particularly if there were financial and social
consequences that affected New Zealand society.

Bowler's desire to get the New Zealanders off Gallipoli was not an isolated
determination: he had co-agitators in the war correspondents Ellis Ashmead-
Bartlett and Keith Arthur Murdoch. [78] (Bowler had met war correspondents
on the peninsula, though he mentioned only New Zealand's Malcolm Ross.)
Bartlett's commendation of the Anzacs was similar to Bowler's: 'the superlative
gallantry of the Colonial troops, and the self-sacrificing manner in which they
threw their lives away against a position which should never have been
attacked'. Like Bowler describing the Otago Battalion's sacrifice in early May,
at Lone Pine and in the attack on Chunuk Bair, Bartlett wrote, 'The muddles
and mismanagement beat anything that has ever occurred in our military
history.' Were it not for the discipline of the British military tradition within

the colonial army, Bartlett continued, an open state of mutiny might well have broken out, for 'the outlook for the troops is deplorable'. He recalled the unburied and lightly covered bodies of the dead that would be swept down to the beach in the coming winter rains. 'The whole army dreads beyond all else the prospect of wintering on this dreary inhospitable coast.' Bartlett also echoed Bowler's description of the Anzacs clinging onto the rim of the eagle's nest: 'At present some of our positions, gained by the Colonial troops high on the spurs of the hills on which the Turks are perched cannot be considered secure'.[79]

Bartlett also shared Bowler's poor opinion of British leadership 'as the dust of poor generalship': 'the confidence of the troops can only be restored by an immediate change in the supreme command'. Both eyewitnesses feared a disaster with the approaching winter. 'If we are to stay here this winter,' Bartlett wrote, 'let orders be given for the army to start its preparations without delay.' Both men agreed on the required course of action: 'If possible... have the Colonial troops taken off the peninsula altogether because they are miserably depressed since the last failure [Chunuk Bair] and with their active minds, the positions they occupy in civil life, a dreary winter in the trenches will have a deplorable effect... [on] this once magnificent body of men, the finest any Empire has ever produced'.[80]

The dismissal of Hamilton probably gave Bowler some hope that the New Zealanders were unlikely to remain on Gallipoli. A fortnight later, he sailed to Egypt, looking forward to a new appointment. Within four days of his arrival, however, he was unceremoniously placed on a vessel bound for Wellington.

A witness denied

In mid-May 1916 Bowler left the office of the Military Secretary in Wellington, aware that his services were no longer required, but in March 1917 he asked Birdwood for an appointment in France: 'I would most gladly do anything I could... if it were... in my power'. Birdwood replied. 'I am sorry... as I have no say... in New Zealand matters.... I will speak to General Godley... but I am not very sanguine that anything I can say will be of much use.'[81] Birdwood's use of the word 'sanguine' was appropriate: he was using colonial 'speak' that really means 'not bloody hopeful'.[82] Bowler never returned to the army.

It would not have taken long for surviving senior New Zealand officers from Gallipoli and France to learn of Bowler's discussions with Mackenzie. His outspoken criticism of the military establishment in Britain and his advocacy of the withdrawal of the Anzac forces was no doubt related to those in authority. Yet his was just one voice among others, stronger and more powerful, campaigning in October 1915 for a withdrawal from Gallipoli.

There is no official mention of Bowler's service with the Anzac staff in his NZEF service records. Nor does he rate a mention in the New Zealand official history of the Gallipoli campaign, though Bean, the Australian official historian, lists him in his biographical index in *The Story of Anzac* as the beach commander. The normally studious John Studholme omits his posting to the ANZAC staff in his 1928 *New Zealand Expeditionary Force: Record of Personal Services*. Bowler's descendants believe that after his return to Gore from Wellington and his release from the NZEF a dark cloud remained over him for the rest of his life.

General Birdwood, who visited New Zealand in mid-1920, recorded that 'Bowler who was with me joined train at Gore'.[83] Following Birdwood's Invercargill visit, Bowler returned to Gore and Birdwood wrote asking him to apologise to the mayor that he was unable to visit Gore because he had made other arrangements. Lady Birdwood, however, would represent him. This was out of character for Birdwood, who had chosen to drive through Central Otago and 'stood up' the citizens of Gore, a visit 'to which I had originally much looked forward'. He hoped Bowler would 'acquit me of any discourtesy in the matter'.[84] Bowler's family are convinced that Birdwood did not wish to renew an association with his assistant provost marshal, whom he believed had acted improperly in seeking political action regarding Gallipoli.

The *Dardanelles Commission Report* of 1917 indicated that Bowler's overall judgment about the dust of poor generalship at Gallipoli was not far off the mark. When the commission delivered its findings, Kitchener was dead and his headmaster-prefect relationship with those generals who were close to him in the Anzac campaign had died with him. That Bowler went unrecognised by any award singles him out as an exception among ANZAC survivors of similar rank.[85]

Bowler's lasting legacy to the Anzac legend are his letters: he was a critical eye-witness to the events at a command level singularly absent among the few published New Zealand accounts of the Gallipoli Anzac story. I am left with the firm impression that the silences in Bowler's papers are filled with the echoes of human argument within the staff corps. Bowler was too much of a gentleman to record everything: he knew more than he ever wrote about. New Zealand has had to wait over 85 years for Bowler's papers to surface. In them he revealed some of the elements of the legend that is now part of the nationhood of both Australia and New Zealand.

12

Devils on Horses:
The New Zealand Mounted Rifles Brigade

Terry Kinloch

Clifton Bellis attended the 50th commemoration of Anzac Day at Gallipoli in 1965. He later wrote:

> In conversation with two Turkish officers who were on the Sinai front, they told me that the Anzacs were always referred to by the Turkish soldiers as 'devils on horses', the reason for this being that they never knew where they would strike next. The Turks' reconnaissance planes would report no movement in the enemy camps at sundown, yet by daybreak the Anzacs would be attacking a position twenty miles away from their base, which the Turks had never thought possible.[1]

When the Main Body of the New Zealand Expeditionary Force sailed from New Zealand in October 1914, a quarter of its men and half of its horses belonged to the New Zealand Mounted Rifles Brigade (98 officers, 1842 men and 2032 horses). It was organised into three regiments – Auckland, Wellington and Canterbury, each with 549 men and 608 horses – and medical, engineering and support units. A regiment contained three squadrons and a machine gun section. A squadron of 158 men fielded four troops, each consisting of eight four-man sections. Within each section, one man was responsible for holding the horses when the other three dismounted for action. The structure of the brigade in 1914 is illustrated below.

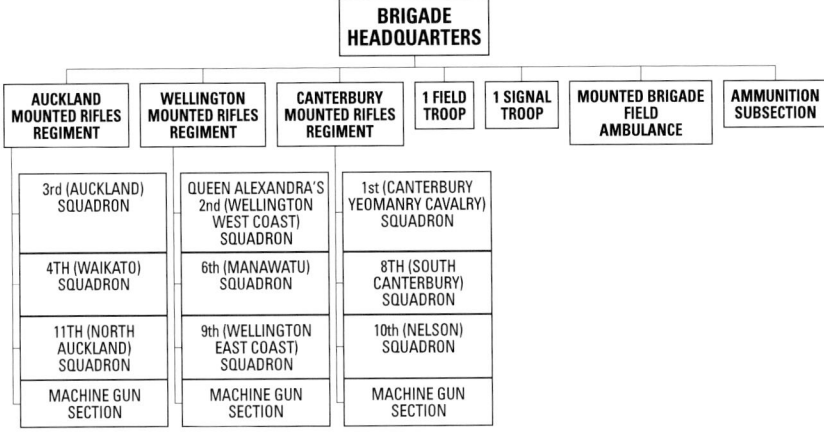

The mounteds, as they were commonly known, expected to win their laurels in a short, sharp, victorious fight against the Germans in Europe. Many of them thought they would be gone for just a few months. Instead, the brigade was away from home for almost five years. During that time, the horsemen fought, not the Germans, but the Turks, in what are now Egypt, Gallipoli, Israel, Syria and Jordan for three and a half years. The timeline below summarises their war.

NZMR BRIGADE WAR DIARY[2]

1914

6 August	Expeditionary Force offered by New Zealand government
16 October	Departure of NZEF Main Body from New Zealand
3 December	NZEF Main Body disembarked in Egypt

1915

12 May	Arrival of NZMR Brigade at Gallipoli
19 May	Defence of Anzac
28–30 May	Attack at Old Outpost No. 3
6–7 August	Capture of Sari Bair foothills
8–9 August	Defence of Chunuk Bair
21 August	First attack at Hill 60
27–28 August	Second attack at Hill 60
13 September–10 November	Resting of brigade on Lemnos

---

20 December	Evacuation of brigade from Gallipoli
1916	
11 March	Formation of Anzac Mounted Division
4–5 August	Defeat of Turks at Battle of Romani
23 December	Capture of Magdhaba
1917	
9 January	Capture of Rafa
26 March	Failure of first attempt to capture Gaza
17–19 April	Failure of second attempt to capture Gaza
30–31 October	Capture of Tel el Saba in Third Battle of Gaza
14 November	Defeat of Turkish counter-attack at Ayun Kara
24 November	Failure to capture bridgehead across River Auja
1918	
21 February	Capture of Jericho
27–30 March	Failure of first attempt to capture Amman
1–6 May	Failure of second attempt to capture Amman
25 September	Capture of Amman
31 October	Turkey signs Armistice
1919	
March – June	Suppression of Egyptian revolt in the Nile Delta
30 June	NZMR Brigade disbanded
23 July	Last NZMR contingent sails from Egypt for New Zealand

The Turks were tough and courageous fighters, and quite effective when on the defensive. They could never be taken for granted, and they inflicted defeats on the New Zealanders throughout the war.[3] In addition to this human enemy, the mounteds also had to contend with venomous snakes, scorpions and centipedes, and giant tarantula spiders, in their beds and in their boots. They lived and fought in blistering heat and numbing cold, often made worse by suffocating sandstorms and freezing rain. They lived for years among indifferent or hostile local populations.[4] Their food was often poor, and clean water was a luxury for much of their war. They enjoyed few of the compensations available to the men in France and Belgium. Leave was available, but almost never further afield than Egypt. Rest periods in friendly French villages, or in England, were an impossible dream for the mounteds. To add insult to injury, their efforts were often belittled at home. Some ill-informed New Zealanders considered them to be little more than tourists in uniform, enjoying the sinful pleasures of the East while the New Zealand infantry fought the 'real' war in France and Belgium.

On the positive side, their casualties were a fraction of what the rest of the NZEF suffered. According to Commonwealth War Graves Commission records, about 600 men in the NZMR Brigade lost their lives as a result of the Gallipoli campaign. Around 400 more mounteds died during the remaining three years of the war. Many more were wounded, and many hundreds of others suffered from debilitating sickness.

At the end of it all, they came home and were quickly forgotten. Today, when one thinks of New Zealanders in the Great War, it is Gallipoli, the Somme, and Passchendaele that come to mind. It is not generally known that nearly one-fifth of the total embarked strength of the NZEF served in the NZMR Brigade in some capacity during the war.

Mounted riflemen – and the Australian equivalent, the light horse – were not cavalry. They were not trained in the traditional cavalry role of attacking enemy cavalry on horseback with swords or lances. Instead, mounted riflemen used their horses to move quickly around the battlefield. When they gained contact with the enemy, they dismounted and fought him on foot with the rifle, the bayonet and the machine gun. They did perform some cavalry tasks such as reconnaissance, but they were not considered to be on a par with traditional cavalry. Compared with infantry battalions, mounted rifles regiments were much smaller and more lightly armed. After taking out horse holders and others, a complete mounted rifles brigade of three regiments could put only as many riflemen into a firing line as a single infantry battalion. The brigade was equipped with modern rifles, but it had only a few Maxim machine guns at first.[5] Its mobility meant that heavy artillery support was not usually available.[6]

The mounteds could travel far and quickly. This high degree of operational mobility had a downside: they could ride into trouble quickly, but they lacked the firepower and numbers to disengage as easily from enemy contact. Mounted rifles units always ran the risk of being isolated and destroyed by superior enemy forces – and it did not take a very large enemy force to outnumber or out-gun a mounted rifles regiment. The need to water the horses meant that a sustained assault was not possible, at least in the desert. The horses were very vulnerable, especially when concentrated under cover during dismounted action. All these factors made the command of mounted riflemen a delicate balancing act of risk versus benefit.

Major-General Sir Alexander Godley, the commander of the NZEF, appointed Colonel Andrew Russell, a Hawke's Bay farmer with formal British military training and some operational experience, to command the brigade. The three regimental commanders, Lieutenant-Colonels Charles Mackesy, William Meldrum and John Findlay, were sound leaders with extensive experience gained over many years, although only Findlay had served in the South African War.

As with the rest of the NZEF in 1914, the men of the brigade were all volunteers. Not all of them came from the land. In the Auckland Mounted Rifles Regiment, for example:

> There were lawyers and schoolmasters and students; there were bushmen and farmers and stockmen; there were tradesmen and labourers and clerks; one single tent in the Epsom camp included a schoolmaster, a barber, a coach driver, an accountant, a carpenter, a farm labourer, a commercial traveller, a farmer and a lawyer.[7]

The decision was taken in November 1914 to land the NZEF in Egypt to help guard the Suez Canal against Turkish attack, and also to gain better training grounds.[8] This was expected to be a short-term diversion, with onward travel to the Western Front expected at any time. Their time in Egypt was indeed brief, but for a different reason.

The NZEF was committed to the Gallipoli invasion in March 1915. After being left behind for the landings on 25 April – the landings were by infantry and artillery only – New Zealand's mounted rifles regiments and the Australian light horse were called forward in early May, without their horses. Most of the men were excited at the prospect of some fighting at last, even unmounted. Generals Ian Hamilton and William Birdwood wanted the mounted riflemen and light horsemen as individual reinforcements to build up their weakened infantry battalions, but they received complete brigades instead. As it turned out, this was a good decision: the brigade staffs proved to be very useful on the peninsula.

From May until December 1915, Russell's mounted regiments had their full share of the fighting on Gallipoli, and they suffered heavy casualties. The original brigade that left Egypt for Gallipoli was effectively destroyed in three and a half months. The mounteds earned a reputation for doggedness, initiative and resourcefulness, especially as scouts. They fought early, hard actions at The Nek and at Outpost No. 3. On 19 May, less than a week after their arrival on the peninsula, the Auckland and Wellington regiments helped to fight off a threatening attack ('The Defence of Anzac') at The Nek. The Aucklanders, who bore the brunt of the assault, lost 23 men killed and about the same number wounded.[9] The reliability and discipline of the mounteds in this action first marked them out as superior troops.

The mounteds made the foothills and valleys of the Sari Bair Range to the north of Anzac Cove their own almost from the day they arrived. Led by Major Percy Overton, Russell's 'patrol master', New Zealand mounted riflemen scouted the ground thoroughly, providing evidence that this area was lightly defended. Their reports suggested that the area was a likely option for a breakout from the Anzac perimeter, and contributed to General Hamilton's decision to stage his next major offensive there.

The mounted brigade played an important role in the battles for the Sari Bair Range in August. Old Outpost No. 3, Table Top, Bauchop's Hill and Chunuk Bair were all fought over by the mounteds, and they suffered heavy casualties. Their work in securing the western foothills of the range was described by the Australian official historian as a 'magnificent feat of arms, the brilliance of which was never surpassed, if indeed equalled, during the campaign'.[10] British praise was equally effusive:

> It would be difficult to praise too highly the conduct of the New Zealand troops engaged in these encounters. Thanks to the dash and initiative displayed, which was never surpassed in the whole Gallipoli campaign, the majority of the Turkish outposts north of Anzac had now been accounted for, and the way was clear for the advance on Chunuk Bair.[11]

The success of the mounted regiments merits further comment. They attacked and seized five enemy posts at the point of the bayonet, at night, entirely without covering fire, and often in the face of heavy machine gun and rifle fire. Only a few of the officers and men had traversed the country before, and the regiments had to make converging attacks in the dark while adhering to very tight timings. This latter aspect was the only one in which the brigade failed: the last of the posts was declared secure two hours late. Nonetheless, the mounteds had once again shown themselves to be reliable and determined fighters.

On 8 August the Auckland and Wellington regiments were called forward to reinforce Chunuk Bair after its capture by Lieutenant-Colonel William Malone's Wellington Infantry Battalion. The two mounted rifles regiments were decimated as they hung onto the crest for another 36 hours in the face of fierce Turkish counter-attacks. They were replaced by British battalions just hours before the overwhelming Turkish attack that recaptured Chunuk Bair.

The NZMR Brigade was 1900 men strong on 5 August. With 500 men of the 5th Reinforcements added, it had 2400 men. Within a week it had lost 151 men killed, 485 wounded and 53 missing – a total of 689 casualties.[12]

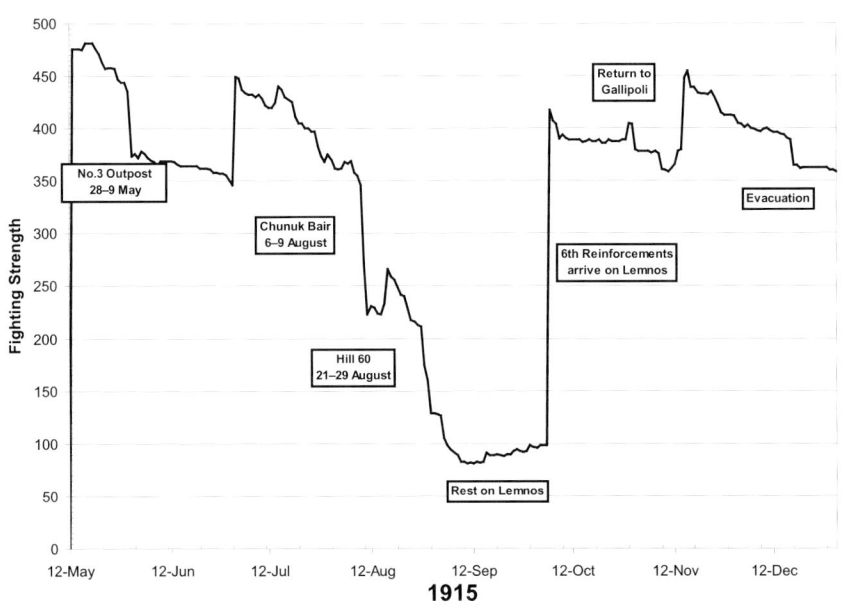

The destruction of the Wellington Mounted Rifles Regiment on Gallipoli
Decreases in fighting strength are due to men being killed, wounded or sick. Significant increases are due to the arrival of reinforcements, with lesser increases reflecting the return of men from hospital.
Source: Wellington Mounted Rifles regimental war diaries, WA Series 42/1, Archives New Zealand[13]

After the failure of the August offensive, the weakened brigade had one more ordeal to endure. At Hill 60, 236 mounteds lost their lives. Their efforts throughout August earned them high praise, and boosted their self-confidence in spite of their terrible losses. When they were evacuated to Lemnos for a month's rest in September, only about 250 men left Gallipoli from an initial strength of 10 times that number. The losses of the Wellington Mounted Rifles Regiment throughout the Gallipoli campaign are illustrated above. The other regiments suffered similar casualty rates.

The NZEF was evacuated from Gallipoli in December 1915 and the survivors returned to Egypt to rebuild their strength. Russell left the mounted rifles brigade to take up the command of the New Zealand Division, and Brigadier-General Edward Chaytor took over the command of the brigade, now remounted on its New Zealand horses. In April 1916, the majority of the NZEF went to France, leaving the NZMR Brigade behind in Egypt to help defend the Suez Canal against the Turks. Many of the riders had already tasted defeat at the hands of the Turks on Gallipoli, and they felt they had a score to settle.

The NZMR Brigade was one of four mounted brigades making up the Australian and New Zealand Mounted Division, commonly known as the Anzac Mounted Division.[14] At first it was the only mounted formation in the Egyptian Expeditionary Force (EEF) under the command of General Sir Archibald Murray. Murray was responsible for the defence of Egypt, which really meant the defence of the Suez Canal, against the Turks, who were expected to follow up their success at Gallipoli with an invasion from Syria (the southern part of which is now Israel). Murray decided that the best place from which to defend the canal was from the Syrian border, and this is what he set out to do in mid-1916. The mounted troops had made the most of the intervening months to learn the art of desert survival.

The Anzac Mounted Division led the way across Sinai in 1916, almost single-handedly defeating the Turks at Romani, Magdhaba and Rafa.[15] Romani was their first fight as a mounted brigade. The battle was won, but a complete victory was denied through stubborn Turkish resistance and poor command decisions at critical times. The New Zealand brigade performed well enough for its first effort, although one British cavalryman described them as 'marvellous fellows, but very slow'.[16] In the finale to the Romani battle at Bir el Abd, the Anzac Mounted Division was launched at a stronger-than-expected and very aggressive Turkish rearguard, and the New Zealanders came close to being cut off and destroyed. They escaped through the execution of a textbook fighting withdrawal, supported by covering fire from their horse artillery and machine guns.

By Christmas 1916, the EEF had reached the southern border of Syria. Along the way, the NZMR Brigade played an important part in two small-scale battles at Magdhaba and Rafa that resulted in the capture of unsupported Turkish rearguard regiments. Rafa has been described as 'New Zealand's day'.[17] General Murray had abandoned the fight when the New Zealand mounteds made a final bayonet charge under intense enemy fire, covering 300 yards 'in two grand rushes,'[18] and captured a key part of the enemy redoubt. One Australian Light Horse brigade commander was reportedly heard to shout to his troopers to 'attack at once or those N.Z. b...s will take the lot!'[19]

In early 1917, Murray's army invaded southern Syria. The Anzac mounted troops played a leading role in the eventual capture of Gaza and Beersheba, and in the pursuit of the defeated Turks across the Plains of Philistine and up into the Judean Hills surrounding Jerusalem. During the first Battle of Gaza, the New Zealand mounted rifles and the Australian light horse were close to capturing the town when Murray ordered them back, fearing a Turkish counter-attack. Before they withdrew, some enterprising Wellington troopers made good use of a captured German field gun to blast an enemy post in a house into submission, by sighting through the open breech. Not being experienced artillerymen, they were as dangerous to themselves as they were to the enemy. The first round ploughed up the ground in front of the muzzle, while the recoiling gun ran backwards over the amateur gun crew and tried to climb a tree.

In the reorganisation of the EEF that followed the failure of Murray's second attempt to take Gaza, Chaytor took over the command of the Anzac Mounted Division. The commanding officer of the Wellington regiment, Bill Meldrum, took over the NZMR Brigade. In the third battle of Gaza, in October 1917, the New Zealanders captured the important redoubt of Tel el Saba, from where they overlooked the famous Australian Light Horse charge into Beersheba.

Two more stiff fights took place at Ayun Kara, south of the modern city of Tel Aviv, and across the River Auja, in what is now a northern suburb of the same city.

The battle at Ayun Kara was the worst single day in the mounteds' war since Gallipoli, with 44 men being killed and 141 wounded.[20] The Auja fight, which took place 10 days later, was characterised by one officer as 'a very pretty little action'.[21] One veteran, Trooper 'Tap' O'Neill, dismissed all of these battles, stating that, as far as he was concerned, the greatest victory won at this time was the capture of the wine cellars at Jaffa 'which they held against all comers for over a week'.[22]

Moving down into the inhospitable Jordan Valley in 1918, the Anzac Mounted Division captured Jericho and secured the western banks of the Jordan River. From the Jordan Valley, the New Zealand brigade took part in two unsuccessful raids across the river against the Turks in the highlands around Amman. The first raid in March 1918 was particularly costly: 38 New Zealanders were killed, 122 wounded and 13 posted as missing.[23] In both raids, the division was extracted from threatening situations by well-conducted fighting withdrawals and by the fighting skill and tenacity of the troopers. On 23 March, the Auckland regiment made a rare mounted charge against Turkish cavalry:

> Without a second's hesitation, Lieutenant Tait with his 20 men, armed only with rifles, galloped at the sabres. The Turks showed some spirit, and attempted to ride the North Aucklanders down, but they broke and fled before the troopers who fired as they galloped forward. The Arab horses of the Turkish cavalry were no match for the swift and powerful mounts of the riflemen.... The Turks seemed to be mesmerised by the suddenness of the onslaught, and they were prisoners before they knew what had happened.... It was a wonderful day.... A total of 50 Turks were killed, 60 were captured, besides four machine-guns, at a cost of one officer killed, and one officer and one man wounded.[24]

Finally, as the First World War drew to a close in the Middle East in September 1918, the New Zealand Mounted Rifles Brigade crossed the Jordan River once again and played a major role in the capture of Amman and the entire Turkish 2nd Corps. With its armies in Syria and elsewhere soundly defeated, Turkey sued for peace at the end of October 1918. As General A.P. Wavell later wrote: 'The Anzac Mounted Division here ended a very fine fighting record. It had taken a gallant part in practically every engagement since the E.E.F. had set out from the Canal two and a half years previously.'[25]

In its hour of triumph, malaria and the influenza epidemic ravaged the New Zealand brigade. Their return home was delayed because of a lack of shipping, and most of the men of the brigade took part in the suppression of riots in Egypt in 1919 before finally being repatriated in the middle of the year: '4th July [1919]: ... this night... glory be, saw a wonderful sight on the starboard horizon, the Southern Cross. It made home seem so much nearer.'[26] They came home without their faithful horses, which were passed on to British Army garrison units, sold to local Egyptians or Arabs, or shot.[27] 'So ended the career of the soldiers' best friends – the lovely horses. It was a sad parting for many of the lads who had had only the one horse throughout the campaign.'[28]

On the mounteds' return to New Zealand, it was acknowledged by some that their war service had not received due recognition:

> These men of ours played a glorious part in the smashing of Turkey, and their name will ever be associated with one of the most brilliant campaigns in history.... The Mounted Brigade has never had from the public the credit that was its due.[29]

The New Zealand Mounted Rifles Brigade received glowing praise from senior commanders during the war, and from many commentators afterwards. The formation was considered by many to be one of the best brigades to fight on Gallipoli; its commander, Andrew Russell, was one of the few senior officers to come off the peninsula with his reputation intact. In Egypt, General Murray considered the Anzac Mounted Division to be the best force under his command. Lord Allenby, Commander-in-Chief of the EEF, wrote in 1926 that none of the troops he commanded during the war were better than the New Zealanders: 'Their discipline in camp, their dash in action, their endurance in retirement and their vigour in pursuit were unsurpassable. Everything they were called upon to do they did with the greatest efficiency'.[30]

The New Zealand Mounted Rifles Brigade performed consistently well in the three and a half years that it took part in combat operations. It fought off one of the heaviest Turkish attacks ever launched on Gallipoli, within just a few days of arriving on the peninsula. Its work in securing the approaches for the infantry in the August Sari Bair offensive is one of the few successes in that overall failure.[31]

From Romani to Amman, the New Zealanders fought in every major battle of the EEF in Egypt and Syria. The brigade did not beat the Turks in every encounter, but, when it lost, it was not through a failure of resolve or of tactical command. There are many factors that contributed to the effectiveness of the brigade, only a few of which can be addressed here.

The New Zealand brigade was particularly fortunate in its commanders, particularly at senior level. Russell was an able commander who led the brigade on Gallipoli with skill and a fine sense of the achievable. Chaytor was a careful planner and a brave commander: as an Australian wrote, he was 'one of those rare soldiers who did everything in this prolonged campaign so surely, thoroughly and yet so quietly and with such apparent ease that it might be said that no task set him between the canal and Amman was big enough to test his full capacity'.[32] Meldrum, the last commander of the brigade, earned a reputation as an aggressive fighting leader who nonetheless tried to secure his battle objectives at minimum cost in lives.

When compared with the NZEF as a whole, the ranks of the mounted brigade included a larger proportion of men with previous war experience.[33] Most of this came from the South African War, where over 6500 men served in 10 New Zealand mounted rifles contingents. Their experience must have contributed something to the effectiveness of the brigade when it began similar mobile operations against the Turks. Too much should not be made of the influence of the earlier war: only 160 men in the Main Body had previous war experience, and their numbers must have declined as the First World War continued. Chaytor's South African War experience was perhaps of the greatest significance. He gained experience in commanding mounted troops in prolonged, long-distance dispersed operations. He also learned how to exploit ground, and how to preserve men and horses in demanding climates. He also forged important relationships with other commanders, most notably Chauvel, and these stood him and his command in good stead in the First World War.

The training of the mounted rifles brigade was another key factor in its performance. Before the war, the mounted rifles regiments were considered to be among the most well-trained troops in the Territorial Force. General Hamilton, the British Army's Inspector-General, wrote of them in 1914:

> New Zealand is fortunate in being able to muster at a very moderate expense
> such a fine body of horsemen as the Mounted Rifles. The higher commands are
> in capable hands, the instructors are able, and all ranks are animated with a
> keenness and initiative that deserve high praise..... I should esteem myself lucky
> indeed if ever I had the good fortune to encounter Continental Cavalry in
> reasonably broken ground with them at my right hand.[34]

This is not to say that the mounteds had nothing to learn. Most importantly, the majority without South African War experience lacked a good understanding of the importance of the care of horses over prolonged operations in harsh conditions. Lieutenant-Colonel Arthur Bauchop, the future commander of the Otago Regiment, wrote in *The Cavalry Journal* in 1914 that 'The New Zealand Mounted Rifleman, although a good rider, cannot be considered a good horsemaster'.[35]

Before and after Gallipoli, the operational tempo permitted thorough and ongoing training of both officers and men. Mainly for logistical reasons, the war in the Middle East proceeded in a very stop-start manner, and there were relatively long periods between active operations. The advance across Sinai to the border of Syria proceeded at the pace of the railway and water pipeline that was being laid across the desert. The mounted brigade's first serious fight at Romani took place four months after the brigade began desert operations, and four more months passed between that battle and the next, at Magdhaba. It took another nine months for the EEF to advance beyond the Gaza–Beersheba line. This operational tempo allowed the regiments to be rotated out of the front line regularly for weeks at a time, for rest and for training.

Men in the NZEF signed up for the duration of the war. In contrast, in the South African War, it was usual for men to serve for one year before they were replaced by a new contingent. This factor, combined with the relatively low casualty rate experienced by the mounteds after Gallipoli, meant that hard-won experience was retained, and there was little need to constantly retrain new men.

In 1918 Chaytor declined the opportunity to re-equip the regiments under his command with swords, thereby avoiding a significant additional training burden for what he believed to be an unnecessary change.

The horse was the most successful weapon in the mounted rifles brigade.

Without the horses, the men were no more than immobile infantry. The mounteds rode New Zealand horses almost exclusively, and they were very well served by them. An efficient remount and veterinary service maintained the horses in good fighting condition throughout the war, although remounts stopped coming from New Zealand in 1917. New Zealand's horses gained a reputation for toughness and endurance that was second to none. In one instance, New Zealand horses went 72 hours without water, and they regularly had to put up with indifferent rations. The horsemastership of the New Zealanders had to be high to preserve the horses. The men got used to the idea of having to keep one horse fit and well day after day, week after week, and the incidence of sore backs and other horse maladies was maintained at a low level throughout the war.

The mounteds were good and they knew it. They were aware that their predecessors had performed well in the South African War, and they considered themselves to be the élite of the Territorial Force. They took this high reputation to the Middle East in 1914. They guarded their reputation jealously, and anyone who let them down was left in no doubt of his error. When they were beaten, they did not blame themselves. When they were successful, their confidence grew. On occasion, easy successes or misleading intelligence led them to stick their necks out a little too far. Each time, they were reminded never to underestimate the Turkish Johnnies.

The men stuck together. Occasional letters from home referring to the 'cold-footed mounteds' enjoying the pleasures and sun of Egypt, while the infantry fought the 'real' war in Europe, caused great offence and served to unite the men. They fought their war in a hostile and alien environment, where the local population either ignored them or took advantage of them. Leave in Cairo or Alexandria lost some of its appeal after the initial novelty wore off, and many men on leave soon yearned to return to the comradeship of the regiment. The small size of mounted units, and their low losses after Gallipoli, allowed the men of the sections, troops and squadrons to develop strong bonds over the years. This cohesion contributed greatly to their morale and their effectiveness.

A low incidence of disciplinary problems is symptomatic of a successful and happy force, and this is true of the mounteds: incidents of crime within the units were relatively uncommon. Adjacent units of other nationalities were less safe from predation by New Zealand 'hunters and gatherers', and most other disciplinary lapses occurred while men were on leave, away from the regimental environment. There were a few notable and serious lapses of discipline, but these occurred either before major combat operations (the Wazza riots in April 1915) or afterwards, most notoriously, in the Surafend massacre[36] after the Armistice in 1918.

The men of the New Zealand Mounted Rifles Brigade, our 'devils on horses', fought a long, hard war against a stubborn and tough enemy, in a difficult environment with few redeeming features, and in the face of public indifference from home. They put up with boredom, extremes of climate, disease, poor food and bad water. They played a full part in the defeat of the Turkish army. They were among the last of New Zealand's men to come home, and when they did return they were forgotten. The cost, in lives lost or blighted, never approached the horrendous casualty lists of Gallipoli and the Western Front, but it was nonetheless significant. Over 1000 New Zealand mounted riflemen lie buried in neat but lonely cemeteries across Turkey, Egypt, Israel, the Gaza Strip and Syria.

The seeds for their success were sown in the South African War, where several key commanders gained valuable practical experience of how to conduct dispersed and prolonged operations in difficult country. The Middle Eastern theatre of war permitted mobile operations, the enemy was not formidable enough to prevent them exploiting their advantages and there was ample time to train between major operations. Their equipment, especially their horses, was up to the job, and the casualty rate and operational tempo were both low enough to allow hard-won experience to be retained.

Of course, the war in the Middle East could have been won without them. In 1918, New Zealand's contribution to Allenby's great army of 140,000 fighting men numbered just over 2000. At the end of the war, they were outnumbered by Australian Light Horse regiments by more than five to one. But our mounted riflemen punched well above their weight, as New Zealanders often do in times of war. They performed consistently well, and they deserved the praise given to them. What they did not deserve was to be forgotten.

13

AN AWKWARD SALIENT: NEW ZEALAND INFANTRY ON THE SOMME, 15 SEPTEMBER 1916

Andrew Macdonald

Amid the grisly First Battle of the Somme in 1916 the New Zealand Division seeded its reputation as one of the finest on the Western Front. At the start of the battle's third phase on 15 September, the division stormed more enemy-held ground than any other, reached all its objectives and helped to defend the village of Flers. This chapter will examine how skilled New Zealand infantrymen overcame confusion, near-disaster and heavy casualties to earn that reputation.

The Somme was the division's first offensive action since arriving on the Western Front in May 1916. The Anglo-French offensive had been spluttering along in Picardy since its bloody opening on 1 July 1916. Although initially conceived to relieve pressure on the French at Verdun with a combined push, it had gradually become a mainly British effort because of the scale of French casualties at Verdun.

With two German defensive lines under his belt General Sir Douglas Haig, the BEF's Commander-in-Chief, decided yet another push in mid-September would break the German defences in the Picardy region of Northern France.

> For the last 2½ months we have been gradually wearing down the enemy. His morale
> is shaken, he has few, if any, fresh reserves available and there is every probability that
> a combined and determined effort will result in a decisive victory.[1]

Haig decreed that the so-called Battle of Flers-Courcelette would start on 15 September and in it tanks, the Allies' new and secret weapon of war, would be used for the first time. The Fourth and Fifth Armies were to renew the offensive on this day, supported by a massive artillery bombardment.

By nightfall on 15 September the New Zealand Division, attached to the Fourth Army's XV Corps, had stormed and held three German trench networks and Flers village. The cost was high: more than 34 per cent of the men who went into the battle were dead, wounded or missing.

Twelve hours earlier some 6000 infantrymen of the division's 2 Infantry and 3 Rifle Brigades were hunkered down in the latticework of assembly trenches between High and Delville Woods near Longueval. They had spent a sleepless night ahead of the 6.20 a.m. zero hour. The day dawned cool and misty, 'a typical autumn morning'.[2] One veteran remembered: 'At last the stars went out and the sky lightened to pale green and then to pink. By six o'clock we had eaten breakfast of bread, cold bully beef and water.'[3]

Since leaving the increasingly dangerous Armentières salient in mid-August, the division had marched steadily towards the Somme battlefield. Its journey was studded with intensive rounds of training in the new tactics it would use in the offensive, namely a creeping artillery barrage and limited objectives. The former was designed to cover infantry as it advanced towards an objective and stop enemy infantry manning their parapet. Laid down by field artillery, the barrage moved forward to timetable in increments of 50 yards, with infantry following close behind. Limited objectives were those a given body of infantry was ordered to capture but not advance beyond. In the case of the Somme, all the New Zealand Division's objectives were limited.

In the lead-up to 15 September, divisional commander Major-General Sir Andrew Russell was busy with XV Corps, preparing plans for the attack. 'Corp. Conference at Vivier Mill,' he noted in his diary on 12 September; 'a more or less final recapitulation of the probable action'.[4] The next day he issued Operational Order 49.[5] 'Everything is I think on a sound footing,' he wrote after discussing it with his infantry brigadiers.[6] Russell was optimistic about preparations for the attack.

The Division had been ordered to seize a 2-mile-deep north-east-facing wedge of land west of Flers village. Within this 875-yard-wide area were four colour-coded objectives each encompassing an enemy trench – Green, Brown, Blue and Red Lines – and a low-lying ridge.

Operational Order 49 spelled out the tactics to be used by the two New Zealand brigades, 2 and 3 (Rifle), that would go into action: they were to deliver a series of leapfrog actions to capture each successive objective.

Broadly speaking, the division's advance had three main acts. The first was the uphill advance by two infantry battalions moving abreast of each other behind a creeping barrage to capture the Green Line (hereafter Switch Trench), which sat atop the low-lying ridge. The next act, or the battle for the downhill slopes, took in the capture of the second and third objectives, the Brown and Blue Lines respectively. The former was a zigzagging chain of interconnected trenches, taken by one battalion advancing behind a creeping barrage. The Blue Line included the strongly held Flers Trench network and the sunken Abbey Road leading into Flers' western entrance. Blue Line was stormed by two battalions advancing side by side and behind a covering barrage of machine gun fire. The third and most confusing act of the day was played out in the flat land north of Flers village. It involved the capture and subsequent loss of the Red Line, or Grove Alley communication trench, and the formation of a defensive line on Flers' northern outskirts.

On the day of the advance the New Zealanders would be sandwiched between two English divisions – 47, on its left, and 41 – that would advance alongside them. Opposing them were battalions of 5 and 18 Bavarian Infantry Regiments.

By 6 a.m. the two New Zealand brigades were ready to attack. Leading the way would be 2 Brigade's 2 Otago and 2 Auckland Battalions; both were in the most advanced assembly trenches. Behind these battalions were all four of 3 (Rifle) Brigade's battalions. Then came the other half of 2 Brigade: 2 Canterbury and 2 Wellington Battalions, which were held in support. The division's artillery, machine gunners, engineers, pioneers and medics would also play significant parts in the advance.

In the assembly trenches morale was solid. Several 2 Auckland soldiers detailed as left out of the battle – no more than 20 officers and 680 other ranks of each battalion were permitted to fight so that a cadre was available for reconstitution in the event of heavy losses – tried to rejoin their platoons, eager to take part in the advance.[7] Sergeant-Major Charles Kerse, of 2 Otago, was frank about his feelings: 'It [the attack] won't be any fun, but we don't worry about it. We have been looking forward to it and are sick of bayonet practise [*sic*].'[8] Private Claude Burley, of 2 Wellington, had asked his mates to send his personal effects home if he died, but 'they laughed and joked at me, and said it may be our turn'.[9]

For three days beforehand, heavy and field artillery had pasted the German trenches, defensive positions, artillery batteries and any sign of enemy life. The 1 and 2 New Zealand Field Artillery Brigades were attached to the 14 Divisional Artillery Group to cover the advance. On the New Zealand sector there was one field gun to every 12 yards of German front.[10] The preparatory bombardment, which had continued at a steady pace day and night since 12 September, spiked to an 'intense and hurricane like' tempo over the German positions at zero hour.[11]

It was the beginning of the first act and Lieutenant George Tuck, of 2 Auckland, was in the assembly trenches:

> some of us could clearly see more Germans on the skyline passing into their trench. We couldn't do much shooting, but the O.C. [Officer Commanding] and I were watching them pass along their trench and occasionally come into view as they climbed over the debris where one of our shells must have struck their parapet. Amid the infernal roar the men were getting their rifles all ready and bayonets fixed.[12]

As the first curtain of the creeping barrage fell in no man's land at 6.20 a.m., 2 Otago, on the left, and 2 Auckland Battalion advanced side by side towards Switch Trench, the first objective. On 2 Otago's left 47 Division had started off one minute early and was quickly held up outside High Wood. As 2 Otago advanced beyond the Londoners' line a 'considerable' part of its left flank became exposed to a withering enfilading fire from German machine gunners and snipers in the wood.[13]

One of the problems with an advance across a wide front involving several units is the scope for catastrophe: any flank advancing beyond its immediate neighbours is exposed to potentially devastating enfilade fire. This was 2 Otago's fate from the outset and by day's end its left-most company had been hacked from 180 men to just 36 commanded by a sergeant.[14]

Small groups of 2 Otago soldiers displayed initiative in countering the enfilade fire. Sergeant Donald Brown and Corporal Jesse Rodgers destroyed a machine gun post checking the advance at Crest Trench, halfway up the incline to Switch Trench. Private Dick Travis, later New Zealand's most decorated soldier of the war, set to work sniping the German marksmen. All three would be decorated for their actions: Brown received a Victoria Cross for this and a later action.[15]

On 2 Auckland's frontage the advance went largely to plan. Most of the battalion's casualties came from a German counter-barrage, or from soldiers advancing into the path of the creeping barrage. However, 2 Auckland and 2 Otago quickly closed on Switch Trench, overwhelming it with a final flurry of hand-to-hand fighting. Tuck recorded his impression:

> our men flood the trench... Almost with the naked hands the fight is waged... As
> soon as they entered the Hun wanted to surrender. I do not blame our men that
> they would make them fight or die – or not fight – but die anyhow.[16]

From their vantage point on Switch Trench the New Zealanders would have realised the importance of the low-lying ridge. They could look over the reverse slope's gentle downward incline and, perhaps, through the clouds of dust and smoke from shell bursts, see Flers about three-quarters of a mile away to the north-east. Perhaps they also saw the earthy parapets of successive trench networks yet to be attacked. If not, the ridge's importance had certainly been emphasised in orders: 'The Switch Line when captured is to be held at all costs; there is to be no giving way as it is the most important line for observation'.[17] The infantry began digging a new trench 60 yards on from Switch Trench to avoid an expected counter-barrage, which came an hour and a half later.

In the 30 minutes it took to capture Switch Trench casualties in the two attacking battalions were horrendous. From the 700 who went into action the Aucklanders lost 324 men (46 per cent) killed, wounded or missing, while 2 Otago recorded 475 (68 per cent) casualties, most of them from the enfilade fire that cut across its ranks.

With Switch Trench in New Zealand hands, the battle for the downhill slopes began and in it tanks featured prominently. About 7 a.m., 4 Battalion, of 3 (Rifle) Brigade, was 'singing and very cheery' as it leapfrogged Switch Trench and advanced towards Brown Line some 700 metres further on.[18] It overcame 'stubborn resistance' to take the trench 50 minutes later.[19] The creeping barrage had worked effectively while the preparatory bombardment had smashed the trench's defensive qualities. The battalion suffered 267 (38 per cent) casualties, mostly from machine guns in the Brown Line and hostile artillery fire.

One of 4 Battalion's NCOs, Lance-Corporal Lawrence Blyth, never forgot the arrival of a tank, one of the first to catch up with the infantry, which broke down near the centre of the Brown Line about 8 a.m.:

> we were very nicely situated there, minding our own damned business, when this tank stopped about a hundred yards behind our trench, with the result that the Germans set to work to plaster it with artillery fire in an attempt to knock it out. And we got really strafed.[20]

If the battle for the downhill slopes had started promisingly, it took a turn for the worse when 2 and 3 Battalions moved into the vanguard. Advancing abreast, they leapfrogged 4 Battalion about 8.20 a.m.

On the left, 3 Battalion quickly ran into trouble in front of Flers Trench network. The preparatory bombardment had not cut the barbed wire entanglements and the trench's garrison unleashed a hail of small arms fire on the New Zealanders. Repeated efforts to break through failed. By 9.30 a.m. the battalion's leading waves had gone to ground, ostensibly waiting for some of the four tanks working in the New Zealanders' sector to move forward and crush the opposition.

Captain Lindsay Inglis recalled the view from Switch Trench:

> Below us, a little to the left front, we could see men of the 3rd Battalion taking cover in shell craters and obviously held up by the uncut wire in front of Flers Trench, in which my glasses showed up the heads of a strong German garrison, whose rifle and machine gun fire was sweeping the ground up to our crest.[21]

Two tanks that lumbered onto the scene at 10.30 a.m. proved decisive in unravelling the Flers Trench network for 3 Battalion. The Machine Gun Corps' historian wrote that the tanks crushed the barbed wire entanglements and 'metaphorically sat over Flers Trench and raked it up and down with their machine guns'.[22] Lieutenant Cecil Lewis, of 3 Squadron, Royal Flying Corps, was in an aircraft overhead:

> When we climbed up to the lines, we found the whole front seemingly covered with a layer of dirty cotton-wool, the smoking shell bursts...We could see them [tanks] sitting across the trenches and enfilading the enemy with four-pounders.[23]

With the barbed wire gone and the German garrison in disarray, 3 Battalion swarmed over Flers Trench network and with the help of a 4 Battalion platoon captured 145 prisoners. The battalion reached Abbey Road about 10.50 a.m.[24]

Meanwhile, 2 Battalion had suffered a different but similarly testing set of circumstances. It had lost men by the score at the hands of German machine gunners firing from the north-west outskirts of Flers village. According to Rifleman Tom Bisman, 'We marched one behind the other, and I could see the lads dropping like flies – the gunners just mowed us down.'[25] Another tank, directed by soldiers of 2 Battalion, rumbled over the German machine gun post, its garrison fleeing in disarray. Again a platoon of 4 Battalion was sent forward from the Brown Line and with the tank 'these men proved sufficient to turn the scale'.[26] In the deep dugouts lining Abbey Road 2 Battalion also encountered stubborn resistance, but had taken control of its portion of the Blue Line by 9.30 a.m.

Soon both battalions were hard at work consolidating the newly won positions. Blocking the left end of Flers Trench network, 3 Battalion put out covering parties and dug a series of north-west-facing strong posts. On the left, 47 Division was still lagging behind the New Zealanders' line of advance and 3 Battalion was acutely aware of the risks this posed. The battalion's war diary noted: 'About 11.15 a.m & within a few minutes of starting work a Machine Gun opened up from the ridge to our left front & caused 8 casualties in 5 minutes'.[27] On the right, 41 Division had also reached the Blue Line,[28] with parties of its infantry and a tank moving into Flers itself during the morning.

Casualty records for 2 and 3 Battalions are sketchy at best. It is known they lost, respectively, 74 (11 per cent) and 72 (10 per cent) men killed during the day, most in their attack on the Blue Line. It is unclear how many were wounded or missing, but evidence points to a lengthy list in both battalions. In 2 Battalion, for instance, one company, about 180-strong before the attack, was slashed to 40 men commanded by a sergeant by nightfall. In 3 Battalion the loss of three of its four company commanders meant subalterns had to take their place and, in turn, NCOs theirs.[29]

The captured ground up to the Blue Line quickly became a hive of activity. The New Zealand Machine Gun Corps brought its Vickers gun teams forward, Maori of the Pioneer Battalion continued carving out a communication trench to the forward area, and the field engineers set to work digging strong points and laying phone lines. On the right, 41 Division's advance was progressing well. However, all along the left flank, from Switch Trench to the Blue Line, strong points and machine gun posts were positioned to guard against counter-attacks and enfilade fire from the area where 47 Division should have been. Consolidation was in full swing.

Enemy artillery was also in full swing and laying down a barrage of heavy explosive and shrapnel shells over the captured ground. Switch Trench was plastered with shrapnel from about 8.20 a.m. onwards, while a grazing counter-barrage simultaneously swept over the forward area. All units moving over the Switch Trench ridge had to negotiate their way through this maelstrom of fire. Second Lieutenant Charles Treadwell, of 2 Wellington, later wrote:

> The real blessing was that the ground was soft from the previous bombardment. There was no more deadly shell than that fired from the German 5.9 [howitzer]. The high explosive has a terrible effect. Its lateral burst was murderous. However, it required some substantial resistance before it exploded, and it did not get it till it had penetrated some distance into the soft ground; then it spent its deadliness more or less harmlessly.[30]

Hostile shellfire was not hampering the advance and consolidation too much, but it was playing havoc with the lines of communication. Telephone lines, run forward from Switch Trench, had reached 2, 3 and 4 Battalions by 10.30 a.m., but were repeatedly cut by hostile artillery fire. Time and again runners wove through the shellfire with progress reports for brigade headquarters in the assembly trenches.[31] Planes of 3 Squadron, RFC, also noted the infantry's positions by observing flares and calico markers, and later offloaded this information at pre-set drop zones in small containers. The time it took to deliver information ultimately caused a communication delay between the forward-most New Zealand units and their headquarters.

The fact that a division's headquarters was well behind the battlefield was not unusual during the First World War, nor that it became isolated from its most forward units. Russell's headquarters were at Meaulte, just over 4 miles behind the battlefield. Although messages from the front line flowed in to his headquarters all morning, they were up to an hour late in arriving.[32] Technology of the day did not allow for faster communication.

Sergeant Arthur Rhind, a clerk, described the pressured situation at headquarters, noting that it was 'beastly being chained here waiting for news.... The General [Russell] is walking up and down outside looking very anxious and dispatch riders are pouring in and out and everybody is on the bustle.'[33]

Russell even described the problems he faced on 15 September in a letter to his sister:

> We are in the middle of a hot day; and heavy fighting going on; hope we manage
> to do all we want. But one's hopes seldom come to full fruition at once. It's
> difficult to see as much of this business as one would like; smoke, enemy fire,
> folds in the ground, etc, all make observation poor.[34]

By 11.30 a.m. Russell knew the first three objectives had been taken, the Blue Line with some trouble. He also knew of the heavy casualties and that a tank had advanced into Flers during the morning. He did not know that 1 Battalion had launched a much-weakened assault on the Red Line, the division's last objective.[35]

Back on the battlefield, the New Zealanders' advance was already losing steam when the third act began shortly before 11 a.m. with a piecemeal attack on Grove Alley (Red Line). Behind the other attack battalions 1 Battalion had advanced on a two-company frontage, but only one company, A, was at the Abbey Road jumping-off line in time for its attack. The other, B Company, had been held up behind 3 Battalion, which was at that time struggling to break through Flers Trench network.

Inglis led A Company in a swinging right hook on Grove Alley at 10.50 a.m.

> Within a few seconds after the leading platoons set out they were in sight of Grove Alley. Heavy rifle and machine gun fire broke out sweeping them from the front and the right flank and giving the impression that streams of bullets were swishing past knee high. I have never been under a hotter small-arm fire. Men were bowled over in all directions. [36]

Leutnant Braunhofer, of 5 Bavarian Infantry Regiment, recalled the weight of 1 Battalion's attack from his position north of Flers:

> I succeeded in holding out [1 Battalion] until mid-day... The attack from the left was led by a tank which, armed with small cannons, came from the flank and fired along our whole position with devastating effect. The attack itself was carried out with hand-grenades and bayonets. The attack on us from the north-west of Flers was carried out with bayonets. Under such circumstances it was quite impossible to hold out any longer; further resistance... would have led to a completely pointless massacre of the remainder of my company. [37]

Inglis's company grabbed a toehold in Grove Alley amid fierce opposition and despite heavy casualties. One platoon faced German field guns firing at point-blank range while another met stout resistance in the form of machine gun nests. But the much-weakened A Company persisted and had won a chunk of the trench by 11.30 a.m. At the same time, the battalion's B Company launched its right hook on Grove Alley, forcing the German garrison to retire. By midday most of the trench was held, albeit sparsely, by 1 Battalion. As Inglis recalled:

> Considering the heavy casualties already incurred the number of A and B Company men holding an isolated four hundred and fifty yards of Grove Alley

> cannot have been many more than one hundred and twenty [out of a combined
> 360]. The left flank was not in touch with any other troops, while the right flank
> was entirely in the air with several approaches to it the enemy might use... we
> knew that the nearest bodies of our own troops were five or six hundred yards
> behind us across an exposed plateau... A considerable volume of rifle fire was
> crackling over the whole position and from Cox we could see increasing enemy
> movement to our right front near Guedecourt [sic].[38]

First Battalion's position was tenuous. Neither of the neighbouring divisions had reached their portion of the Red Line, meaning that 1 Battalion was open to a spectrum of hostile fire – from the west, east and north. On the left, 47 Division had failed to make significant progress beyond High Wood after encountering stiff resistance in its capture. On the right, 41 Division had reached Flers but in the face of strong hostile artillery fire was forced to withdraw to Flers Trench network.[39]

This was another problem with an advance over a wide front involving a large number of units: any unit that advanced too far ahead of its neighbours was at risk of being encircled, then annihilated by the enemy. Good luck rather than good management would spare 1 Battalion this fate.

About 2 p.m. large numbers of German infantry were seen massing and advancing towards Grove Alley from the north-east. Their approach was along dead ground on either side of a country road dubbed Glebe Street, but 'rather to our surprise the attack did not close with us'.[40] Nevertheless, Inglis, who was by this time at Box and Cox, sent a runner back to Grove Alley with instructions to move a platoon and Lewis gun to the head of Glebe Street and cover any German advance from that quarter.

But, as Inglis remembered, something went wrong:

> to my amazement, an extended line of [1 Battalion] men came in succession
> from right to left out of the whole occupied length of the Alley... at once the
> plateau was plastered with German shells... through it they walked slowly and
> steadily in the direction of Flers, the whole movement deliberate, orderly and,
> as it afterwards appeared, reluctant.[41]

Thinking the movement of a platoon was part of a general withdrawal, the battalion abandoned Grove Alley. Inglis and a handful of men raced to stop the withdrawal.

> Once we reached the retiring line and halted a party here and there, the check rapidly communicated itself and the retrograde movement stopped.... For a few minutes my idea was to reoccupy our former salient with a more equal distribution of the available men... but it was now a case of handling a thin line of perhaps a hundred and twenty men spread over a front of eight hundred yards and, so far as I knew, with only two other officers.... I gave up the idea as unlikely to succeed until some reorganization and preparation had been carried out.[42]

In his cumbersome history of the New Zealand Division, Lieutenant-Colonel Hugh Stewart said the withdrawal from Grove Alley had been ordered: 'The officer in command ... decided to withdraw steadily to Box and Cox and the Blue Line'. Stewart went on to state that the tactical correctness of the withdrawal was later confirmed by orders not to advance beyond the Blue Line (see below).[43] However, Inglis, the officer to whom Stewart was referring, flatly denied he had ordered a withdrawal. Instead, he said it was born amid confusion on the battlefield. He later wrote that an enquiry 'made at the time failed to elicit an entirely satisfactory explanation as to how the withdrawal came about'.[44]

Whatever the case, 1 Battalion's new north-west-facing line cut across the northern end of Flers from Abbey Road to Box and Cox. It progressed no further and scattered handfuls of 1 Battalion men immediately set to digging in under artillery and small arms fire. The new line straddled the inter-divisional boundary line, which was Flers-Factory Corner Road, and half of 1 Battalion was in 41 Division's sector where 122 Brigade should have been. It was about 2.30 p.m.

The few surviving junior officers and NCOs of 1 Battalion played a crucial role in consolidating the new line. 'Company-Sergt. Major G.H. Boles early in the afternoon found himself in command of his company, now without an officer... [and] displayed remarkable powers of leadership and organization.' Elsewhere, 'Sergeants A.R. Blackman, R.T. Caldwell and C. Gair proved their ability in grappling with unusual situations, and their independent work was of utmost value'.[45] All four gained decorations for their actions in the defence of Flers.

At 3 p.m. the leading companies of 2 Wellington arrived forward under Captain Hugh McKinnon. In a pressured conference at Inglis's headquarters on Flers-Factory Corner Road, he and McKinnon quickly summed up the situation. They decided McKinnon would command the left of the line, west of Flers-Factory Corner Road, and Inglis the right. On the right, elements of 1 Battalion continued to dig defensive positions under heavy fire, later with help from a composite company of 2 and 3 Battalion men. On the left, 2 Wellington was committed piecemeal. Its companies and platoons were sent to fill weak points in the line.

To quote Private Burley:

> I was one of the few told off to dig a short trench across the [Flers-Factory Corner] road.... This road cut the trench we were in at right angles and we wanted to join up with Taranaki [Company], on the other side of the road, so just had to get up on the road and dig. The Huns put a machine gun on us but luckily we escaped. Thought not one of us would miss being hit. It got so tiring trying to dig like mad in my equipment so took it all off, even my tunic.[46]

McKinnon later reported:

> we had possession of the village and could not leave it... In the village we found a tank which was in working order. After consultation with the Officer i/c [in command] tank he was sent out along Flers Factory Corner road and covered the digging parties with his broadsides of Vickers at the same time firing up the road with his forward gun.[47]

Throughout the late afternoon Inglis and McKinnon acted independently of battalion, brigade and divisional command. There was no phone line from the forward area and runners took too long to relay instructions. '[Lieutenant Neil] Macky was not supposed to move his two reserve platoons from Fort Trench

without orders from battalion headquarters,' Inglis recorded in his diary, 'but...
he agreed to take my orders and bring his men forward... we sent a message to
battalion headquarters informing them of our action.'[48] It was 4 p.m. when both
officers learned the advance was to progress no further,[49] and 4.30 p.m. before
Brigadier General Harry Fulton, commander of 3 Brigade, and Captain Robert
Purdy, of the divisional staff, inspected the lines and reported back to
Russell.[50]

When darkness began to descend on the battlefield at 5 p.m. most of the
fighting and defensive organisation had been done. The forward-most New
Zealanders manned a line that ran from the left end of Blue Line (held by 3
Battalion), along Abbey Road (3 Battalion and 2 Wellington), across the
northern end of Flers (2 Wellington and 1 Battalion) and then to Cox in 122
Brigade's sector (1 Battalion and a composite party of 3 Brigade troops). 2
Battalion was withdrawn from the Blue Line to Flers Trench network where
it remained in support of the front line through the night. McKinnon wrote
later: 'The line by this time was well dug in and covered right round by cross
fire from Vickers and Lewis guns'.[51] By 8 p.m. 1 Battalion had lost some 100
men killed, while 2 Wellington reported 111 men killed, wounded and
missing. The outstanding objective, Grove Alley, would be attacked again on
16 September.

Lance-Corporal Roy Ellis, a 2 Brigade signaller, aptly described the
situation:

> The New Zealand Division had gained its objectives on the 15th September but
> the 41st Division on our right and the 47th Division on our left had not done so.
> We were in an awkward salient, it was difficult to get ammunition and food up
> through the mud, and there was heavy hostile shelling.[52]

Throughout the day the New Zealand Division had outperformed those on
either side of it. The result could be seen in its casualties and the often tactically
weak position it held. The New Zealanders' frustrations were clear in their
criticisms of neighbouring English units.

Lieutenant Tuck was less than impressed by 41 Division:

Lt Hewitt on the right of our line [Switch Trench] had to work to the right &
help clear the trench from inside before the 41st could come in. Yet the English
papers commended them. Rotten![53]

According to Private Burley:

It was scandalous just because we made sure of all we were given to do and not
like the majority of Kitchener's famous army, we heard so much of. Am satisfied
that our boys are not be classed with the English troops and for fighting qualities
are second to none as the General said afterwards, we have been classed as 'A'
fighters... and most of the English units 'C' class.[54]

Although valid, these criticisms must be viewed alongside the New Zealand
Division's performance. Why did the it perform so well compared with other
nearby divisions? The answer can be found in its command and leadership on
the battlefield.

Officer casualties in the principal attacking battalions were horrific. In 2
Brigade, 2 Auckland lost 13 of its officers killed or wounded (65 per cent) and
2 Otago 15 (75 per cent). The brigade's two other battalions, 2 Canterbury and
2 Wellington, which played lesser roles in the attack, lost a combined five officers
(12.5 per cent).[55] The only reliable casualty figures of 3 Brigade are those of 4
Battalion, which lost 13 officers (65 per cent).[56] The other three 3 Brigade
battalions suffered an officer casualty rate similar to that of 4 Battalion.

Despite heavy casualties among officers commanding companies and
platoons, evidence in regimental histories proves surviving subalterns and
NCOs took over their roles. In 2 Auckland: 'Lieutenants Tuck, Cooper,
Senior and Stewart, the platoon commanders, Sergeant Hill, Sergeant
Gordon, the section leaders, men here and there all along the line take the
initiative'.[57] In 3 Battalion, three second lieutenants took command of
companies: '[Second Lieutenant S.J.E.] Closey and [Second Lieutenant W.A.]
Gray, indeed, found themselves the only officers left in their respective
companies'.[58] 2 Otago's 10th Company was cut to just 36 men who were
'commanded with much skill and judgement by Sergt. H. Bellamy'. Many of
these men were later decorated or promoted.[59]

If there is such a thing as a distinctive New Zealand style of command, elements of it were on display on the battlefield on 15 September. One of them was the ability of New Zealand soldiers to lead from the front.[60] Skilled subalterns and NCOs showed initiative in leading their units to capture and immediately consolidate their allotted sections of Switch Line, Brown Line and Blue Line, despite heavy officer casualties. In the fast-moving battle around Flers, Captains Inglis and McKinnon seized on the urgency of this situation, quickly evaluated their options and entered the fighting. They took control of the various platoons and companies and quickly secured the village. In another case, Captain Robert Brydon 'reorganized the remains of two companies, established two strong-points, and beat off repeated enemy counter attacks'.[61]

Even senior battalion officers led from the front. Within hours of their battalions taking an objective they moved forward to take command and supervise consolidation. Invariably they set up their headquarters in or near the captured trench and always under hostile fire, though none was killed or wounded.

It would be wrong to assume, however, that all the division's junior leaders on the battlefield were of a high calibre. Lance-Corporal Blyth was critical of the performance of an NCO he knew:

> And in this shell hole was a sergeant, won't mention his name, and he was scared to death. He wouldn't move. On parade he was one of those arrogant blokes, and here he was shivering in his shoes.[62]

And Inglis wrote:

> As B Company [1 Battalion] advanced it was subjected to further heavy fire. One officer lost his nerve and took part of the company back to the road. The other officers were casualtied.[63]

Afterwards Russell was critical of his officers' performance on 15 September: 'A good many officers… who are returning to New Zealand are not wanted back…. There are quite a few more who must go. They are in a few words not up to the job…. Character first, health next, and experience last.'[64] He also complained about the casualties, particularly among officers, but praised the work of Brigadiers William Braithwaite and Harry Fulton as well as the infantry's gains. Both brigadiers had moved forward during the day and Fulton was slightly injured.[65]

Russell handed out little praise to the junior officers and NCOs who had performed with distinction. Instead, his satisfaction with their work was implied by the decorations and promotions he granted after the battle. For example, Captains Inglis and McKinnon each received a Military Cross for their actions. Others, like Sergeant-Major Boles and Sergeants Blackman and Gair were decorated and promoted for their work in front of Flers. Russell was prepared to recognise those who met his high standards of leadership.

Ultimately, then, both soldiers in action, like Rifleman Blyth, and Russell rated officers and NCOs according to their competence in battle. A large part of this yardstick was based on preparation and training before the battle,[66] two aspects Russell had championed in the lead-up to 15 September.

Even before the battle had started the infantry battalions knew their tasks were to capture and consolidate four successive lines of German trenches. This and tactics – the creeping barrage and limited objectives – had been impressed upon the infantry in mock attacks during pre-battle training. Sergeant-Major Cecil Malthus, of 1 Canterbury Battalion, was one of many who were realistic about training in the new tactics.

> The difficulty was to make training realistic. Rows of flags or men with arm badges made a poor impersonation of a creeping barrage, but at least the need for perfect co-ordination and instant movement when the barrage lifted was thoroughly impressed on us. Provided we got the idea, experience would be quickly gained when we met the real thing.[67]

In short, companies, platoons and sections were well briefed on their specific roles before battle. This is demonstrated by the capture of the first three objectives despite heavy casualties among officers and, at times, obstacles blocking the advance. Those who took command of an otherwise leaderless unit understood the job that had to be done and worked towards it.

The advance to Switch Trench and the Brown Line had gone rather more than less to plan, with both objectives being quickly captured and consolidated. Both the creeping barrage and preparatory bombardment had worked well, while a number of subalterns controlled the speed and line of the advance to ensure it went to plan. As Tuck wrote, 'I yell at Sergt Walker, cursing, to keep the line, as he was getting ahead. He can't hear and I throw dirt at him and he notices, and seeing my signal drops back into line.'[68] Afterwards, Brigadier-General Braithwaite stated that, generally, the advance 'was carried out without a hitch, the direction, pace and general alignment being excellent'.[69]

However, once outside the range of the creeping barrage the momentum of the attack fell off markedly. At the Blue Line both 2 and 3 Battalions struggled to make progress without the creeping barrage to cover their advance. Enemy infantry was able to defend the Flers Trench network and the preparatory bombardment had failed to destroy all of its defensive qualities. Uncut wire blunted 3 Battalion's attack, and well-placed machine gun nests slowed 2 Battalion's. Without the timely arrival of three tanks and help from 4 Battalion the outcome at the Blue Line might have been different.

By contrast, the battle to the north of Flers, after the withdrawal from Grove Alley, was an unstructured battle that called for prompt and confident leadership. This was found among the NCOs and junior officers on the spot who immediately grasped the urgency of the situation and set about organising a defensive line covering the village. Their competence, along with help from tanks operating in the forward area, turned the situation in the division's favour.

Aside from the pressures on the division's command structure, the New Zealand Medical Corps' units were stretched to breaking point by the influx of wounded from the battlefield. The corps had two advanced dressing stations (ADS) immediately behind the battlefield, one at Flat Iron Copse, on the left, and the other at an old quarry in Caterpillar Valley, on the right.[70] From these, wounded were evacuated to hospitals in France and England.

> All wounded were receiving A.T.S. (anti-tetanus serum) injections, the necessary dressings and splints were applied and such surgical interference was made as seemed urgently required. The patients were fed, warmed up and ultimately evacuated to the 36th and 38th C.C.S.[casualty clearing stations], which had been cleared in anticipation.[71]

By 6.45 a.m. the first of the walking wounded were beginning to file their way into the dressing station.[72] Corporal Norman Gray, of 2 Field Ambulance, was at Flat Iron Copse that morning:

> Our A.D.S. was at full pressure. 100 or more stretcher cases were on the road, all the available vehicles were at work, and the wounded were coming in at the rate of one every three minutes. The Captain in charge gave me a corner of a dugout, and for twenty-four hours two orderlies and myself dressed without stop, putting though sixty-nine cases on our 'table'.[73]

By 10.30 a.m. the battlefield up to Switch Trench was practically clear of 2 Brigade wounded, but by midday it was obvious the wounded of 3 Brigade were not making their way back for treatment. The enemy barrage on Switch Trench was blocking the safe passage of stretcher-bearers, and 3 Brigade wounded were cut off in the forward area. Many would remain there until midday on 17 September.[74]

Despite the problems with clearing 3 Brigade wounded, the Medical Corps' historian, Major A.D. Carbery, concluded that arrangements had 'worked well', with most being evacuated within 40 hours. By 8 p.m. the congestion of wounded at the dressing stations was relieved and hundreds were on their way to hospital.[75]

Bald statistics give killed and wounded in 2 and 3 Brigades as, respectively, 798 and about 1200 for 15 September, a total of 1998.[76] If the casualties of the Pioneer Battalion, 12 killed and 40 wounded, are added, the total number of casualties for the division's infantry units on that day is 2050, including 603 dead.[77] In other words, about one in every three infantrymen who went into battle was killed, wounded or missing. As Carbery noted later: 'the wounded of the previous day [15 September] had shown a preponderance of machine gun casualties'.[78]

One 2 Auckland soldier witnessed a burst of machine gun fire near Switch Trench kill four men and wound three others. Among the dead were Sergeant William Cowan and Sergeant-Major Robert Hunter. Cowan left behind his wife and three young children. His only brother had been killed at Gallipoli a year earlier. Hunter was mourned by his wife. His brother Frederick was killed in

June 1916 and their cousin, Captain Joseph Hunter, also died on 15 September.[79] It would be several weeks before their families received official notification.

New Zealand learned that its division had been in action from bold newspaper headlines in the following week. On 22 September the *New Zealand Herald* splashed news of the advance across page 7 in a five-deck headline.

THE CAPTURE OF FLERS

NEW ZEALANDERS ASSIST

AUCKLAND AND OTAGO MEN LEAD

GERMAN ATTACKS ON FRENCH LINE

ROUMANIAN OFFENSIVE IN DOBRUDJA

The article then raced over the bones of the attack in colourful prose:

> The New Zealanders, who have had the honour of being in the new phase of the Somme advance... One armoured car charged slowly right into the village in front of the cheering infantry, a scene unparalleled in war.... All night the Rifle Brigade bravely held on, and even occupied a bit of ground beyond their own area.

What this article and others like it did not give were casualty lists, possibly the most sought-after information in New Zealand. By late October most of the daily newspapers had run columns naming those killed, wounded and missing. Some later published pages of captioned photographs and pen portraits of the casualties. These pages became the most thumbed through in the country as the community searched for news of relatives or friends.

New Zealand's Defence Minister, James Allen, learned details of the division's part in the Somme through letters from NZEF commander Lieutenant-General Alexander Godley. 'What a terrible time our men must have had!' he replied. In another letter he wrote, 'I am delighted to hear about the splendid work the Division has done'. The Somme was the NZEF's first major engagement since Gallipoli and by the time the division withdrew in early October 1916 its casualty lists again ran into thousands of names. Allen, whose son John had been killed at Gallipoli, said: 'Of course we grieve over our losses and simply have to bottle up our grief.'[80]

But it was writer and Somme veteran Ormond Burton who perhaps best caught the mood after news of 15 September hit New Zealand:

> behind the men and about them were the hopes and fears of all New Zealand. But such happenings are costly and when in four years they have surged through the life of the community not once but twenty times there is at the end a mood of exhaustion.[81]

For the New Zealand Division, 15 September 1916 became the cornerstone for its exhaustive 23-day tour on the Somme. It is the successes on this day for which its tour is principally remembered, although there were more successes – and disasters – to follow. After three weeks on the Somme, the division had lost 2111 dead and 5848 wounded.

In the aftermath of 15 September praise was lavished upon the New Zealanders. Writing, generally, about the gains of 15 September General Haig said, 'All this had been accomplished with a small number of casualties in comparison with the troops employed.'[82] General Sir Henry Rawlinson, commander of the Fourth Army, wrote of the New Zealand infantry in glowing terms: 'They showed a fine fighting spirit, and admirable energy and dash'.[83] Godley conveyed to Allen still more praise from Rawlinson: 'They also told me that the thing they liked very much was, that after they got their orders, nothing more was heard of them, till a report was sent that they had gained their objective.'[84] The division's performance had seeded its reputation as a thoroughbred.[85]

Summing up, the division had won more ground from the enemy than any other in the battle on a single day. But the cost was high. Of those who went into action, 2050 (34 per cent) were dead or on their way to hospital. The operation had robbed 3 (Rifle) Brigade of any immediate offensive capability as a unit, and its battalions were thereafter committed piecemeal to the offensive.[86] Before it could once again be used in an attack, 2 Brigade had to be substantially reinforced.

Captain Inglis summed up the effect of the day's casualties:

> We of A Company were 49 all told. The casualties on the 15th had been approximately seventy five per cent.... But it was not simply a question of

numbers. Hitherto its original members had comprised the greater part of the company and our previous casualties had come in small doses, while reinforcements arrived in easily absorbed driblets; and never again would casualties, however heavy, have the same depressing impact as these.[87]

Although the attack had started well, it quickly became confused. Switch Trench and the Brown Line were captured much to plan, while the capture of the Blue Line was comparatively scrappy and the fighting gave way to a soldiers' battle in front of Flers. Most of the division's headaches came after it had advanced outside the range of the creeping barrage or as a result of the preparatory bombardment failing to destroy German defensive positions.

In addition, the division had for the most part forged ahead of its neighbours and was thus forced to fight in a salient of its own making. The dangers associated with exposed flanks were particularly evident on the left throughout the day and, in the afternoon, in the area forward of Flers. For New Zealand soldiers on the battlefield that night it was obvious what had happened. Sergeant-Major Malthus discerned that:

> it was no use advancing on a company or even battalion front if the units on one flank or the other had failed to come abreast. Some of the heaviest losses were incurred through isolation of this nature and consequent enfilading.[88]

Privately, in diaries and letters, others shared Malthus's view.

However, the division could take some positives from its performance on 15 September. Among them was Russell's emphasis on training and preparation, which directly contributed to the capture of the first three objectives. It would, for the most part, become a hallmark of his tenure as commander of the division. Russell would later appraise the division: 'Am I satisfied with the result? Yes.'[89] But, as we have seen, he also saw that there was room for improvement.

Among the other positives that Russell recognised was the emergence of skilled junior leaders. Determined leadership from NCOs and subalterns overcame many of the tactical problems the division faced. Were it not for the high calibre of these soldiers and, at times, good luck in the form of tanks, the division might have returned a different result. Nevertheless, it was evident that

Russell and his division still had much to learn about fighting in an offensive. This would come through experience.

For the New Zealand public, the division's performance on 15 September was proclaimed as an outstanding success. However, the arrival of casualty lists in the weeks and months afterwards conveyed the truth and further dissipated their enthusiasm for war. According to Ormond Burton, 'Somewhere between the bloody ridge of Chunuk Bair in August 1915 and the black swamp in front of Passchendaele in October 1917, New Zealand quite definitely found individuality and nationality.'[90] He was referring to the awkward salient the New Zealand Division had created and grimly clung to on 15 September 1916.

14

'NEW ZEALAND IS BEING BLED TO DEATH': THE FORMATION, OPERATIONS AND DISBANDMENT OF THE FOURTH BRIGADE

John Crawford

The short history of 4 New Zealand Infantry Brigade is in itself of considerable interest, but it also provides insights into a number of key issues relating to New Zealand's war effort in general and support for the New Zealand Expeditionary Force in particular. The picture that emerges from analysis of the formation, service and disbandment of 4 Brigade is of a political and military leadership that generally had a clear conception of the dominion's interests and a commitment to ensuring that New Zealand made a substantial and effective, but not extravagant or unreasonable, contribution to the imperial war effort.

At the beginning of February 1917 New Zealand was asked by the British government to form a second division or, if that was not possible, one or more additional brigades of infantry. The additional troops were to reach Britain no later than July, by which time, according to Walter Long, the Secretary of State for the Colonies, the climax of the war would, at the very least, be imminent.[1] The request to New Zealand and similar requests made to Australia and Canada were part of a wider British drive to find the manpower necessary for major offensives planned for the summer of 1917.[2]

Lord Liverpool, the Governor of New Zealand, Sir James Allen, the Minister of Defence and acting Prime Minister, the Cabinet, and the Commandant of the New Zealand Military Forces, Major-General Sir Alfred Robin, all regarded the British approach as unwelcome and unreasonable. They took particular exception to the implication that New Zealand was not doing all it could for the imperial war effort. There was already significant concern within the government that New Zealand's contribution was not sufficiently appreciated in London and that the dominion was being unfairly exploited. That the telegram conveying the request did not refer to the similar communications with Australia and Canada heightened these concerns. Liverpool warned Long that the request for additional forces had not been well received in Wellington, and that 'New Zealand considers that she has already contributed a larger quota in proportion to our population than any of the other Dominions and it is questionable whether it would be in interests of the Empire for New Zealand to suffer disproportionately to other Dominions because they had not applied compulsion to maintain their obligations'.[3]

At Allen's request, Robin's staff prepared a detailed analysis of New Zealand's manpower situation. This review noted that New Zealand had already provided more than 13 per cent of its male population for service in its expeditionary force or other military forces. It pointed out that because the dominion's economy was based on agriculture, it required a higher proportion of able-bodied men to function than an economy like Britain's, which was based on manufacturing and commercial activities. Robin's report examined options for increasing the number of men being conscripted into or volunteering for service with the NZEF. More men could be conscripted, especially if the minimum age for service in the NZEF was dropped from 20 to 18, but Robin warned that such measures might well generate a level of opposition that would place conscription itself at risk. These considerations and the limited capacity of the military training system meant that raising an additional division to reach Britain by July was utterly impracticable, though it might just be possible to raise an additional brigade. On the basis of the losses sustained by the New Zealand Division in the Battle of the Somme, however, Robin concluded that the New Zealand Division would need all its reserves once it was again committed to major offensive operations.[4]

The New Zealand Cabinet was initially inclined to follow the advice in Robin's report and decline to form any additional units.[5] Such a response would have been consistent with the New Zealand government's long-standing determination not to overcommit its manpower resources.[6] Allen and his colleagues reconsidered their position after the Prime Minister, William Massey, in London to attend the Imperial War Cabinet, informed them that he supported the request for additional units. What prompted Massey to take this position is unclear, but Long had stressed in a personal appeal to Massey that the Allies urgently needed more troops on the Western Front in 1917. Massey may also have been concerned that a refusal would make New Zealand appear unhelpful – especially if he knew that Australia was going to agree to raise an extra division.[7] After receiving this advice from Massey, the Cabinet rather reluctantly agreed to the raising of an additional brigade from the reinforcements currently in Britain. On the same day this reply was dispatched, the Australian government informed the British authorities that it had agreed to form an additional, sixth, Australian division.[8]

Within a few days Allen and his colleagues had a change of mind and asked Massey to do what he could to prevent the formation of the brigade, stressing that it could exist for only a limited period because the additional reinforcements needed to support a four-brigade division could not be provided without serious adverse effects on the New Zealand economy. Massey replied that the formation of the new brigade was contingent on it being used, if necessary, to provide reinforcements for the New Zealand Division, with which it would operate.[9] It is also clear that New Zealand agreed to form the brigade on the basis that it would not send any additional reinforcements to support it.[10]

New Zealand was well placed to raise an extra brigade of infantry because of its highly efficient reinforcement system and the sound organisation of the NZEF. Although volunteers continued to come forward in large numbers, conscription had been introduced in August 1916 and the first ballot under the new compulsory scheme was held in November 1916.[11] By the time the additional brigade was being considered, the reinforcements system was working well. Each month a reinforcement draft of approximately 2200 personnel was sent from New Zealand to the NZEF's bases in Britain, from where they were called forward to France to meet the division's requirements. The regular provision of a sufficient number of trained reinforcements was central to the success of the NZEF. Indeed one officer commented, using a somewhat unfortunate analogy, that 'reinforcements bear the same relation to a fighting army as does a healthy blood supply to the human body'.[12] Because the New Zealand Division had suffered only light casualties since October 1916 and was regularly receiving substantial reinforcements by February 1917, it had accumulated 5000 reinforcements in France and a similar number in England. It was the existence of these reserves that made the establishment of 4 New Zealand Infantry Brigade feasible.[13]

The commander of the NZEF, Lieutenant-General Sir Alexander Godley, did not seem to object to the formation of the additional brigade, and at first Allen even suspected that he had played a part in instigating the request.[14] Major-General Sir Andrew Russell, the New Zealand Division's commander, regarded the formation of the new brigade as a mistake and was concerned about the strain its formation would place on his command's resources.[15]

As soon as the establishment of 4 Brigade was confirmed Russell, in consultation with Godley, appointed the charismatic and able Lieutenant-Colonel Herbert Hart to command it. Godley described Hart as 'a capital New Zealand citizen soldier'.[16] Russell also decided that a nucleus of experienced officers and NCOs should be posted to the new brigade to ensure that it was fit for active service as quickly as possible.[17]

Officially formed on 15 March 1917, the new brigade was based around the third battalions of the Auckland, Wellington, Canterbury and Otago Regiments, all formed on the same date. Some of the brigade's supporting units were also formed at this time, but others were established later. The brigade's headquarters and training camps for the new battalions were at Codford, where the NZEF had its Command Depot. Its personnel were drawn from three sources: men sent back from the division in France, men at Codford who had recovered from wounds or illness and recently arrived reinforcements. The cadres from France were posted to their regiment's newly formed unit, with personnel from 1 and 2 Battalions of the Canterbury Regiment, for instance, being posted to the regiment's third battalion.[18]

The recently arrived reinforcements posted to the new brigade were not all young men like 23-year-old George Wyatt, who had arrived in England in March 1917 as part of the 20th Reinforcements.[19] Private Jesse Stayte, who was posted to 3 Auckland Battalion, was 41. Like anybody going into action for the first time, these men wondered how they would cope with the demands of combat. After seeing a working party of German prisoners of war at Codford, Stayte wrote in his diary that they were 'a very scraggy looking lot. After seeing them my pluck went up 50 per cent for I did not see one that I would not be afraid to meet with the Bayonet. If they are all like these well "hooray".'[20] Comrades who had already seen action were regarded with a mixture of respect and envy. While he was in camp 21-year-old Private Neil Ingram 'gazed with awe at the returned men in the camp, resplendent with their Battalion "patches" Regimental badges, service chevrons and wound stripes. In our eyes they appear Demigods.... Well, it is consoling to me to know that I shall soon be of the intimate company of men who have been "over the top with the best of luck".'[21] The small group of officers who had arrived from New Zealand with no previous active service experience were particularly aware of the need to prove themselves. Second Lieutenant Peter Howden wrote to his wife, after an inspection during which he was questioned at length by Hart, that 'it is very evident that in order to establish one's self at this game one has got to "make good" at the first opportunity. By that I mean that I who have had no previous active service and have only a theoretical knowledge of machine gunning will in the forthcoming "stunt" have to prove to the O.C., to the company and to the brigadier that I'm good enough for my position.'[23]

The officers and NCOs of the brigade's infantry battalions were on the whole an experienced and capable group. The 25 officers of 3 Otago Battalion, for instance, included 14 commissioned from the ranks and had on average more than 16 months' service in the NZEF.[23] The situation of the brigade's supporting units was similar. Its machine gun company, for example, was commanded by Captain (in the Second World War Major-General) Lindsay Inglis MC, who was 'a great student of the machine gun and its tactics'.[24] Virtually all the key positions in the company were occupied by recently commissioned former machine gun corps NCOs. The company's NCOs and men were also of a high standard, leading Inglis to comment that if it did not turn out to be 'a good company it will be no one's fault but mine'.[25]

Hart was particularly fortunate in having the services of Major Thomas Eastwood as his brigade major. As the first brigade major of 3 New Zealand

(Rifle) Brigade, Eastwood had done exceptional work during the formation of that unit. He was also to play a key role in the formation of the new brigade, and its success was 'in no small measure due to his untiring efforts and the magnificent example he had at all times set'.[26] The experience the NZEF had gained through the formation of the Rifle Brigade and the splitting in two of the original New Zealand Infantry Brigade certainly contributed to the well-ordered way in which the new brigade was formed.[27]

New Zealand was at this time an intimate society in which most of the population had a strong network of social relationships. The NZEF reflected that society, with the result that men commonly found themselves serving with men whom they knew or who were known to them. For socio-economic and professional reasons this was especially the case for officers. For instance, Inglis, who came from Otago, had known at least five of the officers in 3 Otago Battalion before the war. The organisation of the NZEF on a mainly territorial basis accentuated this tendency.[28]

New Zealand reinforcements generally had between six and 10 months of training before they reached a front-line unit. They received a thorough basic training before proceeding overseas, then did further training in England and in France before being posted to the Divisional Reinforcement Unit. One of the strengths of the New Zealand system was the way in which men with previous military service, most commonly in the Territorial Force, were mixed in with those who had no previous experience. This seems to have raised the overall standard of proficiency and reduced the time it took inexperienced men to reach the required standard.[29] Because 4 Brigade was a new unit its training did not follow this pattern. Once the new units had been established they settled down to an intensive programme of training. Hart had various frustrating administrative problems to overcome. By the end of March, for instance, Southern Command, which controlled the Codford area, had not been officially informed by the War Office of the formation of the new brigade and would not, therefore, issue mobilisation stores such as rifles, Lewis guns and wagons. This problem took some time to sort out and was not until 12 April that the brigade received its complement of rifles.[30] Initially the infantry battalions concentrated on individual training in such basic skills as musketry (shooting), bayonet fighting and bombing (the use of hand and rifle grenades). This phase of the training finished on 13 May, and two weeks of company field training then began.[31] After several days of tough training that lasted from 8 a.m. to 4 p.m. and from 9 p.m. to midnight each day, a company commander in 3 Wellington Battalion was moved to write in his diary 'damn training and damn the war generally. And especially the Kaiser and his people.'[32]

By mid-1917 the British army had established a vast network of training establishments. Men from the new brigade were sent to a wide range of specialist training courses, and expert British instructors were brought to the New Zealand camps at Codford to conduct specialist training. The NZEF's ability to utilise these substantial resources facilitated the rapid training of the brigade.[33]

Brigadier-General Hart set the overall training programme to be followed. He paid particular attention to the training of officers and was very conscious of the need to develop a strong *esprit de corps*.[34] Hart and his Brigade Major conducted a well-organised staff ride for the commanding officers, second-in-commands and adjutants of the four infantry battalions. The three officers from each battalion worked together on the problems infantry battalion commanders and their staffs were likely to face during operations. Hart and Eastwood reviewed the performance of the officers, and promulgated a detailed paper setting out both problems that had been identified and the necessary corrective action.[35]

During early May the brigade was inspected by a number of senior officers, including Field-Marshal Sir John French, the former commander of the BEF, who were pleased with the progress made by the brigade. Nonetheless, it came as a great surprise to Hart and Southern Command when on 21 May they received orders to have the brigade ready to embark for France in three days' time. Hart was unhappy at the premature termination of the training programme: he had expected to have at least three more weeks to conduct battalion and brigade training. His command still lacked a great deal of essential equipment, while the brigade's machine gun company, field engineer company and field ambulance had not yet arrived at Codford. The decision, the British authorities told Hart, had been made because of the high standard already reached by his brigade, but it may well have been prompted by a desire to get additional combat units to the front on the eve of the Battle of Messines.[36] With the concentration of its units and their equipment rapidly completed, the brigade left Codford in 10 special trains on 27 May and sailed for France the following day.[37] 'Everyone who had not been over before greatly excited and jubilant at proceeding one stage further on the last move to the theatre of the war,' Hart confided in his diary. 'The old hands calm and stoical, proceeding with the others unconcernedly as upon a long constant steady task that has to be seen through to the finish.'[38]

Generally the training programme had proceeded smoothly, but some support units had not had an easy start to their service and were particularly badly affected by the decision to cut short the brigade's training. For instance, 4 New Zealand Field Ambulance was only formed at the end of April 1917, when the NZEF was experiencing a serious shortage of medical officers. Its commanding officer and many of its senior NCOs were experienced men brought back from France. The rest of the unit's personnel came from the New Zealand hospitals in England and from medical personnel who had arrived with recent reinforcement drafts. The personnel from the hospitals were largely replaced by women. The under-strength and poorly equipped field ambulance was sent to a British depot in Blackpool, but there were virtually no facilities for training there. Training had to be directed by the unit's own officers and NCOs. Less than a week before it sailed for France on 28 May, the field ambulance was sent to Codford, where its equipment was completed. Fortunately, after it arrived in France the field ambulance had more than six weeks' service in a quiet sector to bring itself up to a good standard of efficiency. The unit's experienced NCOs played a crucial role in preparing the field ambulance for active service.[39] There can be no doubt that the significant number of experienced officers, NCOs and men posted to 4 Brigade made possible its rapid and successful formation. The historian of 3 Canterbury Battalion, for example, noted that by the end of May what 'had been a mere collection of men was now a well-trained unit ready for war. The admixture of "old hands" gave a splendid stiffening to the later reinforcements, and – most vital thing of all – a genuine *esprit de corps* had developed.'[40]

On reaching France, the brigade was sent to the front, where it was attached to Godley's II Anzac Corps. Its specialist units supported the assault on Messines Ridge, which began on 7 June, and the brigade's infantry battalions also did useful service by providing substantial working parties to repair and construct roads in the Messines area.[41] A few days later the brigade was attached to 3 Australian Division, before at last coming under the tactical control of the New Zealand Division. Given the task of holding a fairly quiet section of the front line south of Messines, the brigade had an excellent opportunity to familiarise its personnel with operational conditions and to further hone its skills. Apart from active patrolling, it staged a number of minor operations, which were designed to keep German attention focused on the Messines area, rather than on Ypres, where the British were about to launch their great offensive. Although generally happy with the way his command had performed, Hart kept a close eye on all this units, identified problem areas and initiated remedial action. He established a brigade school for platoon commanders, which included a model platoon, battalion schools at which Lewis gun, bombing and rifle sections received additional practical training. As a result of these experiences and additional training the brigade emerged from its first period in the front line as a significantly more effective unit.[42] Even as early as mid-June, Inglis had decided that his new machine gun company was 'hardly distinguishable from the old hands now, except when it runs up against some new kind of experience when the difference is more or less apparent'.[43]

At the end of August, 1, 2 and 4 New Zealand Infantry Brigades and their supporting units were withdrawn to a training area near Boulogne. The Rifle Brigade was detached from the New Zealand Division and sent north to provide working parties to support the Allied offensive in Flanders.[44] After the Battle of the Somme, the German Army had adopted new defensive tactics, which were based on defence in depth, with fewer infantry committed to holding the front line and more reliance on strong points equipped with machine guns and the employment of counter-attack units to recapture lost ground. In response the British army developed new assault tactics, which were first used by the New Zealand Division at Messines and which were now, during September 1917, refined by 4 Brigade and other units. They involved, in part, the organisation of assaulting infantry into small columns or 'worms', covered by a screen or advance guard of troops who would locate the main enemy defensive positions. The assault troops were divided into teams of riflemen, bombers (armed with both hand and rifle grenades) and Lewis gun crews. These groups were trained to work together, with support from light mortars, to suppress the fire generated by the German strong points, to outflank and then assault them.[45] Late in the month, the training programme culminated in a series of battalion and brigade exercises. For instance, 3 Otago Battalion conducted two day-long exercises that featured attacks closely mirroring the kind of operation it would shortly undertake.[46] In these exercises much attention was given to methods of responding to the kind of prompt counter-attacks that were a key element of German defensive tactics.[47] The training concluded with two practice brigade attacks, conducted under very realistic conditions. Because the brigade's training in Britain had been cut short, these were the first exercises on this scale conducted by Hart's command. Although they were successful, Russell thought the final exercise was 'rather amateurish'.[48]

By the time this training period ended 4 Brigade was well rested, well trained and generally in a very good state to conduct offensive operations. The commander of 3 Wellington Battalion, for instance, described his unit as being 'in the pink' owing to the combination of experienced men and fresh reinforcements who had formed the battalion, the training in Britain and France, three months' service in the front line and the fact that it had not lost its cohesion because of heavy casualties.[49] The simple fact that the brigade was well rested should not be underestimated. All too often on the Western Front infantry who were exhausted by earlier operations or through carrying out such demanding physical work as burying telephone lines were called upon to carry out attacks. Perhaps the worst example of this in the New Zealand Division was the use of the Rifle Brigade, which had been exhausted by labouring tasks, in the disastrous attack of 12 October 1917.[50]

While the training programme was under way, preparations for the commitment of the New Zealand Division to the Third Battle of Ypres (Passchendaele) were proceeding. As part of Godley's II Anzac Corps, which in turn formed part of General Sir Herbert Plumer's Second Army, it would take part in the attack in early October that would become known as the Battle of Broodseinde. Detailed plans for the division's role were first discussed at a major divisional conference in mid-September. Three days after the brigade moved out of its training area on 25 September, Hart and 24 of his officers went up to the front line for the first time to reconnoitre the ground over which they would attack. With many bodies from previous fighting littering the ground, the stench of death was clearly evident 2½ miles behind the front line.[51] In accordance with standard practice, a proportion of officers and men from each battalion were 'left out of battle'. As in all major operations, preparations for the attack were marked by the production of a series of increasingly detailed orders, which cascaded down the command chain from army headquarters to company commanders. Hart held conferences with his battalion commanders and other senior officers of the brigade and they in turn held conferences with their subordinates.[52]

The attack on 4 October was one of a series of 'bite and hold' operations directed by the capable Plumer and his first-rate staff. Designed to seize the strategically important Passchendaele Ridge, these operations were characterised by meticulous planning, limited objectives and ample artillery support – a combination the Germans found difficult effectively to counter. The main part of the attack, which had as its objective the capture of Broodseinde Ridge, the section of Passchendaele Ridge east of Ypres, was carried out by the Second Army's I and II Anzac Corps and XVIII Corps from the Fifth Army.[53] The New Zealand Division had the task of capturing the Gravenstafel Spur, which ran off the main Passchendaele Ridge and which included a rise known as the Abraham Heights. The New Zealanders were to attack over a front of 2000 yards and to a depth of about 1100 yards. Russell's plan called for 1 and 4 Brigades each to use two battalions to seize the division's initial objectives, known as the Red Line. The other battalions of these brigades would pass through these units to take the final objectives, known as the Blue Line. The German defences in the area centred on numerous, strongly built concrete pillboxes. The ground behind the New Zealand front line and over which they would attack was a shell-blasted wilderness.[54] Ormond Burton described the scene in suitably biblical terms: 'it is a dreadful place, hideously bare of all comfort, with no beautiful, or decent, or pleasant thing anywhere to be seen. It is a field of agony and death. No place on earth has been so desecrated by slaughter, no place, save Calvary, so consecrated by sacrifice.'[55]

The high standard of staff work involved was exemplified by the plan for artillery support. This featured four barrages designed to take the infantry forward to their objectives, to break up counter-attacks and protect the attacking infantry once the objectives had been taken (including the provision of a smoke barrage). Direct artillery support for the New Zealand attack was provided by 180 18-pounder guns and 60 4.5-inch howitzers backed by some of the hundreds of medium and heavy guns available to the Second Army. In addition 60 machine guns, organised into three groups, were to provide a machine gun barrage. On the day of the attack the machine guns would fire nearly 600,000 rounds.[56]

In preparation for the attack 3 Auckland and 3 Otago Battalions took over the sections of the front line from which they were to attack on the night of 2–3 October. The brigade's Canterbury and Wellington battalions, which were to seize the final objectives, were positioned behind the two leading battalions. Their officers and NCOs then completed their reconnaissance of the ground over which they were to attack. The following night the attacking troops took up their final jump-off positions. Conditions 'were enough to try the stoutest hearts' as it was raining and the German artillery was increasingly active. At 5.30 a.m., half an hour before the New Zealand attack, the Germans launched a full-scale barrage, most of which, fortunately, fell away from the assembly areas of the assault troops. This barrage was the prelude to a substantial German counter-attack planned for later in the morning. This, however, was forestalled by the British attack, which opened at 6 a.m. with a ferocious artillery and machine gun barrage. The enemy forces preparing for the assault were caught in their assembly areas by this torrent of steel and high explosive and destroyed. German losses were compounded by a recent change of policy, which had led them to increase the number of troops holding their front-line positions. The attacking troops were full of praise for the weight and accuracy of the barrage: as one New Zealand soldier later wrote 'The noise was indescribable. The spectacle I saw appeared like the edge of a giant rainstorm as it traversed an area of water.'[57]

The fighting during the attack centred on the many pillboxes in the area. The garrisons of some of these positions quickly surrendered, but others resisted desperately. Private Neil Ingram, a member of a Lewis gun team, wrote a good account of one such action in his diary:

> A large pill-box appears immediately before us and a rain of bullets lashes the air all around. Down we flop into a shell-hole, the Lewis Gun is set on the brink and we get into action in earnest.... As fast as the drums of ammunition are used up we refill and hand to the No. 2 of the gun who clamps them on and hands back the empty, while No. 1 peppers away at the loophole of the pill-box. Bullets hit with a WHACK! the earth about us and soon No. 2 rolls to the bottom of the shell-hole, hit in the temple with a ricochet, blood and brain-matter exuding from the hole. No. 3 immediately takes his place and we continue to lay siege,

keeping up a concentrated fire at the loop-hole… from which the stream of lead is directed at us. Meanwhile other parties work around the flanks and suddenly the fire from the pill-box ceases as these parties get to the garrison with bombs through the rear doorway. We rise from our cover and again move forward skirting the now silent pill-box.[58]

The new tactics certainly proved their worth, and enabled the well-trained New Zealand infantry to overcome with their own resources strong enemy positions. Although boggy ground slowed the attacking infantry in some areas, in general the attack made good progress. By 9.30 a.m. 4 Brigade's troops were in possession of all their final objectives.[59] Large numbers of German troops were killed in the attack. Of the more than 1100 POWs taken by the New Zealand Division, 700 had been captured by 4 Brigade. As was almost always the case on the Western Front, such success did not come cheaply – over 300 New Zealanders had been killed and 1300 wounded (in 1 Brigade 192 were killed and 700 wounded; in 4 Brigade 130 died and more than 600 were wounded).[60] Although well satisfied with the performance of both attacking brigades, Russell reserved particular praise for 4 Brigade. Many of those involved were also very proud of what they had achieved. Second Lieutenant Howden told his wife: 'that it was one of the most complete successes our side has ever had and even General Godley has doled out a little praise to the NZers particularly the 4th Bde, for their efforts. A thing which must have given him a severe strain. By jove Girlie it is a thing to be proud of being a New Zealander.'[61] Although the majority of the objectives set for the Allied attack on 4 October were achieved, albeit at considerable cost, the Battle of Broodseinde was not the significant success it was portrayed as at the time. There can be no doubt, however, that the New Zealand Division's part in the operation was a marked success.[62]

During the night of 5–6 October 4 Brigade was relieved by a British unit and withdrawn to a rest area. The brigade was in reserve during the disastrous attack by the New Zealand Division on 12 October. Next day it relieved the decimated 2 and 3 Brigades in the front line.[63] At the end of the month Inglis, the commander of 4 Machine Gun Company, described it as 'a real solid old unit now. Everyone's tried and it knows itself. Of course there will be swags of reinforcements soon; but the solid foundation is here for them, and that makes all the difference.'[64]

These remarks apply equally well to the whole 4 Brigade, which Godley regarded as 'a most efficient brigade and full of esprit de corps'. Nonetheless, the brigade would take part in no more major operations and was in fact coming to the end of its short life.[65]

To understand why it is necessary to review wider political and military developments that affected the strength and organisation of the NZEF. When news of the formation of a new brigade leaked out late in March 1917, it drew adverse comment. In particular, it was suggested that New Zealand must have been sending too many reinforcements to the New Zealand Division if it was possible to form an additional brigade from the accumulated reserves.[66] The decision to form 4 Brigade came at a time of increasing concern about the level and sustainability of the dominion's military commitments. In particular, as Allen commented, it was widely considered 'that New Zealand is being bled to death whilst Australia and Canada are not making fair contributions'. The entry of the United States into the war in April 1917 gave those who thought New Zealand could and should limit its military commitments another powerful argument.[67] This agitation was related to the realisation that New Zealand would soon need to begin conscripting married men, which would have important political and practical implications for the country.[68]

Publicly Allen defended the raising of the new brigade, even though he had opposed its formation, but in private he stressed the agreement that New Zealand would provide no additional reinforcements for the brigade and that it would be disestablished when the New Zealand Division required its personnel. A shortage of manpower had already forced the Australian Imperial Force, in mid-1917, to disband the sixth division it had raised before it had seen any action.[69] Allen was very critical of Australia's failure to implement conscription and was dismayed to discover that the British authorities had, without informing New Zealand, agreed to a substantial reduction in the number of reinforcements provided by Australia. It is indicative of the level of Allen's distrust of both the British and Australian governments that he suspected some kind of deal may have been done to ensure that the Australian divisions did not require too many reinforcements. He considered the British government had not acted openly towards New Zealand and in particular that the Army Council had 'been trying to make things easy for Australia without informing New Zealand'.[70] The reduction in Australian reinforcements left Allen and the rest of the Cabinet in a hopeless political position. They wasted no time in pressing for a reduction in the level of New Zealand reinforcements. In response the British Army Council offered in July, after some negotiation, to cut the rate of infantry reinforcements from 15 to 10 per cent per month and then to 6.5 per cent in December 1917.[71]

It has incorrectly been assumed that the heavy losses suffered by the New Zealand Division at Passchendaele and the reduction in the rate of reinforcement led directly to the disbandment of 4 Brigade.[72] The actual course of events was, however, rather more complicated. After Passchendaele, Russell was certainly keen to break up the brigade and use its personnel as reinforcements. Godley, it seems, initially agreed to this, but at the end of October 1917 he changed his mind after discovering that the reinforcement situation was not as bad as he had earlier thought and that the War Office favoured the retention of the brigade, at least in the short term. Russell continued to strongly believe that for various, mainly practical reasons, a four-brigade division was not desirable.[73] By December he considered 4 Brigade the best brigade in his division and felt that the Rifle Brigade, which had suffered grievous losses at Passchendaele, should be disbanded instead. Robin and his staff opposed this proposal because of the still pressing need to utilise the excess manpower in the larger military districts, which had led to the formation of the Rifle Brigade.[74]

In January 1918 the British army was forced by manpower shortages to reduce the number of infantry battalions in a brigade from four to three. In response Godley, after reviewing the structure of the New Zealand Division, concluded that for manpower and practical reasons it made most sense to move to a three-brigade, 12-battalion structure. Hart was told in mid-January that his brigade would be disbanded in early February. Naturally this decision left him very unhappy, for his brigade had, as he wrote in his diary, 'done splendidly, more than made good, and the *esprit de corps* of each of its units is of the very highest standard'.[75]

The events surrounding the decision to establish and then a year later to disband 4 New Zealand Infantry Brigade clearly illustrate the way in which the dominion's political and military leadership attempted to balance the sometimes conflicting demands of the imperial war effort and New Zealand's interests. The formation of the brigade was a significant departure from New Zealand's sound policy that the

New Zealand Division and mounted rifles brigade in Palestine were the limit of its military commitments. New Zealand could have maintained a four-brigade division at full strength until the end of 1918, but when the future of the brigade had to be decided no one knew that the war would end in November 1918: most informed people were convinced that it would continue into 1919.[76] Certainly with the benefit of hindsight and in the knowledge of the full toll the Great War would take on New Zealand, it seems clear that the decisions taken to limit calls on New Zealand's limited reserves of manpower were very much in the national interest. In fact, it can be argued that in the First World War New Zealand proved better at resisting the temptation to overcommit its resources than it did in the Second World War. Much of the credit for this must go to Sir James Allen whose clear thinking, determination and exceptional capacity for hard work made a major contribution to New Zealand's war effort.[77]

The story of the formation of the brigade and its operations is one of significant success. From the outset the New Zealand military authorities did everything in their power to ensure that the new brigade would rapidly become a highly effective unit. The choice of an exceptionally capable commander, the provision of a strong nucleus of experienced personnel, the mixture of training and experience the brigade received before its major operation and the careful planning and preparation that went into the attack on 4 October 1917 – all ensured that it was thoroughly primed for success. Its experience provides a stark contrast to the way in which many Allied units were raised and first committed to combat.[78] That the organisation of 4 Brigade was such a success is not surprising in light of New Zealand's good record during the First World War of organising and supporting its military forces. The sound pre-war structure, training and planning of the New Zealand military forces were complemented by sensible decisions and policies adopted after August 1914. As a result New Zealand was able to rapidly organise and dispatch a force to capture German Samoa, and later to form, expand and support a substantial expeditionary force, in which more than 10 per cent of the dominion's population served. This great achievement is all too often overlooked when the First World War is discussed in New Zealand.

15

STOPPING THE STORM: THE NEW ZEALAND DIVISION AND THE KAISER'S BATTLE (*KAISERSCHLACHT*) MARCH–APRIL 1918

Glyn Harper

On 21 March 1918, at 4.30 a.m., the German artillery that had been secretly assembled around St Quentin on the Western Front opened fire on the British lines opposite. Nearly 6500 guns of all calibres and more than 2000 trench mortars joined in this bombardment along a 50-mile front, the heaviest artillery barrage of the war. Lasting five hours, the 'Devil's Orchestra', as the Germans labelled it, was designed to stun the defenders, destroy front-line communications and silence opposing artillery by its sheer weight and ferocity.[1] At 9.40 a.m. the bombardment gave way to a creeping barrage behind which specially trained storm troops, equipped with many flame-throwers and light machine guns, advanced. Their tactic was to push forward and bypass centres of resistance.

By the end of the day the British situation was critical. Casualties numbered 38,000, 500 guns had been lost and German storm troops had penetrated the front line to a depth of 5 miles. Two British armies had fallen back in some confusion, and over the next six days they continued to withdraw in the face of renewed attack to a distance of some 40 miles.

In a theatre where gains measured in a few thousand yards were considered successful, the German achievements were regarded as staggering. British withdrawals opened up huge gaps in the lines between army and corps boundaries, leaving the British front in danger of collapsing. As historian Gary Sheffield has noted, the German Spring Offensive of 1918 had 'brought the allies face to face with defeat'.[2]

In order to plug these gaps and to stem the German advance, nine BEF divisions were rushed to the endangered sections of the line. Among them were three Australian divisions and the New Zealand Division. This chapter focuses on the experience of the latter in the Michael Offensive, or the Kaiser's Battle (*Kaiserschlacht*), as the Germans called it.

The military background

Why was this German offensive so successful and why was the BEF singularly unprepared to meet it? The answers to these questions lie in the disasters and defeats of 1917, the Allies' hardest year of the war. The last Russian offensives of the war, launched early in that year, failed dismally. With her armies disintegrating and wracked by revolution at home, Russia signed an armistice with Germany in December 1917. On 24 October 1917 the Italians suffered a disastrous defeat at Caporetto that came close to knocking them out of the war as well. The French had suffered a major disaster in the Neville offensive, resulting in nearly half their army mutinying. Given command of the French armies, General Henri Pétain was determined to nurse them back to health. His strategy was twofold: to make the British do more of the fighting and to 'wait for the USA and the tanks'.[3]

This strategy had serious flaws. For a start the American Expeditionary Force was very slow in arriving on the Western Front. By January 1918, only four US divisions, numbering about 130,000 men, had reached France. American soldiers in 1918 were untrained and ill-equipped; they were also under the tight control of General John Pershing, who opposed their use in a piecemeal fashion. It would be at least the middle of 1918 before the US force in France would be ready for offensive action.

Nor had the year 1917 been kind to Britain, which had suffered catastrophic losses in three failed offensives on the Western Front. With German unrestricted submarine warfare at its height, there were fears that Britain would be starved into submission. As a result, the morale of the nation was at its lowest ebb.

On the Western Front the BEF in early 1918 was in a perilous state. To make up the losses of 1917, Field Marshal Sir Douglas Haig needed an additional 615,000 men. The British War Cabinet agreed to allocate him only 100,000 Category A men, with a further 100,000 men from lower medical categories should they be needed. In order to stretch the BEF's manpower resources as far as possible, Haig was directed by the War Office to reorganise his armies. This involved reducing a standard British infantry brigade from four battalions to three. It meant that 145 infantry battalions would simply disappear. The timing of this reorganisation was disastrous: ordered on 10 January 1918, it was not completed until 4 March, just two and a half weeks before the opening of the Michael Offensive. This reorganisation not only had a destabilising effect but also adversely affected morale and *esprit de corps*. Even after the changes, British divisions in France remained significantly under strength. Those battalions that survived were supposed to number around 1000, but a lack of reinforcements meant that most in 1918 were down to 600 men.

Such measures are understandable if the government wanted to clip the wings of its field marshal. Because of the lack of manpower and the subsequent reorganisation of the BEF, however, the weakened British armies in France were believed incapable of mounting a large-scale offensive in 1918. Less reasonable was the insistence that this weakened BEF hold a greater extent of the Western Front than before. In early 1918 it took over from the French responsibility for a further 26 miles of the line.

It should be noted that of the 10 dominion divisions, only the Australians were forced by severe manpower shortages to disband individual units, a price paid for Australia's refusal to introduce conscription. The Canadians and New Zealanders retained 12 battalions in their infantry divisions, making them significantly stronger than their British counterparts. Although the New Zealand Division did disband its fourth infantry brigade, the troops were used to provide a pool of reinforcements and to form three entrenching battalions as a divisional reserve. This reorganisation made the New Zealand Division the strongest division on the Western Front.[4]

Meanwhile, knowing victory was near on the Eastern Front, and now gifted the initiative by the British and French actions described above, from November 1917 the Germans began transferring men, artillery and experienced commanders from the Eastern Front to the West. By March 1918 46 fresh German divisions plus an additional 1000 heavy guns were available on the Western Front. This left 192 German divisions facing the Allies' 175.[5] This advantage presented the Germans with a military situation that was 'more favourable to us... than one could have ever expected'.[6] The realisation that it could not last increased their determination to make the most of it.

Against the thinly stretched British Third and Fifth Armies with a combined strength of 26 divisions, General Erich Ludendorff, who now controlled Germany's war effort, concentrated 71 divisions. Numbering more than a million men, this force was equivalent to the 1918 population of New Zealand. He also concentrated artillery on a scale five times greater than that possessed by the two British armies. It is little wonder that the British front buckled under this pressure.

The attack of 21 March was the Germans' most successful such effort on the Western Front. Overwhelmed by the devastating firepower and numbers ranged against them, the two British armies fell back to the River Somme with the Germans in pursuit. But the Germans had launched their offensive with no clear objective. Breaking a fundamental principle of war, they now settled on the vital junction town of Amiens as their immediate target. Taking this vital junction town would, they hoped, lead on to the seizure of the French Channel ports.

The New Zealand Division is rushed south

In March 1918, the New Zealand Division had been billeted in pleasant villages about the Cassel and the Hazebrouck district as part of the Second Army reserve. Its focus was on rest and training after its 'winter of discontent' in the Ypres salient. With the glorious spring weather, the training in open warfare instigated by a prescient Major-General Sir Andrew Russell and the chance to rest, the spirit and health of the New Zealand Division, shattered at Passchendaele in October 1917, slowly revived.

On the evening of 21 March, the New Zealanders were placed in the BEF's General Reserve, and next day marked for transfer to the Third Army. On 24 March they began their march to the front. At this stage there was uncertainty as to what the division would be doing or where it would be used. Not until the evening of the 25th, after much confusion, did Russell receive orders that he was able to put into practice. His division was to march to the old Somme battlefield and form a defensive line between Hamel and Puisieux. During the withdrawal of the Third Army on 25 March, a gap of 5 miles had opened between the Vth and IVth Corps and German storm troops were streaming through it. Russell's task was to close this gap.

To carry out these orders, the New Zealand Division had to travel many miles, a fair proportion of them on foot because of the lack of transport. Since the division would initially be without artillery support, the New Zealanders would have to fight the advancing Germans with only the weapons that they could carry. Their flanks would be exposed and, as soon as the marching stopped, the fighting would begin. Russell was conscious that it was a move fraught with risk.[7]

For men who had wintered in the trenches of Flanders, the march to the Somme was very hard. After moving initially by train and being deposited south of Amiens, most faced a march of between 25 and 30 miles. The men marched in light fighting order, which meant that they had to leave their packs, blankets and greatcoats behind. They carried 220 rounds of ammunition, extra ammunition for the Lewis guns and three days' water and rations. For the next two weeks they had to live, sleep and fight in their uniforms. They lacked shelter and warm clothing, and the spring weather, as well as being unpredictable, meant that the nights were bitterly cold.

Every account of this journey left by the soldiers describes it as extremely tough. For example Corporal Gerald Beattie of 1 Otago Battalion recorded in his diary that on 25 March:

> We marched in Battle Order not even carrying greatcoats. Were issued with extra ammo and rations and then marched on until 8.30 when we were billeted in a row of crippled motor lorries along the roadside.... It was a hard frost and we were very miserable without any blankets, but we had to make the best of a bad job.

Next day came a forced march of 25 miles, 'a record for the New Zealand Division'. That night the battalion 'had to doss down in an open field in a heavy frost with only an oilsheet.... Another most miserable night.'[8] Such a difficult journey meant that the New Zealand soldiers arrived at Hédauville, where the division's headquarters had been established, footsore, tired and hungry. It was certainly not an ideal state for soldiers about to meet an enemy flushed with victory. Most of the soldiers were exhausted before they even met the Germans.

As the New Zealand and Australian soldiers neared the front line, they came across thousands of retreating soldiers, mainly from the Fifth Army. They were not at all impressed by what they witnessed. Bernard Cottrell wrote home to his father:

> As we came up everyone was clearing for their lives, many did not know what was doing, others gave very vivid descriptions, but one look at their clothes was sufficient. They had never been in the line. They were told what was thought of them in very forcible language.[9]

Charlie Lawrence from Greymouth, who served in 13 Company, 1 Canterbury Battalion, gave some indication of this forcible language when describing how his battalion came across a large group of retreating British soldiers:

> They said to us: 'Don't go over there chum, you'll get killed.' That's what they said: 'Don't go Chum, you'll get killed.' We said: 'Turn around, you bastards and go the other way.' … It was a bad affair that was.[10]

The widespread judgment that British soldiers were of poor quality and greatly inferior to Australians and New Zealanders, according to the Australian official historian Charles Bean, was derived largely from the experiences of 1918 during this British retreat. Unfortunately New Zealand and Australian soldiers took this harsh opinion back to their respective countries, where it gained a widespread following. Although inaccurate and unfair, as Bean himself recognised,[11] the view has persisted.

An event of significance occurred on this difficult journey. As the New Zealanders marched south and then east, the roads were crowded with stragglers, transport and French refugees fleeing from the advancing Germans. Dressed in their best clothes and carrying their most valuable possessions with them, the refugees were worn out, frightened and in a state of bewildered despair as their world tumbled into ruins. All surviving accounts of New Zealand soldiers comment on their plight. 'We saw some pitiful sights on our march,' Harold Muschamp of the Machine Gun Battalion recorded in his diary. 'Old men and women and children all fleeing for their lives.'[12] Cecil Jepson of 2 Wellington Battalion wrote in his pocket diary of 'Heartbreaking sights' but added that 'many of our boys are wheeling barrows and carts and carrying bundles for the refugees who are passing through here day & night'.[13] The sight of refugees fleeing from a war zone was a new experience for the New Zealand soldiers, and it made a lasting impression on them. According to Ormond Burton, they were filled with compassion for the suffering French; and their determination to halt the Germans hardened.[14]

For many New Zealanders, this was also 'payback' time for their suffering at German hands in the previous year. 'Oh what a target,' James McWhirter wrote in his diary after watching a large group of Germans march into the killing zone of his machine gun crew, 'men & transport in marching order, we were all eager to have a bit of our own back for what we got at Passcendaele [*sic*].'[15]

Closing the gap: 26 March 1918

During the march south to the Somme, the New Zealand brigades had become so mixed up that Russell collected the battalions as they passed through his headquarters at Hédauville, cobbled them together to form makeshift brigades and sent them into action. On the morning of 26 March the first unit of the New Zealand Division encountered the advancing German storm troops at the small village of Mailly-Maillet in the Picardy region of the Somme.

At 6.30 a.m. on that day, 1 Battalion, 3 New Zealand (Rifle) Brigade (hereinafter 1 Rifles), with two sections of machine guns attached, advanced eastwards from Hédauville into the gap in the British front line. They reached Mailly-Maillet just as the German storm troops were entering the town. The Germans had been advancing continually for four days and expected no opposition. The New Zealanders easily drove them out of the town. A race then began to secure the Auchonvillers Ridge, a vital piece of high ground running from Beaumont Hamel through to Hébuterne, which offered excellent observation up the Ancre Valley and could be used as a platform for further attacks. Occupying a portion of the ridge, 1 Rifles sent out patrols that managed to link up with V Corps on the right of their position. However, with the Germans occupying the rest of the ridge, two of the New Zealand rifle platoons on the extreme left had the fight of their lives and suffered heavy losses as the Germans tried to overrun their positions. When in the early afternoon the battalion commander committed his last reserve to hold this flank, the situation looked perilous.

That afternoon 2 New Zealand Brigade, consisting of 1 and 2 Canterbury Battalions plus a machine gun company, arrived to relieve the pressure on the hard-pressed 1 Rifles. At 4 p.m. 1 Canterbury moved through the outpost line established by 1 Rifles and onto the brigade's objective, establishing a line west of Hamel and south-west of Beaumont-Hamel. Although experiencing some light shelling, it easily took its objectives. Lieutenant John Harcourt, a platoon commander of 13 North Canterbury and Westland Company, recorded the experience in his diary:

> On our left we could see the 1st Bde [in fact the 1st Rifles] having a good scrap but we found a few Tommies holding some old trenches (the old British Line on the Somme) in front of us. Occupied these. The Hun could be seen retiring over a hill some distance in front and we peppered him with rifle & MG fire. At the time we could have advanced almost unopposed but the 'Heads' decided to stay there.[16]

Attempting to do the same on the left, 2 Canterbury Battalion experienced considerable problems. At Auchonvillers it came under heavy machine gun fire and light shelling. Nonetheless it took the village, and moved through it and onto the objective, which was the old British trench line of 1916.

Private William Morris of the 12 Nelson Company of this battalion remembered this day more than 70 years later. His comments suggest that the time spent in training for open warfare was well worth the effort. After three days on the march:

> We ended up on a hillside like that one there and it was a nice sunny day.... and we had our first hot food – a plate of porridge. Not much of a feed was it? Then

we started off and it was all rolling downs…. And there were Australians on that side and New Zealanders on this side. All in order, one section here, one here and so on. I said to the bloke in front of me 'Good Lord, it doesn't look like there is a war on'. I just got the words out of my mouth and old Jerry turned a machine gun on us. Well, there wasn't a second and there wasn't a bloke standing up, they all went down like a shot. We were trained to do that you see. We never got any casualties then.

When his company reached the old British trenches, Morris was confronted by a German soldier and forced to bayonet him, an experience he found horrific: 'It was the only time I used a bayonet. I'm glad it was the last. I was nearly sick. It was a terrible thing to do.'[17]

In the early evening, 1 Brigade (consisting of 1 and 2 Auckland Battalions, three companies of 2 Rifles and a machine gun company) carried out an attack to take Colincamps, La Signy Farm and Serre. While Colincamps was cleared of enemy, it proved impossible to take La Signy Farm or to reach Serre beyond it.

By the end of 26 March, the New Zealanders had occupied a continuous line from west of Hamel to north of the Serre Road. Only in the centre, in front of La Signy Farm and towards the Serre Road, did the Germans hold any high ground. Although the southern portion of the gap between V and IV Corps had been filled, the situation remained precarious. There was still a gap of 1½ miles between the Australian 4 Brigade, now at Hébuterne in the north, and the New Zealand Division. And already the New Zealanders had suffered 150 casualties.[18]

Turning point: 27 March 1918

To carry out the vital task of closing the remaining gap, Russell organised his freshest New Zealand troops into a composite brigade, consisting of the 3 Rifles (less a company), 2 Wellington, 2 Otago and a machine gun company. These troops set off from Mailly-Maillet at 1 a.m., passed through Colincamps at 4 a.m. and reached the outskirts of Hébuterne by dawn. German outposts in between the Australians and New Zealanders were surprised and most fled. At one strong point a determined bayonet charge overcame resistance. By 9 a.m. on 27 March the gap between V and IV Corps had been finally closed.

This would be an eventful day on the Western Front. The Germans took Albert in the morning, but it would be virtually their only success. The New Zealanders and Australians faced a day of hard fighting as the Germans, abandoning their cautious infiltration methods, now made frontal assaults by infantry supported by machine gun and some light artillery fire. The change indicated German desperation to restore the momentum of their attack by reopening the gap. In their efforts to prevent such an outcome, the New Zealanders benefited from the fact that 'the enemy's efforts were not well combined' because the position lay on the boundary line of two German armies – the Second and Seventeenth.[19] The Australians and New Zealanders held a position of considerable tactical advantage for they could see for some considerable distance to their front. Everywhere they looked on the morning of 27 March, their front was alive with exposed and vulnerable German troops making ready to resume their advance. It was, the Australian official historian later noted, a sight 'such as Australian infantry had never before watched from their front trenches'.[20] Nor had the New Zealanders: 'Such an opportunity had not come to most of them during the whole war', according to veteran and historian Ormond Burton.[21]

The Germans must have believed that only light opposition faced them. They began advancing towards the New Zealand and Australian positions as if on parade 'without the slightest attempt at concealment'.[22] For a brief moment the watching New Zealanders and Australians were stunned by the sheer audacity of their opponents. 'Look at the bloody bastards coming up the road', a 2 Auckland Battalion soldier shouted as the Germans marched in four columns along the Serre Road.[23] The Germans were allowed to get to within 45 yards of the New Zealand front line before the order was given to open fire. Rifle and machine gun took a fearful toll, inflicting thousands of casualties in the space of a few minutes:

> It was like corn before the sicle [*sic*], machine guns cracked everyone of the
> enemy fell like ninepins, horses struggled on the ground, those who did escape
> flew in a panic and there was congestion all along the road. The dead were
> heaped on top of one another, the German red cross were carrying away the
> corpses for three days afterwards.[24]

William Morris was haunted for the rest of his life by the killing that occurred on that fateful morning. He recalled in 1989:

> The Germans come over three times. Three times the next day in close formation. As close as you and I. And they just wiped them down. Wiped them down. And he sent another lot and he got wiped down the same. Terrible! One lot of Australian soldiers when we were going up there, they met a whole regiment of Germans coming along a sunken road – they had the Colonel right along in the front coming along the sunken road and they came to the top of the hill and there they were. They just wiped the whole lot out. They had four deep, cleared the whole thing. Terrible! A terrible thing to happen isn't it? Just murder.

But, as Morris realised, at the time, 'It was you or them'.[25] That morning it was the Germans who were killed in large numbers.

While the fighting was continuous from midday, the Germans launched four large counter-attacks against the New Zealand positions that afternoon. The first came just after noon, and the others followed at 1, 3.30 and 7 p.m. Only in the last did the Germans, advancing on a front of 1500 yards midway between the sugar refinery and Hébuterne, succeed in capturing any ground from the hard-pressed New Zealanders: 2 Wellington Battalion was forced back a distance of 500 yards from the road. When the reserve company tried to regain the ground at 8.50 p.m., it made little headway against enemy troops now well established on the Wellingtons' old position, protected by machine guns and holding a section of the Hébuterne-Sugar Factory road. This company from Hawke's Bay fought hard, killing about 60 of the enemy and capturing five machine guns but suffering heavy casualties itself. In all 2 Wellington lost four officers and 69 soldiers on 27 March.

The loss of ground could have hugely disrupted the New Zealand line. That it did not was the result of fast and courageous action by the men of 3 Rifle Battalion, whose flank 2 Wellington's withdrawal had left exposed. Only one platoon could be spared to form a defensive flank, however, and it soon came under intense pressure. When its officer was killed in an early exchange of fire, a sergeant and then a corporal took charge and held the Germans at bay. This hard-pressed flank was reinforced first by the reserve platoon, then by the bulk of 3 Rifles' C Company, which had been detained on duty at Amiens. The exposed flank was secured and contact regained with 2 Wellington Battalion.

With the New Zealanders occupying most of the high ground, German casualties mounted steadily throughout the day. Most of these were inflicted by the New Zealand machine gunners, who in the absence of any artillery support, provided the bulk of the fire support for the infantry. For them, 27 March 1918 was a red-letter day. The Wellington Company in support of the composite brigade opened the account at 10.30 a.m. Occupying a superb position on the division's left flank with a commanding view over the whole brigade front, it observed an enemy battalion 1600 metres away moving across the front from near Hébuterne and opened fire. This, the battalion's war diary recorded, had the effect of 'scattering and thoroughly disorganising the enemy'.[26] At 12 noon the situation was repeated.

In the mid-afternoon the next target appeared: two long columns of enemy infantry advancing towards them. The columns, observed at 1600 yards by one gun position, were gradually converging over the Serre Ridge. Although the Germans were well within the range of the New Zealand machine guns, the gunners were ordered not to open fire until the enemy came within 1000 yards. As the Machine Gun Battalion's history commented: 'Probably no better target presented itself to the New Zealand Machine Gun Corps in France, and the fullest advantage was taken of it'.[27] The machine guns played havoc among the advancing German soldiers and their casualties were conservatively estimated as being in the region of 300.[28]

Still the Germans came on. At 3.30 p.m. they again attacked the composite brigade's position, this time taking the precaution of advancing in open order. The advance was observed as it came over the ridge some 1200 yards away. The Wellington company's guns opened up on the targets and immediately many of the enemy fell. The rest took cover. For some time afterwards, isolated groups of Germans were seen trying to crawl back over the ridge. The ground in front of the composite brigade was 'until nightfall littered with dead Huns'.[29]

At 9.10 p.m. Captain George Tuck wrote an entry in his diary that neatly summed up the day's activities:

> a stressing day... The Hun has been attacking us all day by all means. Things
> happened of which I dare not write. Haven't had 10 seconds to myself all the

time. We are just holding the bounder but we have suffered pretty heavily – but
he more so. If he doesn't put in an attack before the next hour I think all will be
well. A thousand pities he was allowed to cross the line of the Ancre.[30]

It had been a real soldier's battle, one in which nearly every New Zealander then
in the line had an opportunity to take part. It was their tenacity and courage as
well as the superb leadership skills shown by junior officers and non-
commissioned officers that held the New Zealand line intact. 'During these
attacks the… Officers and N.C.Os particularly distinguished themselves….',
2 Auckland Battalion's war diary recorded. 'The bravery displayed by all ranks…
during these attacks was beyond all praise and it was purely due to this that the
Hun failed entirely in his efforts.'[31]

Before midnight on 27 March batteries of the New Zealand Divisional
artillery were in action in support of the New Zealand units in the front line.
Breaking this position open now was not going to get any easier for the Germans.
Many Germans regarded 27 March 1918 as the turning point in the great
offensive. This was certainly the view of the Crown Prince Rupprecht of Bavaria,
who referred to it ever afterwards as 'this fateful day'.[32] On learning of the lack
of progress of his Second Army, he requested that the German Supreme
Command (OHL) send him three more divisions to strengthen his right wing.
On learning they were not available, he cried 'in consternation… then we have
lost the war'.[33]

Return to trench warfare: 28 March–3 April 1918

From 28 March until 3 April a pattern of action developed. The Germans
continued to probe the New Zealand lines, searching for gaps or weakly defended
locations. As the New Zealand position grew stronger with each passing day, it
became clear to the Germans that only a full-scale, frontal assault would break
the newly established British front lines. They began gathering the resources
necessary for such an effort.

Meanwhile the Germans were content to harass the New Zealand lines with
bombing attacks and artillery. The dangers of such attacks were demonstrated
when, on the evening of 28 March, a German 5.9-inch shell scored a direct hit
on the headquarters of the Rifle Brigade, killing 11 men and wounding 14

others. Brigadier-General H.T. Fulton later died of his wounds, the third New Zealand officer of this rank to fall in action during the war.

Heavy rain, which had been falling since 27 March, soon flooded the trenches. For the New Zealand soldiers, deprived of shelter and warm clothing, conditions were far from pleasant, as Captain Tuck noted on 1 April while his battalion was withdrawing from the line:

> Tho' we have been in only four days the Battalion has spent just about the hardest week in its history. Practically no sleep from Sunday to Sunday. No blankets or overcoats. Raining the last two days which turned the trenches into clay baths. How the men stood the terrible strain I cannot tell. [34]

With the lull in the enemy activity, the New Zealanders prepared to strike back by seizing areas of the line that would improve their position. Most of the attention focused on taking La Signy Farm, an important piece of high ground that gave miles of observation to the east of their current positions. It offered a much better view over the Ancre valley to Thiepval, Pozières and the Albert-Bapaume Road. After piecemeal attempts to take the position failed on 28 and 29 March, a more determined effort was planned for 30 March, Easter Sunday.

La Signy Farm's defenders, soldiers of the German 20 Division, were tired and short of supplies. On 30 March they were not expecting a daytime attack and sentries were careless. At 2 p.m. a shrapnel barrage by the New Zealand gunners forced them to take cover in the trenches. Emerging after the barrage, they found soldiers of three New Zealand infantry battalions right on their positions. It was too late to organise effective resistance. Within seven minutes 300 Germans were killed, and 300 taken prisoner; the booty included 110 machine guns and 15 trench mortars. The New Zealanders quickly consolidated the position, having inflicted such losses on the German division that it had to be withdrawn from the line and later disbanded.

This attack was the first offensive action taken by the BEF on the Western Front since the start of Michael nine days earlier. Its success stunned the Germans and provided considerable encouragement to the soldiers of the Third Army. Congratulatory messages flowed in from Generals Birdwood, Plumer, Godley, Monash and many others. The New Zealand official history of the division is almost dismissive of the success of this attack and downplays its significance,[35] but the Australian official historian, the astute Charles Bean, recognised its importance: 'small though the operation was, the news of it came in those dark days like a tonic to the whole of the British Army and to the Empire'.[36] Sir James Edmonds, the British official historian, noted that 30 March 1918 was a significant day for several reasons: 'at the time it was said that, simultaneously with the arrival of the Australians and New Zealanders, as a result of the heavy losses inflicted by Fifth and Third Armies the initiative had passed out of the hands of the enemy'.[37] The successful New Zealand attack was the first indication that this was so.

The Germans' last attempt: 4–5 April 1918

It was clear to Ludendorff and the other German commanders that their attack was losing momentum. They planned to make one last supreme effort on the Somme in an attempt to break through to Amiens. If this failed, they would abandon the Michael Offensive and launch another further north. From 1 to 3 April the German Supreme Command rested the troops of three armies before directing them to make a final attempt to reach Amiens. This they would do by attacking south of the Somme on 4 April, then north of the Somme on the following day.

The attack on 4 April was made on a 15-mile front using 17 divisions, six of which were fresh. The bulk of the attack fell on the French army and it petered out in costly failure. Against the BEF the Germans made some progress, taking Hamel and reaching the outskirts of Villers-Brétonneux, less than 10 miles from Amiens. A spirited counter-attack by the Australian 36 Battalion and the remnants of two British companies saved Villers-Brétonneux.

On 5 April two German armies attacked the whole front of the Third Army in a last-ditch attempt to reach Amiens. In the IVth Corps sector, where the New Zealand Division anchored the southern flank, three divisions faced more than six German divisions, two of them fresh.

For the New Zealand Division the day began with the opening of a heavy German artillery barrage at 5 a.m. For just over three hours, the New Zealanders endured intense shelling by guns of all calibres, including massive 12-inch guns. The bombardment reached behind the front line as far as Bertrancourt,

Courcelles and Colincamps. This barrage, which the New Zealand official history described as 'perhaps the severest bombardment that the Division as a whole experienced during the war', cut all communications.[38]

In line that morning were 2 New Zealand Brigade, on the right, and 3 (Rifle) Brigade, which linked with the Australian 4 Brigade on the left. German infantry attacked both brigades on two separate occasions during the day. Synchronising these attacks, as the Germans intended, proved impossible because of the disorganisation on the German front. The last two attacks were in fact separated by as much as four hours.

The first attack was made just after 8.30 a.m., when a regiment of 26 German Division advanced against the Rifle Brigade barring their way to Colincamps. The German infantry suffered heavily from the New Zealanders' withering machine gun and rifle fire – and from the efforts of bombers operating from the saps. But they still came on, managing to reach to within 30 yards of the Rifle Brigade's trenches before being finally driven off.

The next German assault on the Rifle Brigade, at 10 a.m., met with more success than its predecessor. The Germans managed to capture an advanced outpost at La Signy Farm manned by a small garrison from 4 Rifles, as the battalion's war diary explained:

> The enemy under cover of fog rushed an advance post at LA SIGNY FARM. 1 sector with a Lewis gun evaded the flanking movement by the enemy but the remainder of the garrison 14 in all were either killed or captured.[39]

Using this position as a lever, the Germans went on to take the troublesome La Signy Farm. Hoping to use the farm as a pivot to capture the New Zealand trenches, they used trench mortars on the New Zealand positions and then pushed as many parties of infantry as they could up old saps towards the main New Zealand position. The forward posts of 4 Rifles foiled this attempt to get to them, inflicting massive casualties on the enemy. As the Rifle Brigade history states: 'Never before had the Lewis gunners of the 4th Battalion had such targets as on this day and of their opportunities they made full use'.[40] German possession of La Signy Farm exposed 1 Rifles to dangerous enfilade fire. This problem was overcome by having its C Company form a defensive flank along the hedge that ran beyond the farm and another across the main line in case the Germans at the farm launched a frontal assault. Men moving forward along the saps and attacking the enemy there could easily defeat any assault made against the front of 1 Rifles.

By noon the situation was restored, and the Rifle Brigade suffered no further attacks that day. Of its 410 casualties – 96 killed, 311 wounded and three missing – recorded between 1 and 12 April, most were sustained on 5 April.[41] German losses on that day were conservatively estimated to be more than 500.[42] 'The enemy losses appear to have been heavy,' 4 Rifles' war diary recorded, 'as all that day his stretcher bearers were engaged in carrying out wounded.'[43] German accounts of this action claim that New Zealand machine gun fire from the flanks and centre halted the attack, with 10 Bavarian Infantry Regiment recording that:

> The regiment lost 190 officers and men. The attack had no prospect whatsoever
> of success unless the enfilade fire of enemy machine-guns were eliminated by
> the preliminary bombardment and by the barrage.[44]

Although La Signy Farm remained in German hands, it was kept under constant fire by the New Zealand artillery. At dusk on 5 April the New Zealanders struck back with 3 Rifles, south of the Serre Road, advancing their line by some 150 yards.

In the morning and afternoon of 5 April, on the right of the New Zealand line, German infantry attacked 2 Brigade, which was holding the line with its two Canterbury battalions. Of these, only 1 Canterbury was attacked on 5 April. The attack in the morning came just on 9 a.m., with German infantry working up the saps leading to the front line trenches. By establishing blocking positions in the saps, the Canterbury troops forced the Germans into the open where they were overcome with rifle, Lewis gun and machine gun fire. German losses were heavy.

The Germans renewed their attack around 2 p.m., but achieved nothing. The British official historian described it as a 'final but feeble effort';[45] the history of the Canterbury battalions says the attack was launched 'in a half-hearted way'.[46] For a while it seemed as if the Germans might make some progress on the New Zealand right flank, but an enterprising New Zealand corporal quickly organised a bombing party to halt the Germans and check their progress. The attack was easily driven off. When it was clear that this final assault had failed, the German artillery fire died down and from 3.30 p.m. became almost non-existent.

The New Zealand artillery batteries received considerable attention from the German gunners and some suffered heavy losses. Bombardier N. Bailey's diary recorded the fate of one of these unfortunate batteries:

> Fritz started shelling the heavy batteries in the next village of Bertrancourt. He pasted them all the morning. My word the big H.E. [high explosive shells] did come in…. There was heavy artillery fire all day and some of our batteries suffered. The news reached us that the 10th Battery was blown out and some of the others had casualties….Fritz is supposed to have made three separate attacks during the day and sent over three waves of infantry with each attack. Our boys must have stopped him alright though we had a lot of casualties; the ambulances being kept very busy.[47]

It would seem that once more it was the New Zealand machine gunners who inflicted the majority of the casualties on the Germans. The Wellington Company of the Machine Gun Battalion was in support of the Rifle Brigade. At 8.30 a.m. it caught the advancing Germans with 'a perfect hurricane of fire'.[48] The machine gunners estimated that they accounted for about half of the attackers. When the second attack was made on the Rifle Brigade at 10 a.m., the machine gunners once more assailed the Germans with withering fire. One New Zealand machine gun kept firing for more than four hours to deter German infantry from reaching an old communication trench. In the southern sector of the line, the situation was similar. The attack launched in the afternoon received full attention from the New Zealand machine gunners there. Captured German sources testified to the effect of the New Zealand firing. A German officer interrogated by General Headquarters gave two reasons why their attack of 5 April failed:

1. The intensity of our [the New Zealanders'] machine gun barrage.
2. The fact that some of the attacking troops did not leave their front line until ten minutes after the assault had been launched.[49]

The German attack on 5 April 1918 was a significant event for several reasons. First, according to the historian of the Rifle Brigade: 'The attack was unique in the respect that it was the only one of major importance that the New Zealand Division ever sustained'.[50] Second, for the first time in the war, the New Zealanders were not at a disadvantage in terms of the terrain on which they were fighting. On 5 April, they enjoyed the novelty of dealing with an attack in force while occupying a superior defensive position. Their efforts to secure all of the high ground over the previous week had clearly paid off. Third, as a result of the failure of the assaults on 5 April, Ludendorff took the painful decision to abandon the Michael Offensive. As he recorded in his Memoirs:

> These actions were indecisive. It was an established fact that the enemy's resistance was beyond our strength. We must not get drawn into a battle of exhaustion. This would not accord neither with the strategical or tactical situation. In agreement with the commanders concerned, G.H.Q. had to take the extremely difficult decision to abandon the attack on Amiens for good.[51]

Assessment

After 16 days, the German offensive on the Somme ground to a halt. It had experienced spectacular success in the beginning, only to lose momentum and peter out in a series of spasmodic attacks. As in all the Allied offensives that had taken place to date, there was a break-in but no breakthrough, and the situation had deteriorated to the point of stalemate. After the failure of the assaults on 5 April Ludendorff decided that, in order to make any further progress, he needed to attack the BEF elsewhere. This would occur in the north in four days' time. But the Michael Offensive, the *Kaiserschlacht*, 'the most formidable onslaught of the war',[52] was over.

There is considerable variation in the casualty figures given for the New Zealand Division at this time.[53] Carbery's medical history contains a full list of New Zealand casualties month by month in Table II of Appendix B. Of the various casualty figures attributed to the battle, Carbery's are probably the most accurate, especially if measured against the names recorded in the New Zealand casualty returns for these months.[54] The figures for the two months of the Michael Offensive are listed as:

March 1918

Dead 79, wounded 369. Total 448.

April 1918

Dead 885, wounded 2300, missing/POW 16. Total 3204.[55]

The casualty figure for April 1918 is one of the highest for the war. It is surpassed only by the months of September 1916 (the Somme), June 1917 (Messines), October 1917 (Passchendaele) and September 1918. As A.E. Byrne wrote in his history of the Otago Regiment, 'This high total affords some indication of the severity of the period.'[56]

It should never be forgotten that each of these numbers represents an individual, a New Zealand soldier far from home with dreams and aspirations, plans for the future and loved ones to whom he wished one day to return. New Zealand's role in 'stopping the storm' on the Somme in March–April 1918 had indeed exacted a heavy price.

But 'stopping the storm' on the Somme in March and April 1918 was also a fine performance and a major New Zealand success. This was recognised at the time in all quarters but one, and glowing tributes poured in from generals, politicians and even governments. More than a year after the event the New Zealand Division was still receiving accolades for its performance on the Somme in 1918. In the War Ministry of the Republic of France on 28 November 1919, Russell's name was recorded in Army Orders with the following explanation:

> Has led to countless victories a splendid Division whose exploits have not been equalled and whose reputation was such that on the arrival of the Division on the Somme Battle Field during the critical days of March, 1918, the departure of the inhabitants was stopped immediately. The Division covered itself with fresh glory during the battles of the Ancre à la Sambre, at Puisieux au Mont, Bapaume, Crèvecoeur, and Le Quesnoy.[57]

This was high praise indeed.

It is somewhat ironic that Russell was the person named in the French army order above because the only criticism of the New Zealand performance on the Somme in 1918 came from the New Zealand commanders, especially Russell himself and Godley. Russell was the stronger critic, demanding 'something better still....I certainly do expect the New Zealand Infantry both in thought and action, to be at least 50 per cent quicker than the new Armies.'[58] Russell communicated his concerns to Godley, who duly passed them on to the New Zealand government. Writing to Minister for Defence Sir James Allen at the end of April 1918, Godley stated:

> Since I last wrote you will have heard that the New Zealand Division went South, and arrived just in time to help to stem the Boche advance there... I hear very good accounts of what they did, and their first attempt, since the landing at Gallipoli, of what was practically open warfare, seems to have been on the whole quite successful, though naturally after all these years of trench warfare, they were not as quick as they should have been, and Russell very rightly has issued criticisms and instructions on the subject.[59]

It is to be hoped that Russell issued some praise too, but this seems unlikely.

Godley and Russell were wrong. To force march 20–30 miles and fight and defeat a skilled, determined enemy for 11 days without respite in just the clothes you are wearing and in the most appalling of weather conditions is no mean achievement. The New Zealand soldiers who fought on the Somme in 1918 performed a magnificent feat of arms, perhaps their finest of the war. That they also made a crucial difference to the outcome of the battle was acknowledged at the time by all but the senior New Zealand commanders. They deserved better.

HAIG AND HIS DOMINION COMMANDERS: THE EVOLUTION OF PROFESSIONAL CITIZEN ARMIES ON THE WESTERN FRONT

Christopher Pugsley

'I have not got an Army in France, really, but a collection of divisions untrained
for the field. The actual fighting Army will be evolved from them.'[1]

'Some General Officers of the Great War'

In 1922 John Singer Sargent finished his painting of 'Some General Officers of
the Great War' commissioned for the National Portrait Gallery. It shows Field
Marshal Earl Haig surrounded by the commanders of the British armies during
the First World War. The 22 figures include the Chiefs of the Imperial General
Staff during the war, Sir William Robertson and Sir Henry Wilson, Haig, his
predecessor Sir John French, and the army commanders of the British armies in
France and also those of the campaigns in East Africa, Italy, Palestine and
Mesopotamia. There are some prominent commanders who do not make the
group: General Sir Ian Hamilton is missing, as is Air Chief Marshal Sir Hugh
Trenchard of the RAF.

One can imagine that below army level there would have been some intense
jockeying for the few places available and one surmises that the positioning of
each man in relationship to Haig, the man at the centre, would have also led to
certain machinations. Lieutenant-General Sir William Birdwood, for example,

is distinctly divorced from the group of army commanders immediately surrounding Haig. Or am I reading too much into this?

Of particular interest are the dominion commanders of the Western Front: Lieutenant-General Sir Arthur Currie, who commanded the Canadian Corps from May 1917, Lieutenant-General Sir John Monash, who commanded the Australian Corps from May 1918, and Major-General Sir Andrew Hamilton Russell, who commanded the New Zealand Division from its formation in 1916 until the Armistice. Currie stands in the front rank half-turned towards Haig, almost confrontational, as indeed at times he was. Monash and Russell appear as faces looking over the shoulders of those in the front two ranks, almost as if their omission were noted at the last minute and, though it was recognised that they should be in the frame, they were evidently not as important as Currie, who is placed in the forefront.

In this chapter I will examine Haig as Commander-in-Chief of the BEF and his relationship with dominion forces and position New Zealand, Australian and Canadian performance in combat in the context of the British armies in which they served. The 'tyranny of distance' that divides New Zealand and Australia from scholarship in Europe and America sometimes makes it difficult to see comparative performance in context. Monash and the performance of the Australian Corps stand centre-stage in Australian historiography of the war. However, as I will argue, it was the Canadians who set the benchmark for tactical brilliance, at first under the enlightened guidance of Lieutenant-General the Hon Sir Julian Byng, and who sustained it under their Canadian citizen-soldier commander Lieutenant-General Sir Arthur Currie.[2]

The Canadians were at the forefront of the all-arms revolution built upon improvements in artillery techniques and technology, combined with platoon-level infantry tactics that are the keys to understanding the breaking of the trench deadlock on the Western Front. The Canadians also led the way in the evolution of the machinery of a national force, a dominion army within the empire. Haig encouraged the first but was baffled by the second. His frustrations over the question of dominion command explode on occasions within his diaries and shape the reader's perceptions, but this has to be separated from his assessment of the dominion contingents' capabilities as fighting formations.

That is best judged by their employment, and it is here that certain distinct advantages in their organisation and structure gave the dominion forces a basis for combat effectiveness that was confirmed in practice by the quality of leadership displayed by the three figures in Sargent's portrait: Currie, Monash and Russell.

But let me go back to the opening quotation. This is the story of evolving professionalism of mass citizen armies, the first that the British Empire had raised in its history and on an unprecedented and unimagined scale. When Haig assumed command of the British armies in France, the superbly professional BEF that deployed to France in 1914 had vanished in the Battles of First and Second Ypres of late 1914 and early 1915. In its place were new armies consisting of regular divisions in name only manned with wartime replacements and raw but enthusiastic Territorial and Kitchener New Army divisions. Partially trained, fitting into newly raised corps and equally newly raised armies as they arrived, Haig's armies grew from one million men to some 1.8 million by the beginning of 1917. The New Zealand and Australian divisions of the two ANZAC Corps were late arrivals: the last wave of reinforcement divisions of April–May 1916 with Monash's 3 Australian Division did not arrive until December 1916.

Within the ANZAC formations the Gallipoli experience had been diluted by the enormous expansion of the single New Zealand infantry brigade into a division of three infantry brigades and all the accompanying arms and services, and of the two Australian divisions into four divisions with a fifth – 3 Australian Division to make it confusing – being raised in Australia and shipped to England for training. In every way they reflected the standards and experience of the British divisions that deployed to France with them: generally superb material, keen, enthusiastic, but still largely amateur, and committed to the most difficult operation of war, that of driving a skilled enemy of equal mass out of carefully prepared defences.

Sir Douglas Haig

In the public imagination Haig is that 'butcher' isolated in his chateau, never visiting the front, blind to the suffering and the deaths of the hundreds of thousands that he is sending forward to die in the mud. He is the Haig of the Somme and Passchendaele, a traditional cavalryman who could not see beyond the value of the horse and who sent brave men forward needlessly to their deaths. He is a distant figure, inarticulate and unapproachable, feared by his army commanders, blind to the feelings of his officers and men and ignorant of the conditions at the front. As Gerard De Groot has written, he was 'confident that he alone knew the right way to victory…. A man divinely directed [who] did not seek the advice of mere mortals.'[3]

Natural soldiers are rare individuals. The reality of success in war on the scale of the Western Front demands a sustained effort by professionals with the skills to co-ordinate, administer and train vast armies and employ them on operations. To achieve that in wartime with a citizen force is an expensive journey of trial and error involving enormous sacrifice. The evolution of Haig as BEF C-in-C and the evolving professionalism of his armies are integral to understanding the Anzac and empire experience on the Western Front. When first looking at the Haig diaries in the National Library of Scotland some 10 years ago, I was struck by something that Haig said to Lieutenant-General Sir Edmund Allenby on his appointment as an army commander: 'I discussed the merits of the 18 Div[isio]ns and their respective commanders who will be under his orders so that the best commanders may be given the most difficult tasks'.[4]

To put this axiom into practice one has to know one's men and my research indicates that Haig made it his business to know his subordinates. By 1917 he understood that the key to the effectiveness of his armies was at the divisional level, because it was at this level that training was conducted and changes implemented. Having forged effective divisions, he then had to ensure that they fought effectively as corps or groups of divisions and armies. This, too, was a learning process for Haig and his commanders. This chapter offers not just a glimpse into Haig's relationships with his dominion commanders, because he did not see himself dealing with them on those terms, but rather an opportunity to assess Haig and his relationships with his subordinates at the tactical level of command: Currie as GOC Canadian Corps, Monash as a divisional commander until May 1918 and then as GOC Australian Corps, and Russell as a divisional commander. It is a study both of Haig's understandings of the workings of his armies at corps and divisional level, and, because of the nature of the man, in microcosm of his dealings with his corps and divisional commanders throughout his armies.

The British armies in France consisted of a number of corps, 100,000–150,000 strong, each made up of three or four 15,000–18,000-strong divisions. An army corps, except for the Canadian Corps and I ANZAC Corps after September 1917, was a moving feast of constantly changing divisions. Stage managers for the periodic battles, corps commanders were given resources in the form of a number of divisions to do a job; these were then replaced when exhausted or moved as the tactical situation directed.

The New Zealand Division – a typical British division?

Russell's New Zealand Division is an example that reflects the reality of most British divisions. It came to France as part of Birdwood's I ANZAC Corps before joining Godley's II ANZAC Corps on its arrival in late May. It was detached for the Somme in 1916, where it was first earmarked to join I ANZAC Corps but was fortunate that 4 Australian Division went before it, so that it served instead as part of XV Corps in the operations that started on 15 September 1916. As a result it did not have to experience Pozières and Mouquet Farm, which was the fate of Birdwood's Australians in General Sir Hubert Gough's Reserve Army. It then rejoined II ANZAC, remaining with it throughout 1917 until the formation of the Australian Corps in January 1918, when it became part of Godley's XXII Corps. It never fought with Godley in 1918, being detached during the German March offensive, and serving in IV Corps throughout the rest of the year. It was moved as need dictated, perhaps not as often as some British divisions, but its experience reflected more that of a typical British division than those of its Australian or Canadian counterparts.

The Canadian Corps' advantage

The Canadian Corps was at the forefront because it got to the Western Front first. When the Anzacs arrived in France in March 1916, the Canadians were veterans in the theatre who had demonstrated their prowess in holding the line under gas attacks during the Second Battle of Ypres in April 1915 when 1 Canadian Division formed part of V Corps.[5] The 'sideshow' of the Anzac landings on Gallipoli, although occurring in the same week, was not accorded the same significance, being so remote from the decisive theatre. Ironically the drive to form the Canadian Corps, after the arrival in France of 2 Canadian Division in

September 1915, used as its precedent the formation of the ANZAC.[6] It benefited from being solely Canadian in that tactical lessons learned by one of its divisions could be more easily applied corps-wide, an advantage not available to the shifting mass of divisions within British corps.

The closest to the Canadian Corps was Birdwood's I ANZAC Corps which, apart from the brief attachment of the New Zealand Division in April and May 1916, was a *de facto* Australian Corps, its commander always under pressure from the Australian government to achieve a national corps incorporating all five Australian divisions. Birdwood had visions of an ANZAC Army, which Haig refused to contemplate. So the formation of the two ANZAC corps was a compromise.[7] The focus of Australian attention was on Birdwood's I ANZAC, and Monash's 3 Australian Division became the odd one out: it was the last to arrive in December 1916 and served through 1917 in Godley's II ANZAC Corps.

Lieutenant-General Sir Alexander Godley, who commanded the NZEF throughout the war, does not feature in the Sargent assemblage of notable commanders. Yet as NZEF commander he was Russell's national commander on the Western Front, and throughout 1917 both Monash and Russell served as divisional commanders in his II ANZAC Corps. But in this portrait group corps commanders did not make the cut unless they represented their dominion's effort in support of the empire. Administratively Godley did this superbly, but he was always conscious that he was an officer of the British army and in that sense II ANZAC always functioned like any other British corps, containing a mix of divisions, with the New Zealand and 3 Australian Divisions as its bedrock and other British and Australian divisions cycled through depending on the operational need.

The Battle of the Somme, 1916

The British experience on the Somme was the turning point in the professional development of the British armies. It demonstrated the gulf that existed between Haig's ambition to achieve a breakthrough and the practical capabilities of his armies in 1916. The Somme showed that for all the technological development that had occurred with artillery, tanks and the introduction of critical infantry weapons such as the light Lewis machine gun and the 3-inch Stokes mortar, his armies and their commanders at every level were still groping towards an effective combination of these advances.

It was a blunt instrument that paid for its inexperience with enormous casualty lists. The experience of the AIF in 1916 reflects this, first on 5 July at Fromelles where 5 Australian Division, the last raised and least experienced of the Australian divisions, was destroyed as a fighting formation in an ill-considered and rushed assault, losing 5300 men in 24 hours. This unhappy start continued on the Somme in July 1916 where Birdwood's I ANZAC fought as part of Gough's Reserve, later Fifth Army. Major-General Harold Walker, whose 1 Division alone showed a degree of professionalism, resisted Gough's impetuosity, but neither Birdwood nor his other divisional commanders did so. Legge's 2 Division's attack on Pozières was hasty and failed. It drew Haig's criticism of Legge, ('not much good'), his division ('ignorant'), and Birdwood's staff.[8] Only as the battle progressed did Walker's professional skills in the planning and conduct of the attacks, first on Pozières and then Mouquet Farm, filter through to the rest of I ANZAC Corps. The calibre of the soldiers involved was excellent, but once again their standard of training, the tactics employed and Australian staff and command skills at corps and division level did not match this.[9] One could argue that this was also the experience of the Canadian Corps, which replaced the Australians in Gough's Fifth Army, and they, like the Australians, suffered from the demands he made upon them and hated him for it.

It was different for the New Zealand Division. It had an opportunity to learn from the lessons of July and then practised these before its commitment to the Battle of the Somme on 15 September. It earned a reputation as an outstanding fighting formation but at a cost of 7400 casualties. Russell was conscious of how much the division did not know, and how much better it had to get in administrative, staff and tactical skills if it was to survive as a fighting formation.

Learning from the Somme: the infantry revolution

The best of the divisional and corps commanders evaluated the Somme experience and profited from it. This was certainly true of Lieutenant-General Sir Julian Byng's Canadian Corps. Bill Rawling's detailed study *Surviving Trench Warfare* shows the growth in tactical development between the Somme and the Canadian attack on Vimy Ridge in April 1917.[10]

Byng, selected by Haig to command the Canadian Corps, proved to be a practical thinking general who in his eight months with the Canadians was determined to work out how to successfully attack at minimum cost. Equally importantly, he understood the particular nature of the men he commanded. He recognised that a citizen army had to be treated and trained differently from regulars, noting that it was important for senior officers to become involved at levels that would not be contemplated in a regular formation but 'when so many Senior Officers in Battalions are still inexperienced, the interference even of Corps and Divisional Commanders in the training of the Platoon was beneficial'.[11]

Directives from above were not enough when inexperience at every level of command down to private soldier meant that the few professionals who knew what to do had to get involved and, by 'hands on' involvement and advice, teach staffs and units both the management and the business of fighting.

This was the reality in every British and dominion division. Byng was prepared to do this and stuck his nose in at every level it was needed. He also recognised and preached that the key to tactical success in breaking the trench deadlock was to be found at platoon level.

Byng sent his outstanding divisional commander, the corpulent 41-year old auctioneer and estate agent and Militia officer Major-General Arthur Currie, to visit the French at Verdun and assess their organisation and training. As a result he made organisational changes to the platoon structure within the infantry battalions which would anticipate army-wide changes in the months ahead.[12] Currie's report detailed how the organisation, communication and training had to improve within the Canadian Corps in terms both of the infantry who carried out the attack and of what the artillery needed to do to ensure they could get forward.[13] He summarised the primary factors behind successful French offensive operations as 'careful staff work', thorough 'artillery preparation and support', the 'element of surprise' and the 'high state of training in the infantry detailed for the assault'.[14] Currie was impressed by the fact that the French were producing what he termed '"storm" troops on a large scale'. Indeed if one looks at the subsequent adoption of this approach in the British armies, by late 1917 every British soldier was trained in the tactical skills of fire and manoeuvre, and it is this breadth of training that constitutes the critical difference between the Allied and German approaches. In the latter the *Stosstruppen* or specialist storm trooper remained an élite and the German imperial armies suffered for it.[15] The key for the Allies was improving tactical skills within the infantry battalions. Currie noted in his report:

> Too often, when our infantry are checked, they pause and ask for additional [artillery] preparation before carrying on. This artillery preparation cannot be quickly and easily arranged for and is often not necessary. Our troops must be taught the power of manoeuvre and that before giving up [and asking for more artillery support] they must employ to the utmost extent all the weapons with which they are armed and have available.[16]

In essence, the infantry had to be taught how to fight once the supporting artillery fire lifted from the German trenches. This required a change in platoon organisation and the evolution of tactical drills based on the Lewis light machine gun and other infantry weapons such as the rifle, rifle-grenade and hand-grenade.

Byng was not alone. Commanders and staffs from Haig down were assessing the lessons of the Somme fighting and were suggesting changes. It was a combination of directions from top down matched by ideas feeding from the bottom up. Haig, like Byng, recognised the need to intervene wherever it was needed, although it took him time to get it right, critically with his favourite Gough to whom he gave too much leeway. Throughout 1917 he took a critical and direct interest in the tactical preparations and training of his armies.

This platoon-level revolution was adopted army-wide in February 1917. Directives from Haig's General Headquarters led to the introduction of the new platoon structure throughout the British armies, including the New Zealand Division and its Australian counterparts in I and II ANZAC Corps throughout 1917.

The Canadians at Vimy, April 1917

Byng demonstrated the new structure's importance with the success of the Canadian attack on Vimy on 9 April 1917 as part of the Arras Offensive. It showed what an infantry-based army could achieve with detailed preparation and planning and the co-ordination of all the resources available. The four

Canadian divisions advanced side by side in battle for the first time under a creeping artillery barrage, assisted by specially dug communication tunnels that allowed the attacker to move close to the German front lines. Counter-battery fire silenced the German artillery and most of the critical ground except that on which the Vimy Memorial now stands was gained in the first few hours of battle. The toll exacted was high: 3598 killed and 7004 wounded.[17]

The Canadian victory at Vimy showed that it was possible to break in and seize heavily defended ground with platoon-based tactics assisted by engineering skills, and the skilled use of artillery. As Ian M. Brown has argued, it was a 'not glamorous but effective' set-piece attack, which became the model for future Canadian operations on the Western Front. This in turn became a model for British armies through the dissemination by Haig's staff of the lessons learned.

Disaster at Bullecourt, April–May 1917

The lessons learned by the Canadians were not as evident in Birdwood's I ANZAC Corps in the operations it conducted in early 1917. The Australians failed before Bullecourt in the two attacks on 11 April and 3 May 1917. Part of this was undoubtedly due to the determination of the Fifth Army commander, General Sir Hubert Gough, to push on with attacks against what he thought was a retreating enemy, despite growing intelligence to the contrary. Few subordinates in the Fifth Army would oppose Gough's raging zeal to press on at all costs, and Birdwood was certainly not one of them, so his Australians were committed pell-mell to hastily arranged attacks against strong defensive positions, with inevitable results. The Australians blamed Gough, British flanking formations and the supporting tanks, and though the first is deserving of blame the others are more of an excuse to hide Australian deficiencies. I ANZAC had not changed battalion and platoon organisations to effect fire and movement within the platoon, and this tactical ineptness showed in both operations.

The Battle of Messines, 7 June 1917

Godley's II ANZAC Corps was more fortunate in being part of Plumer's Second Army, whose formations were well served by a brilliant staff under the direction of Plumer's Major-General, General Staff, Tim Harington. In 1917 Plumer's Second Army HQ provided a framework of planning and operating procedures in an atmosphere that allowed both ANZAC corps to develop into effective fighting formations.[18] Godley's II ANZAC Corps had the opportunity and the time to assess both the lessons from the Somme and the success of the Canadians at Vimy in its preparation for the attack on 7 June 1917 at Messines. Both Russell's New Zealand's Division and Monash's newly arrived 3 Australian Division adopted the new platoon organisations and benefited from having time to practise and rehearse these changes.

Driving all of this was Haig himself. Like Byng at corps level, he saw the importance of picking up on details in a way that, in a fully professional army, would have been seen as interference. On 24 May 1917 he was on the final day of three days of visits to the corps in Plumer's Second Army, where he discussed in detail corps and divisional planning for the coming battle. In each corps he followed the same pattern. With his Artillery Adviser, Major-General J.F.N. Birch, he would go through the corps plans with the corps commander and his principal staff, usually the BGGS (Brigadier-General, General Staff: the principal operations officer) and the CRA (Commander Royal Artillery: the artillery adviser), after which he would visit each of the divisional headquarters within the corps and repeat the process with the divisional commander and GSO1, the principal operations officer.

After discussions at Godley's HQ Haig noted that 'Everything seemed to have been most carefully thought out'. At the New Zealand Division he noted that Russell 'seems a most capable soldier with a considerable strength of character. His problem is a difficult one, but he and his officers and men are all most confident of success.' Haig went through the divisional plan in detail and 'was well pleased with their arrangements but suggested Messines village should be taken in three "jumps" so as to give artillery a greater chance of producing an effect. His plan results in an awkward salient prematurely!'[19]

I suspect it was this discussion that formed the basis for Haig's comments on Russell's strength of character. Godley had given Russell a degree of latitude in solving the difficult task of securing the village of Messines, the key to the southern sector of the Messines–Wytschaete Ridge. Russell assessed that, once captured, Messines would be both an obvious German artillery target and an obstacle during the attack. He determined to outflank the town, committing into it only sufficient troops to winkle the opposition out of the cellars; these troops would then use the cellars themselves as shelter from the inevitable bombardment. The distinctive bulge in his divisional artillery plan reflected this approach.

A British divisional commander faced with a 'suggestion' from the C-in-C would normally take the suggestion as an order to be followed. Russell, however, argued his case and continued with his original plan, and this registered with Haig. Russell's own diary gives little indication of any debate, noting that 'Douglas Haig came to see Divl. Hq. He looked over plans – discussed one or two details, spoke pleasantly of N.Z.ers work and departed.'[20]

At 3 Australian Division Haig noted that

> The commander is General Monash … in my opinion a clear-headed determined commander. Every detail had been thought of. His brigadiers were equally thorough. I was much struck with their whole arrangements. Every suggestion I made was most carefully noted for consideration.[21]

At the end of the day, a satisfied C-in-C 'had a conference with General Plumer, his C.G.S. (Harington), and Generals Butler, Birch and Davidson.… I told him [Plumer] that of all the attacks which had been made under my orders, I considered the present one was the most carefully "mounted," and that all commanders and troops were better prepared for their work than on any previous occasion.'[22]

Plumer's preparations and Haig's assessment were borne out on 7 June 1917 in the attack on the Messines–Wytschaete Ridge. By mid-morning the ridge, critical to the first phase of Haig's Flanders offensive, was in British hands. Haig went forward and was briefed by each corps headquarters before visiting Plumer and congratulating him on the success. Haig noted in his diaries that the 'operations to-day are probably the most successful I have yet undertaken'.[23] It was Plumer's plan and his and his staff's execution, but in the planning and build-up, as his visits programme indicated, Haig was not a distant commander unaware of the tactical detail. He knew precisely what was planned and would comment, suggest changes and, if necessary, discuss changes in command if he believed the briefings he received showed that the commander was not up to the task. In the preparation for Messines we see a man who had given his army commander a task, but assessed the effectiveness of the planning and constantly monitored the pulse of the preparations. His supervision of the Messines offensive showed that Haig too had learnt from the Somme.

This was consolidated by return visits to gauge performance and assess applicable lessons. On 9 June Haig visited the divisions on the Messines front. Russell at the New Zealand Division's headquarters 'was most interesting regarding his experience. He was holding Messines with many machine guns to great depth, all our troops being in positions around and outside the village to avoid shell fire.'[24] Haig also confirmed his initial impressions of Monash, '(evidently of Jewish descent) and by trade head of a Ferro-Concrete firm. He is a most practical and capable commander, and has done well.'[25] His impression of both commanders was strengthened on each subsequent visit. After inspecting Monash's division on 22 September, he noted that 'Every detail connected with the parade had been carefully thought out before hand, hence the parade was so successful. I think Monash has a good head and commands his division well.'[26] The stage management of a parade was an indication of the staff work of a division and gave the C-in-C an opportunity to assess the training and spirit of the men. Monash was already aware that Haig had marked him out. On 3 August he wrote:

> Birdwood told me the C-in-C had a very high opinion of my Division and of me personally, and had gone out of his way to express himself in terms of praise of my work. B. added that it was rare for the Chief to do this. White entirely confirmed these statements.[27]

Success at Messines did not blind Haig to where things had gone wrong and which divisions had not performed. He noted that Major-General William Holmes, commanding 4 Australian Division, 'does not seem to have the same qualities of character as Russell and others'.[28] Haig had already received reports, by Major-General Sir Guy Bainbridge of 25 British Division, highly critical of 4 Australian Division's performance, complaining that 'detachments of the 4th Australian Division have been wandering about in his vicinity as if they had "no leaders"'. Haig noted in mitigation that the '4th Australian Division was at Bullecourt and lost many officers'.[29]

Haig and the Canadians

Currie succeeded Byng as Canadian Corps commander on 6 June 1917 and became the first non-regular officer to command a corps in the BEF.[30] Currie, a 'very big, tall, heavy fat man', was Haig's choice and the C-in-C pre-empted the Canadian government in appointing him, but Canada acquiesced.[31] Currie first demonstrated his skills at this level in the planning and conduct of the Canadian Corps attack on Lens. The purpose of the attack was to draw German attention away from the next phase of the British offensive in Flanders. It was also designed to draw the German forces into a meat-grinder battle, destroying the combat effectiveness of as many German divisions as possible to prevent their being sent north to Flanders as reinforcements.

Currie's strength of character and determination to do what was best for his corps was evident when, unhappy with the directive and the detailed instructions given to him by General Sir Henry Horne's First Army, he convinced his army commander that both the objective and the method had to be changed.[32] Currie was a man who had to go forward and see for himself, and from a careful study of the ground he demonstrated that the key feature dominating Lens was Hill 70, which had been placed outside the Canadian boundary in the First Army directive. Seizing this hill would leave the Germans no option but to counter-attack it in force.

Currie's plans came in for Haig's close scrutiny on 23 July. Haig wrote: 'I went into the arrangements made for an attack north of Lens (Hill 70). Every detail had been gone into with the very greatest care and all seemed full of confidence, so that I came away with a feeling that the attack would be made under the best possible conditions.'[33] It was also obvious, however, that Currie did not hesitate to state his requirements and in this he showed the same strength of character as Russell before Messines. Haig tetchily noted that the Canadians had a 'considerable number of guns [which] had been damaged in action... and were still in the repair shops. I said I would go into the question and replace them as far as possible. But the Canadians always open their mouths very wide!'[34]

Unlike Birdwood before Bullecourt, Currie refused to be rushed and repeatedly postponed the attack until the weather conditions were perfect. The critical ground was seized and, as Currie anticipated, the Germans counter-attacked furiously over three days, mounting 21 separate counter-attacks, each of which was destroyed by massed artillery fire backed up by machine guns and rifles. Canadian losses were heavy, 9198 for the period 15–25 August against assessed German losses of 25,000–30,000.[35] All the skills that had marked Canadian success at Vimy were repeated at Lens. A successful attack was mounted under a carefully planned creeping barrage while German artillery was suppressed by counter-battery fire, allowing infantry to fight their way onto the objective with fire and movement.

Currie got results and this was enough. Haig inspected the Canadians after an extensive period of rest and training in August and noted:

> The experience and training of the past year has done wonders for the Canadians. Their moral[e] is now very high, and though they have been opposed by the flower of the German army (Guards, etc.) they feel that they can beat the Germans every time.[36]

Passchendaele, August–November 1917

Passchendaele has gone down in history as the nadir of the BEF's experience on the Western Front. The mud and casualties of October and November 1917 have blinded us to the tantalising successes that were gained by the British armies from Messines on. One is struck by the rapid re-evaluation by Haig's GHQ of German defensive tactics. The British army was no mastodon stuck in its ways: from the highest level down there was an ongoing assessment of how the Germans were reacting to evolving British tactics. Haig was the spur to this. Whether it was a live-firing platoon attack demonstration in XIX Corps, whose 'main object was to show all ranks the importance of good covering fire in order to help forward an advance', a brigade attack practice, divisional exercises or detailed evaluation of divisional and corps planning, his notes show an understanding of both the problems and what was needed to solve them. Major-General Henry Thuillier, GOC 15 Division, summed this up when he remarked to Haig that he was 'astounded at the splendid feeling among the troops of confidence and discipline; quite different to the state of the troops when he commanded 2nd Brigade 1½ years ago'.[37]

Both ANZAC corps had time to prepare and rehearse before being committed to Haig's Passchendaele offensive. Exhausted after Bullecourt, the AIF used the period between May and September to good effect in building up its tactical efficiency. It was not the quality of the soldiers alone that made the difference; rather it was how they were moulded into an efficient fighting team with hard training, matched by sound administration and leadership. Birdwood's Ist ANZAC Corps enjoyed the opportunity to adapt platoon organisations, practise drills and conduct rehearsals to solve the practical difficulties of defeating the German defensive system, which they then demonstrated so effectively in the battles before Passchendaele. Haig noted the changes:

> The Australians have never looked better since they came to France than they did this morning. I was greatly pleased with their bearing and evident desire of each one to do his very best to show well at my inspection. These divisions have been out of the line for three months and have benefited from the training which they have undergone. [38]

Working as part of Plumer's Second Army, the Australian divisions achieved a series of successes: by 1 and 2 Divisions in the battles of Menin Road on 20 September; by 4 and 5 Divisions at Polygon Wood on 26 September; and by both I and II ANZAC Corps, involving 1, 2, and 3 Divisions as well as the New Zealanders, on 4 October, the only time both corps were used together side by side on the Western Front. Despite the image we have of Passchendaele, it saw the two ANZAC corps employ in battle a level of command and tactical skills at last equal to those of the Canadian Corps. This proficiency was not confined to the ANZAC corps or Canadians alone, but reflected the Second Army's level of expertise. After detailed discussions with army staff, corps and divisional commanders, Haig wrote:

> In every case I found the officers full of confidence as to the result of the forthcoming attack. Every detail had been gone into most thoroughly, and their troops most carefully trained.... Altogether I felt it most exhilarating to go round such a very knowledgeable and confident body of leaders. [39]

This growing professionalism was, however, matched by an increased determination to group all the Australian divisions together in an Australian

Corps. Haig understood the reasons for doing this on tactical grounds, but dominion nationalism was beyond his comprehension.

> Mr Murdoch, an Australian, a friend of Hughes (Prime Minister), and also a newspaper man, came to see me and lunched. He expressed a wish of Australia to have their five divisions organized as 'an Army!' I pointed out the impossibility of complying with this wish, but said everything would be done to keep the Australian troops together. I could not help feeling that at the back of this fellow's mind there is a desire to be independent of the old country!'[40]

It was an issue that refused to go away. In September Haig agreed that four of the Australian divisions would be grouped in I ANZAC, with 3 Australian and the New Zealand Division in II ANZAC being joined by two British divisions rather than rotating an Australian division through. But the demands for all five Australian divisions to serve together continued.

> General Birdwood with General White (BGGS) and Hawes (Head of Australian Medical Services in England) came to lunch. B is very anxious to have the five Australian divisions grouped into one corps. Tactically such an organization is not workable but I told M I would try and keep all the Australian units together so that he could supervise their units.[41]

This would lead to the formation of the Australian Corps in January 1918, but Haig always saw this as a potential counter to his tactical control and resented it. He was equally perplexed by Godley's appointment as commander of the NZEF, and this puzzlement was evident in a letter to Plumer: 'As the New Zealanders are now all in a division under Russell I don't know how Godley claims special command over the "New Zealand Expeditionary Force"?'[42]

The Second Army's success on 4 October was followed by the failure of Godley's II ANZAC Corps in front of Passchendaele on 9 and 12 October 1917, the latter with heavy losses to Monash's 3 Division and the New Zealanders. Despite the skill of both divisions, lack of corps co-ordination on the part of Godley's staff, particularly in terms of the engineer effort needed to bring up guns and ammunition, saw both Russell's and Monash's divisions attack and fail against uncut belts of German wire. Godley's HQ, despite its success at Messines, did not show the same evolution in staff procedures and planning that was evident in Birdwood's I ANZAC Corps.

Inadequate artillery preparation and planning led to the infantry attacking uncut wire. The creeping barrages were equally ineffective because of insufficient co-ordination and drive by corps HQ to see that the guns, material for platforms, and ammunition got forward. Despite the skills of both the New Zealand and Australian infantry, they could not reach the bunkers and were shot down in the wire. Russell assessed that, had the wire been cut, the attack would have been successful even with limited supporting fire, but the failure of 12 October confirmed that it was the all-arms co-operation of artillery and infantry working together with engineer support that allowed attacks to succeed. Infantry or artillery alone was not enough.

It was now that a reluctant Currie was ordered to attack with his Canadian Corps where Godley's II ANZAC Corps had failed. Currie had discussed with Byng the involvement of his Canadians in a surprise attack with massed tanks that would later be carried out at Cambrai. This was far more attractive than the mud of Passchendaele. Currie made his feelings known to Haig.

> Every Canadian hated to go to Passchendaele…. I carried my protest to the extreme limit… which I believe would have resulted in my being sent home had I been other than the Canadian Corps Commander. I pointed out what the casualties were bound to be, and was ordered to go and make the attack.[43]

Having been given the job, Currie got on with it. Before Passchendaele, Currie did everything that Godley had not: he insisted on time for planning and preparation, co-ordinated the engineer effort, got his guns forward, and committed his infantry to a series of attacks which saw them seize Passchendaele, although at a high price.

Currie and his staff went forward into the quagmire to see the conditions for themselves.[44] At Passchendaele he found that, of the 360 field guns allocated, only 220 were working, but not all were in position. The key to success was his demand that damaged guns be replaced and that the guns allocated, many of which were stuck in the mud, had to be got forward so that they could contribute to the fire-plan for the attack.[45] His planning took into account the conditions that both his artillery and infantry would face fighting in such a swampy desolation against a determined enemy organised in depth. It was important that the artillery creeping barrage did not run away from the infantry squelching slowly forward through the mire. In four bites – on 26 October, 30 October, 6 November and 10 November – the Canadians fought their way forward against stiff resistance until they finally captured the pulverised ridge on which the village of Passchendaele once stood. The gain was a small dangerous salient poking like a finger into the German defensive line, subject to fire from all sides. Currie's corps accomplished this in two weeks at a cost of 15,643 Canadian casualties. Its seizure marked the end of the Passchendaele offensive.

Currie mounted a series of carefully co-ordinated attacks in impossible conditions and succeeded where II ANZAC and other corps had failed.[46] Given the conditions Currie faced, it is hard to see how this wasteland of mud could have been more cheaply gained. As we know, Currie made it clear to Haig that he did not want the task, and insisted on time and effort that the C-in-C was initially reluctant to give. Similar demands by a British corps commander may have been overruled, but Currie by now had a professional formation, valued his men, and knew what was necessary to succeed, and would stand up to his C-in-C if he considered it necessary. It is quite clear that Currie admired Haig as a commander, but the relationship between the two men was always a prickly one, and problems would surface again during the German offensive in March 1918.[47]

The terrible cost of Passchendaele has blinded us to how much the British armies had progressed in combat effectiveness. The tactics employed by I ANZAC and the Canadian Corps exemplified this, but they mirrored those used throughout the British armies. The principal difference was the advantages of homogeneity: the four divisions in each corps benefited from evolving a common corps doctrine based on directives from Haig's GHQ.

1918 – Victory

The Russian collapse saw the balance of numbers swing in favour of the Germans. The seeming success of the March offensive has diverted attention from the way in which Haig's armies consolidated and held ground after the initial gains. They lacked the defensive skills of the Germans, who had perfected them over three years, but the BEF was now a professional hardened organisation with skilled commanders and staffs, who knew how to fight the enemy. It had the flexibility to adapt and, after holding ground, it advanced against a seriously weakened and exhausted German force.

In the Hundred Days Offensive from 8 August 1918, the Canadians, Australians and New Zealanders were at the spearhead of the British assault, and all three were at the cutting edge of tactical doctrinal development on the Western Front. Currie was the first to admit that Canadian skills were drawn both from their own experience and from the dissemination of lessons by Haig's GHQ. 'These documents were carefully studied and, to a large extent, inspired our training.'[48] Monash took those lessons with him when he assumed command of the Australian Corps in May 1918 and demonstrated them in fighting his corps at Hamel, and in the battles of the Hundred Days from 8 August. At last the Australian divisions had a man in command who knew the value of planning and preparation. Both the Australian and Canadian Corps demonstrated the value of having homogenous corps consisting of fixed divisions, and they gained strength from that cohesiveness. It was something that Australian commanders had always recognised, but, although I ANZAC was structured with four Australian divisions in August 1917, it was not until the formation of the Australian Corps at the beginning of 1918 that all five Australian divisions were grouped together.[49] What marked out each corps in comparative terms was sustainability of effort. The Canadians had staying power, which the Australians lacked, and this also dictated relative performance. It was because of a guarantee of trained manpower that the New Zealand Division remained the outstanding division on the Western Front.

The crises of 1918 saw Haig and Currie at loggerheads over Currie's insistence that the Canadian divisions be regrouped under Currie's command after the German offensive had been blocked. Currie was prepared to draw on his government's support to achieve this, as he had done in a skilful political battle to retain his 12-battalion divisional structure and prevent the formation of a second Canadian corps early in 1918.[50] This dominion interference in what he saw as tactical matters angered Haig, and became a point of contention with Monash over the withdrawal of the Australian Corps from the line in October 1918. Despite this, Currie, Monash and Russell continued to feature positively in Haig's diaries: they possessed qualities that he admired and, as commanders, exemplified what he had been striving for throughout his armies. Monash and Currie would demonstrate their skills at corps level, Russell at division. In June 1918 Russell became the only dominion commander to be offered command of a British corps by Haig, though his diffidence and stipulations on choice of staff amounted to a refusal.[51] As leaders Currie, Monash and Russell embodied Second Army Chief of Staff General 'Tim' Harington's maxims for success: 'Trust, Training and Thoroughness'.[52]

In 1918 the British armies in France had developed a combined arms approach based on infantry attacks on foot, supported by artillery, armour and aircraft. In terms of combined arms doctrine it was effective and on a scale that British arms would never equal again. In this performance the cohesiveness of national corps made the Australians and Canadians stand out, but their performance and those of the British formations on their flanks reflected a common doctrine and tactical skill in the offensive generally superior to those of the armies they faced. Despite the exhaustion and strain of four and half years of war, the British armies in France were skilled and professional in 1918. This evolution and overall excellence was due in large part to the efforts of the C-in-C, Haig, who both honed the sword and in 1918 wielded it to effect.

17

NEW ZEALAND AND THE NAVAL WAR

Peter Dennerly

At the outbreak of war in 1914, New Zealand's naval force consisted of a single, obsolete third-class cruiser, HMS *Philomel*. Acquired as a training ship a few weeks earlier, this represented the first step in the development of a New Zealand naval force under the terms of the Naval Defence Act of December 1913. The Pearl-class *Philomel* had been laid down at Devonport Dockyard, England, on 9 May 1889. Displacing 2575 tons and 265 feet in length, she was armed with eight 4.7-inch guns, eight 3-pounder guns and four 14-inch torpedo tubes. She had a speed of 17 knots. First commissioned on 10 November 1891, she spent the majority of the next 21 years around Africa.

Ships of the New Zealand Naval Forces were designated 'His Majesty's Ships' and wore the ensign and jack like other ships of the Royal Navy. The New Zealand government was particular, however, that its vessels should clearly appear in the list of the ships of the Royal Navy as New Zealand vessels paid for and maintained by New Zealand. The maintenance of *Philomel* included all operating costs, for both materiel and personnel.[1]

Preparation for war

Having commissioned the ship on 15 July 1914, Captain P.H. Hall-Thompson RN sailed from Wellington 15 days later for a shake-down cruise in the

Marlborough Sounds, before embarking the first trainees. During the day, a telegram was received stating that war was imminent. After spending the night at Picton, Hall-Thompson took the ship back to Wellington.

The complement of *Philomel* as a training ship was 165. Most were Royal Naval personnel on loan, although a number, such as Able Seaman John Moreton, who later died of wounds received in action, were New Zealanders by birth. The advent of war required the complement to be brought up to its wartime level of about 222. This was achieved by mobilising reserve personnel of the New Zealand section of the Royal Naval Reserve, supplemented by some Imperial Reservists and a small number from HMS *Torch*. As a final measure a few volunteers were engaged for the duration of the war: these men had the distinction of being the first to enlist in the New Zealand Naval Forces.

A thorough inspection of the ship was not encouraging. Hall-Thompson reported that, 'even taking into consideration her age, the ship was suffering considerably from neglect in the past'.[2] Discussions with the Admiralty led to an agreement that the Royal Navy would pay for repairs to the ship, and for a refit at Malta in January 1915.[3]

According to provisions of the Naval Defence Act, *Philomel* came under the operational control of the Admiralty on the outbreak of war. This was a matter of operational utilisation of the ship, not one of command – *Philomel* remained a New Zealand unit throughout the war. An example of the difference between *Philomel* and ships of the Royal Navy was the question of who was to issue death certificates for deceased members of *Philomel*'s crew. Because the Admiralty did not think it appropriate that it issue them, Hall-Thompson did so.[4]

Escort operations

Operationally *Philomel* formed part of the 'New Zealand Division' of the China Station, which comprised the elements of the former Australia Squadron that had been based at Auckland since October 1913. The only other units of the division were two also obsolete third-class cruisers, HMS *Psyche* and HMS *Pyramus*. The division's war orders directed the ships to be deployed individually to South Pacific Islands groups to undertake intelligence work. However the bulk of the German East Asiatic Squadron, commanded by Admiral von Spee, was believed to be in the South Pacific. Rather than invite disaster by deploying them to the islands, the ships returned to New Zealand shortly after sailing.[5]

On the night of 6 August 1914 Britain requested that New Zealand seize the German wireless station at Samoa. (This possibility had already been discussed and agreed within the Admiralty.) Besides acquiring the station, the occupation would protect trade routes in the South Pacific and possibly draw the German cruiser *Leipzig* from the coast of South America.[6] Next day the New Zealand government replied that the task would be undertaken. On the 8th, it indicated that, provided a naval escort could be furnished, the expedition could be dispatched on 11 August.[7]

The ships departed on the 15th, delayed by the need to provide an adequate escort. The New Zealand government sent a telegram to Rear-Admiral Sir George Patey, in command of the Australian Fleet, advising him that the occupation force was ready to start and asking if the route was safe. This message was the first that he had heard of the expedition and, as the New Zealand expedition was already at sea, he was obliged to support it and to delay the departure of an Australian expedition to occupy German New Guinea.

Arrangements were made for the battlecruiser HMAS *Australia*, the cruiser HMAS *Melbourne* and the French cruiser RFS *Montcalm* to meet the expedition off Suva. Later the rendezvous was changed to Noumea, where the New Zealand ships arrived on 20 August. The ships took on coal from two New Zealand colliers, the *Katoa* and the *Koromiko*. The convoy departed on 23 August and, having called at Suva, arrived off Apia in the early morning of the 29th. The town was occupied without resistance. At 8 a.m. on 30 August the British flag was hoisted over the courthouse, and a proclamation read by the officer commanding the troops, while *Psyche* fired a 21-gun salute. At midday *Australia*, *Melbourne* and *Montcalm* sailed, followed later that day by the transports with the ousted governor and other prisoners of war, escorted by *Psyche* and *Pyramus*.

The wireless station had been put out of action and, although it was anticipated that it could be made operational again, *Philomel* remained to erect a wireless installation that had been brought with the troops. This completed, *Philomel* sailed for Pago Pago in American Samoa on the 31st to inform the authorities there of the occupation and then to Vavau in the Tongan Group, to coal from the *Waipouri*.

That the threat from German warships was real was demonstrated by the appearance of *Scharnhorst* and *Gneisenau* off Apia on 14 September. Although the two ships came close up to the harbour, no attempt was made to communicate with the shore or to land and they eventually moved off without firing a shot. There were no warships left to guard the port, but von Spee's ships could not marshall a sufficiently strong landing party and had no desire to waste ammunition or damage German property by a bombardment.[8]

After coaling, *Philomel* visited other islands in the Tongan group and then Nukualofa, the capital, to inform the King of Tonga that Britain was at war. This advice caused much consternation among the local merchants, most of whom were German. The King proclaimed his neutrality and invited the officers of the ship to a banquet, but that morning, after suspicious wireless signals were intercepted indicating that German warships were in the vicinity, *Philomel* sailed for Auckland.[9]

New Zealand's response to a request from the imperial government began its involvement in Samoa and it was appropriate that the country's only warship was involved in the enterprise. Although *Philomel* was a small part of the larger naval force, it was undertaking a national task in a manner that was not again possible until it acted as a depot ship for the sweeping of mines off the New Zealand coast at the end of the war.

While the Samoa Expeditionary Force was being organised the imperial government accepted an offer of an expeditionary force for service in Europe. On 23 September the units from Auckland, Canterbury and Otago embarked in their transports and sailed from their respective ports. The next day the Wellington units were officially farewelled and paraded through the streets to embark in their ships. It was intended that the Auckland ships, escorted by *Philomel*, would join the others in the Tasman Sea, but during the night orders were received to return to Auckland, while the ships from the South Island put into Wellington. Rumours that the German cruisers were in the area caused the recall.

Philomel and her charges left Auckland again on 11 October, joining the other ships at Wellington. At 6 a.m. on 16 October the NZEF's Main Body finally sailed from Wellington, escorted by *Philomel*, *Psyche*, the British armoured cruiser HMS *Minotaur* and the Japanese battlecruiser HIJMS *Ibuki*.

To avoid any possibility of attack from the German squadron, the convoy was routed south of Australia and, after six days at sea, it arrived at Hobart, where *Pyramus* relieved *Psyche*. From Hobart course was set for Albany, which was reached on 28 October. *Philomel* and *Pyramus* parted from the convoy there, headed for Fremantle and, after coaling, sailed for Singapore on 3 November. This passage was of considerable concern to Hall-Thompson, who was not at all sure that it could be completed without incident. There was a serious risk of *Philomel* breaking down and, more importantly, the passage from New Zealand had shown that he had no accurate figures for coal consumption and there was some doubt whether the cruiser could actually reach Singapore if she encountered bad weather. Proceeding independently and by using the stokehold to stow coal, Hall-Thompson thought he would arrive at Singapore with a small amount remaining.[10]

Middle East service

After four days at Singapore, *Philomel* escorted three French troop transports as far as Aden, which was reached on 5 December. There the ship received its first mail since leaving New Zealand. *Philomel* was then employed on patrol work in the Red Sea, with the object of disrupting Turkish communications and hindering any attempts to construct or repair fortifications. At 11 a.m. on 9 December, during her first patrol, *Philomel* fired her first shots in anger as a New Zealand unit. A number of dhows being built or repaired at Mocha were destroyed, but the village was not damaged.[11]

Routine patrols continued until Christmas Day when the ship sailed for Malta, as the escort for nine large transports. At Malta the convoy was turned over to another escort and *Philomel* entered the harbour for docking and repairs. This was the first time since commissioning in July that there had been an opportunity to undertake major repair work on the ship. There was also some modernisation, including the fitting of fighting tops (gun observation platforms) on the masts and anti-aircraft guns.

Philomel sailed for Port Said on 29 January, and at 4.30 a.m. on 3 February departed to relieve HMS *Doris* on patrol off the coast of Syria, in the vicinity of Alexandretta. Underlying operations in this part of the Mediterranean was the possibility of effecting a landing to cut the Baghdad railway, thereby dividing the

Turkish Empire in two. This was a possible alternative to the Dardanelles campaign.[12] Hall-Thompson was cautioned not to be too active since the area might later be occupied by the British; he was not to land any party.[13]

Early in the afternoon of the 5th *Philomel* observed some trenches being dug near Deurt Yol and demolished them with a few rounds of common shell and shrapnel, before proceeding to Alexandretta. The ship anchored off that port at 4.30 p.m. and remained off the coast overnight, watching the road with searchlights and observing a large number of pack animals. The next day the ship patrolled the coast off Jonah's Pillar where some newly constructed trenches were discovered; the ship bombarded them, causing severe damage. That night *Philomel* again anchored off Alexandretta and kept a close watch on the road, where two or three suspicious convoys of mules with large packs and much other traffic were observed, although it could not be confirmed that they were military.

Next morning a note was sent ashore informing the Turkish Governor of the area that the road must be closed for pack animals at night and that any such animals would be considered as military in origin and fired upon. The ship then patrolled along the coast and spotted a large number of pack animals on the road. At 4 p.m. an armed party went ashore to find out, peacefully if possible, what the packs contained.

The landing party of two officers and 15 men set out in the ship's cutter, which was armed with a Maxim gun. They landed at a dry riverbed near Jonah's Pillar, about 4 miles from Alexandretta, which was swept with a few rounds of shrapnel, as trenches were known to exist in the vicinity. Once ashore, the landing party moved inland towards the road, only to be attacked on three sides by Turkish troops in what was a well laid ambush. Although *Philomel's* men retreated down the riverbed, they could not make the beach because of the intensity of enemy fire. One man was killed and five wounded.[13] *Philomel* covered the party with gunfire, but the men had to wait for darkness to be evacuated to the ship.

All except one of the wounded, Able Seaman Moreton, were brought off to the ship. Moreton should not have left the boat, being 'number two' of the Maxim crew, but he had followed the landing party when it moved inland. It was initially believed that he had been killed, but later that night, illuminated by one of the ship's searchlights, he was seen to be alive. A group of volunteers offered to go ashore to rescue him. Under the command of Lieutenant Charles Keily RNR, they left in the ship's whaler, with muffled oars, at 7.20 p.m. but returned two and a quarter hours later without having found Moreton. When the searchlights were turned on, he was again seen to move. A further search party, which left the ship at 1.20 a.m., succeeded in locating him and by 2.40 a.m. he was back aboard. However, his wounds were so serious that he died two days later.[14]

Another of the wounded, Able Seaman William Knowles RNR(NZ), who also died on board, was the first New Zealand naval person to be killed (although a New Zealander, Moreton was a Royal Navy rating). Hall-Thompson reported that the object of the operation had been achieved: one mule had been captured, although it had not proved possible to confirm whether it came from the pack train or what it carried.[15]

Annoyed by Hall-Thompson's failure to observe his specific direction not to land any party, the Commander-in-Chief East Indies demanded to know the reasons.[16] Hall-Thompson responded very briefly, expressing regret that he had misread the Admiral's instruction, having taken it to refer to restrictions on landing parties in the vicinity of Lake Bordowil and El Arish and not near Alexandretta.[17]

From late February until early April, *Philomel* was outer guard ship at Port Said. She then patrolled the Great Bitter Lake at the southern end of the Suez Canal, riding her luck when she almost certainly hit floating mines that failed to explode.[18] In mid-1915 *Philomel* was one of the vessels patrolling the northern coast of Egypt, from Alexandria to Sollum, searching for enemy submarines.[19] These operations appeared to accomplish little, but the enemy made its presence felt shortly after *Philomel* left the area, when a submarine sank two Egyptian gunboats and an armed boarding steamer in the vicinity of Sollum.[20] From mid-July *Philomel* was deployed to Aden as part of the protection of the Suez Canal. The situation was serious and at one stage the Turks had occupied Sheikh Othman, a suburb of Aden.[21] On the orders of the Senior Officer, Southern Red Sea Patrol, *Philomel* landed a Maxim gun detachment and communications section to supplement the defences of the port.[22]

During August and September the ship's crew received a tangible reminder that, although they were a long way from home, the people of New Zealand had not forgotten them. They were delighted to receive a gramophone and harmonium, as well as several cases of food. Despite the climate, they also welcomed the arrival of a quantity of mufflers and socks.[23]

On 25 September the Maxim detachment was involved in a skirmish with tragic results. It took part in a reconnaissance that moved out at 4.45 a.m. to attack the village of Waht, about 11 miles from their position at Sheikh Othman. After coming under Turkish shrapnel fire about 6.30 a.m., the force took up an open formation for the attack. By 9.30 a.m. the small village of Shiraj was in its hands. It was a very hot day, so the men were allowed to rest and shelter from the sun for about an hour.[24] At 10.30 a.m. the Turks began shelling the force. An hour later the *Philomel* detachment was ordered to take up a covering position and to retire with the main force as part of the rear guard. After about a mile the sailors began to straggle, however, and Lieutenant Fitzdam Millar decided that they were unable to carry out rearguard duties. Continuing to retire, they halted about every 20 minutes for five minutes' rest. Although they could feel the extreme heat through the soles of their boots, the men threw themselves down on the burning sand at each stop. Three men had died of heat stroke by the time the remnants of the party arrived at As Sela about 3.30 p.m.[25] In his report on the incident, the Senior Naval Officer, Southern Patrol, was careful to highlight the fact that neither he nor Hall-Thompson had known of the expedition before it was mounted.[26] Perhaps not surprisingly, the Senior Naval Officer was informed shortly afterwards that a naval machine gun detachment was no longer required.[27]

While the ship was providing support to the southern Sinai Peninsula, the situation in Mesopotamia (today's Iraq) was worsening. A British force had been sent to the area at the outbreak of war both to protect the oil supply so essential to the Allied war effort and to counter German moves in Persia (now Iran).[28] Additionally, the telegraph cables to Mesopotamia ran along the northern and eastern shores of the Persian Gulf. The supplies for this force, as well as those for troop detachments guarding the telegraph cables, all came by sea. Supporting these lines of communication was a squadron of cruisers, of which *Philomel* became a part in November 1915. Also in this squadron was *Pyramus,* with a large number of New Zealanders on board. Hall-Thompson's instructions were quite vague. In the event of war with Persia *Philomel* was to assist in the evacuation of British nationals; otherwise she was generally to act as a sort of policeman for the local area. The troubles with the local populace, it was emphasised, were essentially a continuation of normal conditions, rather than related to the war.[29]

Conditions in the ship were most uncomfortable with temperatures in the order of 100° Fahrenheit. On occasions it was 105° at midnight. Double awnings rigged both fore and aft kept the sun off the decks, but the heat was insufferable. Most of those on board suffered from boils, ringworm and prickly heat. Even underwater the situation was unpleasant. Several times a day divers had to endure water temperatures in the order of 95° Fahrenheit in order to clear jellyfish that continually blocked engine intakes when *Philomel* was at Chahbar.[30]

Philomel's and *Pyramus*'s connections with the dominions were again highlighted on 13 November when a cable was received advising that each ship had been granted £28 15s from Royal Australian Navy House, Sydney. The money, a contribution to the men's Christmas comforts, was gratefully received.[31] By now *Philomel* was in need of a maintenance period and docking. Having spent Christmas Day at sea, she arrived at Bombay at 7 a.m. on 28 December. Work immediately began on the defects to the machinery, some of which were outstanding from August 1914. While she was there, another consignment of Christmas gifts arrived from New Zealand.[32]

In mid-January 1916 *Philomel* was back in the Persian Gulf, where the weather was generally bad and communication with the shore cut off most of the time. On 1 February the ship's cutter was sent away with orders to anchor outside the breakers and make the final part of the trip in a local surf canoe. Shortly after the boat anchored, a series of steep waves completely swamped it and the canoes were capsized. All but one of the crew managed to swim ashore. Eighteen-year-old Able Seaman Frank Kivell, one of the New Zealand volunteers, rescued the able seaman in distress; for his efforts he would later receive the Royal Humane Society Bronze Medal.[33]

As the Senior Naval Officer on the Mekran Coast, Hall-Thompson was regularly involved in the general affairs of the area, including the commercial and political activities of the populace. The political management of the local leaders was of considerable importance, requiring a great deal of tact and diplomacy. In an effort to create unrest the Germans and Turks had declared themselves brother Muslims and called for a holy war to be raised against the British. Such a call placed those who wished to remain loyal to the British in a difficult position; it was complicated by the efforts of British politicians to win over those who were hostile to the Allied war effort. In order to pacify some disaffected leaders the British bribed them with a considerable amount of money. Although this achieved the immediate aim, it angered those who professed loyalty to Britain: it was more profitable, they said, to be anti-British than pro-British.[34]

Hall-Thompson and *Philomel* were to become even more closely involved in the politics of the area. A tribal war was in progress on the Trucial Coast, with the local sheik facing a rebellion by one of his subjects. Hall-Thompson wrote:

> Both disputants were short of ammunition, but each possessed one or two old smooth-bore cannon. At regular intervals one side would fire its gun and shortly afterwards the other side would reply. After a shot had been fired the villagers would be sent out to collect the round shot which had probably rolled and bounded away into the plains beyond, to use it to reload the gun and fire back again.[35]

After discussions with both parties Hall-Thompson drew up an agreement and gave them a week to consider it. On 29 March in HMS *Clio* he called both the sheik and his rebellious subject on board, explained the terms of the agreement and invited them to sign it before leaving the cabin. After about three hours of heated discussion, they were told that unless they signed their villages would be bombarded and their towers knocked down the next morning. Both signed.[36]

In May 1916, *Philomel* was again in Bombay for maintenance. Ammunition and stores were disembarked and the ship entered dock, while the ship's company moved ashore into the sailors' home.[37] With the onset of the wet season, the climate was most unhealthy. Many of the men fell sick. One of the New Zealanders, Able Seaman Victor Adlam, died of food poisoning, while two other seamen succumbed to malaria. When the ship sailed on 12 June, 15 sick sailors were left in Bombay.[38]

While in Bombay some of the ship's company made an effort to repay some of the kindness received from New Zealand. Twenty-four men, under Lieutenant-Commander Keily, had formed a concert party and performed shows at the Excelsior Theatre. The proceeds from the shows, £164 12s, were donated to a fund for New Zealand soldiers and sailors who had been wounded in the war.[39]

Return to New Zealand

By August 1916 Hall-Thompson, the Commodore Persian Gulf, the New Zealand government and the Admiralty were in discussion about *Philomel*'s future. Now an old, tired ship, she was in need of a major refit. But would such action be justified? In any case the three-year engagement of the vast majority of the ship's complement would soon expire; the future of the New Zealand personnel called up for the war and the leave entitlement of imperial reservists also had to be considered.[40] In late January 1917 it was decided that *Philomel* should return to New Zealand and pay off in time for the imperial ratings to return to Britain and have six weeks' leave before the expiry of their three-year contracts. When *Philomel* left the Persian Gulf, Commodore D. St A. Wake expressed his keen appreciation of the continuous and excellent work she had performed under his orders. After acknowledging the monotonous nature of the work and the trying climate, he expressed his admiration for the zealous and cheerful manner in which these difficulties had been borne.[41]

On 16 March 1917 *Philomel* berthed in Wellington, where she was met by a guard composed of 50 corporals from the NZEF and various dignitaries. The ship paid off on 19 April. Next day, at 9 a.m., she recommissioned as a depot ship with a nucleus crew of about 30 ratings under the command of Lieutenant-Commander Keily.[42] As she would not again be actively involved in the war, the government approved the use of her guns on defensively armed merchant ships.[43]

When she returned to Wellington, *Philomel* had been in the service of the New Zealand government for two years and eight months. Intended as a stop-gap measure to undertake no more than training duties, the ship had been handed over to New Zealand in poor condition. Even so, she was now in much better shape than she had been in at the outbreak of war, despite needing a refit.

As Hall-Thompson wrote in 1917,

> at the commencement of the war the ship was considered as a training unit. I was informed that she would break down if steamed at over 8 knots for any period (which was true in her state then) and she was in a very bad condition generally. The ship is now in an infinitely better condition than then and has steamed many thousands of miles at any speed desired, up to 15 or 16 knots, thanks to the energy and keenness of my departmental officers and men.[44]

Philomel's active service was confined to the backwaters of the war at sea. For the most part the duties undertaken from 1915 to 1917 were routine, dull and boring, in a debilitating climate. There were only two close encounters with the enemy, both ashore. Neither of these actions involved more than a small part of the crew and only at Alexandretta did the ship itself participate.

Understandably, given the nature of *Philomel*'s employment, rewards were meagre. Lieutenant Fitzadam Millar received a Distinguished Service Cross for his actions at Alexandretta and Aden, Able Seaman Sidney Beagley was mentioned in dispatches and several seamen had a notation for valuable conduct made on their service certificates. Hall-Thompson was made a commander of the Order of St Michael and St George in June 1917. Such awards were generally acknowledged as reflecting the value of the performance of the ship as a whole, rather than just of the recipient.

That *Philomel* was technically a New Zealand unit is unquestionable. However, it remains debatable how much national identity the ship projected. As a unit of the East Indies Squadron, she was an integral part of the Royal Navy and Hall-Thompson was tasked as an officer in the Royal Navy with the implementation of imperial policy. It is notable, however, that the signature block he used varied, depending upon the function of the ship. When he was the Senior Naval Officer, he generally signed himself 'Captain RN'. However, when a 'private ship', he generally used a signature block 'Captain RN, Naval Adviser to New Zealand Government'.[45]

In the projection of a national identity *Philomel* was not unlike units of the NZEF. The New Zealand Division and the Mounted Rifles Brigade formed parts of British armies but were still perceived as part of a national unit, the NZEF.

There was, however, a major difference in scale: an army division comprised about 15,000 men, but *Philomel* was a single, small, obsolete cruiser. Similarly the New Zealand Division, in particular, was at the centre of operations on the Western Front, while *Philomel* was employed in a remote part of the world. Certainly the ship's company felt some affinity with New Zealand. Not only were gifts received from New Zealand from time to time but also there was also some measure of reciprocation: when the ship's concert party performed in Bombay, for example, the proceeds went to the benefit of wounded New Zealand soldiers and sailors.

New Zealand under attack

In December 1917, nine months after *Philomel*'s return to New Zealand, a bottle containing a message was found on a beach on Toli Toli Island in the Celebes. This uniquely nautical means of passing a message was used by Captain T.G. Meadows, the master of the *Turritella*, who was held captive on board the German armed merchant raider SMS *Wolf*. His message warned that *Wolf* had laid mines off South Africa, Aden, India, Australia and New Zealand.

A converted cargo vessel of the Hansa Line previously named *Wachtfels*, *Wolf* had been commissioned in the Imperial German Navy under the command of Corvetten-Kapitan Karl Nerger.[46] She had been built at Flensberg in 1913 and was a single-screw ship displacing 5809 tons, with a top speed of 11 knots. For naval service she was fitted with seven 150-millimetre guns and four torpedo tubes and loaded with 400 mines.[47] Also carried was a seaplane nicknamed *Wolfchen* (wolf cub). Manning the ship were 16 officers and 320 men.[48] After departing Germany on 30 November 1916, *Wolf* encountered atrocious weather conditions. Although most unpleasant for the crew, they were particularly helpful to *Wolf* in breaking through the Royal Navy blockade. Having passed between Iceland and the Faroes, she was in the open sea on 10 December.

The ship's first war-like act took place on the night of 16–17 January 1917 off Dassen Island, South Africa, when 24 mines were laid. Following that she laid other minefields off Cape Agulhas, Colombo, Bombay and Aden. It was ironical that the first British vessel *Wolf* captured was the *Turritella,* a sister ship captured at Port Said at the beginning of the war.

Nerger headed towards the Pacific Ocean, where he hoped to capture enough coal to continue operations and to find a remote anchorage in which to undertake some routine but essential maintenance. On 22 May *Wolf* anchored on the south-eastern side of Raoul Island in the Kermadecs, some 600 miles to north of New Zealand. Ten days later repairs were still in progress when the Union Steam Ship Company's *Wairuna*, en route from Auckland to San Francisco, hove into sight. The officer on watch called Nerger when he sighted the strange ship, suggesting that the stranger could be another German raider and recommended that they keep clear, but Nerger scoffed at the idea. The *Wolf* launched its seaplane, which flew over the *Wairuna* and dropped a message on deck that stated, 'Do not use wireless. Stop Engines.' As a warning a bomb was dropped ahead of the ship. Captain H.C. Saunders complied with the German's order.

From the sub-tropical Kermadecs *Wolf* steamed south into the New Zealand winter. Between 10 p.m. and 2.30 a.m. on the night of 25–26 June, in squally rainstorms and a choppy sea, she laid 25 mines off North Cape, towards the Three Kings Islands.[49] *Wolf* then continued south, to a position off Cape Farewell in the western approaches to Cook Strait, where between 10.30 p.m. and 2 a.m. the next night a further 35 mines were laid.[50] Crossing the Tasman Sea, *Wolf* laid a further field off Gabo Island, on the south-east coast of Australia. On 24 July she intercepted a wireless message concerning the movements of a supply ship from Sydney to Rabaul. After sailing from Sydney on the 27th, the *Matunga* was intercepted by *Wolf* on 6 August.[51] The two ships proceeded in company to a secluded anchorage in Offack Harbour on the island of Waigiu, off the north-western tip of New Guinea. From 13 to 26 August *Wolf* was refitted by the crew, including cleaning the bottom by divers.

Wolf then threaded a passage through the reefs and Maluku Islands into the Banda Sea, passing to the south of the Celebes on 29 August, continuing into the Java Sea and into the shipping routes to Singapore. It was during this time that Captain Meadows threw his last bottle containing a message over the side, the one found on the beach on Toli Toli Island on 9 December. The British Consul-General at Batavia passed it to the C-in-C China Station, who cabled the message to the Admiralty.[52]

Nerger continued on his way back to Germany, taking several other vessels en route. There were, however, other difficulties to be overcome. Should he break through the British blockade there were still the minefields, both British and German, to be negotiated, for which the raider had no up-to-date charts. There was also the submarine threat, again from both the British and German navies, as *Wolf* could not break radio silence to advise her arrival without giving her position away.

Wolf reached the coast of Norway on 14 February 1918 and entered the Baltic on the 17th.[53] In a cruise of 20 months, spent entirely at sea, she had sunk 12 ships; another 12 had fallen, or would soon fall, victim to her mines. For a week she was held off Flensberg while an official welcome home was arranged. Each member of the crew was decorated with an Iron Cross and Nerger received a Pour le Mérite. Once the clamour had died down the crew were posted to other ships and Nerger was appointed officer in charge of armed trawlers in the North Sea.

Following the outbreak of war in 1914 few in the New Zealand government gave much thought to the realities of the worldwide nature of naval warfare. New Zealand seemed remote from the action, and the threat of German raiders seemed to have been removed in the Battle of the Falkland Islands in December 1914. In early 1915 the Naval Intelligence Officer warned the government of the possibility of mines being laid around the coast, urging that a minesweeping flotilla be formed, but the Chief of the General Staff, Lieutenant-Colonel C.M. Gibbon, considered this to be unnecessary and the associated expense unwarranted. As a result nothing was done over the next two years.[54] Within days of the return of *Philomel* from the Middle East in 1917, Hall-Thompson reviewed the threat to New Zealand, concluding that the greatest danger was from enemy mines.[55] However, even the disappearance of the *Wairuna* in June 1917 and the sinking of the *Port Kembla* off Cook Strait in September 1917 did little to disturb New Zealand's complacency.[56]

In October 1917 Hall-Thompson submitted to the Minister of Defence a report by Lieutenant-Commander Keily on the establishment of a minesweeping organisation.[57] Keily noted that there were only four suitable vessels in the country that could be used, and detailed the equipment that would be required. He had also located an invalided petty officer with considerable wartime experience in minesweeping. The necessary equipment should be fitted as soon as possible, Hall-Thompson suggested, and the vessels returned to fishing until such time as they were required, but nothing came of these recommendations.[58]

Once there was evidence that mines had actually been laid around New Zealand, the government quickly approved arrangements to charter two vessels and to have some essential equipment manufactured.[59] Hall-Thompson contacted the owners of the selected vessels, the *Simplon* and the *Nora Niven*, the Auckland City Council and the New Zealand Trawling and Fish Supply Company of Napier respectively. He expected the charters to cost about £200–250 per week,[60] but in fact that for the *Nora Niven* alone was more than £985. The basic wages of the ship's complement were paid by the company, with only the bonus being paid by the Crown. Monthly wages ranged from £27 for the master and £24 for the engineer to £17 for the boatswain, deckhands and cook, and £8 for the boy.[61] When the vessels were ready to begin minesweeping, Hall-Thompson issued sailing orders to Keily on 9 February 1918. He was to take *Simplon* and *Nora Niven* to the position where the *Port Kembla* had been reported to have experienced an explosion and start sweeping operations early on the morning of 11 February.[62]

The two ships duly left Wellington, but foul weather prevented immediate operations. It was not until later on 12 February that the first sweep was streamed.[63] Having spent the night at anchor, the vessels weighed and began streaming the sweep at 6 a.m. next morning. After 15 minutes there was a sudden check on the sweep wire and a few minutes later something was reported floating astern. Approaching as close as possible, *Simplon* identified the red-painted object, which was spherical in shape with four horns around the side and one on top, as a mine. Paint had worn off on one side and small barnacles were forming, leading to the conclusion that it had been in the water about six months.[64]

On 26 June 1918 a tragic, but avoidable incident occurred a few miles off the northern coast. The liner *Wimmera* had left Auckland the previous day, bound for Sydney with 300 tons of cargo and passengers on board. The ship was regularly engaged on this run and Captain H.J. Kell had been made aware of the danger of mines, to the extent of signing an instruction that he was to proceed 'outside', that is to the north of, the Three Kings Islands.[65] After passing North Cape Kell ordered a change of course that would take the ship south of the Three Kings. At 5.15 a.m. there was a loud explosion, followed shortly by another: *Wimmera* had struck two mines. Because the explosions had brought down the aerials, it was not possible to radio news of the event ashore. The ship settled on an even keel for about 12 or 15 minutes, enabling five lifeboats to be launched. These craft set out for shore, and four landed next day. The fifth drifted down the coast, but then made a safe landfall. Of the 116 persons on board, 25 lost their lives, including Kell. [66]

Sweeping for *Wolf*'s mines continued until May 1919. The northern field presented some difficulty because of the depth of water and to overcome it a special Aceton type sweep was acquired from Britain with the intention of fitting it in the government steamer *Tutanekai*. When difficulties were experienced in engaging a crew for the steamer, the whaler *Hananui II* was chartered and equipped to use the Aceton sweep. [67]

In all 46 mines were accounted for, 28 from Cape Farewell and 18 from the Three Kings. Seven from each field had not been found. It seemed likely that the fields were clear, but this could not be guaranteed. As part of a worldwide operation, the Royal Navy therefore dispatched a minesweeping unit to New Zealand to undertake check sweeps of the minefields. [68] Three Flower-class vessels, HMS *Geranium, Mallow* and *Marguerite*, arrived at Wellington at the end of June 1919, and began sweeping off Cape Farewell on 5 July. [69] By this time another three mines had come ashore from this field, leaving four outstanding. Sweeping continued until 20 July, and 10 days later Hall-Thompson declared the Cape Farewell minefield clear. [70] Between 6 and 16 August the minefield off Three Kings was swept twice, without finding any further mines. With the sweeping operations considered to have given 100 per cent coverage, this field was declared clear. The seven outstanding mines were believed to have broken adrift. [71]

Throughout the war New Zealand's major participation had been in Europe and the Middle East, with the NZEF. This tended to focus attention away from the direct threat to New Zealand which, like naval matters in general, was perhaps not really understood. In this light, the lack of preparedness to counter the threat from enemy mines in 1917 is understandable. Less understandable is the government's failure to heed the advice of its naval advisers, initially that of the Naval Intelligence Officer and, after the return of *Philomel* in March 1917, of Hall-Thompson. Given the lack of preparedness and equipment, Keily performed creditably in fitting out the two trawlers and operating them, manned by their normal crews, as a team in the difficult task of minesweeping. His ability proved to be the major factor in the success of the operations.

Intelligence operations

New Zealand's active part in the naval war of 1914–18 was not just confined to its cruiser *Philomel* and the men who served in the Royal Navy. From the outset, the Senior Naval Officer, New Zealand Division, Captain J.M. Marshall RN, gave attention to the part that intelligence would play. He appointed a retired officer as Naval Intelligence Officer (NIO) on 4 August 1914.[72]

Commander Robert Newton established a Naval Intelligence Centre in Defence Headquarters, Wellington, which reported intelligence to the C-in-C China Station and other similar centres, such as those at Melbourne, Esquimalt (Canada) and the Cape of Good Hope, as necessary. By the end of 1917 there were six New Zealand officers reporting to the Wellington centre, as well as one at Apia, which was also a New Zealand responsibility. At that time a re-organisation of the Admiralty intelligence network resulted in the New Zealand centre reporting directly to the Admiralty.[73] In addition to purely intelligence matters, the Naval Intelligence Officer also had responsibility for some administrative matters, such as arranging supplies of New Zealand coal for the Admiralty.[74]

The Naval Intelligence Centre organisation, which included three watchkeeping officers and a coding section, was a 24-hour operation. It co-ordinated reports on all Allied shipping arriving at or departing from New Zealand ports and disseminated information received from overseas. Some difficulties had to be overcome. For example, at the outbreak of war the NIO did not have access to any ciphers. His only point of contact for the reception or transmission of classified material was through the Governor. Indeed, at that time, even if the NIO had been provided with an appropriate cipher, he had no means of keeping it secure.[75]

Although Newton was instrumental in setting up the organisation, he soon left the country as transport officer of the troopships taking the NZEF's main body overseas. By mid-September 1914 Paymaster W.J.A. Brown of *Torch* had taken up the position. It was left to him to develop the skeleton organisation. He continued in the role until the end of the war.[76]

One of the most significant advances of technology employed for the first time during the First World War was radio. This facility was, and remains, a two-edged advantage, because there is the possibility that the enemy will also receive the transmissions. Before the outbreak of war several powerful shore radio stations were established in New Zealand – at Wellington, Awanui, the Chatham Islands and Awarua – under the control of the Post and Telegraph Department. Following the occupation of Samoa in August 1914, the former German station at Apia also came under New Zealand control. These stations were part of a worldwide empire network, with particular importance for naval communications.[77]

Even before war had been declared the New Zealand radio stations were making reports of German activity, the first recorded being on 2 August when Awanui reported that the German Telefunken station at Apia was on the air, working with Nauru. The Australian stations were also intercepting radio traffic, with Thursday Island reporting German warships working with Yap on 4 August. Two days later the Australian Commonwealth Naval Board was sending reports of the positions and courses of German warships, together with their call signs.[78] The New Zealand stations did what they could, but the Royal Australian Navy achieved a major coup when it secured the secret codes of a German merchant ship captured off Melbourne in early August.

Intercepted enemy radio messages were passed between the various authorities, and to Navy Office Melbourne, which was the major intelligence centre of the region. Even at this early stage the distinctive features of individual radio sets and operators were being exploited. On 28 September New Zealand was advised how to recognise and distinguish transmissions made by the German cruisers *Scharnhorst* and *Gneisenau*.[79] By October the German codes acquired by Australia were enabling intercepted messages to be deciphered. From this time the individual stations passed all intercepted messages to Melbourne as soon as they were received.[80] Not only were the shore radio stations providing intelligence, but New Zealand ships were also involved from an early date. On 15 September the *Marama*, off Christmas Island, reported hearing German radio signals and call signs, which were reported when the ship arrived at Suva. Similarly the *Talune* reported intercepted messages in the Cook Islands area in October.[81]

On 14 October the Naval Intelligence Officer received a copy of the German HVB code, used between German warships and merchant ships, from the Australian Naval Board.[82] This enabled Brown to analyse intercepts, and only those that could not be satisfactorily explained were transmitted to Melbourne. Any intercept indicating the presence of an enemy was given to the Governor and the Chief of the General Staff (as Military Intelligence Officer). Additionally, all British and Allied shipping was warned and telegrams dispatched to the Admiralty, the Commonwealth Naval Board, the C-in-C China, the Director of the Naval Service in Canada, and the Intelligence Officer at Montevideo.[83]

In early 1916 the newly established French radio station in Tahiti was requested to become part of the organisation and to report any suspicious signals intercepted through the British Consul at Papeete.[84] Although the French were only too happy to oblige, there were some severe practical difficulties, so the Consul suggested that the radio station communicate directly with the French Consul at Auckland or Wellington.[85] At the end of July Brown suggested that, because the value of intercepts was entirely dependent upon the time taken for them to be received by a scrutinising officer and of the fact that in their original form the messages were intelligible only to a trained officer, the French Consul in Auckland should be authorised to pass them direct to him, in the French language. This would enable messages to be analysed quickly. Any technical explanation could be transmitted through the French Consul to the Governor of French Oceania.[86] This suggestion was approved.[87]

In most respects an organisation for reporting enemy wireless transmissions was in place, but some serious problems remained. On 2 May 1916 Brown, in his capacity as Acting Senior Naval Officer, warned Gibbon that the Admiralty was under a misapprehension that the New Zealand stations were keeping a practically continuous naval watch: most of their time was in fact occupied in handling other military traffic, leaving little time for listening for enemy transmissions. If this could not be rectified, he suggested, the Admiralty should be informed of the true situation.[88] This resulted in the issuing of a memorandum on 9 May informing all concerned of the need to reduce traffic.

Still pursuing the matter, Brown wrote to the Secretary of the Post and Telegraph Department seeking information about the efficiency of the watch possible at each station.[89] He learned that Awarua could maintain an almost continuous watch; that Awanui seldom handled messages with ships but kept a listening watch for a considerable period; that more work was done at Apia than at Awanui but that there was still a 'fair amount' of listening watch and the station was probably troubled with jamming; that there was not much traffic at Wellington and listening watch for enemy signals was continuous, though its reception range was not as great as those of Awanui and Awarua; and that at Chatham Islands a close watch was kept for enemy signals on varying wavelengths during the hours of attendance at the station (not stated) and that the situation of the station was such that it could read signals over a wide area. Overall, good attention was given to listening for enemy signals and, except at Awanui and Apia, a greater portion of the time was devoted to that purpose.[90]

By November 1917 there were six reporting officers in New Zealand and Apia, all reporting to the Naval Intelligence Centre in Wellington. That centre then forwarded intelligence to the C-in-C China, the C-in-C Good Hope, the Navy Offices in Melbourne, Esquimalt, Panama and Callao. The Naval Adviser was also in direct communication with the Admiralty in respect of the detailed arrangements of the centre.[91]

In mid-November it was proposed that an intelligence centre be established in Suva, a suggestion that seemed to duplicate the organisation already in place. The situation was explained in some detail to the Admiralty, which then determined that Wellington should be retained as the Admiralty Intelligence Centre for the central Pacific and that a centre at Suva was unnecessary. The arrangements for reporting were also redefined: New Zealand, Suva, Fanning Island and Ocean Island were to report directly to the Admiralty in London and to Wellington, while Tulagi and Vila were to report to the Admiralty and Navy Melbourne.[92]

Although intelligence was a product of the advent of radio, a more practical contribution for New Zealand was allowing the use by the navy of the stations themselves. Radio technology was still relatively primitive and there was a great need for assistance from shore stations to facilitate communication, both between ships and between ships and distant shore stations.

By late 1915 it was noted that although the Royal Navy had its own radio stations in Australia, Canada and Hong Kong, the central Pacific was not fully covered. Royal Navy warships could no longer fill this gap, but New Zealand could. As a cost-effective solution, approval was sought from the Admiralty for the operators at the New Zealand stations to be trained in naval procedures, not to full naval standards, but to a level that would allow them to handle naval traffic. Thus the stations became a part of the naval network, taking instructions from naval authorities.[93] Besides this significant step, other measures had been taken from early in the war. From October 1914 New Zealand had agreed to accept telegrams for Allied warships at the British government rate, rather than the normal commercial rate. At the beginning of 1916 the government agreed to waive charges entirely for naval telegrams.[94]

The arrangements developed from scratch by Newton and Brown continued until the end of the war. Unfortunately the veil of secrecy that surrounds all intelligence matters has prevented a full assessment of the New Zealand contribution.

One of the more important considerations for the Admiralty when war broke out in 1914 was to ensure a regular supply of coal for the ships of the fleet, in all corners of the globe. This meant having sufficient supplies available and being able to give them to ships at sea. The size of the Pacific made it one of the more difficult areas in which to arrange supply.

The Admiralty had been particularly concerned for many years about the quality of coal used in its warships' boilers. Coal from some places, such as Australia, reduced speed and produced more smoke and an inordinate amount of residue, besides causing structural damage to the boilers. An example of the relative value of coals was provided by a trial in HMAS *Australia* before the war. To keep the propellers turning at 186 revolutions per minute required 16 tons of New South Wales coal, 12.5 tons of New Zealand coal, or 10 tons of Welsh coal.[95] Not all New Zealand coal was suitable for naval use, and coal for Admiralty use came from only two mines, Denniston and Granity, both near Westport.

From early in the century the Admiralty had stationed an officer responsible for inspecting supplies of coal in both Australia and New Zealand on the staff of the C-in-C Australia Station in Sydney. By 1913, however, the importance of coal from Westport had been recognised by the stationing of an officer there whose sole task was the inspection of the coal shipments as they went into the colliers.[96] After the outbreak of war this officer was assisted by a leading seaman, two stokers and two able seamen until he was posted away in 1915.

The Admiralty also chartered ships of the Union Steam Ship Company, a New Zealand concern, for use as colliers. This followed pre-war practice: in 1913, for example, the *Katoa* was hired to coal HMS *New Zealand* in Melbourne.[97] Apart from the ships of the New Zealand Division, these chartered ships met the needs of ships both of the China Squadron and the Japanese Navy operating in the area.[98]

The quantities of Westport coal required by the Admiralty, combined with the requirements for the Royal Australian Navy, created problems with the supply of coal for domestic use within New Zealand during the war. To overcome this it was necessary to import coal, mainly from Australia, for domestic use. Nearly 350,000 tons was imported in 1914, but, mainly through lack of shipping, imports for the next three years steadily decreased to just over 200,000 tons in 1918.[99]

By mid-1916 the Admiralty's coal requirements from New Zealand were approximately 7000 tons per month. The Australian Commonwealth Naval Board also obtained coal from Westport for ships operating off Australia. As the war progressed, the Westport Coal Company experienced serious problems in meeting the demand. Production suffered from miners enlisting in the NZEF: by early 1916 some 250 men from a workforce of 1100 had volunteered. The monthly output of the mines decreased from about 53,000 tons in January 1915 to around 36,000 tons in early 1916. At this point the Admiralty asked whether anticipated production from Westport would still be reliable, what alternatives were available and what steps were being taken to prevent further depletion of the workforce.[100] The New Zealand government responded that although, under the Military Service Act, it was not possible to grant exemption from enlistment by occupational class, employers of men in important industries could apply for exemptions, which would not be refused.[101]

Despite these assurances, the output of the mines continued to diminish, primarily as a result of insufficient labour. The Westport Coal Company was also concerned that continuing to supply coal to the Admiralty would diminish its ability to supply other customers, who were turning to its competitors and might be permanently lost. The Senior Naval Officer was sympathetic, temporarily discontinuing shipments of Westport coal to Singapore until early 1917.[102] This went some way towards alleviating the the company's concerns, but there was still an acute shortage of coal for domestic use in New Zealand. In January 1917 the government sought the use of four Admiralty colliers inbound to New Zealand for one or more trips to Newcastle to import coal, which was urgently needed to supply troop transports and the ships carrying primary produce to Britain.[103]

Less than two weeks later the Senior Naval Officer told the Governor that the Germans were perhaps intending to establish submarine bases near the Dutch East Indies and that there were reports of an enemy raider operating off Chile. Should these prove to be accurate, he warned, Westport coal, in adequate quantities, would be needed for Royal Navy ships. The present situation did not warrant resumption of the export of coal for the Admiralty, but this would be reviewed in early 1917.[104]

Noting the domestic situation, the Senior Naval Officer was able to reduce the quantities ordered for the Admiralty. Still, some 34,200 tons were shipped for naval use during 1917, although this was down on the 58,141 tons shipped in 1916.[105] There were still serious difficulties in meeting domestic demand, as the shortage of shipping constrained importation of coal from elsewhere. To add to the difficulties of both the government and the navy, the miners went on strike for three weeks in April 1917.[106]

In January 1918 the imperial government was asked to help arrange a few cargoes of coal to be brought from Newcastle, New South Wales, to New Zealand.[107] This request elicited the unexpected response that the Admiralty knew of New Zealand's difficulties in meeting internal requirements and had not shipped coal from Westport for many months.[108] One can understand the somewhat mystified reaction to this statement, given the export figures already quoted and the fact that up to mid-February 1918 2486 tons of coal had been shipped during the current year and a further 3336 tons had also been requisitioned.[109] And these quantities were for Admiralty use only and do not reflect the total picture, which included the requirements of the Australian Commonwealth Naval Board.

To overcome the supply difficulties, the government strictly regulated the coal industry: the output of every mine was directed to specific areas and uses. Although unpopular, these measures, combined with additional imports, meant domestic requirements could be met in 1918 and 1919. New Zealand certainly 'did its bit' for the naval war effort in the supply of coal for the ships, but it could have done more if measures had been implemented to maintain production from Westport at pre-war levels and adequate imports for domestic use had been arranged.

Although the mines laid by *Wolf* brought the naval war to the shores of New Zealand in 1917, a considerable number of men had made their way to that war overseas, serving with the Royal Navy. Some were in the service before the outbreak in 1914, but most joined for the duration of the conflict. They served in every theatre and in every type of craft, from ships of the Grand Fleet in the North Sea to motor launches in the Mediterranean, in the air with the Royal Naval Air Service, beneath the waves in submarines and even in a naval armoured car unit in Russia from 1915 to 1917. A number of these men were decorated for gallantry, including Lieutenant-Commander W.E. Sanders RNR, who was awarded a Victoria Cross for his work in Q ships, camouflaged warships designed to destroy U-boats that were lured into their vicinity.

18

FROM BURN TO BANNERMAN:
NEW ZEALAND AIRMEN COME OF AGE

Vincent Orange

Somewhere in his numerous writings Sir Winston Churchill reflected on luck in wartime. Two soldiers crawl towards a tree, he wrote: one decides to go around it to the left and is at once shot and killed; the other makes his way around it to the right and survives to enjoy a long, successful career full of private joys and public honour. True enough, although in many cases, including the two New Zealanders I will talk about, their choices were made *for* them. Also, one of them fell victim to that ancient military maxim: 'Don't get involved in the early stages of a defensive war. Wait until realistic training and effective equipment permit you to mount a massive offensive.'[1]

I do not know what the unlucky William Burn, murdered in Mesopotamia (then 'Turkish Arabia',[2] now Iraq) only a few days after his 24th birthday, could have done to avoid finding himself at the left of the tree, given the inadequate aeroplane he was obliged to fly. He was the first of our military air casualties – and the first to receive official recognition for exploits in the air, being twice mentioned in dispatches. As for the more fortunate Ronald Bannerman, who died at home in his 88th year, I doubt if his courage and skill – and he had plenty of both – were greater than Burn's, but Bannerman was able to fight his war from the cockpit of an infinitely superior aeroplane. He became our most successful combat pilot of the Great War, earned the Distinguished Flying Cross twice and during the Second World War rose to the rank of air commodore, became a member of the Air Board responsible for personnel and was appointed a commander of the Order of the British Empire.

William Burn, an airman of limited experience, was involved in one of the greatest military disasters in British history; Ronald Bannerman, carefully trained over a long period, played a significant role in one of Britain's greatest military triumphs. The aeroplanes they flew illustrate just as starkly the contrast in their fortunes. The two-seater Caudron G. 3 biplane flown by Burn was fragile, slow, unarmed and already obsolete even for training purposes when the Great War began, [3] whereas the Sopwith Dolphin flown by Bannerman 'was probably the RAF's best operational fighter' when that war ended. [4]

Although he was born in Melbourne in July 1891, Burn's parents were New Zealanders and the family, apparently without William's father, was back home in time for him to be educated at Christchurch Boys' High School. Even for that tragic generation, the family's suffering was exceptional: William was killed at 24; his brother Robert, serving with the Canterbury Mounted Rifles, was killed at Gallipoli only a week later, aged 27; his other brother, John, remained a civilian, but died at 30 in January 1919, a victim of the influenza pandemic; and a foster-brother, Jack, a 15-year-old pupil at St Andrew's College, Christchurch, was lost off the ferry *Maori* only a few days later. [5]

William Burn was commissioned as a regular officer in the New Zealand Staff Corps in Wellington in August 1911. A confidential report in May 1912 described him as 'tactful, energetic and resourceful and likely to make a good officer'. Like so many young men of his generation, he was enthralled by the newly discovered wonders of powered flight and persuaded his superiors to send him to England, where he arrived in September 1913. He began to master this dangerous art at the Central Flying School, Upavon, Wiltshire, and earned his 'wings' in April 1914. Among his fellow pupils were several who became famous airmen: Amyas Borton, Lionel Charlton, Wilfrid Freeman, Hugh Dowding – and one who became a notorious daredevil: Christopher Draper, 'the Mad Major'. [6]

Burn returned home in September 1914 and despite his hard-earned flying skill was employed as Adjutant of 3 Auckland Infantry Regiment. In the following April, however, he was lent to the Indian government, in response to a request for trained pilots to serve in the Mesopotamian campaign. He was at that time 'the only qualified aviator belonging to the Defence Forces of the Dominion'.[7] On arriving in Bombay, he was attached to the Royal Flying Corps in what became known as the Mesopotamia Flight on 1 May.

Mesopotamia (now Iraq) was of acute interest to the British Empire from about 1900, partly because of growing German commercial and political influence there, and partly because of the discovery of oil in the region. This discovery led to the creation in 1909 of the Anglo-Persian Oil Company (APOC). A site for a refinery was chosen on Abadan Island, on the Shatt-el-Arab south of Mohammerah. Early in 1914, the British government obtained a controlling interest in APOC, and the Ottoman Empire's decision in November to side with Germany in the Great War caused intense alarm for the safety of the oilfield and its pipeline (only 35 miles from Ottoman territory) and for the vital link with India and Australasia through the Suez Canal.

An 'Indian Expeditionary Force, D' occupied Basra in November and set up a strong base there. Although the Turks failed to drive out the IEF in January 1915, a need for aerial reconnaissance was obvious, so during April an aerodrome and supporting facilities were set up on a site close to Basra. Captain Hugh Reilly,[8] a New Zealander serving with the Indian Central Flying School, arrived to command a small unit of Australian pilots and observers, plus William Burn. Equipped at first with four Maurice Farman Longhorns and one Shorthorn – all in poor condition, some lacking even engines – this ramshackle outfit was reinforced by two Caudrons in July.[9] Tragically, a sensible plan to protect the oil refinery at Abadan and its pipeline to the coast was escalated by ambitious generals into a campaign to occupy Baghdad, nearly 300 roadless miles from Basra, using the Tigris, 'a tortuous and uncharted river of reefs and sandbanks flanked by marshes and inhospitable desert'. The result was 'a military disaster so total yet unnecessary, so futile yet expensive, that its like did not occur again until the fall of Singapore in 1942'.[10] Mercifully, it was also one of the few major British campaigns in either world war that did not cost the lives of a host of New Zealanders.[11]

And yet, even before the tragedy began, one of its principal advocates, Major-General Charles Townshend, had written these words:

> All these offensive operations in secondary theatres are dreadful errors in strategy: the Dardanelles, Egypt, Mesopotamia, East Africa – I wonder and wonder at such expeditions being permitted in violation of the great fundamental principles of war, especially that of Economy of Force. Such violation is always punished in history.[12]

Burn's last flight was as an observer in a Caudron piloted by George Merz, an Australian who had received 'a scientific training' at Melbourne University and was the only officer of his training course to earn a distinction in the theory of flight.[13] But the Caudron's air-cooled Gnome rotary engine was unable to cope with the very high temperatures in that part of the world; worse still, the aeroplane was unarmed.[14]

Between 5 and 6 a.m. on the morning of 30 July 1915, both Caudrons were returning separately from the Nasiriya area (at the point where the Euphrates and Shatt al Hai rivers join) to Basra, a distance of about 110 miles: a very long way for uncertain engines of no more than 80 horsepower. One machine, piloted by the flight commander, Major Reilly, lost power and, unsighted by the other, landed near a village that happened to be friendly. Reilly made repairs and flew safely on to Basra. Meanwhile, the other machine was forced to land in the desert some 20 miles south-east of Nasiriya. Merz and Burn were immediately attacked by a number of well-armed Marsh Arabs. They fled on foot for several miles towards Basra, to a place where British and Indian soldiers guarded a fuel dump. Armed only with revolvers, Merz and Burn fired at their pursuers whenever they came within range, killing one and perhaps wounding five more. Then one of the airmen – we do not know which – was wounded and fell and the other gallantly stood over him until the Arabs came up and murdered them both. Later, search parties sent out from the fuel dump and from Basra found no trace of either man, but their Caudron, badly damaged, was found and taken by truck into Basra. Their names were – and I hope still are – commemorated on a memorial in Basra. William Burn was the first New Zealand airman to lose his life on active service, George Merz the first Australian. A street is named in his honour at the Royal Australian Air Force base, Point Cook, where he learned to fly.[15]

Major Reilly wrote to a friend in India on 6 August, when he still hoped that Merz and Burn were prisoners, explaining that his flight had done all it could during the fighting for Nasiriya. 'It was a pity we had no wireless,' he added, 'we could then have given the artillery some very useful information about their fire. But we had only smoke balls, and they can only be used to signal results if the artillery are prepared to cease fire and then let us have one round at a time on previously selected targets.' Although Reilly found the Caudrons 'slightly faster' than the Farmans and better climbers, he thought them 'very bad for observation purposes' and useless as bombers.[16] Duncan Grinnell-Milne, a notable pilot who wrote a delightful account of his war service, thought the Caudron 'was a nice little machine' which 'could do about sixty miles an hour when hard pressed'. Compared with the Longhorn, it 'climbed remarkably fast', but the Dolphin of 1918 far outclassed it in every aspect of performance.[17]

Burn had written to his mother on 25 June 1915. The letter, which she made available to the Christchurch *Star* early in August, after he was reported missing, echoes the sentiments of so many young New Zealanders and Australians of that generation.

> If we all try to do our job we can't help winning but I am very much afraid that the people of New Zealand are too far away from the war areas to realise the real state of affairs…. I little realised when I was in Auckland how much men were needed, and I believe that if the average man in New Zealand heard some of the tales I have heard the whole male population would clamor to enlist. The New Zealand soldier when he enlists only has a very hazy idea of how much he is needed, and thinks that soldiering is a rather sporting way of serving his country. When a parent loses a son, or a sister a brother, in this war, the more dear he was to them the prouder they should feel in the knowledge that he gave his life to his own country.[18]

His mother received from Major-General G.V. Kemball, Chief of the General Staff, Indian Expeditionary Force, 'a very valuable' map made by her son during a reconnaissance in June, 'as a memento of him'.[19]

As a marked contrast to Burn's short and unlucky career, let us turn to the long and altogether better favoured life of Ronald Bannerman, born in

Invercargill in September 1890 and thus 10 months older than Burn.[20] Bannerman was educated at Otago Boys' High School and Otago University College, where he studied law. By 1916, he was a company sergeant-major in 1 Battalion of 4 Otago Regiment. Like Burn, he wished to make his mark in the air and enrolled at the seaplane school, in Kohimarama, Auckland, in March 1916. He obtained his Royal Aero Club certificate on a Curtiss flying-boat in December – the last of his class of 12 to qualify – and sailed to England.[21]

Bannerman was commissioned in the Royal Flying Corps in March 1917 and spent the rest of that year learning to handle a wide variety of aeroplanes, all far more advanced than Burn's Caudron. In February 1918, he was posted to the freshly formed 79 Squadron, equipped with a new fighter, the Sopwith Dolphin, which was very fast in level flight and able to reach a very high ceiling quickly; it could also carry four 25-pound bombs under the lower wings. Modern though the Dolphin airframe was, its stationary 200 horsepower water-cooled Hispano-Suiza engine had serious defects that needed numerous modifications. In fact, many were put into service 'on the plea that engines of incomplete efficiency were better than none at all', in the words of H.A. Jones, the British official historian. 'A pilot who knows that he must mistrust his engine,' Jones sagely remarked, is in a 'bad plight because he is aware that when the engine fails, all his qualities, no matter how brilliant, will avail him little.'[22] Bannerman's logbook records numerous engine failures, and in such circumstances his achievements in combat, as well as on patrol, escort or ground-strafing duties, are all the more remarkable.

According to an account of 79 Squadron, 'The Dolphin was a most unusual aircraft. A complete change from the other ships of the family line, the Pup, Triplane, Camel and Snipe', it looked 'more like a whale than a sleek dolphin' and many pilots disliked the placing of the upper wings slightly behind the lower wings. It could be armed with no fewer than four machine guns – two Vickers on the engine cowling and two Lewises above the cockpit – making it Britain's first multi-gunned fighter.[23] In service, however, the Lewises were often dumped because the extra weight, including ammunition, impaired performance and they were impossible to aim accurately.

Oliver Stewart, who flew the Dolphin, agreed that in 'general layout' the plane 'was extraordinary', but, in his eyes at least, 'it was not an ugly aeroplane, and it certainly looked like an efficient fighting machine', giving its pilot 'the best possible outlook upwards' and a 'reasonably good outlook forwards and downwards', but not to the rear and downwards. When the engine functioned properly, the Dolphin had an excellent top speed of nearly 130 miles an hour.[24]

The squadron flew to France and settled in at Estree Blanche, south of Dunkirk, on 22 February to get ready for active service.[25] The commanding officer was Major Maurice Noel,[26] a noted pre-war pilot who has been credited with the famous reconnaissance in August 1914 that reported General von Kluck's change of direction away from Paris, which resulted in the Battle of the Marne – that wartime rarity, a *decisive* battle. The squadron made a long move (some 80 miles) to Champien, south-west of St Quentin, early in March to join two Camel squadrons and form No. 9 Wing.

On 21 March 1918, the Germans began their Kaiser's Battle, a huge offensive that cost both sides a total of 30,000 casualties a day for the next 16 terrible days.[27] The onslaught forced 79 Squadron to move north again, to Beauvois, west of Arras, where it stayed for about seven weeks. Bannerman was promoted to lieutenant on 1 April, the day the Royal Air Force was created.

Willie Fry, an experienced pilot, was posted to 79 Squadron, arriving late in April 1918. The squadron, he recalled, 'was not yet fully functioning owing to engine troubles'. Also, the pilots 'were nearly all inexperienced and were making frequent forced landings, which affected the squadron's use as a fighting unit'. Its performance only began to improve, thought Fry, when a capable warrant officer arrived to organise the workshop and iron out the engine troubles. The squadron was based some distance behind the front and Fry

> found the complete isolation from the war, except when in the air, to be depressing … at Beauvois we were in touch with nothing and I feel that had a dispiriting effect on morale…. One of the first things I found out was that we were expected to stay up longer on patrol, the Dolphin having greater petrol capacity and longer endurance, and that we were expected to escort bomber and reconnaissance formations for longer distances over any part of the front. All the same, we could not get going as a really efficient unit.[28]

The squadron made its fourth move in three months from Beauvois on 16 May to Sainte Marie Cappel, close to the Ypres salient, where it was one of seven squadrons in No. 11 (Army) Wing. 'Things began to look up when we got there,' recalled Fry, 'for we were nearer the war and more in touch with events, and were at last beginning to get on terms with our Hispano engines.' Fry, however, crash landed on the aerodrome on 27 May, his last flight with the squadron, and was later diagnosed as suffering from 'Flying Sickness D', a bland way of saying that his body and mind had had enough.[29]

A month later, on 23 June, Maurice Noel was succeeded as commanding officer by Major Anthony Arnold, who soon proved himself a dynamic commander, earning the affection of his air and ground crews.[30] Within a month, on 18 July, the Allied armies, at last under a single commander, had begun a counter-offensive that drove the Germans back in increasing disorder and achieved a complete victory by early November.[31] Both before and after that exhilarating offensive began, Bannerman was in the air on most days, training, testing engines, 'showing a new chap the line', escorting bombers, firing at ground targets, and dropping a few light bombs as well as engaging in aerial combat. His name appeared in 'comic cuts', more reverently known as official communiqués, far more often than that of any New Zealander, apart from the legendary Keith Caldwell.[32] Bannerman, wrote Arnold in May 1919, 'shewed himself to be a thoroughly efficient and reliable officer, and a very good pilot indeed'.[33]

Bannerman's combat reports, like most others, are carefully drained of colour, but one at least is worth quoting as an example of what can be read between the dry lines. About 9.45 a.m. on 22 August, he spotted west of Bailleul a DFW. This was one of Germany's most effective two-seaters, in performance and armament, as that great pilot James McCudden ruefully testified, after pulling out of a fight with one in December 1917.[34] Bannerman dived, but both guns jammed, and the DFW fled eastward. 'I remained about the line until I saw the enemy aircraft coming back. I went down again to his level, having got my guns working again, and met him head on and opened fire at fairly close range. I followed him down to 2,000 feet, firing about 300 rounds in all. He went down out of control … but I did not see him crash.' Bannerman hurried home, grabbed another Dolphin and returned to look for his victim. 'He was lying very badly crashed,' he reported, 'and his tail was broken.' Bannerman thereupon took the opportunity to practise his ground shooting by firing at the wreckage: if the two Germans had still been alive, he left them very dead indeed.

For fighting in Flanders at the end of September, No. 11 (Army) Wing, now of eight squadrons, was attached to General Sir Herbert Plumer's Second Army and in October 79 Squadron made its fifth and last wartime move, to Reckem, south-west of Courtrai, to support Plumer's advance.[35]

During the last eight months of the war, Bannerman flew the Dolphin for more than 330 hours. Allowing for leaves and 'dud days', that figure amounts to at least one and a half hours every flying day. He drove down 'out of control' 22 aeroplanes and had 16 confirmed victories, including one observation balloon, to his credit. These successes, better than one every week, were all achieved in just seven months, from April to November. The most recent research confirms these figures.[36]

Only four squadrons flew the Dolphin on operations and 79 Squadron proved to be the pick of them,[37] credited with a total of 73 confirmed victories (64 aeroplanes and nine observation balloons), setting aside their many 'out of control' claims. Bannerman and an American pilot, Lieutenant Francis Warrington Gillet, from Baltimore, Maryland, were by far the star performers, being credited with 32 of those victories between them. They were also awarded four of the squadron's six DFCs.[38]

'During recent operations,' reads Bannerman's first DFC citation, awarded on 16 September, 'this officer has done gallant service. While on an offensive patrol with two other machines he was attacked by several Fokker biplanes and, in the engagement, he shot down one. In addition, he has destroyed four other enemy machines.'[39] According to the citation of his second DFC, awarded on 9 October, he was 'A bold and resolute leader, whose ability inspires confidence in those who serve with him. During the operations in September he accounted for six enemy machines, displaying marked courage and judgment.'[40]

Bannerman returned to England in December 1918; he served with the Army of Occupation in Belgium and then as an instructor in fighter tactics and aerobatics in Britain. He was back in New Zealand by early September 1919. He became a successful lawyer in Gore and found time for serious fishing and gold prospecting in Otago, Southland and on the West Coast. He also continued his military service, first with the Otago Regiment and then with the Southland Regiment until May 1924, when he transferred to the Territorial Air Force, retiring as a flight lieutenant in June 1930. A decade later, in September 1940, then 50 years old, Bannerman returned to regular service with the RNZAF, enjoying high office and retiring as an air commodore at the end of the war. He died in Gore on 2 August 1978, in his 88th year.[41] He thus outlived William Burn by more than 60 years, receiving, in Hamlet's words, fortune's 'rewards' and not her 'buffets'. But both men, like so many of their contemporaries, were exactly equal in the *quality* of their service: they gave all they had to New Zealand's distinguished role in resisting the aggression of Germany and her allies.

PART 3

ASPECTS OF SERVICE OVERSEAS AND AT HOME

19

A DIFFERENT SORT OF WAR:
THE EXPERIENCE OF NZEF TRANSPORT DRIVERS

Graham Langton

The usual images of war in France and Belgium between 1915 and 1918 focus on the difficulties, destructiveness and futility of the trenches. This is encapsulated in titles such as Chris Pugsley's *On the Fringe of Hell*, or more ironically in *The Great Adventure* edited by Jock Phillips and others. Ben McIntyre, in *A Foreign Field*, describes the First World War as 'an obscene war of mud, lice, excrement, of death in stagnant ditches, meaningless sorties and courageous, long-forgotten raids, pointless offensives and counter-attacks'.

But for some soldiers involved in supply activities behind the front lines, the experience of war was rather different. Les Collis and Andy Jamieson from the Manawatu district of New Zealand were two ordinary soldiers in the Army Service Corps (ASC) whose hard work as transport drivers helped to maintain the front lines. Julia Millen's *Salute to Service* outlines the general story of the Army Service Corps in the First World War, but it does not include much detail from the transport driver point of view.

The diaries of Collis and Jamieson, transcribed for their families, show a different sort of war from that experienced in the front-line trenches. The tiny and difficult handwriting of the brief diary entries made by Collis and Jamieson reveals a war of horses and GS (General Service) wagons, of frequent and repetitive movement behind the lines. It was often a monotonous and tiresome war, with the occasional unexpected danger. But in some ways their wartime tasks were not too dissimilar from their farming activities at home. They were sustained also by their faith, regular letters from home and frequent meetings with neighbours and relations from the Manawatu. All these made their war bearable and their transition to life after the war relatively straightforward. Les Collis was from Kairanga and Andy Jamieson from Longburn, both small settlements outside the main Manawatu town of Palmerston North. These two men were fairly typical of soldiers from rural backgrounds, young, active and practical. Neither was very big, even by the standards of the day. Each man was about 5 foot 5 inches, strong and wiry, with Collis over 9 stone in weight and Jamieson a little under.

Jamieson enlisted first, after the initial enthusiasm for the war, on 26 May 1915, at the age of nearly 24. He left New Zealand on 9 October 1915 and saw brief service in Egypt before being transferred to the Western Front. He kept a sporadic diary from 1915 to 1918 and was finally discharged from the army in New Zealand on 24 June 1919.

Collis enlisted on 27 January 1916, aged 21, and left New Zealand on 19 August 1916. After further training in England, he served in Belgium and France before returning to New Zealand for discharge on 7 June 1919. He made a diary entry for every day in 1917 and 1918, and also summarised his military experience before and after those years.

These men had much in common before their wartime service and they were probably acquainted. Both had served in the Territorials before the war, and enjoyed riding motorbikes for recreation. They were brought up on farms, the children of hardworking, second-generation Pakeha settlers. Each was from quite a large family, with other relations nearby. They were all church-going people, and Collis and Jamieson were sincere Christians. Neither was intensely interested in sport, though Collis records watching and playing football. Drinking alcohol, gambling and chasing women were not part of their nature. Indeed, the boozing he saw in the war put Collis completely off alcohol.

Andy Jamieson had left the family farm and qualified as a cabinet-maker by the time war started, while Collis worked on his father's farm after he left school. Both had good practical skills. The one significant difference between the pair when they went away to war was that Les Collis had a sweetheart to whom he was strongly committed. Jamieson was a much more retiring man. Both had a quiet acceptance of the need to contribute to the war effort. They knew this was a war that had to be won and they were prepared to serve.

Transport in the First World War was a huge business, as it is in any war. Each driver had just a wagon and usually two horses, but they were part of an increasingly organised war effort – cogs in a huge war machine. Neither Collis nor Jamieson, however, seems to have felt overwhelmed by the scale of supply and organisation, and they kept diary comments on the work at a fairly personal level. They often did not mention that they were working as part of a larger group, though that may have been because of the limitations of space in their army-issued 'shirt-pocket' diaries. Nor did they comment much on French or Belgian people.

However, the lack of detail about the course of the war was usually because they did not really know what was going on, even close at hand. Les Collis was completely oblivious to the three main days of fighting at Passchendaele in October 1917:

4 October 1917	Went to dump for rations and to water station for water. A bit wet and sloppy. One good thing no bombs while this weather lasts.
9 October 1917	Nothing much doing. Went down to Watou to buy some cards to send home. Rum issue.
12 October 1917	Stayed in all day. Cleaned harness etc. Wet day.

Collis, Jamieson and other transport drivers conveyed a variety of material from dumps, usually at railheads, forward to advanced dumps just behind the front lines. The main 'stores' carried were food or rations, munitions and unit equipment. The troops in the front lines needed all three, and on a very regular basis. Only occasionally did Collis and Jamieson transport water, because that essential was usually loaded on specialist wagons if it was not available locally.

Other supplies contributed directly to the trench warfare. Guns and barbed wire were carried from time to time, while wood and bricks were common loads. Bricks were used not just in dugouts, but to build platforms on which guns could be stood. The horses used so extensively for transport also needed food. Collis and Jamieson record carrying chaff, straw, hay, oats and clover. A load of horseshoes was also necessary occasionally.

Then there were the less pleasant consignments. Coal, and occasionally coke, were brought up for the cookers, special wagons set up for other ASC personnel to cook on. Less commonly, coal was used for heating. Some of the fuel managed to find its way into the drivers' camps. Metal and cement were brought forward for making more permanent establishments. Ashes and manure, from the horses, were both loads taken away from the front lines to be disposed of further back. Neither Collis nor Jamieson records carrying sandbags, empty or full, though tens of thousands were used in the trenches and camps.

The main activities for the transport drivers were loading, conveying and unloading, but such a brief summation does not portray the hard physical work, the often poor conditions or the hassles and frustrations so frequently encountered. Early starts were common, as were late finishes, sometimes on the same day. The distance travelled in a day could be up to 30 miles, though usually it was much less. Shorter trips might be done two or three times in a shift, which put a lot of strain on both men and horses.

The weather was a factor that constantly affected their work. Sometimes it was too hot and dry. More usually it was cold, wet weather which made their work unpleasant. Even a day off could be unpalatable. On 25 February 1918 Les Collis wrote: 'Day in camp cleaning harness, wagons, etc. Cold miserable day.' 'Miserable' was an adjective he used fairly often. Conditions overall were not as bad for the transport drivers as in the trenches, but they faced plenty of challenges. At either end of the winter, rain and mud were the great difficulty; at the height of the frosts, wagon wheels could be frozen into the ground.

One of the difficulties for the transport drivers was boredom. There could be quite a lot of waiting around – for orders, for loads, or for people to shift what was to be carried. Les Collis often wrote letters while he waited, if it was fine, but in poor weather there was little the drivers could do except cultivate stoicism. There was also frequent repetition of tasks. On seven days out of eight in May 1916 Jamieson wrote 'Stores from Steenwerck' or its equivalent. Collis recorded long periods of carting bricks. On the other hand, some regular jobs, such as brushing the horses or working the harness, could be relaxing, even therapeutic, in their regularity and action.

A feeling of frustration was also common. Too often for their liking the drivers were sent to pick up certain materials, only to find when they got to the dump that the items had not yet arrived. On 26 February 1918 Collis recorded, 'Went to Reninghelst railhead for straw. Carted to 49th Div dump then to Ouderdon for coal but the train did not come in.' Three months later he wrote ironically, 'Up at 5 am. Went for a tour round France but did not do any work.' Sometimes they were sent home, not needed, or the fatigue party detailed to load the wagon did not turn up. Occasionally the drivers did all the work themselves, but they were more likely to return to base empty if help was not available to load. Fortunately for the war effort, there were usually men around to give assistance. There are also a few diary entries which show that the attitudes of British soldiers could be troublesome. On an autumn day in 1918 when he was tired from carting two loads of bricks, Collis 'Had a row with Tommy sergeant who took the number of my wagon', but nothing ensued.

Accidents, injuries and illnesses were never far away, but both Collis and Jamieson escaped fairly lightly. Their hands were vulnerable in the loading and unloading; the horses trod on their feet, and fairly often pushed them over. They preferred not to go to hospital, even when they fell ill, though Jamieson had eight days in a field hospital at the end of December 1916. There were plenty of bugs around in the dirt and filth, and the water was not of high quality for drinking either. Collis seemed to record every bath he had, and there were not many in two years. But the main problems for both men were the driving conditions and the horses. It could be very difficult to keep control of a heavily loaded wagon on a downhill slope. The edges of the roads were usually broken, so that horses and wagons ended up in the ditches that usually bordered the roads on either side. The horses reacted to the noise of shells and guns. On 20 January 1918 Collis wrote, 'Horses bolted about ¼ of a mile but managed to pull them in.' Sometimes it was the load that was the danger. On 23 December 1915 Jamieson recorded, '16 boxes loose shells which ran hot so had to transfer load to rear wagon' in case they exploded.

Guard duty was a common chore, usually on top of a full day. For Jamieson it was 'picket' duty, but Collis wrote it in the French way, 'piquet'. More of a burden was the frequent shifting of camp. Seldom did either of them stay based in one place for more than a fortnight, at the most; often it was much less. This unsettled aspect to their work did sometimes irritate them, but generally it was accepted as just part of the job. Collis often slept in or under his wagon. Both men used their practical skills in establishing bivvies and creating horse lines. A number of times Jamieson recorded working for a few days as a carpenter.

Their horses were a major part of the lives of Collis and Jamieson in wartime: they needed daily attention, feeding, watering, brushing and checking of their health and hooves. Less often, but still quite frequently, their wagons needed maintenance or repair. In fact Jamieson had mules most of the time until August 1916, but after that it was always horses, which were given names like Tom and Darky. A frequent diary entry was 'cleaning harness' but this involved more than just cleaning. The metal had to be polished but the leather had to be both cleaned and have some sort of softening agent worked into it.

Transport drivers such as Collis and Jamieson also faced an ever-possible danger from German attacks. In 1916 it was the 'Huns' who attacked, but by 1918 the common term was 'Fritz'. Sometimes the hazards came when the Germans were trying to push forward, but threats to the safety of the drivers were most likely when the enemy feared an Allied attack and attempted to disrupt supplies and communications. Danger could be frequent behind the lines. Jamieson was nearly shelled by guns and then bombed from aeroplanes on 8, 9 and 12 August 1917. A few months earlier Collis had come close to death a number of times. His diary included:

1 March 1917	Anti-aircraft guns in action. Large piece of shrap fell 5 yards away.
13 April 1917	Nose cap fell through hut about 3 yards from where I was standing.
22 April 1917	narrow shave with German shrapnel fired at captive balloon. Large piece landed 3 feet away.
23 April 1917	to railhead. 2 men injured with bomb from aeroplane and 1 dead.
24 April 1917	Shell case from anti-aircraft gun fell about 3 feet from team.

So, compared with the soldiers in the trenches, transport drivers faced less immediate danger, though their job was not without many different hazards.

Carting with horses and wagon was a regular job, unlike trench warfare where there could be periods of inactivity or training, interspersed with frenetic times of attack or defence. Transporting was not always pleasant, but it was not as wet and muddy as life often was in the trenches, nor as psychologically damaging. The drivers had rifles, but never fired them: they were not active in the fighting and killing. Life as transport drivers was closer to their ordinary existence back home than was war in the trenches, and this is one of the key factors which helped them cope.

There was nothing unique about Les Collis and Andy Jamieson, but they seemed to cope with the war fairly well, and after it they were able to get on with their lives, which turned out to be long, happy and productive. Like most soldiers they seldom talked about the war, though Jamieson carved a board with Dickebusch, the name of a village outside Ypres, near which he, and Collis, were based for a time. Other artefacts also generated questions and answers, but on the whole the two men kept their war private. Les Collis's son did not even know his father's diaries existed until they were found after his death in 1974.

Not talking about their military service overseas was one way of coping, but other aspects of their wartime experience helped them handle it, both in Europe and later at home. Some were aspects of their work as transport drivers, others were common to many soldiers. There were also factors more peculiar to these individuals.

The needs of the horses have been mentioned. Such animals were innocents in warfare, and animate beings to which the drivers could relate. Caring for the horses also occupied the men at times when they might otherwise have dwelt on their problems and difficulties. For Collis and Jamieson, both raised on farms, working with horses and wagons was quite similar to the farm work they had been brought up with, so in this way their wartime lives were not totally dissociated from their normal lives.

The postal service to the troops in Belgium and France was superbly efficient: both Collis and Jamieson received an enormous amount of mail, and wrote many letters. This correspondence ensured that they stayed in touch with life back home, and with friends and relations. On one page of his diary Andy Jamieson recorded 87 letters received. In the first six months of 1917 Les Collis recorded the receipt of 100 letters, plus two uncounted mails, one large, making a likely total of about 115 letters. In other words, he was receiving two letters every three days on average. Most of the mail was from home in New Zealand, but some was from soldiers elsewhere in the battle zone or in camps, and a few letters were from people in Britain. In the same six months Collis recorded writing 54 letters, but he actually wrote more, since by the end of the six months he was not always noting his outward correspondence. Communication by letter, and parcel, continued at almost this rate throughout the war.

A sense of humour was almost a prerequisite for survival in the First World War. Both Jamieson and Collis were quiet men, but they had an understated sense of humour that enabled them to observe their world with a wry smile. In a letter to his father dated 31 July 1917, Jamieson began: 'I am just sending you a few lines to say that I got through my leave in England quite safely. I never got lost and I was not robbed so that is not too bad is it.' After illness on the voyage to England Collis was sent to the Command Depot on the Salisbury Plains for those not fully fit. Less than a mile from the camp lay the little old-fashioned village of Codford, from which the camp derived its name. This was the only oasis of interest in the midst of a drab environment, but Collis was not particularly impressed. In late 1916 he sent his sweetheart a postcard showing the main street of the village, and on the back he wrote ironically: 'This is the main street of Codford. You will notice the Electric trams and also the uptodate buildings of the great Metropolis.'

Leave during the war was brief and infrequent, but was most welcome and important in providing some balance in life. On his one break Collis went to London and Scotland. Jamieson's diary records only one trip, to London and Edinburgh, but given the length of time he was overseas it is possible that he had another break as well. After the war, but while they were still in camp in England, each had another holiday in early 1919. Andy Jamieson ventured as far as the Shetlands where the Jamieson family originated, while Collis travelled to Cornwall to visit his sweetheart's family, including her grandfather. The holidays after the war helped to prepare them for civilian life. By the end of it all they had had enough overseas experience and were more than ready to settle down in New Zealand.

Both Collis and Jamieson had a strong Christian faith which gave them a steadfast assurance that all would be well. Services led by a padre on Sunday were important to them, especially Collis, and he seems, quite often, to have been able to use Sunday as a rest day and a time to meet people he knew. The YMCA was also important to these men.

Family back home in New Zealand were always vital to Jamieson and Collis, as they were for most soldiers, and the frequent connection through letters was important. The news from home gave a sense of the normal amid the abnormality of the war. Most family members wrote, siblings as well as parents. Since his mother had died before the war and his brother was also serving, Jamieson's main links were with his father and his sister Barb. Collis received considerable mail from both his parents, but his sister Alice, closest to him in age, was perhaps a more important correspondent. But for Collis, the most significant figure at home, whom he clearly thought about more than any other, was his sweetheart Edith Teague, known as Edie. He wrote to her often, as she did to him, and she received the most elaborate postcards.

Perhaps the most striking aspect of the war to come out of the diaries of Les Collis and Andy Jamieson was the family and community dimension to war in Belgium and France. These men kept meeting their relatives and friends there, so that the war always had a neighbourly dimension. In the first six months of 1917, most of which he spent in Belgium and France, Collis met 25 relatives and friends, mostly from the Manawatu. Some encounters were accidental, some arranged. Although the rate of meetings decreased a little after that as the war intensified, Collis seldom went more than 10 days without direct contact with someone he knew from home. Most frequently he met his cousin Jim Print, who was in the artillery and seemed to be able to leave the lines fairly often. Jamieson's diary is much more episodic, but among various similar occasions, he records meeting his cousin Jack a number of times in 1916–17 and then his brother Jim quite regularly through December 1917 and January 1918.

Through these meetings, through the mail they received and through their work with horses, Les Collis and Andy Jamieson were never out of touch with their ordinary lives. Given the dislocation of the war, and the negatives of so much of that experience, they came out of it in reasonable shape. In the juxtaposition of the normal and the abominable which gives any war, but especially this one, its peculiar, horrific character, the balance of the war experience, for Les Collis and Andy Jamieson, was clearly towards the normal.

Epilogue

After the mobility and uncertainty of war Collis and Jamieson were content to stay anchored in the Manawatu when they returned home to New Zealand. Les Collis married Edith Teague on 20 November 1920. Andy Jamieson, a much shyer man, did not marry Ellen Shailer until 1930. Collis was helped onto a farm near Kairanga by his father, while Jamieson, with other family members, purchased a property at Orua Downs in the Manawatu through the agency of the Patriotic Board. Collis was forced off his farm by the economic downturn of 1921, but with his father's help, again, he was on another farm by 1923. Later in the 1920s he developed hydatids, and had a major operation to remove the cysts, but in time he recovered fully. Both Andy Jamieson and Les Collis lived full, happy and satisfying lives, working hard on their farms and enjoying family life. Collis died in 1974 and Jamieson in 1980. Their diaries were published by their families in 1999 and 2001 respectively.

20

ON THE TRIANGLE TRAIL:
THE NEW ZEALAND YMCA AND THE GREAT WAR

Ria Keenan

Before the YMCA became known to a generation, via a collection of gay stereotypes, as a place where 'You can get yourself clean, you can get a good meal, you can do whatever you feel'[1], it was a service organisation known for its religious and recreational activities. The Young Men's Christian Association was started in England in 1844 by George Williams. One of the men who attended its London meetings, R.B. Shalders, emigrated to New Zealand and advertised the first programme of YMCA lectures in Auckland in 1855. The organisation spread to Christchurch in 1862, Nelson and Wellington in 1866, Dunedin in 1874 and Invercargill in 1876. These groups in each city were independent of each other until the formation of a national council in 1886. The activities of the early New Zealand YMCA consisted of Sunday afternoon Scripture groups, fortnightly Bible study lectures, choirs and evangelical meetings. In 1860 the Auckland YMCA imported gymnasium equipment from the United States and the organisation started the sport and recreation courses for which it is best known today.[2]

In the years leading up to the Great War the YMCA became involved in providing canteen services, writing and recreational rooms for young men at military service camps (referred to, rather unfortunately, by the National

Committee as 'Concentration Camps').[3] When war broke out the New Zealand government permitted the YMCA to continue their work in the Main Body camps at Auckland, Christchurch, Wellington and Dunedin and at the permanent training camp established at Trentham, but was initially reluctant to let them go overseas with the troops. It was not until after the Main Body of troops had arrived in Egypt and their off-duty recreational activities began to worry the authorities that the value of the YMCA's services was recognised. The British YMCA had established itself in Egypt with help from the Red Cross, and the New Zealand organisation helped to convince the New Zealand military authorities that field secretaries for New Zealand troops would help provide a more wholesome distraction for the troops than the fleshpots of Cairo.[4]

James (later Sir James) Hay was the first New Zealand YMCA field secretary to go overseas with New Zealand troops, leaving with the 4th Reinforcements in April 1915. Hay later went on to YMCA duties in France and finally in England.[5] In the next two to three years many more New Zealand YMCA representatives joined him overseas, sailing on the same troopships as the men or, in some cases, making their own way to wherever they felt they were needed.[6]

Although many different groups provided welfare workers for the New Zealand troops behind the lines, particularly the Salvation Army, which had its own huts near the lines, the most organised, and widespread, and the only one officially sanctioned by the NZEF, was the New Zealand YMCA.

The YMCA and the New Zealand Expeditionary Force

Although they were directed to get on with and be helpful to the commanding officer of the unit to which they were assigned, YMCA workers were not part of the NZEF hierarchy and their main purpose was to serve the men, of any rank or denomination. They were not commissioned officers, and until 1918 were technically not even part of the NZEF. They were either civilians whose pay was subsidised by the New Zealand army but who were medically unfit or too old for service, or men who had been on active service and invalided home.[7] In July 1918 the YMCA National Executive convinced NZEF Headquarters in London to attest all overseas YMCA secretaries and they became members of the NZEF, receiving army numbers. Not all YMCA secretaries, however, could get New

Zealand authorities to recognise the attestation,[8] a source of some concern for those who had served overseas and were unable to get pensions or the same benefits as returned soldiers.

The New Zealand National Council of YMCAs supplied money for the field secretaries' uniforms and paid for life insurance policies for each man. A total of 70 YMCA representatives served overseas during the First World War, including seven who travelled from New Zealand at their own expense to serve as honorary commissioners on the YMCA Executive in London. In addition 25 officers and non-commissioned officers acted as YMCA representatives on troopships returning to New Zealand. Although YMCA literature gives the impression that its field secretaries could be found in the front lines almost as often as chaplains, its casualties were lower. No New Zealand YMCA workers were killed in action; one YMCA representative died of sickness, one was accidentally killed in camp and two others were seriously wounded.[9]

By comparison, of the 140 chaplains on active service in the First World War, four were killed in action, one died of wounds, one as a result of an accident while on active service, one of sickness and one in 1921 as a direct result of his war service.[10]

The YMCA at the front and behind the lines

The YMCA's work was mainly behind the lines but they did take services up to the firing line, mainly what were called 'buckshee stunts' near the front: providing hot drinks, sweets and cigarettes to soldiers coming out of the front line. They worked from dug-outs or small lean-to shacks and barns if they were available. A popular piece of soldier slang that widened to mean a variety of things, buckshee initially meant a good, lucky thing such as free cigarettes, coffee, tea, chocolate, oranges or eggs and other treats rarely seen near the front. A modern-day equivalent slang term would be freebies or loot. YMCA field secretaries also helped with stretcher-bearing when needed, and burial details, they would even stand in for a chaplain at funeral services if no ordained man could be found. In France, if there was an attack planned, the YMCA co-operated with the Medical Services by caring for the walking wounded in tents or at refreshment stalls once a doctor had tended to them. They would sit the wounded down and give them food, drink, chocolate and cigarettes and offer a friendly ear to listen to tales of escape. In his history of the New Zealand Medical Services during the First World War A.D. Carbery noted that the food and attention made the wounded 'an easily managed and very patient crowd'.[11]

Coffee and tea were often in short supply and it was not always possible for soldiers to light a fire and brew their own, so the YMCA huts were often the only places to get a warm drink and a break from the war. As Ormond Burton mentions in his Auckland Regiment history, a well-remembered event during the campaign in France was a burst of German shellfire that ended the troops' two-up gambling rings but 'also destroyed the Y.M.C.A. Hut, quite a dastardly thing to do, considering that there, and there only, was the supply of hot coffee'.[12] Coffee, tea and cocoa were comforting, especially after being out in the cold and wet, or in a muddy, stinking trench. Hot drinks were a quick morale booster for troops and a tie to the comforts of home, a shred of civilised society amid the death and mud of the battlefront. They drew the men of a fighting unit back together again, reinforced social ties and gave the soldiers the impetus to get through one more day or night.

Behind the lines, the YMCA provided canteens and buffets where cheap and often free meals were available, as well as luxury items such as chocolate and cigarettes. There were reading rooms with the daily papers and writing materials for the troops to send letters home, bath houses and, in France, a Divisional Library that by 1918 contained more than 3000 books.[13] The YMCA also provided voluntary religious services, sporting equipment and organised games, events, opportunities for Bible study and, in conjunction with the British YMCA, arranged for visits by concert parties and lectures on 'general educational topics'.[14] When men were on leave, the YMCA provided cheap accommodation at hostels, sightseeing tours of towns or historical places of interest nearby, families to visit in London for a bit of normality, night patrols who would escort lost or drunken soldiers back to their lodgings, and information bureaux.

The YMCA also did a lot of work in military hospitals: most New Zealand troop hospitals and camps in England and France had a YMCA hut and free cinema unit attached to them. The YMCA helped to house the relatives of wounded soldiers who came to visit, though this was rare for New Zealand soldiers. Instead they often sent visitors on behalf of relatives who would report back, usually via a short note published in a newspaper or newsletter, but, if requested, a letter could be sent home with a full report of the visit. The YMCA provided recreational rooms for soldier hospitals, as many of the wounded, although requiring hospitalisation, could walk around and were often bored. Later in the war the YMCA also provided rehabilitation and arts and crafts programmes, aimed at preparing wounded or sick soldiers for work in civilian life through teaching them draughting, painting, weaving, carpentry and pottery.

The YMCA, military discipline and morale

The NZEF and the NZ YMCA developed a symbiotic relationship – the army needed the YMCA to supply welfare services and morale-boosting activities for its troops in order to maintain discipline during a long war, and the YMCA needed military assistance to transport its workers and supplies both at the front and in England.

The YMCA's no alcohol stance meant there was less drunkenness and more order and control at YMCA venues and events. Their safe recreational activities, such as sports, concerts and films, were an attempt to keep the troops from drinking, getting into fights, looting or harassing the local populace. Although these 'clean' activities did not appear to stop many New Zealand soldiers from contracting venereal disease,[15] the YMCA huts and events did encourage sobriety and a moral climate, and attempted to reintroduce the social controls that prevailed back home in normal New Zealand society.

Night patrols in London, conducted by many different national YMCA associations, were primarily aimed at discouraging soldiers from spending time with prostitutes, both to prevent venereal disease and to ensure that the soldiers did not lose all their pay at once: some could be sent home to wives and families. The New Zealand public, however, was protected from this side of the Kiwi diggers' wartime experience so the night patrols were often portrayed as helping soldiers lost in London find their way back to their lodgings. The patrols also helped drunken soldiers to avoid getting robbed – they were easy targets when inebriated – and discouraged pub crawls and fights.

The YMCA acted as a welfare safety net for troops on leave in London or Paris who did run out of money through spending it on women, liquor or both. The YMCA was one of the few cheap sources of accommodation and food in

London or Paris. The YMCA night (or morning) patrols would also act as clean-up squads to prevent, as far as possible, civilians from seeing soldiers lying in gutters with no place to go, causing embarrassment to the military.

The YMCA assisted with the maintenance of military discipline by encouraging troops to send word home to their families that they were well, and provided the materials and space to read and write quietly. These reading rooms were often the only peaceful places near the front. Contact with relatives and the world outside helped to distract soldiers and reassure them about family members fighting elsewhere. Letters and gifts from home, often distributed by the YMCA, boosted troop morale. The YMCA also ran a coupon scheme through which relatives in New Zealand could safely send money that could be redeemed at YMCA canteens to purchase food, cigarettes, matches, candles and other conveniences that made life in the trenches more bearable.

Because until mid-1918, YMCA workers did not hold a rank as chaplains did, some men found it easier to approach them for advice about personal or spiritual matters. The YMCA national association in New Zealand, however, was continually lobbying the NZEF to give YMCA field secretaries the same honorary rank as chaplains lest their service not be taken seriously.[16] If troops could get advice or confidential support from someone they trusted they were less likely to engage in drunken binges, or to wound or even kill themselves when they had personal problems. Such responses which could have a bad effect on other troops' morale and discipline. Through its huts and activities the YMCA created a homely atmosphere designed to help the troops to feel less isolated and unhappy about their time at the front and more as if they were part of a surrogate family within the military.

Relationship with the churches and army chaplains

The YMCA was careful to work with the churches, not against or in competition with them. The organisation realised, too, that it was much easier to conduct its activities with the support of chaplains and churches because they helped to provide resources and official sanction. A non-discriminating and non-denominational attitude to religion also helped to bring in money for the YMCA's work, as in the case of a Jewish congregation in London fundraising for a hut.[17]

Although the YMCA said it was not a church or religion in itself, it did have as its stated aim the reclamation of men back to their own churches and also evangelising to the unaffiliated, thus claiming souls for Jesus.[18] Some churches were suspicious of the YMCA's motives, thinking that the organisation wanted to take soldiers in a more evangelistic, dissenting direction rather than back to established denominations such as the Church of England. These suspicions would have been further deepened by the creation of an organisation called the Brotherhood of Men of Goodwill where Christians within army units gathered together for social events and discussion of religious and social issues. The brotherhood had several conferences during the war and relied on the YMCA for help in getting established and organised. Although it was also non-denominational, the brotherhood did emphasise evangelising and pledges, which were not common to some of the more traditional churches.

Many chaplains were glad to have the help of the YMCA, especially in providing such services as making hot drinks or supervising writing rooms, which were too time consuming and which some chaplains may have felt beneath them. They were also grateful for the use of the rooms, tents and Bibles provided by the YMCA when conducting their own services for the men. Some chaplains, however, suspected the YMCA was trying to take troops away from established churches and convert them to a more evangelistic brand of Christianity.[19] The YMCA for its part, was always very careful to point out in its literature that its workers were there to supplement regular churches, not replace them.[20] The New Zealand YMCA knew, too, that in order to implement its post-war plans, which included spreading the organisation throughout New Zealand and embarking on community work, it must gain the support of the church.

Troop reactions to the YMCA

YMCA literature, such as fundraising or awareness-raising pamphlets and newsletters, was filled with positive comments from soldiers. The YMCA was usually at pains to say that these comments were unsolicited, in order to overcome cynicism about the reasons behind the lavish praise and to counter any charges of self-promotion. One regular New Zealand YMCA publication was a newsletter called the *Triangle Trail*, which was published during the campaigns on the Western Front and distributed to troops and supporters in

England and France. The triangle is the international symbol of the YMCA: the three corners represent mind, body and spirit.

Much YMCA literature purporting to be by soldiers was anonymous or signed with a nom de plume. An example can be found in a *Triangle Trail* article by 'a muddied oaf, weary, tired and hungry' who came across a group of New Zealand soldiers gathered round a YMCA dugout, writing their home towns and comments on a map of New Zealand stuck to the outside wall. Every man, the writer reflects,

> will retain in his heart an everlasting gratitude to the YMCA. This institution caters for his needs and enjoyment in the camps, on the troopships, and, vastly more worthy still, it is the only patriotic association in existence that follows us right up to – and often into – the trenches.[21]

The Salvation Army and the Anglican Church Army might have begged to differ on this last point, as they also had welfare officers near the front lines and recreational huts in some soldier camps.

Ormond Burton's impressions of the YMCA were always positive, in stark contrast to the way he wrote about army chaplains, whom he described as mouthpieces for war.[22] Burton mentions the YMCA in every work he wrote about the Great War. This is probably because he took a personal interest in the association, serving as a YMCA secretary on the troopship that brought him back to New Zealand and becoming involved with the running of the YMCA's activities for boys in Wellington.[23]

A very different opinion of the YMCA and its work is expressed in the semi-autobiographical novels of John A. Lee, *Civilian into Soldier* and *Soldier*, in which his soldier characters react with disgust to the YMCA workers while on leave in London. They feel the YMCA offers cheap tea and scones only in order to lure men into taking part in boring and sanctimonious religious services. Lee portrays the YMCA as a place of last resort – once soldiers had spent their pay on drink and prostitutes it was the only place where they could afford to eat and sleep for the rest of their leave. In *Soldier* Lee makes it clear that he resented the YMCA for trying to take advantage of the situation to evangelise and thought even less of the literature available at their canteens: 'I reached for one of the saintly tracts lying around. The leaflet made war godly, saintly; trench-life tracts omitted the lice and the lethal obscenities. If there were lice on a soldier's body there was obviously none on his soul.'[24]

Most surviving soldier diaries are fairly neutral on the topic of YMCA field secretaries. For example, Private William Malcolm, writing from France in June 1918, describes in his diary how YMCA field secretary Horner gave him a map and 'was good enough' to help to find the location of his brother's grave. Once they had found the approximate location, Horner asked the pioneer sergeant of his battalion to build a cross to mark the gravesite and advised Malcolm that he could apply to have a photo of the grave taken and sent home.[25]

Some troops wrote equally negatively about YMCA field secretaries and army chaplains in their diaries and letters,[26] but others preferred the informal YMCA prayer services to the compulsory church parades run by the army and conducted mainly by chaplains (although YMCA secretaries would often also take part). The church parades were viewed with disgust and lack of interest by many troops who did not want to be forced into religious ceremonies.

The New Zealand YMCA needed the military for transport, assistance with logistics and for the official sanction that it gave to their activities, which helped the association to continue raising money. The YMCA also saw the troops as a source of many potential new members: it had high hopes of playing an expanded role in New Zealand society after the war with the help of large numbers of returning troops who would either become members or support the YMCA out of gratitude for its wartime services. The YMCA misjudged soldier enthusiasm, however. Once home and faced with a wider choice, most returned servicemen found their socialising needs better met at the pub, sports clubs or the new Returned Soldiers Association clubs which sold alcohol and had no religious function beyond the annual Anzac Day commemoration of the war dead.

Conclusion

YMCA workers went to war with a genuine desire to help soldiers and to see if they could impress upon them the importance of religion. The NZEF permitted YMCA workers to accompany troops and become part of the general workings of the army because it recognised the valuable morale-boosting services they offered and their contribution to discipline through trying to prevent troops from overindulging in drink and gambling or frequenting prostitutes.

The YMCA, in turn, benefited from its relationship with the military, as we have seen. The New Zealand public could feel that they were contributing to the comfort of soldiers at the front by giving money and goods to organisations such as the YMCA which distributed socks, sweets, cigarettes and other treats to soldiers. Families at home were also comforted by the impression that YMCA workers were keeping their boys out of trouble, visiting them in hospital and assisting with Christian burials for those who had died.

The success of the YMCA's work among the troops during the Great War was reflected in the decision that, in the Second World War, the YMCA and the Church Army should be the only organisations to administer patriotic funds from the public for the welfare of troops, as opposed to the confusing number of organisations during the First World War.[27] In the Second World War the YMCA was also given permission by the Catholic Church and New Zealand Jewish Congregations to act as their official troop welfare agency.[28]

'COME BACK WITH HONOUR': PROSTITUTION
AND THE NEW ZEALAND SOLDIER, AT HOME AND ABROAD

Bronwyn Dalley

Five hundred newly enlisted soldiers at Trentham getting ready to sail to Egypt in late 1914 found in their mail a copy of a pamphlet addressed 'To the Men of New Zealand from the Women's Christian Temperance Union of New Zealand' discussing the 'White Slave Traffic'. Chances are that these young men had never heard of the union, let alone white slavery – the enforced prostitution of women. There may have been a few raunchy comments about the pamphlet's subjects: 'immoral houses', prostitution and venereal disease were bound to raise nudges and winks among a group of single men, some barely out of their teens. The pamphlet's message may have generated loud guffaws: 'We make this appeal to the men of this country that for the sake of their women-kind, some of whom must inevitably be drawn into this traffic; for the sake of their unborn children; for their own sake, to do all in their power to stamp out this evil in all its branches'; 'Of those who have contracted disease we would ask that… they will now lay on the una for the fun of life alanger for the mer, but a most ann gaols and mental hospitals are being filled and overcrowded by the children of the dissolute.'[1]

The pamphlet was part of the WCTU's long quest to make men moral. War injected its rhetoric with a new urgency. A wartime issue of its magazine *The White Ribbon* implored soldiers departing New Zealand's shores:

Lads, come back with honour, or come not at all…

Protect every girl, ne'er cause one to fall,

Oh, come back with honour, or come not at all.[2]

Neither prose nor poetry worked. Perhaps the soldiers eventually came back with honour, but before that many certainly came back with something less desirable. Brothels were riskier than battlefields; soldiers were more likely to catch the clap than a bullet. The shifting debates about the First World War, white slavery, and prostitution and venereal disease are my focus. I am particularly interested in how the WCTU depicted and responded to these issues. The war offered a new context for the union's moral position. Heightened debates about the fitness of the fighting population highlighted the dangers of prostitution and the wastage to the war effort that venereal disease caused: 'The State has to be saved by service within New Zealand as well as overseas; the fight has to be against the social plague as well as against the Prussian plague'.[3] Inevitably, arguments turned on sexual and gender relations. The WCTU had once framed prostitution as a story of male aggressors and female victims. Such an analysis was not as straightforward, or as politically acceptable, when New Zealand men went to war.

Little white girls of tender years

The topic of white slavery recurred periodically in New Zealand between the 1890s and the 1920s. Internationally, there had been an interest among social reformers and feminists since 1885 when London journalist W.T. Stead published in the *Pall Mall Gazette* the sensational 'The Maiden Tribute of Modern Babylon', detailing organised child prostitution rings in England and France. An ensuing outcry, also in New Zealand, looked for and found white slavery in many places. There was a flurry of reform organisations and legislation to combat white slavery, as well as surveys to investigate its extent. Melodramatic novels, short stories and films – titillating, soft-porn accounts of women inveigled into a life of prostitution, misery and eventual death – added a spicy jolt to official reports.[4]

Considerably more words were expended on white slavery than the evidence warranted. Yet there was an established trafficking in women, to use the modern term, primarily from Central and Eastern Europe down through the Balkans, across to the Middle East, where Cairo was a stopping point, and on to Asia or the United States. Some women, like those today, worked unwillingly as prostitutes, while others were aware of what they were doing even if they had been forced into the work through lack of economic choice in their homelands.

There was a handful of white slavery cases in New Zealand in the first two decades of the 20th century. A few young women were duped into working in brothels either in New Zealand or overseas. Police kept a close eye on a group of French and Italian men pimping and operating brothels in Auckland and Wellington in the 1910s, and some of these men were convicted of white slavery offences elsewhere.[5]

Local interest in white slavery was primarily confined to the WCTU and religious organisations such as the Salvation Army. From the late 1890s the latter published stories illustrating the dangers facing women and girls. 'Motherless Maud: A New Zealand Rescue Story', for example, appeared in the March 1897 issue of *The War Cry* and recounted the tale of an 'innocent and unsuspecting girl' duped – and doped – into prostitution.[6] The WCTU periodically ran similar stories in its magazine, but preferred more investigative pieces. From about 1910 members explored the issue in depth. A series of articles in *The White Ribbon* discussed the situation in India and Asia before moving on to the local scene. The union concluded that there was no 'white slavery proper' in New Zealand, by which it meant large-scale trafficking rings, but its members knew of cases from Frankton to Dunedin. More importantly, the union believed that there was the potential for organised white slavery to occur, and that was motivation enough for it to act. In 1914 the president read a particularly emotive paper at the annual convention, and this led to the establishment of a committee to investigate the extent of white slavery in New Zealand and to suggest preventive measures. One of these was the pamphlet issued to soldiers: 10,000 of these were circulated within three months of printing.[7]

As with other scares about morality, crime and sexual behaviour, it was the idea of white slavery, its imagined extent and effects rather than its actual occurrence, which motivated social reformers. To groups such as the WCTU, the concept of white slavery was a powerful and flexible emotional tool. The union used the phrase to refer to anything they interpreted as women held in thrall. Barmaids, for example, were spoken of as the 'white slaves behind the bar', at the mercy of the drink trade. Attempts to regulate prostitution through legislative measures that penalised women but not men were seen as white slavery. It was, in effect, part of men's oppression of women: 'white slavers, brewers, sweaters of woman and child labour all opposed the enfranchisement of women', according to one WCTU member.[8]

The red plague

The WCTU's growing interest in white slavery coincided with public discussions about prostitution and venereal disease. The repeal in 1910 of the Contagious Diseases Act 1869 prompted much of this. The legislation had allowed for the compulsory medical inspection of women working as prostitutes, though not the clients who frequented them. New Zealand women opposed the legislation, just as women did in other countries that had enacted similar measures. By 1910 the local act had not been enforced for many years but its repeal renewed questioning of how to combat prostitution, viewed as the primary cause of the rising levels of venereal disease. As Minister of Justice John Findlay argued in the repeal debates, something had to be done to check the 'black plague' of disease: he wanted venereal disease made notifiable and incorporated into public health legislation.[9] The union would have nothing to do with compulsion: it applauded the opening in 1914 of the Christchurch Hospital Board's venereal disease clinic but urged that attendance should not be mandatory.[10] Over the next few years some commentators promoted the compulsory inspection of prostitutes, and their detention if found to be suffering from venereal disease. A few even suggested that affected men be detained as well.[11]

War changed everything, for venereal disease could seriously undermine the health of New Zealand's fighting men.[12] Even before the soldiers had left, military authorities confronted rising levels of venereal disease, and throughout the war – either at home or abroad – New Zealanders had the dubious reputation of the highest rates of venereal disease among the empire's soldiers. The exact levels were difficult to determine, but medical personnel estimated about one in six New Zealanders contracted venereal disease; others put it at 134 per 1000 men.[13]

When it became evident that soldiers were contracting venereal disease even before they departed for overseas, attention turned to their sexual partners.

Rather than acknowledge that the men may have made a conscious decision to visit brothels, military authorities, women's groups and the general public blamed women – and alcohol – for leading men astray. Newspapers, police, the public and military and women's organisations lambasted diseased women who enticed soldiers from the path of good conduct and good health. Prostitutes, or women earning money from casual sex work, were targeted in police clampdowns.[14] Military authorities worked in unison with police in Wellington in particular to identify and then close brothels that soldiers visited.[15]

Even though the WCTU was among those who sought to downplay the responsibility of soldiers in the state of their own sexual health, it looked carefully at attempts to police brothels and monitor prostitution lest, in its view, vice be made safe. Members met periodically with politicians to discuss measures to counter venereal disease. New Zealand politicians were careful not to offend women's groups, but some became impatient with the union. In 1915 WCTU representatives met Minister of Defence James Allen to discuss ways of preventing the spread of venereal disease among soldiers. The minutes of the meeting show Allen becoming exasperated with the union's uncompromising position on dealing with prostitution. He pleaded for advice, suggestions and information beyond what he interpreted as facile ideas such as stationing women outside the doors of brothels to shame men from entering. He was quite willing to listen to any feasible suggestion, 'but unless you have practical advice it is no good'.[16]

The union also roundly condemned the work of safe-sex campaigner Ettie Rout, who urged that soldiers be given prophylactic packs. Rout imagined what would happen when women's groups learned of her suggestions: 'This is what happens.... Everything is going on quietly and sweetly, and you think they're a rather sensible crowd of women after all, and suddenly somebody says something about "white slaves" or "licensed houses" and the whole lot go mad on the spot.'[17] Her prediction came true: a headline in *The White Ribbon* screamed 'The Maiden Tribute to Modern Mars' in a play on Stead's 1885 report. The article spoke of the shame in a New Zealand woman asking for thousands of young girls to be 'immolated' on the 'altar of Mars' to satisfy the needs of soldiers: 'she is practically asking for the White Slave Trade'.[18] Such measures were, for WCTU members, simply white slavery in another form. Chastity for both sexes, and the abolition of the drink trade which led men to visit prostitutes, were the best remedies, whether soldiers were at home or abroad. 'Continence is regarded now as feasible and good.... Most men can get on all right without sexual intercourse. So we want to say this to our boys: Purity is possible. This power is intended by nature for reproduction, and that alone. If you break this law you will suffer.'[19]

Feminist debates over white slavery and prostitution posited a polarised view of male and female sexuality. Men were sexually aggressive and demanding, subject to their strong urges; women were sexually passive or at least able to control their desires. The emphasis was not on pleasure but on sexual danger and protection for women from that. The challenge to men was to become more like women, taking charge of their sexual urges and being held to the same moral code; chastity was the most desirable state for all in the world of social purity.

Theatre of sensuality

For many years, Egypt enjoyed a reputation among Westerners as a mysterious land. It was 'a place at the very limit of the European imagination': a 'glorious idea, a splendid cultural fantasy. Egypt was the orient, a country of the mind, a grand theatre of sensuality, despotism, slavery, polygamy, cruelty, mystery and terror.'[20] The West found this mystical East both exciting and dangerous.

Egypt also had the more dubious reputation as a land of dirt and pestilence, and for the New Zealand and Australian troops, these two sets of perceptions came together. Poor sanitation went hand in hand with suspect morals: Cairo was, an Australian correspondent noted, 'home of all that is filthy and beastly'.[21] Towards the Egyptian men, New Zealanders and Australians could be racist, cruel and ready to believe that the 'niggers' were out to get them; contemporary accounts indicate that the Australians were worse in their sense of superiority over and cruelty towards Egyptians.

Dirt, disease and suspect morals did not stop the men from frequenting the local brothels. Prostitution had been legalised in Egypt since 1882, but before that Egyptian and French women worked openly as prostitutes. From the 1880s there was a stream of European sex workers, either 'amateur' or professional. Some of these worked on an involuntary basis, for both Cairo and Port Said were known as 'turnstiles' on the human trafficking routes from west to east. In *The White Slave Market*, published in 1912, Port Said was considered 'the deadliest spot on earth' with all nationalities 'intermixed in an unhealthy conglomeration of lazy lawlessness'.[22]

Contemporaries noted that the European woman had distinct advantages over her Egyptian and African peers in the sex industry. She was immune from a number of the regulations that governed the trade, including where she lived and worked. Most large Egyptian centres had clearly designated red-light areas with women working from the rooms in which they lived; European women could live and work outside such zones.[23]

The distinction between white women – Europeans – and non-white – Egyptians or Africans – was an important element in narratives of white slavery. Anti-white slavery campaigners emphasised how much worse white slavery was than 'ordinary' slavery, for the qualifier 'white' evoked a particularly monstrous relationship where white women were at the mercy of non-white men. Commentary on prostitution in Egypt drew this distinction, too. Here is the British vice-consul describing Cairo just after the First World War when he made a tour of its red-light district:

> Most of the women were of the third-class category for whom Marseilles had no
> further use, and who would eventually be passed on to the Bombay and Far East
> markets, but they were still European and not yet fallen so low as to live in the
> one-room shacks of the Wasaa which had always been the quarter for purely
> native prostitution of the lowest class. Here in the Wasaa Egyptian, Nubian and
> Sudanese women plied their one shilling trade in conditions of abject
> squalor.[24]

This was a pecking order of race and geography depicted through a sexual lens. Marseilles was the lowest rung on the European ladder of the organised sex trade before the plunge to the East. Cairo was the first, and therefore 'top' stop on that slide before the great descent to the cities of the East – Bombay, Singapore, Shanghai, Peking.

Egyptian authorities tightened up brothel regulations in 1905, defining a brothel, detailing the number of its exits and entrances, putting a minimum age limit of 18 years on the workers and requiring the women to have a weekly health check.[25] Local authorities had no control over European women and it was left to the foreign powers and the women themselves to attend to medical issues. By the end of 1915, however, all European women working as prostitutes were required to register and submit to an examination for signs of venereal disease that was growing at an alarming rate. Any woman working outside the recognised brothel zones in Port Said, Cairo, Ismalia and Alexandria was liable to arrest.

The rules were relatively easy to flout. Examinations could be very cursory, and certainly in other areas where there were similar health checks, doctors boasted of how many examinations they could get through: one claimed he could examine a dozen women in 30 minutes, while 'the record' was 120 in an hour. There is no reason to suspect Egypt was any different, and given the speed at which examinations took place, the opportunities for cleanliness were marginal and the risk of spreading infection high.[26] Women could also get their own doctors to issue a certificate for a clean bill of health, regardless of their condition. Cairo women, whatever their nationality, ran a brisk black market in certificates, selling and circulating them among themselves.[27]

With the arrival of foreign troops from the end of 1914, the trade in drugs, alcohol and prostitution increased, and local authorities had enormous difficulties in regulating prostitution when demand was exceedingly high. Egyptians viewed the British, Australian and New Zealand soldiers as sources of corruption in their country. They may have attributed the sudden growth in the number of prostitutes to the effects of the Allied soldiery – and bewailed it as one of the ill-effects of British occupation – but Egyptian men were content to reap the profits that women earned. The murder of one pimp in 1922 revealed the extent of trafficking over a number of years by Egyptian men with the connivance of senior British officials.[20]

Temptations of the flesh

The first batch of New Zealanders arrived in Egypt in Christmas week, 1914. Major-General Sir Alexander Godley, in overall charge of the NZEF and responsible for the training of the New Zealand troops in Egypt, took a realistic view of the situation he would experience in Cairo. He expected to lose about 10 per cent of his manpower to venereal disease in Egypt, so on the journey he prepared the New Zealanders for what lay ahead. He warned of 'the extreme danger of having any intercourse with native women' and said bluntly that 'syphilis in a most virulent form is most virulent in Cairo, and men having connection with prostitutes are running the gravest possible risks. Forms of venereal disease are far more severe in Oriental countries than in New Zealand or England, and such diseases are certainly far more common.'[29]

Godley may as well have saved his breath. Alcohol, drugs and sex were in cheap and plentiful supply and the soldiers wanted rest and recreation after the long voyage. The majority in the Main Body was young: 95 per cent of them declared themselves unmarried, 56 per cent were under 25 and 85 per cent under 30. No doubt there were those for whom training camp was the first time they had been away from the confines of home and family, and Egypt the first foreign place they had stayed in for any length of time, for diary accounts reveal their sheer wonder at the ancient land in which they found themselves.[30]

There was a veritable charge on the brothels. From the respectable confines of the YMCA's canteen at Esbekia Gardens, where tea and biscuits, fruit and other refreshments were on offer, soldiers flowed into the Wazza (Wazir) or Derb el Wasa'a quarter immediately behind. Known colloquially as the fish-market, it was also called the bull-ring by the New Zealanders. This name echoed that of their army training ground, but also evoked the macho pursuits conducted in the quarter, where an estimated 30,000 Egyptian, Nubian and Sudanese women, along with others from African states, worked as prostitutes. Another 20,000 or so women – mainly Europeans – worked in unlicensed, but officially tolerated, brothels, cafés or bars, all of which sold alcohol. Other estimates put the combined number of prostitutes as high as 60,000.

Two days after Christmas 1914, the ANZAC commander, General William Birdwood, noted that many of the Australians and New Zealanders were 'sodden with drink or rotten from women'. Within two weeks of their arrival, Godley reported that the bulk of his men in hospital – 174 – were venereal disease cases. For the Allied troops in general, Egypt meant a swift rise in the levels of venereal diseases, with the Australians and New Zealanders, always needing to be first, leading the way, and continuing to do so throughout the war. The New Zealand government and military authorities were loath to make public acknowledgment of the level of venereal disease.[31]

W.H. George, a Wellington executive member of the YMCA in Cairo, conducted his own investigation of the situation.[32] With chaplain Guy Thornton he visited the Wazza one evening and was horrified by what he saw: women 'shamelessly exposing themselves' with their pimps lounging beside them, and hordes of men in 'sodden stupefied condition' in the drink shops, 'ready victims of touts in wait to guide them to one or other of the innumerable low brothels of the most filthy and repulsive character situated in narrow, ill-lighted lanes running off the main street'. Outside the large brothels he saw queues of 30 or 40 soldiers waiting their turn. George and his companion were accosted several times, with one woman offering to expose her person for a shilling. The entire area, in George's view, was given over to 'an orgy of unrestrained licentiousness'.[33]

Accompanied by representatives of the Australian forces, George and Thornton visited the area again within weeks. In the following month, George toured the quarter with Ettie Rout, who had arrived in Cairo early in 1916. Rout made an early evening visit, between 6.30 and 7.45 p.m., and found the place already crowded with soldiers. They gathered in bars, drinking shops and dance halls, and formed long queues outside brothels waiting their turn. 'Bedizened and lustful women thronged the streets and doorways, many of them being embraced by soldiers.' Soliciting and enticing were openly carried on, and through the narrow partitions and thin curtains in some of the brothels Rout could see women and soldiers moving about in makeshift bedrooms.[34]

Soldiers themselves were, unsurprisingly, reticent about their sexual habits: the story of a visit to a brothel was hardly going to appear in a letter home to Mum. But there were discussions of prostitutes and visits to brothels in diaries, sometimes by men the writer 'knew', or the writer himself. One or two of the soldiers were blatant in their descriptions of the women. Trevor Noel Holmden, who at the end of the war married a daughter of Sir Robert Stout, referred in his diary to his sexual adventures in Cairo and Alexandria. Within the space of a week in January 1916 he reported the 'dirty little bitch cats' of Alexandria who demanded £5 for the night; he preferred to go elsewhere to be 'rather pestered' by 'painted tarts'. A week later he was at the Kursal in Cairo in the 'forbidden part of town' where he was frank about his sexual preferences: 'we do not roger the dirty little bitch cats but made them do the Cancan and then the 69'.[35]

Other soldiers were upset by what they saw in Cairo. They disapproved of any steps the New Zealand authorities took to try and prevent the spread of disease, such as giving soldiers early treatment. Lieutenant-Colonel William Malone wrote in horror and dismay of his fellow New Zealanders:

> many of them go off into Cairo and get into sore temptation... Then to my horror the G.O.C. (ours) [Godley] has approved certain measures for preventing certain frightful consequences of vice, so as to enable them to indulge in the vice with no fear of disease. At present we appeal to the man's better nature and to his morality at the same time letting him know the awful punishment of certain vice in this country. To do what is proposed is to destroy all moral restraint and lead to worse things... Right and not Expediency is the only sound rule in life.[36]

Godley claimed to be doing everything in his power to contain the level of venereal disease by trying to deter the men. He marched his troops through the Wazza in daylight so that they would see the place stripped of its night lighting; he opened a wet canteen at base in an effort to stop the men from travelling to Cairo for alcohol, that natural ally of cheap sex. Weekly 'dangle parades' were held to check for signs of disease among the soldiers.[37] Lieutenant-Colonel Percival Fenwick, the senior NZEF medical officer in Cairo, informed the Minister of Defence that he had visited many of the local brothels and, more importantly, made suggestions to the army that could, in his view, mitigate the growing evil. He had addressed the troops and warned them that venereal disease was rampant in the town, but he believed it wrong to issue preventatives as Godley had done when he ordered that the soldiers carry tins of ointment that could be used before or during intercourse. This, he considered, was an insult to the women of New Zealand, although he recognised the 'absolute need' to stop syphilis from returning to the 'clean country' of New Zealand.[38] The efficacy of the ointment was dubious anyway. Some women refused sex with men who used it because it caused vaginal blistering; enterprising New Zealanders sold the tins to Egyptians who used it to kill lice.[39]

Good keen men

Lying behind the reluctance to supply the New Zealanders with prophylactics until near the end of the war – and certainly not while they were in Egypt – was the possible implication that New Zealand's soldiers were less than respectable. Throughout the war, and beyond too, the New Zealand soldier was generally depicted as a shining personification of colonial masculinity: gallant, valiant, kind to women, children and animals, brave, cool under pressure, loyal, hard-working, true to the values of home and hearth even when separated from the domestic circle.[40] Even contracting venereal disease was not a crime, one military official noted in 1917, adding that afflicted soldiers were 'patriots, not prisoners'.[41]

The New Zealanders' involvement in some of the seamier sides of leisure time during the war were explained away or minimised. Among these episodes were two riots in the prostitutes' quarter of Cairo in 1915, when Australian and New Zealand soldiers ran amok, trashing brothels. The first riot, in April 1915, was presented as the troops' desire to 'clean up' the area and combat the high levels of venereal disease encountered there; the second, in July that year, was in retaliation for prostitutes robbing Australian soldiers, some of whom had refused to pay for the sexual relations they enjoyed.[42] The New Zealand version of the events has the Australians leading the way, but prostitutes giving evidence at a court of inquiry convened following the April riot did not distinguish between the men as they related the fear they experienced as their homes and workplaces were destroyed.[43]

The perception of soldiers as good blokes became difficult to sustain given the wastage incurred through venereal disease, but for the most part the image remained intact. The WCTU shared the view, even when soldiers were sent home from Egypt suffering from venereal disease. When it became known that 'our boys' faced temptations in Egypt, the union called for them to be protected from the immorality and disease rampant in the lowest quarters of the cities. It asked the government to bring pressure to bear on the Cairo authorities to prohibit solicitation, and to place the brothel area out of bounds to soldiers.[44]

The union emphasised the ill-effects of alcohol, for it believed that drink lay at the root of social problems and certainly played no small part in leading soldiers to visit brothels, whether they were in New Zealand or overseas. Union members preferred to see soldiers as prey to drink, and young innocents who were the unwitting victims of the false charms of evil older women. In New Zealand and overseas, importuning, painted women waylaid them in the streets, bars and hotels: 'it was not a fair thing', declared union member Lily Atkinson, 'to have innocent country boys exposed to temptation'.[45] Other groups echoed this. The RSA protested in 1917 that all the talk of venereal disease had caused unpleasantness between soldiers and their 'lady friends'. It took issue with public discussions of soldiers' health when everyone knew venereal disease existed among the civilian population.

In 1917 the WCTU published the story, perhaps fictitious, of Jack Frazer from Cargill's Harbour, a member of the NZEF in Egypt, a teetotaller who gave in to a desire for drink. Under the byline of 'The Widow's Only Son' the story noted: 'One drink was followed by another, and then with brain bemuddled and passion inflamed by alcohol he followed a fair-haired, painted and bedizened woman to her quarters. The "strange woman" had Jack in her clutches. Next morning, thoroughly ashamed of himself, Jack resolved never to touch a drop of drink again.' Jack contracts an incurable disease, and is invalided home where his long-suffering mother receives him 'with open arms'. Jack ascribes his downfall to the rum ration: 'Had I never had that I would not have touched the stuff in Egypt, and had I been sober that woman would never have got me'.[46] Military authorities themselves took this view too: 'Time after time', a medical officer from Trentham noted, men said 'that it was because they had been drinking that they fell prey to enticements which, if they had been sober, they would have been able to resist'.[47]

The union had made strong connections between prostitution, venereal disease and white slavery for several years, so its lack of commentary on the conditions of the women servicing the New Zealand troops, either at home or abroad, is noticeable. The place of Cairo in the international sex trade attracted no comment in discussions about prostitution during the war. As the war went on, and the venereal disease rate among soldiers rose – with all the wastage that implied – the union held fast to the line that purity was the only answer, that soldiers were basically good men who were falling for the temptations put in their way by bad women at home, in Egypt and then in London. Given the union's support of the war effort, such a stance is not necessarily surprising. These women had sons, husbands and lovers in the forces and it would have been a significant step for them to condemn their menfolk; better to see their predicament caused by alcohol than a desire to have cheap sex with strangers.

The WCTU's insistence on sexual purity and a moral interpretation of prostitution and venereal disease placed it out of step with public opinion. Both issues were being reinterpreted as medical rather than moral problems, with the answers lying in medication, education and treatment rather than injunctions to live a morally pure life. With the encouragement of Ettie Rout, the military authorities finally appreciated this at the end of the war and issued soldiers with prophylactic packs. Meanwhile, the union continued its moral stance after the war ended; in 1919 Nurse Chapelle wrote of women 'lying in wait' for tipsy soldiers who then contracted venereal disease, through the fault of others rather than their own choices.[48]

The union was certainly not averse to talking about sex, or gender relations. Indeed, aspects of its discussions about white slavery and prostitution were either potentially liberating for women – they should be free to walk the streets without being accosted by men looking for sex – or broke down some of the common perceptions of women as either respectable or fallen. But its emphasis on social purity was inherently conservative and, in the end, reinforced the idea that sexuality was about risk and danger, for all parties. And even though much of the union's creed had been to show that sex was most dangerous for women, in the difficult years of the war it was men, specifically military men, who were seen as the victims. In the interests of the war effort, ideas of sisterhood could become less important in the face of patriotism and loyalty to 'our boys', and the WCTU members' own roles as mothers of such men.

22

PREPARATION FOR A RURAL FUTURE: AGRICULTURAL TRAINING OF NEW ZEALAND'S FIRST WORLD WAR SOLDIERS

Ashley Gould

> Farming more than any other occupation demands knowledge, experience, and a certain degree of adaptability, and it is only courting failure to undertake a new and intricate business without serving some apprenticeship to it.[1]

The subject of this chapter is the military component of an almost forgotten part of our military history, namely the preparation and instigation of an education programme in agriculture and other subjects for New Zealand soldiers who were serving in Europe and the Middle East during and immediately after the First World War. The primary focus is agricultural training/instruction and education, but some comment is made on the broader aims of the NZEF educational programme. This story had a strong civilian and post-service component, the details of which are the subject of another study.

The dominions of the British Empire, Britain and its colonies and the United States all looked towards soldier land settlement as a means of both reincorporating returning soldiers in civilian life and continuing to develop rural economies or to reinvigorate reverted or waste lands. The New Zealand wartime authorities were not unaware of the difficulties of dealing with potentially inexperienced soldier settlers, and an agricultural training component formed a somewhat tangential part of its land settlement plans. Such a concern was not an isolated one within the empire or among the Allies generally.[2] Public and official debate concerning soldier settlement during the war had touched on the likely rural inexperience of returning soldiers, though this discussion was also partly related to longer running concerns about the establishment of institutional agricultural education in New Zealand.[3]

Despite positive utterances from the authorities in New Zealand, very little appears to have been achieved during the course of the war to provide training facilities for the 25,000 wounded and ill men and women who had been returned to New Zealand before the Armistice. The official view was that these soldiers and nurses, for a variety of reasons, did not wish to avail themselves of the facilities, albeit limited, that were being provided. Following the Armistice, discharged soldiers who sought training in agriculture were dealt with under two schemes provided by the newly created Repatriation Department.

The first involved subsidised attendance at 'State Farms', properties devoted to scientific research. The second option provided a subsistence allowance for soldiers to find positions with farmers on the understanding that they would acquire practical experience in the course of their paid employment. Dovetailing into this second scheme were the initiatives of several patriotic organisations providing funds to buy land for specialised training farms. The Repatriation Department also established a farm dedicated to the instruction of infectious tubercular patients.

An independent initiative came from the NZEF authorities in France and Britain and this is the primary focus of this chapter. Early in 1918, a diverse educational programme was put in place for New Zealand soldiers, including instruction in agricultural subjects. These formal classes were continued on the troopships returning soldiers to New Zealand. Those who, on arrival in New Zealand, remained in the NZEF for reasons of health recuperation were offered short instructional courses at hospitals, while more extensive facilities were eventually provided at sanatoria for longer stay tubercular patients. The 'guiding motto' of the army education initiative, according to the officer in charge, Captain J.R. Kirk, was 'the greatest good for the greatest number'.[4]

During debates on the Discharged Soldiers' Settlement Bill in 1915 and its 1916 amendment, MPs raised concerns about the need to train those men who might return disabled and whose best prospects for the future lay in light farming. Activities such as orcharding and vegetable growing, beekeeping and poultry-raising were considered appropriate and it was anticipated that the existing state farms could provide the necessary training.[5] In April 1916 the Department of Lands sought information about the arrangements, 'if any', that the Department of Agriculture was making 'to teach discharged soldiers farming'.[6] The Minister of Agriculture, W.D.S. MacDonald, outlined a role for the department in what appeared to be a substantial programme both for training returned soldiers on state farms and for providing practical training on special development blocks of Crown land. At the outset it was expected that inexperienced soldiers would be used to clear and fence virgin land.[7] Prime Minister Massey had informed James Allen, the Minister of Finance, that under 'an arrangement' with the Department of Agriculture a limited number of soldiers would receive training at the seven state farms, provided a class of instruction to suit the soldiers' requirements was available and local accommodation could be found.[8] According to *The Soldiers' Guide*, an information booklet for returning soldiers, the department 'would provide free of charge, instruction in all forms of farming experience'.[9]

Massey had certainly been aware of the shortcomings of the inexperienced soldier settler, who was no different to any inexperienced civilian settler, and, in 1917, chided those parliamentarians who 'imagine that it would be possible to make a farmer out of every man that returns'.[10] In 1917 William Ferguson of the National Efficiency Board (NEB) had outlined the central difficulties of settling soldiers without adequate farming experience. For Ferguson the issue was one of economics: how to bear the burden of the cost of the war and ensure that New Zealanders' standard of living was not endangered. To do this would mean operating existing farms 'on improved methods with less loss of time and energy than has been the custom in the past'. Land settlement of the kind proposed required that the settlers be 'properly trained, so as to produce in a scientific manner, and not as in the past, to stumble into a method of production through their own practical experience with very little real or scientific guidance'.[11] In June 1918 Ferguson informed Allen, then acting Prime Minister, that

> the method adopted of placing soldiers upon the land without having had previous experience and training, is faulty, and [the NEB] believes that in this

view they are supported by those who are best able to judge as to agricultural and pastoral matters. They trust that the question of the training of soldiers for country life will not be over-looked, as they feel satisfied that in many cases the settlement of soldiers without previous training will not have satisfactory results, and will not be as economical as if the men had previous training in farming matters.[12]

The NEB favoured a two-year training programme in practical farming for inexperienced soldiers, and considered that its own nationwide local boards of trustees should obtain positions for novice soldiers with established farmers. Concerned primarily with the government's wartime financial efficiency, the NEB considered that applicants for government assistance should have a minimum of two years' experience on the land.[13] The board also hinted at support for a colony-type development scheme, suggesting that soldiers would be more content and successful if placed on lands where there had been a considerable amount of development work.[14] Such projects may have been perceived as providing basic training for bush clearance, but they were hardly preparation for modern commercial farming. The development colony proposal remained as a contingency policy of the Department of Lands until 1920.[15] Despite not progressing beyond discussion, it was regularly alluded to by the Minister of Lands as an example of the breadth of the government's thinking on the subject in the face of mounting public and political criticism.

During 1918 the Defence Expenditure Commission, in a report on land settlement, observed that 'A popular cry is to put returned soldiers on farms: but before putting men on the land, their fitness for that work should be thoroughly tested'.[16] In testimony before the commission RSA General-Secretary D.J.B. Seymour, in a concession that connoted a reward on the basis of more than just war service, observed that prospective soldier settlers had to be carefully 'selected'.[17] As with other interested parties, the military authorities also saw the existing state farms as the basis of a training scheme that, though not providing a thorough agricultural education, would serve to show whether the soldiers had the aptitude and persistence to succeed.[18]

Independent of the domestic debate over the issue of agricultural training were the plans and policies of the NZEF in Europe. This military concern for the civilian future of soldiers was motivated by a number of factors, including the impact of conscription imposed on men in August 1916. Efforts by the authorities to provide agricultural training fell into two categories. First, a type of training activity was used to help wounded and ill soldiers recuperate. This was carried out at NZEF hospitals and military depots in Britain, and in hospitals and sanatoria in New Zealand. Second, able-bodied men were provided with instruction in agriculture to prepare them for a civilian vocation. Before the Armistice an initiative to provide training for the soldiers' post-war vocations had come from the NZEF structure based in Britain under command of Brigadier-General G.S. Richardson. From April 1916, when the bulk of the NZEF was transferred from the Middle East to France, New Zealand hospitals and depots had developed small garden plots to provide fresh vegetables for messes and canteens. The scope of these activities eventually was extended to provide light therapeutic work for recuperating soldiers. At the New Zealand Mechanical Transport Depot at Oatlands Park in Surrey, disabled soldiers raised pigs, poultry and rabbits and sold them on the open meat market. Added impetus to the programme was given by urgent calls from the imperial government to increase domestic food production after the importation of food was affected by the 1917 U-Boat campaign against Allied shipping. As a result the NZEF authorities extended the hospital garden concept. In September 1917 Richardson considered sending agricultural experts to all the camps and depots to advise on the best methods for maximising crops.[19]

The first formal agricultural classes given to soldiers began in early 1917 at part of the No. 2 New Zealand General Hospital at Walton-on-Thames.[20] These classes, for rehabilitation of limbless men, included wool-classing, pig and poultry husbandry, and rabbit-breeding. The Commandant of the New Zealand Convalescent Hospital at Hornchurch reported in February 1918 that the 'work on the farm was carried out almost entirely by "blue men" [hospital patients] although it was necessary to have a few "khaki men" as a permanent staff'.[21] Hornchurch had also been running excursions for soldiers working on the farm to places of agricultural interest with, reportedly, 'considerable pleasure and profit'.[22] From March 1917, the New Zealand YMCA had been assisting with classes at the New Zealand hospitals and convalescent depots, to counteract what Colonel Hugh Stewart, Director of Army Education, described as 'hospital spirit'. These classes provided the initial impetus for the subsequent educational scheme.[23] The Canadian military authorities with the assistance of the YMCA established a 'Khaki University' in October 1917.[24]

By early 1918 the number of wounded and ill New Zealand soldiers convalescing in British hospitals and depots had risen to such an extent that the authorities were prompted to initiate a more broad-ranging educational scheme. It was hoped that this would improve the employment opportunities for soldiers on their return home. The implementation of an integrated educational programme began with a conference held in London between 29 April and 6 May 1918, attended by New Zealand soldiers with pre-war teaching experience at all levels of education.[25] The underlying ideal, according to Richardson, was 'to produce a scheme that would stimulate in each individual soldier ideas of good citizenship and assist to make him a useful member of society'.[26] The inspiration for the conference appears to have been the Inter-Allied Conference for the study of Professional Re-Education held in Paris in May 1917.[27] The imperial government's reconstruction efforts were also seen in a concern for furthering adult education generally.[28]

As a result of the London conference of New Zealand representatives, courses were created in purely educational as well as vocational subjects. Funds and equipment were to be provided by regimental funds and the YMCA.[29] Following an initial trial at Hornchurch Convalescent Camp, teachers were appointed for all New Zealand military hospitals and depots in Britain.[30] Richardson also reported in 1918 that 'classes have been established in English and arithmetic for the Maoris under a Maori instructor... A special agricultural class for Maoris has also been inaugurated under L/Cpl Hinaki.'[31] Classes were also offered at the New Zealand base camp at Étaples in France.

Beyond the immediate vocational training, it was hoped that the provision of the skills and knowledge would ensure the protection of the state by the successful reincorporation of the men.[32] Stewart later reported that the 'citizenship' component of the education course, taught through compulsory lessons in civics and economics, was 'the primary object of the scheme', and that 'it is hoped to drive home generally some measure of acquaintance with economic principles, and inculcate an attitude of sanity in a subject where extremist notions have vociferous partisans'.[33] The spectre of revolution in

Eastern Europe appeared to be having an impact, at least in the general sphere, but these comments were apparently aimed specifically at the increasing popularity of the Labour Party in New Zealand.

In South Devon the various camps and bases known collectively as the Torquay Discharge Depot became the Central School of Agriculture. Established in April 1917,[34] it was the largest NZEF agricultural operation in Britain. By early 1918, three farms totalling some 500 acres were being operated under the direction of Captain Henry McGowan. Interestingly, the increasingly technological war was echoed in new agricultural developments. Special classes were established in mechanised tractor work, using two 'wheeled' tractors and a Cleveland caterpillar, the latter a development for towing heavy artillery pieces across muddy terrain in France and Flanders. The Fordson tractor used on Heathfield farm was supplied, along with a civilian instructor, by the District Agricultural Committee – Food Production, and was reportedly the first such tractor to be seen in the region.[35] The New Zealand Council of Agriculture had recommended that tractor training be part of any training curriculum because of the more advanced state of development of this technology in Britain.[36]

The curriculum at Torquay accommodated classes of instruction in most branches of farming, included visits by expert lecturers, and allowed for trips to research and instructional facilities around southern Britain. By September 1919 some 30,000 men had passed through the depot.[37] The degree of 'training' success that may have accompanied the activities on the various farms is questionable. A report on the educational activities carried out at various bases in Britain between March and April 1919 indicated that of the 1265-man average daily strength of the Torquay camp only some 470 attended classes.[38]

Some officers also appear to have sought information unofficially for the benefit of their men. One individual wrote to the Minister of Lands in June 1918, on behalf of his brother, Lieutenant-Colonel G.C. Griffiths, requesting up-to-date information on land settlement in order to offer lectures to his men.[39] Briscoe Moore, a notable farming sector leader and author in New Zealand after the war, recalled giving a lecture on the subject of sheep farming to an audience of 400 men of the New Zealand Mounted Rifle Brigade at Rafia camp in Palestine before their embarkation for New Zealand. His lecture was part of an educational course which, 'was set up in a number of subjects designed to help the troops on their re-entry into life at home. This was quite popular and served to mitigate the boredom of the men throughout several months.' Moore, a graduate of Lincoln Agricultural College, was officially a member of the Army Education Staff appointed from within the brigade, and his course was part of an official series of lectures.[40] His interest in education was clear: of his own decision to seek a degree in agriculture before the war he wrote that 'the general farm view was that a young fellow should learn his business the hard way, on the farm, and this newfangled idea that books and learning could help was scoffed at by many'.[41]

The New Zealand troopers were provided with tractor and truck driving courses at Ramleh, while some also attended the Jewish agricultural college at Mikwe Israel, near Jaffa in Palestine, where at least three four-week courses were run for the New Zealanders, presumably in orcharding and viticulture, these being the primary activities of the Rothschild-supported proto-kibbutz settlement.[42] A total of 30 troopers completed the third course. Those attending were provided with army rations. All were armed,[43] understandably given the reported threat posed by Palestinian Arabs, particularly following the Surafend village incident, which occurred nearby (see Chapter 12). George Ranstead, an NCO with the brigade's signals section, observed in a letter to his parents in December 1918 that, as more of joke than anything else, he and several friends had put in for an 'afforestation' training programme to be held in Britain.[44] In a further letter to his father later in the month he observed:

> The educational scheme is greatly talked of here & information with rules regarding all the different subjects pretty well fill the daily orders. For all that I don't think the business will be of much practical value. If they can teach a man typewriting, electrical engineering, architecture or any of the other things they skite about while he is looking after horses or doing two or more hours drill a day, they are pretty clever. And studying is out of the question. It is hard enough to write a letter.[45]

Courses, including agriculture science, fruit farming, and wool-classing, were also provided at the New Zealand base camp located at Ismailia in Egypt. Educational work in the brigade was halted in March 1919 when it was ordered to Egypt under active service conditions to help quell civil unrest.[46]

Following an initial trial, the activities of the education section in Britain were progressively expanded throughout 1918, although control of the programme was not centralised until November, with the establishment of the NZEF Education Department.[47] Its primary function was to provide educational services to men awaiting repatriation, in the hope that soldiers' thoughts would, according to Captain Kirk, be focused 'not on war but on peace, not on destruction but on production and construction'.[48] J.B. Condliffe, an eminent post-war economist, after recovering from wounds received at Ypres, acted as an education instructor at the Hornchurch Convalescent Hospital during 1918. For him, the most important feature of the education scheme was its compulsory nature; he thought it unlikely that soldiers could be exposed to the benefits of the scheme once they had been discharged in New Zealand.[49] This comment was an informed one: with his Canterbury University College mentor Professor James Hight, Condliffe had founded the Workers Education Association (WEA) in Christchurch, and before volunteering for overseas service he had taught at Canterbury University College. As to the soldiers' attitude towards the scheme, Condliffe noted:

> While I have no doubt that there is a certain amount of inertia and growling (a common habit among soldiers) there is no trace of it in the class room.... I believe the fellows are genuinely interested, and while one never hopes for any revolutionary results, the stimulation of interest cannot altogether be void of effect.[50]

At the conclusion of hostilities it had been anticipated that New Zealand troops would be used for garrison duty in Germany at least until the end of 1919, with troops being trickled back to Britain for demobilisation. They would pass through Torquay camp and receive advanced instruction in agriculture, after having preliminary instruction in their unit depots or at the large New Zealand 'Reception Camp' at Rouen in France, to which the education establishment at Étaples had been transferred in January 1919.[51] The New Zealand infantry and artillery who had, in some cases, marched 170 miles into the Cologne occupation zone occupied some of their time taking educational classes.[52] Classes for the Canterbury Regiment battalions began on 17 January 1919. But the imperial government's decision, at the request of the various dominion governments, to quickly repatriate dominion soldiers called for a change of policy in the NZEF spirit'. These classes provided the initial impetus for the subsequent educational scheme.[23] The Canadian military authorities with the assistance of the YMCA established a 'Khaki University' in October 1917.[24]

By early 1918 the number of wounded and ill New Zealand soldiers convalescing in British hospitals and depots had risen to such an extent that the authorities were prompted to initiate a more broad-ranging educational scheme. It was hoped that this would improve the employment opportunities for soldiers on their return home. The implementation of an integrated educational programme began with a conference held in London between 29 April and 6 May 1918, attended by New Zealand soldiers with pre-war teaching experience at all levels of education.[25] The underlying ideal, according to Richardson, was 'to produce a scheme that would stimulate in each individual soldier ideas of good citizenship and assist to make him a useful member of society'.[26] The inspiration for the conference appears to have been the Inter-Allied Conference for the study of Professional Re-Education held in Paris in May 1917.[27] The imperial government's reconstruction efforts were also seen in a concern for furthering adult education generally.[28]

As a result of the London conference of New Zealand representatives, courses were created in purely educational as well as vocational subjects. Funds and equipment were to be provided by regimental funds and the YMCA.[29] Following an initial trial at Hornchurch Convalescent Camp, teachers were appointed for all New Zealand military hospitals and depots in Britain.[30] Richardson also reported in 1918 that 'classes have been established in English and arithmetic for the Maoris under a Maori instructor... A special agricultural class for Maoris has also been inaugurated under L/Cpl Hinaki.'[31] Classes were also offered at the New Zealand base camp at Étaples in France.

Beyond the immediate vocational training, it was hoped that the provision of the skills and knowledge would ensure the protection of the state by the successful reincorporation of the men.[32] Stewart later reported that the 'citizenship' component of the education course, taught through compulsory lessons in civics and economics, was 'the primary object of the scheme', and that 'it is hoped to drive home generally some measure of acquaintance with economic principles, and inculcate an attitude of sanity in a subject where extremist notions have vociferous partisans'.[33] The spectre of revolution in

Eastern Europe appeared to be having an impact, at least in the general sphere, but these comments were apparently aimed specifically at the increasing popularity of the Labour Party in New Zealand.

In South Devon the various camps and bases known collectively as the Torquay Discharge Depot became the Central School of Agriculture. Established in April 1917,[34] it was the largest NZEF agricultural operation in Britain. By early 1918, three farms totalling some 500 acres were being operated under the direction of Captain Henry McGowan. Interestingly, the increasingly technological war was echoed in new agricultural developments. Special classes were established in mechanised tractor work, using two 'wheeled' tractors and a Cleveland caterpillar, the latter a development for towing heavy artillery pieces across muddy terrain in France and Flanders. The Fordson tractor used on Heathfield farm was supplied, along with a civilian instructor, by the District Agricultural Committee – Food Production, and was reportedly the first such tractor to be seen in the region.[35] The New Zealand Council of Agriculture had recommended that tractor training be part of any training curriculum because of the more advanced state of development of this technology in Britain.[36]

The curriculum at Torquay accommodated classes of instruction in most branches of farming, included visits by expert lecturers, and allowed for trips to research and instructional facilities around southern Britain. By September 1919 some 30,000 men had passed through the depot.[37] The degree of 'training' success that may have accompanied the activities on the various farms is questionable. A report on the educational activities carried out at various bases in Britain between March and April 1919 indicated that of the 1265-man average daily strength of the Torquay camp only some 470 attended classes.[38]

Some officers also appear to have sought information unofficially for the benefit of their men. One individual wrote to the Minister of Lands in June 1918, on behalf of his brother, Lieutenant-Colonel G.C. Griffiths, requesting up-to-date information on land settlement in order to offer lectures to his men.[39] Briscoe Moore, a notable farming sector leader and author in New Zealand after the war, recalled giving a lecture on the subject of sheep farming to an audience of 400 men of the New Zealand Mounted Rifle Brigade at Rafa camp in Palestine before their embarkation for New Zealand. His lecture was part of an educational course which, 'was set up in a number of subjects designed to help the troops on their

Education Department.[53] There would be more instruction carried out at unit level, including special instructional tours to various agricultural shows, stud farms, wool sales and other similar institutions in Britain and Ireland. Some soldiers appear to have received leave without pay to travel to Holland to observe the Dutch dairy industry.[54] More talented men were given special training at facilities in Torquay before taking up scholarships at the West of Scotland Agricultural Collage in Glasgow.[55] The Overseas Soldier and Sailor Scholarship Fund and Kitchener Scholarship Fund assisted access to universities in general. The New Zealand government reportedly provided funding of £50,000 for the educational scheme and had authorised 50 scholarships for university training.[56] Up to 30 April 1919 70 men were attending, or had attended, agricultural courses at educational institutions in Britain.[57]

The London-based NZEF Education Department, concerned over the lack of teaching material relating specifically to New Zealand agricultural conditions and methods, compiled a series of booklets on agricultural and related topics.[58] These, almost the first of their kind to be produced by the New Zealand government, appeared to provide sound advice on a large range of issues relating to farming, particularly on the subject of land valuation and the dangers of speculation. For the young farmer, the two main essentials were experience and capital. The prospective soldier farmer was also reminded that energy and perseverance were vital for success, and that time wasted was money lost. Farming 'was not the vocation for the tired man; but it offers splendid prospects to the man who is prepared to put his shoulder to the wheel'.[59] Booklets were distributed to units and placed aboard homeward bound troopships.

The military authorities' concern for training in agriculture appears to have been justified. Lieutenant-Colonel E.H. Northcroft, successor to Kirk as NZEF Director of Education, observed that, 'the greater number of the men had reached a settled determination to "go on the land" when they return to New Zealand'.[60] Such was the enthusiasm to farm, 'often with very unsound basis of experience, capital, or even of ideas', that the military authorities felt compelled to appoint an itinerant instructor to provide lectures focusing on the practical realities of farming and explaining the nature of the legislation that had been passed to assist the returning soldiers.[61] Richardson later reported that the troops were extremely enthusiastic about classes in agricultural science and related areas.[62]

To help keep the men occupied on homeward-bound troopships, the education programme was continued under the direction of appointed instructors. The first troopships to provide education classes left Britain in August 1918.[63] Attendance at classes was voluntary on the *Ayrshire,* but no record remains of the effectiveness of this approach.[64] Late in 1918 attendance was made compulsory on troop transports, as it had also been in British camps, with students subject to normal army discipline. Approximately three hours per day were set aside for educational classes. Regardless of these strictures, as Christopher Pugsley has clearly shown, discipline aboard many of these vessels broke down almost completely, so the effectiveness of the official shipboard programmes may be questioned.[65] The shipboard courses suffered from a lack of resources, space and time. Many of the men working in key areas such as the mess did not get time to attend, while many others found reasons not to attend or, if they did, not to co-operate with the instructors. The records of classes on troop transports indicate that in many subjects the level of attainment by the soldiers was not high.[66] On 8 March 1919 the *Dominion* in Wellington reported that the officers responsible for classes on the *Port Melbourne* were disappointed in the results and critical of the lack of resources. The officer in charge observed that 'instructors were compelled to take classes of sometimes 200 or even 300 men, and as there were on the vessel not more than two text books on any one subject it was impossible to make much progress'. After the first week of the voyage the classes were made voluntary and there was an improvement in attitude among those attending. Officers also complained that the classes did not meet the specific vocational requirements of many of the soldiers.

Reporting on the education classes conducted on the troopship *Westmoreland,* Lieutenant-Colonel William Ennis, commanding officer of the Maori Pioneer Battalion, noted that

> a fair degree of success was obtained, but owing to the difficulty of arranging classes that would be suitable to [the] peculiar temperament and nature of the Maori, the system has not received the support one would wish – however, most intelligent men have shown a great interest in their work which augurs well for their future success... Owing to the lack of proper facilities for carrying on the work on deck, it was found most difficult at times to do justice to a most ambitious scheme.[67]

Above: Women volunteers at the Nelson Red Cross depot preparing parcels to be sent to the NZEF. [Alexander Turnbull Library, F.N. Jones Collection, G-9356-1/1.]

Left: 'Hush, hush! here comes the bogey-man.' [*New Zealand Free Lance*, 16 March 1917.]

EFFICIENCY BOARD

BOOKIE

BREWER

FILM

AMUSEMENTS

Hush! Hush! here comes the Bogey-man

Above: Cadets taking part in the 1917 Anzac Day parade through Nelson. [Alexander Turnbull Library, F.N. Jones Collection, G-25635-1/2.]

Below: Brigadier-General Herbert Hart inspecting his brigade in France, on 6 July 1917. [Alexander Turnbull Library, RSA Collection, G-12832-1/2.]

Above: The first German soldiers to be captured in the attack on 4 October going back through the old New Zealand front line. [Alexander Turnbull Library, RSA Collection, G-12934-1/2.]

Below: Wives and children feature prominently in this photograph of the Te Kuiti Defence Rifle Club's opening shoot of the 1917 season. [Peter Cooke Collection.]

TE KUITI DEFENCE RIFLE CLUB
OPENING SHOOT, SEASON 1917

Top: The first wool-testing and wool-classing course for women was run at the Masterton Technical School late in 1917. [*Auckland Weekly News*, 15 November 1917, Alexander Turnbull Library, N-P 1090-36.]

Above: The fast 19-knot interisland ferry *Maori* (3399 tons, 1907) was one of the high value units that made the Union Steamship Company's fleet a strategic asset for the British Empire. [Gavin McLean Collection.]

Right: The *Ysabel* (149 tons, 1874) was one of several elderly sailing vessels bought by ship agent Geo. H. Scales for coal hulking, but given a new lease of life by wartime demand for shipping space. [Scales Corporation.]

BEYOND A JOKE.

OFFICER: "Hullo! anybody hurt there?"
THE VICTIM: "Nobody hurt, sorr, but look wot the——s 'ave done to my stew!"

GERMANS GROWING TIRED OF THE WAR! *See any Newspaper.*

Picture of five happy Anzacs (snapped during stand-to) who absolutely revel in it.

Above: 'Beyond a Joke' and 'Germans Growing Tired of the War!' [*Fourthoughts: Being the Journal of the Fourth New Zealand Infantry Brigade Group* (London: Argus Printing Company, 1918).]

Above: Children raising money for returned soldiers. [Peter Cooke Collection.]

Left: 'Aotearoa'. [*New Zealand at the Front* (London: Cassell and Company, 1917).]

Above: 'The modern infantryman: "a thing to hang things on" drawn by Private J. O'Grady.'
[*New Zealand at the Front 1918* (London: Cassell and Company, 1918).]

Above: A portrait of Lieutenant-Colonel Thomas Todd, CMG, DSO, which he sent to his sister in 1917. He was born in Christchurch in 1873 and served with the Second New Zealand Contingent in the South African War. Todd was an accountant in Perth before enlisting in the AIF in November 1914. He was a capable and popular commander of the 10th Light Horse Regiment from 1915 to 1919. His health was not good after he was badly wounded in the Second Battle of Gaza and he died of illness in January 1919. [Alexander Turnbull Library, C-16570-1/2.]

The difficulty of maintaining the troops' interest in education programmes was not confined to New Zealanders and Australians. A British officer recalled that the imperial authorities saw education schemes as a means of occupying the soldiers' time before demobilisation, and that he had given a poorly received talk to his men though it 'was when the boot was rather on the other foot and the men were educating their superiors'.[68]

The NZEF's educational programme was intended to meet two specific needs. The first, of a purely military nature, was to keep the men occupied during convalescence and, later, to provide positive distractions while the troops awaited repatriation following the end of hostilities. Unlike the British, troops from the Dominions were not able to return quickly to their homes and kin, and delays arranging return passage resulted at times in violent riots.[69] It is difficult to establish the success of this part of the scheme. The second aspect seems to have been motivated by a genuine belief in the benefits of a broad-ranging education programme, albeit under the compulsion of army discipline. A report at the end of April 1919 recorded that the average daily attendance at education classes in six of the larger camps and hospitals was 2237, or 19.9 per cent of the average daily strength. These ranged from 10.5 per cent for Codford through to the highest, 37 per cent, for Torquay. Such attendance figures were, according to the Director of Education, indicative of failure. He did, however, emphasise that the 232 instructors were highly motivated and that the various camps' administrations had failed 'to apply the scheme firmly' so that the soldiers were decidedly hostile.[70] However, some of the fit men in the camps may simply have wished to place the experience of war and discipline behind them as quickly as possible. The available information suggests the surroundings of many of the camps at Torquay were more pleasant and salubrious than, for example, Sling Camp, which was located on the Salisbury plains and associated with the tough wartime combat training regime for various reinforcements to the New Zealand Division.

Opportunity for training when the soldiers returned to New Zealand was dependent upon whether they remained under army discipline while recuperating from wounds and disease, or were discharged from further service. Theoretically the NZEF would not discharge soldiers until their health was satisfactory. This directed the pre-Armistice training policy in New Zealand towards the provision of training facilities at army hospitals and sanatoria, where agricultural training focused on the therapeutic value of light work. Almost all of the 25,000 men who had returned home by the end of 1918 were categorised unfit, and so spent a period of time in health institutions, either in Britain or New Zealand.

In January 1918, the military medical authorities asked if the Department of Agriculture was to have 'neurasthenia' (shell-shock) cases trained in farming at Ruakura State Farm. The Director of Military Hospitals believed that state farms should be used for these cases: 'there is no doubt that many cases of this sort might benefit from having to do light work and thus keep their minds occupied'.[71] This approach was independent of the discussions taking place between politicians and the Agriculture and Lands departments over the training of discharged soldiers. Although initially hesitant, the agricultural authorities consented to the placement of four enlisted soldiers at Ruakura as an experiment to gauge the effectiveness of such a training programme for their health. In June 1918 the Agriculture Department was suggesting that work, and 'some' training, in various agricultural pursuits could be provided so long as transport could be arranged to bring selected soldiers to Ruakura each day. By August 1918 some 20 soldiers had attended Ruakura and, according to an army report, 'some of these completed their courses'.[72]

In the belief that light outdoors work was a cure-all for TB and shell-shock cases, the military authorities established small farming operations at four of their special hospitals: Te Waikato near Cambridge, Pukeora in Hawke's Bay, Hanmer in Canterbury and Cashmere near Christchurch. Pukeora and Cashmere were dedicated TB sanatoria, while both TB and neurasthenia cases were dealt with at Hanmer. The training farm there was established so that, to quote the Director of Sanatoria Medical Services, 'soldiers would not be wholly without experience if they decide to go on the land after discharge'.[73] Attempts to persuade the director of Ruakura State Farm to allow military TB patients to attend classes were, however, unsuccessful and prompted the military authorities to increase their farm operations at the three sanatoria hospitals. In a separate move the Repatriation Department (a hybrid department created late in 1918) also established a training farm at Tauherenikau in southern Wairarapa, on what had been an army farm producing supplies for the NZEF camps, especially for infectious and discharged tubercular soldiers. This farm was operated initially in conjunction with the army hospital at Featherston.[74] The Department of Agriculture took over the running of Tauherenikau, on behalf of the Repatriation Department, in October 1919.[75]

The Military Forces attempted to provide agricultural instruction as part of the general educational and vocational scheme at all hospitals and camps where soldiers were housed. W.H. Montgomery, Officer-in-Charge of the Education and Vocational Training Section, thought highly of the agricultural training plan as 'it is essential that as many soldiers as possible be "induced" to settle upon the land'.[76] The practical provision of agricultural training at general hospitals and camps was, however, beset by problems, including a lack of qualified instructors. In June 1918 the military educational authorities reported that it was difficult 'to do anything more than toy with agricultural instruction because the instructors of the Agricultural Department and the Education Board can attend us only in their spare time'. It appears that agricultural instructors provided this service on a voluntary basis and the military authorities suggested that some capable men should be employed for the purpose.[77] As was the case with the attempts by other government agencies to provide agricultural training courses during the war, these authorities complained about the men's apparent apathy towards the help that was being provided for them.[78]

The army called a halt to agricultural education as the soldier 'problem' appeared to decrease with the passage of time. Notwithstanding the soldiers' attitudes, the government was not properly prepared for the scheme nor did it understand the soldiers. Two contradictory forces were in operation, yet the paradox is that both aimed at efficiency. Training soldiers in agriculture to be the shock troops in a campaign to more closely settle the abundant land of New Zealand was justified by the need for increased production to improve the nation's income and promote self-sufficiency in the empire, but at the same time economic efficiency justified the provision of only a short course of instruction. This was succinctly articulated by J.L. Bruce in November 1919 when he observed that 'the real object of the [Agriculture] department is to get these men through as quickly as possible so that they may have an opportunity if [sic] either obtaining employment with private owners to further improve their knowledge, or of going out on their account, and, further no doubt, the Repatriation Department is desirous of reducing this enormous expenditure as soon as possible'.[79] It was reported early in 1916 that soldiers were not enthusiastic about training and that no returned soldiers had requested agricultural training at the 'experimental farms'.[80] This early lack of expressed enthusiasm coloured official reaction to the provision of training in the period up to the Armistice. The Under-Secretary of Lands noted in the Department of Lands' 1918 annual report that 'the discharged soldiers at present have shown no inclination to submit to training before taking up the land…. Offers by the Department of Agriculture to train men on their agricultural farms met with little or no response.'[81]

The fundamental reason for soldiers objecting to training may have related to their war experiences. Once discharged, few would have been willing to subject themselves to the kind of institutionalised training and control offered on the state farms and, particularly, under the draconian discipline suggested by the Department of Agriculture. The trauma of combat had temporarily left many soldiers with little initiative. They needed time before they could make decisions concerning their directions in life. The value of army training courses was also affected by the soldiers' attitude and respect for the instructors. Front-line troops had only scorn for those, in or out of uniform, who they thought were shirkers and, during wartime, instructors fitted neatly into this category. Also 'book learning' did not fit well with the image of the tough antipodean soldier. Some of the soldiers resented the paternalistic attitude of the education authorities.[82] The very nature of the immediate post-war economy did not encourage those with a serious bent for the land to indulge in 'time-wasting' study.

The training debate revealed a sharp philosophical division between those individuals and organisations who favoured modern 'theoretical' training, and those supporting 'practical' 'on the job' training, either on private farms or special blocks of Crown land. In each case the agenda being followed had little to do with preparing the returning soldiers and nurses for a rural future. Deep-seated beliefs concerning the nature of the New Zealand rural environment and the message, implicit in any call for agricultural 'training', that a rural Arcadia was unavailable to the novice and required more than just innate skills – and more immediate issues related to the booming land market – worked against the successful implementation of an effective agricultural educational programme.

The military authorities may have perceived agricultural training as contributing to the maintenance of discipline, and to recuperation. Vocational training could be seen as a concrete attempt at recivilising the returned soldiers and bringing them back into peacetime society. The authorities seemed to be ambivalent about the value of educational training in terms of improving soldiers' employment prospects. Following an administrative decision to maintain a record of the soldiers' educational attainments, the Director of Base Records noted that,

> although the entries re education etc. will be most useful for statistical purposes and proof of the government's consideration for our soldiers future welfare, the actual value in assisting soldiers to obtain employment will be practically nil.… The fact that a soldier has taken a few hours course in numerous subjects is unlikely to assist him in obtaining employment.[83]

What had appeared to be a substantial programme to assist soldiers before and after discharge was in reality a flimsy affair, poorly co-ordinated, beset with problems caused by administrative indecision and lack of resources, and undermined by the attitudes of the prospective soldier students. Success was negligible, with only a small minority of returned soldiers taking up the limited opportunities offered. It is difficult to estimate the number of soldiers who took part in the various post-discharge agricultural initiatives but in March 1922 David Guthrie, the Minister of Lands, reported that to date only 962 men had received agricultural training.[84] This figure represented approximately 10 per cent of the total number of soldiers assisted under the Discharged Soldiers' Settlement Act, but little information survives as to how many took up farms after receiving training. Nor can a clear estimate be made of those serving soldiers who received agricultural training as part of the demobilising process overseas. Brigadier-General Richardson noted in 1923 that 6834 soldiers in France, 13,152 soldiers in Britain and 1127 troopers in Egypt had attended classes of some type and that the most popular were those which taught agriculture.[85]

23

NEW ZEALANDERS IN THE AIF:
AN INTRODUCTION TO THE AIF DATABASE PROJECT

Peter Dennis and Jeffrey Grey

The Great War continues to cast a long shadow in both our histories and our societies. Anzac Day remains the *de facto* national day in Australia, a role that it does not play in New Zealand because of the complexity surrounding Waitangi and everything that flows from it. Anzac Day nonetheless remains the single most important popular symbol of the Australian–New Zealand relationship, even if many New Zealanders believe, with justification, that in the Australian vernacular the 'NZ' is largely silent – or, perhaps, frequently mispronounced? Anzac has justly been called Australia's 'civic religion', and as with the Civil War in the United States, any attempt to understand Australia and Australians is imperfect without serious consideration of Anzac's mythic role in our culture. Although the war's impact was, if anything, greater and more severe in New Zealand than in Australia, the study of that impact and of the events that gave rise to it has had a much lower profile in New Zealand than has been the case across the ditch.

There are a number of reasons for this. Although military history has found little favour and even less support in the university history departments of both countries, the relatively larger publishing market in Australia has meant that some forms of military historical writing have nonetheless flourished because they have a popular readership to sustain them. Although its contribution to the fostering of military history, outside the official histories, is a relatively recent phenomenon in its own history, the Australian War Memorial did a great deal in the 1980s and early 1990s to encourage research and publication through conferences, grant schemes and its journal; it has and has had no equivalent in New Zealand. Finally, and perhaps most importantly of all, the academic study of military history has been supported by the history department at the Royal Military College Duntroon, and then at the Australian Defence Force Academy, over a period of nearly 40 years; in that time a whole generation of military historians has mapped the history of the Australian army, in particular, in some detail, with some work on the other two services appearing as well. Although New Zealand students have attended both institutions since the Royal Military College's foundation, they have not benefited from this resource because their own service's policy has precluded their enrolment in either honours or research degrees in history.

One sign of the greater opportunities that have been available to military historians in Australia is the greater and more varied work available to the student or interested lay reader. In too many cases, what might be accounted as the basic work in the field has still not been done in New Zealand, and though this presents the next generation of historians with numerous and exciting challenges, it also means problems for the teaching and dissemination of New Zealand's military history at various levels. In terms of the First World War, the inadequacy of the 'official history' of New Zealand's involvement, even when not contrasted with C.E.W. Bean's history of Australian participation, means that we lack a basic and authoritative record, one containing knowledge and information now lost to us through the death of the generation that experienced these events. New Zealand was by no means unique in this after 1918, and the failure was redressed in spectacular fashion for the next world war in the decades after 1945, but the intersection of these various lost or missed opportunities presents us with particular problems, not least when we wish to embark on the sort of comparative cross-national work that represents the next stage in our developing understanding of the impact on the British world of the great wars of the 20th century.

Having noted that Australia benefits from a larger and more sustained body of historical writing, it is only fair to note too that much of this work is repetitive, and at times uncritical and relatively unsophisticated, and that there are still enormous gaps in our knowledge. Bean's romantic and even simplistic notions of the nature of the Australian soldier and the elements that combined to produce him and the force of which he was a member still hold considerable sway despite attempts, themselves not always convincing, to chip away at the edifice he created through his writings. With the last Gallipoli veterans now gone, and with a mere handful of Great War veterans still among us, we can do little more than generalise about the nature, composition and experience of the Australian Imperial Force, despite the importance that we, as a nation, have accorded these men and their deeds.

The size of the AIF has proven both help and hindrance in all this. On the one hand, Bean was able to employ his 'democratic' method in recounting the individual exploits of ordinary soldiers and junior leaders in small groups precisely because the AIF was relatively modest. He may have wished to do otherwise, but the British official historian, Brigadier Sir James Edmonds, was forced to treat his subject at the formation level and higher by the sheer scale of the British endeavour. Bean's judgments and conclusions were impressionistic, even if based on wide experience of the Australians and the campaigns. Conversely, the sheer volume of records generated by the army has frustrated attempts at a more precise and 'scientific' approach to the analysis of the AIF: even a 'small' army by Great War standards generated records at a level impossible to utilise systematically before the advent of computers. Lloyd Robson's attempt in the early 1970s to sample the force, resulting in a capture of just 0.05 per cent of the total, was arresting enough but too small to be statistically valid. So Bean's conclusions and assertions concerning the nature of the AIF have proven enormously influential over decades, but have been incapable of being tested.

For the last 15 years a small, and at times embattled, group of colleagues at the Australian Defence Force Academy has been constructing a database containing the basic information on all 331,000 members of the AIF who embarked for overseas service between 1914 and 1918. The material we are using has in almost all cases been available for many years (the exception being the personal dossiers of individual soldiers), and in all cases is on the public record. The database project has 'added value' to these records by making them searchable in an interconnected manner, and by enabling us to provide a census, not a sample. The four major groups of records used are:

1. The Embarkation Rolls, compiled from 1916 and which provide data at the point of attestation (names, occupation, marital status, stated age, religion etc.) and at the point of embarkation (date and place, together with the name of the ship). These are organised by unit.

2. The Nominal Roll compiled in 1919. This is organised by surname, alphabetically and provides an 'end of war' snapshot of each man or woman. Many details of service changed over the war's length, especially for men who had enlisted early: regimental number (which unlike its Second World War equivalent was not a unique signifier), rank (through promotion), unit (especially in 1916 with the massive expansion of the infantry divisions and the later breaking up of light horse units and reinforcements for service in the artillery and other arms), and fate (most commonly 'returned to Australia', 'killed in action', 'died of wounds or disease') and the date.

3. The Roll of Honour circulars, which were sent out to the next of kin by the Australian War Memorial at the end of the war in the form of questionnaires. These were designed to elicit personal details for the use of the official historian, such as schooling, place of birth, details of migration if born elsewhere, and so on. About 40,000 were returned, many with enormous amounts of detail, some poignantly brief and unforthcoming.

4. The Office of War Graves records, which provide additional details for those buried overseas, and which sometimes provide details such as age and date of death for men who returned to Australia and died later.[1]

These are the core records, reflected in every entry on the database. There are additional, supplementary sources available, some of which we are still attempting to utilise: the London and Commonwealth *Gazettes*, which provide details of awards and decorations; the *Army List*, which enables us to track commissioning and subsequent promotion of officers, and which also provides some limited details of prior military experience before 1914; cemetery records, for men who died much later but whose headstones frequently have unofficial details of their war service inscribed; and 'war books', popularly produced on a subscription basis in each state and which list the men (and occasionally women) who served overseas. Their value varies widely: some contain large amounts of pre-war information on individuals, while others, though more general, contain photographs of the individuals themselves.

The final major set of records, alluded to briefly already, are the personal dossiers. For decades the Central Army Records Office in Melbourne retained these, and access to their contents was strictly controlled. In the course of the 1990s these have been transferred to the National Archives of Australia and are now available for public perusal at the reading room in Canberra and, to a limited extent, in digitised form. Containing details not available elsewhere, such as place and date of birth, these are the only records that enable one to reconstruct the movements of individual soldiers in and out of their units, on leave, attending courses, transferring and for periods of hospitalisation or confinement as a result of misconduct.

It is important to understand that, even with this seeming wealth of material, the record is incomplete. There are names missing from the nominal roll, and we estimate that a very small percentage of the personal dossiers have been misplaced over time. There are sometimes errors of fact, either because the clerk at the time wrote what he heard (thus misspelling surnames) or what an enlistee chose to tell him (accounting for switches in religious affiliation or the mysterious disappearance of a spouse), or through simple human error. Our favourite example of the latter was an outraged letter we received several years ago from a descendant who pointedly informed us that his father had in fact returned from the war and was buried in his town's local cemetery. The accompanying photograph of the grave certainly confirmed the point, but did nothing to explain how he came to be enrolled among the legions of the missing, his name engraved in the Australian section of the Menin Gate memorial at Ypres and this 'fact' reflected on the database.

But as with any undertaking of this kind, we need to be aware that the Australian military authorities, and indeed the Australian War Memorial after the war, kept records and gathered information for their own purposes, not ours. The army spent a lot of time collecting details of next of kin for notification purposes, and in order to establish entitlement not only in the event of a soldier's death but also in order to make the allotment ordained by regulation for the support of a spouse and dependants while a man was overseas. It had no interest at all in a man's ethnic background, and simply did not ask the question. We are thus unable, for example, to determine with any precision the number of Aborigines who served, because they were not entitled to enlist under the terms of the 1903 Defence Act, though we know, from other sources, that several hundred at least did so. The army was interested in prior military service, especially early on, since it needed a means of selecting NCOs with some experience, but until very late in the war did not bother to ask for date of birth, contenting itself with a statement of age attained. For every pink-cheeked schoolboy of popular imagination, manfully adding several years to his age in order not to 'miss out', there was another, older man who put his age down in order to meet the maximum enlistment age for private soldiers of 38. The discrepancy often became known only after a man was killed.

Various things historians would like to know about these men can probably never be known, at least from the public and official record. But computerising those records, with the greatly enhanced search capacity thus provided, does allow us to examine some interesting questions, even if by somewhat indirect means. We have noted already that the army then, unlike the army now, had no interest in a man's nationality – what today would be termed a 'non-English speaking background', or NESB. The regulations stipulated that he must be 'substantially of European descent' while the attestation form enquired whether he was 'a British subject' by birth or naturalisation, the absence of which was clearly no barrier to enlistment. Bean sought to emphasise the Anglo-Australian character of the AIF, and most of us would probably date Australia's increasingly diverse migration heritage as a largely post-Second World War phenomenon. But if we search the database for place of birth or address of next of kin, we find some interesting results. From a base figure of 285,000 (about 86 per cent of the whole), we find the number of British-born to be around 43,000:

England	26,000
Scotland	13,000
Wales	900
Ireland	3200

No surprises there. We know that almost half the first contingent of the Canadian Expeditionary Force consisted of recently arrived, British-born migrants. From the empire in the AIF, we find:

New Zealand 2213 (this includes those born in New Zealand and those whose next of kin address is in New Zealand)

South Africa	312
India	306
Canada	407
Ceylon	25
Fiji	54

together with 276 wayward citizens of the United States, and:

France	103
Sweden	149
Norway	97
Finland	134
Russia	211
Latvia	34
Poland	26
Italy	70
Belgium	34
Netherlands	84
Switzerland	32

Not to mention a significant number of Australians of Chinese descent whose ethnic background must be inferred from their surnames. The Reverend John Tong Way's two sons, whom he tried to dissuade from enlisting, told him that they would serve 'because they were Australians'. Nor have we included the 88 'Yugoslavs' recruited from Australia for service in the Serbian Army in 1917. Just as recruiting officers in some parts of Australia ignored the requirements of British racialism and enlisted some fit and willing Aboriginal men, so the imperatives of British race nationalism proved flexible in the face of Australia's diverse migrant population: men from lands encompassed by the Russian Empire, for example, were allowed to enlist in the AIF in response to the Tsar's general mobilisation decree, and their files often contain letters from the Russian Consul-General endorsing their enlistment.

In a recent article on New Zealand soldier experience in the Great War, James Bennett has suggested that the marked distinctions sometimes drawn between Australian and New Zealand soldiers are overstated, and that 'Bill Massey's tourists', while certainly not regarding themselves as 'honorary Australians' nonetheless drew increasingly keen distinctions between themselves and their British, especially English, counterparts in much the same way as the Australians did (which did not prevent Lieutenant-Colonel William Malone from claiming that the Australians looked 'a loose beery lot' with a 'Garibaldean, boy scout, scally wag look').[2] This process of differentiation between the various Dominion contingents and their Imperial counterparts was common to all, albeit at different rates of development. As Bennett, again, notes, 'After their initial stand-off in Egypt, soldiers from both New Zealand and Australia worked together cooperatively for the most part, learned to trust each other and, at times, even sang each other's praises.'[3] And some found themselves serving in the ranks of the other's army.

The best-known Australians in the NZEF, certainly in New Zealand, are undoubtedly those sentenced to be shot by capital court martial, Privates John Joseph Sweeney and John King. Both were serving in South Island regiments and both were found guilty of desertion, one of the besetting sins of Australian soldiers in the eyes of both their own and British senior officers. What can we say about their Kiwi counterparts, who found themselves enlisted in the AIF, where, of course, they were in no danger of being shot by judicial process?

We have so far identified 2533 men who qualify as New Zealanders through place of birth. They were aged between 18 and 45 – no surprise given the eligible age range for enlistment was 18–38 – and 353 of them were married, or at least admitted to being so. The breakdown by age favours men in their twenties, as might be expected of a migrant group, but a little over a third were 31 or older. The great majority were Protestants (Anglicans 825, Presbyterians 293, Methodists 79) with 254 Catholics, seven Jews and one claiming no religious affiliation. We as yet know nothing of their educational backgrounds, although we can infer that the professionals among them had probably been to university and one, Percy Storkey, VC, born in Hawke's Bay in 1891, enlisted in May 1915 while a law student at the University of Sydney: he had been educated at Napier Boys' High School and Victoria College, Wellington.

Blue-collar employment categories, semi-skilled and skilled workers are heavily represented – 241 labourers, seven farm labourers, nine shearers, 13 blacksmiths, 62 carpenters, five carters and eight bricklayers – and no fewer than seven jockeys join five drovers and 10 stockmen working with horses. White-collar workers and professionals are represented as well, though not in the same proportions: six bank employees, six teachers, four law clerks, but only one solicitor, 93 clerks, three bookkeepers, six architects and two clergymen (one of whom served as a chaplain, as you might expect, but the other of whom, John Stafford Farrer, enlisted as a bombardier in the field artillery and was subsequently commissioned in the artillery). There were also 13 professional soldiers.

Most lived in New South Wales and Victoria (833), with few in the outlying states of Tasmania and South Australia; the 125 resident in Western Australia had probably joined the movement of internal migration to that state begun in the 1890s with the discovery of gold and reinforced by severe drought and economic downturn in the decade before 1914.

The overwhelming majority, 1114, enlisted as privates, since after January 1915 the route into the AIF, other than for graduates of the Royal Military College and those holding pre-war commissions or specialist appointments, was generally through the ranks. The pattern of enlistment matches that of the AIF as a whole, with the great majority, 1358, enlisting between the outbreak of war and the end of 1916; enlistments in 1918 total just 37. One of the things we have noted in working on sub-groups within the AIF is the relatively higher incidence of previous military service among men who were born elsewhere: discernible among former subjects of the Russian Empire, many of whom had done their conscription service before migrating, but also among Irish-born men for whom the same explanation does not hold.

The New Zealanders conform to this finding, with 83 claiming prior military service. Some, like Alfred John Shout, born in 1882 and arriving in Australia at the age of 23, had served in the Australian Militia. This must have served him in good stead: commissioned a second lieutenant on enlistment in the 1st Battalion, he was awarded a Victoria Cross, a Military Cross and a mention in dispatches for his service on Gallipoli, where he was killed at Lone Pine during the August offensive. Shout had also served in the South African War with one of the New Zealand contingents. Private Thomas Vincent, born in Oamaru, served in the Stratford Mounted Rifles in New Zealand before he migrated; enlisting in 9 Battalion at war's outbreak, he died of natural causes in February 1917 at Tidworth. His age at death was 39, belying his stated age at enlistment of 33. Clarence Sydney Smith, who was born in Waipara and migrated to Australia with his family at the age of 12, had served in the Queensland Mounted Rifles in South Africa; he enlisted in August 1914 at the age of 45 and died of disease in England in May 1917. Others brought regular service in the British army in their wake. Joseph William Conolly Shaw, born in Tauranga in 1877, served in South Africa with 2 Dragoon Guards. He enlisted in 1915 at the age of 38 in 12 Light Horse, survived the war and died peacefully in Sydney at the age of 84 in 1961. But like many of the younger men, whether Australian or New Zealand, Napier-born Frank William Banner Hopkins, who enlisted at the age of 19 in May 1915 in 23 Battalion, could only claim membership in the cadets, which had been made compulsory under the military training scheme introduced in 1910. He was in fact in the first draft intake. He was killed at Ypres in September 1917, aged 21.

As some of the above might suggest, and as knowledge of the two dominion armies would confirm, most of the New Zealanders found themselves in the combat arms. There were 991 infantry, 95 artillery, 120 light horse, 83 engineers, plus 20 signallers. The figures tell their own tale: 321 were killed in action, 99 died of wounds, 35 died of disease. This total of 455, or roughly a third of the group, is proportionally much higher than for the AIF as a whole: 60,000 dead from 331,000 overseas, or 17.5 per cent. It is much higher than the figure for the NZEF: roughly 18,000 from 100,000 dispatched. Casualties fell heavily among those commissioned as well. Commissions were granted to 108 of the group, and most remained junior officers (i.e. subalterns) by the end of the war: the highest rank achieved being colonel by one individual. Of these, 32 were killed in action, died of wounds or died of disease – again, nearly a third of the total. So 14 per cent of our group served as officers, compared with 5 per cent in the AIF as a whole, while the casualty rate for officers overall in the AIF was 23 per cent (though higher still for Royal Military College graduates at 28 per cent).

Nor did the New Zealanders' efforts go unrecognised. Three of the Victoria Crosses awarded to the AIF in fact went to New Zealanders: Shout and Storkey, whom we have already encountered, and Thomas Cooke, born in Kaikoura in 1881 and a builder by trade, who was killed at Pozières in the ranks of 8 Battalion, and who is commemorated on the Australian memorial to the missing at Villers-Brétonneux. In addition the AIF's New Zealanders won 17 military crosses, 47 military medals, 13 distinguished conduct medals, four meritorious service medals, and a clutch of mentions in dispatches, including the award of no fewer than seven mentions to the one individual, Colonel Alfred Joseph Bessell-Browne. Born in Auckland and a pre-war citizen soldier in Western Australia, by the war's end he was in command of 5 Division artillery. The wartime paths of the small group who reached senior staff or unit command – Bessell-Browne, Lieutenant-Colonel Thomas John Todd of 10 Light Horse and Lieutenant-Colonel William Reginald Rogers Ffrench of 1 Machine Gun Battalion – faithfully reflected the experiences of their peers: all joined up at the beginning of the war, were commissioned by the time they embarked and had prior military service. Todd had been made a DSO in South Africa and received a bar to the award in Palestine in 1918, while Bessell-Browne was a pre-war fortress gunner, like John Monash. All three came from more affluent backgrounds: Bessell-Browne was a 'merchant', Todd an accountant and Ffrench a station overseer working for the big pastoral company, Dalgety.

What, if anything, may we conclude from this brief introductory foray into the potential of the database project? Are we likely to fundamentally overturn and rewrite the received image of the AIF? Displace Bean's great history as the received wisdom on the subject? Probably not. But the database does yield some very interesting prospects for refining and extending our understanding of the AIF and the wartime experience of Australian soldiers. The Australia of 1914–18 was scarcely the multicultural entity it became in the last years of the 20th century, but the AIF was clearly a more varied and multinational force, and less relentlessly Anglo-Celt, than previously believed. It is possible, for example, to study the recruitment and experiences of individuals or units in a way not possible previously, and to test assumptions about the allegedly more egalitarian nature of the dominion armies through analysis of commissioning patterns across the war and between branches of the service. And this small snapshot of New Zealanders in the AIF might suggest additional underpinning for James Belich's argument for the existence of an Australasian, trans-Tasman world of interaction and interdependence between Australians and New Zealanders, of similarities as well as rivalries.

Appendix

The digitising programme of the National Archives of Australia will eventually result in all personal dossiers of members of 1 AIF being available on the worldwide web. The only material that is withheld are documents less than 30 years old (usually letters from individuals enquiring about a relative who served in the war). To look at preliminary details of those identified as New Zealand-born, go to the NAA website at www.naa.gov.au. Click on RecordSearch. In the enquiry box on the first line, type in 'pob New Zealand' or 'pob Auckland' (pob = place of birth). In the fourth line (Reference Number) type in b2455, and press Search. After a minute or two, the list of New Zealand-born members of the AIF will come up. Scroll down until you see one entry with the icon 'View digital copy'. Click on the icon and the complete file on the individual will be produced. NAA is gradually digitising all First World War personal files, but this will take time. In the meantime, enquirers can request that a particular individual's file be digitised. There is no charge for this process, which takes about four weeks. In order to request a particular file to be digitised, go to the home page of NAA, click on RecordSearch, and register as an enquirer (no charge; two minutes to complete). Having registered, either call up the whole NZ-list, or enter the details of a particular individual. At the bottom left of the entry there is a box marked 'Request digitised copy'. Click on the box and follow the simple instructions. It is important to keep a note of the date of your request. NAA does not contact you when your request has been fulfilled; instead it is necessary to check the NAA homepage, which at the bottom states 'Requests received on dd/mm/yyyy are now being processed'. When your date of request comes up, check RecordSearch, and enjoy the result. There is a limit of about five requests per individual enquirer per year.

24

THE FOURTH SERVICE:
THE MERCHANT MARINE'S WAR

Gavin McLean

In April 2003 Ted Coggins finally got his wish. 'About bloody time,' the 81-year-old pensioner told the *Press* as workers from the Christchurch City Council prepared to add a new plaque to the Citizens' War Memorial.[1] This, which gave equal billing to the four armed services, may have surprised people used to hearing only about the army, navy and air force. That was just the point Ted wanted to make. The merchant mariners had a plaque down at the city's Bridge of Remembrance, but Ted and others wanted them to have equal billing with the soldiers, air crews and the grey funnel line on the city's most prominent memorial. At first not everyone had shared this enthusiasm. Christchurch's heritage planners had suggested adding the new plaque to the bridge, but applicant Earle Crutchley refused; like Ted, he thought the merchant marine deserved the equal status that its British counterpart enjoyed. So on 23 April 2003 officials unveiled a plaque bearing the inscription 'The Combined Services' that gave equal place to the emblems of the army, navy, air force and merchant marine.

An ancient, blood-soaked history lies behind that 'fourth service'. For hundreds of years the British merchant marine, or merchant navy as it is often – and quite significantly – called, has served in times of crisis as an extension of the nation's fighting forces. Press gangs, privateers and letters of marque are outside the scope of this chapter. Instead, let us pause only to observe that before the industrialisation of warfare and strategic bombing effectively placed everyone in the firing line, when the distinction between merchant and naval vessels was not so pronounced, merchant ship crews were the civilians most likely to feel the heat of battle. In times of war the men and the ships of Europe's merchant fleets and their fisheries were bribed, beaten or robbed to augment the state's fighting forces and its supply trains.

This chapter surveys the impact of the First World War on New Zealand's merchant marine. It is not the story of the 'New Zealand merchant marine' in wartime, since, as we shall see, British and New Zealand ships were as interchangeable as the men and women who served aboard them. Instead of dilating on allegedly prolonged bouts of national adolescence, I have taken guidance from the title of that invaluable reference tool, M.N. Watt's *Index to the New Zealand Section of the Register of All British Ships*, remembering that until as recently as 1992 New Zealand did not have its own specific ship registration legislation.[2] That did not imply subservience, at least in late Victorian and Edwardian times. The sheer size of the Union Steam Ship Company enabled New Zealand's maritime entrepreneurs to foot it fairly equally with all but the very richest British shipping barons. Sir James Mills, the New Zealand-born founder of the company, had lived in Britain since 1907. He and Union's managing director, Charles Holdsworth, knew the major British shipowners, and with a fleet the size of theirs they could hold their own. The company's Dunedin board had subsidiary boards in London and Hobart and a design office in Scotland and was also listed on the London stock exchange. Both the New Zealand Shipping Company and Shaw Savill & Albion, the dominant players in British–New Zealand trade, had local boards of advice in New Zealand. A Union Company director, J.M. Ritchie, also sat on Shaw Savill's New Zealand board of advice and, thanks to cable and family connections, knew many of the British shipowners and shipbuilders. The New Zealand directors watched their own interests, of course, but they would have found it almost inconceivable to draw a distinction between New Zealand's shipping interests and those of Britain's, so long as profits remained good, and the Old Country's lines did not offend local sensitivities by employing 'Lascar', or coloured labour, on their ships trading here.

Sinews of steel or tender tendons? New Zealand's trade routes

Then, as now, few nations were as dependent on overseas trade. Everyone and everything that entered or left the dominion did so by sea. Although there were many trade lanes, this chapter will draw a broad distinction between the blue-water trades (principally the 'Home trade' to Britain) and the short-sea trades, then known as either the intercolonial (i.e. trans-Tasman), Pacific Islands or coastal trades.

The 'Home boats' of the British lines dominated New Zealand's blue-water trades. Two lines in particular had become household names. They were the New Zealand Shipping Company ('the Shipping Company' to industry insiders), founded at Christchurch in 1873, but under British control since the late 1880s, and the Shaw Savill & Albion Company. Most New Zealanders were familiar with their ships, especially the Shipping Company's 'R'-class liners, and Shaw Savill's. Their names were then a mixture of the older Maori ones and the newer ones ending in '*-ic*', a nomenclature system inherited from the White Star Line. The other significant British lines were the Federal Steam Navigation Company, owned by meat baron Allan Hughes (who also owned the Shipping Company, although for local reasons this was always given as the dominant line), and the companies that merged in 1916 to form the Commonwealth and Dominion Line (the Port Line). The link between meat processors and shipping was especially strong in the New Zealand trades, where the high cost of providing refrigerated tonnage contributed to a high level of collusion over freight rates, ports of loading and steamer schedules. A pool, codenamed Davis, which set rates, had tightly controlled the trade since late Victorian times and in 1897 the Shipping Company and Shaw Savill virtually divided the meat trade between themselves. A new pooling agreement, or conference, was on the verge of being negotiated just before the war.[3] Within the industry, the main companies were known as the Liners, a term later replaced by 'the Conference Lines'.

Only one locally owned venture ran between New Zealand and Britain, and it did not own any ships. Geo. H. Scales, a farmer-owned business, dated from 1897 and chartered a few wool ships every wool season. Although it never carried more than 10 per cent of the wool clip, Scales's rates had a knock-on effect on the Liners, whose wool charges were kept down as a consequence. Although a public company since 1912, Scales had one curious feature: to protect against hostile takeovers, it required shareholders to be registered sheep farmers with brand marks registered in the *Sheep List*.

Other deep-water trades were minimal. The Union Company ran to India and across the Pacific to Vancouver and in 1912, for appearances' sake, Hughes had allowed it to buy the four-ship 'Irish Counties' service to British west coast ports. Taken together, the hundred or so Home boats formed the centre span of James Belich's so-called 'protein bridge', linking London to its 'new town-supply district, 12,000 miles to the south'.[4] They carried more than protein, of course, but that protein made the Home boat fleet special. Meat and dairy cargoes, a disproportionate part of exports, required the Liners to provide an equally disproportionate large number of refrigerated freighters ('reefer' ships in today's jargon). Reefer vessels cost more than dry cargo ships to build. Because they were used so promiscuously on only the South American and the Australasian routes, they could not be replaced as easily as dry cargo ships.

Small numbers of American, Scandinavian and other ships plied to and from New Zealand on scheduled liner routes. Equally modest numbers of foreign-owned tramp ships carried grain, Marseilles tiles and other cargoes. But the figures spoke for themselves. In 1914, of the 1,781,981 tons of shipping entering New Zealand ports, 826,358 or 46 per cent was 'British', 867,184 tons, or 49 per cent was 'colonial' and a mere 88,439 tons or 5 per cent was 'foreign'. In 1905 the corresponding percentages had been 41, 44 and 15 per cent respectively. Clearly commandeering and wartime patriotism for all things British would only build on an already well-established trend to greater reliance on Britain.[5] Indeed, the 1918 figures, even with German and Austro-Hungarian ships cleared from the seas, were remarkably similar to those of 1914, if allowance is made for the largest colonial ships now being registered in Britain for insurance purposes: 65.5 per cent British, 29 per cent colonial and 5 per cent foreign.[6]

The short-sea trades were important. The principal ones were the 'inter-colonial', or trans-Tasman trade, the Pacific Islands and the coast. The Union Steam Ship Company dominated them all. Formed in 1875, it began as a successful fusion between Otago and Scottish capital, although the capital base had quickly diversified as the company built up its monopoly of Australasian and Pacific Islands services. By 1914 the Union Company, with 75 ships of 240,553 tons, was larger than its five Australian rivals combined.[7] Indeed, it more or less matched the combined tonnages of the Shipping Company (21 ships, 166,775 tons) and the Federal Steam Navigation Company (11 ships, 84,959 tons). In 1914 there were 384 steam vessels (totalling 135,838 tons gross registered tonnage) and 197 sailing vessels (22,714 grt) on the local register. Dunedin, thanks largely, but not entirely to the Union Company's dominance (some of its ships were registered overseas), was the homeport for 87,315 tons of steam and 7132 tons of sail tonnage.[8] A year earlier the dominion's shipping had provided work for 5477 'seamen and boys' (a few women served in the larger ships as stewardesses), up significantly from 4983 in 1912.[9] These figures came down with a thump at the outbreak of war when the registries of 19 ships, principally the Union Company's biggest and best vessels, were transferred to London to take advantage of the British government's war risk cover.[10]

But whatever the changes to ages, size and composition of the fleets, the cargo kept moving. The number of overseas steamers entering the country's ports fell from 567 vessels of 1,676,840 tons in 1914 to 385 of 867,729 tons in 1918, the last year reflecting the impact of the 1917 U-boat tonnage war, but the total value of overseas trade (tonnages were not given), worth £48,117,543 in 1914, was still £52,707,441, after peaking at £59,626,220 in 1916.[11] Clearly tonnage was being used more efficiently.

Government response

The Marine Department issued some certificate exemptions, for passenger loading on vessels, to get the Defence Department-requisitioned Samoa Expeditionary Force transports away in August 1914. The government also insisted on Britain and her allies providing an adequate escort for the convoy. But unlike the Second World War, when there was a Shipping Controller, the government intervened only lightly in shipping matters. Before then it had subsidised mail services, particularly the Vancouver segment of the imperial round the world 'All-Red Route', as well as several Pacific Islands trades. New Zealand had also participated in the 1907 Imperial Shipping Conference but, apart from meeting international obligations for ship safety, the government largely let the market look after itself.

Shipping services were generally first class and although the public complained from time to time about service quality and fares and freights, there was no political mandate for change. That *laissez-faire* attitude prevailed even after war broke out. Unlike the Second World War, for example, the government did not centralise overseas loading at the key ports. Thus the Home boats continued to work the smaller outports such as Picton, Nelson, Oamaru and Gisborne. The principal harbour boards enforced an elementary examination service and old coastal defence sites were manned. The government waited until 17 January 1916 before giving itself the power to requisition ships in local ports as transports. It was even more dilatory about censorship. Only in January 1917 did it prohibit the publication of information about the movements of ships, and even then the ban applied only to vessels whose voyages would take them north of the equator.[12] Otherwise the newspapers continued to report other comings and goings. Other government activities were ad hoc and small-scale. Minister of Defence James Allen hired Wellington ship charterer George Scales to advise officials on hire costs for troop and horse transports.[13]

As we shall see, keeping the Home boats running was the government's primary concern. Coastal services largely escaped the direct effects of requisitioning or sinkings, although the coal trade, which could be affected by the state of the Greymouth and Westport bars as much as anything else, remained a major concern for the Defence Department, which monitored coal stocks closely. The Marine Department's annual reports dwelt little on the war. Like most institutions, it noted the loss of men to military duties and the long hours being worked by those who remained at home. The department's officers also provided additional service to the Defence Department in connection with the crews of transport and hospital ships 'without any additional remuneration', but mostly it was a case of business as usual as far as possible in very unusual times. In 1918 the Chief Inspector of Machinery reported that war conditions had given ship owners incentive to fit labour-saving machinery. 'A great many inventors out of pure patriotism have submitted to the Department during the year suggestions for the solution of the submarine problem,' the same gentleman reported. 'Several of them were of a very ingenious nature,' he noted, with appropriate bureaucratic diplomacy. 'It has been interesting to read through their specifications and to peruse their plans.'[14]

Wellington had little to do because London was running the war. The British government's Board of Trade began allotting those ships that it had not requisitioned for war purposes – as troop transports, auxiliary cruisers etc. – to specific trades.

The dominion's unusual dependence on reefer shipping led to quite a bit of juggling about. If the authorities diverted too much high-quality Shipping Company or Shaw Savill passenger/cargo tonnage into trooping duties, the dominion's cool stores started to fill up rapidly. Consequently there was a great deal of cable traffic between Whitehall and Wellington over shipping. A 1916 dispatch from the Governor, Lord Liverpool, gives some indication of the lengths to which the New Zealand government had to go in its negotiations with the imperial authorities in order to maintain a regular flow of reefer tonnage and keep up with the storage capacity of the country's cool stores. That year it had had to arrange the discharge of some steamers at Egypt en route to Britain so they could be returned to load up again in New Zealand, and it had also paid some of the cost of bringing other ships out in ballast. The vice-regal cable traffic shows that New Zealand officials kept in close touch with their Australian and Canadian counterparts.[15]

Studies of British shipping companies have shown that despite the carnage caused by U-boat sinkings, which peaked in the northern spring of 1917, the shipping industry boomed during the war. The British government's need to transport troops to France brought on 'the most prosperous financial period ever known' for shipping lines, as David Burrell observed:

> The key to this was not freight rates, although free market prices spiralled, but ships were fully employed… [the British] Government chartered and requisitioned ships were paid 'Blue Book Rates' [fixed, publicly advertised] on time charter. An important tool in getting back to sea was the inauguration of the State Insurance Scheme against war risks, which in the course of the conflict received £80.2 million in premium, paid claims of £64.2 million and made a profit to the Government of £16 million.[16]

The British government began softly, taking over only refrigerated steamers and the wheat carrying space in trans-Atlantic liners. From 1915 the 'Blue Book' rates dictated what the rest of the industry could charge.[17] By 1917, however, with German and Austro-Hungarian U-boats sinking ever more Allied freighters, the British government had to requisition more freely and to establish the office of the Shipping Controller, which by 1917 had taken control of virtually all carrying capacity.

Consequences and casualties

New Zealand-owned or operated ships would come under fire, especially once the U-boat campaign intensified in 1917, but most commonly they did this as merchant ships and not as auxiliary warships. Here, too, the hand of the state moved lightly. In general, and unlike the situation during the Second World War, when many small coasters were taken over by the New Zealand authorities for service in its navy or with those of allies, few local merchant ships were requisitioned as naval vessels. There was no local navy to speak of. The only ship operated by New Zealand was the old third-class cruiser *Philomel*. After the early destruction of the German units in the Pacific, African and South American waters, along with the sole Austro-Hungarian cruiser, there was no need to augment the handful of small craft monitoring the port entrances. No fleet of auxiliary minesweepers, patrol craft and training vessels patrolled our waters until 1918, when the government belatedly chartered three trawlers to sweep mines laid by the German raider SMS *Wolf*, a converted merchantman.[18]

That raid, conducted a year earlier, was the only enemy incursion into New Zealand waters. In June 1917, while off the Kermadecs, *Wolf* used her seaplane to halt and then sink the Union Company's big trans-Pacific freighter *Wairuna* and the American schooner *Winslow*. Fortunately, there were no casualties. The *Wolf* had already skirted the New Zealand coast and had laid mines off Cape Farewell. On 18 September one shattered the forehold of the 4700-ton Port Line freighter *Port Kembla*, which sank rapidly, again fortunately without loss of life. Local officials were so confident of the security conferred by the tyranny of distance that they initially put the sinking down to an internal explosion. But they had to revise that opinion in later months as 11 mines were discovered. Then, in June 1918, the Huddart Parker inter-colonial liner *Wimmera* hit a mine from another of the *Wolf*'s fields, this time 18 miles north of Cape Maria Van Diemen. Twenty-six of the 151 passengers and crew aboard the *Wimmera* drowned, the only wartime casualties in territorial waters. Her master, Captain H.J. Kell, who went down with his ship, had disregarded Admiralty warnings to keep clear of an area known to have been mined by *Wolf*.[19]

Even the Royal Navy made few demands on New Zealand tonnage. It requisitioned one unfinished Union Company trans-Pacific liner, the *Aotearoa*, building in Britain, and completed her as the auxiliary cruiser HMS *Avenger*. In

1915 it also commissioned the high-speed Wellington–Lyttelton ferry *Wahine* as a dispatch vessel. Her master, Captain Edwin, was commissioned as a lieutenant in the Royal Naval Reserve and the rest of the crew became RN reservists. For eight months from October 1915 HMS *Wahine* shuttled back and forth between Malta and Mudros, a support anchorage for the Dardanelles, her high speed and then rare bow rudder drawing much favourable attention. In May 1916 the ship was rebuilt as a minelayer. Naval personnel replaced the deck officers, but most of the former Union Company engineers remained with the ship, as did some of the able-bodied seamen. From ports in the east coast of England, *Wahine* carried out 76 mining operations in the North Sea and laid 11,378 mines.[20] But that was the extent of government requisitioning for naval purposes. True, the *Wahine* was a prestigious ship taken from an important run, but the Union Company plugged the gap by partnering the *Maori*, the other modern Lyttelton ferry, with the old, but still adequate *Mararoa*. The demands on the coastal fleet were minimal.

That did not mean that New Zealand ships were idle. The Union Company's *Moeraki* and *Monowai* formed part of the fleet used to carry the New Zealand expeditionary force to Samoa, when the New Zealand government had briefly held fears about the cruisers of Germany's East Asiatic Squadron.[21] Overall, the company's fleet must be seen as a strategic asset of immense significance to the dominion's war effort. According to an old company history, its steamers 'made 86 of the 125 [troop] embarkations in New Zealand and carried 61,813 men, or 61 percent of the total of 100,444 New Zealand servicemen who went overseas'. Its steamers carried another 45,000 Allied soldiers, American doughboys, across the Atlantic and British soldiers across the English Channel.

In 1915 two of the company's newer liners, the *Maheno* and *Marama*, were fitted out at Port Chalmers as hospital ships, a project overseen personally by Lord Liverpool. Between them they made 17 voyages bringing sick and wounded servicemen back home to New Zealand, as well as many shuttle voyages between Mediterranean ports and European base hospitals. They carried 47,000 men and were the poster girls of the New Zealand merchant marine's contribution to the war effort. Fortunately none of the passenger ships was lost. But travellers noticed a reduction in service, and the war brought a temporary suspension of the historic passenger service between Melbourne and Hobart and Dunedin and Bluff.

The British civilian authorities did most of the requisitioning. In 1915 they took the Union Company's incomplete *Aotearoa* and its *Aparima*, *Waitemata* and *Waitomo*; in May 1917 they requisitioned the *Waihemo*, *Waikawa*, *Waimarino* and *Wairuna*. Most were big trans-Pacific freighters. In 1914 the company had 270,646 tons of shipping in service or on order. Eight ships were lost to enemy action and two to other causes during the war. Despite some purchases and new orders, the fleet fell to 213,266 tons by war's end.[22]

Shipbuilding and ship repair

The Union Company's status and its participation in blue-water trades enabled it to get some new tonnage. But smaller lines had to make do with what they had. In contrast to the Second World War, there was no local wartime shipbuilding effort. The history of building European-style ships here preceded colonisation, but as large iron and then steel ships took over from wooden sailing vessels, New Zealand, like most other nations, became almost entirely dependent on British and European shipyards for its foreign, inter-colonial and even coastal ships. By 1914 shipbuilding was principally concentrated in and around Auckland, which specialised in, but was not limited to, wooden craft, and Dunedin, which largely built steel ships. Dunedin also had the Union Company's Port Chalmers Marine Repair works and the harbour board's two dry docks, which together constituted a strategic asset capable of repairing or refurbishing ships up to 10,000 tons. Dry docks at Auckland – Calliope and the smaller Auckland Dock – and Lyttelton also offered some succour to blue-water shipping. But no one built ships of anywhere near 10,000 tons. The 1911 census had shown that the dominion's 29 shipyards employed a mere 589 people; 1910's launchings amounted to 95 vessels under 50 tons, five between 50 and 100 tons and a mere three over 100 tons.[23] The largest ships built before the war, the lake steamer *Earnslaw* (330 tons, 1912) and the tug *Dunedin* (345 tons, 1914), both assembled largely from imported steel and engineering plant, only emphasised the country's near-total dependence on foreign shipyards for all but the very smallest of coastal vessels.

So there was no special wartime shipbuilding programme. Indeed, by 1915 employment in the yards had fallen nearly 50 per cent to 402. The supply of vessels from other sources dried up almost entirely. The Union Company, which had taken over, bought or built 16 ships of 80,640 grt between 1910 and 1913, added only nine of 43,284 grt between 1914 and 1918.[24] Since no German or

Austrian ships were caught in local ports at the outbreak of war, and both price and availability severely restricted the opportunity to purchase new tonnage, the country's shipping lines made do with what they had. Here the coastal lines, as we have seen, were relatively unaffected by requisitioning, as they would be during the Second World War, which, because of the fighting in the Pacific Islands and in South-east Asia, was much more a war of small ships. But it did mean holding onto vessels that might otherwise have been discarded.

That in turn also led to the maritime equivalent of graverobbing: recommissioning ancient hulks from 'Rotten Row' and returning them to seagoing service. At Port Chalmers, for example, Miller Brothers recommissioned the former Oamaru Harbour Board steam dredge *Progress*, an iron-hulled relic from 1883. They rebuilt it first as a schooner and then as a motor vessel. As we have already seen, Geo. H. Scales was the most ambitious resurrectionist. Squeezed out of the wool trade to Europe by the Conference Lines, the company decided to tide itself over by entering the coal hulk business. In 1916 it bought two old barques and a barquentine, intending to moor them in Wellington Harbour. But after a survey showed that it would cost as much to strip them as to refit them for seagoing service, Scales entered the shipping business again, and with sail instead of steam. The *Raupo*, *Rona* and *Ysabel* were joined shortly by the even smaller *Rira*. Thanks to the war, the tonnage of sailing vessels on the New Zealand register, which had nearly halved from 40,894 grt (254 vessels) in 1910 to 22,714 grt (197 vessels) in 1914, actually rose slightly to 25,700 (178 vessels) by 1918.[25]

Repairs and refits kept the Union Company's Port Chalmers Marine Repair Works busy. In 1915 the yard converted the two hospital ships, *Maheno* and *Marama*. Benefiting from their experience with the *Maheno*, in September/October the workers took just 23 days to convert the larger *Marama*. The work involved overhauling her engines, repainting her hull and superstructure and removing all internal bulkheads and fittings to make room for 600 hospital beds, storerooms and offices for the medical staff.[26]

Seafarers

If the three or so pages devoted to the First World War in the official Seamen's Union 1968 history are an accurate yardstick, New Zealand seafarers felt relatively untouched by the direct impact of war. That may have been because they had been through a war of another kind just a year earlier, the 1913 waterfront strike, which had shattered union power and left their union deeply divided. The wartime labour shortages certainly helped trade unionists to recover from that setback and strengthened their bargaining position. During the war years the Court of Arbitration increased seafarers' wages by 45 per cent, compared with just 10 per cent between 1897 and 1914.[27] But the same pressures made it harder for the union to enforce the preference clause for crews for the troopships. It campaigned for a general exemption from conscription for seagoing staff. British seafarers had been granted a general exemption, but it took concerted lobbying by the unions representing deck officers, engineers, seafarers and cooks and stewards to persuade the New Zealand government to empower the secretaries of the unions to make exemptions for union members and for the Military Service Boards to understand that it 'would give effect to these applications'.[28] Even so, boards tended not to see pursers as irreplaceable. That may have intensified seafarers' basic hostility to conscription and their willingness to smuggle what may have been several hundred draft evaders and deserters out of the country to Australia. Many men did, of course, volunteer for the land and sea services, but their desertion rate (8.1 per cent) was disproportionately high.[29]

Improved pay and freedom from employer harassment helped union members, but wartime service was not an entirely positive experience for seafarers. The war did little to disrupt the coastal fleet's schedules and conditions, but older ships stayed in service longer than they might have otherwise done, and the Rotten Row relics that re-entered the trade must have been uncomfortable. Further afield, the troopships and hospital ships were worked hard, steaming fast between ports and spending only minimal time alongside. In an age of stokeholds and shovels, this made for very gruelling work. On the troopships the military authorities assigned soldiers to help the crew, but on the hospital ships the firemen and the trimmers went without such assistance. Conditions would have been particularly bad on the *Maheno*, always a notoriously heavy coal eater. In September 1915, a few hours out of Malta, some of her firemen and trimmers refused duty, forcing the master to turn back to port, where the strikers were sentenced to three months' hard labour.[30]

Nearly 360 Union Company employees, sea staff as well as shore workers –

about 10 per cent of the men on its payroll – enlisted in the New Zealand and imperial forces. We have no idea how many New Zealand seamen perished aboard British-flag blue-water traders, tramp vessels as well as the reefer vessels and passenger/cargo liners from the established companies. Most Shipping Company and Shaw Savill crews were British, but New Zealanders had always signed on and off these ships to replace dead or deserted crewmen and of course New Zealanders sailed aboard them as passengers. Some New Zealanders must have gone down aboard household names such as Port Line's *Port Adelaide*, *Port Curtis*, *Port Hardy*, *Port Kembla* and *Port Nicholson*, Shaw Savill's *Delphic* and *Tokomaru*, Federal's *Middlesex* and *Somerset* and the Shipping Company's *Hurunui*, *Kaipara*, *Otaki*, *Rotorua* and *Turakina*. The most celebrated story was the sinking of the *Otaki* by the German armed merchant raider *Moewe*. The freighter had a mere single 4.7-inch gun against the German ship's four 5.9-inch and three smaller guns, but Lieutenant Archibald Bissett Smith RNR held the raider off for some time and damaged it before succumbing to her superior firepower. Smith won a posthumous VC for his bravery.

The worst local casualty was the Union Company's cadet training ship *Aparima*. She had been the biggest vessel in the company's fleet when she was commissioned for the Calcutta trade in 1901, but by the middle years of the war she was considered too slow for trooping duties and was returned to more mundane freighting duties after making three voyages transporting men and horses to Egypt. In November 1917 the ship was steaming from London to Cardiff when a submarine torpedo blew off her stern, sending her to the bottom in just eight minutes. Fifty-four of the 100 crew and cadets, including 24 New Zealanders, lost their lives. One of the luckiest was cadet Thomas Bevan. He was asleep when the ship was torpedoed, but the explosion compressed the air in his compartment, shot him up through a ventilator and dumped him virtually unhurt in a life raft floating in the sea.

Ownership

The war's impact on the ownership of the shipping industry was profound. First, it generated extraordinarily high profits for owners and second, largely because of this, ownership within the industry consolidated. Although there was a dizzying merger spree throughout the empire's shipping lines, in New Zealand the consolidation trend showed itself when P&O took over one of the country's two major blue-water lines, the Shipping Company/Federal combination, and the major short-sea operator, the Union Company.

We will deal with profits first. The table below shows the return made on capital by selected New Zealand shipowners and operators during the war years. It should be treated with some caution since, as we shall see, the Union Company used an accelerated depreciation policy and created secret reserves to conceal profits. Richardsons and Canterbury Steam were coastal lines, both secretly part-owned by the Union Company. Perhaps the most profitable business was that conducted by Geo. H. Scales. After being evicted from the British wool trade by the Liners in 1916, Scales bought some old coal hulks, rerigged them and ran them across the Pacific, to the Islands and across the Tasman. Low-value, bulk cargoes such as coal, cased benzene and flax filled these old and uneconomic ships' holds, but they ran full from 1916 until shortly after the war. In 1919 the company earned £43,666; after deducting £16,621 expenses, Scales made a profit of £27,055, or 26 per cent on shareholders' assets that had more than doubled from £48,431 in 1915 to £105,873. In 1919 the Scales directors gave staff a bonus of 20 per cent of their annual salaries and shareholders dividends amounting to 70 per cent on ordinary shares and 75 per cent on preference shares. Indeed, the business was too profitable for company chairman Sir Walter Buchanan's conscience. He ordered the sale of the ships and 'the withdrawal by the Company of operations that have produced profits out of all proportion to the Capital invested'.[31]

Return on capital for selected New Zealand shipping lines 1914–19[32]

	USSCo	Richardson	Canterbury Steam	Geo. H. Scales
1914	n/a	13.5%	13.7%	n/a
1915	16.7%	9.8%[33]	13.7%	12%
1916	17.3%	18.4%	8.4%	26%
1917	11.7%	21.5%	8.4%	n/a
1918	n/a	13%	25.3%	n/a
1919	n/a	11.3%	26.5 %	26%

The trend towards consolidation had been marked since 1910, with six to eight major lines acquiring smaller firms. But the war gave British lines additional incentive to go shopping for shipping. The excess profits duty (EPD), introduced in 1915 and by 1917 levied at 80 per cent above profits at pre-war levels, could be avoided if taxable income was spent on capital goods. Since shipyards were clogged with naval construction, thereby restricting the amount of new mercantile tonnage that could be ordered, the major groups scrambled to buy whatever ships and fleets they could lay their hands on.[34] Gordon Boyce estimates that the concentration ratio (CR) of British tonnage controlled by the eight largest firms rose from 18.5 per cent in 1910 to 32.9 per cent in 1914 and 42.5 per cent in 1919. While this was a lower CR than for some other industries, he argues that the CR for the liner trade – about 40 per cent of British overseas shipping – went from 44.6 per cent to 100 per cent by 1919.[35]

That was, as noted earlier, a continuation of an established trend, and one that had been evident even in New Zealand. The Union Company had been strengthening its control of local shipping from about 1904, frequently taking secret shareholdings in other lines and binding them with strict trade agreements. By the end of the first decade of the 20th century it had shares in all the minor coastal lines apart from the Northern Steam Ship Company and it also took a quarter share in the large Melbourne line Huddart Parker. But New Zealand was a small place and, as the Edwardian era drew to a close, there had been some feeling that the company was becoming too big and might become a target for monopoly-busting politicians, as had happened earlier in the United States and in Australia. Senior company managers, nervous of government intervention and the prevailing farmer-led suspicion of shipping rings, even contemplated breaking up the line and registering parts of it overseas. But British shipping magnates, less concerned with the whims of colonial politicians or taunts about shipping octopuses, continued to consolidate ownership. In 1914 Allan Hughes, who had taken control of the Shipping Company through his Federal Steam Navigation Company, sounded out the Union Company for a merger or at least a closer form of association. Only the outbreak of war put plans on hold.

But not for long. The process of consolidation was widespread, but the growth of two groups, P&O and Cunard (which snapped up Shaw Savill), had a particularly important impact on New Zealand. P&O had become a major player in 1914 through its purchase of the British India Steam Navigation Company, whose chairman and soon-to-be P&O managing director, Lord Inchcape, went on to build up the business produced by the 'fusion'. The following table, taken from Boyce, shows their acquisitions (* = New Zealand trade lines):

P&O	Cunard
	1915 Well Line
1916 New Zealand Shipping Company*; Federal Steam Navigation Company*	1916 Donaldson Line; Royal Line; Commonwealth & Dominion Line*; Watson Line (with Ellerman)
1917 Union Steam Ship Company of New Zealand Ltd*; Hain Steam Ship Company; Nourse Line: Mercantile Steamship Co	
1919 Khedevial; Orient Steam Navigation Co (51%)	1919 Brocklebank

The Shipping Company/Federal takeover was less controversial. The Shipping Company had been under British control for 30 years and comment was brief. The Union Company was a different matter. Again the initiative had come from Hughes, although Sir James Mills, now 70 and a decade into his London-based retirement as chairman, had told managing director Charles Holdsworth on hearing the news of P&O's takeover of the Shipping Company that 'we are to some extent left standing by ourselves'.[36] As Inchcape would later tell his board, 'I think probably at the back of the mind of Sir James Mills is also a desire to hide away the profits which have been and are being made by the Union Company of New Zealand from the public in that country.'[39] He may also have worried that if things ever turned nasty, P&O might enter the coastal and trans-Tasman trades to create feeder services for its blue-water businesses.

Hughes had a lot at stake. The Union Company's presence in every port in the dominion and many of the Pacific Islands offered the Shipping Company a valuable agency network for its steamers there and business as Union's agent in Britain. He was also troubled by the creation of the new Australian government shipping line and by Cunard's purchase of the Commonwealth and Dominion Line, both bringing the potential for increased competition. Throughout 1916 and early 1917, therefore, Hughes acted as Inchcape's frontman in the negotiations with Mills and Holdsworth. On 30 May 1917 the takeover was announced publicly, although then, as now, people seemed reluctant to call a takeover a takeover: it was called 'the shipping fusion'.

The offer looked good to shareholders, who were offered 30s in cash and 10s nominal value in P&O deferred stock for each £1 Union Company ordinary share; the market value of the P&O stock gave them more than 60s a share, a tempting premium on shares that had been trading at 45s lately (although they had leaped to 52s the day before). As a further sweetener, they knew that P&O's deferred stock had been paying 18 per cent dividend compared to Union's 10 per cent.[38]

But as Mills and Holdsworth anticipated, the reaction was not entirely positive. The 'shipping fusion' alarmed those businessmen who worried about losing control of the dominion's shipping services, despite P&O's assurance that there would be no alteration in the management, personnel or the operations of the Union Company. Some reaction was sentimental and nationalistic. Dunedin's *Evening Star*, for example, wailed that 'a great opportunity will be missed if the country does not step in and outbid the present bid of the P&O company… [government intervention] would prevent the establishment in our midst of a powerful shipping combine which might not, our readers can easily conceive, be entirely in the public interest'.[39]

The Reform–Liberal wartime coalition government had its reservations. Prime Minister Massey favoured the deal, but two of his ministers supported a state takeover. The greatest opponent was Minister of Internal Affairs and Minister of Public Health, the Canterbury Liberal George W. Russell. In June 1917 Russell reminded his Cabinet colleagues of P&O's behaviour in 1910 when it had put its big liners on the Sydney–Auckland run in brief competition with the Union Company. 'The experience of 1910, when an Act passed by the New Zealand Parliament, to fight the P&O regarding coloured labour, was vetoed by the Home Government, shows that against a powerful English Company, lobbying at headquarters, the Parliament of New Zealand will not count for much.' Three days later he warned that 'with a loss of control will probably come higher rates of freight and fares, while this country will not be in a position to control its trade with the Pacific Islands, Australia and America'.[40]

Russell lobbied hard. 'It would greatly strengthen my hands if you were to hold a public meeting in your Borough and pass a resolution in support of [the] suggestion you have made,' he told the mayor of Devonport.[41] Soon appeals for government action were flooding in from the Auckland branch of the Federated Seamen's Union, Auckland newspaper publisher T.W. Leys and chambers of commerce both large and small. Dunedin's chamber, where Union Company directors would have held great sway, stopped short of recommending rejection, but urged 'great watchfulness'.

The Solicitor-General reported that there were no insuperable difficulties to acquiring the Union Company's shares or to legislating against the takeover. (Acquiring just the ships would be slightly more difficult, but not impossible if a new state agency was established.) On 19 June he got Cabinet to agree to cable London that:

> The Government of New Zealand therefore suggests that the consent of the British Treasury to the merging proposal be deferred until the New Zealand Government has had a reasonable time to fully consider the important questions involved. If the Imperial government has strong reasons to the contrary and considers its consent should be given the New Zealand Government would be glad to learn the reasons therefor.[42]

From London Sir James Mills reassured fellow Dunedinite, and acting Prime Minister, James Allen, that the company's position would not be altered. The majority of shares had been in foreign hands for decades and even now New Zealanders held only about a third of them. Mills seems to have acted adroitly. Government permission was granted on 7 July and by the end of the year 97 per cent of shareholders had sold to P&O.

P&O had certainly got a bargain. As a memorandum prepared for its board in 1918 noted, P&O had paid Union Company shareholders £1.5 million in cash and £1.75 million in stock for assets that Union's books publicly showed as being worth less than £1.3 million. That is because 'Union had followed a policy of accelerated depreciation for its ships, and in the years of the First World War had been able to conceal substantial earnings through creating secret reserves'.[43] But by valuing the ships at cost price and by allowing a 5 per cent per annum straight line depreciation, producing a figure of £6,387,935, P&O had come out £3,137,935 ahead. Its takeover of the Shipping Company had been equally favourable. The empire had struck back.

Conclusion

The merchant marine successfully carried out its task of conveying the dominion's regular imports and exports in addition to meeting the special needs of wartime, troop transport, casualty evacuation and the transport of bunker supplies. It came through the Great War with far lighter losses in ships and in seafarers than it would sustain during the next global conflict. Indeed, by 1920 the lines had largely replaced their losses with a mixture of new construction, ex-German ships or the wartime 'standard' ships built for the British government, enabling them to pay off their overage vessels and the wartime expedients such as the Scales sailing vessels. The real scars were less visible. It is possible that the Union Company ownership would have changed even if there had been no war, but recent studies in accounting history have shown that the P&O dominance of our trade lanes came at a price. The Union Company managed to fund its publicly declared dividends and to keep its fleet up to date between the wars, but 'the impact on the New Zealand economy… was more serious', accounting historian Christopher Napier argues. The millions extracted from the Union Company by P&O 'in ways that concealed the transactions from the preference shareholders of Union and the New Zealand public' between 1917 and 1936 represented 5 per cent of gross national capital formation during that period.[44] It was a heavy price to pay.

PART 4

HOME FRONT
PERSPECTIVES

25

THE POOR COUSIN:
NEW ZEALAND'S HOME DEFENCE

Peter Cooke

The extensive reforms of New Zealand's military forces recommended by the British authorities in 1909–10 were geared towards an expeditionary force which, in an emergency, would take the cream of New Zealand's military forces offshore. The dominion accepted this imperial advice 'with very little idea of how it was to be put into practice,' complained Major-General Alexander Godley, who had been sent out from Britain to implement the new scheme. It involved replacing the ramshackle Volunteer Force with a new Territorial Force to be manned largely by a system of compulsory military training. After the imperious Godley arrived in Wellington, he set about building New Zealand's scheme 'on which they had rather lightheartedly embarked'. He inspected the fixed defences and toured the Dominion as if standing for Parliament, making 'speeches to large audiences, and explain[ing] the working of the defence scheme. I also interviewed deputations of business men, farmers, clergymen, anxious mothers, and all classes of the community and explained to them how the scheme was going to affect their particular interests.'[1]

The reforms meant standardising New Zealand units, equipment and arms with those of Britain. The purchase of mountain guns caused an early ruction, as will be noted below. Godley's reorganisation of the New Zealand Military Forces took most of his first year in the dominion. By 1912 the regiments and battalions, restyled from their Volunteer days, were attending their first camps. Previously camps only up to strengths of company or squadron had been the norm. Although equipment and uniforms were in most cases lacking, these camps produced interest and enthusiasm that Godley found remarkable.

He went on to hold brigade camps in 1913 'despite a good deal of opposition from my staff, who insisted, with some reason, that we were trying to fly before we could walk'.[2] Godley was keen to form and test the higher formations 'before we should be called upon to furnish an Expeditionary Force'. All these efforts tested the mobilisation capacity of a citizen-based army with regular cadres. Although the manoeuvres were based on defending the shores of New Zealand – with the briefing notes showing, chillingly, enemy warships anchored off Timaru – Godley expected that the only fighting the troops would ever do would be overseas.[3]

By the time divisional camps were being held in 1914 – and inspected by General Sir Ian Hamilton, Inspector General of the Overseas Forces, the call for an expeditionary force was very near: Godley had discussed the possibility only weeks before on a trip to Britain.[4] In August–September 1914 the NZEF was assembled, trained and dispatched with remarkable speed, enthusiasm and efficiency. With it went virtually all the staff officers who provided the energetic foundation of New Zealand's military forces.

So what was left behind for home defence? The rump of the New Zealand Military Forces was provided by the Territorial Force units and a recruiting and training system designed to feed manpower overseas as reinforcements. The defence of New Zealand was on paper the job of a field army of two divisions, one in each island. Each division would be formed from two infantry brigades, one mounted rifles brigade, two artillery brigades and support troops of engineers, services and field ambulances. Another mounted brigade in each island was to be kept independent, as were the coast defence and line of communication troops (consisting of railways engineer and Post & Telegraph battalions). Under the Defence Scheme, in the precautionary stage the home regiments had to deploy detachments to guard vital points, such as the radio and cable stations, rail tunnels and magazines, and also respond to suspicious activity, such as the many instances of mysterious signalling to seawards that occurred. If the alerts advanced through the mobilisation stage to the war stage, each division would assemble at its predetermined war station. In the North Island this was to be Palmerston North, and Waimakariri in the south, with the independent mounted rifles brigades going to Hamilton and Taieri Plain respectively.

This was all very well in theory, but the units making up these formations soon ran into trouble. The listed strength of the New Zealand Military Forces in 1914 – 66,738 – is misleading, as under half were trained soldiers (Territorials); the rest were instructors, teenage cadets or rifle club members.[5]

Having sent away over 11,800 men by Christmas 1914, including the 2nd Reinforcements, the military authorities looked to the NZEF's next intake. The mobilisation camps around the country received volunteers, gave them a bit of drill and sent them in batches to Wellington and Featherston for further training. Each intake left the country in bi-monthly reinforcement drafts, starting with the 3rd Reinforcements from February 1915 and increasing to monthly in August. Of the men feeding the NZEF, about 8000 to 10,000 men each year came from the Territorial Force, which was in turn supplied by the Senior Cadets (about 8000 18-year-olds a year) with the balance coming from volunteers and, after 1916, conscripts. And herein lay the problem – the NZEF was a completely different organisation from the Territorial Force-based home defence units. The New Zealand Military Forces family furnished a stout son, in the form of the NZEF, for collective imperial defence, but it did so at the expense of its poor cousins, the home defenders. According to the official historian Lieutenant H.T.B. Drew:

> The strain placed upon the Territorial and Cadet forces was considerable. Not only were these forces unexpectedly called upon to supply large numbers of officers and other ranks for immediate service abroad, but they were continually drained throughout the war of large numbers of trained officers and non-commissioned officers for instructional and administrative duties in the Expeditionary Force training camps and in the four military districts.... The training, in these circumstances, was carried on under conditions of exceptional difficulty.[6]

So the Territorial Force was required to furnish men both for the NZEF and, if need be, for the two home defence divisions. It consisted of 17 infantry and 12 mounted regiments, 18 field and fixed batteries, and a bevy of engineer, signal and service units based around the country. In the annual camping season of March–April 1915 these units came together in encampments on government property, land lent by patriotic citizens, or showgrounds. Much denuded by the NZEF, they were hurriedly training up raw volunteers and graduating cadets. Also by now their role had subtly changed because the NZEF had been formed and dispatched: despite preparing to provide reinforcements to the NZEF, they had no formal link with it apart from unit nomenclature. There was no conduit for feeding those new Territorial recruits to the NZEF, in contrast to the Main Body, which did have formal connections, with each Territorial battalion, for instance, contributing a company to its corresponding NZEF composite battalion. Recruits merely joined the NZEF and at best resigned from their Territorial unit or at worst failed to appear for their next weekly parade. The home defence units suffered an institutional loss of experience and know-how throughout the war.

Shortages characterised the home defence units. Having handed in anything of value to the NZEF, the Territorial units had to make do with older equipment and arms. The field batteries, for example, lost their new 18-pounder guns, received in the previous two or three years, and were left with a section of old and undercapable 15- or 16-pounder guns, taken from Senior Cadet artillery units or stores. Rangefinders were rare, but even low-tech supplies were in short supply: pole-draught harness for instance had to be made locally.[7] Despite a shipment of rifles having been imported from Canada just before the war, 'rifles and other essential equipment were taken from the home units for the Expeditionary Force'.[8] In planning recruitment for the 5th Wellington Regiment, which had to establish posts in six locations surrounding the city in late 1914, the commanding officer first had his rifles counted then instructed the regiment to recruit 'a man for each rifle available.'[9]

The fixed home defences

The fixed defences during the First World War were based largely around old equipment and suffered the same manpower shortages that plagued the field force. Except for the 6-inch Mk VII batteries erected recently in Auckland and Wellington and some 3-inch 12-pounder guns bought about 15 years earlier, the fixed armaments dated from the 1880s. Armstrong 6- and 8-inch breech-loading guns were mounted in works built following a Russian war scare, but suffered from poor range and accuracy. While the old 6-inch guns were relegated to reserve status, the 8-inch were felt to still have some value. In 1914–15 some were converted to cordite, the propellant used by the newer Mk VII guns. In the two southern ports, which relied exclusively on these old guns, the artillery redistributed 6-pounder Nordenfelts among hastily erected pedestals. In all ports except Lyttelton the 12-pounder guns formed the examination battery, manned by regulars, throughout the war. The 12-pounder examination battery at Fort Dorset was the only new battery built during the war. The job of these batteries was, by threat of their presence, to induce merchant ships entering harbour to display the correct recognition signal, and to cover the examination vessel as it checked the *bona fides* of ships that failed to do so and which had been moored for inspection in the examination anchorage.[10]

To augment the fixed defences, small numbers of field guns were allotted to mobile coast defence troops on the outbreak of war. Coast defence companies in Lyttelton and Otago had two 15-pounders each until mid-1915.[11] Wellington's D Battery had this role on paper, but most of its personnel and all its guns were in Samoa.

A special case was Westport. Because it was the source of the best steaming coal in the South Pacific, the Admiralty considered its defence to be vital. So two 12-pounder quick firing guns, which had earlier been mounted on railway wagons, were shunted out to the Buller rivermouth's eastern mole and parked for several wet weeks. A new call on the limited resources of the fixed defences, including Westport's, came later in the war when a number of forts were robbed of their quick-firing guns to arm troopships or government steamers.[12]

To man the fixed defences small numbers of Garrison Artillery Territorial gunners were called up in August 1914, as was a company of their supporting infantry battalion in each port. Such was the strain on manpower that the GOC, Godley, asked if Territorial gunners could attend the forts at night but go to their normal work during the day.[13] This was impractical, especially where the forts were miles from town, but still the batteries, examination service and port war signal stations had to be kept fully manned, day and night.

In this crisis of late 1914 New Zealand's solid tradition of citizen soldiery came to the fore when former soldiers offered themselves. Some of these offers were accepted. In Wellington, for example, former Wellington Naval Artillery Volunteers gunners, probably members of the rifle club they had formed 20 months before, offered their services on 5 August. They mustered enough old gunners to provide reliefs for those manning Wellington's 8-inch guns by day and night. The men were described as physically fit, strong and mostly of long service. Their only condition in volunteering was that they be kept together as one unit. The Wellington Coast Defence commander accepted the offer to man Forts Gordon, Halswell and Kau Point, for which he had no detachments. He was husbanding his trained Garrison Artillery Territorials at the Fire Command Station at Fort Ballance.[14] Similar offers were made in Auckland, where the ex-gunners were embodied into an informal reserve. In both cases these volunteers relieved the Garrison Artillery Territorials at nights and weekends, but attendance fell off within a couple of months as the novelty of sitting idle in damp concrete holes wore off.

Although the departure of the NZEF's Main Body in October 1914 had allowed a slight relaxation, it was not until von Spee's German East Asiatic Squadron was brought to account in the Battle of the Falklands in December that the level of threat receded enough for a stand down to be considered. By April 1915 the strength at the forts had been reduced to infantry guards only, though regular gunners continued to man the examination batteries. In this time, and for the rest of the war, the fixed defence units were 'embarrassed', to use the Commandant Major-General Sir Alfred Robin's word, by so many of their men volunteering for the NZEF.[15] Cadets filled some of the gaps, but their inexperience and lack of specialist training hampered the efficiency of the forts. A home service section NZEF attached to the Garrison Artillery early in 1917 also failed to reverse the losses. By 1918 the problem was acute enough for Robin to complain publicly about this drain in brawn and brain.[16]

Although the fixed defences remained serviceable during the war, albeit with strained manpower, from 1915 they lacked the best incentive to efficiency – a viable threat. Even the visit by a mine-laying German raider in mid-1917 did not have a noticeable effect on the defences because its visit was not confirmed for six months, by which time the Allied naval response to raiders in general had been stepped up to lessen their threat to New Zealand.

Standardisation – the mountain battery débâcle

Part of the process for New Zealand accepting her place in imperial defence was standardisation, which in theory would help New Zealand units meld into larger imperial forces at the front. The dominions received instructions on 17 October 1910 on the adoption of imperial service patterns of war-like stores.[17] With these New Zealand forces were cemented into the .303 calibre Lee Enfield rifle, a particular style of uniform and webbing equipment, and 18-pounder and 4.5-inch artillery pieces. But a strong vein of stubborn southern independence permeated elements of local decision-making. Tension over this move towards standardisation is illustrated by the mountain battery débâcle in the period leading up to the Great War. In it the Dominion's process of acquiring arms was brought into line, but only after much kicking and struggling.

The affair focused on Wellington's D Battery, New Zealand Field Artillery, which had been formed from a Volunteer unit that dated back to 1867. In 1911 it was converted into a mountain battery because the hilly terrain of Wellington was thought best defended with very high-angle weapons. It handed in its old 15-pounders, but the process of conversion was stymied by problems in obtaining suitable guns.

For a start, the decision to convert it to a mountain gun battery was a local one. Major G. Napier Johnston, a British artillery officer who been brought out by Godley to help with the reorganisation of the forces as Director of Ordnance, did not approve of the change. He dismissed mountain artillery as both unsuitable to New Zealand conditions and expensive. In his view howitzers were 'sufficiently mobile to move over most country in New Zealand where operations would take place'. However, his real beef against mountain artillery related to the skill level required to handle it: 'the transport being all pack and difficult to train, more especially with short service men'. In India, the principle stamping ground of the mountain artillery, 'the drivers are all native', he noted.[18]

Johnston nonetheless dutifully directed attention to the Vickers Maxim 2.95-inch quick firing Mk I, the only available mountain gun. The government's long serving Military Adviser in Britain, General E. Harding Steward, concurred with this choice.[19] Based in the High Commissioner's office in London, the veteran Harding Steward had been advising New Zealand on arms purchases and attending test firings of coast defence pieces intended for the colony since the 1880s. He had also acted for other authorities in such matters, for example supplying mountain guns of this calibre to Egypt and the West African colonies of Nigeria and the Gold Coast since 1897. The British army had adopted this model for colonial use in 1901 and some had served in the South African War.[20] Notorious for bucking like a bee-stung mule, its violent recoil was only partially checked by the on-board hydro-spring recoil system.

At the War Office's request, Vickers had been preparing another design. Of 2.75-inch calibre, it was an improved version of the old breech-loading 10-pounder jointed gun, in which the barrel was in two parts. The parts were joined by screwing them together, hence the generic term screw-gun, immortalised in poetry by Rudyard Kipling with a chorus that went 'For you all love the screw-guns, the screw-guns they all love you'. Although this breech-loading gun had been under planning since 1908, a certain amount of confusion existed over its designation. Vickers finished a prototype of it in the same month that New Zealand's High Commissioner Sir William Hall-Jones placed orders for four of the only gun then under manufacture, the 2.95-inch version.

After Harding Steward observed their proof firing, the mountain guns with their pack saddlery were shipped to New Zealand. They arrived in January 1912, along with the first of the other new field guns and howitzers, and went into storage at Shelly Bay while the D Battery was geared up to receive them.[21] Wooden rounds and leather knee pads were made for drill purposes, and the depot at Mount Cook in Wellington was modified to accommodate the battery, with the old powder magazine on Tasman Street becoming stables for the 15 pack mules purchased.[22]

Before the guns had actually been issued to D Battery, though, the Army Council in Britain got wind of the purchase.[23] The British authorities immediately advised New Zealand that the gun was obsolete and queried why it had been ordered when the latest weapon, the 2.75-inch BL gun, 'is now being manufactured for the regular army'. The government's attention was drawn to the 1910 instructions sent to the dominions on the adoption of standardised arms and stores.[24] This led Godley to ask why correct procedure had not been followed.

Johnston thought the guns received *were* Vickers' new design, the 1908 pattern as he called it. To confirm he went to Shelly Bay, physically unpacked the guns from their crates and manually inspected them. Finding them not to be this new version but the older Vickers 2.95-inch model, manufactured in 1903, he furiously blamed Harding Steward and called for them to be exchanged.[25]

Harding Steward in turn blamed Johnston for the mix-up. Even so, he defended the 2.95-inch gun, maintaining that it was still the latest pattern because the other model was not actually yet in production, despite London's assertion to the contrary.[26] In fact the prototype had been sent to India for trials but had not yet been adopted when New Zealand placed its order. New Zealand ironically had an officer in India, Captain R.B. Smythe RNZA, serving with 8 Mountain Battery at Quetta, who probably saw the new design there and sent Wellington information on Indian mountain batteries.[27]

Things now got personal. Johnston, writing drafts for Godley to sign, attacked Harding Steward as 'too old for this work'. Some of his recommendations 'have not, in my opinion, been made in the best interests of the Dominion'. Delay in sending the guns 'must be attributable in some measure to want of energy or touch with the War Office on the part of our Military representative'.[28]

Godley blamed the High Commissioner for not following procedure: he had, he complained, not sought advice from the War Office or obtained the latest pattern, and had ordered direct from a commercial supplier rather than through the War Office, 'which is the correct procedure for service pattern weapons'.[29] Hall-Jones also claimed, disingenuously, that he had thought the ordered guns to be the later model. Godley said Harding Steward's experience had been in Africa and Egypt 'some years ago', and that the technology in artillery had 'moved on since then'. The GOC even lambasted as evasive a claim by Vickers that a gun manufactured in 1903 *was* up-to-date: 'We are now saddled with nearly obsolete guns costing £4,000.'[30]

After the Cabinet in Wellington agreed that this had been a bugger's muddle, Johnston penned the *coup de grace* for Godley to sign and the Minister of Defence was urged to dispense with the services of Harding Steward, who was 'not in touch with modern developments in gun manufacture' and whose age 'now unfits him for the work'. He was duly relieved of his duties by the new High Commissioner, Thomas Mackenzie, in November (sadly, while suffering after having had a leg amputated).[31]

Clarifying that the adviser's duties should henceforth be carried out by a New Zealand officer, Godley suggested that Major George S. Richardson, then at the

Staff College in Britain, could 'help out' Colonel Robin 'on weekends'. Robin had been appointed in February 1912 to represent New Zealand on the Imperial General Staff in London. This arrangement would overcome such confusions as had occurred over the mountain guns and provide the High Commissioner with better advice. Not wanting to lose the sale, Vickers offered to repurchase the guns if they could supply their new version instead. New Zealand accepted this proposal, selling the guns back to Vickers for around £1495 less than the purchase cost.[32] The deal was contingent on the guns being returned to Vickers by a certain date, as a resale was already under negotiation. Although they were dispatched from New Zealand in January 1913, the supply of replacement 2.75-inch pieces was delayed by other demands and the outbreak of war; the order for them would eventually be cancelled in March 1916. D Battery remained without weapons until most of its personnel embarked with the Samoa Expeditionary Force in 1914 armed with two 15-pounder Mk IV and two older 6-pounder Nordenfelts on field carriages 'from odd corners of the Defence Stores'.[33] The new owners of the only mountain guns ever bought by New Zealand had soon made themselves known – according to the Australian official historian Charles Bean, the guns reappeared on the Gallipoli Peninsula in Turkish use.[34]

Defence rifle clubs

Although the military forces that emerged from the reforms of 1910–11 were designed to defend New Zealand as well as the empire, the country soon gained a second line of defence in the form of rifle clubs. Such clubs were a vestige of the frontier spirit produced by New Zealand's pioneering period, particularly the fighting role for new settlements attempting to wrest their livelihood from hostile Maori. As the internal threat receded, though, the popularity of hunting and guns maintained a number of shooting clubs that had been formed in the 1860s. Others were formed when Volunteer Force rifle corps dissolved into a state too inefficient to be considered military units. In 1902 they came under the wing of the New Zealand Military Forces as Defence rifle clubs. Although their reputation among military sticklers was poor, they were seen as a way of improving overall marksmanship and keeping tabs on a body of skilled men who would be useful should the defence of the country be tested. After a government grant to the national body, the Dominion Rifle Association, had nearly been withheld because of differences of opinion, the clubs' defence role was recognised in 1912 when they were formally described by Godley as the second line of home defence.[35] As such they entered the Great War with much promise.

All rifle clubs were told in March 1912 that they and their affiliated training sections were to form the second line of defence, the first being the Territorial Force and Reserve.[36] (The training sections became the General Training Section, which was absorbed into the Territorial Force in 1915.)[37] 'Rifle Clubs exercise a very important function in the defence scheme,' Godley explained. The separation between rifle club and Territorial Force was confirmed in the Defence Amendment Act 1912, which provided that no Territorial soldier could become or remain a member of a rifle club.[38] Essentially, those who could joined the Territorial Force, those who could not became rifle club members. The clubs themselves 'promised their cordial support and co-operation in enabling us to make the training universal by means of their organisation'. Two thousand Magazine Lee Enfield (MLE) rifles were ordered for the rifle clubs that year.[39]

In the compulsory military training scheme rifle clubs were to absorb those men classed as unfit for service in the Territorial Force. Medical examinations sorted recruits into three classes, with the fittest – about 60 per cent – being good for active service in the Territorial Force. About a third were deemed 'fit to serve in a Rifle Club'.[40] Only around 5 per cent were rejected outright. Provision was made for existing and new clubs to absorb these men, who had to train in their clubs for a minimum of 18 afternoon or evening parades at 'convenient' drill centres and undertake prescribed courses of musketry, including at least six attendances at a rifle range. Army officers and NCOs undertook this instruction. The term 'convenient' was defined as not more than one hour's walk or ride from the homes of members – hence the spread of rifle ranges throughout the country: there were 170 by 1912.[41]

Rifle clubs were intended to provide drill of a 'refresher character only' for young men who had had up to four years' experience in the senior cadets. 'Rifle Clubs will be given a place and function in the defence scheme, and their movement in time of necessity provided for in the mobilisation instruction of the Dominion.'[42] Clubs would be formed to provide a territorial spread throughout each army area, of which there were 56, in 16 groups spread across the four military districts.[43] Four clubs were planned for each area, with each club intended to provide a 30-man platoon of armed men, out of its maximum strength of 100. This in theory would furnish a company to the defences in each area, or 22,400 men for the home defence forces. Those aged between 25 and 30 who had finished their Territorial training had the option of joining either the Reserve or a rifle club – as could any man up to 55 years old as a voluntary member. Members had to be British subjects, have a clean police record and be willing to take an oath of allegiance.[44]

Progress towards rifle clubs becoming militarily efficient was slow. The new regulations drawn up in 1912 were to make the Dominion Rifle Association 'of real assistance to the new scheme'. These included organising shooting of a strictly military character, conducive to the training of the force. Rifle club representatives would serve on the association's executive. Points of detail were thrashed out in a conference in August 1912, attended by 16 club representatives, four from each military district.[45]

The rifle clubs were active in lobbying politicians, much to Godley's annoyance for it 'ignored proper and definite channels of communication' as laid down in the regulations.[46] An executive of rifle club members in Wellington, representing about half the rifle clubs in the dominion, lobbied Parliament for favourable conditions, including access to government rifle ranges, representation on the association and keeping the free railway passes that Godley wanted to stop.[47] Presided over by long-standing MP William Field, himself a former patron of the Karori Rifle Club, the executive first discussed the issue with 20 parliamentarians; then a deputation organised by Field met Prime Minister Sir Joseph Ward to try 'to secure in the new defence regulations some practical encouragement for these organisations'.[48] In this Field was successful, but at that stage he was lobbying only to have voluntary rifle clubs maintained in order to give men who had completed their compulsory military training 'an opportunity of keeping up their marksmanship' once they left the service. He noted, however, that Australia provided far better assistance to its rifle clubs in the form of free ammunition, cash payments and subsidised replacement barrels.[49] Rifle clubs maintained direct pressure on the authorities through their own organ, *Bulls Eye,* and the press.[50]

The military authorities had two main gripes with rifle clubs: the class of target they shot at and the fact that they did not do any field work. Rifle club members fired at and liked the bulls-eye target, but when they were taken into the defence scheme 'the Military people took charge and introduced a class of target that was not popular with shooting men… a fancy coloured Military target'.[51]

Quantitatively, progress towards this second line of defence moved quickly: by 1913 there were 199 clubs, 29 of them new;[52] by the outbreak of war there were 205 clubs with 4849 members. Qualitatively, however, relations between the military and rifle clubs were still cool at best, and hostile at worst. Relations had not been helped, moreover, when the Defence Department scheduled the annual camp for Wellington's Garrison Artillery Territorials on days in February 1914 that clashed with the Dominion Rifle Association's annual shoot at Trentham, thus preventing men from the Royal New Zealand Artillery from acting as markers on the ranges.[53] Godley was confident, though, that the willfully independent rifle clubs could be made 'of use if my authority over them is established'.[54]

Assistance from area group officers and NCOs may not have been as forthcoming as Godley had wanted, for in 1913 he instructed them to offer more help to rifle clubs. Disdain for what were perceived as amateur target shooters may have influenced some professional soldiers.[55] Presidents of the clubs were charged with liaising directly with area group officers to provide 'discipline and steadiness, which is the most essential and difficult part' of the training of men posted there. While officers on the Military Forces' active list were barred by legislation from joining a rifle club, those on the reserve list had no such obstacle – so long as they were still available for posting should the need arise. A number joined as a way of having more involvement.[56]

By 1914 the military usefulness of the clubs was being questioned, not for the first time. 'If Rifle Clubs are to be considered a second line of defence to the TF,' Godley stated, 'more should be done by them in the form of field training to fit themselves to take the field if required.' Although 205 clubs existed, 13 had been disbanded during the year. In 1914 they paraded for Sir Ian Hamilton, who urged them to 'qualify themselves to take the field with the rest of the Citizen army'.[57] The enrolment of compulsory military training members in rifle clubs had broken down by 1914, with the clubs themselves not knowing who their compulsory members were because those members were in fact 'now being put back into the Territorials'.[58]

Already, too, Godley recognised that urban-based rifle clubs had significant advantages over those in rural areas. It was easier for urban than rural men to get together, travel to rifle ranges that were nearer at hand and shoot more often. But the reality of New Zealand's very small population made its mark: the minimum membership for a rifle club soon had to be halved from 30 to 15. By 1913 over 5500 service rifles had been sold to club members. These represented about 13 per cent of the rifles available in the dominion. (A similar number was on issue to cadets, with the rest being used by the Territorial Force.)[59]

The fact that rifle clubs were placed firmly under the Directorate of Military Training highlighted their training role. Initially, the Inspector of Rifle Clubs, Drill Halls and Rifle Ranges, Colonel G.C.B. Wolfe, had the task of overseeing them. Later Captain J.A. Wallingford assumed the role as a secondary function to his duties as the general staff officer responsible for musketry.[60]

The war produced a surge of membership for the rifle clubs, including new mounted rifle clubs. The number of clubs rose to 240 in 1915, 33 of them new, with 8770 voluntary members, i.e. not including those posted from Territorial recruitment. On 8 August 1914, when von Spee's squadron was thought to be nearby, Godley instructed rifle clubs to be armed and mobilised, but rescinded the order two days later to keep priority focused on preparing the NZEF.[61] The threat nonetheless had a galvanising effect on men 'who could not go into camp [and who were] determined to use their utmost effort to repel an attack upon our shores'. According to a colourful post-war account, 'They decided that they would band together for home defence, even if they could only stand on the shore and fire a bullet towards the far horizon in the event of a raid or an attempted invasion.'[62]

As the NZEF sailed, but while the German squadron was still unaccounted for in the Pacific, rifle clubs were organised into home defence units. Without incurring any costs and without having any arms or uniforms issued to them, they were to form into their platoons of about 30 men each under their presidents. In lieu of uniforms, their unique coloured hatbands would identify them. When formed into companies of four platoons each, they would be under and take orders from the army group commander.[63] Godley saw this going 'some way to filling up vacancies caused by the departure of the Expeditionary Force'. In the Canterbury Military District, where the extant records are fullest, we know that such rifle club companies were formed in North Canterbury, Christchurch, Banks Peninsula, Akaroa and Timaru. Clubs in the Wellington area acted as a reserve company of 5 (Wellington) Regiment, under Karori club president Henry Marshall. In these heady months of 1914 some of the clubs, such as Marlborough's Sounds Rifle Club, took to the field to conduct realistic exercises under army instructors.[64]

By forming into their platoons for military service the clubs 'rose to the occasion', the Wellington Military District hierarchy thought.[65] Such units were voluntary and were assisted by overworked staff officers (mostly from the Territorial Reserve) or their own elected officers 'in some cases with great vigour. An organisation was achieved which had not hitherto existed and which would be very useful if the Rifle Clubs were required as a second line of defence.'[66] Some rifle clubs evinced 'much interest… in drilling and fitting themselves, as far as possible, to take the field if required'.[67] This involved being 'put through in rifle exercises, platoon drill, and extended-order work'. But these would seem to have been the exception. In November 1914, despite the now departed Godley having said that 'Senior Cadets Rifles are not to be interfered with', the clubs asked the Minister of Defence if even 10 per cent of senior cadets' rifles (approximately 2500 rifles) could be called in for use by rifle clubs.[68]

Immediately after the outbreak of war a number of organisations requested assistance from the military to form defence units. To all such enquiries the Defence Department responded by urging the formation of a rifle club, provision for which existed in the defence scheme. Groupings of old naval artillery volunteers or other ex-Volunteer Force members petitioned for rifles and ammunition. Groups as diverse as Auckland watersiders and Auckland yachtsmen formed corps for home defence.[69] The paramilitary Legion of Frontiersmen, which formed nine clubs, was one of the strongest. These 'decided to co-operate with the Defence Dept by registering as Rifle Clubs. In some instance, and notably on the West Coast of the South Island, sections of the National Reserve have formed Rifle Clubs, and have been accepted by the Department.'[70]

Some of the new clubs formed were mounted rifle clubs. Waiuku, for instance, offered 50 mounted men, but mustered 57, and Te Puke 20. Such offers were accepted so long as the members provided their own mounts and imposed no additional costs on the government. One of the most interesting such units was the Auckland Mounted Rifle Club, which had 65 members in 1915. This club also had a history: it was the vestige of the Auckland Farmers' Union Mounted Yeomanry Force, a group of special constables formed by former Volunteer and permanent soldier Major D.H. Lusk and others in November 1913 to oppose striking maritime workers in the bitter and violent strike of that year.[71] 'With the inception of the movement in which I took a leading part,' Lusk said in September 1914 when offering his men to Prime Minister Massey for the second time, 'I had 1500 mounted men with me in camp and under my control. This force was officered and organised as if [it was] a regular military brigade.' The Defence Department had helped to run this camp on Auckland's Domain.[72] Originally created to help provide 'for internal peace and order', under the motto of 'God and Our Rights', the force was now offered for defence against external attack.[73] Since its men had ceased to be special constables, the unit's name had been changed from a Constabulary to Yeomanry Force. Lusk also met Allen and Godley in search of recognition and rifles.

The commander of the Auckland Military District supported Lusk's application, saying that his corps had previously 'procured' personnel 'at short notice, and of a very good stamp' for the Territorial mounted regiment and drivers for the field artillery brigade. While insisting that they still form themselves into 100-man mounted rifle clubs, Godley accepted Lusk's suggestion that each could become a 'nursery and depot' for men to join the NZEF.[74] Few of these Farmers' Union clubs actually formed outside Auckland, Waiuku, Maungaturoto and Te Puke. The Onewhero branch, for instance, asked if it could form a unit other than a rifle club but, like others, it did not form anything before men and interest started to fall away.[75]

Another body that pestered the Defence Department for rifles and status was the Christchurch Citizens Defence Corps. It formed in October 1914 after an upwelling of enthusiasm from respectable citizens, prompted and guided by members of various chambers of commerce. It first met at King Edward Barracks on 29 October, after which 252 names were published of keen men willing to enrol.[76] The local MP, Heaton Rhodes, who had been lobbied by the group, said 'even if you do nothing more than enroll, you will thereby form an organisation of men who can immediately be mobilised should their services be required'.[77] The corps asked to be considered part of the National Reserve, but instead was told to form rifle clubs. When, in December 1914, the numbers involved had, they claimed, reached 2000, the elected commander of the corps, J.J. Dougall, told Allen that 'Rifle Clubs do not offer any inducement to businessmen nor under existing organisation would they be of much value for the purpose of defence'. He preferred to see the corps regarded as an active militia, something the government would not countenance. A better description might be that it was a 'great patriotic defence movement'.[78] This should be contrasted with existing rifle clubs, such as Christchurch Working Men's, Christchurch Defence, Veterans and Lincoln, which were meanwhile forming platoons and doing field work. From early 1915, the defence authorities regarded the Citizens Defence Corps as 'ephemeral' and, after 'the need of the CDC as a fighting unit passed away', it saw the war out as a good Samaritan – a recruiting and soldiers' welfare organisation.[79]

The demise of the rifle clubs

This enthusiasm and martial spirit at the beginning of the war soon faded: in 1915 the Otago Military District's commander reported that his rifle clubs 'continued to parade every week for the first four months. At the end of that time the parade was abandoned.'[80] The removal of threat contributed to this, but the growing call of the war on numbers of men for the NZEF, first identified through national registration late in 1915, then balloted into compulsory service from November 1916, sapped the will of those providing home defence. One role the clubs had up to the middle of the war was keeping tabs on potential manpower. By 1916 the Defence Department had experienced 'extreme difficulty' in keeping trace of men in the General Training Section, which, together with an unrelenting need for more personnel, led to the Military Service Act and its compulsory provisions.[81]

For most clubs the war brought an end to rifle shooting competitions, the normal activity for rifle club members. The competition shooting by the Dominion Rifle Association at Trentham stopped, because the camp was devoted fully to NZEF training.[82] The Ballinger Belt (the rifle champion), teams and district challenge shield, and the Collins Challenge Cup were not competed for during the war.[83] Expeditionary Force and Territorial Force units had an 'outstanding claim' on the use of government rifle ranges, and could therefore book them ahead of rifle clubs or even cadets. Prizes for shooting, however, continued to be awarded within the Defence Department's musketry training, competed for by Territorial Force, Cadet and Rifle Club members.[84] Some clubs, such as Linton, continued to shoot their own annual musketry course using .22 calibre rifles, the ammunition for which was not in limited supply.[85] Apart from 1916–17, the Petone Rifle Club shot its own club championship throughout the war, which was won each year by members of the Ballinger shooting dynasty.[86] Clearly some service ammunition was available.

The supply of rifles to clubs dried up, the Territorial Force and Senior Cadets having priority after the NZEF had been armed.[87] Despite ammunition being in short supply its delivery to clubs continued, even if that for 1917–18 was delayed several months or patchily distributed.[88] Clubs received the usual free grant of 150 rounds per member and with more to sell at discounted rates.[89]

The newer rifle clubs, which had formed in the fervent early months of the war, did not last. The Wellington Military District commander recommended the disbandment of seven such clubs in Group 8 (Taranaki) in 1918 because 'no rifle practice has been carried out for the past 2 or 3 years by these clubs'. Their presidents had reported 'that there are now insufficient members to carry on and that the Clubs should be disbanded'.[90]

The older clubs, in contrast, are the ones that lasted longer and did more for the war. Canterbury District reported in 1915 that 'the older clubs have been carrying out the Musketry Course and in some cases a large amount of Field work'.[91] Many of these clubs had been formed years before the war, and lasted years after it. Some clubs chose to temporarily amalgamate to get them through the bad times: for instance, five clubs in Wellington formed the Wellington City & Suburbs Rifle Club Union late in 1915.[92] The 100-man limit on membership was not enforced: half a dozen clubs returned figures in 1915 of over 100, with others much higher – Opaki 250, New Plymouth 266, and Marsden (near Whangarei) 581 members.[93]

Rifle club members could join the NZEF, and many clamoured to do so. By mid-1915 the national body asked clubs to keep it informed of numbers joining up: 70 members of the Wellington union had already offered themselves, and hoped (in vain) that a 'stated number of commissions in the NZEF [would] be offered to Rifle Clubs'.[94] Even officials did so, such as the middle-aged secretary of the Ngapara club, John Roberston, who downplayed his age by 6 years in order to join in 1916.[95] This had a similar effect on Rifle Clubs as it did on other home defence units, robbing them of manpower. The Commandant, Robin, expressed surprise that 231 rifle clubs existed in 1917 'considering the number of members who have volunteered and enlisted in the Expeditionary Force, and the abnormal strain of the present time'. Men not eligible to serve actively were encouraged to offer themselves as musketry instructors.[96]

Surviving clubs contributed to recruiting, providing a pool of trained men who, although beyond the age limit for the Reserve, still wanted to serve their country. 'All the clubs have evinced a patriotic endeavour to help the Dominion,' the Military Forces' annual report said, 'and have in many ways given expression to this desire.'[97] This may have been a reference to fundraising and similar patriotic activities, or taking part perhaps in parades for Allies Day or for the Belgian Relief Fund.

Musketry standards dipped slightly in 1916, reflecting the lesser emphasis on shooting practice than on drilling for the broader requirements of war. Although some clubs continued to hone their shooting skills, musketry courses recognised by the Military Forces were not available.[98] Robin talked of the 'disability' under which clubs carried on their business from 1917, 'owing to the abnormal conditions incident on the war' – by now, effectively, they had no defence role.[99] The clubs saw their role as keeping up shooting practice for returned men, and stiffening the NZEF Reserve's Second Division, which constituted married men eligible to serve and who were called up from October 1917.[100]

The heavy demands of the NZEF and a draw-off by essential industry led to the curtailment of all Territorial and cadet training in November 1917. Rifle clubs were henceforth incorporated in the National Reserve, as the NZEF Reserve was more often called.[101] The Garrison Artillery Territorials had already missed out on their annual camps earlier that year. Ironically this coincided with a resurgence of normal rifle club activity, as men were now freed up to spend their Saturdays shooting for prizes. The annual meetings of a number of clubs, resuming normal activity, made the news in 1917.[102] Although regular shooting resumed and the military force started planning for a national match in 1918, it did not take place until March 1919.

The competing needs of the NZEF versus those of the home defence units caused strain. In contrast to the encouragement of men to join the NZEF in 1914, the problem by 1918 was to *stop* men volunteering, thus weakening the home defences.[103] With so much of New Zealand's able-bodied manpower overseas, a scheme arose whereby home service men of the NZEF would replace Territorials in the home defence role. But by 1918 the quality of these men was described as 'poor … indifferent… either lacking physically or morally'.[104] In the rifle clubs, specifically, the New Zealand Military Forces also saw problems in the quality of men. Before the war Godley had expressed disgust at 'money being wasted on the travelling expenses of [rifle club] men who are thwarting our efforts to promote military efficiency'.[105] He had been pessimistic about the clubs' ability to shape up as part of the military forces, thereby justifying the money spent on them, and a good number of his professional military colleagues shared his view. When members for the Dominion Rifle Association executive came up for appointment after the war, nominated by the rifle clubs themselves, General Headquarters looked hard at their character. Two were long-standing members who had served overseas: Henry Marshall had been awarded the MC and the 1914 Ballinger Belt winner William Masefield had been wounded.[106] GHQ found no fault, either, with other members who had tried to join up – F.J. Silvius of Dunedin's Kiwi Rifle Club had volunteered for Samoa but at 49 was rebuffed as overage and W.G. Fellingham of Wellington Suburbs, who was the same age and had a family. But with S. Elliot of the Akarana Rifle Club, however, the Inspector of Rifle Clubs, Captain Wallingford, did not hold back, noting that he

> had nothing to prevent him enlisting or at least trying to do so, further he had been enjoying the privileges given to a rifle man for many years and had won a good deal in hard cash. He is not a good type. He seems to me to be a shy bird but a grumbler behind the scenes. As a matter of fact there are a large proportion of this kind in the Auckland Rifle Clubs. They think that heaven is made for the man who can hit a standing target.

Elliot was, in the end, given the benefit of the doubt because Auckland District Headquarters had no problem with him and he was a first-rate shot, and he was duly appointed to the national body.[107]

The experience of rifle clubs as part of the home defences was sobering. In

1920 the GOC, Major-General Sir Edward Chaytor, reported that 'while serving a useful purpose by creating an interest in rifle shooting, these clubs cannot be used in war as an integral part of the Military Forces'.[108] While acknowledging that the rifle clubs saw themselves as having 'done so much to make the splendid army sent overseas,' and that they had played a part in 'developing among the youth of the country a love of the use of the rifle', the Defence Department removed them from the order of battle, reduced the clubs' control over the Dominion Rifle Association executive, and scaled down its subsidy to rifle clubs and their annual shoots.[109] To be a 'great old enthusiast' for shooting, like Colonel R.J. Collins, who had started shooting in 1867 and retired from chairing the Dominion Rifle Association in 1921, was not enough to make rifle club members into useful soldiers.[110] While the tension between the clubs' national body and the Defence Department continued, not everyone in the shooting fraternity saw this divorce as a good move, one commentator describing it as the 'beginning of the rot' for rifle clubs.[111]

From 1919 to 1923, 71 clubs were disbanded.[112] This was in part to remove the cost of subsidising them from the Defence Vote, but also because they had not measured up. Colonel Heard's words in 1914 that 'their value as a fighting force is a negligible quantity' had proved to be prophetic.[113]

Enthusiasm for shooting, however, did not diminish with the end of the war: 168 clubs remained on the books in 1921. In future all members would be required, like other citizens, to join a proper military unit in time of emergency but rifle clubs would never again constitute military units in their own right.[114]

Perhaps seeing them as anything other than schools for marksmanship was the mistake. One stalwart said the military men 'made a great mistake' when they took over rifle clubs and 'pushed to the fore… a class of target that was not popular with shooters'.[115] In reality the threat to New Zealand was not great enough to warrant their mobilisation, and their response to the needs of the country in 1914–18 was not as keen as Godley had hoped it would be. For a very brief time in the first few months of war, some rifle clubs were the Home Guard of the First World War. Most, however, wanted to only 'smell powder without paying a high price for it'.[116] They were, after all, the poor cousins.

26

NEW ZEALAND CHURCHES
AND DEATH IN THE FIRST WORLD WAR

Allan Davidson

Private Alfred Charles Young was born at Kaiapoi and was killed at Messines on 8 June 1917.[1] His name is among the over 800 NZEF soldiers who are commemorated on the memorial at Messines Ridge, 6 miles south of Ypres, which remembers the men 'who fell in or near Messines in 1917 and 1918, and whose graves are known only to God'. In the nearby cemetery on the memorial altar the words are carved: 'Their name liveth for evermore'.[2] The New Zealand High Commissioner in London, Sir Thomas Mackenzie, wrote what was no doubt a form letter to Alfred Young's widowed mother in Kaiapoi, expressing condolences and 'the admiration we feel for our brave soldiers, and for all they have done for the Empire'. Using the euphemistic language typical of the war, Mackenzie concluded: 'Your son has gone to the Great Beyond, and our one hope is that sacrifices such as he has made will not be in vain'.[3] The King's Scroll, sent to the relatives of soldiers killed in the war, commemorated 'those who at the call of King and Country, left all that was dear to them, endured hardness, faced danger, and finally passed out of the sight of men by the path of duty and self-sacrifice, giving up their own lives that others might live in freedom'.[4]

As Pierre Berton wrote, 'Nations must justify mass killing, if only to support the feelings of the bereaved and the sanity of the survivors.'[5] The rhetoric surrounding death in the First World War was part of this justification: only by making sense of the conflict could society give some meaning to the loss of life and some comfort to the relatives of those who had been killed. The role of the churches, in using, supporting, and reinforcing war rhetoric in general, and death rhetoric in particular, has received little detailed attention in New Zealand compared with other countries.[6] Churches were in the business of giving meaning to both life and death. In 1916 over 77 per cent of New Zealanders identified themselves, at least nominally, as Anglicans, Presbyterians and Methodists, and a further 14 per cent were Catholics, making more than 90 per cent of the total population.[7] Through their publications, in the pastoral comfort they offered to the bereaved and in their services of worship, the churches articulated, reflected and shaped attitudes towards death.

In his last letter, from 'Somwhere [*sic*] in France', Alfred Young wrote as the dutiful son:

> Well mother a Church parade at the front always seems very sacred and I always like them. It is not often we get the chance. Now and again we have them. Sunday as a rule is the same as any other day. A chap sees things out here that make him stop and think but mother you need never worry I am prepared to die if it is the Almighty[']s wish.[8]

Like so many parents, family and friends, Mrs C. J. Young had to live with the uncertainty and anxiety of war. She received news of her son's death by 29 June 1917 when his name appeared in the Roll of Honour in the Christchurch *Press* alongside the names of three other soldiers. His death notice concluded with the patriotic ascription, 'For King and Country'. The brief personal note in the paper mentioned his birthplace of Church Bush, Kaiapoi, his attendance at the district high school, his work as a farmer and his enthusiastic membership 'of the 13th Regimental Band for fourteen years'.[9] For his widowed mother, a loyal member of the Presbyterian congregation in Kaiapoi, words of comfort were offered in a memorial sermon. 'Alf', the minister indicated, had 'paid the price of supreme sacrifice'; he had left 'the proud record and cherished memory of a hero in the fight for freedom against oppression and for right against might'. Mrs Young was commended to the 'God of all comfort and hope'.[10]

There was nothing exceptional or notable in this one death, but Alf Young is representative of the over 17,000 New Zealanders who died during the war. The soldier was killed on the other side of the world. There was no body over which to grieve. In this case, as in so many, no corpse was ever identified and interred in a named grave. A.C. Young's memorial is a name on a monument far away. There was an attempt, through civic memorials, and honours boards in churches, schools and workplaces, to give some local physical expression to remembrance, and these monuments became functional substitutes for the graves and headstones in local cemeteries. Kaiapoi, where Alf Young had lived, erected a notable public memorial to the more than 100 soldiers from the community who were killed in the war. The marble sculpture of a New Zealand soldier by William Trethewey was described by the Mayor of Kaiapoi at its unveiling as 'a soldier in full kit ... complete in every detail, even to the broken boot-lace!... The face was lined and careworn, and bore the marks of what the soldier had experienced: it was the face of a man who had looked into the face of hell and had yet been undaunted.' As Maclean and Phillips comment, 'the sculptor had succeeded in capturing the popular mythology of the Anzacs'.[11]

The development of the rituals associated with Anzac Day, to which the churches made a significant contribution, along with the words used by officials and clergy, were all part of the attempt to give meaning to death in the First World War. But in surrounding these deaths with sacrificial language and theology was something of the reality of death itself lost? To critically examine that language and the theology undergirding it is a subversive undertaking, for it calls into question the meaning that has been given to the soldiers' deaths.

The churches and war rhetoric

Ecclesiastical war and death rhetoric, as part of the association between the church and the military, has a long history. The intimate connection between the Crusaders and the church, the so-called 'religious wars', the involvement of clergy as military chaplains, the just war theology, the lodging of battle colours and the erection of war memorials in cathedrals and churches, the Christian pacifist voices of dissent – all point to this long and complex inter-relationship. The way in which the churches saw death in the First World War needs to be placed in the context of the way in which they saw the war itself.

From the outset, all the major churches sanctified the Allied cause. Anglicans, Presbyterians and Methodists, and to a lesser extent Baptists, were vocal in their support, not surprisingly given their British roots. An editorial in October 1914 in the Auckland Anglican diocesan monthly, the *Church Gazette*, declared that:

> The Empire is indeed united, calm resolute, and we enter into the mighty conflict trusting in God. England enters into this war with clean hands and a clear conscience. She has striven for peace, and only enters into the war in the defence of the rights of the smaller nations of Europe.... There is such a thing as national morality, and England stands for that. We believe in a moral God, and to Him we appeal: 'We have heard with our ears, O God, our fathers have told us, what Thou hast done in their time of old.... Through Thee we will overthrow our enemies, and in Thy name we will tread them under that rise up against us.'[12]

Imperial loyalty, patriotism and jingoistic rhetoric were combined. The Methodist Conference in 1915 regarded 'the British Empire, with all its defects, as being, in practical righteousness, the largest instalment of the Kingdom of God that has yet arisen among men'. They rejoiced 'in the valour and growing strength of the King's forces' and joined 'earnestly in prayer that God will defend the right, and cause the grinding militarism of Germany to cease from the earth'.[13] Anglican sentiments on war were not surprising, given their English established church origins, and the *de facto* role they often played as chaplain to the nation. Methodists, in defining themselves against the Church of England in the late 18th and early 19th centuries, repeatedly protested their loyalty to the Crown. This, combined with their enthusiastic commitment to single issues, contributed to their patriotic fervour.

Baptists, in contrast to Anglicans and Methodists, had a long history of asserting their independence in matters of secular authority. In September 1914, H.H. Driver, the editor of the *New Zealand Baptist*, gave a very considered judgment on the war, but nevertheless asserted that Britain had never before 'waged war with purer motives and nobler aims. She may safely make her appeal to the righteous Lord, whose right hand is full of righteousness, to vindicate her and her Allies in this tremendous conflict.'[14] Under Driver's successor, J.J. North, the *New Zealand Baptist* from 1916 continued to support the war effort.

North, however, reflected Baptist concerns about individual conscience and gave much more room to discussing the rights of conscientious objectors and the question of conscription than other church publications.

In the first period of the war, from 1914 to mid-1915, many perceived the conflict as a religious crusade, almost a holy war. Professor John Dickie, in his sermon to farewell students from Knox College, Dunedin, who were going to the front, chose as his text the Psalmist's reference to the God of battles: '[Through], God, we shall do valiantly; for He it is that shall tread down our enemies'. For Dickie, 'The righteousness of our cause is a guarantee that the principles for which we stand must ultimately, in God's own time and way, prevail.' Those who were going to war were told that they were following 'the path of Christian duty'.[15] There was criticism of the church and its ignominious failure to 'win the world for Christ and the Kingdom of God,'[16] but William Gray Dixon, Presbyterian minister at Roslyn, Dunedin, claimed that 'The war has made us gloriously one in heart and aim – one and invincible, one… [in] potential as never before for the universal Kingdom of God'.[17] There were some hopes that war might bring about a religious revival: the editor of the Presbyterian publication, the *Outlook*, noted in February 1915 that:

> The war is quietly but surely doing wonderful things for the British nation; and this altogether apart from what is happening on the battlefields or on the sea. People everywhere are evincing a desire for prayer, and the Church should miss no opportunity of encouraging that desire.[18]

At the opening service for the Presbyterian Theological Hall in March 1915, the chosen hymn was 'Fight the good fight with all thy might!', a reminder of the ambiguity of Christian hymnody and the way in which militaristic imagery could easily be used to refer to both spiritual and secular warfare. 'Onward Christian soldiers, marching as to war' is another hymn of the many with this double connotation. Speaking on 'War and Christianity' at the Knox opening, R.E. Davies, the minister at Knox Church, Dunedin, declared, 'The day of the pacifist is for the present over…. Academic discussions are over, and the sword now decides.' Davies criticised Germany's 'confusion of the Old Testament god Jehovah with their war god Odin' and their abandonment of 'moral restraint' and contrasted this with the 'clean hands' with which the Allies had entered the war. At the same time he was concerned 'that in our condemnation of Germany we may not engender a spirit of self-righteousness.'[19]

The Catholic church, as Hugh Laracy has pointed out, 'was at one with itself, and with the nation at war'.[20] In August 1914 the editor of the *New Zealand Tablet* commented on the 'unanimity of feeling and sentiment throughout every portion of the Empire in regard to the Mother Country's action and attitude'. Sir Joseph Ward, former Prime Minister and a Catholic, told the departing troops, 'The war you are about to engage in is a just war.' Henry Cleary, Catholic Bishop of Auckland, who served for three months as a chaplain in France, viewed the war as 'more than merely a just war or a patriotic duty; it was a sacred cause'.[21] While James Kelly, who became editor of the *Tablet* in 1916, was more concerned in its columns with Irish independence, Catholic education and combating Protestant bigotry than the successful outcome of the war, throughout the war the paper had pages titled 'Roll of Honor' with photos and brief descriptions of Catholic soldiers killed in the conflict. For Kelly to oppose the war would have been to question the motives of the thousands of Catholics serving overseas. The *Month*, founded in Auckland in July 1918, was Cleary's counter to Kelly's extremism and included more personal reflections on the war than its southern counterpart.[22]

Moderating voices in a context in which the enemy was demonised were few and far between. A statement from the Society of Friends spoke about the 'vital importance that the war should not be carried on in any vindictive spirit, and that it should be brought to a close at the earliest possible moment'.[23] Brethren, who identified as conscientious objectors, pointed out that 'Many true Christians will undoubtedly be engaged in the war, and the Christians in the German Army are as dear to God as those in the British Army'.[24] Smaller groups such as Seventh Day Adventists and Jehovah Witnesses generally opposed the war.[25]

One contributor to the Presbyterian Women's Missionary Union's magazine related the war to the union's own specific interests: 'our soldiers are fighting for the ideals of Christ Jesus as surely as their forefathers did' and they were 'presenting their bodies – a living sacrifice' in order to keep the seas open so 'that we may carry on our work in the extension of Christ's Kingdom'.[26] The Women's Christian Temperance Union, while advocating peace, linked the deaths of soldiers with 'the foe without', and identified their own work with 'the deadlier forces of evil within'.[27] The ongoing battle for prohibition was expressed in militant language.

Although all the larger churches held onto the justice of the Allied cause throughout the war, the crusading language employed in the first 18 months sounded increasingly hollow as the war literally became bogged down on the Western Front and weariness began to overtake all those involved in the fighting. Churches were faced with the task of trying to help a grieving community make sense of the mounting number of overseas war dead and injured. The horrors of war and the dreadful circumstances in which many soldiers died were largely hidden from public view. An exception in church publications was the letter from the Methodist Chaplain-Major John Luxford which appeared in the *New Zealand Methodist Times* in July 1915, describing the awfulness of Gallipoli:

> I have witnessed the wounded by hundreds, and some of the scenes have been heartrending. For days I have seen pilgrimages of pain and death, and in some cases have been able to minister consolation in the Name which is above every name. I have been obliged to read or recite the burial service in the grave, kneeling with the dead bodies, because of the bullets flying around.[28]

The need to uphold public morale, to recruit more soldiers, and to support the war effort was reinforced by the war rhetoric used in newspapers and in the churches. In 1915, for example, the WCTU noted that the Women's National Council of Canada was 'urging the people of that Dominion who have lost loved ones in battle not to wear black as mourning' but to wear a purple arm band as 'a mark of honour, indicating the one mourned for had given his life for his country'.[29] Luxford softened the horrors of death and battle by pointing to comradeship, bravery, endurance, patriotism and the values of blood sacrifice:

> The battlefield is very different in reality from descriptions in books and papers. It is an Inferno in one sense, and a comradeship in another. Doubtless New Zealand has wept tears of bitter sorrow because of the loss of her brave sons, but she must rejoice for their bravery, endurance and patriotism. She has helped to cement the Empire with her best blood![30]

The war and patriotic duty

Because many church leaders defined the war as a sacred cause, soldiers were encouraged to see their patriotic duty in religious terms. For James Gibb, the leading Presbyterian minister in New Zealand, it was 'the urgent duty of all men of age and physical fitness to offer themselves at once to their country, and it is the duty of all women to surrender their men, nay, to bring pressure to bear on them to do their duty to the flag'.[31]

The churches tried to give significance to the deaths by ennobling the way in which the soldiers had joined up and gone to fight out of a sense of duty. In an editorial in July 1915, responding to the early casualties lists coming from Gallipoli, the *Church News* questioned:

> Are we all at the mercy of cruel necessity that first creates and then destroys our dearest? Are we to acquiesce in death? Play our funeral march, put on mourning, cherish fond memories of the past, until we and our memories alike have passed into death and oblivion?

In answering this question the editor addressed the soldiers' parents:

> Then came the war. You knew he would want to go. The call of duty came to him, the call of his country, the call of comradeship. Of course he must go.... Was it not all God's call to his soul? – from that first opening of the eyes when he became a child up to the higher call to be a man and a patriot, and right on to this last call to lay down his life bravely, at its best?[32]

The idealisation of the call of duty was used in recruiting rhetoric in an extreme way by Chaplain-Captain Sullivan in a sermon at St Paul's Methodist Church in Palmerston, in January 1916, using the text, 'I am the door: by me if any man enter in, he shall be saved' (John 10.9). Enlisting in the King's Army was, in Sullivan's view, the highest Christian duty. In what sounds like a perverted altar call, he declared that 'Today Christ's way led straight to the firing line and into the bayonet charge. Christ asks you to come in His name to avenge intolerable wrongs.... He wants you to come and enlist in the service of your country.'[33]

Christian commitment was identified with patriotic duty. There was a strong element of theological coercion and compulsion in this kind of rhetoric with no room for dissent. J.S. Ponder, a Presbyterian, preaching in May 1915 to the Waitahuna volunteers departing for the front, endorsed the 'privilege of patriotic self-sacrifice' and referring to the 'call of duty', said that 'we ministers are in the glad position that we can send the young patriots to do or die with our best "God-speed," for the war we are waging is undoubtedly a righteous one'.[34]

At the first Anzac commemoration at St Patrick's Cathedral in Auckland, Monsignor George Gillan articulated sentiments similar to those heard from Protestant pulpits. Reading from a chaplain's account of the Gallipoli landing, Gillan described how, 'Amid scenes of horror beyond description, the men did their duty with unswerving loyalty and devotion, with a sure faith in God that led them to face death unflinchingly'.[35]

Many of the early volunteers went to war out of a sense of adventure. The slowing down of volunteering and the introduction of conscription in November 1916 made the sanctifying of duty seem rather hollow as other people defined duty for those conscripted. Comforting the grieving by telling them that the one they mourned had done his God-given duty as a way of justifying his death also seemed rather shallow. This kind of rhetoric from the pulpit or the pen avoided the bigger questions and somewhat blindly endorsed the values associated with warfare. The uncritical identification of duty to God with duty to country, undergirded by a belief in the righteous cause of the Allies, meant that churches were in danger of being seen as not only supporting but also sanctifying the war. This made it very difficult for any prophetic alternative to be heard.

War and the sanctifying of sacrifice

The sanctifying of duty contained the implication that death in battle was also death in God's cause. This led to a third dimension in the church's understanding of war, the sanctifying of sacrifice.

As the first anniversary of the Anzac landing at Gallipoli approached, the Christchurch Anglican monthly *Church News* drew together the themes of Good Friday and the war. The 'Cross of Christ' was seen as 'a cruel symbol of the world's enmity' but also of love. 'In that self-sacrifice', the writer believed, lay 'the answer to the tragedy of Europe'. The cross symbolised the 'world-old conflict of good and evil in which Christ died'. Just as Jesus had won, so 'in the end the right will win' in the war 'and we know that the man who bravely lays down his life for country and comrades, for love and duty, for others and not for self, is so far in the footsteps of Christ'. The claim was made that 'The sufferers – like Christ – are suffering for the sins of the world.' The battle that Christ fought at Calvary was being refought in the trenches of Europe: 'It is God's battle; and those who know how to suffer willingly and to die can claim His comradeship who died in like manner for them.'[36]

There were murmurings in some church circles about the identification of Christ's sacrifice with that of soldiers. This particularly revolved around the application of the text from John 15:verse 13: 'Greater love hath no man than this, that a man lay down his life for his friends'. In September 1915 W.J. Williams, the editor of the *New Zealand Methodist*, recognised the 'supreme sacrifice' being made by soldiers, but questioned whether this text was not 'sadly overworked when it is made to apply to conditions of death on a field of war?'[37] But by 26 December 1916 Williams, while recognising that 'War to-day is a hideous anachronism', embraced these words:

> In hundreds of thousands of cases the supreme sacrifice has been consummated. It was Christ Himself who pronounced a benediction on such a sacrifice by saying, 'Greater love hath no man than this that a man lay down his life for his friends.'… Men by the million are discovering the truth of what Christ taught by example and precept, that the best use that can be made of life for the benefit of others is to give it away.[38]

Wilkinson, in his study of *The Church of England and the First World War*, indicated that 'doctrinally, and therefore pastorally, the ministry of the Church of England to the dying and bereaved was confused'.[39] In the context of war and faced with the vast scale of death that confusion was accentuated. Theological language referring to the cross and sacrifice and giving one's life for others was easily stretched to try to incorporate both those within and without the church. John Arkwright, in his hymn 'For the fallen', written during the war, distinguished between the cross and the death of Christ and the 'lesser Calvaries' endured by others. He nevertheless made the identification between the death of the soldier and the death of Christ:

These were her servants, in his steps they trod,

Following through death the martyred Son of God:

Victor he rose; victorious too shall rise

They who have drunk his cup of sacrifice.[40]

As the war was drawing to its close, an editorial in the *New Zealand Methodist Times* reflected on the significance of 'The Cross in War': 'It is not meaningless that at the head of each soldier's grave is a white cross. It is the mute sign that through the Cross Christ overcame death and for those who believe in Him has robbed the grave of all its terrors.'[41] Churches sought to give meaning to death in wartime by associating it with the cross and death of Christ. The Imperial War Graves Commission, however, used a headstone rather than a cross to mark soldiers' graves, although a large 'Cross of Sacrifice' was erected in many of their cemeteries. As Maclean and Phillips explain, the cross was absent from many public war memorials in New Zealand on the grounds that 'people wanted the war memorial to be a unifying monument…. It was feared that if such an avowedly Christian symbol as the cross was chosen as the dominant motif, it might give offence.' They do note, however, that 'since the cross was so perfect an expression of the dominant ideology of the war memorial – the concepts of sacrifice and death for others, and the hope for eternal life', it was used in some monuments 'as a sculptural detail'.[42] Although the cross figured prominently in the theology and language of evangelical Protestant churches, they disputed its use in symbolic form. Some saw the cross as too Catholic, so its absence from public monuments may also indicate sectarian pressure rather than secular influences.[43]

Theological language referring to the cross, sacrifice and giving one's life for others was easily stretched to try to make sense of the enormous carnage. Behind these sentiments was pastoral concern for the grieving families. A memorial service was hardly the time to raise questions about the war strategy of generals who sent tens of thousands of soldiers to their deaths for a few hundred yards of territory. Yet by using the language of sacrifice and patriotism and endorsing the war effort, churches were complicit in helping it to continue unquestioned. Dennis McEldowney has written that 'what was seen as the Christian concept of sacrifice made the carnage possible, as well as acceptable'.[44]

War and the promise of heaven

Some extended the theology of sacrifice by appealing to the concept of a heavenly reward in order to further legitimate and make sense of the death toll in the First World War. After Gallipoli, the editor of the *Church News* had crudely used belief in the world to come to comfort the grieving:

> We must think of our brave soldiers marching on, in advance of us, mustering in the greater world that comes next to this. What greeting of comrades there! What new enterprize, new understanding, new light, among the great multitude whom no man can number! They are not sadly looking back, unless it may be that we make them sad. And if your very best and dearest is among them, how would he like you to pity him now?[45]

With an insight into the next world that went beyond orthodox theology, the author makes those mourning guilty for feeling sad about their lost ones. While this approach was intended to comfort and bring hope, there is a question as to how much it was 'pie in the sky when we die' theology.

Following the Battle of Messines in June 1917, the *Church News* referred to 'The brilliant victory', 'The cost of this last advance', and the consequent sadness brought to many homes. The editor suggested that:

> 'We learn to take the larger view of life' and the way in which 'in the light of Christ we are coming to look with steadfast faith on the larger life, of which this is only the first act; we can hold fast to our friends who have passed the gates, and entered, with honour, on the higher career beyond... It is this certitude that redeems the world from all its sordidness and failure.'[46]

The war challenged the churches' understanding of eternity and salvation. Universalism became much more attractive than the narrow selective salvation taught by some before 1914. The communion of saints and prayers for the dead became much more widely acknowledged during and after the war.

The Methodist minister H.L. Blamires struggled more carefully with the question of heavenly rewards than the editor of the *Church News*. Within the context of the liberal Protestant teaching of the 'Fatherhood of God' and the

'Brotherhood of man', he recognised that what he called the 'Larger Hope of the Life Beyond' appealed 'to modern views of justice and of the love of God for the souls of men'. He cautioned, however, against the teaching that 'the men who die in battle, because of their death in a righteous cause, necessarily go straight to Heaven'. In a carefully nuanced article, Blamires resisted universalism, salvation for all, but he did offer the 'possibility of probation' for some who had died. He concluded that there was 'no loophole' and emphasised 'the importance of availing ourselves of Christ's saving grace and fellowship here and now'. At the same time he left the final judgment to God, telling his readers that 'we are to remember that God's heart yearns over all'.[47]

At the Anzac memorial service at St Paul's Cathedral in June 1915, Randall Davidson, the Archbishop of Canterbury, took a cautious line: 'that it would be untrue to claim that all who gave their lives were stainless saints. But we should pray that they may "pass onward in the new and larger life from strength to strength".' Wilkinson noted, 'The pressures of bereavement and patriotism made any mention of hell or even an intermediate state rare on the lips of preachers.'[48] Instead, many preachers pointed to salvation and the possibility of immortality in the world to come.

Anglican Archbishop A.W. Averill, was more explicit than Blamires, telling an Auckland Anzac Day service in 1916 that 'the brave men who will not come back to us have not finished their life of devotion, but have gone into God's higher training camp of service, where he has special work for each one of them'.[49] Matthew Brodie, the Catholic Bishop of Christchurch, in a sermon preached at the 1916 Anzac Requiem Mass, declared that:

> The mourners would be consoled by the fact that the separation was only for a time, that the lost ones, by their deaths for their country and their God, had inherited the crown of eternal reward, which would be shared by those who had made the great sacrifice of sending them forth.[50]

Father McCarthy offered a more nuanced perspective when speaking at 'a solemn High Mass for the repose of the souls of soldiers killed at the front' in Auckland in 1918. 'Although patriotism is of itself but a natural virtue, and therefore incapable of obtaining the supernatural reward of heaven, yet when offered to God it is raised to a supernatural order and it is rendered pleasing to God.'[51]

Driver, in the *New Zealand Baptist*, rejected the 'post-mortem salvation' advocated by the Reverend Percy Wainwright of Gisborne, who contended 'that those who had no fair chance of knowing Christ and His saving power in this world would have new chances afforded them in the next'. Driver argued that it could not 'be reasonably held that the mere fact that men sacrifice their life in battle alters the case' and suggested 'we must be careful lest we encourage men to live carelessly now on the off chance that new opportunities will be afforded them in the world to come'. Automatic salvation for soldiers was denounced in forthright language as 'erroneous teaching' and 'fallacious comfort' to those who 'write and speak as if the soldiers' sacrifice were akin to the redeeming sacrifice of Calvary, and ensured eternal safety whatever their previous attitude towards Christ had been'.[52] An editorial in the Salvation Army paper soon after the landing at Gallipoli was aghast at the suggestion that the 'noble and patriotic conduct' of 'our brave boys' was 'worthy of being named by the sacred word "atonement", or that such an act was reconciling them to God'.[53]

In contrast, Anglicans seemed more open to embracing universalism, which in the context of war became much more attractive than the narrow selective salvation taught by some. Noting the death of Captain M.W.C. Sprott, eldest son of the Bishop of Wellington, the *Church Gazette* quoted from the English poet, John Oxenham:

> He died the noblest death a man may die,
>
> Fighting for God, and Right, and Liberty –
>
> And such a death is Immortality.[54]

The Auckland Catholic paper, the *Month*, noted in 1918 that 'the war is … gradually bringing home more of the inner significance of the familiar, immemorial Catholic doctrine of the Communion of Saints'.[55] J.J. North, however, reacted with characteristic anti-Catholic rhetoric in rejecting prayers for the dead as 'Popish and utterly Christless' and without the warrant of Scripture.[56]

For some soldiers, living with the reality of death, the universalising of salvation to incorporate all those who were killed was rejected as a sham. One soldier wrote:

> I don't hold myself up to be a plaster saint.... Here am I, I swear like blazes; there is not a blamed thing that the Bible is up against that I don't do; and to say that we, if we get a bullet through our heads or hearts, go straight to Heaven is more than I can swallow.[57]

Many soldiers understood death in terms of fate and the bullet that had their name on it. The churches were unable to develop an adequate theological response to the enormous ongoing tragedy with which it was trying to cope. Its theology of life and death was found wanting.

Memorialising the dead

Churches have a long history of memorialising the war dead. The large numbers of dead, the lack of bodies for funerals, the distance from the conflict and the demands of recruiting and morale led the churches in the First World War to adapt their ministry to the grieving. As early as June 1915, the *Church News* noted that 'At the beginning of the fight we had thought of recording in these pages something of those who should fall, but now that the heavier lists come in we see it to be impossible'.[58]

Memorial services became one way of helping individuals, families and communities to mourn publicly. Churchill Julius, Anglican Bishop of Christchurch, spoke on 6 June 1915 at 'A special memorial service for the New Zealand soldiers fallen on the battlefield in the Dardanelles'. The use of euphemistic language, such as 'the fallen' or 'those who had passed over', was a rhetorical way of softening the brutality and reality of war and death. 'Why,' Julius questioned, 'should they mourn for those who had died gloriously for their King and country?' For him, the service was 'a thanksgiving for those who had done their part; it was a service of prayer for those who had lost their lives, and it was an appeal to those who remained behind to do their duty'.[59] Memorial services, with their reverential music, hushed tones, patriotic hymns and sanctifying language, contributed to the growing mythology surrounding the war.

Parishes held their own special memorial services. At St Barnabas's in

Christchurch, four 'Fendalton men' were particularly remembered in a service on 27 June 1915. The same news item describing this service noted that the parish had lost two more 'of its well-known sons'. In extending sympathy to the relatives, the parish gave 'thanks to God for those who have died so gloriously for their King and Country'.[60] In October 1915 the *Church News,* noting the death of one of the regular communicants from Fendalton who had died from wounds received at the Dardanelles, referred to 'his promotion from the Church Militant to the Church Expectant'.[61]

The division of the churches became all too apparent as they were faced by the growing impact of death on the community. In 1915 Bishop Julius warned against joint memorial services as 'neither necessary nor desirable': it was 'not lack of charity that makes me dislike them, but a hatred of sham and inconsistency'.[62] By the end of the war, however, speaking at the day-long ecumenical service of intercession in May 1918, he noted 'How much had been lost during the Churches' separation and division' and hoped 'It might be that the Church restored to unity and fellowship in the coming ages would be better because of the sorrows experienced through division'.[63]

Because of their lack of unity the churches tended to be bypassed as New Zealand began to develop its own civil rituals associated with Anzac Day commemorations. The *Auckland Star* reported in April 1916 that returned soldiers 'did not want to be "split up among twenty or thirty different churches on Anzac Day"' but preferred 'a simple, combined service conducted by one of the popular army chaplains'.[64] Civic or public Anzac Day services overshadowed denominational services. While hymns were sung and prayers were said on these occasions, they focused on the values of patriotism, nationalism, sacrifice and honouring the war dead: by default they could easily be seen as glorifying war. The laying of wreaths at public war memorials, the firing of volleys and the treating of Anzac Day as a holy day were features of what John Harré referred to in 1966 as New Zealand's 'most important indigenous religious ceremonial' occasion. 'It is coincidental that this is associated with Christianity.... It is a memorial cult which mobilizes more people into a ritual expression of togetherness than any conventional religious observance.'[65] It can be argued, however, that the cult of the war dead was in fact deeply influenced by the blending of Christian theology about duty, sacrifice, rewards and remembrance with patriotic virtues and a public ideology. Secular interpretations can very easily miss the pervasive influence of Christian language, thought and symbols on the understanding of death in the First World War.[66] Although institutional Christianity was increasingly rejected, account must be taken of the significant connections between Christian theology and what American scholars have identified as 'civil religion'.[67]

Physical memorials in churches also were used as a way of helping people remember those who had gone to serve overseas and particularly those who had died. The *Church News* advertised in 1915 a framed 'Roll of Honour and Record of Men who are serving at the Front'.[68] Reflecting on the importance of church memorials, one article in the April 1916 issue referred to the way in which 'our children will gain their first lesson in the history of these years of sacrifice, from the consecrated names and memorials, among which they are taught to worship God'. The writer did question whether individual memorials should be erected: 'it is greatly to be desired that when this war is past, its heroes should be commemorated in our churches in such a way that all alike have due honour, and that any purely personal memorial should take a form which will be something of permanent beauty and use'. The recommendation 'that the erection of memorial tablets or brasses should be deferred until the Roll of Honour is complete' was not heeded.[69] For example, at St Barnabas's in Fendalton, on 8 March 1917, a brass memorial tablet was unveiled in memory of Lieutenant William John Marriott.[70] People without a grave to visit needed physical monuments to help them to remember and to grieve.

The process of memorialisation was seen in churches in honours boards, gifts of church furniture, communion vessels, memorial windows and church buildings. The Catholic church in Feilding advertised that it was 'erecting a MEMORIAL CHURCH' and asked supporters to 'Ensure a weekly Mass for the souls of your gallant dead by sending their names, regiments, and date and place of death' to the parish secretary.[71] St Andrew's Church in Epsom, Auckland, has a number of memorials, including a window based on James Clark's famous painting 'The Great Sacrifice', dedicated to the memory of a Gallipoli casualty.[72] The dead soldier, in his clean uniform, with a small bullet wound in his forehead, lying at the foot of the cross, sums up much of the ambiguity about the church's depiction of death in the First World War. The chapel at King's College in

Auckland was dedicated 'To the glory of God and in memory of the Old Boys who gave their lives in the Great War, 1914–18.'[73] The church and public memorials helped keep alive the names of those who had died. Through civic services, Anzac commemorations in schools and denominational worship, a new generation was inculturated into the overlapping public ideology and Christian theology about war and honouring the dead.

Conclusion

In identifying themselves so closely with the war, in sanctifying duty, sacrifice and death, and promising heavenly rewards, had churches compromised their theology? Ormond Burton, a noted soldier and New Zealand's leading pacifist after the war, thought so:

> The greatest debacle of the war was without question that of the Christian Church. She was subservient everywhere to the national governments. All over the world Christian ministers closed their New Testaments, preached more paganism and became the recruiting sergeants of the armies.[74]

Churches left so little room in their preaching and teaching for the God of peace during the war that the small number who tried to voice the pacifist cause were ostracised and persecuted. Only towards the end of the war did some church leaders come forward to speak out for fairer treatment for conscientious objectors.[75]

Values such as patriotism, duty, sacrifice and imperial loyalty were overworked in a secularised theology which in an extreme form went as far as seeing the war as restoring Christendom.[76] Bishop Averill, speaking to the Anglican General Synod in October 1918, claimed 'We have not assimilated the spirit of militarism as some of our pacifist friends seem to imagine; we hate war to-day as we never hated it before'. At the same time he declared that 'Not until arrogant militarism is crushed by the power in which it has trusted, viz., the sword, can peace be possible.'[77] Averill pointed to the unresolved tension facing churches during the war: how to hold together the gospel of peace with the sword of war – the age-old Christian dilemma of how to render to Caesar the things that are Caesar's, and to God the things that are God's

This ambiguity was reflected in resolutions passed by the Presbyterian General Assembly in February 1919. In a resolution on the Armistice they gave 'thanks to God for the victory that has attended the Allied arms, and the triumph of the principles of righteousness, truth, and freedom for which we have been contending'. In a subsequent resolution on the League of Nations, the assembly declared 'its deep and abiding hatred of war, as an immeasurable evil in itself, and the fruitful source of other evils, and prays God that the war now ended may be the final war'. In attempting to bring comfort to the bereaved, the assembly commended 'them to the compassion of Him Whose grace never faileth and Whose mercy is over all His works'.[78] Methodists were even more explicit, noting that 'after more than four years of struggle and sacrifice, during which time there have come to the homes of our Dominion much suffering, bereavement and sorrow, God has graciously granted to the Allies a glorious victory, achieved in the interests of justice, freedom and humanity'.[79] The God thanked for victory and the God of mercy were held together, without any attempt to address the unspoken issues of theodicy.

After the war W.E. Leadley, a Methodist minister, asked 'Why is it that the Church is utterly failing to reach and to hold the men who have returned to this country from the various battlefronts?' He pointed to a 'new type of manhood' having been bred by the war:

> 'Our old time religion' ... is not good enough for the majority of men who are returning after fighting for Truth, Freedom and Justice! They are not attracted by our heaven, nor are they afraid of our hell! ... Do you think that any appeal which was based on the ground of the fear of death would reach these men? I tell you they don't fear death.

Leadley suggested that returned soldiers needed to be presented with 'Christ, not as an awful Judge, who consigns the wicked to everlasting fire ... but as their Comrade and Friend ... their Greatest Pal'.[80] Strong negative reactions greeted Leadley's letter, rejecting the idea of bringing 'the religion of Jesus down to the returned soldier's level'.[81] Leadley, however, was unrepentant, concluding the correspondence by declaring that:

> If our Church doctrine bids us tell that brokenhearted mother who gave her only boy, that she will never see him again because he did not believe a particular creed, or was not a member of any particular Church, then I say it is time that doctrine was scrapped.[82]

Jon Davies, in an article on 'War Remembrance as an Elementary Form of Religious Life', concluded that 'All religions are syncretism, and nowhere more so than when dealing with war and death in war, one of the centrally powerful myth-creating experiences of all societies.'[83] The churches in New Zealand engaged in and supported the myth-making process. The civic and ecclesiastical rhetoric and powerful mythology that developed around death in the First World War showed how deeply scarred New Zealand society was by this experience. Those returned soldiers who knew the reality of fighting, dying and death in Europe found it almost impossible to question this rhetoric and mythology, even if they had wanted to.

For the churches, the acceptance of the war as a righteous cause, and pastoral expediency in the face of the demands of war and the vast number of those who were killed and injured, helped to shape their response to death. One of the consequences of the churches' triumphalistic endorsement of the war was their inability to criticise either the way in which the war was being waged or the very nature of war itself. The churches' teaching about God and the cause of both suffering and the war reflected the difficulty they had in providing satisfactory answers to people's questions. Having identified the war as a righteous cause, with God on the side of the Allies, churches could not explain why it dragged on for so long with so much suffering. After 1918 a struggle emerged between those who wanted a world in which there would be no more war and those who maintained and supported the status quo.[84] In using the language about 'supreme sacrifice' to make sense of death in the First World War, the churches allowed their theology to be co-opted and thereby contributed to the secularisation of their own message.

Above: Maori and Pakeha soldiers examine a wounded dove. [Alexander Turnbull Library, G-13078-1/2.]

Below: New Zealand mounted riflemen on the move between the Jordan River and Bethlehem, probably in March 1918. [Alexander Turnbull Library, L.F. Wilson Collection, F-66833-1/2.]

Above: New Zealanders in the front line near La Signy Farm, 6 April 1918. [Alexander Turnbull Library, RSA Collection, G-13089-1/2.]

Below: A New Zealand Vickers machine gun team in a front-line position near Colincamps, 27 April 1918. [Alexander Turnbull Library, RSA Collection, G-13733-1/2.]

Right: Major-General Sir Andrew Russell in May 1918. Russell commanded the New Zealand Division from its formation in 1916 until the end of the war. [Alexander Turnbull Library, RSA Collection, G-2064-1/1.]

Below: Chaplain David Herron conducting a funeral for members of 2 Otago Battalion at Gommecourt, 26 July 1918. On the same day Herron also conducted the funeral of the battalion's most famous soldier, Richard Travis, VC, DCM, MM. [Alexander Turnbull Library, G-2074-1/1.]

Above: British Whippet light tanks advancing through mist on the morning of 24 August 1918 during the New Zealand Division's attack on Grévillers. [Alexander Turnbull Library, RSA Collection, G-13524-1/2.]

Below: During a period of rest behind the front line, Maori soldiers help French peasants with their harvesting, 17 September 1918. [Alexander Turnbull Library, RSA Collection, G-9520-1/4.]

Above: The bodies of American soldiers killed on 29 September 1918 at Gillemont Farm in an attack against the Hindenburg Line by 27 American Division. The bodies are being prepared for burial in a nearby cemetery. [Australian War Memorial, E04942c.]

Below: The End of the War, Starting Home (1930-33) by Horace Pippin. [Philadelphia Museum of Art.]

Above: The well-used library at the New Zealand YMCA in Beauvois, northern France, 12 October 1918. [Alexander Turnbull Library, RSA Collection, G-13635-1/2.]

Below: A New Zealand mortar firing in support of the assault on Le Quesnoy, 4 November 1918. [Alexander Turnbull Library, RSA Collection, G-13798-1/2.]

H 1308

Above: Soldiers participating in one of the agricultural rehabilitation schemes. [Alexander Turnbull Library, Making New Zealand Collection, F-945-1/4-MNZ.]

Below: A procession through Stratford during the town's peace celebrations early in 1919. [Alexander Turnbull Library, J.K. Wall Collection, G-12998-1/2.]

THE LONELY GRAVE
"Here sleeps an heir to glory"

Drawn by Pte. J. Weeks

Above: 'The Lonely Grave: "Here sleeps an heir to glory"' by Private J. Weeks. [*New Zealand at the Front 1918.*]

27

FIRST WORLD WAR RELIGION

Peter Lineham

New Zealand churches were the first to admit that the First World War went badly for them. Caught up in currents of opinion, naively pursuing imperial and nationalistic goals and seeking formal respect from the state, they came out with their reputation tarnished. This chapter seeks to understand what went wrong.

Disruption

The Great War had a huge effect on the shape of the New Zealand churches. They were unavoidably implicated in the first total war, which disrupted religion and other aspects of society from the outset, when the planned centenary celebration of Marsden's planting of Christianity was cancelled. Salvationists lamented that 'the most titanic struggle in the history of our world is shattering the foundations of our civilization'.[1] For Anglicans, 'The dreadful war that is being waged in Europe appears to overshadow everything'.[2]

So from the very beginning people were forced to grit their teeth in the face of 'the awful tragedy of war'.[3] As W. J. Williams, editor of the *Methodist Times* commented, 'The chill of despair has already fallen upon the hearts of many.' Many clergy felt the difficulty of explaining the purposes of God in allowing such evil. 'All that is tender in humanity... sacred in religion, seems to be rudely questioned by the events,' wrote Williams.[4] One report early in 1915 noted that 'this war has placed Christianity on its trial as it never has been placed within living memory'.[5] Especially for denominations with German links the sense of war's tragedy and futility was strong.[6]

A new agony surfaced with the news from Gallipoli early in May 1915. Some tried to find the bright side in the tragedy, pointing out examples of sacrifice, but the dark side was strong: 'the war god has held and still holds his cruel riot of blood'. It was a powerful and pagan metaphor, suggesting the alienation of war from religious experience. A few weeks later the same writer lamented, 'Yes, but if ever peace is restored one of its first articles must be that the man who ever again proposes war as a solution of international difficulties should be shot down like a mad dog.'[7]

There was also a growing sense after Gallipoli that the church had failed to prevent the war.[8] In an editorial in July 1915 Williams asked whether the war would be worth its cost, and recognised the 'tremendous sacrifices' involved in it.[9] Monsignor Gillan in a sermon in Auckland 'referred in a feeling manner to the war and to the many casualties among the New Zealand soldiers and whose mothers were denied the consolation of comforting and helping their sons in their dying moments.'[10] A Christchurch Anglican invoked the thought of a 'harvest of death'; the soldiers were 'cut down in the flower of their age', but offered the consolation that 'it was life wrought to its noblest and willingly offered up in response to the call of God who gave it'.[11]

This perception remained throughout the war. At Christmas communion in 1917 Dean Peter Regnault, Provincial Secretary of the Marist Brothers, prayed for a speedy end to 'the present cruel and devastating war'.[12] The new editor of the *Tablet* found plenty of copy to back up his concerns. 'Hideousness and unparalleled splendour meet every day in and behind the battle line. Civilization stands over its own grave....'[13]

Catering for religious needs

Initially the churches were hopeful that concern about the war would draw people 'flocking to God's house', and they wanted war mentioned in every service.[14] Denominational leaders constantly exhorted people to prayer lest the evil enemy should win. 'We must pray every day this year, as we never prayed before.'[15] The Anglican Bishop Thomas Sprott chaired a meeting of all denominations in Wellington on 18 January 1915 at which it was agreed to copy an English precedent and ring church bells and open church buildings daily at midday to encourage prayer for the war. The practice was quickly adopted in other centres, although attendance was never high at these services.[16]

New Zealand was a society without a state church but the circumstances of the war inspired state sponsorship of religion. There were royal requests for days of prayer, beginning on the first weekend of January 1915, and at frequent intervals thereafter, and churches took these up with alacrity. Churches were often crowded on occasions of national crisis. The first anniversary of the landing on Gallipoli, 25 April 1916, provoked intense religious commemorations.[17] The Governor attended a service at St Matthew's in Auckland,[18] and many other churches had services arranged with local town authorities. The Catholic Church held parallel but separate services. Christchurch Bishop Matthew Brodie's words were as fervent as those of any Protestant that day: 'The mourners would be consoled … that the lost ones, by their deaths for their country and their God had inherited the crown of eternal reward, which would be shared by those who had made the great sacrifice of sending them forth'.[19]

The war rhetoric aroused initial hopes of a revival of religion. Methodists brought the Reverend Val Trigge from Australia to hold a revival campaign.[20] With occasional exceptions, however, church attendance did not rise during the war, and war could be very disruptive, for example if the vicar or minister had gone abroad with the forces.[21] The pattern was similar to that for German churches, where low levels of attendance were doubled at the outset of the war, but not sustained.[22]

Helping

The churches threw themselves into support for the war effort. At the military training camps the churches erected huts for church services and facilities for soldiers. The Salvation Army set up a tent and then a hut in Trentham Camp in December 1914, and sought to convert soldiers before they went overseas, even including a 'motherly' talk which made some soldiers 'weepy'.[23] The Methodist Home Mission Department from 1915 stationed a minister, the Reverend William Walker, at Trentham.[24] Soon most churches were in on the act.

Churches also encouraged fundraising for the war effort, and especially its compassionate aspects. Thus the Bible in Schools League gave to the government £1000 for field ambulances at the very outbreak of war.

Supporting the soldiers drove some more evangelical churches into a frenzy of activity. The Salvation Army, seeking to relegitimise its ministry for a new generation, was delighted when the Minister of Defence approached it to support those in overseas hospitals: 'Even war, the most frightful of all catastrophes, has certain compensations'.[25] The *War Cry* gleefully reported the soldier who asked; 'I say, chaplain, how can I change to Salvation Army?'[26]

Volunteering

Before conscription was introduced the churches encouraged their members to join up: every denomination took pride in its level of volunteers. Some ministerial candidates were not content to volunteer as chaplains but they wanted to go to the front line.[27] Archbishop Francis Redwood, greeting the Apostolic Delegate in 1916, commented that New Zealand was:

> the favored land, and already the mother of heroes, for had she not sent her sons, and had they not sacrificed themselves in the fight for justice, truth and civilisation, which had won for her the admiration of the whole world.'[28]

Catholics referred proudly to the Irish contribution to the war effort.[29] The Presbytery of Dunedin urged that kirk sessions display rolls of honour of those who had volunteered, while Anglicans displayed the names of the dead from their parishes.[30] The Church of England Men's Society commented that 'the burden of justification rests not on the call to go out, but on the desire, if it exists, to stay behind'.[31] The churches felt duty-bound to achieve the same levels of volunteering as in England.[32] Some of the clergy became virtual 'recruiting officers' and sometimes they took it too far. The culprits included the Presbyterian leader, James Gibb, and the Anglican vicar, Reverend W.E. Gillam, who used five sermons to explain the message of the Allies, and appeal for recruits.[33]

W.J. Williams, the *Methodist Times* editor, inconsistently argued that nobody should be coerced to enlist, 'But we have now reach a crisis in which every young man should be challenged to show cause why the call for service leaves him unresponsive.'[34] Similarly one of the Methodist chaplains declared that 'the man who said he was a Christian and was fit and free, and did not enlist, was a coward and a cad, and was unworthy of the name of Britisher'.[35]

So conscription tended to undercut the moral cause of the Allies, awakening divisions between religious groups.[36] And there was a great deal of defensiveness in the face of public criticism that clergy were exempt from the draft.[37]

Competition between churches

Recent research has demonstrated how in Scotland the war initially induced a sense of unity.[38] The same was true of New Zealand. The chaplains operated together harmoniously at first.[39] Support for church union was aided by the need to ration resources. At Featherston Camp all the Protestant churches combined with the YMCA to make joint provision for soldiers.[40] 'One thing that the war is doing finely,' a Salvationist volunteer noted, 'is the breaking down of barriers between the different branches of the Church of Christ.'[41]

Yet the war had broken out at a time of acute sectarianism in the dominion. Ferocious disputes were raging over the demand for a referendum on Bible in Schools, which Catholic Bishop Henry Cleary of Auckland fiercely opposed, and over the prohibition of alcohol. Canon David Garland, an Anglican from Queensland, responded to the war by wisely asking that the Bible in Schools Referendum Bill be withdrawn, so as not to introduce 'anything of a controversial character into our politics'.[42] The issues had not, however, gone away. Bible in Schools supporters sought the election of sympathetic MPs in the December 1914 election while Bishop Cleary maintained his caution.[43] The prohibition debate took on a fresh momentum in the context of war.

So churches soon returned to their instinctive competitiveness. The selection of chaplains awakened intense concern as denominations jostled for their fair share. Most non-Anglican Protestants were prepared to be treated as a single grouping, and also co-operated with the YMCA. Anglicans and Catholics, however, expected separate treatment and were prepared to pull rank to get it. The first significant complaint came with the selection of chaplains for the troopships. Methodists claimed that some of their boys were being recorded as Anglican.[44] The government for its part resisted sending a chaplain with every ship that took troops to the front until the demands became insistent.[45]

Some Anglicans felt strongly that their church should operate quite separately from Protestants and were concerned about Anglican troops being sent to the united Protestant services in the camps.[46] Anglican leaders felt that at Trentham they had been 'completely outdistanced' by other denominations, despite being the 'Mother church'.[47] And the result would be serious: 'If the church will not assert herself she will be lost in the increasing tide of nonconformity'.[48] They complained that they had too low a proportion of the chaplains.[49] In 1915 Christchurch's Bishop Julius opposed the holding of joint services of memorial for the fallen.[50] Other denominations were outraged by this attitude, particularly when some Anglicans in camp refused to share communion with Protestants.[51] At home there was annoyance when Anglican leaders generally would not join in the first civic commemorations of Anzac Day.[52] Ordinary Anglicans seem to have disliked this denominational prissiness, and in the final crisis of May 1918 the Bishop of Christchurch welcomed ministers of all denominations to participate in a day-long service of intercession at the cathedral. Lay Anglicans were now able to rejoice that 'there was no rivalry of ministries: all that was forgotten'.[53] Thus the war and its aftermath was a critical factor in leading the Anglican church to view other Protestants more positively.

Missions

The war profoundly disrupted church life and activities. The overseas missionary effort was immediately threatened.[54] Missionaries reported that indigenous peoples were baffled by the war fever in the Christian community and asked some sharp questions about it.[55] The Bishop of Auckland, A. W. Averill, remarked at a meeting in September 1915:

> ... he was perfectly certain the war, righteous and just as it undoubtedly was, would prove a hindrance to missionary work .... The difficulty was that when the natives saw Christian nations engaged in a terrible war, they were prone to think that there was something wrong.[56]

The religion of patriotism

From the first, church people wanted to demonstrate their loyalty. So in Christchurch Father Cronin 'felt assured that Catholics were firmly determining to be second to none in recording ... an instance of practical loyalty'.[57]

Presbyterians rejoiced that war had revived the spirit of patriotism, although they worried about 'the street-corner variety' with its emphasis on hatred of the enemy.[58] Robert Francis of Opotiki wrote a loyal poem for the Presbyterian magazine *Outlook*, in which he dreamed that 'the Britisher's heart beats loyally wherever his footstep may roam. / So we stand or fall together'.[59] A speech at a Bible in Schools League meeting declared: 'We are all patriots, and we are all prepared to make self-sacrifice for the preservation of the Empire'.[60] Particularly in the Anglican context, patriotism was embraced without reserve. Curiously, there was constant reference to the 'fatherland' and the 'motherland', with New Zealand and Great Britain included under both categories. For example, an Anglican editorial written just after news of the first casualties from Gallipoli, took pride that they were soldiers for the motherland, but also commented: 'It causes the pulse to throb with pride to read how our boys, fresh from the fields of peace, faced the foe with a courage equal to any the most famous regiments have displayed'.[61] Methodists similarly noted that 'in an age when selfishness had become so marked in so many departments of life, men in such large numbers can be found prepared to make this supreme sacrifice'.[62]

In 1914 the churches were bemused by the power of patriotism, and anxious to understand its relationship to religious aspirations. Dr James Gibb, the great Presbyterian leader, sought to determine a 'higher patriotism' in which honour and respect made it a spiritual value, a patriotism shown by Jesus himself.[63] Another Presbyterian, the Reverend J.S. Ponder, preaching to troops departing for the front, declared that a patriotism based on the fear of God had more profound roots than selfish nationalism.[64]

But a year later patriotism had become less discriminating, and war was seen as a purifying force. In July 1915 the Anglican bishops issued a pastoral letter, offering their loyalty to the government and urging their people to fresh penitence, prayer and service in the face of the shocking pain of war.[65] The Methodist preacher P.W. Fairclough, in a sermon delivered to his preacher peers, declared that 'in the bible the partition between religion and patriotism is thin indeed'.[66] And in 1916 the Anglican Bishop of Auckland, in a sermon to the General Synod of the church, asked, 'Has the church fully realised the sacred nature of the nation, or its executive, the state?'[67] Bishop Samuel Nevill's statement to the same General Synod that the war was unifying the empire, and would lead logically to Irish unity was quoted approvingly by the Catholic newspaper.[68]

The righteous war

Initially justifications for the war reflected English explanations. As Albert Marrin has indicated, immediately before August 1914 English Anglicans frequently expressed feelings of kinship with German Lutherans and German Christians in general. This outlook changed almost overnight.[69] New Zealand preachers were not necessarily anti-German in the first few weeks of the war. Bishop Averill acknowledged that the Germans too were children of God, and some took great encouragement from early signs of fraternal feelings between the two armies of Germany and Britain.[70] Dr Gibb recognised that Germans and English were 'blood brothers', and claimed that 'our mood towards the German people has not been lacking in that breadth of view and that consideration of others which most assuredly is always a factor in true patriotism'.[71]

Yet now they were at war. Why? The Reverend J. W. Shaw, in the Presbyterian magazine, the *Outlook*, took the view that war was a tragic aspect of modern life. No Christian could be comfortable with war and 'in any international dispute the right may be difficult to determine'.[72] As late as April 1915 the editor of the *Outlook* indicated that although the moral righteousness of the British case was strong, 'there are grave questionings in the minds of many as to the right attitude of the Christian world towards war as a whole'.[73]

So clergy felt the need to assure their parishioners of the righteousness of the war. As a Presbyterian minister insisted, 'If we cannot believe that our cause is just, and that the right shall prevail... then the religious nerve is cut, and the mightiest impulse to fight and not to yield is taken from us.'[74] At the Methodist conference early in 1915, the Reverend Fairclough moved the resolution that:

> While deploring the appeal to brute force in differences between rational beings, and mourning over the horrors and miseries of the present world-wide conflict, this Conference is profoundly convinced that Great Britain, is absolutely innocent of the awful guilt of letting slip the dogs of war, and has a cause transparently just before God and the nations.[75]

Several justifications of the war appealed to the churches. Honouring treaty commitments seemed a Christian act. One Anglican magazine commented: 'Seldom has Britain entered on any war in a cause more righteous. ... the children of Israel regarded a treaty with an ally as binding in the sight of God'.[76] This comment applied to France but especially to Belgium. As Marrin notes, Belgium had been much criticised before the war because of its treatment of its African colony in the Congo, but this view rapidly turned in New Zealand as much as England.[77] Soon the whole community was passionately sympathetic to the invaded Belgians. Many churches took up a collection for Belgium in September 1914.[78] On 14 August 1914 the Clutha Presbytery regretted the war but affirmed that 'Britain has been forced to defend by arms the rights of weaker nations against the aggression of a stronger power and treaty obligations'.[79] The issue had a special significance for Catholics, given Belgium's Catholicism. Bishop Cleary made much of this in sermons and lectures: on 27 August he changed his lecture topic at the Leys Institute to a description of Belgium.[80] At the same time the prominent Presbyterian minister Gray Dixon claimed Belgium deserved protection as a one-time Calvinist centre.[81]

Overall clergy welcomed the defensive approach that Britain took to war. Bishop Averill said in a significant sermon at the outbreak of war:

> Thank God we have not rushed into this fray .... Stern necessity has forced us to unsheathe the sword, because all our overtures on behalf of peace and neutrality were rejected, and because our very national existence was threatened. We are not aggressors, our hands are clean, our consciences are unsullied, our motives are pure, our duty is clear, and the terrible crime of kindling the war-flame cannot be laid at our door.[82]

But at the beginning of May, just before the news of Gallipoli, the editor of the *Methodist Times* recognised that there were Methodists in Germany praying for the success of their troops.

> As Britons we naturally wish that British arms should be victorious, because we believe that those arms are only exercised in the interests of a righteous cause. We must give credit to our fellow-Methodists in Germany for being equally

sincere in their belief that it is the German army that is fighting for justice and freedom. Who is to decide which is right? Who but the one God to whom both Germans and Britons pray?[83]

So by 1915 the defence of war had become more difficult as its horrors necessitated stronger defences.[84] It therefore followed, as Dr Gibb declared in an ecumenical service in the Wellington Town Hall on 8 August 1915, that for the sake of justice there could be no compromise peace: it had to be war to the bitter end.[85] An Anglican editor made the same point:

> We believe that we are on God's side in this conflict; we believe that the real contest is between the spiritual and the material, between Christ and anti-Christ, and therefore we can pray earnestly for victory and that God's will may be done. Our prayers cannot be half-hearted and spasmodic if we are absolutely convinced of the righteousness and justice of our cause. In praying for victory for the Allies we are also praying for the regeneration and purification of the heart of Germany and the dawn of a truer and more Christian international relationship.[86]

These views led churches to take an interest in the conduct of the war. The vicar of Kaikoura, for example, complained that the First Echelon was sent to the front with inadequate training, because of the pressure of 'hysterical excitement'.[87]

Imperial responsibility

The church leaders were given to imperial arguments. Bishop Winnington-Ingram of London had suggested as much in a sermon extolling England as the mother of free countries (not mentioning Ireland) with a mission to preserve freedom from tyranny.[88] Bishop Averill led the way in voicing this imperial Anglican outlook in New Zealand: 'England, the mother of us all, calls us in her hour of need to maintain her honour, which is also ours. Above all, God calls us to fight his battle for liberty, justice, mercy, truth, and we will send the answer back to heaven: by God's grace we will.'[89] To his synod in November the bishop urged the unity of the British Empire, and brotherhood of people as linked to the fatherhood of God.[90] Christchurch Anglicans took the same line.[91] Catholics praised 'that nobler, saner type of imperialism' which motivated the war, although the editor of the *Tablet*, reflecting on the Irish Home Rule campaign, expressed surprise that the dominions were still subject to British governors.[92] The Reverend Gray Dixon rejoiced at 'the wonderful empire'.[93] The Methodist resolution quoted above continued:

> We rejoice in the unanimity and loyalty in all parts of our far-flung Empire, and particularly of New Zealand, in supporting the Motherland in the hour of her need. We also rejoice in the valour and growing strength of the King's forces, and we join earnestly in prayer that God will defend the right, and cause the grinding militarism of Germany to cease from the earth. We regard the British Empire, with all its defects, as being, in practical righteousness, the largest instalment of the Kingdom of God that has yet arisen among men, and we earnestly pray that Almighty God will avert calamity from that dispensation of righteousness and liberty which it has been the glory of our Empire to spread over the world.[94]

The Gallipoli campaign changed attitudes to the war. A Christchurch Anglican report noted that the Dardanelles were once the scene of the Crusades and now New Zealand, 'no longer a distant and isolated community', was united to Christendom in a grand defence of the empire.[95] When Jerusalem fell to the Allies, even some Anglicans interpreted it in apocalyptic terms.[96]

Creating ideals

One of the strange features of the era was the creation of various symbolic figures, such as noble motherhood.[97] The Salvation Army Hall in Trentham Camp had a huge sign at the front: 'For God and Empire: We fight to win: Don't forget to write to mother'.[98] The Reverend J. Dukes preached at the Dominion Road Methodist Church from the text about Rachel weeping for her children. In his sermon, Rachel is transmuted into a colonial mother witnessing her son enlist despite her fear of losing him. When he goes to war she sits at home wondering what is happening to him. And then comes the 'ominous telegram', and soon the New Zealand Rachel is weeping: 'Our womanhood, Rachel, is weeping, and we are weeping with her, for nearly three thousand of the flower of our manhood are more or less put out of action'. But what is her consolation? Only this:

> there will often come to the lonely heart a feeling of intense satisfaction that the boy died A REAL HERO, a sustaining thought that he died for principles dearer by far than life. They were worth dying for, and generations unborn will arise and call these dying heroes blessed. O there comes from the death of these men, a solemn inspiring message to all laggards in the rear.[99]

The country had to be made worthy of the soldiers, with rather less 'made in Germany' religion (presumably meaning too liberal).[100] At Christ Church, Ellerslie, the gospel theme of setting the spiritual above the material was used as a basis to urge people to enlist for the army.[101] The Battle of Jutland led the editor of the *War Cry* to urge people to more courage; victory was sure, however ugly the present experience was.[102] And the Christchurch Anglican newspaper exhorted readers that endurance in a righteous cause was essential: 'No nation or group of nations ever had a more holy and rightful and inevitable task than ours to-day, to be carried on and on to the utmost end with the certainty that generations unborn will bless those who set the world free from an unholy doom'. Underlying this was the belief that, unlike the Germans, the British and their Allies were committed to democracy and freedom, and ironically, as it later turned out, to voluntary service.[103]

The issue of how to pray for the fallen worried the Protestant community, though not Catholics.[104] From mid-1915 thinking was reshaped by interpretations of the text, 'greater love hath no man than this'. Deaths as sacrifices had religious merit. Given the growing sense of the suffering and pain of war, this vision of sacrifice made the soldiers 'the flower' or 'the cream' of 'our manhood', inspired by the righteousness of the cause, ennobled by their endeavours.[105] Occasionally this interpretation was challenged, for example in a Salvationist editorial denying that soldiers fighting for their country thereby made atonement for their sins.[106]

The war exposed the inadequacy of the optimism of Victorian religion, both mainstream and evangelical. Methodists' liberal notion of evangelism, as the meaning of the war – 'to bring all nations into a brotherhood of co-operation in righteousness and peace' – seemed somewhat optimistic.[107] The Reverend G.P. Hunt undercut the argument in a brutal manner. He thought that liberals had expected the kingdom of God to grow by peaceful evolution. On the contrary, a struggle was necessary. Everyone needed a sword, and they needed to use it.[108] The Presbyterian newspaper reprinted an article by a Cambridge chaplain, insisting on the place of the sword in faith, for 'Christianity endorses the law of struggle'.[109] Chaplains had little truck with this language: the Australian Salvationist chaplain at Gallipoli called war 'the most damnable insensate folly of which mankind could be guilty'.[110]

The failings of German 'Kultur'

At the outset of the war, religious commentators were emphatic that 'we are not fighting the German people' and they valued their links with their counterparts in Germany.[111] Hostility focused on the Kaiser, the 'modern Caesar', as Bishop Averill called him in a sermon in September 1914.[112]

The German churches leaped, like the English, into defending the German case for war. Prominent scholars were among the signatories to the September 'Appeal to Evangelical [Protestant] Christians Abroad', and to the October 1914 *Proclamation of the Ninety-Three German Professors to a Cultured World*, defending Germany's cultural mandate as the land of Goethe, Beethoven and Kant, and as the foe of Russian barbarity. On the 400th anniversary of Luther in 1917, grand words again flowed freely from German pastors.[113]

In response to the German appeal numerous British Anglican, Presbyterian and Non-conformist leaders issued a letter on 23 September 1914 which sought to demonstrate that Britain had sought to avoid war and focused on the breach of the neutrality of Belgium.[114] Anglican writers issued *To the Christian Scholars of Europe and America* in answer to the German academic statement. Such replies increasingly focused on German apostasy.[115] The German self-defence may indeed have encouraged a growing English focus on the sins of Germany. New Zealand religious writers reported the debate.[116]

The steady change of tone from defensive to offensive was very evident in New Zealand commentaries. Bishop Cleary in August identified the culprits of the attack as a selfish clique in Germany, and went further in September, saying that the good German spirit had been crushed and Germany had become a mere fighting machine.[117] Father Richard Coffey expressed the opinion in late August that Germany should have been attacked ten to twelve years earlier.[118] The first tentative suggestion of flaws in German values expressed in the *Methodist Times* was an exposure of the philosophy of Nietzsche and then of Treitschke.[119] Then the German opposition to everything English was noted with concern.[120] Presbyterians moved onto the attack more quickly. Their first analysis felt that 'Germany alone has made ready for war to gratify a narrow national pride'. Her passion for dominion meant that she must be taught a lesson. Germany, as Professor Dickie of the Theological Hall told volunteers at a service on 23 August 1914, was an 'unscrupulous enemy', and it was 'a war of aggression pure and simple, a deliberate bid for the mastery of the world'.[121]

There was also a growing feeling that the German scoffing at the British appeal to the 'bit of paper' (the 1830 Treaty with Belgium) revealed the failure of German values. She had chosen, as the eloquent Gray Dixon told the Presbyterians of Roslyn in Dunedin, 'to play ruffian among her sister States'; she was guilty of 'wanton aggression' against brave little Belgium; she was convicted of 'international criminality' and must be punished as any criminal individual should.[122] The Women's Christian Temperance Union described Germany as 'mad with the lust of power, drunk with the blood of the slain'.[123] There was, perhaps, concern at the initial German success and a sense that the Allies might be dependent on divine intervention against German militarism. Certainly that emphasis was apparent in the address of Bishop Churchill Julius to the Christchurch Diocesan Synod in October 1914.[124]

Gradually the moral focus broadened into an analysis of German society and values. Given the *Kulturkampf* of the 1880s, Catholic preachers were particularly critical of the German creed of 'might is right', but the Dunedin Presbytery early in 1915 declared its mind: 'assuredly believing that Germany's unhallowed ambition to become supreme in the world's affairs, and make her own form of civilisation the standard of all excellence, is a distinct menace to the civil and religious liberty of other races'.[125] This view gained huge publicity when the Anglican Bishop Winnington-Ingram of London, 'the Bishop of the Battlefields', in a notable series of sermons in June 1915 identified the war as a holy war. His views reached a disturbing climax with the exhortation to kill Germans 'lest the civilization of the world itself be killed'.[126] The essence of this argument was that the German Empire was unnatural, built not upon healthy nationalism but upon Prussian militarism. John Moses has analysed the impact of these ideas in the Australian context.[127] The same approach was rapidly adopted in New

Zealand, particularly by Anglicans. One spokesman commented that 'In ideals Germany stands for might against right, for despotism against democracy, for violated faith as against honourable performance of treaty obligations'. Another Anglican wrote of Germany as 'the Warrior State', and Bishop Julius lamented that 'Germany has returned to the religion of the Hun'.[128] Non-Anglican Protestants agreed. Ross Anderson has noticed the way in which Methodists 'diabolised' Germany from early in the war.[129] Such an enemy would oblige the Allies to achieve total victory, so that, as a Methodist commentator argued, 'that masterpiece of consummate devilry represented by German militarism is so smitten to earth that it can never rise again'[130] The Reverend J. Gibson Smith at St Andrew's (Presbyterian) in Wellington chose National Intercession Sunday to accuse Germany of paganism, of becoming 'a barbaric horde – the willing instruments of a ruling class which has played the Judas not only to Christianity, but to civilization'. For him this overcame the 'degree of doubt' which he had first felt about the war.[131]

As German atrocities were exposed during 1915, the just war gradually became holy war. At his valedictory service before leaving as chaplain on a troopship, the Reverend W.E. Gillam, vicar of St Matthew's Church in Auckland, preached that New Zealand was sending its best manhood to war 'to aid the crushing of the animal spirit in prussianised Germany'.[132] This description of the Germans as displaying something primitive is apparent in a Methodist description of 'this costly freak of barbarism' in April 1915.[133] The Reverend R.E. Davies, in the opening address of the Presbyterian Theological Hall on 30 March 1915, used the text on resisting the devil, and then diabolised Germany: 'They have abandoned moral restraint, and let loose in their national life a spirit which is demonical in character, and which is driving the nation outwardly towards destruction ....'[134]

Another Presbyterian, the Reverend J.W. Shaw, wrote a long study of 'the modern Hun' in which he severely castigated German values. In contrast, the then editor of the *Tablet* insisted that Catholic priests would never call Germans 'dogs'.[135] Perhaps a sense that Britain was not winning led to these disturbing reflections: 'no gold can stain Germany's criminality; no territory acquired can outweigh the terrible burden of a lost soul'.[136] The Anglican Bishop of Auckland A.J. Averill acknowledged tacitly that his argument had changed:

> It is not German humanity but Prussian spirit which calls for destruction, and we can only regard the German nation as Jesus regarded a man possessed with the devil, viz., a subject for pity and restoration to its true self. The devil must be exorcised, in order that the true nation may reappear and make its proper contribution to the world's well-being and progress. It is certainly unchristian to return hate for hate.... If the British empire can carry this war through without resorting to fiendish methods, she will not only honour God, but exalt the principles and ideals of Christ in the eyes of the whole world.[137]

Because Christianity itself was threatened by Germany, a crusade was justified. If German culture was pagan, then no blame attached to Christendom for failing to stop the war. At the Auckland Diocesan Synod in November 1915 the bishop called Germans to account for 'nothing less than a lost God and a spurned Christ'.[138] Presbyterians, somewhat ashamed of their link with the Reformed Church in Prussia, and the influence of liberal German theology, began to use this to explain the weakness of the churches' hold on the people. They began to note by the end of 1914 that 'we have given in too much to Germany already in the domains of theology and practical religion'. Modernism was emptying the German churches, as it deviated from the evangelical faith.[139]

As the cost of the war rose, so the justification became more passionate. This is very evident in the resolution of the Auckland Anglican Synod after Averill's address in 1915:

> that this synod while fearing that there is no apparent prospect of an early termination of the great war for liberty and righteousness in which the empire is engaged, desires to reaffirm its loyalty to the king and empire and expresses its profound confidence that New Zealand is prepared to support the Empire to the very uttermost in this great struggle.[140]

In July 1915, Catholic Archbishop Francis Redwood, newly returned from Europe and the United States, declared that the issue of the war was 'the question whether militarism, despotism, and barbarism are to triumph over civilization'.[141] Churches joined the call to abandon the use of German terms and rejecting German *Kultur* became an act of national conviction.[142] By 1916 the church newspapers were citing accounts of the evil things supposedly said in German churches.[143] In his 1918 charge to his synod, Averill traced the false German views to the influence of Darwin: only when Social Darwinism's quest for power was denied could true civilisation dawn.[144]

The introduction of conscription revived these arguments, yet people grew more leery of them, and J.T. Pinfold for one commented that 'the sins of Germany, which most of us are now ready to acknowledge, are only the common denomination of all those sins which beset men everywhere'.[145] An Anglican editor, in far-sighted words, cautioned about 'the wild vindictive talk that one sometimes hears in the street or reads in the press of what is to be wrung from Germany.... If we talk of creating fresh grievances, Europe will never be at peace.'[146]

Later discussions of these issues moved in the direction of eugenics, with newspaper discussions of German racial inferiority.[147] This theme survived after the war, most notably in the intensely anti-German views developed by Dickie of the Presbyterian Theological Hall, who rapidly backtracked on his German theological training and at the outset of the war removed Luther's portrait from the hall's chapel. He began to insist on the collective guilt of all Germans, and even 20 years later was unable to work with a German refugee brought to the hall, Helmut Rehbein, taking the attitude that the problems of Europe could not be solved until Germans, even refugees, ceased to exist.[148]

British and colonial failings

Why had the war happened? Despite the belief that Germany was at fault, there was still a feeling among Protestant preachers that the moral responsibility was broader than this. Dr James Gibb, eminent Presbyterian minister at St Andrew's on the Terrace in Wellington, felt that, in the deepest sense, 'the nations have forgotten God and turned their backs on His will and commandments'.[149] Gibb felt that the church must therefore call the nation to repentance. Britain would only deserve to win the war if it became a more righteous nation.

Clergy were inclined to use the war as an occasion to condemn the secular world of the dominion. In Auckland Bishop Averill urged voters in the 1914 general election to choose candidates who sought national righteousness. Similarly, the editor of the Presbyterian *Outlook* saw the need for the country to recover its Christian faith and commitment. In June 1915 the Bishop of Nelson complained both of 'national' (British) and colonial failings, and the 'flaccid self-indulgence and frivolity of the times'.[150]

By the end of 1915, with no sign of victory, the language became more concerned. In the *Methodist Times* W.J. Williams complained of the low moral standards of Parliament, with its laxness about gambling, and Averill felt that the nation had not reflected on the underlying causes of the war. If only Britain had held its ideals more strongly things would have happened differently: 'Has not the spirit of service and sacrifice, consequent upon those uncertain ideas, been sadly wanting?' It was time to examine national failings – in particular the glorification of material progress at the expense of a spirit of generosity.[151]

In 1916, as the war showed no signs of ending, the calls for self-examination and penitence became urgent. The British churches launched a National Mission of Repentance and Hope, and this theme inspired copyists in New Zealand.[152] Gibb identified the recrudescence of paganism in the colony, along with the decline of the European race and the waste of money on the totaliser. As a people, he felt, 'we have ignominiously failed'.[153] Averill saw it as a failure of a sense of duty: 'What must God think of us when He sees us growing weary and slack and indifferent, instead of calling up all our reserve power and religious enthusiasm to meet the present day of trial.'[154] The strongest statement was probably that by the Reverend W.A. Sinclair during the Sunday afternoon gathering at the 1916 Methodist Conference:

> The war had proved the reality of sin, and Britain had yet much to do to make herself fit for the position as a leader of the nations of the earth. The liquor traffic and gambling must be suppressed. … Only vice could destroy a nation. History proved this. New Zealand was paying a great price, but we were not yet ready for victory. We had not yet risen to the required standards of righteousness. Love for the nation must lead us to sacrifice our sons and forsake our sins. We must find God again, for no nation could survive the loss of its religion. New Zealand needed a prophet to lead the Dominion to the feet of God in true penitence.[155]

Eventually these calls fed a deep concern about a vague sense of public corruption. In 1918 the Kirk Session of Dunedin's North East Valley Presbyterian Church produced a pamphlet on 'How to end the War', which argued that the conditions of victory were Sabbath observance, reverence for the sanctuary and obedience to the commands of God.[156] It was a very clear statement for an election year.

For many Protestants, God's support for the nation was in doubt if there was no Bible instruction in schools, as the Auckland Diocesan Synod spelled out in November 1914:

> the present distress of nations should be regarded as a call to all God's people to pay more attention to those things which make for national righteousness, …
> the necessity in the present sad times, of placing … the building up of national character upon those foundations which have given in times past the British empire its place among the nations.[157]

For others the hot issue was alcohol. Buoyed by the King's decision not to drink alcohol during the war, the Methodists regarded the drink trade as lacking in moral responsibility, and the editor of the *Methodist Times* was concerned for the nation: 'If in this great testing hour of sacrifice it chose the baser part and surrenders itself to a craven fear of the most corrupt form of Mammonism it will brand itself as unfit for … moral leadership ….'[158] Salvationists used much the same rhetoric, and pestered Defence Minister James Allen with concerns over the 'wet canteens' in the camps.[159] The Dunedin Presbytery debated whether to ask the government to introduce national prohibition during the war, for some felt that 'drink was a more serious menace to the nation than their armed foes'.[160] Some Presbyterians hoped that moves against alcohol and waste were clearing the ground for 'a great advance in national righteousness' and therefore victory. Considering this and the associated issue of gambling, the Presbyterian General Assembly of 1915 felt that the government was being hypocritical in its statements and actions.[161] Even Anglicans provided ardent support for the early closing of bars.[162]

Britain was often compared unfavourably with France and Russia, which had taken steps to curb the use of alcohol at the outset of the war. One Methodist correspondent suggested that there were three enemies in the war: Germany, Austria and the liquor traffic.[163] The Reform Party clumsily allowed the proposal for 6 p.m. closing to turn into a raging religious dispute, which triggered

Protestant acrimony towards Catholics. As the columns of the *Methodist* Times showed in 1915 and early 1916, a campaign against 'treating' (shouting) soldiers was conducted by the pro-temperance elements, some of whom even wanted it declared a criminal act. Allen tried to defend the lack of regulation against much huffing and puffing from the Methodists. Wet canteens got even non-prohibitionist Bishop Averill excited.[164] By the time of the Methodist and Presbyterian conference season in February 1916 six o'clock closing, treating and wet canteens had become a cause that some thought would determine the outcome of the war. Resolutions and speeches on the subject filled these conferences, and a deputation met the Prime Minister in April but got only a reassurance that wet canteens were not likely in New Zealand. But the campaign continued and focused increasingly on the 6 p.m. closing issue. War regulations about shouting seemed to satisfy the concerned public, although the wowsers felt let down by the Cabinet.[165]

In the Methodist view, drinking and gambling were a disgrace, especially in wartime because they were a shameful waste of money. So the issue was one of rationality. A war fought by drunken people was a 'blood-drunken orgy'; sober, sensible people fought a more moral war.[166]

A series of other issues also emerged. Methodists condemned the gambling spirit, horrified by the continued occurrence of race meetings during the war. The introduction of the movies just before the war offended some. The growth of the 'red plague' of venereal disease was even more disturbing. Some people even reacted to the introduction of trams on Sunday in Auckland in 1916.[167]

And then there was the matter of British conduct of the war. The most daring complaint about British war methods was issued by W. J. Williams, the Methodist editor, in 1915: 'But – frankly we could wish that the use of asphyxiating gases as a weapon of war had been left to the Germans. Because it represents the very climax of devilish cruelty we regret exceedingly that the war lords have deemed it expedient to retaliate on the Germans in kind…. What will the Germans say of our indignation now?'[168]

In a very real sense the old liberalism had failed the men and the churches, and left-wing politics grew in its place, as the *Methodist Times* explained in August 1916:

the present parliament and notoriously the present Government is one of the worst that New Zealand has ever known.... It is nothing short of a tragedy that those in this country who are fighting the forces of unrighteousness, who are struggling towards the ideals of national purity, honesty and sobriety, should be antagonised at every turn, by the action of our own government.[169]

Catholics participated rather less in the condemnation of the nation in the early years of the war, although Bishop Henry Cleary asked soldiers in August 1914 that there be no exhibitions or dissipations that would incur the anger of God.[170] Admitting that the war showed that 'we had a great deal to atone for',[171] Catholic commentators were generally sensitive to the need to defend the Irish contribution to the war effort and the neutrality of the papacy, and so did not copy this Protestant rhetoric. But after 1917 James Kelly, as editor of the *Tablet*, was passionate in exposing the failings of the dominion: 'As a people the New Zealanders are simply irreligious' – and this included Catholics who had missed out on religious training in the godless nation.[172] Father Coffey at the Dunedin Cathedral made the same point eloquently: 'there was abroad a spirit of recklessness, of unbelief, of disobedience, love of money, worldly ambition, a seeking after pleasure and luxury that belied the Christian name. The war may recall us to our senses; but we have a long road yet to travel before we can logically claim to be a Christian nation.'[173] Such statements reached a climax in Kelly's editorial in February 1918:

> Have we done a single thing since the war began to merit a mitigation of the punishment which God has inflicted on a sinful people? ... All over the empire iniquity hangs like a cloud. Never was there more pride and less humility.... The poor are forgotten. Profiteers grow fat on their plunder. Patriotic funds go astray. Gifts for soldiers have been sold by corrupt officials.[174]

Protestant feeling

There was clearly a growing divergence in the Protestant and Catholic interpretations of the war. The first reported instance of sectarian conflict came when the Reverend A. Macdonald, Presbyterian Minister of Otautau, claimed early in 1915 that Catholics had made no significant contribution to the war effort.[175] The same theme suddenly surfaced in the Methodist magazine in September 1915 with reports of a new Protestant federation, and an editorial complaining of the Pope's approach to the war.[176] A few months later the prominent Baptist, J.J. North, complained about the Pope's neutrality, and the refusal of the secular newspapers to ask for an explanation of this from the apostolic delegate who had visited in May 1915.[177] This was a problem that Catholic preachers constantly had to address. In mid-1915 an offensive letter was posted to many Wellington Catholics, alleging Catholic complicity in the war, and there were increasing allegations that Catholics were not volunteering to the same degree as others.[178] Catholics were outraged at such views: as the *Tablet* emphasised, 'Not only in money, time, and energy, but in life blood also, the Catholics of the Dominion are bearing their full share of sacrifice for the Empire'.[179] By 1916 rumours and innuendo were especially intense in Auckland – some of them ironically accused the Methodist mayor of being pro-Catholic – criticising papal neutrality and raising questions about the loyalty of Irish troops in the British army.[180] The 1916 Easter Rising was very bad news for Catholic apologists, and their initial response was horror that this 'made in Germany rebellion' had been able to undermine the will of the vast majority of the Irish – in New Zealand Catholic eyes, anyway.[181] James Kelly and the Protestant Political Association moved the invective onto new levels in 1917, but that story is well known.

Minority voices

This chapter has focused on the dominant tone in the New Zealand churches. A few people saw things differently, but there was little scope for dissent. When the Methodist conference recorded its resolution in 1915, it was carried without discussion.[182] No-one dared to air alternative points of view. There was no political protest from New Zealand Protestants as there was in England and Scotland, and there were few equivalents to those English Anglicans who sought to moderate the warmongering tone.[183] Methodists, who in the Second World War included many pacifists, were much less critical of the government in the First World War. In early 1915 one anonymous correspondent to the Methodist newspaper complained of the failure to pray for the Germans:

… there is too much of a spirit of hatred and revenge towards the German people. Now, if this supposedly righteous war is not to leave an awful aftermath in the shape of racial animosity, the Church must at once set about teaching both children and adults to love the sinner even while hating the sin.[184]

The same publication quoted Reverend Arthur Guttery in July 1915 as suggesting that people must somehow hate German *Kultur* but not hate Germans. Some regarded the number of enlisted soldiers as a sign of spiritual decadence, presumably because they had joined the forces of the world and its corruptions. The smart C.H. Laws warned the March 1916 Methodist conference against being swept away by a wave of patriotism.[185] But that was as far as dissent went.

It was only when James Kelly became editor of the *Tablet* that a significant new tone was introduced into the debate in New Zealand. His much-quoted remarks on the British royal family were only a part of his challenge. He also queried the strategy and ideals of the war, exposed its harsher side and challenged the righteousness of New Zealand and its moral right to win the war. Passion reached new heights with statements of this kind, in a January 1918 editorial:

In all its works and pomp the Government of New Zealand is frankly on the side of Antichrist, and neither religion or morality seems to have the slightest influence on our legislators. But parents have not forgotten God; they know that they and not the State, are responsible to him for the souls of their children; and because they know that they are becoming every day more determined that a government of unprincipled men shall not pervert the children.[186]

Sympathy for the conscientious objector

Given the tone of religious response to the war, there was little sympathy for those who had religious objections to killing: not surprisingly, few pacifists came from the mainstream churches.[187] At a church parade on 6 June 1915, the vicar of Te Aroha urged everyone to help with the war effort, but criticised the posting of white feathers to people who may have had valid reasons not to volunteer. A Methodist correspondent felt that there was no respect for conscientious objectors, but others rejected this argument.[188] Just occasionally there were hints of concealed pacifist opinion even in the ranks of Methodists and Presbyterians, who allowed Charles Murray and the Quakers one opportunity to state their case.[189] The other churches were sometimes willing to speak privately on behalf of religious objectors with the government, but the hysterical atmosphere in the House of Representatives seems to have prevented a more reasonable measure.[190]

The religion of the soldier

The mythology of the just war was accompanied by a belief in the heroism of the soldier, who was idealised as someone who had been purified through witnessing so many acts of courage. Father James McMenamin, arriving back from a term as Catholic chaplain, spoke of 'the wonderful fervor of the Catholic troops. Being under fire all the time, the men were naturally anxious to keep in the state of grace.'[191] Dean William Burke, a Catholic priest from Invercargill, similarly spoke of 'the courage, the unselfishness, the almost reckless daring of the Irish Catholic regiments in the present war'. Such statements were intended to counteract complaints that 'The Catholics have no honest principles; they are a dangerous, disloyal lot'.[192] A much reprinted British article, 'War and Religion', described soldiers as having a new sense of the importance of religion, and early accounts of Gallipoli emphasised the heroism of the 'boys' in the face of the pain.[193] The Reverend W. Hay at Hanover Street Baptist Church in Dunedin believed the best of the soldiers: 'They are looking over the edge of things into eternal realities. Their eyes will be filled with the sight of such things as will have given a new direction to their minds.'[194] But comments like this were chiefly intended to console those who had remained behind.

The reality was more uncomfortable. Even in Trentham, Chaplain William Walker admitted that 'Clear-eyed young fellows came to the camp, met men with foul tongues, sank, and were debauched'. And salvationists noticed abuse of alcohol. Keen Christian soldiers who wanted to say their prayers were sometimes 'chafed'.[195] As early as mid-1915 a shrewd Methodist soldier reported that the only military values were 'play the game' and 'stand up for your pals'. Soldiers did not pray, and they did not like chaplains who put on 'airs'.[196] The *War Cry* identified prostitution in Egypt in a veiled reference: 'This particular sin, which horrified the writer of the letter quoted, flourishes in connection with art, lovely forms, exquisite garments, and most attractive conditions; for all that the end is degradation and death'. [197] In a vivid letter from Gallipoli, Chaplain Captain John Luxford described the horrors and peculiarities of war: 'The battlefield is very different in reality from descriptions in books and papers. It is an Inferno in one sense, and a comradeship in another'.[198] The *Tablet* reported the loss of sensitivity among soldiers, and the *War Cry* noted that the expected wartime Christian conversions had not occurred.[199] In a remarkable interview, the Methodist chaplain Henry Blamires indicated that the chaplains were only respected if they were in the hard places; that the soldiers were hard and alcohol abuse was rife. He still held, however, that there were more serious views of religion.[200]

Increasingly as soldiers were repatriated their reaction to their brutal experiences confused commentators. As early as July 1915, the Salvation Army noted the severe temptations facing returning heroes,[201] and even W. J. Williams had to admit the reality:

> To the hell of actual warfare has been added the hell of temptations of a nature and on a scale that represented the most fiendish assault conceivable on a pure and virtuous manhood. The twin devils of liquor and lust have represented foes infinitely more dangerous and deadly than any they have met on the field of battle.[202]

Catholic soldiers had fraternised so much with Protestants that the war had changed their outlook. James Kelly defended the ordinary soldier, much to the anger of the *Otago Daily Times*, which accused him of lack of patriotism.[203]

A church for the future

Clergy gradually realised that the war had changed the face of religion, especially for the soldiers, and that returned servicemen might not be so interested in religion in the future. They noted a growing national unity and camaraderie across social divisions, and the decline of traditional sectarianism. As in Germany, former soldiers typically believed in a vague sense of fate but were antagonistic towards organised religion [204]

As the war came to an end the churches had to rethink in a way they had never expected. At first they argued that the church had to be made good enough for the soldiers. By 1916 the Reverend A.B. Chappell argued at the Methodist conference that people needed a new theology to cope with the war. Similarly an Anglican commentator asked if the soldiers who 'seem to have little formal religion, but hold their lives in their hands, ready to die for friend or country, are nearer to Christ than we who are so respectably punctilious in our cultured lives?'[205] When the ex-President of the Methodist Church gave the ordination address at the 1916 Methodist conference, he replaced love, in the famous biblical passage in 1 Corinthians 13, with 'manliness' as the need of the hour for the church of the future: 'You may be trained in all the arts of elocution, speak with the tongues of men and of angels, have the gift of prophecy and know all mysteries and all knowledge, yet if you have not strong manliness, they profit you nothing'.[206] The dream of 'the higher career above' became the new hope.[207] An Anglican layman in Auckland insisted that the church had to reconsider its emphases: 'How can the Church expect the average man to take it seriously while so many of its prominent members fritter away their time and waste their energies on ritual trivialities and fruitless doctrinal disputations?'[208] In 1917 Bishop Averill insisted that the church had to recognise that 'religion as a corporate power is painfully weak'. He urged a higher ideal of the kingdom of God and of a church with a stronger sense of service, social involvement and commitment to education.[209]

The First World War did bring a change to the churches of New Zealand, which showed much more willingness, after 1918, to experiment with new ideas and to embrace new visions of the contribution of religion to society. But the soldiers did not come back to church, and that had great consequences for the place of religion in New Zealand society.

28

'KEEPING NEW ZEALAND HOME FIRES BURNING': GENDER, WELFARE AND THE FIRST WORLD WAR

Melanie Nolan

The First World War is usually regarded as having given an impetus to women's paid employment, although the extent of this is debated. Similarly, the war is considered to have promoted a post-war push for women's rights, although, again, the extent is debated.[1] Gail Braybon summed it up: 'The demand for women's labour during... wars may suggest that at this time, if no other, views of women's position and role might change – such has been the conviction of many a social historian when describing the granting of women's suffrage'.[2] In Britain, for instance, the proportion of women in paid employment rose from 24 to 37 per cent during the war. However the almost two million women working for the duration did not make up for the number of men away and there were still acute labour shortages. Furthermore the development of a female-oriented society after 1918 is encapsulated in book titles such as *Out of the Cage*.[3] Francoise Thebaud notes that the 'idea that the Great War had done more to redefine relations between the sexes and emancipate women than years or even centuries of previous struggle had accomplished was widespread during and immediately after the conflict'.[4] Certainly the post-war extension of women's suffrage dominates discussions about change: women's suffrage was extended to United States women in 1920; and to British women over the age of 30 in 1918 and between 21 and 30 in 1928. Although suffrage was the most significant signal of change, other pieces of legislation are also cited. British anti-discrimination laws regarding employment were enacted in 1919, new divorce laws in 1923 (adultery became grounds for divorce on the behalf of women) and inheritance legislation in 1925 gave women a better legal deal than before.

Jan McLeod has written one of the few sustained accounts of the activities of New Zealand women during the First World War.[5] Her 1978 university honours essay examines women in the peace movement as well as the positive and negative aspects of women's patriotic work, but she also concentrates on women's economic participation and broadening interests. Like Thebaud, she distinguishes between rhetoric and change: there was certainly plenty of talk of revolution and the 'whole new, exciting era' unfolding for them after the war. Nonetheless, she notes signs of New Zealand women's wartime activities and confidence. For instance, she regards the growth in political activism and the massive wave of female institution building as evidence of the increasing self-confidence felt by many women.[6] Women were elected to hospital boards in critical numbers during the war: three women to the Dunedin Hospital Board in May 1915 and six (out of 12 women candidates) to the Wellington Hospital and Charitable Board in May 1917. In 1919, under the Women's Parliamentary Rights Act, women were able to stand for Parliament.[7] The movement for women to organise themselves during the war culminated in the re-formation of the National Council of Women (NCW). By 1920, 50 societies had joined forces with the six original branches. McLeod believes, however, that change regarding paid work was only for the 'duration'.

Despite some changes in confidence that historians have pointed to, almost all agree that 'the assumption that a woman's first responsibility was to her home and family remained remarkably resilient, and acted as a brake on the opening up of opportunities for women'.[8] There were important limitations in the long-term effect of war. Above all, the gender order did not change. McLeod, too, follows the developing consensus that the First World War did not liberate, emancipate or 'modernise' women.[9] It only accelerated trends that were already in progress.[10] Moreover, she and others emphasise a conservative, even reactionary, post-war imposition of a 'cult of domesticity', which negated any 'liberation' that war had brought.[11]

I want to argue, however, that 1914–18 was critically important for New

Zealand women's history and gender relations, but not in the way that is usually considered important. New Zealand is a not a good example for either of those 'home front' developments commonly regarded as the main results of the First World War: increases in women's paid employment and political rights, however evolutionary. We need to emphasise that there are particular reasons not to see the First World War as a turning point in traditional measures for New Zealand women. But there were important socio-political implications for women's role as wives and the attention given to their maternal material subsistence.[12] These implications are very important for the expansion and gender dynamics of state welfare several decades before it is usually considered significant.[13]

The general context: absence of 'typical' wartime changes?

One of the main reasons why New Zealand is a not a good example of wartime paid employment change or post-war political gains is suffrage. New Zealand women, Maori and Pakeha, won the vote in 1893, significantly earlier than their counterparts in Britain, in 1918, and the United States, in 1920. Moreover, the New Zealand census data suggests a strange quirk. As Louise Simich has shown, the percentage increase in the employment of women was greater between 1901 and 1911 (43.21 per cent, from 63,049 to 90,295) than between 1911 and 1921 (26.42 per cent, from 90,295 to 114,152).[14] The war decade did not see a massive increase in women's paid employment or even a rise and fall (with a couple of small exceptions which will be discussed below).

Clearly the First World War did not result in a complete disruption of New Zealand society. New Zealand was not geared for war as European countries were, and it experienced moderately – some suggest very prosperous times.[15] The state did not assume powers to commandeer for war purposes the lives and labour of the entire adult population. There were no heavy munitions factories in the dominion. There was demand for clothing, boots, and saddlery goods for the troops; some ammunition was manufactured; shipwrights and carpenters were employed in preparing troopships.[16] But there was no large government department involved in war production. This is important because Martin Pugh and other British historians have isolated significant change in women's employment in Britain to 'government-controlled workplaces'.[17] Sheila Rowbotham notes that, by October 1916, 'the number of women working in such places had increased by nearly 300 per cent', whereas the figure elsewhere was only 36 per cent.[18] The August 1915 establishment of the New Zealand Base Records Section within the Defence Department was important, but by May 1917 only 62 out of 162 employees were women, which pales into insignificance when compared with the British experience. The number of women in the public service rose from 1826 to 4153. The New Zealand government had made its position on women in general advisory and administration work clear: from 1913 girls were excluded from public service entry examinations and were offered only low-paid and low-status positions. The number of government-employed female clerks was dropping before the outbreak of the First World War.[19] Questions were asked in Parliament about how the government might use female labour and an enquiry was made in relation to the Railways Department. In the end, however, only 60 women were employed in the Railways from 1917 to 1919 as cleaners of the interiors of carriages.[20] During the war the New Zealand government was a most reluctant employer of women in its civil service, or more generally.

Above all, there was no direction of women's labour – 'manpowering', to use the Second World War term. The National Efficiency Board (NEB) was established in February 1917 as a result of concerns about the shortage of labour; it was held responsible for the study of the question of female labour and the extent to which it could replace that of men.[21] The board published a pamphlet in 1917 exhorting women to offer themselves for employment, suggesting that there were perhaps not sufficient women available for the job vacancies, but the NEB's recommendations to use female labour were never implemented,[22] and there were no post-war implications. As McLeod notes, these was nothing like the British Cabinet paper *Report on Women in Industry during Wartime* of April 1919.

Prominent citizens established the Women's National Reserve (WNR) in August 1915. Originally a branch of the Men's National Reserve, it shared the aim of performing 'any available work for King and Country'.[23] It urged home front conscription of women and established a voluntary register of women prepared to free men for overseas service. But by June 1916 the WNR had the names of 850 Wellington women who were ready to take up clerical employ-ment. In 1917 representatives of Christchurch women's organisations informed J.A. Frostick, Efficiency Commissioner for Canterbury, that there were 'about 500 women in the city not engaged in essential industry or not employed at all who are willing to do any work they might be asked to do in order to release men of military age'. Although appreciative of the women's offer, Frostick 'did not think it was fair to take advantage of it until men qualified for work had been absorbed in essential industries'.[24] The WNR attempted to 'establish clubs throughout the Dominion for the wives of soldiers and sailors serving the Empire'.[25] As Jane Tolerton has pointed out, the WNR achieved limited 'piecemeal and local' organisation. It 'seems to have been more written about than used'.[26]

The Women's Employment Bureau (WEB), to whom both employers and women seeking employment could turn for aid, was instrumental in finding suitable positions for the wives of soldiers at the front – usually in farmhouses.[27] The 'Men's' Labour Bureau had been established when the Department of Labour was founded in 1891, and by the outbreak of war there were 15 principal and 170 sub-agencies throughout New Zealand. The WEB was established in 1895, and after a chequered history there were six branches at the outbreak of war. After 1915 the Labour Department reported more applications from soldiers' wives wishing to do domestic 'day work' to supplement their allowances.[28] Significantly, however, the WEB had less work to do during the First World War than before 1914: the number of women workers the WEB assisted fell from 2192 in 1915 to 1692 in 1917, 1552 in 1918 and 1406 in 1919.

Table 1: Jobs Secured for Women and Men by the Labour Bureaux[29]

Year to March	Women's Employment Bureaux	Men's Employment Bureaux
June 1908–9	2542	10,391
1909 10	2655	8506
1910–11	2244	7102
1911–12	2215	5735
1912–13	2072	5848
1913–14	2163	5645
1914–15	2165	7515
1915–16	2192	5978
1916–17	1957	2966

1917–18	1692	2952
1918–19	1552	3199
1919–20	1406	4205

Indeed during the war, the Labour Department reported employers resorting to a range of labour sources other than women, and considered women suitable to substitute in clerical work, 'notably in banks', an occupation they were colonising before the war.[30] The vacancies caused by the number of men withdrawn from industry were filled in various ways:

> (1) The employment of women and girls in occupations hitherto filled by male workers, especially in offices, etc.; (2) the absorption of workers from unessential industries to essential work, and the postponement of various kinds of non-urgent work; (3) the employment of persons who had retired from active work; (4) the employment of boys and girls on leaving school to a greater extent than usual; (5) longer hours of work, and the assistance rendered by one farmer to another.[31]

In particular, the Labour Department noted the doubling of the overtime hours from 1914–15 to 1915–16 by females and boys (it did not record male overtime worked but suspected it was 'large').[32] Women were not the vital group in filling the employment gap. Indeed the Women's Employment Bureaux were closed as separate offices in 1921 on the grounds that the number of engagements did not justify the expense involved,[33] The closure of the bureaux is further evidence that women were content with domestic duties concerned with the home.[34] In 1921, only 3.15 per cent of all married women were engaged in outside paid employment, which was a conspicuously low figure internationally.[35] The official view was that there was no female unemployment or need to manage women's labour in war or peace.

The state was at least consistent in this view. When Agnes Bennett offered her services as an experienced doctor to the New Zealand Military Forces, officials simply did not know what to do, so she turned to the French Red Cross instead.[36] No unit of nurses was contemplated 'until members of the New Zealand Registered Nurses' Association made representation': more than 500 nurses eventually served overseas.[37] The government went so far as to oppose Ettie Rout's New Zealand Volunteer Sisterhood. As Tolerton notes, 'Women in New Zealand fought hard to get into the Great War'.[38] Even on the home front women were not 'resorted to'. Newspapers published women's complaints about not being used. In 1917, for instance, a 'strong demand by the women of New Zealand that they should have an opportunity to become more directly associated with war work' was noted as having come to the notice of Minister of Internal Affairs G.W. Russell, but to no avail.[39]

Of course, some women did serve in the forces during the war and some did war work. Women delegates to the February 1916 United Federation of Labour (UFL) conference 'resented the endeavour of employers to exploit female labor as a result of war conditions; they protest against the female labour being called in to displace the higher-paid male worker'.[40] At the 1918 UFL conference, too, there were complaints about the lack of organisation among women workers. Jane Runciman, a tailoresses' union leader, said that the 'difficulties in the way of organizing workers were very palpable to her, especially during the present crisis.... She thought that unorganized women always menaced the conditions of those that are organized and called upon the Conference to endeavour to do something in this matter.' Runciman was supported by William Moxsom, a tailoring leader, who claimed to know of cases where women were doing work for 25s that men had been doing for £3. M.J. Savage, F.R. Cooke and J.T. Paul also spoke on the same lines.[41] The Returned Servicemen's Association drew attention to the 'very large number of women who are now in posts formerly occupied by men'.[42] But female labour was not a burning issue for the labour movement during the war.

All historians agree, moreover, as McLeod concludes, that 'No permanent change in women's basic economic status resulted' from changes during the First World War.[43] Conditions for women in the public service deteriorated and they made up just 5 per cent in the inter-war period, again a very low rate internationally.[44] The major change was some redistribution away from domestic service into shops and offices. And the number of women in industry dropped: women made up 25.6 per cent of factory employees in 1895–6 but only 21.3 per cent in 1914–15.[45]

Table 2: Percentages of all Females in Paid Employment By Sectors[46]

	1911	1916	1921
Primary produce	8.30	9.66	8.06
Transport & communication	1.35	2.26	2.33
Professional & public administration	13.91	17.26	19.34
Commerce & finance	14.28	16.67	18.05
Domestic service	36.88	31.72	28.71
Industry	22.29	19.83	17.80
Unspecified	2.99	2.60	5.71

Given this absence of change for New Zealand working women, it is perhaps not surprising that there has been little work on women and the First World War. Indeed, there has been no debate over the effect of war on women's work and, consequently, gender relations: such work as has been done in New Zealand has concentrated upon the effect of the Second World War.[47] New Zealand was a male breadwinner country in which most married women were labelled 'dependent'. That very characteristic leads us to look for change in areas other than the workplace or the political realm. But first, let us review the state's provision for women dependants during war. It was substantially more involved than it was in managing women's war work.

Did state measures stymie efforts to mobilise women?

It could be said that the state stymied women's mobilisation because it intervened to help keep the home fires burning and permitted women to continue in domestic roles. New Zealand was a nation that put a premium on male breadwinning so the state stepped in when the lads were 'far away'. It certainly supplied four main provisions: it made pensions available, it protected married men from going to the front, it facilitated allotments for grass widows and dependants and it established the Soldiers' Financial Assistance Board.

Providing pensions for soldiers was an ancient state responsibility, and there were 19th-century precedents in New Zealand: the Militia Act 1858 provided disabled soldiers with pensions and land grants based on Imperial precedents and the Military Pensions Act 1866 set out a schedule of pensions, according to rank, race and injury, for colonial soldiers who fought in the New Zealand Wars. Widows and dependants received pensions according to the rank of the soldier, and whether he died of injuries or sickness, although a payment could not be claimed as a right. And such pensions were restricted to Europeans. In 1900, these provisions were extended to men serving in the South African War. The Defence Act 1909 substituted daily or annual payments for lump-sum payments. Means testing ensured that only 'deserving' cases received pensions.[48]

War pensions changed in degree and kind as a result of the First World War, partly because of the sheer numbers involved. Of the 6500 New Zealand troops who fought in South Africa, 228 soldiers died and 166 were wounded. By contrast, of the 100,444 New Zealanders who served overseas in the First World War, 16,317 died and 41,262 were wounded.[49] The New Zealand government responded with more than 'flag-flapping'. The War Pensions Act 1915 established a pension, based on rank, for the wives and children and other dependants of soldiers who died in the war. The basic rate, that for the widow of a private, was £1 5s, with 5s for each child. Indeed, the government claimed that the war pensions of 1915 were among the most generous 'proposed in any Parliament in the world', a claim the RSA continually challenged.[50] Indeed, the government was subject to massive lobbying to increase the rates:[51] deputations from the First Division Mothers League, the Soldiers' Wives, Mothers and Dependants' League and other women's organisations called for the 'betterment of the financial conditions' of dependants.[52] By 1923 the RSA was seeking a 75 per cent increase in all rates and cost of living adjustments. Its pressure led to the appointment of a royal commission, which resulted in moderate increases.[53]

By protecting married men from the front, the state indirectly reinforced the male breadwinner ethos. Ninety-five per cent of those who served in the NZEF declared themselves unmarried. Before conscription, married men comprised 6.9 per cent of volunteers to the end of 1915, and 7.6 per cent to June 1916.[54] These figures may be slightly understated as some recruits hid the fact that they were married. Balloted conscription for married men was first introduced in October 1917. As a result of their own protests, and the government's reluctance, only 796 married men without children, and a handful of others (widowers, divorced or separated men also without children), reached Britain. The government managed to keep all married conscripts from front-line service.

There were of course even fewer women, with or without dependants, who went to the front or died for King and Country.

The allotment scheme facilitated by the state, which 'obliged' a soldier to give his wife and dependants a portion of his pay and allowances, embodied the aims of a broad maternalist campaign. Unlike civilian wages, a soldier's pay and allowances were based upon the number of those dependent upon him. In 1914 a soldier with dependants was paid more than those without any. In June 1915 the government introduced 'separation allowances' for soldiers with dependants or with widowed mothers and other relatives who had relied on their income before the war. In all Allied countries payments to soldiers were based upon the number of dependants but New Zealand was the most generous. The allowance was increased on several occasions and by 1918 a New Zealand private could be granted up to 11s if he was married, making their income £2 16s and 10s 6d for each child per week.[55]

Initially the government did not prescribe that a portion of a soldier's pay and allowances be paid to his dependants, but the embarkation of the NZEF late in 1914 prompted the introduction of a scheme that became known as the 'allotment'.[56] Although the government established the allotment system for those overseas, it was clearly reluctant to extend the principle further and insist that male breadwinners at home provide for their dependants.

Through their support for the allotment system and continued agitation to extend it, women's groups were in the forefront of promoting the male breadwinner ethos for the benefit of wives and children. Groups concerned about 'grass' or temporary war widows agitated for remedies to three problems: the fact that allotment was not automatic, that men in camp before embarkation did not have to allot and that soldiers sometimes forfeited their allotment before it could be sent back to their families.

The Society for the Protection of Women and Children (SPWC) played an important role in attempting to strengthen the allotment system. The society cared for a number of unmarried women and deserted wives whose former partners were in the armed forces. When the Minister of Defence announced that the government would not insist that soldiers made provision for their families, the Wellington Branch of the SPWC sent him a copy of the more enlightened 'Orders for Australian Forces'. It then claimed the credit for new 'stringent orders making it compulsory for men joining the Expeditionary Force to make provision for the wives and children (legitimate or illegitimate) or any relative dependent upon them'.[57] The SPWC was less successful in getting the minister to require men to obtain their wives' consent before enlisting, or to require them to allot from the time they entered camp but before going overseas. It joined patriotic committees in demanding that the state go much further in its allotment policies.

Apparently, camp commandants threatened men with discharge if they heard they were not providing for their wives and dependants. A system of direct deductions was tried out when the 2nd and 3rd Reinforcements were mobilised at Trentham, but 'owing to the trouble it caused' the trial was abandoned.[58] Moreover, the logistics were against direct deduction. Because of the incidence of discharge, detention, fines and even absence without leave, final pay had to wait until the Aquittance Rolls were closed, that is receipts signed by soldiers recording that all pay owing to them had been paid in full. It took up to a week for that to be 'squared', and then for allotments to be processed.

The government issued a guide to the rate of allotment, recommending that soldiers supporting mothers allot 3s per day or £1 1s per week and those with wives 4s per day or £1 8s per week. It believed that the pay rates in its armed forces were 'the most liberal of all schemes', but to its embarrassment there were allegations in Parliament that the rates were still too low. Just as the Second Division League, a lobby group formed by married men in 1917, was about to hold a conference to discuss its demands for increased pay and allowances, the government held a 'round table' meeting of all MPs. The existing separation allowances of £18 4s annually for a wife and £13 for each child were raised to £54 12s and £26 10s respectively. This still fell short of the league's demands. It wanted £150 12s for the wife, and for the state to provide some of that independently of the soldier's pay so that families could accumulate nest eggs. When these claims were not met, thousands of league members rioted at the Christchurch army barracks in April 1918 in an unsuccessful attempt to prevent balloted men from going into camp.[59] It is important to note that a high proportion of those in the armed forces did make allotments. There were 30,906 warrants for allotments and dependant allowances in March 1916; 53,013 in March 1917; and 61,198 in March 1918. The numbers were maintained at about this level until November 1918, when they dropped from 61,670 to 40,424 in March 1919 and 25,486 in May 1919.[60]

The final major state initiative for dependants during the war was the establishment of the Soldiers' Financial Assistance Board (SFAB). The drop in family income on mobilisation was sometimes considerable. The SFAB won the formal power to increase a widow's pension if she and her children were not able to maintain themselves 'in accordance with the standard of comfort to which they were accustomed before the war'. Regulations in January 1917 provided for the payment of rent, interest and instalments of loans, rates and taxes, insurance premiums and expenses incurred in keeping a business going during the breadwinner's military service, to a maximum of £2 per week.[61] This assistance was not means tested, and sometimes amounted to substantial subsidies. Overall, the SFAB considered 10,409 applications for assistance during the First World War.[62]

Patriotic societies' welfare work: Otago Soldiers' and Dependants' Welfare Committee

Nonetheless, the income from soldier allotment and state assistance was often insufficient to support the family, and here the private sector played a role. It is unclear how many employers were like Kaiapoi Woollen Mills:

> There is one other matter the Directors desire me to mention, and it is that they feel proud to report that 31 of our boys have already gone to serve their King and Country, and four others are making preparations to do likewise. Some were among the first in this county who responded to the call of duty. Your directors had no hesitation, acting on your behalf in making provision for them on the following basis: married men two-thirds wages for six months; single men one third wages for six months, such grants being subject to the reconsideration and probable renewals for further period[s of] six months each during the war; maximum payment to any one man, two pounds per week, but always subject to the condition that no grant be more unless the man has been in the company's service for at least two years.[63]

By 1916 the company had paid £1,780 in wages to employees on active service, 'contributed a further sum of £1,478 to various patriotic funds' and paid a subsidy of £1 for £1 on 'all moneys collected by officers and staff of any class of workers for a similar purpose'. At the war's end 91 men were on the company's Roll of Honour: 12 of these men were killed and nine wounded. In 1919 69 men returned to work at the firm, which apparently recouped its investment with loyal and long employee service. However, Kaiapoi Woollen Mills was an extraordinary employer by New Zealand standards, with an Employees' Welfare Committee revamped in the wake of the First World War, a weekly free medical clinic and a superannuation scheme.[64] From September 1921 the company established a hostel for the women workers whose homes were not in Kaiapoi and built company cottages for workers with families.[65] The government and banks were among the few employers that were also systematically contributing to absentee workers: the government, for instance, paid half the contributions of superannuation fund members who enlisted in 1914–18.[66]

The role of patriotic societies is much clearer. These had been established throughout the country from 1915, with locally organised committees collecting funds on behalf of sick and wounded soldiers and their dependants. It was estimated in 1916 that there were about 350 societies collecting war funds, 120 of them patriotic societies.[67] In total, New Zealanders subscribed nearly £5 million to various war funds and at the end of the war various patriotic bodies still held about £1.5 million.[68] Patriotic societies saw their role as being, 'to assist State, civic and public effort in connection with patriotic and relief funds, especially to alleviate the distress caused to widows and children by the present war'.[69] Certainly responsibilities were demarcated: the state provided the 'average necessaries' through soldier pay, separation allowances, allotments or pensions; the voluntary funds were used for supplementary aid.[70]

The RSA objected to patriotic societies as a matter of principle, arguing that the state and not charity should provide for soldiers, and that the societies were inefficient – 'Charitable Aid by Hocus-Pocus', it called them. The state would continue to 'shirk' its responsibilities while patriotic society funds remained important sources of family income.[71] There were many complaints about the inadequacy of government provisions. A private's pay with an allowance for a dependent wife or mother was very low compared with the lowest arbitration award rate: in 1916 the private received £89 9s 3d a year while the award rate was £132 2s.[72] Moreover, many men had earned above award rates in civilian life. Furthermore the cost of living was increasing rapidly and fell heavily upon those with 'fixed' incomes like soldiers and their dependants.[73] The military authorities were quick to point out that many other men had been outside the arbitration system, and had earned less, or less regular, pay than in the army. In addition, soldiers were fed, clothed and given medical care. The Public Health Department paid their dependants' hospital bills while they were overseas. If a soldier's wife was confined or needed other medical care, she could apply to the SFAB.

The War Relief Association, the SPWC, the Defence Department, the Honorary Soldiers' Pensions and Allowance Board and the patriotic societies all offered assistance to soldiers' families over and above state provisions.[74] The Otago Soldiers' and Dependants' Welfare Committee, like a few others, preserved the details of its support, especially for 'grass' or temporary widows.[75] The OSDWC had three main purposes: farewelling soldiers, entertaining them in camp and welcoming them home; providing rehabilitation and comfort; and endeavouring to 'cherish the disabled, to succour the orphans, to sustain the widows, to uphold the mothers'. It vowed to protect soldiers' homes 'from the wolf of want… their children from hunger', to shield 'their wives from privation'.[76] The committee's most time-consuming function was to assist the wives of married soldiers, particularly those still in camp. Its main activity was fundraising and then dispensing funds. It was 'showered with almost £1000 within a few days of the outbreak of war; its largest and most successful venture, a 1915 Queen Carnival, crowded out the biggest hall in New Zealand (the Otago Drill Hall) for ten days, and cleared an extraordinary £104,000'.[77] For a carnival, businesses and organisations picked a woman to represent them as 'a queen', who had a duty to attract donations. The queen who raised the most money was then declared winner and her crowning was the highlight of the carnival.[78] Nineteen-fifteen was the year of the big fundraising carnivals throughout New Zealand. Between 1915 and 1919, the OSDWC of the Otago Patriotic and General Welfare Association dispersed to soldiers and their dependants £61,735 4s 9d, which it had raised in various ways. In the inter-war years, it went on to disperse £122,445 5s 1d in relief and £16,192 16s 8d in advances.[79]

The OSDWC case files suggest that most soldiers allotted the government-recommended 4s a day. On average, the OSDWC supported soldiers' dependants for just under eight months, paying them £18 3s or a little more than 11s weekly in cash during that time. But its support was variable. Different combinations of rent, cash orders and goods were distributed. Most payments were weekly grants of 5s to 10s, which do not appear to have been tied, but many payments were, including grants for the grazing of two horses.[80] More commonly, grants were of coal (usually half a ton at a time for winter), grocery vouchers and orders, doctor's appointments made and paid for by the patriotic society, Christmas allowances for women with large families and rent payments.

Like all charities of the day, the OSDWC was moralistic, though perhaps slightly less than average.[81] Fourteen per cent of applications to the OSDWC between 1914 and 1919 were declined, some because the applicants moved to a different city, some because they had no dependants, and others because their income was considered sufficient, or because it was felt that sons ought to be supporting them, or they were receiving half pay from their husband's ex-employers. Mrs Thirza A. had one child aged 13. Her husband allotted £1 1s with the separation allowance of £1 8s. The committee discontinued her allowance of 10s 6d when they discovered that she was earning £3 3s per week from private nursing.[82] 'Suspect character' was always grounds for refusing an application. Mrs Hannah H.'s character was considered 'unsatisfactory': she was a separated woman and 'Police reports as to her character and mode of living' meant she had 'forfeited all right to receive support from her husband or the Defence Authorities'.[83] Very occasionally prostitution was suspected and proven. Mrs Rosina H., a married woman with a child, was charged with 'loitering and importuning passers-by'. She denied the charge, although she admitting she had been convicted in Wellington for the same offence. She was convicted and bundled off to the Salvation Army Reformatory Home for six months and her application for assistance was denied.[84] Three women had their relief withdrawn because they had turned to prostitution to supplement their income. But even women who had taken this step could return to the OSDWC's good books. Jessie B., mother of four children, was brought before the court for 'keeping a house of ill fame'. She would lock her children in her house and go into the 'city at night' to the house where police arrested her. The Patriotic Association immediately stopped her allowance of £1 8s. Francis Cumming of the Patients and Prisoners Aid Society sent her to her sister in Oamaru and, once it was clear that she was keeping on the 'straight path' after her 'act of indiscretion', the association began payments again.

The OSDWC records reveal two general things. First, they show the extent to which a range of members contributed to a family's support, what is known as the family economy. It contrasts with the male breadwinner idea of a family being dependent upon a single male's earnings. The original census scripts for New Zealand have been destroyed so these records give us a rare view into homes around the time of the First World War. Second, the records demonstrate how the system drew reformers' gaze to the inadequacy of income for families, even those of soldiers who were making allotments. Respectable hardworking families were struggling financially. The experience of the OSDWC visitors and their allied societies led to a campaign for more state and private family support.

Family economy

Between 1914 and 1919, the OSDWC received 919 applications from soldiers' dependants.[85] Each was investigated and received a home visit and a dossier was compiled. Married women without dependants initially received support, but in 1917 the committee decided that it would decline to grant them further allowances.[86] The OSDWC records show that most of the 792 cases the society supported were soldiers' wives and their children, the second largest group were soldiers' mothers and the remainder a mixture of relatives. Although children were the most common single dependant, most dependants were other family members.

Table 3: Numbers of Soldiers' Dependants Assisted by the Otago Patriotic and General Welfare Assocation

	Total of all dependants assisted: 1930	
Soldiers' wives	534	28%
Children	853	44%
Mothers	253	13%
Fathers	90	4%
Sister/brother	178	9.2%
Grandparents	6	
Aunt	3	
Father-in-law	2	2%
Nephew/niece	13	
Grandchildren	8	

Soldiers' mothers were eligible if they could prove their sons regularly supported them, wholly or in part, throughout the 12 months before enlistment. A different indication is given by the annual returns of relationship of dependant applicants for war pensions to 31 March 1917.[87] Here fully 50 per cent of applicants were soldiers' mothers. War dependency certainly shows that New Zealand male breadwinners were responsible for more than nuclear families.

The OSDWC records also show how families survived at the time of the First World War. Take for instance the 'A' family. Before the war Mrs E. A., a widow, worked for five years cleaning and washing under Miss Mollison at Knox College. During the war:

> One daughter is in the Otago Steam Laundry earning £1 a week giving her mother 10/- and the other a tailoress earning 12/6 giving her mother 9/-. Both living at home. Mrs. A ... gets 17/6 a week from an uncle's legacy. Two sons 'helped'.[88]

She did not apply for a widow's pension, which had been established in 1911, because her family contributed more than the means-tested criteria allowed. In 1921 58 per cent of widows were similarly not receiving a widow's pension and the OSDWC files record their family struggles.[89]

Respectable families struggling

The OSDWC reports are also a valuable social history resource because the visitors went into, and reported on, a cross-section of poor and relatively well-off homes, including those of solicitors' and skilled tradesmen's wives.[90] All too often alternative records such as charitable aid reports refer only to the poorest homes. The reports of OSDWC visitors Jane Runciman, Annie Park and Mary Downie Stewart reveal their surprise at the extent of need.[91]

A substantial number of families with breadwinners were struggling. As Mrs M. pleaded, 'My Husband's pay is not enough.'[92] Mrs McL.'s husband 'has been working on boats at Port Chalmers but has had a lot of broken time — was out for one month' and they were not coping well before their son went to war.[93] Indeed, many families found they had never been so well provided for as they were during the war. This was certainly the case for Mrs C. According to Park, she had 'been in many homes in Dunedin but this is the saddest one I have ever been in'. There was absolutely no furniture in the home, and the woman with three children was in a destitute condition. For two years the OSDWC met the family's needs by weekly orders and paying the rent.[94] There were a number of letters on file, like that from Mrs C., in which the recipient wrote that I 'believe every day I thank God for your society because if not for you I do not know how I would have existed'.[95]

Some families had debts at the outbreak of war:[96] 'All the income Mrs. R. has is 15/- Old Age Pension and 10/- a week for minding child 6 months old. The property is her own but rates for 2 years owing £8.'[97] Some had 'heavy mortgages' or insurance payments.[98] Some had invalid, sick and delicate children or spouses or were themselves laid up with medical expenses.[99] Mrs B. 'has been able to go out and work herself earning sufficient money at her profession as a nurse but at the present moment it is quite impossible for her to do this, and the husband is a chronic invalid'.[100] Mrs M. was 'an elderly widow lady with 1 daughter age 12. She was induced to come to NZ by her brother, now enlisted… She is rather frail and cannot do washing – she has tried. They are really poor.'[101] Many lived hand to mouth and mobilisation wiped them out financially: one man 'drew all his money right up to the day of sailing, consequently his wife was left with nothing',[102] while another 'spen[t] ready money available to make husband presentable for Trentham, household would have starved'.[103] The size of the family was always noted: 'five little children' or 'seven'; one had 15.[104] Miss J., a 'most deserving case' was left with nine brothers and sisters; one sister 'who helped maintain the family… lost her reason under the strain & is in Seacliff Mental Hospital'.[105] Mrs H. 'is a very hard working woman. She has had eleven children' with three left at home, one an invalid son requiring 'little extras', and a daughter who lost 'an eye and was ill for a year (no compensation). The father is over sixty… It is really a deserving case – only the splendid constitution of the mother who works late really has saved the family from present want.'[106] Runciman visited Mrs J. with five children and 'found house clean – woman very nice and grateful for what we have already done for her'.[107] Of another woman with two little children Park wrote 'An extremely fine woman and in order to get their home together I have personally on my own behalf guaranteed the payment of certain articles of furniture – the latter has nothing to do with the Committee'.[108]

The soldier allotment and patriotic society systems drew reformers' attention to the inadequacy of provisions for large families and inspired them to seek more state provision. The state supported women on an unprecedented scale during the war. Many women received allotments and a state allowance, sometimes an employer subsidy, yet they still required supplementary assistance. No other group of women temporarily without breadwinners had been given the level of assistance these temporary widows received during the First World War. Their plight gave reformers an inkling of the vulnerability of all widows and deserted women or women with incapable male breadwinners. The financial difficulties of wartime grass widows and soldiers' mothers led reformers to press for even more generous state support. The visitors were labour activists and feminists who believed that society should support women in the home, but increasingly they looked to state support. As Downie Stewart, addressing a meeting of the Otago Women's Reserve, declared,

> The home is the very formation of the state, that round the home cling the
> highest influences that go towards building up the character of our citizens. This
> we know is women's best and highest sphere. It is most natural and the most
> ideal.[109]

The women involved in visiting the homes of women without breadwinners provide the link between wartime lobbies and post-war developments. The experiences of Runciman, Park and Downie Stewart led them to actively lobby for support for families in need in the post-war period through organisations with which they were associated: the New Zealand Labour Party, formed in 1916, the SWPC and the NCW.

Labour women led by Dunedin's Runciman and Mary McCarthy promoted a motherhood endowment along the lines of that advocated by British reformer Eleanor Rathbone, but based on their own wartime experiences of worthy families in need.[110] McCarthy noted the 'accidental precedent' offered by the First World War, when 'no one made any objections to the payments made to the wives of soldiers'. But like the good pacifist that she was, her main point was that the soldiers were paid to kill whether they were in the trenches or on furlough. No one begrudged them or their dependants these payments. Indeed

£1 million per month was found for the war. 'Surely, those who gave life ought to be similarly supported? They had created the means of wealth … It is not too much for the women of this country to ask of those at the helm of the state to find a similar sum, if need be, for the vital needs of the nation'.[111] The money could be raised by a land endowment to the 'mothers of the nation', or by nationalising mineral wealth or shipping. McCarthy spoke throughout New Zealand and published articles in the press.

The SPWC, which had linked poverty with alcohol abuse and mismanagement, had also changed its tune by the war's end. The society had often stated its belief that the drinking and general habits of parents resulted in maltreated and neglected children and families in poverty. In its annual report for 1916–17 the Wellington branch noted:

> However during the year we have come across many cases in which the neglect is attributable to the high cost of living which renders it impossible for the mothers to secure comfortable conditions for their families on wages obtainable by their husbands. Under these circumstances the poor women lose heart and let things drift.[112]

Drink or mismanagement was not the culprit. 'In all cases the homes were clean and the mother and father hard-working and good-living and the children of the quality and upbringing which the country requires.'[113] The problem was simply the size of families and the cost of living. These large families were penalised, for landlords did not like to let them houses and there was usually no domestic help for the mothers. The societies pointed out that 'as women are urged to keep the cradles full some provision (as is proposed in Australia) for grants for every child after four should be given to women who are bearing heavy burdens for the State'. The separation allowances paid to New Zealand soldiers' wives proved a boon for many women and the SPWC's work decreased. The society's workload eased during the war with fewer maintenance cases and because its members were being diverted into patriotic work.[114] Runciman, a member of the SPWC, was fully aware of this.

The SPWC urged the state to assist all mothers of large families trying to cope with a 'high cost of living'. From 1918 the Wellington branch began to 'beg' that the United States model be adopted: the American 'mothers' pension' fostered 'true motherhood and the conservation of the home'. The New Zealand government, the society suggested, should pay 5s each week to mothers 'for every child above four in families'.[115] This soon became a plea for a mother's pension for each child after the first on a graduated scale based on income. In 1919 the Wellington branch sent a resolution proposed by Mrs A.R. (Lily) Atkinson to the Prime Minister William Massey and all MPs:

> That in consideration of the high cost of living and the extreme value of child life, this society begs the Government to formulate and carry out as soon as possible some scheme whereby, say 5s weekly shall be paid to the mother for each surviving child after the first (up to the age of fourteen years) and the average weekly income, exclusive of overtime, if the family income is £3 or under; to the mother for each surviving child after the second, if the income is £3.10s or under; to the mother for each surviving child after the third, if the income is £4 or under; to the mother of each surviving child after the fifth, if the income is £5.5s or under.[116]

Several members received favourable replies, but Massey rejected the recommendation on the grounds of the 'heavy expenditure entailed'.[117]

A public meeting of 1500 people in the Wellington Town Hall on 4 June 1919 resulted in representatives of the Wellington RSA and the NCW unanimously demanding state intervention over the cost of living on behalf of family welfare. The meeting had major demands. First, it called on the government to reduce paper currency, to 'pay a yearly bonus of at least £19 for each child to families with incomes under £250' and to tax all war profits.[118] Second, it asked the government to ensure the 'necessaries of life' by policing profiteering, to fix reasonable rates of profit, to reduce customs on the 'necessaries of life' and specifically to cheapen the price of butter and meat and woollen goods through export taxes and tax breaks to companies producing the 'necessaries of life'. Third, it wanted the government to attend to land and housing to prevent land aggregation by increasing land tax, stopping speculation and concentrating upon 'private homes for the people'. The President of the RSA pointed out that these demands, 'coming as they do from a moderate and loyal section of the community which never has made, or desired to make extravagant or unreasonable demands, … are, I suggest, deserving of your most earnest and serious attention'. Indeed, the 'moderacy and loyalty' of the lobby made the state take the suggestion seriously. The government priced the option of a 'family allowance', discovering 'a bonus of five shillings per week for all children under fourteen and exceeding two in number whose parents have small incomes would amount to approximately one-and-a-quarter million pounds per annum'.[119] It refused to act in 1920, but there were seamless demands along these lines until the family allowance was introduced in 1926.

Increasingly economic rights were sought. Family rights were the issue, but glimmers can be seen of new demands for subsistence rights for women in their own right. 'Wahine' in the *Maoriland Worker* declared that:

> Until women demand as a right something more than bare subsistence we will continue to witness scrambles at jumble sales where the wives of honest working men fight to snatch up the left-off garments of other people's …. My own view is that the present position is largely due to women who acquiesce in the present conditions instead of insisting that they and their children should fully participate in the good things of life.[120]

There was a challenge to the differential whereby war widows and those bereaved by the 1918 flu epidemic got a higher pension than civil widows: the independence and standard of living provided by war pensions was increasingly seen as the benchmark.[121] The Women's Christian Temperance Union wrote to the government urging 'the necessity for giving all widows and young children as a basis of pension not less than [is] granted to the epidemic widows or widows of soldiers'.[122] Women's groups and reformers wanted to ensure that any widow and her children were 'provided for and her children educated, just exactly as though her breadwinner was not taken away'.[123] They found an ally in the New Zealand Labour Party, which adopted a policy clause in 1923 calling for a pension to include 'all widows and incapacitated citizens and an increased rate of payments'. It also called for all state pensions to be 'universally obtainable as a right of citizenship' and to be based on the prevailing standard of living.[124] As Stephen Garton and Margaret McCallum have noted, 'Once the idea of welfare payments as a right became accepted for one group, it could be transferred to others'.[125] In this way the war served to expand expectations and ideas of state welfarism. The state and patriotic support offered to women during the war set off a wave of demands for similar support in the post-war period.

Conclusion: subsistence provisions, gender and the transformative nature of the First World War

During the First World War women previously dependent on men's financial support negotiated the means of survival for themselves and their families from the state, their husbands' employers and patriotic societies. Family issues came to define social policy and rested on an intensified identification of 'woman' and 'family'. The war turned the spotlight on the fact that the male breadwinner wages by themselves might not be sufficient to support all families. This was a critical welfare development in a male breadwinning country.

Until recently, New Zealand historians emphasised the labour and feminist origins of its welfare state.[126] Theda Skocpol has characterised the United States in the wake of the Civil War and the rise of feminism as a wartime-maternalist welfare state which protected 'soldiers and mothers'.[127] It is instructive to examine New Zealand as an imperfect wage-earners' welfare state that was exposed during war. Welfare expanded around the time of the First World War and we can see the influence of maternalist and defence lobbies at work.[128] The state granted war and grass widows unprecedented financial support and some employers pitched in too. Private institutions such as the patriotic societies deemed this provision insufficient. Leaders in the welfare associations and those involved in visiting 'soldiers' homes' went on to call upon the state to provide more. The strength of this lobby makes us reconsider the First World War as a turning point for women's history and New Zealand gender relations.

29

BLUEPRINT FOR THE FUTURE?
'NATIONAL EFFICIENCY' AND THE FIRST WORLD WAR

John E. Martin

National efficiency became the catch-cry in Britain at the turn of the 20th century, as public opinion was dismayed by the performance of troops in the South African War.[1] The war changed British politics fundamentally, exposing the fragility of British imperialism, the degraded condition of the working class and the need for the social organisation of its citizenry. The German example was widely held up as a model, with its army, social insurance system, highly organised education system and an organic link with industry. The concept of national efficiency presupposed organised central state intervention in the interests of national survival and prosperity. The application of compulsion and 'scientific' principles to industry and social organisation lay at the core of the concept.

The practical equivalent of the British concerns for national efficiency in New Zealand around the turn of the century was the perpetuation of a healthy, thriving colonial society in which the evils of the old world – classes, poverty and the poor law – were absent and in which self-reliant colonists predominated. The preservation of a land of opportunity with a high standard of living, high wages, access to land, healthy factories and healthy children was the motivating force here. In this sense the concern for physical or racial degeneration, which surfaced in Britain about 1900, had always existed from the early days of settlement because it was seen to relate to the infection of the 'new world' by the 'old'. There were neither the same imperialist factors nor a war that had had the same enormous impact as the South African War.

Just as the South African War had been formative for Britain, so too was the First World War for New Zealand. It provided a test for New Zealand's bonds with Britain and for its 'frontier' manhood, and it also elicited endeavours that sought to follow the 'national efficiency' movement in Britain. The adoption of national efficiency would keep the country in the antipodean vanguard of the British Empire.

The impact of national efficiency has largely been discussed in terms of the strengthening of social control over the population, particularly in relation to drinking and gambling. Paul Baker, in *King and Country Call*, regards compulsory military training, introduced in 1909, and conscription that followed it during the First World War, as manifestations of the power of the state and its capacity to exert social control.[2] He also provides a brief account of the National Efficiency Board, appointed in February 1917, but does not explore its wider impact or examine its demise in any detail, confining himself to the rejection of industrial conscription by the government. Here we take a closer look at the NEB in the context of wartime manpower developments, in an attempt to assess its broader influence.

Voluntary recruitment

In the early months of the war many thousands volunteered and there was no difficulty in dispatching the NZEF's Main Body in October 1914.[3] Efforts to raise troops were strengthened in early 1915 as it was realised that the war would not be over soon and the reinforcement rate was increased. The experience of Gallipoli strengthened resolve and resulted in another flood of volunteers and by mid-year some were suggesting that conscription might be unnecessary. (Casualties from the Gallipoli campaign are indicated in the graph on page 533 covering the period May–September 1915.[4]) In the latter half of 1915 the numbers coming forward slackened, however, and by October New Zealand had reached a crisis point in its voluntary recruitment as its commitment to supply troops exceeded those of the other dominions on a per capita basis. Calls for conscription strengthened, as the government raised the reinforcement rate from

15 to 20 per cent (dropped again to 15 per cent in January 1916). Minister of Defence James Allen acknowledged the mounting opinion that compulsion might be required and felt that New Zealand had contributed its fair share and was reaching its limits. The major constraint was fear over the opposition to the introduction of conscription, especially from the more radical wing of the labour movement.

Meanwhile, persuasion was exerted to continue the flow of volunteers and the 'shirker' who would not contribute became the butt of public disapproval. Equality of sacrifice became increasingly important and the volunteering ethic declined under the moral pressures. The necessity for conscription was increased by fears of dire labour shortages in the rural economy and the loss of skilled labour in industry. This was because under the voluntary approach there had been no system of organising the flow of recruits and monitoring its impact on the economy.

A register of those of military age was taken in November 1915, under the National Registration Act of that year. This indicated that nearly 60 per cent were prepared to volunteer for overseas service, but also that a substantial minority would not volunteer for any kind of service. The fact that there seemed to be substantial reserves in theory encouraged perseverance with the voluntary approach, but such confidence collapsed when it became apparent that, despite Allen's announcement that he would ask those who said 'yes' to actually volunteer, the flow of volunteers continued to dry up.

Following similar shifts in opinion among the British, Allen conceded that conscription now had to be considered, given that the last-resort recruiting campaign had failed over the summer. More than two-thirds of those eligible for military service had failed to volunteer. Allen conceded: 'we are face to face with the recruiting problem, and there can be no doubt about it that the bulk of opinion in the Country is in favour of compulsion, and has been for some time'. Only the 'fear of what might happen in Labour circles, prevents it being adopted here, with also a desire not to embarrass the Home authorities by doing so before they are right for it there'.[5] And he commented as he desperately toured the country during the recruiting drive, 'the willing horse cannot be worked till it drops'.[6]

Conscription

In March 1916 Prime Minister William Massey announced that legislation for conscription would be introduced into Parliament. In the middle of the year the Military Service Bill, providing for conscription of men aged 20 to 46, was introduced and enacted rapidly with general support. Only three Labour MPs and an independent Liberal voted against its third reading.[7] The small contingent of Labour members battled against the bill to the bitter end, forcing division after division until it went through in the early hours of 10 June, upon which the House rose and sang the National Anthem.[8]

The Act brought in conscription by means of monthly ballots to top up volunteering in the military districts, based on the enrolment through the National Registration Act of all men of military age into a First Division (single men, widowers and recently married men) and Second Division (others). Military service boards, which would hear cases of exemption on the grounds of public interest or personal hardship, were formed in preparation for implementation of the scheme. Paradoxically, preparing for conscription improved the flow of volunteers at first, with men preferring to avoid the connotations of being conscripted. But by September 1916 the flow had begun to dry up again. The Somme offensive produced a huge increase in the casualty rate for September and October 1916 (as shown in the graph), but unlike Gallipoli did not give rise to an increased volunteering rate. By now the demand for equality of sacrifice was overriding and men would no longer volunteer to the extent required without knowing that others would do so also. Compulsion was needed.

The first ballot under the Military Service Act took place in November 1916. Over the 1916–17 summer the Act was in full operation and a number of ballots were held. As further reinforcements were sent, the proportion of those conscripted would rise from about a third to three-quarters of the reinforcement drafts by the latter half of 1917. Conscription would keep the New Zealand Division up to full strength.

Massey and Finance Minister Sir Joseph Ward had left the country in August 1916, after the passage of the Military Service Act, and would remain away until June 1917, leaving Allen in charge. In December 1916, following a conference between ministers, the military service boards and the military, the Minister in charge of Munitions and Supplies, Arthur Myers, stressed to the Cabinet that it was now necessary for the military service boards to be guided by the needs of what should be regarded as essential industries.[9] It was becoming increasingly difficult to deal with exemptions of those voluntarily enlisted as well as appeals under the Military Service Act. The military service boards operated meanwhile on the basis of *ad hoc* understandings of essential industries and the issue of certificates from the Minister of Munitions recommending exemption.[10]

Appointment of the National Efficiency Board

In January 1917, amid growing weariness over the war, the government announced that it would need to establish a nationwide organisation that would allow it to supply greater numbers of soldiers than it had been committed to.[11] The introduction of conscription greatly magnified demands that the war effort be organised, most particularly industry and manpower. Allen himself complained of how the country had 'bungled along' with no 'satisfactory organization of industry'.[12]

Allen appointed a National Efficiency Board, with a brief to consider the organisation of industries, industrial efficiency and the development of scientific research after the war.[13] It was to function as a royal commission and would continue working for one year after the war had ended. It was intended not only to organise the process of recruiting in the face of competing demands for manpower but also to consider broader issues of economic and social organisation that might be vital to post-war reconstruction. It set about recommending a host of measures that would both deal with the immediate military manpower and labour problem and assist in the reconstruction of New Zealand society.

Board members were appointed for each of the four military districts: James A. Frostick (Canterbury), J.H. Gunson (Auckland), W.D. Hunt (Otago) and Thomas Moss (Wellington). Each district commissioner had his own office in the main centre in his district and would meet monthly in Wellington under chairman William Ferguson. The board, which held its first meeting in Parliament Buildings on 2 February 1917, immediately made clear its interest in exploring how the award-based industrial relations system might be modified or suspended, the rationalisation of businesses, restriction of amusements and reduction in alcohol consumption.

In February 1917 news came through of a request for a further division, or at least one or more brigades, from New Zealand as Britain planned a 'big push' in the search for victory.[14] At the Imperial War Conference in London in March

Massey agreed to provide additional units of troops, which would take the form of a fourth brigade formed from the accumulated reserves already in Britain; it would not be reinforced, however, and would eventually be broken up to supply other brigades. Massey drew the line at 100,000 men sent overseas – about 40 per cent of the roughly 250,000 men of military age in 1914.

The board set about its task with gusto. Ferguson, a leading engineer who had been responsible for the development of the capital's harbour facilities through the Wellington Harbour Board, took a very active role.[15] Frostick was a well-known Christchurch businessman who manufactured boots and was active in the Chamber of Commerce, the Employers' Association and the Industrial Association. Gunson was Auckland's mayor, having entered local politics through involvement in the Auckland Harbour Board. Hunt was managing director of Wright Stephenson's, had chaired the ground-breaking Royal Commission on the Public Service of 1912 and was a known advocate of prohibition as a leading figure in the Businessmen's Efficiency League, which pushed for prohibition on the grounds of 'efficiency'.[16] Moss, a farmer from Eketahuna, was at one time a carpenter and trade unionist before taking up land and becoming active in farmer and local body politics. All, aside from Hunt, had been involved in harbour boards – a matter of some significance given the attention the NEB devoted to reducing casual waterfront employment.

The board argued that the elaborate system of committees initially suggested was unnecessary, being unwieldy, slow and costly. It envisaged instead a network of voluntary groups, supplemented by experts as needed. Formed as 'boards of trustees' and 'committees of advice' in business and farming sectors in the military districts, these were appointed to manage soldiers' farms and businesses while they were away at the war. But immediately the NEB got to work the popular perception was of a 'bogey-man' controlling the pleasures of the populace.[17]

The board's work

In June 1917, as Massey and Ward returned from their trip to Britain, the board delivered a long list of recommendations for the government to consider. In July it submitted its substantial first annual report and included a major report on liquor.[18] Parliament had already enacted legislation that increasingly disciplined and controlled what were seen as the less desirable aspects of social behaviour

– drinking, horse racing and gambling – in the interests of 'economy and efficiency' as the prohibition movement seized on the opportunity offered by the war. In 1914 the drinking age had been raised from 16 years to 21 years, and in 1916 'shouting' of drinks was prohibited in public bars.

Now the NEB argued that the greatest efficiency would be attained by complete prohibition – of the importing, manufacture and sale of liquor – but that this was a decision for the people by means of a referendum. The restriction of drinking was important not only during the war but also to promote 'permanent national efficiency'. The loss of productivity was most important. Meanwhile the board recommended restricted hours of sales – 8 a.m. to 6 p.m. on four days and to 9 p.m. on the fifth day with 8 a.m. to 1 p.m. on the half-day holiday – confinement of consumption to licensed premises and a reduced strength of spirits.

The move by the NEB was supported by the largest ever petition presented to Parliament up to that time, with 177,000 signatures in support of early closing. In a generally polarised atmosphere Massey declared that the matter would not be a party one. Although the government favoured a more limited compromise restriction to 8 p.m., he admitted defeat and accepted an amendment for general 6 p.m. closing, initially for the duration of the war, but in fact made permanent in 1918. Liquor could also no longer be served with meals after that time.

The NEB's major work in relation to recruiting was the classification of industries. In its first month of operation it prepared a draft classification of 'essentiality', which the Cabinet discussed on a number of occasions before it was approved and gazetted in July.[19] The 'most essential' industries included the rural sector and associated primary industries, coal mining, railways and shipping. Manufacture of ammunition – after some controversy and pressure from the Colonial Ammunition Company to raise its status – was in the end graded as merely 'essential', since New Zealand-produced ammunition was now used only for practice purposes. The board then got to work scheduling more detailed lists of essential occupations. This was in line with its declared objective in its 1917 annual report that direction and control of all persons be accomplished so that labour could be commanded as 'national industrial service'. In July the NEB exhorted Allen to introduce this by means of a national register of those employed. The lists, finalised by September 1917, were adopted by the government and used extensively by the Military Service Boards in assessing exemptions and appeals. They proved a vital classification device.

As has been mentioned, the NEB was also particularly interested in employment conditions on the waterfront.[20] In its view, removing casual labour would go a long way towards solving the perennial instability and unrest as well as making the work more organised. There was a special investigation of Wellington's waterside employment and consideration was given to putting the control of all labour under the Wellington Harbour Board. The scheme did not go ahead, however, in the face of competing shipping company interests and waterside union resistance.

Such moves were in response to an increasingly serious shortage of labour in industry. To compensate, overtime hours had been increased, particularly in clothing, boot and shoe manufacture and biscuit and confectionery making. Munition workers also worked long hours in the early part of the war, when New Zealand supplied its own troops with ammunition. Industries reduced staff to a bare minimum and those in essential industries worked at high pressure. From 1915 the numbers of factories and those employed in manufacturing began to contract as the demand for military manpower took effect. This situation was to remain until the end of the war.

In 1916, after much pressure for an acknowledgment of the impact of wartime inflation on wages, the Arbitration Court devised a 'war bonus' scheme. By now labour shortages had reached serious proportions and in conjunction with shortages of materials were disorganising industry. In addition to increased hours, the problem was dealt with by the employment of women, retired men and boys and girls on leaving school. Women's employment expanded considerably in the public service, with many employed in the Defence Department and other wartime departments for clerical and administrative work. Numbers of women were also taken on in offices and banks for similar work.

Fears that the rural economy would suffer greatly through manpower demands were not realised.[21] Large numbers of farm workers volunteered for the NZEF in the early days and the number of employees fell away somewhat – by 6 per cent from 1915 to 1917 – but this did not check production. Classification as an essential industry proved effective as more than one-third of those exempted from service were from farming occupations.[22] The volume of primary products was maintained or even increased as export prices rose with the securing of bulk purchase arrangements – the commandeer – with Britain. There was concern that the harvests of 1916 and 1917 might not be got in, but this proved groundless. A NEB survey in Canterbury and Marlborough in December 1917 found that farmers were somewhat short of men, but those affected were only scattered and in ones and twos.

The board attempted to encourage the greater involvement of women in the labour-force. It produced a pamphlet, *Women's War Work*, which adopted the British approach to the employment of women and exhorted New Zealand women to follow suit. 'The necessity for the active service of every woman not engaged in some useful or essential work towards victory is very urgent.'[23] The pamphlet listed a multitude of jobs undertaken by women in Britain that should be considered in New Zealand.

Unfortunately the NEB got unduly excited by a report of a woman observed to be ploughing with a horse and team in Canterbury and handling them well.[24] This example of patriotic womanhood was exalted to the skies before it was realised that the report was misleading in that the woman did not regularly handle the horses at all. The embarrassment was compounded when it was discovered that the man employed to do the farm work had just been balloted for military service. The women on the farm appealed against this and pleaded for the NEB to act on their behalf.

The board was particularly keen to involve the labour movement in its deliberations.[25] Conscription and the war effort more generally were reliant upon getting the labour movement onside. The NEB recognised from the start that it would not be able to co-opt a labour representative directly onto the board, since that would divorce the person from the labour movement and render him ineffective.[26] Frostick urged the board to encourage the regional industrial associations to work alongside the trades councils and began to broach matters quietly with leading moderate labour leaders. He wanted 'councils of labour' to be formed in the major centres. Meanwhile the NEB was coming under pressure from the New Zealand Employers' Federation, led by William Pryor,[27] who urged the placing of industries affected by strikes under 'war conditions' if agreement was not reached. Regulations should be issued to compel workers to accept employment under award conditions. The board did not feel that the time was right to take such draconian steps.

But when Frostick got together with a group of labour representatives much scepticism was expressed. At the subsequent Labour Congress in Wellington in July 1917 (the New Zealand Labour Party's first conference), it was said emphatically that 'the only National Efficiency Board which can safeguard Labour interests is a board composed of Labour representatives elected from the Labour organisations'.[28]

Nonetheless the NEB resolved that the government would have to in some way obtain the co-operation of the trade unions in its planned amendment or suspension of awards, and set about approaching individual moderates who might be co-operative. Frostick believed there was a gulf between the old type of trade unionist who could be approached, on the assurance that industrial conditions would be restored after the war, and the younger militants influenced by the ideas of the Industrial Workers of the World. 'Councils of advice' in each military district, including five employer and five trade union representatives, were advanced as a means of involving labour that would facilitate the amendment of working conditions. But it seems that this idea was not taken further. Certainly the 'Red' Federation of Labour, led by M.J. Savage, was strongly opposed to such interventions and actively agitated against the NEB's plans for the government to direct industrial labour.[29] The NEB continued to pursue the freeing up of regulation of working conditions and wages.

Political problems

With the return of Massey and Ward in June 1917 the NEB lost the sympathetic ear of Allen.[30] Massey said bluntly that he was not going to be 'dictated to by the Board' and Ward likewise warned that he would not allow the NEB to 'take the position of the Government of the country'.[31]

The NEB felt it was getting nowhere. In spite of its energy and enthusiasm it came up against a brick wall in Cabinet. In private correspondence Ferguson complained of a 'very narrow political aspect, and that there is a risk that either the Board may be made a scapegoat or that its recommendations may be ignored'.[32] He wrote to Allen in August advising that the board had concluded that 'its advice is not generally acceptable to the Government' and that it wanted to resign.[33] In spite of entreaties to continue, resignation followed. Ferguson wrote: 'The Board realised that the Government was not in earnest in employing them and that largely we were the child of only one of the Ministers [Allen] and were treated as a step-child or even not so well by the other Ministers'.[34]

Allen conceded that some ministers and their departments were not sympathetic to the NEB and argued for retention of its terms of reference. After negotiations, these were confirmed. When Gunson and Hunt refused to withdraw their resignations, they were replaced by George Elliot, company director of Auckland, and James Begg, sheepfarmer and company director of Dunedin. Allen and Massey were in theory co-opted onto the board, on the understanding that they would not interfere with its deliberations by attending meetings. The new board presented its recommendations again in October 1917.[35] Massey muttered that what they had to propose was 'a pretty big proposition'. He did not think Parliament would entertain the prospect.

The amendment or suspension of awards proved the crucial issue upon which the NEB foundered. Massey finally replied in November that the War Legislation Act 1917 already gave the government powers to control labour, the National Registration Act 1915 allowed the creation of a national register and the Regulation of Trade and Commerce Act 1914 allowed modification of awards in the public interest. Legally this might have been so, but mustering up the political will was another thing altogether – and this the NEB began to realise after its deputation had interviewed Massey. The board's observations on the state of industrial relations in the country and their enquiries into employment in the two crucial parts of the economy – the coal mines and the waterfront – had underlined the fact that the government had decided on quite a different strategy in spite of the legal provisions theoretically available to them.

The government was determined to avoid confrontations in the coal mines, on the wharves and over shipping. Allen, who was sympathetic towards keeping the miners in their essential work rather than allowing them to be conscripted, wanted to give them a blanket exemption and although this was not possible he assured them that appeals would be heard favourably.[36] He negotiated with the miners and bent over backwards in appeasing them, but when he acted to arrest the leaders of a 'go-slow' and suspended the exemptions from conscription in early 1917 a serious strike that would cripple the economy loomed. Allen sought a compromise, which was accepted, involving increased rates of pay, dropping the charges and restoring the exemptions, in return for no further strikes. Turbulence in the mines continued into 1918, now over wage increases, leading Massey to threaten to implement the war legislation.

In other instances the government intervened. A threatened drivers' strike late in 1916 resulted in the government overruling the Arbitration Court and mediating towards a settlement. When the watersiders became agitated over a new award in early 1917, the government issued regulations banning 'seditious strikes and lockouts' that interfered with the war effort. Later that year the government intervened in a shipping dispute to secure a return to work.

Direction of labour?

In June 1917 the fighting at Messines resulted in huge casualties and this was followed in later months by the slaughter around Ypres, especially at Passchendaele. Allen complained to NZEF commander Sir Alexander Godley that 'There has been a feeling growing in New Zealand that the willing horse is being worked to death'.[37] He was finding it increasingly difficult to hold the line on supplying reinforcements.

From this time onwards New Zealand's casualties continued to climb until near the end of the war. From mid-1917, as American troops began to arrive in France in large numbers pressure was exerted to reduce New Zealand commitments, which were higher than Australia's on a pro rata basis. Some wanted a halt to the mobilisation of the Second Division of men of military age, before married men with children were taken in. The Second Division League agitated for improved pay and allowances. Allen sought to reduce the reinforcement rate below 15 per cent. In July it fell to 12 per cent, then 10 per cent and dramatically to 6.5 per cent in December. As the reduction in the reinforcement rate took place, 4 Brigade was disbanded.[38] The overall effect of reduced reinforcements was that the numbers of men sent in 1918 tailed off markedly and pressure on manpower and the application of conscription eased considerably.

As Germany's major offensive was launched in March 1918 Britain appealed for more troops, mobilisation was accelerated again and more reinforcements were sent as the reinforcement rate doubled.[39] Massey foresaw the shutting down of non-essential industries and transfer of labour to essential ones in response as Allen envisaged an exhausting of manpower reserves if mobilisation continued. These developments motivated the government suddenly to respond to the NEB's blandishments. The NEB persuaded the government to include far-reaching measures in the Finance Act passed during the emergency short session in April 1918, just before Massey and Ward left again for Britain. Section 25 provided for regulations that would introduce 'national service', in the sense of controlling all services, employment and industries and regulating wages and salaries (subject to awards) when they were deemed to be 'essential to the public welfare'. At first the NEB felt it could not draft such regulations because the government had not obtained statutory authority to provide for suspension of awards, but after meetings with the law draftsman and with Allen and William Macdonald, the Minister of Agriculture, it agreed to do so.[40] Ward dramatically described the provisions in Parliament as creating 'a system under which the country can be organized, because such organization is essential for the preservation of the whole body politic … in this time of unprecedented trial'.[41]

Thus it appeared for a time that direction of labour, so characteristic of the Second World War, might become a reality in the First World War, although Massey conceded that it would not happen immediately. In the end the only regulations actually promulgated concerned the control of employment of aliens. Reinforcement rates were soon reduced to the previous level as the Allied forces absorbed the German attack and themselves took the offensive from July 1918.[42]

Demise of the NEB

As the war neared its end negotiations began on the continuation of the work in the interests of national efficiency. The NEB was encouraged by Massey's exhortatory declaration, in response to a deputation of trade unionists, that 'the nation that was most efficient was going to be the nation that would win in the great competitive struggle which would follow the years of war; and they hoped that nation would be the nation to which we belonged'.[43]

But when the NEB prepared its second annual report in 1918 and sent it to the government it failed to get a response or even an acknowledgment.[44] The lengthy report detailed the travails of the NEB in the latter half of 1917 and the rearrangements. It frankly acknowledged that the changes had not worked, with departments continuing to take a narrow viewpoint rather than a 'broad national standpoint'. The report outlined the board's achievements, limited though they were, and concluded that 'although much has been attempted… in respect of many of the most important items nothing of moment has been accomplished'.[45]

Since the report remained unpublished, a large part of the NEB's work remained undocumented, including some of its constructive proposed post-war initiatives. A lengthy appendix concerned the proposal to establish a Board of Science and Industry, following the NEB's request for the New Zealand Institute to form a committee to discuss the issue. Government promotion of scientific and industrial research had come onto the agenda during the war, with Britain urging the dominions to follow its example in setting up a department. The report was submitted to the government in January 1919 but shelved.

The NEB also investigated moves in other countries towards greater worker participation in industry. In Britain the Whitley reports of 1917 led to the forming of Joint Industrial Councils or 'Whitley Councils' in many industries at the end of the war. Such councils attempted to provide a new framework for industrial relations incorporating worker representation and promoting industrial efficiency. After the war New Zealand also looked at overseas profit-sharing (also known as 'co-partnership') schemes and encouraged their establishment here by the Companies Empowering Act 1924, in the interests of industrial peace. The emergence during the war of an informal system of collective bargaining alongside the arbitration system had brought into question the latter's effectiveness and long-term viability.[46] The NEB recommended to the government that similar joint committees of employer and worker representatives be formed in New Zealand to recognise the place of industry in national life and encourage the co-operation of labour, management and capital.

The NEB had always understood that its broad terms of reference extended to the post-war period. As it moved to consider apprenticeship and post-war education, it asked the government whether it should continue. Ruminating with Godley on the ending of the war, Allen noted that New Zealand's spirit had been wonderful throughout, that the public had accepted compulsion and the Military Service Act, and that the military service boards had gained the confidence of the public in their fairness. 'Now we have the future before us, bringing the men back to their homeland, dealing satisfactorily with the sick and wounded, and re-establishing all our men in civil life again.'[47] But the government's scheme for post-war reconstruction would not include the NEB. It was disbanded.

Allen had acknowledged that he thought the NEB should be made permanent and deal with post-war reconstruction, but the hostility of other ministers had proved insurmountable.[48] The planned education report would be the board's last activity. Completed in March 1919, this included recommendations concerning the development of technical education and modernising of apprenticeship training and was passed on to the Industries Committee.[49] It also urged the government to take up its draft apprenticeship and vocational training legislation appropriate for industrial reconstruction after the war.

In a letter to a correspondent Ferguson reflected that perhaps the board had suffered from being given such wide powers. It should, he felt, have investigated specific issues upon which the government was already agreed. Its second report was probably too forceful and antagonised the government, which suppressed it – 'apparently our plain speaking instead of doing good has thrown upon us the hostility of the Cabinet'.[50] A cartoon, published as the first board resigned, expressed only too well what the problem was.[51] In the public mind the NEB had a swollen head in that its ambitions extended well beyond the tendering of advice to government. It wanted in effect to take over the government.

Reflections on the NEB's impact

But were the NEB's efforts in vain? Were its proposals beyond the realm of the possible? Had Allen encouraged it to think that it could provide a manifesto for a new social order?

During the war the NEB perhaps accomplished more than it was given credit for. And its enquiries sowed seeds, or at least reinforced emerging strands of thinking, that would bear fruit in the future. Moreover, if the war had not taken the course that it did, and if the final German offensive had succeeded, the kinds of measures proposed by the NEB would rapidly have come to the top of the agenda. It is clear that by the last year of the war New Zealand was on the verge of exhausting its manpower reserves. The perennial labour shortages that had up to that time been manageable could well have disrupted the economy very quickly.

What did the NEB accomplish? It provided the means by which the conscription scheme and the military service boards could function effectively, so that an equality of sacrifice was seen to apply, essential industries were protected and appeals were considered in a fair and organised manner. It also provided farmers and others with some surety that their farms and businesses would be kept operating in their absence. The board is perhaps chiefly known for its role in introducing the 6 p.m. closing of bars, which would remain in place until 1967. Although the moral rationale for this can be debated, its effect on social patterns must be acknowledged. And in 1918 the NEB made a potentially crucial intervention in preparing the way for possible direction and control of manpower. These measures were not taken advantage of, but their importance cannot be denied.

What broader developments might the NEB be associated with? Its educational proposals were consistent with 'social efficiency' thinking, as propagated by Inspector-General of Education George Hogben in the first decade and a half of the 20th century.[52] This stressed the modernising, functional dimension of schooling as preparation for citizenship, in which vocational education was emphasised. During the war some of these concerns were displaced into the instilling of patriotism in schools. Following an NEB recommendation in 1917 many schools took up flag-saluting ceremonies.[53] After the war the 'social efficiency' doctrine in the post-primary sector became largely concerned with a curriculum differentiated by ability and gender, according to the anticipated vocational destination.

In 1919 the NEB's report on scientific research was passed on to the Industries Committee, which made a wide range of recommendations, including the establishment of a board of science and industry, increased hydro-electric development, reform of apprenticeship provisions, dealing with the housing shortage and the opening up of immigration.[54] Such elements of post-war development were to come about during the 1920s. The Department of Scientific and Industrial Research was formed in 1926.[55] A network of electricity generating stations was built in the North Island, establishing the beginnings of the national grid. The Apprentices Act 1923 greatly modernised the decayed apprenticeship provisions, which dated back to the archaic legislation of 1865. The state housing scheme was reactivated and a new phase of assisted immigration to New Zealand began.

The NEB's existence was consistent with the much greater state intervention in and control of the economy that developed during the war. The Board of Trade, established in 1915 because of concern at the rising cost of living, was motivated by a concept of 'fairness' in conditions of perceived profiteering. The prices of domestic commodities were fixed or controlled, as were house rents; coal was rationed; and the state became the direct provider of meat and boots.[56] The Board of Trade had its powers strengthened by legislation in 1919. In conjunction with the Department of Industries and Commerce, it began to consider the development of industry to absorb returning servicemen. It also investigated the coal mining industry in detail in 1919, motivated by concern at miners' conditions and instability in the industry.[57] While the NEB's detailed investigation of employment conditions on the Wellington waterfront was not directly taken further, during the 1920s the development of co-operative stevedoring would come under consideration. The initiative looking at worker participation in industry was also to bear fruit: in the early 1920s the Department of Labour encouraged such initiatives, which received Massey's personal endorsement in the passage of the Companies Empowering Act 1924 that facilitated such worker participation.

The NEB had looked hard at the arbitration system and wanted to make it more flexible in wartime conditions. Although it was unsuccessful, the more direct role taken by government in industrial relations during the war, together with the increased power exercised by key unions such as the miners, contributed to fundamental changes after 1918. As a result of wartime inflation and the prevalence of strikes the arbitration system had lost credibility. The government began to cast around for solutions that might bring wages into line with the changing cost of living and create state machinery to ensure that the public interest was not damaged by strikes.[58]

As the war ended the government modified the Arbitration Court's role so that it could amend awards during their currency and, more importantly, could explicitly take into account both conditions affecting industry and increases in the cost of living. This crucial change opened the way for a much enlarged role and led to the general wage order system. It created an element of judgment of the national interest that was to become central in the period after the Second World War. In 1922 the forerunner of the general wage order system, either to raise or lower wage rates, was created. At the same time, as a result of overseas experience (and more than likely the work of the NEB here) showing that overtime was 'inimical to the health, efficiency, and contentment of workers', the Arbitration Court stipulated overtime rates that were intended as a penal measure. It also formally articulated for the first time the principle of the family wage – in terms of the dignity of the worker as a citizen and head of a family – that was to guide later wage fixing.

In conclusion, the optimistic plans of the board proved too much for the cautious and conservative wartime coalition government, even if the board managed to retain Allen's sympathetic ear. But the NEB needs to be seen as part of a wider movement associated with the strengthening of interventionist powers of the state in New Zealand. Its vision stands as a statement of wartime exigencies and the potential swelling of the place of the state that in many ways would come to pass in following decades. The state's strengthening powers accelerated during the First World War, particularly as its fiscal basis was enlarged through wartime taxation increases, and the way was prepared for many initiatives that were to take place during the 1920s and beyond. The experience of dealing with manpower issues during the First World War would largely be replicated during the next world war. This time the government, now more accustomed to assuming extraordinary powers, would work closely with a department specifically set up to organise manpower, which would institute the direction of labour and orchestrate the modification of working conditions.

Recruitment and Casualties, 1914–18

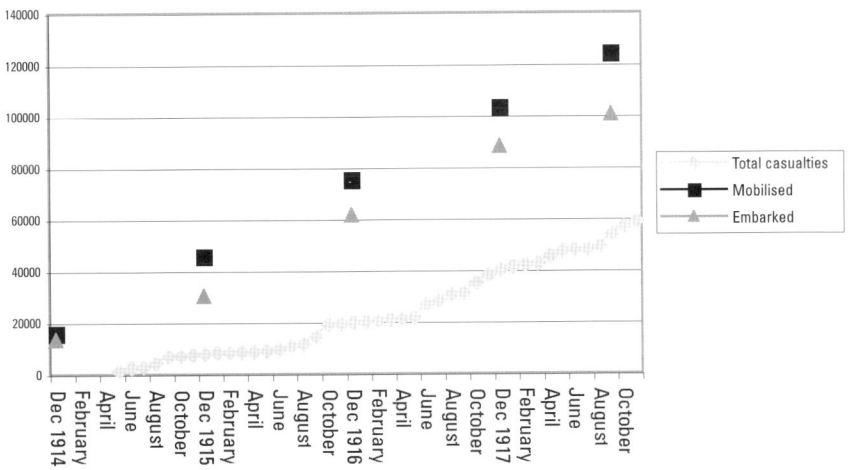

30

PATRIOTISM, PROFITS AND PROBLEMS: NEW ZEALAND FARMING DURING THE GREAT WAR

James Watson

Most attention in the New Zealand historiography has focused on this country's role in the Great War as a supplier of high-quality soldiers to support the Allied military effort. However, New Zealand's other main role, as a supplier of food and fibre, principally to Britain, was at least as significant. Indeed, if we accept Avner Offer's 'agrarian interpretation' of the war, it was in large part the farm production of the dominions and India that enabled the Allies to hold out until Germany provoked the United States into open belligerency.[1] Offer argues that a strategy of starving out the Central Powers while maintaining supplies to the Allies had been adopted in Whitehall before the war. Certainly there is an echo of such a strategy in Prime Minister William Massey's appeal of September 1914 to New Zealand's farmers to grow more grain:

> It is quite possible that if the war is prolonged it may be found that the side possessing the largest food supply will have a highly important advantage over its enemies, and as no one can foretell with any certainty whether campaigns conducted with the colossal armies of the present day will give decisive results, it may even happen that ample supplies of food will be the ultimate determining factor in the struggle.[2]

Comparatively little has been written on the experience of New Zealand farming during the Great War. Numerous commentators have noted in passing the high prices paid for farm exports and have linked this to the commandeer, the compulsory acquisition of the exportable surplus of farm products on behalf of the imperial government.[3] Problems with securing enough shipping space to export the commandeered produce have also been noted and attributed to sinkings, particularly by German submarines.[4] Loud complaints from farmers about the impact of volunteering and conscription on farm labour and farm ownership were noted in Paul Baker's outstanding study.[5] Aside from these difficulties and of course the anxiety and grief of families with members at the front, the picture is generally one of satisfaction within the farming industry after the storms of industrial confrontation in 1913 and the concerns arising from the depression of 1921–2.

This chapter will look first at patriotism and profitability within the wartime farming industry in New Zealand. It will go on to argue that there was actually a surprising amount of discontent in farming, and that some of it was related to the commandeer itself.

From the outbreak of war, farming leaders certainly sought to emphasise the patriotism of their sector. In September 1914 a South Island farming correspondent declared that:

> The splendid response that has been made to the different Patriotic Funds has been truly British. A large number of farmers have presented horses, many, indeed, giving the best animals they possessed…. A large number of rural territorials have shown their loyalty by joining the expeditionary forces, farmers' sons being among the first to show their patriotism.[6]

A Wairarapa farmer cast a slightly different light on what was happening when he remarked the following year that 'All the young fellows are leaving the farms. They got a taste for soldiering during the big strike [in 1913], and are keen to get away as soon as they can.'[7] This could perhaps be rephrased as 'How do you keep them down on the farm now that they've charged down Lambton Quay?'

Arguably one of the best means of objectively assessing patriotic commitment is through comparative enrolment figures. Certainly farmers and farm hands volunteered in large numbers, well over 18,000 of them joining up by March 1917.[8] Yet the only contemporary estimate of their relative contribution to volunteering, made by the Social Democratic Party MP James McCombs, presented them as grossly underrepresented, with 18.5 per cent of volunteers as against 28.5 per cent of male breadwinners in the 1911 census, as presented in the 1914 *Year-book*.[9] However, his calculations were limited to the 4th Reinforcements and rather generalised industry groups. In a much more sophisticated and certainly more accurate analysis, Paul Baker compared what he determined to be the farmer and farm employee proportion of all recruits to March 1917 with their proportion of those balloted under conscription. He concluded that 'farmers were barely underrepresented'.[10] Indeed, if one puts these figures together with his assertion that rural volunteering as a whole dropped off disproportionately in 1916, it is possible that farmers and farm workers were substantially overrepresented among the volunteers in 1914 and 1915.[11]

Ultimately it is probably impossible to be precise about the contribution of the farming industry using census figures,[12] particularly because there are no detailed age profiles of specific occupations or even industries. At the 1911 census men employed in agricultural and pastoral production were underrepresented in the 21–45 year cohort and overrepresented in older cohorts, suggesting that they were less likely to be in the main age groups to volunteer and possibly more likely to have family responsibilities.[13] Nevertheless, comparing the figures of enlistments to March 1917 by occupations with the totals for individual occupations in the 1911 census, it appears that farmers and farm workers were represented in rough proportion to their numbers in the workforce. In other words, they were neither strongly underrepresented, like miners, nor greatly overrepresented like bushmen and clerks.

The low proportion of farmers and their employees who defaulted following the introduction of conscription might also be taken as indicative of a high level of patriotism.[14] However, the waters were greatly muddied by the decision of the government-appointed National Efficiency Board that the 'last man' available to work a farm should be exempted. Clearly if you were exempted you did not need to default.

Whatever the difficulties faced by individuals, the war was extremely profitable for New Zealand farmers as a group. After an initial short spell of gloom and confusion, the prices of farm products began to rise. A month after New Zealand's entry into the conflict, a number of commentators were speculating on which commodities would get the biggest boost. Wool, grain, tinned meat and cheese tended to be among the favourites. Wool certainly proved the best bet in the short term, with an 'unparalleled boom in New Zealand crossbreds' being reported in London by the end of 1914.[15] The dairy industry found by the end of the 1914–15 season that cheese was another front runner, and many companies switched from butter to cheese production.[16] As D. Ross Hunter, chairman of the South Island Dairy Association, explained, 'The whole point was that the Home Government, instead of giving the soldiers tinned meat, had decided to use frozen meat and cheese, and cheese was, apparently, having a good effect in making the soldiers take such a stand against the Kaiser's barbarian armies.'[17]

The prosperity being enjoyed by farmers during the war became proverbial. The Government Statistician, Malcolm Fraser, told the 1917 Conference of the Council of Agriculture of one farmer who sent in a cheque for £20 after being threatened with prosecution for not returning statistics. When a prominent farming leader asked whether that represented the farmer's opinion of the value of statistics, Fraser replied to loud laughter, 'No; I think the farmers are doing so well, that it was rather his idea of the value of £20.'[18]

Given that vast numbers of young men were being called on to risk life and limb in the struggle, farming representatives tended to be surprisingly unselfconscious about maintaining that profit should not be sacrificed to patriotism. Thus Massey's call to grow more grain included the assurance that 'I need not add that if a general shortage of cereals does occur farmers who have endeavoured to help their country by providing this class of produce may find that in serving the Empire's interests they have also served their own.' At the end of the year a member of the executive of the North Canterbury Farmers' Union declared:

> They as farmers did not want to fatten on the woes of the nation, but it was said
> of the working man that he sold his labour in the dearest market, and the farmer

was entitled to the same privilege with his produce. Yet as Britishers they did not want to take advantage of the nation's necessities, and if the Government would guarantee 5/3 per bushel there would be nothing to grumble at.[19]

Earlier in the meeting it had been claimed that most wheat had been sold for around 40 per cent less than 5s 3d per bushel.

S. Boulton of Woodville played on the interaction between profit and patriotism when he amused his fellow farmers in 1917 by declaring 'My country is bush land, and last year for patriotic purposes I put in eight acres of wheat, and received 36 bushels to the acre. This year I am putting in 17 acres for patriotic purposes.'[20]

Not all New Zealand farmers felt comfortable with their wartime prosperity. At the annual general meeting of the Whangarei Dairy Company in 1915, the chairman captured the ambivalent feelings, even guilt, that many farmers, especially those with sons or other relatives serving overseas, must have experienced, particularly as the casualty lists from Gallipoli rolled in. He declared that 'high prices of butter fat were like blood money. They knew what was the cause of the high prices – to their sorrow.'[21] A few months earlier a supplier to the Okato Dairy Company had managed to combine guilt and concern for the company's future commercial prospects if it built a cheese factory: 'These high prices ... were the reward of iniquity and the blood of soldiers. Millions of consumers were being wiped out, and would not want feeding.'[22] Late in 1917, following the New Zealand tragedy at Passchendaele, the chairman of the Awapuna Dairy Company was moved to declare that:

> Those who remained at home, protected by the British fleet, with the great privilege of having boats to carry their produce Home, and get over 20d. for it as against nothing, should be prepared to do their utmost in assisting funds such as the Wounded Soldiers' fund....Their taxes had increased ... but at present they all knew that they really did not amount to much compared with the extra amount farmers were at present receiving.[23]

Despite their general patriotism and the high prices they received for their produce, New Zealand farmers faced considerable difficulties during the war and were frequently very critical of those they saw as exacerbating or even deliberately causing their problems. Furthermore, patriotism and the pursuit of greater profitability tended to make uncomfortable bedfellows. Three major issues that caused agitation in the New Zealand farming sector were the official attempts to keep the prices of exports to Britain down through requisitioning at fixed prices, the shortage of shipping space, particularly in refrigerated vessels, and the shortage of labour. This chapter will also deal briefly with two other causes of farmer concern – shortages of imports, particularly early in the war, and attempts to hold prices to the New Zealand consumer down later in the conflict.

From early in 1915 the imperial government began buying all New Zealand's exportable surplus of particular commodities through the government at prices set after consultation with merchants and producers. This process, popularly known as 'the commandeer', led to the creation of a special Department of Imperial Government Supplies in Wellington. Frozen meat was the first product to be requisitioned in this way, on 3 March 1915. From October of that year about a third of New Zealand's cheese production was purchased at a set price. In 1916 most cheese exports were purchased in this way and in 1917 and 1918 all were. The whole export wool clip was commandeered in the 1916–17 season, and butter finally joined the list of requisitioned commodities in November 1917. It should be noted that as early as the spring of 1914 the New Zealand government had placed its own sort of commandeer on wheat grown in New Zealand, establishing a fixed price and banning exports. This was designed to encourage production of wheat, which had been falling sharply before the war. Although wheat growing did expand, reversing the pre-war trend, the government found itself obliged repeatedly to buy grain from Australia and Canada during the war to keep prices down.

As mentioned earlier, the commandeer itself has generally been associated with high prices, but this is a misreading of the situation. The prices offered by the imperial government were indeed far above those of pre-war days, but so were virtually all prices in wartime. Commandeer prices were generally lower than those being paid immediately before the controls were imposed and lower than the prices that continued to prevail in 'free' markets. It was the war that brought the high prices; the commandeer kept those prices down and assured supplies for the empire and some of its allies at the expense of other markets. The post-war fall in prices following the belated removal of the commandeer has helped to encourage the impression that prices under it were higher than the market would otherwise sustain. They certainly were higher than open market prices would have been in 1920 and 1921, but by then, of course, wartime market conditions no longer prevailed.

There was certainly a widespread belief in the farming community during the war that the commandeer was depressing prices, and this view was supported by overseas observers. A conference of dairy company representatives, who were of course overwhelmingly dairy farmers themselves, was held at Hawera in the spring of 1915 when the War Office indicated that it wished to purchase a thousand tons of cheese a week at 6½d per pound.[24] Attempts were made at the meeting to demand a considerably higher price, on the grounds that 7d was already being paid by the market and

> that last year their prices averaged as nearly as possible 8d., that the Imperial Government commenced buying last year at a price equal to 9d. in New Zealand, that the cost of manufacture would be higher this year, and from a business viewpoint factories could not be expected to consider 6½d.

The meeting eventually settled on 7d per pound, but not before officials appealed to the farmers' patriotism and warned them against overplaying their hand. D. Cuddie, the Director of Dairy Production for the Department of Agriculture, was extremely diplomatic. He pointed out that Canada was selling to the War Office at 6½d and obliquely raised the sensitive issue of patriotism by declaring, to applause, that:

> It would… be quite out of place to stress the point of patriotism, because they were all patriots in New Zealand to the last man and the last shilling; this was purely a business proposition, and he took it that if the factories received what they considered to be a fair market value for their produce they would be willing to supply the War Office what was needed for the gallant soldiers who were fighting their battles at the front.

J.G. Harkness, the secretary of the National Dairy Association, was somewhat more blunt:

> It was a business proposal on the part of the Imperial Government which could stand on a business foundation, but the Imperial Government would not again be pushed, absolutely pushed, into giving such high prices for cheese. Let the producers be honest with themselves and admit that not one of them expected last year that their cheese would realise anything like 90/-, 95/- or 100/-. (Hear, hear.) They must all admit the prices were too high, and whilst they put money into individual pockets it was questionable whether it would be a good thing for the colony in the future... [S]upposing the Imperial Government said: 'The price has gone too high for us; we have all the meat from Australia, New Zealand, and the Argentine at 4½d.... We'll not give this high price for cheese; we'll cut the cheese ration.' What was going to be the price of cheese then?... Less than 6d.[25]

Separate reports from Southland dairy factories at the same time indicated that they were already receiving more than 7d a pound.[26] Hence the dairy companies were to get less for the cheese they supplied to the War Office than they were for private sales to Britain. Nevertheless, T.W. Foster, the chairman of the South Island Dairy Association, declared the following year that all cheese production should be commandeered at such a discount: 'In the great trouble such as the Empire was in at present money counted in the end, and everything that the Empire could save was bound to tell in the final issue'.[27]

However, the full commandeer of cheese was imposed that year only after a somewhat unseemly haggling about price. Whereas the South Island Dairy Association was prepared to accept 8½d per pound, the North Island companies held out for a farthing extra.[28] Angered at official delays, the chairman of the National Dairy Association's negotiating committee declared that he would refuse to accept even 10½d, if that were offered. When the dust settled the price was set at 9½d, still lower than private buyers had been paying at the start of the season and almost certainly much lower than they would have paid later.

Criticisms of the price paid by the imperial government were also heard from sheep and cattle farmers. In November 1915 a meeting of such farmers in Poverty

Bay opposed the continuation of the commandeer on meat exports.[29] They questioned the need to requisition sheepmeat when the imperial authorities then sold it through Smithfield. They also contradicted claims that producers were paid more under the commandeer: 'those farmers who will take the trouble to ascertain the position can readily learn that they are now obtaining less for their commandeered meat than they were obtaining prior to the commandeering'. The meeting attacked the 'middlemen' who were so often a target of farmer criticism and suspicion. For example, they wanted the retail price of requisitioned meat to be controlled to prevent British butchers profiteering.

By the same token, it was clear that the imperial government faced spiralling prices as long as markets for produce remained open. Thus at the opening of the 1915–16 wool season the representatives of the British taxpayer were probably less enthusiastic than the New Zealand farming correspondent who noted that 'The resumption of buying by American operators on local markets has led to an advance in values which must mean an appreciable increase in individual and national wealth'.[30] Not surprisingly, a commandeer was in place for the opening of the following season. A knowledgeable commentator then noted that 'one reason among others why the Colonial clips have been commandeered was to be able to deal more effectively with the applications for purchase on behalf of Japan and Italy, and to prevent the latter country especially from obtaining more wool than it has machinery to operate'.[31] Later the same commentator declared that 'it must be frankly acknowledged that had their clips been marketed in the usual way, they would certainly have realised still more than they have done'.[32] In April 1918 it was noted that 'In Buenos Aires, Monte Video, and South Africa wool has been selling at pence per lb above the Department's fixed values'.[33]

Forms of production not controlled by the commandeer also enjoyed very high prices. In 1917 it was maintained that 'no industry in this country... has benefited in such large measure by the war' as the flax industry. 'Under these circumstances, every flax mill in New Zealand is working at high pressure, and mills which have been closed down for eight or nine years are again in commission.'[34] The market for this flax was largely for binder twine in the United States. British demand for binder twine never seems to have required a commandeer to shut out the Americans and keep prices down.

A number of historians have noted the problem of lack of shipping space during the Great War and they have tended to attribute it to enemy sinking of ships previously engaged in the trade. However, the problem was regarded as serious as early as the beginning of 1915, long before the Germans had sunk much merchant shipping tonnage at all.[35] By 1917 angry complaints about the shortage of shipping had been regular features of farmer meetings for years, and shore-based cold storage capacity had been vastly increased to take the frozen produce that had been held up. If anything, the prominence of 'the submarine menace' in 1917 and 1918 seemed to quieten farmer complaints.

It is difficult to escape the conclusion that the imperial authorities responsible for allocating shipping to the various countries supplying Britain made the decision that importing from Canada, Argentina and the United States permitted a more economical use of ships. This was certainly the perception of the farmers at the Poverty Bay protest meeting in 1915. They wanted representatives of both the shipping and meat trades excluded from committees controlling requisitioned ships. Those committees should be instructed to direct insulated shipping to New Zealand and prevent it from being 'diverted to the Argentine and other foreign countries as at present'. By the winter of 1917 even Sir Walter Buchanan, Wairarapa runholder and 'staunch conservative',[36] a man with considerable knowledge of the shipping industry, was advocating that the government purchase its own vessels, particularly following the takeover of the New Zealand Shipping Company by the P&O line the previous year.

> If the Government did buy the ships, they would be able to make money with them during the war, and would confer important benefits locally through owning them. They knew that otherwise the control of shipping would be out of their hands, and would be at the mercy of the parties to the new merger. The Government could purchase the ships, and sell them after the war. He did not believe in state ownership in such cases, except in the present exceptional circumstances.[37]

Thus can war make socialists of us all.

Shortages of labour on farms were being noted as a problem as early as 1915. Arable farmers were hit particularly hard as their operations were especially labour intensive.[38] Not until after the war would large numbers of suitable tractors start to free them from dependence on ploughmen and eventually harvesters. The dairy industry was somewhat more fortunate: the general manager of the Avon Dairy Company noted that 'the danger was being met by a remarkably active demand for milking machines. Many of these had been installed this winter and no scarcity of the machines was likely to occur, because many of them were made in New Zealand and Australia.'[39] By the winter of 1915 a Wairarapa sheep farmer had concluded that because of the labour shortage 'we will all have to work a bit harder than we have done for some years to keep the flocks in something like order and condition'.[40] The following year a sheep run in Northland was advertised with the note that 'The owner's only son has gone to the war, and the property must be sold, hence the low price at which it is quoted'.[41] The agent concluded that 'A man and a lad can work the place, and the labour question is thus reduced to a minimum', a somewhat optimistic assessment of the needs of a property of almost 3000 acres. More sadly, another advertisement read 'The owner has lost his son at the war, otherwise it would not be on the market today'.[42]

Conscription cut still deeper into the farm workforce and led to demands that farm workers and particularly farmers should be granted exemptions. A Taranaki correspondent declared that:

> Each ballot takes its toll of the farmers, and everywhere the farms are short-handed. Great is the discontent thereat. It is an exciting experience to strike a dairy farm when the milking machine goes wrong, and everyone has to turn out and do their 'bit' with, say, 80 cows night and morning. On one farm the sheep were turned into 60 acres of oats because no labour was available.[43]

From Otago it was claimed that a shortage of shepherds was leading to the complete destocking of some stations.[44] On the low country getting ploughmen was a problem, as a Canterbury correspondent reported:

> The chief difficulty will be to get men for the teams after the harvest is over, for while it is comparatively easy to get men for fancy jobs, such as shearing and harvesting, it will not be easy to get men for the constant work that will have to be done later on if we are to keep our production up.[45]

However, the greatest concern was over farmers losing their farms. During the winter of 1917 a member of the Board of Agriculture who was also a member of a military service board claimed that 'a number of farmers who are drawn in the ballot for military service, more especially in the back country, had to dispose of their farms, and that in numerous cases they sell at a loss'.[46] By that stage the recently established NEB and its local, often farmer-dominated, trustee boards were urging, usually successfully, that the 'last man' available to run the farm should not be conscripted.[47]

Shortages of materials required on farms were certainly an issue early in the war, particularly where farm development was involved. Thus a real estate agent selling properties in Auckland noted in 1915 that 'Fencing wire has gone to a prohibitive price, so has corrugated iron required for buildings; grass seed is abnormally high and also manures. In normal times land could be grassed and fenced for £3 per acre, now it would cost over £4, and probably £5 per acre.'[48] However, shortages of farm equipment and other manufactures due to diversion of British industry to war production were largely overcome by imports from the United States, paid for by the high returns for farm produce on the British market. By the second half of 1915 one Canterbury merchant was noting that all the bar iron he was selling was foreign and expressed himself 'afraid the war and its results will help the Americans to oust the products of Britain – at least temporarily'.[49] Certainly advertisements for British equipment largely disappeared until 1918.

Imports of phosphatic fertilisers dropped during the war and it is unlikely that local production made up for the drop in superphosphate imports and the disappearance of imported basic slag. This probably had a limited impact on farm output, however, given that imports were small in comparison with what they were to be in subsequent decades.

Two attempts by the government to hold down prices for New Zealand consumers caused a major outcry in two significant farm sectors. The local commandeer of the wheat crop became the focus of criticism from growers in the middle of 1917, when a fixed price was established. This criticism was particularly directed at the Liberal elements in the Coalition government, which were seen as trying to keep the cost of living down for urban voters at the expense of graingrowers. An editorial in the *New Zealand Farmer* declared:

> We cannot help thinking that Cabinet in fixing the price of wheat at first gave greater consideration to the views of the Board of Trade, whose aims were to reduce the cost of living, than it did to the producer, who was entitled to have his views given equal consideration with those of the consumer.[50]

The Board of Trade tended to be regarded even more as the illegitimate brainchild of Sir Joseph Ward when it persuaded the government later in 1917 to release some commandeered butter onto the local market at reduced prices. The money the imperial government paid for that butter was then skimmed to pay for the whole exercise and the reduction spread across the dairy companies. There was outrage from many dairy farmers at this 'butter tax'. For example, the chairman of the Manutahi Dairy Company denounced it while providing a glimpse into how the labour shortage was being coped with on some farms:

> He had in mind the case of a widow not many miles from Manutahi, who was sharemilking 120 cows. She was an elderly lady who worked 16 hours a day, and was assisted by one son and two daughters. She had to contribute £25 towards the so-called butter tax in order to allow Mr. MacDonald [the Minister of Agriculture, a Liberal member of the National Ministry] and his following to have cheaper butter. Not only did this widow contribute £25 towards this inequitable tax, but she has also contributed three sons to fight for the Colours.[51]

Returning to the earlier question about patriotism, it seems impossible to determine whether the farming community on balance responded in a particularly patriotic way by making a special effort to produce more. Above all, there is no obvious way to distinguish between the impetus of patriotism and the attraction of the high wartime level of prices. Cheese production surged at the expense of butter, but was this in response to a desire to strengthen British soldiery against 'the Kaiser's barbarian armies' or to capture the extra money that the War Office was spending on the cheese ration? The evidence suggests that the latter was the more prevalent motivation.[52] After the commandeer was imposed, cheese production stagnated, then fell back somewhat. Overall, there was little increase in farm production, no sign that farmers as a whole were extracting extra from their land in order to supply more to the embattled empire. But perhaps simply maintaining existing production represented a Herculean effort, given the problems of securing labour. For instance, cheese-making tends to involve more skill and experience than butter-making, and dairy factory workers seem to have enlisted in droves.[53] Quite possibly shipping difficulties discouraged greater production.

Perhaps the continuation of at least existing levels of production under commandeer prices, despite the widespread appreciation that they were below market prices and the great difficulties involved, could suggest some acceptance of a patriotic duty. It was, after all, an option to produce less, though this would seem contrary to what Tom Brooking has characterised as the basic productive ethos of the Pakeha farmer of the time.[54] Farming tends to be a difficult sector to control, as the great dictatorships of the 20th century, particularly those of Stalin and Mao, found to their own cost and that of the populations they ruled. Heavy industry in particular, because it is centred on large work sites, is much more vulnerable to close surveillance over its inputs, outputs and processes. Most agriculture, on the other hand, is carried out over a vast area, on a myriad of sites, with decisions taken locally. Trying to monitor each farming family or village community, endeavouring to ensure that they invest their resources, not least their labour, in the way the authorities want, is a monumental task and one that it is probably impossible to carry out at an acceptable cost. A more efficient and probably more successful strategy is to persuade farming populations to co-operate and in New Zealand's case a mixture of profit and patriotism seems to have facilitated this. Erik Olssen has claimed that 'The price for requisitioned produce was fixed at a level designed to encourage productivity', and he maintains that it succeeded.[55] Leaving aside the paucity of evidence of increased production, his statement should be rephrased to read that prices were fixed at a level designed not to discourage production, given the patriotic and productionist values predominant among New Zealand farmers.

There is evidence that patriotism had an effect on some individual decisions. Despite repeated references to the setting of cheese prices as a business proposition and the dangers of pushing the imperial government too far, the decision of dairy factory representatives in 1915 and 1916 to accept a price lower than that on the open market seems to have been influenced by patriotic sentiments. Perhaps the farmer from Woodville mentioned earlier struck a typical balance. He went to the trouble of growing eight acres of wheat in response to the call of patriotism, but was prepared to grow 17 acres for profit (and possibly some patriotism) the following year.

It is noticeable that comparatively few of the complaints made by farmers during the war were targeted directly at the imperial government. Faced with a steep increase in freight rates in the winter of 1915, A. Morton, president of the National Dairy Association, declared, to applause, 'If it turned out that the Imperial Government was responsible for the increase, then there was no remedy, as they must recognise what the Imperial Navy had done to protect their produce and their freedom… and take it as part payment for the protection so afforded'.[56] H.A. Knight, chairman of the Christchurch Meat Company, had earlier taken a similar approach to the shortage of refrigerated shipping at the company's annual general meeting:

> We are, I am sure, whether actual producers or exporters, all prepared to suffer any loss or inconvenience, no matter how great, caused by a shortage of steamers if such shortage is really the direct result of deflections for Imperial work. If, however, the dislocation with which we are unfortunately now faced is, as we have reason to believe, largely the result of a lack of appreciation on the part of certain shipowners of their obligations to the producers of the Dominion, out of whom they have built up their business, then it is essential that every possible step should be taken to prevent both ourselves and the producing community from again being placed in such a position.[57]

Institutions like shipping companies, meat companies and military service boards took the brunt of the criticism. The New Zealand government, and particularly the Liberal element within it, certainly came in for some stick as well. Much of this involved criticising, obliquely or directly, the farmers' fellow citizens in town who wanted the cost of their bread and butter kept down by holding wheat prices and subsiding local butter from export returns.

To conclude, the response and experience of New Zealand farming during the Great War demonstrated a somewhat confusing mixture of imperial patriotism and concern to maximise profits, all in an environment of shortages that increased farmers' difficulties. Profits increased a lot while production increased only a little, tending rather to shift between products. Discontents with aspects of the imperial linkage that already existed before the war, notably over shipping and marketing, were greatly magnified during the conflict and eventually required resolution by the creation of producer boards in the early 1920s. Labour shortages posed increasing challenges. Continued resentment at what was seen as urban exploitation of farmer productivity was also evident. The evidence suggests lots of patriotism, lots of profits and substantial problems.

31

DEBATING THE WAR: THE DISCOURSES OF WAR IN THE CHRISTCHURCH COMMUNITY

Gwen Parsons

Historians have generally assumed that the New Zealand home front supported New Zealand's participation in the First World War.[1] This assumption has been suggested by the lack of public opposition and debate in the public arena and more specifically in New Zealand newspapers during the war years. However, a closer analysis of the content of the local Christchurch media during the war years reveals that there was debate regarding participation in the war and, moreover, suggests that support for the war was class-divided. This chapter will identify the basis of support for and opposition to the war in Christchurch. It will analyse how supporters and objectors attempted to define the way in which the war was debated and therefore to influence the wider community. It will do this by locating those who promoted rival pro-war and anti-war discourses within the social structure, and by analysing the discourses themselves, identifying their recurrent ideas, themes, motifs and forms of language.

Discourse and power

Within the Christchurch community two clearly delineated groups of protagonists debated the war: members of the Christchurch élite were in favour of the war, whereas anti-war discourse was promulgated almost exclusively by the leaders of organised labour. The attitude toward the war reflected both groups' interests and world views, while the dominance of their competing discourses reflected their relative power and status within the wider Christchurch community.

The pro-war stance of the middle and top strata of the Christchurch élite – the wealthy businessmen, merchants, manufacturers, lawyers, farmers and their families, whose influence and business links extended beyond the region, and, in the case of the top strata, overseas to Australia and Britain[2] – reflected their close identification with Britain. Enthusiastic British imperialists, they were founding and executive members of the Christchurch branches of the Navy League and the Victoria League. During the war membership of the former included the merchant H. J. Marriner and the stock and station agent Alex Boyle, while the membership of the Victoria League included Marriner, A. E. G. Rhodes and the Anglican Bishop of Canterbury, Bishop Churchill Julius, all of whom actively supported the war. Many members of the élite had been born and educated in England, including the Christchurch mayor Henry Holland and Dr Edward Levinge, who chaired the two most influential patriotic funds in Christchurch. The New Zealand-born sons of the wealthy often attended university in Britain, as did Sir Robert Heaton Rhodes and his cousin A.E.G. Rhodes, both of whom where prominent in the wartime activities of the Red Cross. The links to Britain were maintained via trips back 'Home' to visit relatives or make or renew business contacts. The élite were also involved in the British constitutional infrastructure of the country as representatives of local and national government: during the war they represented five of the six central Christchurch electorates in Parliament, and held two-thirds of the seats on the Christchurch City Council.[3] The Christchurch élite also dominated the legal profession in the city, including in their number George Harper, the son of the former Anglican bishop, and Maurice Gresson, son of the prominent Christchurch lawyer J.B. Gresson and the son-in-law of wealthy businessman Charles Gould.

Perhaps more important than these social and cultural ties was the élite's economic dependence upon Britain, which was the major export market for New Zealand: just before the war around 80 per cent of all New Zealand exports were destined for Britain.[4] The imperial commandeer ensured that Britain's monopoly of all the dominion's primary products continued and intensified during the war years. Jim McAloon has calculated that 56 per cent of the wealth-holders in Canterbury were farmers, and concluded that agricultural and pastoral production was the basis of the wealth of the Canterbury élite.[5] The remainder derived their wealth largely from servicing the primary producers: wool-brokers, such as William Hill; stock and station agents, such as Alexander Boyle of Pyne & Company; accountants, such as C. J. Treleaven; manufacturers of farm equipment, such as Henry Holland, and the directors of the Canterbury Frozen Meat Company and the New Zealand Shipping Company, such as George Gould of Gould, Beaumont & Company. During the early part of the 20th century the dominion was also dependent on Britain for the bulk of its imports – approximately 60 per cent up to 1910.[6] Many of the Christchurch élite had substantial importing interests, including Marriner. Given the strength of their ties to Britain, members of the Christchurch élite had no hesitation in supporting Britain when she went to war in Europe in 1914: they saw her war as New Zealand's war.

The dominance of pro-war discourse in the public sphere reflected the élite's power and influence within the Christchurch community. These were people who dominated the municipal government and national representation of the city and, as publicly elected officials, claimed both to speak for and lead the community. And those who held public office used their status to support the war. The patriotic demonstrations, recruiting meetings and commemorations they organised were official civic events. With the exception of one or two labour leaders who held public office, the Christchurch élite dominated the speakers' platform at these events, speaking in support of the war. Mayor Henry Holland spoke at almost every public patriotic activity reported in local newspapers.

The Christchurch élite also instigated, organised and led an array of patriotic organisations within the community. Ten of the 11 members of the executive of the Canterbury Patriotic Fund who can be identified were members of the élite, as were nine of the 11 members of the executive of the Belgium Relief Fund, nine out of the 11 members of the executive of the Citizens Defence Corps and seven of the nine members of the executive of the Women's National Reserve.[7] These organisations quickly acquired a quasi-official status and their leaders gained access to the platform at civic patriotic functions. The élite in effect made patriotism synonymous with support for the war, and support of the war synonymous with the support of those home front activities they organised. They stressed the need for national unity and denounced those who did not support the home front war effort as 'disloyal' and 'unpatriotic'. The charge of 'disloyalty' or lack of patriotism was made almost exclusively against working class men who publicly opposed the war.

The élite's control of all the local newspapers provided them with perhaps the most powerful means of influencing the wider community.[8] Pro-war discourse pervaded the city newspapers, and was embodied in the propaganda copied from British, Australian and American newspapers, the extensive coverage of national and local patriotic activities and the coverage given to the Coalition government.

Underpinning the dominance of pro-war discourse was wartime censorship, which, as John Anderson has noted, 'gradually increased in severity and in political rather than military significance from 1916 onwards'.[9] In December 1916, in the face of growing dissatisfaction with the government's management of the home front, anti-sedition war regulations made illegal any public utterance or action that might 'discourage the prosecution of the present war to a victorious conclusion'.[10] During the next two years 208 men were convicted and 71 imprisoned for making public seditious or disloyal remarks, including Christchurch unionists Tim Armstrong and E.E. Langley.[11]

In contrast, those who opposed war and conscription in Christchurch between December 1916 and April 1917 were almost all leaders of organised labour.[12] For these men and women socialism was the basis of their opposition to the war. They offered an alternative world view where society was divided not by national boundaries but by the class divisions of worker and capitalist: the aggressor menacing the worker was the profligate capitalist class. Socialists deemed international war to be beneficial only to the capitalist class and believed nothing would be gained by the worker of one nation fighting the worker of another. The leaders of organised labour therefore opposed the war, and in support of their socialist-inspired claims that war exploited the worker, broadened the scope of their opposition to include the government's management of the rising cost of living and war profiteering, and apparent unwillingness to increase soldier remuneration.

The labour movement was strong in Christchurch at the start of the war and the leaders of both the industrial and political branches of organised labour were publicly opposed to the war, conscription and the government's management of the wartime economy. Union leaders included Ted Howard, the secretary of the Canterbury General Labourers' Union, Hiram Hunter, the national secretary of the United Federation of Labour, and Fred Cooke, the secretary of the Christchurch Tailoring Trade and Christchurch Tailoresses' Union. The Canterbury Trades and Labour Council, through the membership of men like Howard, Hunter and Cooke, was active in the campaign against conscription and the government's management of the wartime economy.[13] Politically, labour had strong representation both locally and nationally.[14] During the war years about one-third of the Christchurch city councillors were representatives of the Social Democrat Party, and after 1917 the New Zealand Labour Party, and included the anti-conscription campaigner Dan Sullivan, and the pacifist and anti-militarist Ted Howard, Hiram Hunter and Ada Wells. James McCombs, the MP for Lyttelton, was one of the six labour representatives in Parliament during the war.

It is important to note that both because of the range of issues involved and the existing divisions within the various organisations, organised labour's opposition to the war was not entirely unified. For example, James McCombs supported the war but opposed conscription and campaigned for increases in soldier remuneration, while Ted Howard opposed the war and therefore all aspects of the government's management of the war. However, those who supported aspects of the war, such as McCombs, refrained from explicitly and overtly challenging organised labour's opposition to the war.

Labour had far less ability to influence the wider Christchurch community. Relatively few labour leaders held public office and, unlike their élite counterparts, claimed to speak only for a section of the community – the working class. Their opposition to the war naturally excluded them from many official patriotic activities, such as recruiting rallies. They were able to use the industrial and political labour organisations to present their views to their working class constituency, but were limited in their ability to reach other sections of the community. They were unable to disseminate their views through the city's newspapers, which gave little or no coverage to activities or speeches that expressed opposition to the war or conscription. When reports were included they were brief, designed to demonstrate the disloyalty of those involved and suggested only marginal support for such views. The national newspaper of the United Federation of Labour, the *Maoriland Worker*, did provide organised labour with a means of reaching a wider audience, but as a sectional newspaper it did not enjoy the high readership of the local papers and it emphasised labour's class focus.[15] Only limited opposition to the war was therefore visible in the public sphere.

Pro-war discourse

In the early part of the 20th century there was significant opposition to war within New Zealand. Between 1909 and the start of the war Christchurch was the anti-militarist centre of the country, leading the campaign against the 1909 Defence Act which had introduced compulsory military training.[16] In Christchurch, members of the middle class, motivated by liberalism, along with members of the working class, motivated by socialism, had campaigned hard for the repeal of compulsory military training. Supporters of the war therefore needed to ensure that those who had formerly opposed war as a means of resolving international disputes overcame their anti-militarist qualms. They therefore utilised a range of pro-war discourses to assure both the liberal-minded middle class and the working class that war was the most appropriate, if not the only, response to German aggression. Pro-war discourse presented the military conflict as justifiable and legitimate within the accepted notions of Western (Christian) Just War theory.[17]

Anti-German discourse

The primary means of justifying a military reaction to German aggression was by presenting the enemy in such a way that nothing but war would be an appropriate response. Anti-German discourse therefore attempted to differentiate the British from the German, and to establish Germany as an inherent threat to Britain and her empire. Using ideas of racial categorisation established in the 19th century, pro-war advocates suggested that the Germans were racially different from the British – an idea that was contrary to established racial categories grouping Britons and Germans as Caucasian. In 1914 British patriots dropped the term Anglo-Saxon, which credited the British race and the German race with a common origin, and the term is almost entirely absent from the Christchurch newspapers during the war years. Germans were instead categorised as barbarians. The term 'Hun' was adopted, grouping Germans with the warlike Asiatic nomadic people who invaded Europe in the 4th and 5th centuries.[18] Likewise, Germans were described as 'Teutons', linking them to the barbarian Germanic people who lived in Jutland in the 4th century.[19] The German soldier was therefore a barbarian – an uncultured and uncivilised warrior,[20] whose brutish and unreasoning nature set him apart from the rest of Christian Europe.

Pro-war discourse emphasised German brutality towards innocent Christian civilians. News stories from Britain, reproduced in the Christchurch papers, highlighted reports of German 'atrocities and crimes against civilisation'.[21] The German aggressors practised 'pillage, rape, arson, and murder' against 'helpless women and innocent children'. The German soldiery were said to mutilate children and kill babies. Women in occupied Belgium and France were 'outraged' and herded off, the victims of 'Slave Raids'.[22] Indeed, the fate of Belgian women and children at the hands of the German barbarians was the specific focus of the advertisements placed in local newspapers by the Belgium Relief Fund.[23] At the extremity of anti-German discourse, the German soldier 'lost the last traces of humanity'. The enemy was not just another nation pursuing its own interests at the expense of other nations; rather it was an army of 'inhuman monsters' and 'wild beasts', which perpetrated 'every imaginable refinement of cruelty and bestiality' on innocent victims.[24]

James Allen, the Minister of Defence, considered that by such 'brutal and inhuman' actions the Germans had broken 'all the laws of God and man' and shown themselves to be the enemies of civilisation and beyond the realm of God.[25] The German disregard for civilisation and humanity could be explained only in terms of wickedness. The war was something more than just a border or a political dispute, or even the fending off of barbarian hordes: it was a war against 'the powers of darkness, represented by Germany' – it was a 'Holy War'.[26] Propagandists presented the head of the German state, Kaiser Wilhelm, as either the devil himself or at least working in league with the devil. Christians who supported this righteous war proclaimed, in the Reverend A.C. Lawry's words, that 'even Jesus Christ could lead a bayonet charge to deliver the helpless from the brutal in this war between heaven and hell'.[27]

Many members of the Christchurch élite were, however, aware of the difficult implications of this anti-German discourse on the home front. The élite included a number of Germans, many of whom, such as Heinrich von Haast, son of Sir Julius von Haast, Percy Hallenstein and Hugo Friedlander, had made considerable contributions to the local community. In recognition of their contribution, many members of the Christchurch élite followed the government's lead in giving British citizenship primacy over patriotic anti-Germanism. Christchurch mayor Henry Holland noted that many businessmen of German descent trading in Christchurch 'had proved themselves good citizens for many years', while the editor of the *Lyttelton Times* noted that 'the alien percentage of our population is extremely small, but includes a few hundred Germans and among them some excellent colonists'.[28] The accolade of 'citizenship' was bestowed most readily on naturalised Germans, or those of German descent, when they had the status of 'pioneer', 'settler' or 'colonist', implying long residence and participation in the establishment of Canterbury society.

The discourse of British liberty

Those supporting the war also presented Germany as the enemy of British constitutional liberty. The British liberal tradition had evolved over a 200-year period, during which time it had made a substantial impact on the British sense of identity. By the start of the war, liberalism stood for personal freedom and limited state regulation of individuals.[29] Appealing to these liberal ideals, those who supported the war described the war as a fight for 'liberty and freedom' and, more specifically, for 'personal liberty'. Indeed, those soldiers who lost their lives did so 'fighting for our liberties'.[30]

Those supporting the war contrasted the constitutionally constrained authority of the British monarch and state with Germany, which was subject to the rule of an autocrat, despot or tyrant who held absolute authority over his subjects and governed by his will.[31] The British emphasis on the 'freedom of the individual' was compared with 'the complete subordination of the individual' to the Prussian military state.[32] Prussian militarism was the denial of personal destiny and the supremacy of the state over individualism — the antithesis of everything that British liberalism had been fighting against for the previous two centuries. Therefore, in the language of those supporting the war effort, the war was being fought against 'despotic militarism which [was] threatening the very basis and ideals of [British] civilisation'; it was Britain's attempt to avoid Prussian enslavement and to ensure that her citizens remained 'free men'.[33]

The independence of the British government, the civil service and the judiciary from military influence was one of the triumphs of liberalism. The German military, however, had allegedly hijacked both the government and society, crushing the constitution and the people so that the army was the focus rather than a tool of the state. In the absence of a constitution and an independent government, Germany suffered from 'the supremacy of military authority over civil law'.[34] Without the supremacy of civil law, Germany under Kaiser Wilhelm had, in effect, no law; and her people, like those in the lands that she occupied, had no means of protecting their rights and freedoms. This depiction of the German military as outside the accepted laws of Europe, and therefore criminal, complemented the atrocity argument. Reports of German atrocities against civilian victims were described both in moral and legal terms. The German U-boats were 'U-pirates' and their torpedoing of civilian ships was 'one of the foulest crimes ever recorded in history'. The sinking of the *Lusitania* was a 'foul and dastardly crime', and a British inquest brought the charge of 'wilful and wholesale murder against the Kaiser, the German government, and the submarine'. The 1915 execution of English nurse Edith Cavell was likewise described as 'murder'.[35]

The discourse of duty

Just as the British state guaranteed the liberty of its citizens, those Christchurch identities supporting the war reminded the community that 'citizenship implies obligations, and, when the safety of the State is threatened, it has a right to expect its citizens to rally'.[36] The good citizen became the individual who did all within his or her power to support the war effort.

The obligations that the citizen owed to the state were described as duty, and the discourse was explicit: it was the 'duty of every able-bodied man to go to the front'.[37] Those supporting the war, particularly those actively involved in encouraging young men to enlist, were unanimous that 'a man cannot die better than fighting for King and Country. It is but his duty.'[38] The discourse of duty was primarily concerned with young men without financial or familial commitments. Like the government, the Christchurch élite was not keen for married men to volunteer, fearing the associated financial and social cost to the country. Only when forced to introduce conscription did the government confirm that a married man's duty to the state superseded that to his family – although that duty would not be required until all the single men had been balloted.

Men who were unable to go to the front owing to health reasons, family obligations or employment in a vital industry had a duty to keep vital home front industries operational.[39] Indeed, Dr Henry Thacker, the Liberal MP for Christchurch East, felt that 'the worker who did his duty at home was fighting just as good a fight as the soldier'.[40] Those who remained in New Zealand also had a duty, particularly in the absence of a specific war tax, to support the voluntary patriotic funds.[41]

Patriots reinforced the importance of duty by attacking those men who were not seen to be fulfilling their obligations to the state. After the introduction of conscription, those who supported the war generally described the issue of conscientious objection as the rejection of duty. Those not in uniform were 'shirkers', 'deaf to all obligations' and 'shamefully failing to do their duty'.[42] Objectors were described as 'selfish': their unwillingness to fight was seen as the elevation of their own well-being above that of the rest of the community, the country and the empire.[43] It was in response to this rejection of the obligations of citizenship that the government, in the Expeditionary Forces Amendment Act 1919, withdrew the civil rights of military defaulters and objectors for ten years following the war.

'Duty' was rarely used to describe the obligations that women owed to the state. Using language suggestive of the New Zealand rhetorical tradition of the colonial helpmeet, women were urged to consider 'the countless ways' in which they could 'help' the war effort.[44] Their obligation to the state was to 'help' the war effort through patriotic work – specifically manual labour using such domestic skills as sewing and knitting. Such 'work' formed the backbone of the voluntary war effort.

The discourse of sacrifice

Those who supported the war co-opted Christian language and terminology to promote the morally justifiable nature of the military response to German aggression. The discourse of sacrifice complemented that of duty. It ennobled participation in the war effort and alluded to the just nature of the war — the defence of Christian civilisation. From the outset, those supporting the war gave the conflict religious significance. Belgium was applauded for her sacrifice: by refusing the German demand to allow passage of their troops through to France, she had suffered invasion and occupation. The severity of Belgium's sacrifice was stressed by the use of the language and imagery of crucifixion, which was unique on the Christchurch home front during the war years. The Belgium Relief Fund vigorously promoted the notion of sacrificial Belgium in a series of advertisements that linked the sacrifice and crucifixion of Belgium inextricably with the heathen barbarianism of the enemy.[45]

The sacrifice concept was used to support recruitment. The new recruit was praised for his self-sacrifice: like Christ he went 'freely' to the war prepared to die for 'those whom he has never seen, who are not yet born'.[46] His willingness to offer his life to win a victory for following generations was proclaimed in biblical terms: as Christ had demonstrated his love for mankind, so the soldier demonstrated his love for his fellow countrymen.

Appeals were made to the parents, and especially to the mothers, of eligible men. Mothers were urged to 'be unselfish' and to 'give' their sons to 'help maintain the prestige of our glorious Empire', to sacrifice their sons so that the Allies might be victorious.[47] With regard to Australia, Joy Damousi has noted that the promotion of stories about 'sacrificial mothers' in the media allowed 'mothers to share the honour of their sons: mothers gained status and respect through an association with their men', and the same was true of New Zealand. The 'sacrificial mother' could take pride and joy in a son who had done his duty and in her own 'self-sacrifice'.[48] Acknowledging the anguish and sorrow that many such mothers would experience, those who supported the war noted their stoical courage and went as far as describing them as 'Spartan mothers' of warriors, taking pride and solace from their sons' achievements in battle.[49]

The language of sacrifice was also used more prosaically particularly with regard to the material sacrifices made on the home front in support of the war. Fundraisers appealed to citizens' patriotism and sense of duty, urging them to recognise both the sacrifice that others had made and their obligation to make a sacrifice themselves. In October 1916, for instance, the promoters of Self-Denial Week urged citizens to 'deny themselves little luxuries to which they have been accustomed' and to make 'temporary minor sacrifices… [to] assist… in alleviating the suffering of those who are making the greatest of sacrifices'.[50]

Functions of pro-war discourse

Through pro-war discourse the Christchurch élite also addressed the doubts of those who had espoused pacifism and anti-militarism before the war. By presenting the enemy as a threat to Christian civilisation, they attempted to undermine the humanitarian and peace-loving sentiments that were prevalent in the pre-war community and in early 20th-century Christianity. Pro-war discourse also attempted to silence public opposition to the war: to oppose the war publicly was to risk being labelled as disloyal and unpatriotic, and to set oneself against the interests of the community and state. It was not possible to silence all opposition to the war, but its supporters attempted to set the terms of the debate about the conflict: to oppose the war was to oppose the defence of Christian civilisation and individual freedom, and to deny one's obligations to the community.

Anti-war discourse
Socialist discourse

Socialism was both the basis of labourite opposition to the war and the core component in anti-war discourse. Used in relation to the war and the home front, socialist discourse focused on 'the class struggle'.[51] Socialists did not see the war as the defence of liberty against militarism, or Christianity against barbarism, but rather as a 'mere industrial war' waged, like all wars, 'for economic ends, for the capture of new markets' and to the 'benefit of the exploiting class'.[52] The labour élite presented the rising cost of living, allegations of war profiteering, and the apparent unwillingness of the government to increase soldiers' 'wages' as evidence of the exploitation of the working class. They emphasised the overrepresentation of workers in the NZEF.[53] They described the introduction of conscription not as a necessity for winning the war but rather as a tool to be used against organised labour – memories were still fresh of the clashes between strikers and police at Waihi in 1912 and the 'special constables' who were used to break the 1913 waterfront strike.

Addressing a crowd in Victoria Square, Christchurch unionist Tim Armstrong asserted that conscription was wanted not to win the war but 'to keep you and I and the rest of the working people of the country in subjugation'.[54] The socialist viewpoint was encapsulated by Social Democrat Party president Hiram Hunter, who asserted that the 'industrial classes of the community' were being made to 'fight the battles of the Empire' and 'foot the bill' while being robbed of the freedom which they were told 'they are fighting and paying to uphold'.[55]

The discourse of Christian pacifism

Many socialists held strong Christian beliefs and viewed the political aims of socialism as 'applied Christianity': they saw social ownership of industry as the realisation of the 'Biblical vision where swords will be turned to ploughshares'.[56] So, while the mainstream Protestant churches invoked a fierce Old Testament-based Christianity in support of the righteous war, the labour élite adopted a pacific New Testament-based Christianity in support of their opposition to the war. Basing their interpretation of Christianity on the New Testament, which chronicled the life of Christ as the Prince of Peace, they saw war very simply as a violation of God's teachings. God had commanded that Christians must not commit murder, and socialists insisted that to kill another in war was 'murder, even if the blessing of the church and the sanction of the state were appended'.[57] They emphasised the 'meek and lowly Jesus of Nazareth, who resisted not his enemies and rebuked his disciple who drew a sword', and were unable to reconcile this with the pro-war suggestion that even Jesus Christ would lead a bayonet charge. The dissenters contrasted Christian love, hope and the promise of salvation with the destruction, despair, and inhumanity of war.[58]

It is significant that the discourse of Christian pacifism had some appeal to the wider community. While those who supported the just war believed that a pacifist interpretation of Christianity was 'incorrect', they generally recognised that the New Testament message of 'Peace on Earth' had some legitimacy.[59] As a result, although the government had little sympathy with conscientious objectors whose objections to conscription were based upon socialism or Irish nationalism, they did extend limited acknowledgment to the legitimacy of objections based upon religious scruples.[60]

The discourse of British liberty

For the labour élite the introduction of conscription and the anti-sedition war regulations were evidence of an attack on the freedom of the working man and they argued against these government actions via the discourse of British liberty. In doing so they appealed to the same liberal ideals as those supporting the war. Whereas patriots focused their attention on the evil of Prussian militarism in Europe, those opposed to war concentrated on the threat of Prussian militarism within the home front. Anti-conscriptionists described the introduction of conscription as the importation of Prussian militarism – the antithesis of British liberty – into New Zealand.[61] Labour MP James McCombs asked whether the country had 'kept the Prussians outside our gates only in order to adopt the spirit of Prussianism within them'.[62] The Military Service Act, which introduced conscription, and the Parliamentary Elections Postponement Act, which deferred national elections until after the war, were described as 'edicts ... framed on the pattern of Bismarck's edicts in Germany'.[63] In response to the government's refusal to put the issue of conscription to the people via a referendum or national election, the representatives of organised labour described the members of the government as 'military despots' who were acting in an 'absolutist' and 'autocratic' manner.[64] More generally the legislation, along with the anti-sedition war regulations, were a 'violation' of 'every democratic principle' of British liberty. Through them the government removed individual freedom and curtailed citizens' right to act, speak and think without the regulation of the state.[65] To illustrate its concerns, the *Maoriland Worker* included a blank box on its front page entitled 'A striking picture – our measure of freedom in New Zealand'. Without the liberal trophy of personal liberty and freedom, the people of New Zealand were dragged back 'into a feudal servitude' and 'reduced to a position worse than that of serfdom'. Indeed, 'shackled' and 'fettered' by militarism, the citizens of New Zealand were little more than slaves.[66]

The discourse of equality of sacrifice

By focusing on home front inequalities, the leaders of organised labour were able to illustrate their socialist world view of a society divided into an exploiting and an exploited class. They used the discourse of equality of sacrifice to criticise the rising cost of living and the levels of soldier pay, allowances and pensions, whereas the Christchurch élite used it to justify the introduction of conscription, describing it as the most fair and equitable means of raising reinforcements. Conscription was, the Christchurch élite claimed, a means of creating 'equality of sacrifice'.[67] Those opposed to the war used such discourse to highlight the inequalities – particularly the economic inequalities – caused by the war.

In New Zealand the cost of living increased by 39.35 per cent between July 1914 and July 1918. While Christchurch did not experience the highest increase, the rise was on a par with the other major cities.[68] The rise in prices eroded the buying power of wages as many workers found themselves locked into three-year awards negotiated before 1914. The rising cost of living was in contrast to the seemingly exorbitant prices paid to primary producers for the meat, wool, cheese, butter and hides commandeered by Britain. For example, the price paid for the 1916 wool crop was 55 per cent higher than pre-war prices.[69] This sharp rise fuelled concerns about equality of contribution and claims of exploitation. The leaders of organised labour condemned the capitalists for making a profit out of the war at the expense of the workers. For them, the biggest 'inequality' was between those who were making little or no sacrifice while making a profit out of the war, and those who had made sacrifices, such as the enlistment or conscription of a breadwinner, and were suffering financial disadvantage as a result.

The capitalist 'exploiters' were described using terms previously applied to organised crime: 'the wheat and flour ring, the shipping ring, the butter ring, the oatmeal ring, and the meat ring'. The 'exploiters' were 'food pirates' who 'held up the Dominion and Imperial Governments'.[70] Placing the 'exploiters' outside the law and against the citizens, the representatives of organised labour designated those making war profits not just 'unpatriotic' but 'traitorous'. They went further, describing the 'exploiters' as 'the enemy', 'the Huns in our Midst'. In an illustration the *Maoriland Worker* depicted the capitalist 'exploiter' being acknowledged by the Kaiser as his '"stout" ally' and 'very good friend' who caused 'thousands to die slowly from starvation'.[71]

Labour leaders asked how the families of the men fighting for the empire were to be kept from 'want, homelessness, and starvation' when faced with both the economic exploitation of the war profiteer and 'the loss of their breadwinner'.[72] They urged the government to increase soldiers' pay, allowances and pensions so their dependants could meet the price rises. They claimed that families were being forced to rely on the charity of the Canterbury Patriotic Fund. To support their demands for increased soldier remuneration, the representatives of organised labour utilised the negative attitudes towards charitable aid, describing the assistance offered to the soldiers' dependants by the patriotic funds as inappropriate and outrageous. It was the soldiers' act of sacrifice, not moral ineptitude, that was the direct cause of the financial difficulties, and yet the patriotic funds were administered in the same manner as charitable aid funds. Applicants for assistance were caught by the 'blighting hand of charity' and forced to endure the humiliation of the invasion of their homes 'by female searchers or detectives' who busied themselves 'prying into the soldier's home affairs', just as if they were examples of the undeserving poor. As charitable aid organisations, the patriotic funds were, labour leaders claimed, 'pauperising' the men and their dependants.[73]

To the representatives of organised labour, inequality was the increasing chasm between the financial well-being of the exploiter and the hardship of soldiers' dependants, whereas equality was their improved financial well-being at the expense of the wealthy. To make their claims palatable to the wider community, labour argued that the responsibility for adequate soldier remuneration lay with 'all classes' of the community, both 'equally and proportionately'.[74] To ensure that those growing rich from the war contributed their share, labour demanded that conscription of wealth be a concomitant of the conscription of men. They made their demand that 'the nationalisation of capital' be introduced in tandem with the 'nationalisation of flesh' more palatable by using pro-war discourse: the wealthy must make 'a compulsory monetary sacrifice'; while the workers were compelled to sacrifice their bodies, the rich must sacrifice their wealth.[75]

The strategies of anti-war discourse

Those opposed to the war responded to pro-war discourse by attempting to redefine the debate about the war. With the exception of its socialist components, anti-war discourse appealed to the same assumptions, ideals and language as pro-war discourse. The labour leadership attempted to win over the rest of the community by appealing to commonly held ideals – pacific Christianity, British constitutional liberty and equality – but subverted and manipulated them in order to justify their opposition to the war. The debate about the war within the Christchurch community was therefore carried out by two groups which had different views on property ownership and the distribution of wealth, but which on other issues shared many common principles and ideals.

Élite discourse or public opinion?

As noted at the beginning of this chapter, the lack of public debate and the pervasiveness of pro-war discourse in New Zealand newspapers has prompted the assumption that the public generally supported the war. But, as has been demonstrated, the pro-war discourse of the local newspapers represented the views and interests of a specific group within the Christchurch community – the élite – and was publicly challenged by a different group – the labour élite. Is it possible to draw any conclusions regarding the attitudes towards the war of others in the community outside these two groups? Did the élite succeed in defining the way in which the rest of the Christchurch community saw the war? Did they place those who opposed the war outside the New Zealand citizenry, and label them as unpatriotic traitors?

The results of the municipal and national elections held in 1917 and 1919 suggest that the Christchurch élite failed to influence the attitudes of at least one section of the community: members of the working class who in previous elections had supported labour candidates. Support for organised labour in working class electorates remained strong during and immediately after the war, despite organised labour's public anti-war stance. The 1917 Christchurch City Council elections, for which the labour candidates ran on an anti-war, anti-conscription and anti-exploitation ticket, returned five New Zealand Labour Party candidates – a loss of just one Labour seat on the previous election.[76] Elizabeth Plumridge has argued that the loss of the seat was the result of standing a candidate who was largely unknown outside union circles, rather than a reaction against the anti-war platform.[77] Labour candidate James McCombs lost the mayoral race to sitting mayor and arch-patriot Henry Holland by a large margin. However, as polling was consistent with the previous two elections when the Labour candidate won around a third of the vote, there is little evidence that McCombs' defeat was the result of his opposition to conscription.[78]

The municipal elections held in April 1919, five months after the Armistice, resulted in Labour increasing its representation on the council to six councillors. All three elected by the voters of the working class Linwood ward were Labour Party candidates, including the anti-war and anti-conscription campaigner Hiram Hunter. Three of the four councillors elected in the working class Sydenham ward were Labour candidates, including Tim Armstrong and E.E. Langley, both of whom had spent time in prison for sedition. James McCombs won only 16 per cent of the vote in the mayoralty race, but this was the result of a three-way campaign that was preoccupied with the issue of port development.[79]

When the national elections were held in December 1919, the first since 1914, the war still cast a long shadow over New Zealand society. Non-religious conscientious objectors were still serving prison sentences – they would not be released until the last servicemen were repatriated in November 1920.[80] In December 1918 the Expeditionary Forces Amendment Act had disenfranchised these military defaulters for 10 years. Despite their public opposition to the war, Labour candidates won three of the six central Christchurch seats in the national elections. James McCombs retained Lyttelton, while his fellow moderate Dan Sullivan won the seat of Avon, beating the sitting Liberal MP and Coalition Cabinet minister G.W. Russell. Perhaps more tellingly, the pacifist, anti-militarist and anti-conscriptionist Ted Howard won the working class Christchurch South seat, beating former mayor Henry Holland, who stood as an independent Liberal candidate. Christchurch South was traditionally a close contest between the Liberal and Labour candidates, and had been held by the Liberal H.G. Ell since 1905, so Holland could reasonably have expected to win the seat.[81] Yet Holland, who had done so much in support of the local war effort, was well beaten in the two-horse race by one of the key opponents of the war in the Christchurch community. It appears that Howard's opposition to the war had not damaged his acceptability for public office among the working class voters of Christchurch South and that Holland's patriotism had not enhanced his chances.

The other three prominent anti-conscriptionists who contested Christchurch seats in 1919 on behalf of the Labour Party were unsuccessful. All three – Tim Armstrong standing for Christchurch North, Hiram Hunter standing for

Christchurch East and J. Robertson standing for Riccarton — were defeated by incumbent Liberals: L.M. Isitt, Dr Henry Thacker and George Witty respectively. Although supporting the war effort, Thacker had voiced concern about the rising cost of living and war profiteering and, in doing so, may well have 'upstaged' his Labour opponent, Hiram Hunter.[82] Both Armstrong and Robertson stood in affluent electorates that were unlikely to vote Labour, regardless of the candidates' war records.

These election results suggest that the pro-war rhetoric that pervaded the local newspapers during the war was not reflected in the voting of many working class constituents, who were unmoved by the Christchurch élite's condemnation of those who opposed the war. Although anti-war discourse remained subordinate to pro-war discourse in the public arena it does not necessarily follow that the Christchurch élite's support of the war was representative of the views of other sections of the community. Rather, I would suggest, the vigour with which the Christchurch élite promoted support for the war represented its attempt to address persistent opposition and apathy towards the war within sections of the community.

32

THE ARMISTICE: RESPONSES, UNDERSTANDINGS AND MEANINGS FOR A RURAL REGION

Graham Hucker

In a letter to Florence ['Florrie'] Journeaux in Hawera, south Taranaki, New Zealand, Private Frederick Voitrekofsky told her about Lone Pine at Gallipoli: 'it always put me in mind of the "Lone Pine" on the old South Road, Hawera'. In the same letter he expressed hope that 'some day when the war is over, and peace comes to the world once again, we will renew the old acquaintance once again, won't we?'[1] Nearly two years later in another letter to Florrie from 'somewhere in France', Voitrekofsky hoped that 'the time will arrive when we will be able to walk together again along the old road, and then forget the past in the happiness of the present under the old pine tree'.[2] In Voitrekofsky's imagination the 'Lone Pine' is a striking symbolic representation of peace, home and happiness. Equally striking is the interplay of past, present and future. Voitrekofsky was not alone though in thinking about the end of the Great War. In a letter to her daughter in September 1914, Annis Hamerton, a resident of Inglewood in north Taranaki, asked a question that exercised the minds of contemporaries for the duration of the war: 'when will it end?'[3] Contemporary journals and newspapers asked similar questions. The *New Zealand Farmer* queried in an article in 1915, 'When Peace is Restored. What Will Our Soldiers Do?' In a veiled, yet dour thought about the end of the war, the *Stratford Evening Post* news headlines asked insensitively on Christmas Eve, 1915, 'WHAT IF THE WAR LASTS UNTIL 1917?'[4]

When hostilities eventually ceased, they did so suddenly. On 1 October 1918, people in Taranaki received news that Bulgaria had surrendered to the Allies. Exactly one month later the Ottoman Empire (Turkey) surrendered, followed by Austria-Hungary three days later. And on 12 November, they learned that Germany had signed an Armistice with the Allies. At last Annis Hamerton had her answer. For just over four years the people of Taranaki had endured what Hamerton described as 'terrible times', then it took just over one month for the fighting to end.[5]

Attention by historians to how New Zealand reacted to the collapse of the Central Powers has focused primarily on soldiers in the front line.[6] How civilians in New Zealand responded to such news has received little, if any, analysis, and that has been consistent with the international situation. Writing on the 50th anniversary of the ending of hostilities, C.N. Barclay observed that, 'the circumstances of the Armistice which ended the fighting had escaped close attention'. Over 30 years later another writer still found 'a paucity of effort to understand and explain the causes of war *termination*.'[7] However, an international literature focusing solely on the ending of the Great War has begun to emerge.[8]

This chaper will examine how, and in what ways, people in the predominantly rural region of Taranaki on the west coast of the North Island of New Zealand responded to the surrender of the Central Powers in 1918. It will ask a number of questions. What did these New Zealanders understand about the surrender of Germany and its allies? Also, what did the Armistice actually mean for them? Furthermore, this chapter will argue that the surrender of the Central Powers and the subsequent Armistice celebrations provided a unique social experience during a time of jubilation, sorrow and misery.

In Taranaki, the collapse of the Central Powers and the cessation of hostilities were publicly acknowledged on four separate occasions over a six-week period. Bulgaria, which had entered the war late in 1915, surrendered first. 'ON TO VICTORY' headlined the *Stratford Evening Post* boldly on 2 October 1918 at 'BULGARIA'S SUBMISSION'. Yet the day in Stratford had been quiet with little or no celebration except for an 'impromptu band' in Broadway 'tooting patriotic and martial airs' in an attempt to 'stir up the majority from a state of unimaginable lethargy on such an auspicious occasion.' Stratford's mayor, J.W. McMillan, believed Bulgaria's submission to be 'our finest achievement since the beginning of the war, and the forerunner of further capitulations', and at the King's Picture Theatre he found a captive audience to express his views. McMillan trumpeted familiar themes of self-sacrifice and righteousness in a confident, congratulatory address: 'the men and women left at home must not let up for one minute', he said, 'but keep up the pressure with men and money until Germany was broken'. God, too, it seems, was on the side of the Allies because 'in His merciful providence, [He] has guided us to the end of one act in the horrible drama of the last four years'. At a thanksgiving service 'for recent Allied victories' held a week later in Stratford's town hall, the Reverend Howard suggested that, 'though the end was not yet, ... they could say, with some measure of security, that the end was immensely nearer'.[9] The significance of Bulgaria's exit lay in the hope it gave people that perhaps the end of the Great War was near.

The submission of the Ottoman Empire one month later had a greater impact on the people in Taranaki. The empire in 1914 had been considered 'long crumbling and effete' by the region's press, and yet the Gallipoli campaign of 1915 proved differently.[10] The fighting on the peninsula had claimed the lives of at least 19 soldiers from central and eastern Taranaki, including the commander of the Wellington Infantry Battalion, Lieutenant-Colonel William George Malone of Stratford, so news that a second enemy power had collapsed was considered a 'great historical event'.[11]

Shortly after 10 a.m. on 1 November, Taranaki received unofficial news of the Ottoman acceptance of an armistice. Train whistles blew in response, and fire-station, school and church bells rang out to let people know that 'something glorious had happened'. In New Plymouth and Hawera, newspaper 'extras' were 'rushed by pedestrians, who stood about in small groups and eagerly discussed the news'.[12] About midday Taranaki's mayoralty received official telegrams informing them of the Ottoman submission. Public celebrations then began at 2 p.m. in accordance with arrangements made by the region's borough councils. All business was temporarily suspended, including local government. The Clifton County Council, for instance, adjourned its meeting because of the 'momentous news'. Government offices too, were directed to close for the rest of the day 'in celebration of the armistice with Turkey'.[13] Schools also closed throughout the region: in Manaia, children 'took charge of the town with a tin-can band and marched through the streets; in Normanby, children celebrated in a manner that reminded one correspondent of the end of the South African War, noting that they 'mafficked to their heart's content.'[14] Throughout Taranaki, bands playing patriotic airs headed processions that made their way to public venues where local élites addressed the crowds on a day of 'great rejoicing'.[15]

The public response to Turkey's surrender had barely subsided when news was received on 4 November that Austria-Hungary had sued for an armistice. In scenes reminiscent of the previous Friday, people in Taranaki ventured into the streets to celebrate the collapse of yet another Central Power. In Hawera, 'the whole scene was an animated one, and was perhaps unique in the history of the town'. Eltham, too, 'was "right out" yesterday – drunk – with enthusiasm. Never were [there] such scenes in our quiet little borough before.'[16] In New Plymouth, 'all the whistles in town started at 2.15 to make the same joyous noise as marked the downfall of Turkey'. 'When we met here last Friday to celebrate the fall of Turkey, though events pointed to the early collapse of Austria, I hardly expected that I should be announcing this news today,' stated New Plymouth's mayor.[17] With Germany now alone and without allies the 'great peace' that people hoped for seemed imminent.

Reminders that a great war still existed contradicted the celebrations and optimistic hopes for peace in late 1918. Soldiers from Taranaki destined for the NZEF's 47th Reinforcements were farewelled shortly after the festivities celebrating the collapse of Bulgaria. They departed amidst jubilant scenes reminiscent of earlier farewells, even though much sadness and anxiety prevailed throughout the region. Nowhere, perhaps, was that more poignant than in the death notices of soldiers published by grief-stricken relatives. On the day following the Ottoman surrender, Lance Corporal Albert Henry Chard's grieving parents published a thank you notice in the *Taranaki Herald* 'to all kind friends and relatives for letters and cards of sympathy received in their recent sad bereavement, in the loss of their dear son and brother'.[18] Chard, a farmer from Egmont Village, had been killed in action somewhere in France on the day Taranaki had celebrated the surrender of Bulgaria. Conversely, while the Chard family grieved, the family and friends of Sergeant E.C. Stanley celebrated his homecoming with an evening of dancing and euchre at the Hillsborough Hall. And for those soldiers, like Albert Chard, who would not be coming home, a meeting had been arranged to decide on a memorial. Wives, too, expressed their loss and sadness. On the day Taranaki 'celebrated' the armistice with Austria-Hungary, Gertrude Chapman had a notice of thanks printed in the newspaper to 'her many friends for kind messages of sympathy received upon the death of her husband [Private James Walter Chapman, age 41], killed in action in France' on the day that Bulgaria had actually surrendered.[19] Similarly, Private Robert Rowse's wife expressed her loss with sorrowful sentiments in the fortnight following news of Bulgaria's surrender:

ROLL OF HONOUR

ROWSE – On October 5th, in France, died of wounds,

Robert John Rowse, late of Kotuku, West Coast.

Deeply regretted.

'A painful shock, a dreadful blow; Dearest one I

miss you so.

The loss is great – we will not complain,

But trust in God to meet again'

(Inserted by his loving wife and child)[20]

The contemporary historical record does not show what happened to Private Rowse's wife and child, but death or incapacitation of a husband serving with the NZEF would have also created economic stress. Perhaps such a situation prompted a woman from Mahoe in central Taranaki to place an advertisement in the *Stratford Evening Post* on 2 November 1918; 'WANTED – By soldier's wife with two children, position as housekeeper'.

Rolls of honour were another salient reminder, amidst the heightened expectation of peace, that sacrifices were still being made to win 'the war in the interests of humanity'.[21] So, too, were the hospital progress reports that often accompanied the Rolls of Honour. On 1 November, the day Taranaki learned of 'THE GOOD NEWS' about the Ottoman surrender, a Roll of Honour and Hospital Progress Report was published in the *Hawera and Normanby Star* alongside news of 'CELEBRATIONS IN HAWERA'. It was a striking contradiction. The roll for the Wellington District listed the names of soldiers who had 'previously [been] reported missing, [and were] now reported killed in action', and there were names listed of soldiers from the region who had 'DIED OF WOUNDS', or 'SICKNESS', or were 'MISSING', or 'WOUNDED' and admitted to hospital. The hospital progress report listed 10 soldiers from Taranaki who had either been 'removed from [the] dangerously ill list', or were 'still dangerously ill', or were 'removed from [the] seriously ill list', or were considered 'severe cases'.

In the days immediately following the celebrations marking the demise of the Ottomans and Austria-Hungarians, a contradictory, yet ominous development made its appearance and gathered momentum in Taranaki. Dr Doris Gordon, a medical practitioner in Stratford, recalled in her autobiography that:

> The joy bells for the peace with Turkey rang out when we had probably twelve to twenty severe influenza cases in our region of ten thousand people. But no one had authority to stride down the street shouting 'do not foregather, do not celebrate – death is round the corner'. So collectively we celebrated, and danced in the Town Hall on a warm November night, and within twenty-four hours nearly a third of the revellers were rigoring.[22]

On 7 November, Charles Henry Rowson, a 22-year-old returned soldier, was admitted to hospital after being ill for a week. The following day he became Stratford's first influenza fatality.[23] On 10 November, the day of Rowson's funeral, a second influenza fatality was notified in the Stratford district. Bessie Bayly, aged 51, died at Toko, possibly alone because she had no children and her husband, Lieutenant Charles Bayly, was overseas with the NZEF.[24] Irony surrounded both deaths. Rowson died of an illness in seemingly safe surroundings, not from a bullet on the battlefield. Lieutenant Bayly, alive on the Western Front, with all its implications of death, learned that his wife had died of influenza while safely at home. In a time of increasing medical knowledge, 'germs' were still more potent agents of death than war itself. If soldiers like Rowson and Bayly survived war, *who* would be safe during an epidemic, especially when Gordon believed that 'we're dealing with something unknown'? Far from having been a joyous time, she considered the closing month of the Great War to be 'dark November' because of 'the holocaust which had descended'; it was a period of 'Black Death Plague'.[25]

Contemporaries could be forgiven for such apocalyptic thoughts. Deaths from disease and war continued – seven more soldiers from the Stratford district were killed during October and early November[26]– and in early November came another warning. 'Unhappily the germ of Bolshevism has been found recently in a more or less developed form in all countries,' reported the *Hawera and Normanby Star*. 'While we celebrate the Allies' victories and the downfall of the ruthless enemy, let us remember that there is a serious danger keen and ready to spoil the freedom so hardly won.'[27] Motivated by the thought of a new threat, Marc Voullaire, a farmer from Riverlea in south Taranaki, wrote in his diary that 'Austria seems to be going the way of Russia & Bolshevism appears to be getting the upper hand'. A few days later, in a rare conciliatory comment about Germany, he wrote: 'I only hope the horrors of Bolshevism will be spared the country'. Voullaire expressed his private, fearful thoughts on grim happenings abroad while experiencing grimness around him at home, and even on the farm. Stock in his region were 'getting a rough time, and the milk returns [were] suffering accordingly' because of the bleak showery weather.[28] The meteorological report noted that 'October was a most miserable month, high, cold winds prevailing and rain falling on no less than 22 days'.[29] It seems even the weather had the potential to cloud the celebrations.

Early in the morning on 8 November – the day Private Rowson died – Taranaki received news that Germany had sued for an armistice. New Plymouth

> proceeded to 'go mad' with excitement and joy. Never before had there been such an occasion as this, and never before had such scenes as ensued been witnessed here. The news spread with lightning rapidity, everybody trooped into the streets and schools, shops and offices were closed. For two hours several thousands of men, women and children rejoiced. Steam whistles and the fire-bells were, of course, sounded as soon as the news was received and then, as fancy-goods shops and garages were rushed toy trumpets, squeakers, kerosene tins and any other things that had a noise in them were added to the clamour, in which human voices also joined.

Two hours into the festivities, however, 'it began to be whispered that the news of the armistice was not official and the sounds of rejoicing gradually died away'.[30] In Stratford, disappointment followed similar scenes of rejoicing. Acceptance of the lack of official confirmation of an armistice 'was like a cold douche to the proceedings, and the crowd melted into other avenues'.[31] In New Plymouth, 'many of the sobered rejoicers regretfully wended their way homewards or back to a neglected work-a-day world', while some still gathered in the main street until about mid-afternoon, keeping a vigil outside the *Taranaki Herald* office.[32]

Not everybody would have been able or willing to attend that false victory celebration. Stratford's mayor was 'confined to his home owing to influenza'.[33] The Rowson family on Flint Road had a military funeral to arrange. The Babbage, Cleaver and Linn families of Rotokare, Te Roti and Normanby respectively were in mourning, having all recently lost sons.[34] Rifleman Frederick Babbage's parents received news of his death on the day before the most recent 'celebration'. 'He was only 22 years of age,' lamented the *Hawera and Normanby Star's* Own Correspondent in Eltham.[35] And Opunake's chairman of the town board would probably not have attended either. His loyalty and patriotism had been called into question for not arranging earlier victory celebrations but his inaction could have been explained by his grief for a son killed in action and anxiety about another who had returned home wounded. 'Surely this is sufficient answer to the noisy who parade their patriotism', claimed a 'CITIZEN PATRIOT'.[36]

Four days later the much-anticipated 'DAY OF DAYS' replaced disappointment. It was official: Germany had signed an armistice with the Allies. The 'GREATEST DAY IN HISTORY' had arrived.[37] The *Stratford Evening Post* news headlines announced boldly 'END OF THE WAR', printed alongside a column-long casualty list and news about the influenza epidemic. In scenes reminiscent of those only days before in Stratford,

> The ringing of the fire-bell, whistles blowing, the tin-can band of the boys, and the other devices with which to make a noise joyfully, soon spread the great news over the countryside. There was such a sigh of relief that it could be almost felt. People beamed in each other's faces. Not much was said. There were a few silent hand-shakes. The pent-up feelings of years could not be expressed in

words all at once. Perhaps, it was the thought of a dear one for ever gone, of the empty sleeve, maimed limb, or disfigured feature of a relative or close friend; may be, the thought of the Hell of the past four years welled up in the heart and made all else matter nothing for the time being. It almost seemed good to be sad for a moment, and then Joy won, and the rest of the day was spent with the spirit of thankfulness uppermost, and with an exuberance of pleasure, tempered with the remembrance of the dignity of Victory.[38]

The region's press reported similar rejoicings throughout Taranaki from Otakeho's 'picnic in a paddock' to the beach picnic at Opunake, to the procession in New Plymouth and 'A GLORIOUS PAGEANT' in Hawera.

The Armistice celebrations had no precedent in Taranaki's past. Not even the end of the South African War and the coronation of King Edward VII, both of which took place in 1902, could match the scale and intensity of the Armistice celebrations in 1918. By analysing the region's newspapers, historians can uncover the meanings that lie within the discourse of that unique event. Historians Robert Rutherdale and Jeffrey Verhey examined newspapers in their respective studies of Canadian and German crowds that gathered in August 1914,[39] and because some historians have made connections between the so-called 'enthusiasm' of August 1914 and the 'celebrations' of November 1918, it is appropriate to analyse the public discourse using Rutherdale and Verhey's methodology.[40] The ensuing analysis reveals five broad themes – inclusiveness of community, the ambiguous nature of victory, an absence of agreement on how to act, remembrance and future expectations – that characterise a rural region's understanding of and responses to the cessation of hostilities in 1918.

Inclusiveness of community characterised the Armistice celebrations. Everybody, it seems, had played some part in the Great War and deserved public recognition for their efforts. Praise went to children because of their 'cheerful optimism' which 'had done much to lessen' the 'grief' of their parents.[41] Praise went to Maori because they 'had mingled their blood in gaining this victory', stated the Reverend Koroneho Hemi Papakakura on Armistice day in Opunake.[42] Praise went to 'brave' women for having made the sacrifice in letting sons and husbands go to war. Praise went to the 'returned heroes' of the NZEF. Praise went to the Allies, their armed forces and their leaders. Praise and thanksgiving also went to God. The celebrations were, therefore, a shared event, but not necessarily a shared victory.

Ambiguity over *who* had actually been responsible for the defeat of the Central Powers led to different interpretations of the Allied victory. Church ministers thanked God for the victory; civic leaders were inclined to thank others. 'I believe that there has been the hand of Almighty God behind it all – or the hand of Providence', claimed the Reverend Gordon Gavin at a gathering in Waitara following the surrender of Austria-Hungary.[43] In Stratford following the armistice with Germany, mayor McMillan told the cheering crowd that, 'we must thank God that the war with all its frightfulness is practically over' but also pointed out that 'had it not been for the Navy there would have been no peace to-day as we are celebrating it.'[44] At an Armistice celebration in Opunake, people may have been confused when the chairman of the town board told them that 'If it had not been for that army and the workers of the British Empire Germany would never have been defeated'. When C.W. Rogers, the clerk of the county council, spoke, he said: 'It was the British Navy that saved New Zealand'. The Reverend Palmer, however, told them that God must be thanked 'for giving the Allied armies the victory; he was sure that God had been with them otherwise it would have been impossible for the Allied armies to have stopped the German hordes'.[45] *Who* had actually been responsible for the victory may not have mattered so much because *their* side – the British Empire and the Allies – had won, and that was cause for celebration.

The jubilation and sorrow that characterised the mood of society in early November 1918 did give the authorities some cause for concern over how people should act. Circumscription was needed because those celebrating could upset those in mourning, and crowds could spread influenza. In a 4 November editorial on 'PEACE PREPARATIONS', the *Hawera and Normanby Star* acknowledged that there were 'reasonable and unreasonable ways of celebrating such a great event' as the Armistice and 'unseemly conduct' would be inappropriate on a day of 'sacredness' because the 'great conflict had cost millions of lives, and there are few families in our nation who cannot point to some dear one killed by the enemy'. The Reverend Madill reminded a crowd in Stratford following news of the Ottoman surrender to be 'careful how they rejoiced on these occasions. Lest they injured the feelings of others who simply could not rejoice, and who were beneath a dark cloud of sorrow, mourning for their departed loved ones.'[46] The presence of influenza in the region complicated matters. When news arrived of the signing of the Armistice with Germany, distinctions between responsible and irresponsible behaviour, self-preservation and the need to celebrate became blurred. For instance, local authorities in the south-western settlement of Kaponga took no chances and postponed the Armistice celebrations indefinitely because of the 'flu'. In Inglewood, 'owing to so much sickness the firebell rang only for a short time, and the tin-can band was conspicuous by its absence', but an 'open-air thanksgiving service' was held at 11 a.m.[47] In Stratford, jubilation overcame caution as Doris Gordon recalled:

> Unfortunately many moderately infected cases got out of bed on that Armistice day; for youth in full flush of adolescent enthusiasm could not remain in bed for an ache and a cough when Stratford's Broadway was *en fete*. As a result mild cases developed complications, and as the disease leapt on from case to case it enhanced its virulence until many people were stricken from the outset with a lethal infection.[48]

Why then, did people in Stratford, whether they were ill or not, defy municipal and health authorities by celebrating in Broadway and dancing in the town hall during an influenza epidemic? An immediate answer lies in the desire to mark the ending of hostilities, but the celebrations also represented a lack of public understanding about the epidemic and the anti-flu measures instituted by the authorities.[49] The epidemic cannot be separated from the Great War itself: the virulent influenza brought death to people at home just as war brought death by bullets and shrapnel to soldiers in the front line.

The misery that accompanied the influenza epidemic deepened that felt by the people of Taranaki, and New Zealand, as they remembered the Great War: '[F]or four years they have been treading the path of self-sacrifice and pain, and had met with many bitter disappointments,' stated Reverend R.B. Tinsley in Stratford following Bulgaria's surrender. In Waitara Reverend Gavin wondered 'if it really comes home to us all the price we have had to pay for the victory. New Zealand alone had given 15,000 lives'.[50] The recall of specific events highlighted the Great War as a 'ghastly nightmare'.[51] At Opunake, the Reverend

Stroud stated that 'we shall remember with contempt when one of the greatest acts of inhumanity was perpetrated [in] the sinking of the Lusitania' and the Ottoman Empire, too, would not be forgotten, in part, because of the Armenian atrocities.[52] In Stratford, 'groans and hooting' accompanied councillor Walter's mention of conscientious objectors. In essence, the war had been a time of grimness, of 'dark days'.[53]

Yet, people recalled some aspects of the war with pride. At the celebrations marking the Ottoman surrender, there were positive speeches about Gallipoli and the New Zealand soldiers or, more collectively, the Anzacs. In the popular mind the Gallipoli Peninsula was a 'sacred tract of land on which were buried the brave Anzac soldiers', who had displayed 'heroic courage, sublime devotion and unselfish sacrifice' in the Dardanelles campaign of 1915.[54] Contemporaries revered the ANZAC soldiers, whether returned, or 'fallen', because in the popular mind they had been 'fighting for liberty and justice'.[55] For example, in the Armistice day procession in Hawera, 'a shower of flowers descended upon the gallant soldiers' as they passed a building in Princess Street, and the mayor evoked a poignant image when he asked people to 'remember those brave men who had laid down their lives for the Empire, and whose last resting places were marked by little crosses in Egypt, on Gallipoli, in France and in other parts of the world'.[56] Even though 'disappointment' accompanied the strategic outcome of the Dardanelles campaign, not all contemporaries considered Gallipoli a failure. New Plymouth's mayor, for instance, preferred to wait, believing that 'time and history will tell'.[57]

In remembering the past, contemporaries also looked to a future in which returned and fallen soldiers featured prominently. Soldiers had made 'great sacrifices' in helping secure victory, and what contemporaries hoped would be 'everlasting peace'. Gratitude abounded. The public must 'deal with them as well as they dealt for us', a crowd in Eltham was told on the occasion of the Ottoman surrender. 'Nothing could be too much to do for them when they return.' Gratitude also extended to the 'fallen'. Memorials had to be erected so that 'their memory would ever be as green as the green grass of Taranaki'.[58] A noteworthy example of a proposed memorial came from Hawera where local citizens had recently observed the fiftieth anniversary of the Turuturu Mokai engagement during the New Zealand Wars. Contemporaries felt that Maori 'have nobly done their duty in the titanic conflict in Europe, and they have, side by side with their British friends and neighbours, worthily helped in the cause of freedom'. In a conciliatory gesture, in which memory of past conflicts converged with the present need to commemorate, contemporaries wanted 'this great historic fact [to] be immortalised in a Turuturu Mokai Peace Memorial Park, for Maori and Pakeha have, we hope, in the common cause of liberty and freedom dissolved their old differences in the blood of sacrifice'.[59]

The proposed memorial was a symbolic representation of hope for peace. Ideal as the proposal may seem contemporaries were realistic about future problems. The war against Germany was still being fought, yet they were confident of victory, after which 'tremendous tasks would have to be faced, questions of international finance and of a social nature'.[60] A peace settlement would also have to be successfully concluded. The future, therefore, 'is full of difficulty', as a *Hawera and Normanby Star* editorial stated. 'Enormous tasks have to be faced, and there cannot be a return to the old order of things. Men have had their outlook on life entirely changed, and we live in a totally different atmosphere from that of the few years preceding the war.'[61]

What did the ending of the Great War actually mean for people in a rural region of New Zealand? For Doris Gordon, hearing the 'joy bells' signalling the Armistice with Germany meant her husband would be coming home – alive. For years Gordon had 'lived and prayed' for that moment:

> and now it found me pickled in toxins, aspirins, and quinine. In the next bedroom was my sister-in-law equally ill with gastric influenza. I staggered into her room and pitched myself on to the foot of her bed – I had just enough humour left to think what a queer pair of jubilant soldiers' wives we looked – and croaked, 'Dot, that's peace, and they are not killed yet!'.[62]

For Annis Hamerton, the Armistice meant 'a turmoil of joy & sorrow, thankfulness too deep for words, that God in his great mercy has sent us Peace, though there is & will be for long great turmoil'.[63] For Stratford's mayor, John McMillan, speaking to a crowd on the day of the Armistice, it meant 'Our war weary soldiers will soon be returning'.[64] The cheering crowd agreed. The *Hawera and Normanby Star* noted that 'millions of anxious human beings hourly awaiting news of relatives and friends facing the horrors of the modern battlefield are to-day released from the long strain'.[65] The breadth of meanings is indicative of the impact that the Great War had on people in Taranaki and it helps to explain why, during a time of sorrow and misery brought about by the ubiquitous casualty lists and influenza epidemic, the region desperately wanted to celebrate the victory and the peace.

A distinctly 'British', *not* New Zealand, minded community in Taranaki celebrated the cessation of hostilities in 1918. Speakers at Stratford's Armistice celebrations spoke collectively of 'being Britishers' and even acclaimed David Lloyd George as 'our national hero', *not* somebody from New Zealand like Sir James Allen, Minister of Defence, or even the late Lieutenant-Colonel William Malone. Mayor McMillan even referred to Herbert Asquith's reasons for why they went to war, which, in short, were 'for Liberty and Justice.' Therein lies a key to understanding the reasons for the celebrations: they were about freedom and a just cause. Contemporaries had been told, and had understood since 1914, that the rights of countries like 'brave little Belgium' had to be defended. Failure to do so would mean dishonour. Had Germany won the war, a crowd in Hawera was told, 'slavery, degradation and absolute ruin' would have followed.[66] To the Great War generation in Taranaki the taking-up of arms had *not* been futile. The Reverend W.A. Sinclair made that clear to a crowd in New Plymouth on Armistice Day: 'when these boys and girls were grown up they would tell their children and their grand-children of these four years from 1914 to 1918 when the whole world united to overthrow the greatest military power and menace the world had ever known'.[67] With the Central Powers defeated the Armistice meant 'the beginning of a new age', the Reverend C.H. Grant Cowen told a crowd in Hawera, and 'The Empire, the world, was now free'.[68] The celebrations at the close of the Great War did not so much mark the end of a past, but the start of a future for the generation of 1914–18, much in the same way that Private Frederick Voitrekofsky had imagined his post-war world.

NOTES

Note: All AD (Army Department), WA (War Archives) and Allen Papers references are to these series at Archives New Zealand, Wellington.

Introduction

1   *The Great War, 1914–1918, New Zealand Expeditionary Force, Roll of Honour* (Wellington: Government Printer, 1924), ii; Jeffrey Grey, *A Military History of Australia* (Cambridge: CUP, 1999), 116.

2   *NZEF Roll of Honour*, ii; John Studholme, *New Zealand Expeditionary Force: Record of Personal Services during the War of Officers, Nurses, and First-Class Warrant Officers; and Other Facts Relating to the NZEF* (Wellington: Government Printer, 1928), 383.

3   Malcolm McKinnon (ed.) with Barry Bradley and Russell Kirkpatrick, *New Zealand Historical Atlas* (Auckland: David Bateman in association with Historical Branch, Department of Internal Affairs, 1997), 77.

4   Percival Fenwick, *Gallipoli Diary: 24 April to 27 June, 1915* (Auckland: David Ling and in association with Auckland War Memorial Museum, 2000), 5 May 1915, 18.

5   *Dominion*, 6 Aug 1914, 6.

6   Ibid., 6 Aug 1914, 4, 6–7; C.A.L. Treadwell, *Recollections of an Amateur Soldier* (New Plymouth: Thomas Avery & Sons, 1936), 7–12.

7   H. Hart, diary, 11 Nov 1918, Micro MS 552, ATL.

8   *Dominion*, 12 Nov 1918, 4, 13 Nov 1918, 8.

9   Ibid., 12 Nov 1918, 6; H. Ennor, diary, 8–11 Nov 1918, qMS 0684, ATL.

10 Ennor diary, 12 Nov 1918.

Chapter 1: Gary Sheffield

I would like to thank the New Zealand Ministry of Defence for sponsoring my visit to New Zealand.

1   'Introduction' to Jay Winter, Geoffrey Parker, Mary R. Habeck (eds), *The Great War and the Twentieth Century* (New Haven, CT, and London: YUP, 2000), 1.

2   J.M. Bourne, *Britain and the Great War 1914–1918* (London, 1989), vii; Jenny Macleod, *Reconsidering Gallipoli* (Manchester: MUP, 2004).

3   For a recent example, tinged with Australian nationalism, see Jonathan King, *Gallipoli: Our Last Man Standing* (Milton, Queensland: John Wiley, 2003).

4   John Keegan, *The First World War* (London: Hutchinson, 1998); Niall Ferguson, *The Pity of War* (London: Allen Lane, 1998).

5   Gary Sheffield, *Forgotten Victory: The First World War – Myths and Realities* (London: Headline, 2001).

6   Maurice Shadbolt, *Voices of Gallipoli* (Auckland: Hodder & Stoughton, 1988), 13.

7   David Horspool, *Guardian*, 21 Jul 2001.

8   Jeff Keshen, 'The Great War Soldier as Nation Builder in Canada and Australia', in B.C. Busch, *Canada and the Great War* (Montreal and Kingston: McGill-Queen's UP, 2003), 3–4, 19–20.

9   Glyn Harper (ed.), *Letters from the Battlefield: New Zealand Soldiers Write Home 1914–18* (Auckland: HarperCollins, 2001), 14.

10 Tom Frame, *The Shores of Gallipoli: Naval Aspects of the Anzac Campaign* (Alexandria, NSW: Hale & Iremonger, 2000), 13.

11 A.J.P. Taylor, *The First World War, An Illustrated History* (Harmondsworth: Penguin, 1966), 140.

12 Richard Curtis *et al., Blackadder The Whole Damn Dynasty* (London: Michael Joseph, 1998), 442.

13 For hostile reviews, see Frank McLynn in *Independent,* 29 Jun 2001; Ian Ousby, *Spectator,* 30 Jun 2001; J. Keegan, *Daily Telegraph,* 25 Aug 2001.

14 Brian Bond, *Times Literary Supplement*, 31 Aug 2001. See also Sir Michael Howard, *Journal of the Royal United Services Institute*, Vol. 146, No. 5 (2001), 70. To his great credit, Niall Ferguson reviewed the book favourably: *Sunday Times,* 8 Jul 2001.

15 Alfred Duff Cooper, *Old Men Forget* (London: Rupert Hart-Davis, 1953), 185–6.

16 *Socialism Today*, 74, Apr–May 2003.

17 *Morning Star*, 28 Apr 2003.

18 Alan Clark, 'Douglas Haig: The Greatest Betrayal', *Daily Express*, 11 Nov 1998; Alan Clark, letter to *Sunday Telegraph* quoted in Brian Bond, 'Editor's Introduction', in Brian Bond (ed.), *The First World War and British Military History* (Oxford: Clarendon, 1991), 11; Alan Clark, speech in House of Commons, reported on 13 May 1999 on news.bbc. co.uk/hi/english/uk_politics/newsid_341000/341713.stm; 'Alan Clark – a unique politician', news.bbc.co.uk/hi/english/ uk_politics/ newsid_441000/441268.stm

19 Niall Ferguson (ed.), *Virtual History, Alternatives and Counterfactuals* (London: Macmillan, 1997), ch. 4; Ferguson, *Pity*, 457–62.

20 John Charmley, *Splendid Isolation? Britain and the Balance of Power 1874–1914* (London: Hodder & Stoughton, 1999), x, 1–2, 7.

21 For a recent assessment, see T.G. Otte, '"Almost a Law of Nature": Sir Edward Grey, the Foreign Office, and the Balance of Power in Europe, 1905–12', in Erik Goldstein and B.J.C. McKercher (eds), *Power and Stability: British Foreign Policy, 1865–1965* (London: Frank Cass, 2003), 77–118.

22 Sheffield, 33.

23 Annika Mombauer, *The Origins of the First World War: Controversies and Consensus* (London: Longman, 2002), 211.

24 Ibid., 212.

25 Graydon A. Tunstall, Jr, 'Austria-Hungary', in Richard F. Hamilton and Holger H. Herwig (eds.), *The Origins of World War I* (Cambridge: CUP, 2003), 136, 146; Annika Mombauer, *Helmuth von Moltke and the Origins of the First World War* (Cambridge: CUP, 2001), 283–9.

26 David Alan Rich, 'Russia', in Hamilton and Herwig, 213–14.

27 David G. Hermann, *The Arming of Europe and the Making of the First World War* (Princeton: PUP, 1996), 209.

28 Rich, 214, 223–5.

29 Holger H. Herwig, 'Germany', in Hamilton and Herwig, 183.

30 Jeremy Black, *Why Wars Happen* (London: Reaktion, 1998), 180.

31 Charmley, 1–2.

32 J.P. Harris, 'Great Britain', in Hamilton and Herwig, 299.

33 R. Prior and T. Wilson, *The First World War* (London: Cassell, 1999), 23, 25–6.

34 Richard Schweitzer, *The Cross and the Trenches: Religious Doubt among British and American Great War Soldiers* (Westport: Praeger, 2003), 1, 19–20.

35 John Horne and Alan Kramer, *German Atrocities, 1914: A History of Denial* (New Haven and London: YUP, 2001), 424.

36 Colin S. Gray, *Modern Strategy* (Oxford: OUP, 1999), 66.

37 www.gg.govt.nz/media/speeches.asp?type=current&ID=235, accessed 7 Jul 2004.

38 Cecil Malthus, *Armentières and the Somme* (Auckland: Reed, 2002), 14–15.

39 Jock Philips, 'Was the Great War New Zealand's war?', in Craig Wilcox with Janice Aldridge (eds), *The Great War: Gains and Losses – Anzac and Empire* (Canberra: AWM, 1995), 69.

40 Nicholas Boyack and Jane Tolerton, *In the Shadow of War: New Zealand soldiers talk about World War One and their lives* (Auckland: Penguin, 1990), 25.

41 Geoffrey Blainey, 'If Australia had not participated in the Great War, what kind of society would have emerged?', in Wilcox and Aldridge, 172.

42 For recent studies on this theme, see Chris Coulthard-Clark, 'Australian Defence: Perceptions and Policies, 1871–1919'; Craig Wilcox, 'Australian Involvement in the Boer War: Imperial Pressure or Colonial *Realpolitik?*'; Christopher Pugsley, 'At the Empire's

Call: New Zealand Expeditionary Force Planning, 1901–1918', all in John A. Moses and Christopher Pugsley (eds), *The German Empire and Britain's Pacific Dominions 1871–1919* (Claremont, California: Regina Books, 2000). See also Nicholas Lambert, 'Economy or Empire? The Fleet Security Concept and the Quest for Collective Security in the Pacific, 1909–1914', in Keith Nielson and Greg Kennedy (eds), *Far Flung Lines* (London: Frank Cass, 1997), 55–83.

43   *Guardian*, 27 Nov 2003; bbc.co.uk/go/pr/fr/-/1/hi/uk_politics/3888581.stm, accessed 13 Jul 2004.

44   Niall Ferguson, *Empire: How Britain Made the Modern World* (London: Allen Lane, 2003).

45   For the diplomacy of the war, see David Stevenson, *The First World War and International Politics* (Oxford: OUP, 1988) and David Stevenson, 'War Aims and Peace Negotiations', in Hew Strachan (eds), *The Oxford Illustrated History of the First World War* (Oxford: OUP, 1998).

46   For recent scholarship on Versailles, see Manfred F. Boemeke, Gerald D. Feldman and Elisabeth Glaser (eds), *The Treaty of Versailles: A Reassessment after 75 Years* (Cambridge: CUP, 1998).

47   Peter Simkins, *Kitchener's Army* (Manchester: MUP, 1988), xiv.

48   Figures from Robert Holland, 'The British Empire and the Great War, 1914–1918', in Judith M. Brown and Wm. Roger Louis (eds), *The Oxford History of the British Empire*, Vol. IV, *The Twentieth Century* (Oxford: OUP, 1999), 117–18.

49   Ross Anderson, *The Forgotten Front: The East African Campaign 1914–1918* (Stroud: Tempus, 2004), 296.

50   W. David McIntyre, 'Australia, New Zealand, and the Pacific Islands', in Brown and Louis, 671.

51   Holland, p.126; Ian Miller, '"A Privilege to Serve": Toronto's Experience with Voluntary Enlistment in the Great War', in Yves Tremblay (ed.), *Canadian Military History Since the 17th Century* (Ottawa: Directorate of History and Heritage, 2001), 151.

52   One example of this was the coercion of conscientious objectors. For the New Zealand experience, see Paul Baker, *King and Country Call: New Zealand, Conscription and the Great War* (Auckland: AUP, 1988), 170–201.

53   B.H. Liddell Hart, *The British Way in Warfare* (London: Faber, 1932).

54   George H. Cassar, *Kitchener: Architect of Victory* (London: Kimber, 1977), 389.

55   See Brock Millman, *Pessimism and British War Policy 1916–1918* (London: Frank Cass, 2001).

56   TS diary, in War Diary of RHG, Household Cavalry Museum, Windsor.

57   H.P. Holt, *History of the 3rd (Prince of Wales's) Dragoon Guards 1914–1918* (Doncaster: D.P. & G, 2001, first published privately in 1937), 109.

58   I find the argument that Maori played a major role in inventing trench warfare unconvincing. See James Belich, *The New Zealand Wars and the Victorian Interpretation of Racial Conflict* (Auckland: Penguin, new edition, 1998), 297–8, 315–18; Christopher Pugsley, 'Maori did not invent trench warfare', *NZ Defence Quarterly*, 22 (1998), 33–7.

59   See, e.g., Cuthbert Headlam, *History of the Guards Division in the Great War 1915–18*, Vol. I (London: John Murray, 1924), 251, 255.

60   Jonathan Bailey, *The First World War and the Birth of the Modern Style of Warfare*, Occasional Paper 22 (Camberley: SCSI, 1996); James R. Fitzsimonds and Jan M. Van Tol, 'Revolutions in Military Affairs', *Joint Force Quarterly*, spring 1994, 25–6; Robin Prior and Trevor Wilson, *Command on the Western Front: The Military Career of Sir Henry Rawlinson 1914–18* (Oxford: Blackwell, 1992), 309; G.D. Sheffield, '*Blitzkrieg* and Attrition: Land Operations in Europe 1914–45', in G.D. Sheffield and Colin McInnes (eds), *Warfare in the Twentieth Century: Theory and Practice* (London: Unwin-Hyman, 1988).

61 Ian Malcolm Brown, *British Logistics on the Western Front 1914–1919* (Westport, Connecticut: Praeger, 1998), 197–8

62 H. Stewart, *The New Zealand Division 1916–1919* (Auckland: Whitcombe & Tombs, 1921), 73–90.

63 Ibid., 159.

64 See '4th NZ Infantry Brigade, Narrative of events…October 4th 1917', Sir Herbert Hart Papers, 1990.1026, KMARL.

65 Hart, diary, 12 Oct 1917, Hart Papers, 1990.1021.

66 'Administrative Report…1st Canadian Division at Passchendaele…', 7 Dec 1917, MG30 E54, Vol. 2, file 15, Phelan Papers, National Archives of Canada.

67 Hart, diary, 24 Aug 1918, Hart Papers, 1990.1021.

68 3rd NZ (Rifle) Brigade, 'Report on the Capture of Le Quesnoy, 21 Nov. 1918', Hart Papers, 1990.1047.

Chapter 2: Ian McGibbon

1 'Their sacrifice has helped form the nation', *Dominion Post*, 25 Apr 2003.

2 On this aspect see Ian McGibbon, 'The abuse of history', *New Zealand International Review*, Vol. 26, No. 1 (2001), 28–9.

3 Richard G.H. Kay, 'In Pursuit of Victory: British-New Zealand Relations During the First World War' (PhD thesis, University of Otago, 2001), 31.

4 Baker, 15.

5 Hew Strachan, *The First World War, Volume 1, To Arms* (Oxford: OUP, 2001), 162.

6 Baker, 11.

7 See, e.g., Jock Phillips, *A Man's Country? The Image of the Pakeha Male – A History* (Auckland: Penguin, 1987), 139.

8 CID102-C, II, 'Imperial Naval Policy', Apr 1913, read by Churchill to the Committee of Imperial Defence on 11 April, quoted in Ian McGibbon, *The Path to Gallipoli, Defending New Zealand 1840–1915* (Wellington: GP Books, 1991), 221.

9 See Jürgen Rampke (ed.), *'Ruthless Warfare', German military planning and surveillance in the Australian-New Zealand region before the Great War* (Canberra: Southern Highlands Publishers, 1988), 17.

10 McGibbon, *Gallipoli*, 6.

11 Ibid., 49.

12 John Crawford with Ellen Ellis, *To Fight for the Empire, An Illustrated History of New Zealand and the South African War, 1899–1902* (Auckland: Reed, 1999), 9.

13 James Belich, *Paradise Reforged, A History of the New Zealanders from the 1880s to the Year 2000* (Auckland: Penguin, 2002), 95.

14 'Naval and Military Defence of the Empire 1909', *AJHR*, A-4A, 1909, 19.

15 Ward to Nicholson, 7 Aug 1909, in 'Scheme for the Reorganization of the Military Forces of New Zealand', 23 Aug 1909, 11, ANZ, Allen Papers, Box 11.

16 'Scheme for the Reorganization of the Military Forces of New Zealand', 23 Aug 1909, 5, ANZ, Allen Papers, Box 11.

17 Ibid., 9.

18 Belich, *Paradise*, 109.

19 McGibbon, *Gallipoli*, 239–41.

20 Ibid., 242.

21 *NZPD*, Vol. 169 (31 Jul 1914), p.369.

22 McGibbon, *Gallipoli*, 239.

23 *NZPD*, Vol. 169 (8 Aug 1914), 488.

24 Ibid., 811.

25 Belich, *Paradise*, 111.
26 McGibbon, *Gallipoli*, 230.
27 See Belich, *Paradise*, 110: 'New Zealand itself did very little to protect its recolonial lifeline'.
28 McGibbon, *Gallipoli*, 248.
29 Ibid., 242–3.
30 Michael King, *The Penguin History of New Zealand* (Auckland: Penguin, 2003), 294.
31 W.D. Stewart, *Sir Francis H.D. Bell, PC, GCMG, His Life and Times* (Wellington: Butterworth, 1937), 115.
32 See, e.g., King, 294.
33 McGibbon, *Gallipoli*, 249.
34 Ibid.
35 Kay, 66.
36 Sergeant S.J. Smith, 'The Seizure and Occupation of Samoa', in Lieutenant H.T.B. Drew (ed.), *The War Effort of New Zealand* (Wellington: Whitcombe & Tombs, 1923), 27.
37 Stewart, *Bell*, 116.
38 King, 294.
39 I.C. McGibbon, *Blue-water Rationale, The Naval Defence of New Zealand 1914–42* (Wellington: Historical Publications Branch, 1981), 21.
40 King, 294.
41 Strachan, 508.
42 Baker, 15.
43 McGibbon, *Blue-water*, 22.
44 Ibid., 24, n32.
45 Ibid., 27.
46 Ibid., 26, n45.
47 Ibid., 26.
48 Lieutenant-Colonel J.L. Sleeman, 'The Supply of Reinforcements during the War', in Drew, 2.

Chapter 3: Pierre Purseigle

1 *Press* (Christchurch), 7 Oct 1914, 'The Maori and the Belgians. Honouring the Belgian flag'.
2 Archives Générales du Royaume, Brusselles (hereinafter AGR), T.533, 9–16.
3 Notable exceptions are Peter Cahalan, *Belgian refugee relief in England during the Great War* (New York: Garland, 1982), Peter Gatrell, *A whole empire walking. Refugees in Russia during World War I* (Bloomington and Indianapolis: Indiana UP, 1999), Tony Kushner and Katharine Knox, *Refugees in an age of genocide. Global, National and Local Perspectives during the Twentieth Century* (London & Portland: Frank Cass, 1999).
4 John N. Horne (ed.), *State, society, and mobilization in Europe during the First World War* (Cambridge: CUP, 1997).
5 Stéphane Audoin-Rouzeau and Annette Becker, *14–18: Retrouver la guerre* (Paris: Gallimard, 2000).
6 Archives Départementales de l'Hérault (hereafter ADH) 2 R 729, *Appel du Ministre de l'Intérieur aux maires de France*, 1 Dec 1914.
7 *Le Petit Parisien*, 17 Aug 1914 ; *Petit Méridional*, 2 Sep 1914, and *Bulletin mensuel de l'association amicale des instituteurs et institutrices de l'Hérault*; Archives Municipales de Béziers H 43.
8 Préfecture de Police de Paris, DB 323.
9 *Bulletin mensuel de l'association amicale des instituteurs et institutrices de l'Hérault,* Feb 1915.

10   AGR Brusselles, T.533, 9–16.

11   Miss A. Essington-Nelson, 86/48/1, Imperial War Museum (IWM).

12   *Le Petit Parisien*, 31 Aug 1914.

13   *The Times*, 10 Sep 1914.

14   Horne and Kramer; Jay Winter, 'Propaganda and the mobilization of consent,' in Strachan, *Illustrated*, 216–26, 218.

15   Michael Jeismann, *La patrie de l'ennemi. La notion d'ennemi national et la représentation de la nation en Allemagne et en France de 1792 à 1918* (Paris: CNRS Editions, 1997), 301.

16   *The Times*, 14 Sep 1914.

17   ADH 3 R 30, telegram from the Interior Minister to the Prefects, 2 Dec and 3 Nov 1914.

18   ADH 2 R 729, *Appel du Ministre de l'Intérieur aux maires de France*, 1 Dec 1914.

19   ADH 3 R 31.

20   'Instructions portant fixation du régime des réfugiés', *Journal Officiel de la République Française*, 17 Feb 1918.

21   Ibid.

22   Roger Chartier, *Au Bord de la Falaise: L'histoire entre certitudes et inquiétude* (Paris: Albin Michel, 1998), Antoine Prost, 'Sociale et culturelle indissociablement,' in Jean-Pierre Rioux, Jean-François Sirinelli and Annette Becker (eds.), *Pour une histoire culturelle* (Paris: Le Seuil, 1997), 131–46.

23   Horne and Kramer.

24   Ibid., 175f.

25   *Le Petit Parisien*, 27 Aug 1914.

26   *The Times*, 2 Sep 1914.

27   Ernest Gaubert, *Scènes et types de réfugiés (notes d'un sous-préfet)*, in *La Revue de Paris*, n°10, 22ème année, 15 May 1915; J. Wallon, *Une cité belge sur la tamise* (Brusselles-London, Librairie Moderne, s.d.); *Reports of the Newport (Mon.) Belgian refugees committee, and forty other Belgian refugees committees in Monmouthshire and neighbourhood*, Bibliothèque de Documentation Internationale Contemporaine (hereafter BDIC), O 8947; William H. Holloway, *Northamptonshire and the Great War* (Northampton: Northampton Independent, c.1920).

28   ADH 2 R 729, *Appel du Ministre de l'Intérieur aux maires de France*, 1 Dec 1914.

29   ADH 10 R 43.

30   *Petit Méridional*, 8 Sep 1914.

31   Stéphane Audoin-Rouzeau, 'Violence et consentement: la « culture de guerre » du premier conflit mondial', in Rioux, Sirinelli and Becker, 251–70, 259.

32   Gaubert, passim.

33   *The Times*, 14 Sep 1914.

34   Cahalan, 170–1.

35   *Reports of the Newport (Mon.) Belgian refugees committee, and forty other Belgian refugees committees in Monmouthshire and neighbourhood*, BDIC O 8947.

36   *Le Petit Parisien*, 29 Aug 1914.

37   Armand Varlez, *Les Belges en exil* (Brusselles-London: Librairie Moderne, 1917), 40.

38   Holloway, 220.

39   Miss A. Essington-Nelson, 86/48/1.

40   Varlez, 40.

41   Miss A. Essington-Nelson, 86/48/1.

42   *Report on the work undertaken by the British government in the reception and care of the Belgian refugees*, 1920, BDIC O 10164.

43   ADH Par 2267, *Bulletin mensuel de l'association amicale des instituteurs et institutrices de l'Hérault.*

44 'Memorandum (n°2) for the use of Local Committees for the Care of Belgian Refugees', in *Report on the work undertaken by the British government in the reception and care of the Belgian refugees*, 1920, BDIC O 10164, 94.

45 And in the British case, ministers were happy to leave philanthropy to bear the burden of the support needed by the refugees. See the debate held in the Commons on 31 August 1914, *UK Parliamentary Debates*, 1914. PM: 'We all have the greatest sympathy with these destitute refugees from a country for which we feel so much as we do at this moment, but there is a certain number of funds which are being raised by private action for the purpose, and I would rather wait and see how that works out before answering the Noble Lord's question'. For a broader perspective, see Pierre Purseigle, '1914–1918: Les combats de l'arrière. Etude comparée des mobilisations sociales en France et en Grande-Bretagne', in Nicolas Beaupre, Anne Dumenil and Christian Ingrao (eds.), *Experiences de guerre, 1914–1945* (Paris: Agnès Viénot Editions, 2004), 131–51.

46 *Report on the work undertaken by the British government in the reception and care of the Belgian refugees*, 1920, BDIC O 10164, 15.

47 MH8/7, UKNA, and Cahalan, 86.

48 *Report on the work undertaken by the British government in the reception and care of the Belgian refugees*, 1920, BDIC O 10164, 99.

49 Horne.

50 ADH 3R33.

51 Mrs E. Fernside, Con shelf & 92/49/1, IWM; 23 May 1916.

52 Miss Coules, M 97/25/1, IWM.

53 George Mosse, *Fallen Soldiers: Reshaping the memory of the world wars* (Oxford: OUP, 1990).

54 Pierre Purseigle, 'Beyond and below the nations. Towards a comparative history of local communities at war', in Jenny Macleod and Pierre Purseigle (eds), *Uncovered fields. Perspectives in First World War studies* (Boston & Leyden: Brill Academic Publisher, 2004), 95–123; Eve Rosenhaft, 'Restoring moral order on the Home Front: Compulsory savings plans for young workers in Germany, 1916–1919', in Frans Coetzee and Marilyn Shevin-Coetzee (eds), *Authority, identity, and the social history of the Great War* (Providence & Oxford: Berghahn Books, 1995), 81–109.

55 John N. Horne, 'Soldiers, civilians and the warfare of attrition. Representations of combats in France, 1914–18', in Coetzee and Shevin-Coetzee, 223–49.

56 Cahalan, 13.

57 Varlez, 10.

58 Gaubert, 377.

59 ADH 3 R 2*.

60 *Glasgow Herald*, 7 Nov 1917.

61 For a Swiss example see *Les réfugiés belges en Suisse. Réception et hospitalisation dans le Canton de Vaud* (Lausanne: Ed. Léon Martinet, 1915) and *Reims à Paris*, Bulletin des réfugiés de la Marne, 3 Nov 1915.

62 A Flemish-speaking refugee recalled how he was arrested, in Alton, Hampshire, along with a group of fellow Belgians by a Scottish officer who had wrongly identified them as Germans. See Kushner and Knox, 61.

63 Service Historique de l'Armée de Terre, Vincennes 16N1536 'L'état de l'opinion du 15 juin au 15 juillet' and 7N868.

64 Cardiff Refugee Committee, *Report on the work undertaken by the British government in the reception and care of the Belgian refugees*, 1920, BDIC O 10164.

65 Annette Becker, *Oubliés de la Grande Guerre. Humanitaire et culture de guerre 1914–1918. Populations occupées, déportés civils, prisonniers de guerre* (Paris: Noesis, 1998).

66 Gatrell, 2.

67 Stéphanie Claisse, *La mémoire de la guerre 1914–1918 à travers les monuments aux morts des communes d'Etalle, Habay, Léglise et Tintigny*, *Etudes sur la Première Guerre Mondiale* (Brusselles: Archives Générales du Royaume, 2002).

68 Kushner, 49.

69 In accordance with the most recent discussions of the concept, 'total war' is here understood as an 'ideal type' *à la Weber*, insofar as it emphasizes specific dimensions of warfare while making possible diachronic and comparative analysis. See Manfred Boemeke, Roger Chickering, and Stig Förster (eds), *Anticipating total war: the German and American experiences, 1871–1914*, *Publications of the German Historical Institute* (Cambridge: CUP, 1999); Roger Chickering and Stig Förster (eds), *Great War, Total War, Combat and mobilization on the western front, 1914–1918* (Cambridge: CUP, 2000), Roger Chickering and Stig Förster (eds), *The shadows of total war: Europe, East Asia, and the United States, 1919–1939*, *Publications of the German Historical Institute* (Cambridge: CUP, 2003), Stig Förster and Jörg Nagler (eds), *On the road to total war: the American Civil War and the German Wars of Unification, 1861–1871*, *Publications of the German Historical Institute* (Washington DC-Cambridge: German Historical Institute; CUP, 1997).

70 Chickering and Förster, 13.

71 Jane Kramer, *Unsettling Europe* (New York: Vintage Books, 1981).

Chapter 4: Megan Hutching

1 *NZ Truth*, 8 Aug 1914, 7.

2 Ibid.

3 *Press*, 6 Aug 1914, 8.

4 *NZH*, 6 Aug 1914, 9.

5 Charles Mackie to Egerton Gill, 2 Sep 1914, Papers of Charles Mackie, Series 47, Canterbury Museum.

6 Photocopy of letter from Sarah Saunders Page and Ada Wells to Jane Addams, 14 Dec 1915, in Box 23, folder 11, WILPF Papers, Norlin Library, University of Colorado, in Women's International League for Peace and Freedom Papers, ATL.

7 Manifesto of the Woman's Peace Party, cited in Anne Wiltsher, *Most Dangerous Women: Feminist peace campaigners of the Great War* (London: Pandora Press, 1985), App 1, 218.

8 Carmel Mary Shute, 'Heroines and Heroes: Sexual Mythology in Australia 1914–1918', *Hecate*, Vol. 1, No. 1 (1975), 11.

9 Carmel Mary Shute, 'Australian Women and the Great War: Aspects of Ideological Change, with Particular Emphasis on Queensland' (BA (Hons) thesis, University of Queensland, 1973), 64.

10 Malcolm Saunders and Ralph Summy, *The Australian Peace Movement: A Short History* (Canberra: Peace Research Centre, 1986), 19.

11 The first verse went as follows:
    'I didn't raise my son to be a soldier
    I brought him up to be my pride and joy,
    Who dares to put a musket on his shoulder
    To shoot some other mother's darling boy.'

12 Shute, 'Heroines and Heroes', 12.

13 Ibid., 11.

14 'Now I Dare To Do It', an interview with Dr Aletta Jacobs, in Blanche Wiesen Cook (ed.), *Crystal Eastman on Women and Revolution* (New York: OUP, 1978), 238.

15 Ibid.

16 *MW*, 10 May 1916, 3.

17 Emily Hobhouse to Kate Sheppard, 27 Sep 1915, photocopy of letter from Box 23, folder

11, WILPF papers, Norlin Library, University of Colorado, in WILPF Papers.

18 *LT*, 15 Mar 1916, 3.

19 The figures from a total response of 187,593 men between 19 and 45 were: 109,683 (58%) were prepared to volunteer for overseas service; 43,425 (23.2%) would volunteer for civil service in New Zealand; 34,386 (18.3%) would volunteer for neither. Figures from Baker, 58.

20 *LT*, 29 Apr 1916, 4.

21 Russell's letter was published in ibid., 28 Apr 1916, 5.

22 Ibid., 29 Apr 1916, 4.

23 Page's letter was published in the *MW*, 17 May 1916, 3.

24 Ibid.

25 Ibid., 6 Oct 1915, 2.

26 See Baker, ch. 4, for a detailed discussion of the Act.

27 *MW*, 14 Jun 1916, 2.

28 Ibid.

29 Ibid.

30 Ibid.

31 *EP*, 10 Jun 1916, 6.

32 *LT*, 12 Jun 1916, 9.

33 *MW*, 29 Mar 1916, 3.

34 Ibid., 13 Dec 1916, 13.

35 Ibid., 7.

36 Ibid., 12.

37 Ibid.

38 Ibid.

39 Ibid.

40 Ibid.

41 Ibid.

Chapter 5: Monty Soutar

1 *Te Kopara,* No. 12, Sep 1914, 8.

2 Sir Apirana Ngata, 'The Maori in the Second World War,' unpublished manuscript, 1943, MS-Papers-6919-0234, ATL.

3 James Cowan, *The Maoris in the Great War: a history of the Native Contingent and Pioneer Battalion – Gallipoli 1915, France and Flanders 1916–18* (Wellington: Whitcombe & Tombs Ltd, 1926).

4 Christopher Pugsley, *Te Hokowhitu a Tu: the Maori Pioneer Battalion in the First World War* (Auckland: Reed Books, 1995), 36.

5 J. B. Condiffe, *Te Rangihiroa: the life of Sir Peter Buck* (Christchurch: Whitcombe & Tombs, 1971), 132.

6 *Pipiwharauroa: he kupu whakamarama,* No. 26, 1 Apr 1900, 5.

7 Ngata, op. cit.

8 Ibid.

9 Ibid.

10 P.S. O'Connor, 'The Recruitment of Maori Soldiers, 1914–18', *Political Science,* Vol. 19, No. 2 (1967), 81.

11 Ngata, op. cit.

12 Ibid.

13 Ibid.

14 Ibid.

Chapter 6: Jennifer D. Keene

1   The total force raised during the war numbered 4,412,533, including 3,893,340 soldiers, 462,229 sailors, 54,690 marines and 2294 Coast Guard troops. Of the 3,893,340 soldiers, 2,810,296 (72%) were conscripted. Office of the Provost Marshal General, *Second Report of the Provost Marshal General to the Secretary of War on the Operations of the Selective Service System to December 20, 1918* (Washington, DC: GPO, 1919), 227.

2   Harold Wool, *The Military Specialist: Skilled Manpower for the Armed Forces* (Baltimore, Maryland: Johns Hopkins UP, 1968), 17, 195.

3   Secretary of War Newton E. Baker to President Woodrow Wilson, 1 May 1918, and undated May letter. Both in 'W, May 1918' folder. Newton E. Baker Papers, Library of Congress, Washington, DC.

4   John M. Lindley, '*A Soldier is Also a Citizen,*' *The Controversy over Military Justice, 1917–1920* (New York: Garland Publishing, Inc., 1990), 109.

5   Jennifer D. Keene, *Doughboys, the Great War and the Remaking of America* (Baltimore, Maryland: Johns Hopkins UP, 2001), 83–98.

6   Memorandum for the Chief of Staff, 6 May 1919, file # 8142-199, Entry 296, RG 165, USNA.

7   Mark W. Van Wienen (ed.), *Rendezvous with Death, American Poems of the Great War* (Urbana: University of Illinois Press, 2002), 190.

8   Second Lieutenant D. Dinsome, undated letter to mother, 103 Field Artillery, 26 Division, World War I Survey, US Army Military History Institute, Carlisle, Pennsylvania.

9   Memorandum for Chief of Staff, 4 Feb 1918, file # 10288-10, Entry 296, RG 165, USNA.

10   Sergeant A.J. Hanna, 20 Sep 1918, reprinted in J. Stuart Richards (ed.), *Pennsylvanian Voices of the Great War: Letters, Stories, and Oral Histories of World War I* (Jefferson, North Carolina: McFarland & Co., 2002), 164.

11   Private J. Maleski, 30 Infantry Regiment, 3 Division, 1 Aug 1918, in ibid., 108.

12   Horace Pippin, 'My Life's Story,' in Selden Rodman, *Horace Pippin: A Negro Painter in America* (New York: The Quadrangle Press, 1947), 79.

13   Unpublished war memoir, 54, reel 138, Horace Pippin War Memoirs, Letters and Photographs, Archives of American Art, Smithsonian Institution, Washington, DC.

14   Undated letter to 'My Dear Friends,' Pippin Papers.

15   Lieutenant J. Brown to his wife, 23 Jun 1918, after his participation in the battle of Belleau Wood. Quoted in Mark Meigs, *Optimism at Armageddon: Voices of American Participants in the First World War* (New York: New York UP, 1997), 49.

16   'Appréciations des troupes françaises sur les troupes américaines d'après le contrôle de la correspondance du 15 juin au juillet 1918,' Série 17N 47, Service historique de l'armée de terre, Château de Vincennes, Paris.

17   Private P. Maxwell, memoir, 314 Fd Arty, 80 Division, World War I Survey.

18   R.B. Rathbun, quoted in *Des Moines Register*, 5 Jul 1978, in Bill Douglas, 'Wartime Illusions and Disillusionment: Camp Dodge and Racial Stereotyping, 1917–1918,' *The Annals of Iowa*, No. 57 (1998), 127.

19   The 317 Infantry Regiment of the 80 Division advanced 1½ miles with the New Zealand Division on 14 August 1918 to occupy the villages of Serre and Puisieux-au-Mont in the Somme, an easy advance over territory that the Germans had recently evacuated. American Battlefield Monuments Commission, *American Armies and Battlefields in Europe* (GPO: Washington, DC, 1938), 407.

20   Chaplain J.R. Laughton, 80 Division, 'The Cross in the Tempest: Personal War Experiences,' World War I Survey.

21   Edley Craighill, *History of the 317th Infantry* (n.p., n.d.), 46–8, and Memorandum to Commanding General, 159 Brigade, 15 Dec 1918. Both in Entry 270, G-3 Operations Reports, RG 120, USNA.

22   Anson Eldred, *Overseas Diary of Company "G" 317th Infantry, France, June 1918–June 1919* (n.p., 1919), 4.

23   Joseph Morris, *Revised History of Company "F" 317th Infantry, 80th Division, World War I* (Suffolk, Va, n.d), 7.

24   Commission contrôle postal militaire, 27 Oct 1918, Série 16N 1397, Vincennes.

25   Contrôle postal militaire, 10e Armée, 8 Dec 1918, Série 16N 1447, Vincennes.

26   'The American Military Factor in the War,' 14 Jan 1918, file #811.20/I; Entry 27, RG 256, USNA.

27   Stéphane Audoin-Rouzeau and Annette Becker, *14–18, Understanding the Great War* (New York: Hill & Wang, 2002), 22. Audoin-Rouzeau also points out that the daily losses for the Americans in the First World War exceeded that of the Second World War, during which the United States lost 123 soldiers per day. Stéphane Audoin-Rouzeau, 'Au Coeur de la Guerre: La Violence du Champ de Bataille Pendant les Deux Conflits Mondiaux,' in Stéphane Audoin-Rouzeau, Annette Becker, Christian Ingrao, Henry Rousso (eds), *La Violence de guerre, 1914–1945* (Editions Complexe, 2002), 79.

28   Private Hervey Allan, quoted in Ronald Schaffer, *America in the Great War: The Rise of the War Welfare State* (New York: OUP, 1991), 158.

29   Edward Coffman, *The War to End All Wars: The Military Experience in World War I* (New York: OUP, 1968), 289.

30   Noble Sissle, 'Memoirs of Lieutenant "Jim" Europe,' (1942), 168, box J-56, National Association for the Advancement of Colored People Papers, Part II, Library of Congress, Washington, DC.

31   Harry Haywood, *Black Bolshevik: Autobiography of an Afro-American Communist* (Chicago: Liberator Press, 1978), 58.

32   Memorandum for Inspector General's Office, 11 Dec 1918, folder #123; Entry 22, RG 120, USNA.

33   Memorandum for General Spinks, Office of the Inspector General, 11 Oct 1918, file # 1008, Entry 588, RG 120, USNA.

34   Timothy K. Nenninger, 'American Military Effectiveness in the First World War,' in Allan R. Millett and Williamson Murray (eds), *Military Effectiveness*, Vol. 1: *The First World War*, (Boston: Allen & Unwin, 1988), 116–56.

35   Meirion and Susie Harries, *The Last Days of Innocence: America at War, 1917–1918* (New York: Vintage Books, 1997), 382.

Chapter 7: Richard Kay

This paper is a shortened version of 'Chapter Seven: New Zealand and the Paris Peace Conference' that appears in R.G.H. Kay, 'In Pursuit of Victory: British-New Zealand Relations During the First World War' (PhD thesis, UO, 2001), 227–95.

1   B.H. Wall, 'William Ferguson Massey and the Paris Peace Conference, 1919' (MA thesis, VUW, 1946); V.B. Lo, 'New Zealand, the British Empire and the Paris Peace Conference of 1919' (MA thesis, UA, 1967); R.C. Snelling, 'Australia, New Zealand and the British Empire Delegation at Versailles', *Journal of Imperial and Commonwealth History*, Vol. 4, No. 1 (1975), 15.

2   Snelling, 'Versailles', 15.

3   SS Cols to GGNZ, 11 Nov 1918, Governor's records (G)43/2, ANZ.

4   *NZPD*, Vol. 183, 823.

5   Ibid., 12 Nov 1918, 342–3; Geoffrey Rice, *Black November: The 1918 Influenza Epidemic in*

New Zealand (Wellington: Allen & Unwin/Historical Branch, 1988), 74–5, 88–9.

6 SS Cols to GGNZ, 28 Oct 1918, G43/2; Lloyd George to Massey and Sir W.F. Lloyd (Newfoundland PM), 27 Oct 1918, Lloyd George Papers, F/36/4/4, House of Lords Record Office, London.

7 SS Cols to GGNZ, 24 Nov 1918, G43/2.

8 *NZPD*, Vol. 183, 538. See also *ODT,* 29 Nov 1918, 4.

9 *ODT*, 11 Dec 1918, 6.

10 *NZPD*, Vol. 183, 537–40.

11 Ibid.

12 Ibid., 1035–6; Massey to Lloyd George, 5 Jan 1918, G41/32.

13 *NZPD*, Vol. 183, 1036–41.

14 See Imperial War Cabinet, Meeting 48#, 31 Dec 1918, External Affairs records (EA)11/5, ANZ; SS Cols to GGNZ, 10 Jan 1918, G41/42.

15 Hankey to BED, 13 Jan 1919, William Morris Hughes Papers, MS1538/24/13, NLA.

16 *NZH*, 30 Jan 1919, 5; *NZ Times*, 8 Feb 1919, 1; Massey to Allen, 13 Feb 1919, Allen Papers, Box 9a, ANZ; *ODT*, 21 Jan 1919, 5.

17 *ODT*, 24 Jan 1919, 5; Godley to Allen, 21 Jan 1919, War Archives (WA)252/5, ANZ; see L.F. Fitzhardinge, 'W.M. Hughes and the Treaty of Versailles, 1919', *Journal of Commonwealth Political Studies*, Vol. 5, No. 2 (1967), 132–3.

18 *ODT*, 3 Feb 1919, 5; *ST*, 25 Jan 1919, 5.

19 D.L. George, *War Memoirs of David Lloyd George*, Vol. II (London: Odhams Press, 1938), 2006. Baker, 138.

20 BED, Meeting 3#, 23 Jan 1919, in M. Dockrill (ed.), *British Documents on Foreign Affairs: Reports and Papers from the Foreign Office Confidential Print: Part II: From the First to the Second World War: Series I: The Paris Peace Conference of 1919: Volume 3: Supreme Council Minutes, March–July 1919; British Empire Delegation Minutes, January–March 1919* (Frederick: University Publications of America, 1989), 333.

21 *ODT*, 31 Jan 1919, 5; Hankey, *Supreme*, 36. US Department of State, *Papers Relating to the Foreign Relations of the United States 1919: The Paris Peace Conference* (hereinafter *FRUS:PPC*) (Washington: US Govt Printing Office, 1942–3), Vol. 3, 13; Massey to Allen, 26 Apr 1919, Box 9a, Allen Papers.

22 Massey to Allen, 13 Feb 1919, Massey to Allen, 26 Apr 1919, Allen Papers, Box 9a.

23 Long to Balfour, 8 Jan 1919, Long Papers, FO800/207/3; Long to Balfour, 8 Jan 1919, ibid., WRO947/532/8a; Long to Liverpool, 7 Nov 1918, ibid., WRO947/615/95; SS Cols to GGNZ, 30 Oct 1918, G2/47.

24 Imperial War Cabinet, Meeting 44#, 20 Dec 1918, EA11/5; War Cabinet 459# (Imperial War Cabinet, Meeting 32#), 15 Aug 1918, EA11/5; GGNZ to SS Cols, 16 Nov 1919, G41/40.

25 See R.H. Fifield, *Woodrow Wilson and the Far East: The Diplomacy of the Shantung Question* (Hamden: Archon Books, 1965), 125–39.

26 WCP 42#, 'Mandatory System of the League of Nations', by A.J. Balfour, 27 Jan 1919, FO608/242/1634/1/1. See also D.L George, *The Truth About the Peace Treaties*, Vol. 1 (London: Victor Gollancz, 1938), 554–7.

27 BED, Meeting 4#, 27 Jan 1919, Garran Papers, CP351/1/4/7, Australian Archives, Canberra.

28 S.P. Tillman, *Anglo-American Relations at the Paris Peace Conference of 1919* (Princeton: PUP, 1961), 70.

29 W.R. Louis, *Great Britain and Germany's Lost Colonies 1914–1919* (Oxford: Clarendon Press, 1967), 133. For a more positive assessment of Massey's speech see Hankey, *Supreme*, 59.

30 *FRUS:PPC*, III, 749–52.

31   H. Borden (ed.) with A. Meighen, *Robert Laird Borden: His Memoirs*, Vol. 2 (London: Macmillan, 1938), 906.

32   *FRUS:PPC*, III, 752–3. Also see SS Cols to GGNZ, 2 Feb 1919, G44/1; GGNZ to SS Cols, 11 Dec 1918, G41/41; George, *Truth*, I, 522–3.

33   Hankey, *Supreme*, 60; George, *Truth*, I, 538.

34   See J.G. Latham, 'Reviews: *Prosper the Commonwealth*. By Sir R.R. Garran', *Historical Studies: Australian and New Zealand*, Vol. 9, No. 33 (1959), 105; S.W. Roskill, *Hankey: Man of Secrets, Volume II 1919–1931* (London: St Martin's Press, 1972), 54; P. Spartalis, *The Diplomatic Battles of Billy Hughes* (Sydney: Hale & Iremonger, 1983), 133.

35   Hughes to Watt, 29 Jan 1919, CP360/8/1/3, AA; A.S. Link *et al.* (eds), *The Papers of Woodrow Wilson, 69 vols* (Princeton: PUP, 1966–94), Vol. 54, 347.

36   George, *Truth*, I, 541.

37   Link, Vol. 54, 386; P.H. Kerr to Milner, 31 Jan 1919, Milner Papers, MS. Eng. hist. 700/193, Bodleian Library, Oxford.

38   Lord Riddell, *Lord Riddell's Intimate Diary of the Peace Conference and After 1918–1923* (London: Victor Gollancz, 1933), 16–7; Borden, II, 907. See also P.H. Kerr to Milner, 31 Jan 1919, Milner Papers, MS. Eng. hist. 700/193.

39   See, e.g., W.J. Hudson, *Billy Hughes in Paris: The Birth of Australian Diplomacy* (Melbourne: Thomas Nelson/AIIA, 1978), 26; Spartalis, 138–9.

40   *FRUS:PPC*, III, 797–800.

41   Ibid., 804–17.

42   For contrasting views on this point see Tillman, 97; H.J. Hiery, *The Neglected War: The German South Pacific and the Influence of World War I* (Honolulu: University of Hawai'i Press, 1995), 209; Fitzhardinge, 137.

43   Godley to Allen, 7 Feb 1919, WA252/5, ANZ.

44   BED, Meeting 9#, 20 Feb 1919, Milner Papers, MS. Milner dep. 389/17.

45   Tillman, 98; Allen to Massey, 17 Jan 1919, Allen Papers, Box 9a.

46   Hall, 360; Hughes to Watt, 10 Feb 1919, CP360/8/1/3; WCP 71#, 'Australia and the Pacific Islands', by W.M. Hughes, 6 Feb 1919, Cook Papers, MS762/3; 'Minute', 31 Mar 1919, FO608/211/642/2/1; Cecil to Balfour, 10 Mar 1919, FO608/211/642/2/1.

47   WCP 745#, 'Mandates. Note for British Empire Delegation', by Hankey, 7 May 1919, Milner Papers, MS. Milner dep. 389/63; Massey to Allen, 26 Apr 1919, Allen Papers, Box 9a.

48   Taken from Spartalis, 172.

49   Borden, II, 926–7; Tillman, 302–3; Spartalis, 175; Fitzhardinge, 139.

50   S. Brawley, *The White Peril: Foreign Relations and Asian Immigration to Australasia and North America 1919–78* (Sydney: University of NSW Press, 1995), 17.

51   E.M. Andrews, *The ANZAC Illusion: Anglo-Australian Relations During World War I* (Cambridge: CUP, 1993), 209.

52   P.S. O'Connor, 'Keeping New Zealand White, 1908–1920', *NZJH*, Vol. 2, No. 1 (1968), 41–65.

53   'Minutes of the Sub-Committee of the Imperial War Cabinet on Territorial Desiderata in the Terms of Peace', Meeting 1#, 17 Apr 1917, PM14/34.

54   O'Connor, 'White', 41.

55   Spartalis, 178.

56   Ibid., 164.

57   Fifield, 168; ibid., 166–7.

58   GNZ to SS Cols, 22 Jan 1915, G25/28; GNZ to SS Cols, 22 Jan 1915, *AJHR*, 1915, A-1, 33.

59   Massey to Long, 24 Aug 1918, CO209/299/764; Long to Hughes, 3 Sep 1918, CO209/299/761–2.

60 Milner to Massey, 30 Jan 1919, MS. Eng. hist 700/246, Milner Papers.

61 Massey to Bell, 17 Mar 1919, Bell Family Papers MS5210/102, ATL.

62 Massey to Milner, 8 Apr 1919, FO608/175/555/2/2.

63 Ibid., Milner to Lloyd George, 22 Apr 1919, F/39/1/14; Milner to Lloyd George, 22 Apr 1919, Milner Papers, MS. Eng. hist. 700/208; Kerr to Milner, 26 Apr 1919, Lloyd George Papers, F/39/1/15; Watt to Hughes, 28 Apr 1919, Watt to Hughes, 1 May 1919, CP360/8/1/4.

64 Hughes to Watt, 22 Apr 1919, CP360/8/1/4; Hughes to Milner, 3 May 1919, Lloyd George Papers, F/28/3/34; Hughes to Watt, 7 May 1919, CP360/8/1/4.

65 'Question of the Distribution of the Mandates Meeting', 5 May 1919, MS1538/24/1003, Hughes Papers.

66 Hughes to Watt, 7 May 1919, CP360/8/1; Hughes to Milner, 9 May 1919, Cook Papers, MS762/3; Hughes to Watt, 4 Jun 1919, CP360/8/1/4; Watt to Hughes, 9 May 1919, Hughes Papers, MS1538/6/2094; Spartalis, 149–50.

67 WCP 745#, 'Mandates', by Hankey, 7 May 1919, FO608/152/509/1/1; Massey to Lloyd George, 8 May 1919, Lloyd George Papers, F/36/4/13.

68 Hughes to Watt, 10 Jun 1919, CP360/8/1/4. Also see Lloyd George to Milner, 14 May 1919, Lloyd George Papers, F/39/1/18; Massey to Milner, 23 Jun 1919, Milner Papers, MS. Eng. hist. 700/264.

69 ODT, 5 Jul 1919, 9; 'Agreement Between His Majesty's Government in London, His Majesty's Government of the Commonwealth of Australia, and His Majesty's Government of the Dominion of New Zealand with Regard to the Island of Nauru', AJHR, 1919, H-29C, 1–2.

70 J.F. Willis, Prologue to Nuremberg: The Politics and Diplomacy of Punishing War Criminals of the First World War (Westport: Greenwood Press, 1982), 68.

71 NZPD, Vol. 183, 822; Pollock to Massey, 30 Mar 1919, Massey Papers, MS1398; Otago Witness, 12 Mar 1919, 35.

72 Massey to Bell, 17 Mar 1919, Bell Family Papers.

73 Michael Bassett, Sir Joseph Ward, A Political Biography (Auckland: AUP, 1993), 243; Allen to Stewart, 26 Mar 1919, William Downie Stewart Papers, MS985/1/1/3, Hocken Library, Dunedin; GGNZ to SS Cols, 5 Jun 1919, CO209/300/457.

74 E. Goldstein, 'Great Britain. The Home Front', in M.F. Boemeke, G.D. Feldman, and E. Glaser (eds), The Treaty of Versailles: A Reassessment After 75 Years (Cambridge: CUP, 1998), 162.

75 Massey to Allen, 26 Apr 1919, Allen Papers, Box 9a.

76 M.L. Dockrill and J.D. Goold, Peace without Promise: Britain and the Peace Conferences, 1919–23 (Hamden: Archon Books, 1981), 56; Massey to Lloyd George, 23 Jun 1919, Lloyd George Papers, F/36/4/19.

77 See 'Peace Conference Protocols', FO608/156/511/1/5.

78 NZH, 9 May 1919, 6; NZH, 10 May 1919, 9–10; George, Truth, I, 690.

79 Hughes to Munro-Ferguson, 17/19 May 1919, MS696/2800, Viscount Novar Papers, NLA.

80 Massey to Allen, 26 Apr 1919, Allen Papers, Box 9a.

81 BED, Meeting 33#, 1 Jun 1919, Garran Papers, CP351/1/4/7.

82 Ibid., and Meeting 28 #, 23 Apr 1919, Meeting 9#, 20 Feb 1919, Garran Papers, CP351/1/4/7.

83 George, Truth, I, 718–20.

84 Tillman, 356–64.

85 'Versailles Peace Treaty, 1919', Internal Affairs Department records (IA)20/5, ANZ.

86 N. Mansergh, The Commonwealth Experience: Volume One: The Durham Report to the Anglo-

Irish Treaty (Toronto: Toronto UP, 1982), 207.

87 Bell to Massey, 2 May 1919, Bell Family Papers, MS5210/049. Bell described Massey as a 'force'; B.K. Gordon, *New Zealand Becomes a Pacific Power* (Chicago: Chicago UP, 1960), 48.

88 *NZH*, 9 May 1919, 10.

89 Massey to Allen, 26 Apr 1919, Allen Papers, Box 9a.

90 As quoted in M.P. Lissington, *New Zealand and Japan 1900–1941* (Wellington: Government Printer, 1972), 47.

91 Godley to Allen, 7 Feb 1919, WA252/5; Godley to Allen, 7 Feb 1919, Allen Papers, M1/15/6; Massey to Allen, 13 Feb 1919, 26 Apr 1919, Allen Papers, Box 9a; Massey to Guthrie, 3 Mar 1919, PM9/49.

92 Ann Trotter, 'Friend or Foe? New Zealand and Japan, 1900–1937', in Roger Peren (ed.), *Japan and New Zealand, 150 Years* (Palmerston North: NZ Centre for Japanese Studies, Massey University on behalf of the Ministry of Foreign Affairs, Tokyo, 1999), 77.

93 Massey to Guthrie, 3 Mar 1919, PM9/49.

94 Massey to Milner, 3 Feb 1919, Milner Papers, MS. Eng. hist. 700/243; Milner to Massey, 11 Feb 1919, Milner Papers, MS. Eng. hist 700/244,; WCP 157#, Massey to Balfour, 27 Feb 1919, WCP 246#, Balfour to Massey, 12 Mar 1919, FO608/175/555/1/1; Massey to Milner, 28 Mar 1919, FO608/175/55/1/1.

95 Massey to Milner, 3 Mar 1919, Milner Papers, MS. Eng. hist 700/257; Milner to Massey, 15 Mar 1919, Milner Papers, MS. Eng/ hist. 700/260.

96 Sheffield, *Forgotten*, 226.

97 See McGibbon, *Blue-water*, 93–114.

98 Massey to Lloyd George, 23 Jun 1919, Lloyd George Papers, F/36/4/19.

99 Massey to Bell, 17 Mar 1919, Bell Family Papers, MS5210/102; Massey to Allen, 26 Apr 1919, Allen Papers, Box 9a. *NZPD*, Vol. 184, 2 Sep 1919, 43.

100 Massey to Lloyd George, 23 Jun 1919, Lloyd George Papers, F/36/4/19.

101 *NZPD*, Vol. 184, 43.

102 'Department of Imperial Government Supplies: Review of Operations Covering the Period From the 1st April, 1918, to the 31st March, 1919, Including An Appendix Showing Results to 23rd August, 1919', *AJHR*, 1919, H-38, 2.

Chapter 8: Jenny Macleod

1 Mike Hamilton and Shekhar Bhatia, 'Raging Istanbul', sundaymirror.co.uk, 12 Oct 2003.

2 Mark Ray, 'Gallipoli visit puts tourists in picture over teamwork', *Sydney Morning Herald*, 30 May 2001.

3 Joyce Morgan, 'Battlefield the wrong pitch for the baggy greens', ibid., 30 May 2001.

4 'Waugh enamoured by visit to Gallipoli', 28 May 2001 www.thatscricket.com/2001/test_series/ashes/280501afp-waugh.html. In November 2000, New Zealand's All Blacks visited the battlefields of the Western Front. They followed in the footsteps of the 1924 All Blacks who paid homage at the grave of David Gallaher, the former All Black captain, one of nine All Blacks who died on the Western Front. Ian McGibbon, *New Zealand Battlefields and Memorials of the Western Front* (Melbourne: OUP, 2001), 14.

5 Most notoriously, on the eve of the England versus Germany game at Euro '96, the *Sun*'s headline was 'Blitz Fritz', while the *Daily Mirror*'s front page read 'Achtung Surrender'; Mark Christopher Watkin, 'Hooligans and hacks, what's the real story?', www.hooligansfootball.homestead.com/articlesanddocs.html. This phenomenon is discussed by Martin Conboy, 'Heroes and Demons as Historical Bookmarks in the English Popular Press', in Helen Brocklehurst and Robert Phillips (eds), *History, Nationhood and the Question of Britain* (Basingstoke: Palgrave, 2004), 399–410.

6   Dennis Shanahan, 'The risky business of PM's secret trip', *Australian*, 26 Apr 2004.

7   Peter Wilson, 'Young ignore terrorist threat', ibid., 26 Apr 2004.

8   'Last Post to sound for Australian and Kiwi soldiers', *Edinburgh Evening News*, 22 Apr 2004. I am grateful to Dr Colin Faulkner and to Colonel Shepherd of the SNWM for this information.

9   David Fickling (reporting from Sydney), 'Veterans say call off Anzac Day', *Guardian*, 27 Apr 2004; Nick Squires (reporting from Sydney), 'Gallipoli pilgrims defy terrorist threat', 'Gallipoli's new heroes', *Daily Telegraph*, 26 Apr 2004.

10 Ellis Ashmead-Bartlett, 'Great attack on the Dardanelles. Fleets and armies. Allied troops land in Gallipoli. Success of operations. Large forces advance', *Daily Telegraph*, 27 Apr 1915. Kevin Fewster, 'Ellis Ashmead-Bartlett and the Making of the Anzac Legend', *Journal of Australian Studies*, Vol. 10 (1982).

11 C.E.W. Bean (ed.), *The Anzac Book* (London: Cassell & Co., 1916). Bean edited the 12-volume Australian official history of the war, and wrote six of the volumes himself, including the two covering the Gallipoli campaign: C.E.W. Bean, *The Story of Anzac*, 2 vols (St. Lucia, Queensland, 1981; first published 1921–4); K.S. Inglis, 'A Sacred Place: The Making of the Australian War Memorial', *War and Society*, Vol. 3, No. 2 (1985), 99–126.

12 E.K. Bowden, 'Australian war histories. Renewal of engagement of Official Historian (Mr C.E.W. Bean)', 4 Jun 1924, Bean Papers, AWM38, 3DRL 6673, item 11, AWM.

13 C.E.W. Bean, 'The writing of the Australian Official History of the Great War – sources, methods and some conclusions', *Royal Australian Historical Society Journal and Proceedings*, Vol. 24, No. 2 (1938), 91.

14 Jenny Macleod, 'The Fall and Rise of Anzac Day: 1965 and 1990 Compared', *War and Society*, Vol. 20, No. 1 (2002), 418–41.

15 Many of Inglis's articles have been collected in two recent volumes, John Lack (ed.), *Anzac Remembered: Selected Writings of K.S. Inglis* (Melbourne: University of Melbourne Department of History, 1998) and Craig Wilcox (ed.), *Observing Australia 1959 to 1999, K.S. Inglis* (Melbourne: Melbourne UP, 1999); Bill Gammage, *The Broken Years: Australian Soldiers in the Great War* (Canberra: Penguin, 1974).

16 This endeavour is discussed in Stuart Macintyre and Anna Clark, *The History Wars* (Melbourne: Melbourne UP, 2003), 102–7.

17 Debbie Kruger, 'A Future in History' (Interview with Jonathan King), *Melbourne Weekly Magazine*, 9–15 Nov 2003, www.debbiekruger.com/writer/freelance/king.html.

18 Jonathan King, *Gallipoli: Our Last Man Standing, The Extraordinary Life of Alec Campbell* (Milton: John Wiley & Sons, 2003).

19 Ibid., 1, 2–3, 21, 25.

20 Ibid., x.

21 Ibid., 7. In fact the Campbells were not conspicuous in fighting the English, taking part with them in defeating the Jacobite forces at Culloden in 1746.

22 Ibid., 93.

23 Jonathan King, 'Charge of the rewrite brigade', *Australian*, 20 Dec 2002.

24 'Anzacs "should say sorry" for Gallipoli', *NZH*, 18 Jan 2003; Martin Johnston, 'Apology absurd for "invasion"', ibid., 20 Jan 2003; Christopher Pugsley, 'Did historians have too much to drink?', ibid., 24 Jan 2003.

25 Christopher Pugsley, 'Stories of Anzac', in Jenny Macleod (ed.), *Gallipoli: Making History* (London: Frank Cass, 2004), 44–58.

26 Les Carlyon, *Gallipoli* (Sydney: Macmillan, 2001).

27 This argument is more fully developed in Jenny Macleod, *Reconsidering Gallipoli* (Manchester: MUP, 2004).

28 John Masefield, *Gallipoli* (London: Heinemann, 1916); A.P. Herbert, *The Secret Battle*

(Oxford: Methuen, 1982 [1919]); Ernest Raymond, *Tell England: A Study in a Generation* (London: Cassell & Co, 1922); Winston Churchill, *The World Crisis, 1915* (London: Thornton Butterworth, 1923).

29 Ian Hamilton, *Gallipoli Diary*, Vol. 1 (London: Edward Arnold, 1920), 28.

30 Ibid., 144.

31 Ibid., 158.

32 Hamilton to Spenser Wilkinson, 27 May 1921, Hamilton Papers, 13/113, LHCMA.

33 *Gallipoli Diary*, I, 14.

34 Brigadier-General C.F. Aspinall-Oglander, *Military Operations, Gallipoli,* 2 vols (London: Imperial War Museum in association with Battery Press, 1992; first published 1929–32).

35 This episode is also discussed in Andrew Green, *Writing the Great War: Sir James Edmonds and the Official Histories 1915–1948* (London: Frank Cass, 2003).

36 Proceedings of Meeting, i.e. sub-committee for the Control of the Official Histories, COH 5, 9 Mar 1928, 9, Cabinet Office records (CAB)16/53, UKNA.

37 Aspinall-Oglander to Liddell Hart, 31 Dec 1957, Liddell Hart papers, LH 1/23/5, LHCMA.

38 Alan Moorehead, *Gallipoli* (London: Hamish Hamilton, 1956).

39 John Connell, 'From Imbros Over the Sea', *Time and Tide* (5 May 1956), Moorehead Papers, National Library of Australia, Canberra, box 13, folder 107.

40 Robert Rhodes James, *Gallipoli* (London: B.T. Batsford, 1965).

41 Shannon Mikunda, quoted in 'Bold crowd remembers the brave', *Sydney Morning Herald* (www.smh.com.au), 26 Apr 2004.

Chapter 9: Stephen Clarke

1 The total number of deaths, including those who died after discharge from disabilities due to or aggravated by war or while training in New Zealand, was 18,166: *Roll of Hono*ur, 1.

2 Stephane Audoin-Rouzeau and Annette Becker, *1914–1918: Understanding the Great War*, trans. Catherine Temerson (London: Profile Books, 2002), 166. The impact of the First World War on combatants has been a subject of some interest over the last 30 years beginning with Antoine Prost, *In the Wake of War, 'Les Anciens Combattants' and French Society 1914–1939*, trans. Helen McPhail (Providence: Berg, 1992, orig. pub. 1977); Eric Leed, *No Man's Land: Combat and Identity in World War 1* (Cambridge: CUP, 1979); Robert Whalen, *Bitter Wounds: German Victims of the Great War 1914–1939* (Ithaca: Cornell UP, 1984); Desmond Morton and Glenn Wright, *Winning the Second Battle: Canadian Veterans and the Return to Civilian Life 1915–1930* (Toronto: University of Toronto, 1987); George Mosse, *Fallen Soldiers: Reshaping the Memory of the World Wars* (Oxford: OUP, 1990); Kent Fedorowich, *Unfit for Heroes: Reconstruction and Soldier Settlement in the Empire between the Wars* (Manchester: MUP, 1995); Stephen Garton, *The Cost of War: Australians Return* (Melbourne: OUP, 1996), and Jennifer Keene, *Doughboys, the Great War, and the Remaking of America* (Baltimore: Johns Hopkins UP, 2001).

3 *ODT*, 6 Dec 1915, 8.

4 *Press*, 23 Dec 1915, 8; *QM*, Nov 1918, 3, 10 Feb 1920, 53.

5 C.R. McLean, 'The Dunedin Returned Services' Association', 6–8, Dunedin RSA Collection, Hocken Library, Dunedin, and *QM*, Dec 1919, 45–6 (Dunedin RSA), and *Dominion*, 6, 8 Jan 1916, 4, 7 respectively (Wellington RSA).

6 Captain D. Simson, Personal File, ANZ.

7 D.J.B. Seymour, 'Inception of the NZRSA', 1, enclosed with Seymour to Sir Howard Kippenberger, 23 Jun 1949, Historic File, RNZRSA National HQ, Wellington; see statement by Simson in *Dominion*, 22 Apr 1916, 12.

8 The following description of the conference is based on handwritten minutes 'Conference

of Delegates to form Returned Soldiers' Association, 28 April 1916', RNZRSA; *Dominion*, 29 Apr 1916, 6.

9   G. Wootton, *The Official History of the British Legion* (London: Macdonald & Evans, 1956), chs 1–3, B. Harding, *Keeping Faith: The History of the The Royal British Legion* (Barnsley: Leo Cooper, 2001), ch. 1, and J. Hale, *Branching Out: The Story of The Royal Canadian Legion* (Ottawa: Royal Canadian Legion, 1995), chs 1–2.

10 DEC meeting, 26 Sep 1916; *New Zealand Returned Soldiers' Association* (Crown Print, Moray Place, Dunedin), in Historic File, RNZRSA.

11 *QM*, May 1918, 3–4; Seymour, 2. At a Christchurch race meeting back in November 1915, Simson had caused a 'sensation' when he chastised those present for enjoying themselves while their fellow New Zealanders were fighting at Gallipoli: *Star*, n.d. [c. 15 Nov 1915], reprinted in the *RSA Review*, Sep 1966, 7; see also cutting from *Dominion*, 15 Nov 1915, together with correspondence by the Minister of Defence showing his concerns, in Simson's NZEF Personal File, ANZ.

12 *QM*, Aug 1918, 18, Oct 1918, 3. The framed registration papers hang at the RNZRSA HQ in Wellington.

13 Seymour, 2. Simson departed for England, where he was linked with the Comrades of the Great War and its battles with other veteran organisations before the merger of these factions as the British Legion in 1921, of which he was a foundation executive member. He was appointed inaugural honorary secretary of the British Empire Services League in 1921, a position he held until 1944. Sir Donald Simson returned to New Zealand during the late 1940s and died in Auckland in 1961.

14 Major-General Sir Alexander Godley held a low opinion of his abilities, but Pitt was actually sent back for medical reasons, having suffered some form of heart failure: Pitt's Personal File, ANZ; O'Connor, 'Recruitment', 59.

15 DEC Sub-Committee meetings, 24 Jun, 29 Jul 1919.

16 DEC meeting, 30 Nov 1917, DEC Standing Sub-Committee, 10 Jul 1922; Seymour, 3.

17 Personal Files: Sergeant J.D. Harper, Corporal C. Batten, Major E.A. Boxer and Major-General Sir A.H. Russell, as well as obituaries in *RSA Review*, Aug 1927, 5–6 (Boxer), Jul 1950, 19 (Batten), Aug 1959, 3 (Harper), Dec 1960, 1 (Russell); also Christopher Pugsley, 'Russell, Andrew Hamilton 1868–1960', *DNZB*, Vol. 3 (Wellington, 1996), and R.F. Gambrill, 'The Russell Saga', Vol. 4, qMS 0823, ATL.

18 'NZRSA First Annual Report for the Year Ending April 30th, 1917', 1–2, printed with the proceedings of the NZRSA Conference, 25 May 1917.

19 Seymour, 3; *QM*, Jul 1918, 19–21, May 1922, 21–3.

20 Annual Report, 1917–18, printed in *QM*, Jul 1918, 19–26.

21 NZRSA Annual Conference, 27 May 1918, 9.

22 Bronwyn Dalley, 'RSA Women's Sections', in Anne Else (ed.), *Women Together: A History of Women's Organisations in New Zealand* (Wellington: Daphne Brasell Press/Historical Branch, 1993), 317–19.

23 *QM*, Jan, Feb 1919, 16–17, 23 respectively; Rice, *Black November*.

24 Drew, 164.

25 N.P. Webber, *The First Fifty Years of the New Zealand Returned Services' Association 1916 to 1966* (Wellington: NZRSA, 1966), 6.

26 *QM*, Oct 1919, 21–3, 77; *Dominion*, *EP*, 11 Sep 1919, cited in J.O. Melling, 'The New Zealand Returned Soldiers' Association 1916–1923' (MA thesis, VUW, 1952), 51–5.

27 NZRSA Annual Conference, May 1918, 10; *QM*, Jul 1919, 55–6.

28 *QM*, Oct 1919, 73–5; Melling, 45–7.

29 For the conference see *QM*, Nov 1919, 17–23, and for final organisation see ibid., Oct 1920, 31.

30 Ibid., Apr 1918, 1.
31 '[Auckland RSA] was from the beginning an organisation closely aligned with Simson's policy of hostility to the Government and favouring political action', claimed Seymour, 3.
32 *QM*, Mar 1919, 13–15, Apr 1919, 21–3.
33 For the lengthy debate see NZRSA Report of the Annual Conference, 26 May 1919, 21–74.
34 *QM*, Aug 1919, 41–4.
35 NZRSA Report of Special Conference, 17 Oct 1919, 19; *QM*, Dec 1919, 17.
36 *QM*, Dec 1919, 49–51.
37 NZRSA Annual Conference, 29 May 1920, 6; *QM*, Jul 1920, 69.
38 *QM*, Apr 1921, 57, May 1921, 43, Jul 1921, 48; DEC meetings, 7, 12 Jun 1921.
39 Melling, 42–3; for biographies of Coates and Lee see Michael Bassett, *Coates of Kaipara* (Auckland: AUP, 1995), and Erik Olssen, *John A. Lee* (Dunedin: Otago UP, 1977).
40 G.L. Kristianson, *The Politics of Patriotism: The Pressure Group Activities of the Returned Servicemen's League* (Canberra: ANU Press, 1966).
41 *QM*, Jul 1920, 69.
42 Ibid., Oct 1919, 77–9; see also NZRSA Report of Special Conference, Oct 1919, 18.
43 NZRSA, Annual Report, 1919–20, 6. The 1920 membership would not be surpassed until 1945.
44 *QM*, Jul 1920, 69.
45 DEC meeting, 26 Sep 1916.
46 In Auckland, e.g., the Women's Patriotic League gave the RSA £14,000 to build a permanent club and the council presented a site on Anzac Avenue at a nominal rental of one shilling per annum: Melling, 32.
47 *Star*, 29 Aug 1919, clipping in Internal Affairs records (IA)1, 154/70, ANZ.
48 *QM*, Sep 1920, 71.
49 For the formation of the Dunedin RSA Choir see QM, 10 Jun 1922, 9–11.
50 NZRSA Report of Special Conference, Oct 1919, 20.
51 *QM*, Oct 1920, 47–8.
52 Ibid., Aug 1920, 31.
53 See, e.g., interview with William Murray Morriss, conducted by N. Boyack and J. Tolerton, 4 Jul 1989, tape 3/B, 300–16, New Zealand World War One Oral History Archive, ATL.
54 Melling, 102.
55 'Statement of the Aims and Policy of the New Zealand Returned Soldiers' Association', 3 Sep 1917.
56 NZRSA Annual Conference, 1917, 153.
57 *NZPD*, Vol. 183, 776 (Downie Stewart).
58 *QM*, 1 Jul 1918, 9.
59 Repatriation Act 1918, *NZ Statutes*, 1918, 128–31.
60 'Repatriation Department (Memorandum regarding the Organization and Operations of the)', *AJHR*, 1919, H–30, 1; see also W.H. Montgomery (Director, Repatriation Department), 'Repatriation', in Drew, 163–75.
61 *QM*, Jan 1919, 3–9.
62 Ibid., Jun 1919, 57–9; Melling, 109–10.
63 *QM*, Jan 1923; W.R. Mayhew, 'The New Zealand Returned Services' Association 1916–1943' (MA thesis, OU, 1943), 59.
64 Melling, 60–1.
65 'Report of the War Pensions Commission', *AJHR*, 1923, H–28, 15.
66 *QM*, May 1920, 1.
67 Ibid., Jul 1920, 35.

68   NZRSA Annual Report, 1921–22, 38.

69   *QM*, Oct 1921, 39.

70   Ibid., Jul 1921, 61.

71   See report of a meeting at the Auckland Soldiers' Club in *Auckland Star*, 5 Apr 1916, 6, cited in Maureen Sharpe's 'Anzac Day in New Zealand, 1916 to 1919: Attitudes to Peace and War' (MA thesis, UA, 1981), 35, and 'Anzac Day in New Zealand, 1916 to 1919', *NZJH*, Vol. 15, No. 2 (1981), 97–114.

72   *NZG*, No. 93, p. 2893 (31 Aug 1916); DEC meeting, 28 Apr 1917.

73   DEC Sub-Committee meeting, 23 Mar 1917. For the government's decision to observe 23 April see Decision of Solicitor General, 21 Feb 1917; minute by Under-Sec Internal Affairs, 22 Feb 1917, and Cabinet minute, 22 Feb 1917, IA1, 13/2/20.

74   DEC meeting, 28 Apr 1917; Gen-Sec NZRSA to Min IA, 14 May 1917, IA1, 13/2/20, also in this file correspondence from local councils indicating their intention to observe 25 April.

75   DEC meeting, 4 Jul 1917.

76   *QM*, Apr 1919, 37. For the government's subsequent proposal for one commemorative day see GGNZ (Jellicoe) to SS Cols, tel, 30 Jan 1920, Min Internal Affairs to NZRSA, 11 Feb 1920, and reply of 7 Apr 1920, IA1, 13/2/20, DEC Sub-Committee, 30 Mar 1920.

77   *QM*, May 1919, 30; Sharpe, 44–5.

78   *QM*, Apr 1920, 51.

79   Ibid., Mar 1920, 73–5.

80   *ODT*, 26 Apr 1920.

81   See *NZPD*, Vol. 187, 126–32, Vol. 189, 891; *NZ Statutes*, 1920, No. 78.

82   *QM*, May 1921, 36.

83   Gen Sec NZRSA to Acting PM, 8 Jul 1921, IA1, 13/2/20; *NZPD*, Vol. 191, 385, Vol. 193, 697–8; *NZ Statutes*, 1921–22, No. 44.

84   DEC Sub-Committee meetings, 5 Sep, 27 Oct, 5 Dec 1921.

85   *QM*, May 1922, 24.

86   Christopher Pugsley, *Gallipoli: The New Zealand Story* (Auckland: Reed, 1998), 354.

87   *QM*, Apr 1919, 55.

88   Chris Maclean & Jock Phillips, *The Sorrow and the Pride: New Zealand War Memorials* (Wellington: GP Books/Historical Branch, 1990), 74–82.

89   Sharpe, 64.

90   In fact, *Quick March* itself looked to promote itself as a magazine of general interest in an attempt to halt the steady decline in subscriptions, but without success. It folded in 1923, its demise another indication that most returned soldiers had successfully rehabilitated and no longer required a paper specifically tailored to their needs.

91   Webber, 6.

92   DEC meetings, 1, 2 Nov 1922.

93   *QM*, Jan 1922, 28.

Chapter 10: Peter Stanley

Dr Peter Stanley is Principal Historian at the Australian War Memorial – Peter.Stanley@awm. gov.au. This paper is a by-product of research undertaken for his book, *Quinn's Post, Anzac, Gallipoli* (Sydney: Allen & Unwin, 2005). Research in New Zealand in September–October 2003 was made possible by an award under the Australian War Memorial's Major Research Program.

1   Sergeant J. Milburn, diary, 2 Apr 1915, MS-Papers-4559, ATL.

2   Captain E. Cox, diary, 2 Apr 1915, CA316, Box 2, item 8, Museum of New Zealand.

3   Quoted in Kevin Fewster, 'The Wazza riots, 1915', *Journal of the Australian War Memorial*, No. 4 (1984), 48, 50.

4   Private F. Scarborough, memoir, 1999.759, KMARL.

5   Private A. Smith, memoir, 'Gallipoli', c. 1978, MS-Papers-1542, ATL.

6   James Bennett, '"Massey's Sunday School Picnic Party": "The Other Anzacs" or Honorary Australians?', *War and Society*, Vol. 21, No. 2 (2003), 23–54.

7   Private J. Bayne, diary, 23 Oct 1914, MS-Papers-1418, ATL; Lieutenant A. Rhodes, diary, 28 Oct 1914, MS-Papers-1690, ATL; C.E.W. Bean, *The Story of Anzac* (Sydney: Angus & Robertson, 1938), Vol. I, 129.

8   Diary, 29 Oct 1914, in J.L. Treloar, *An Anzac Diary* (Armidale: Privately printed, 1993), 8.

9   The phrase comes from Jock Phillips's *A Man's Country?*, quoted in Bennett, 27.

10 *NZEF, Alphabetical Roll of New Zealand Expeditionary Force, 1914–1915* (Wellington: Marcus F. Marks, 1917).

11 Lieutenant-Colonel P. Fenwick, diary, I Jun 1915, MS-Papers-4656, ATL.

12 Bennett, 33.

13 Lieutenant C. Algie, diary, 27 Dec 1914, 1990.595, KMARL.

14 Letter, 2 Jan 1915, Private M. Spencer, MS-Papers-1515, ATL.

15 *Masterton Daily Times*, 11 Aug 1915.

16 Trooper Roderick McCandish, letter, 5 January 1915, cited in Pugsley, *Gallipoli*, 81. Pugsley discusses the relationship and argues that the competition reflects a growing New Zealand sense of identity.

17 Cyprian Brereton, *Tales of Three Campaigns* (London: Selwyn & Blount, 1926), 53.

18 Major-General Sir A. Godley to Colonel C. Wigram, Cairo, 5 Feb 1915, 1/5-29, GB99, Godley Papers, LHCMA.

19 Private G. Bollinger, diary, 3 Mar 1915, MS-Papers-2350, ATL. So did Lance-Corporal C. Comyns of the same battalion in his diary: MS-Papers-1417, ATL.

20 Sergeant-Major W. Foster, diary, 26 Apr 1915, 1998.2648, KMARL.

21 Lieutenant-Colonel W.G. Malone, diary, 25 Apr 1915 [and subsequent days, undated], Peter Liddle Archive, University of Leeds (PLA).

22 Sapper E. Clifton, diary [nd but c. 5 May], MS-Copy-Micro-0549, ATL.

23 Private R. Baker, 'Four months at Gallipoli', MS-Papers-1560, ATL.

24 Hamilton to Chauvel, 14 Jun 1915, Hamilton papers, 7/1/16, LHCMA.

25 Godley to Allen, 29 May 1915, War Archives (WA)252/2, ANZ.

26 Malone, diary, 22 May 1915, PLA.

27 Cecil Malthus, *Anzac: a Retrospect* (Auckland: Whitcombe & Tombs 1965), 83.

28 Clifton, diary, 12 May 1915, MS-Copy-Micro-0549, ATL.

29 A.M. Wilson, interview with Peter Liddle, 1974, PLA.

30 Ernest Williams, *A New Zealander's Diary: Gallipoli and France 1915–1917* (Christchurch: Cadsonbury Publications, 1998), 129.

31 Diary, 23 Jun 1915, Charles Bean, AWM 38, 3 DRL 606, item 9, AWM.

32 Lieutenant T. McSharry (15 Battalion), diary, 14 Jun 1915, 3 DRL 3250, AWM.

33 Lieutenant-Colonel J. Beeston, diary, 2 Jul 1915, PR 264, AWM.

34 'Formation of Mining Company', AWM27, 303/100, AWM.

35 Clipping attached to Robin to Allen, 21 Apr 1917, Allen Papers, Box 7, D1/6/3, ANZ.

36 It is my pleasure to be able to thank the many colleagues and archivists in New Zealand who assisted my research in October 2003: Alexander Turnbull Library: Sean McCawley and his colleagues; Archives New Zealand, Paul Frawley and his colleagues; Queen Elizabeth II Army Memorial Museum: director Major Chas Charlton, curator Windsor Jones, Faith Goodley and especially archivist Dolores Ho; New Zealand Defence Force Headquarters: the Defence Force Historian, John Crawford; in Masterton, Gareth Winter of the Wairarapa Archives; National Museum of New Zealand: Jennifer Twist; the reference staff of the Wellington City Library.

Chapter 11: Frank Glen

1   *Mataura Ensign* (Gore), 16 Dec 1927.
2   Defence Act, *NZOYB*, 1914, 264.
3   Field Marshal Lord Birdwood (1865–1951): commanded the ANZAC at Gallipoli and in France; known as 'Birdie'.
4   *Mataura Ensign*, 18 Feb 1927.
5   Lieutenant-General Hon. Sir Fredrick W. Stopford (1854–1929): commanded the Suvla landing of August 1915 and was relieved of his command a week later by General Hamilton.
6   *Minutes of the Methodist Conference of NZ*, Christchurch, Apr [1915], 117. See also J. Ellison & G.H.S. Walpole, *Church and Empire, Essays on the Responsibilities of Empire* (London: Longmans Green & Co., 1908), 21–41.
7   Bowler to Ethel, 11 Apr 1915, Bowler Papers, in private hands.
8   A net consisted of a series of telephones linked through an exchange.
9   Bowler, letter, 31 Mar 1915, AWM, 4.777. Ga.4077.162.
10 Bowler, letter, 18 Apr 1915, AWM, 4.777. Ga. 5428.
11 Commander Charles Cabry Dix RN: retired to Tasmania where he died in 1945.
12 Alan M. Dix, *A Beach Landing Officer's Account* (Melbourne: Privately published, 1996), 3.
13 'Distribution of Beach Equipment to Transports', 10 Apr 1915, AWM, 4.777.
14 Letter, 23 Apr 1915, quoted in Dix, 44.
15 Ibid.
16 Bowler, letter, 16 Apr 1915.
17 Ibid., 9 May 1915.
18 Ibid.
19 Ibid.
20 Ibid., 8 May 1915.
21 Ibid., 9 May 1915.
22 Ibid.
23 Carlyon, *Gallipoli*, 178.
24 Bowler, letter, 8 May 1915.
25 Ibid., 1 May 1915. An estimate similar to the total reported in the corps war diary; Ibid., 5 May 1915.
26 Ibid., 9 May 1915.
27 Pugsley, *Gallipoli*, 181.
28 Bowler, letter, 8 May 1915.
29 Ibid., 9 May 1915.
30 Ibid., 8 May 1915.
31 Ibid., 9 May 1915.
32 Staff Corps Routine Orders, 7 Jul 1915. See also Bean, AWM, 38.3DRL.6673.
33 J.M. Spaight, *War Rights On Land* (London: Macmillan & Co. Ltd, 1911), 267–8.
34 Bowler, letter, 12 May 1915.
35 Ibid.
36 Ibid., 17 May 1915.
37 Ibid.
38 Ibid., 19 May 1915.
39 Ibid.
40 Ibid., 26 May 1915.
41 Ibid., 28 May 1915.
42 Ibid., 31 May 1915.
43 Ibid.

44   Ibid.

45   Ibid.

46   Ibid., 6 Jun 1915.

47   Lieutenant-General Sir J.J.T. Hobbs (1864–1938). See Peter Dennis *et al.*, *Oxford Companion to Australian Military History* (Melbourne: OUP, 1995), 293–4.

48   J.J.T. Hobbs, diary, 20 May 1915, AWM, PR. 82\153. Their shells were landing outside the designated zone of fire

49   CGS to Godley, 21 Jun 1915, AWM, 4.777.

50   Carlyon, 244.

51   Bowler, letter, 6 Jun 1915.

52   Bowler, letter, 13 Jun 1915. Col E.J. O'Neill (1875–1962): Surgeon, 6th Contingent; South African War POW; CO 1 Field Ambulance, Gallipoli; CO 2 Field Hospital, France; Surgeon to NZ merchant navy 1939–41.

53   Ibid.

54   Ibid.

55   Ibid., 21 Jun 1915.

56   Ibid.

57   Bauchop, diary, 19 Jun 1915, Bauchop Papers, Misc MS1152, Hocken Library, Dunedin.

58   Bowler, letter, 21 Jun 1915.

59   Bowler, letter, 31 Jul 1915.

60   Myra Willard, *History of the White Australia Policy* (Melbourne: Melbourne UP, 1923.) See also P.S. O'Connor, 'Keeping New Zealand White', in Judith Binney (ed.), *The Shaping of History* (Wellington: Bridget Williams Books, 2001), 284f.

61   Bowler, letter, 14 Aug 1915.

62   Ibid.

63   Ibid., 17 Aug 1915.

64   Ibid., 20 Aug 1915.

65   Ibid., 11 Aug 1915.

66   Ibid., 26 Aug 1915.

67   Ibid., 17 Aug 1915.

68   Ibid., 26 Aug 1915.

69   Ibid., 9 Sep 1915.

70   Ibid., 14 Sep 1915.

71   Sir Thomas Mackenzie (1854–1930): MP for Clutha; Minister Industries & Commerce; explorer of Fiordland; President NZ Bird Protection Society; High Commissioner, London 1914–20; Member of the Dardanelles Royal Commission of Inquiry and Imperial War Graves Commission.

72   Lord Plunket (1864–1920): 5th Baron; GNZ 1904–1910; politically conservative and remembered for presenting New Zealand cricket's Plunket Shield; had strong Freemasonry links in New Zealand; widow of Harry Parker, mother of Commander Parker RN of Elephant Hill, Waimate, Otago; Lady Gertrude, wife of 4th Baron Decies.

73   Sir James Mills (1847–1936): born Wellington; MP for Port Chalmers.

74   Bowler, letter, 6 Oct 1915.

75   Ibid., 17 Oct 1915.

76   Ibid; William Ferguson Massey(1856–1925): born Northern Ireland; Prime Minister of New Zealand 1912–25.

77   G.H. Scholefield (ed.), *Dictionary of New Zealand Biography* (Wellington: Department of Internal Affairs, 1940), Vol. 2, 68–9.

78   Ellis Ashmead-Bartlett (1881–1931): press correspondent; served in South Africa and covered six wars 1907–1913; following the Dardanelles campaign lectured in United

States and Australia; Keith Arthur Murdoch (1885–1952): journalist sent to investigate mail services on Gallipoli; Australian Director General of Information in Second World War, resigned December 1940.

79 E. Ashmead-Bartlett, *The Uncensored Dardanelles* (London: Hutchinson, 1928), 240–2.

80 Ibid., 243.

81 Birdwood to Bowler, 28 Mar 1917, Bowler Papers.

82 W. Little (ed.), *The Shorter Oxford English Dictionary on Historical Principles* (Oxford: Clarendon Press, 1950), Vol. 2, 1788, col.1.b.

83 Birdwood, diary, 14 Jun 1920, AWM, 3DRL 2316.

84 Birdwood to Bowler, 19 Jun 1920, Bowler Papers.

85 An attempt by MP Jim Anderton in 1997 to have Malone awarded a posthumous VC was unsuccessful. Regulations surrounding the award made this impossible.

Chapter 12: Terry Kinloch

1 Clifton Bellis, 'The Role of the Horse in the Sinai and Palestine Campaign during the 1914–18 War', in D. Holden, *The New Zealand Horseman* (Wellington: A.H. & A.W. Reed, 1967), 56.

2 Adapted from Lieutenant-Colonel C.G. Powles, *The New Zealanders in Sinai and Palestine* (Auckland: Whitcombe & Tombs, 1922), 282–3.

3 Not counting their greatest success on Gallipoli, the Turks prevailed in five of the 12 principal battles or actions fought against the Egyptian Expeditionary Force (EEF) from 1916 to 1918.

4 In general, only persecuted minorities (mainly Jews and Christians) freed from Ottoman oppression were genuinely pleased to see the New Zealanders and their allies.

5 In 1916, the regimental machine gun sections were grouped into a single squadron, and the regiments received Lewis guns, then Hotchkiss light machine guns to replace them. These changes greatly increased the firepower of the brigade.

6 A single battery of horse artillery, provided by the British army, was attached to the brigade.

7 Sergeant C.G. Nicol, *The Story of Two Campaigns: Official War History of the Auckland Mounted Rifles Regiment, 1914–1919* (Auckland: Wilson & Horton, 1921), 3.

8 The training areas in England were overcrowded, and becoming very unpleasant as winter closed in.

9 Nicol, 47.

10 Bean, *ANZAC*, II, 576.

11 Aspinall-Oglander, *Gallipoli,* II, 188.

12 Pugsley, *Gallipoli*, 315.

13 The fighting strengths for 28 May and 22–30 August 1915 are missing from the war diaries, so strengths for these dates are estimated from other sources. Any slight inaccuracies in the daily records do not affect the overall impression.

14 The other three brigades, later reduced to two, were Australian Light Horse brigades.

15 Through no real fault of their own, the infantry divisions of the EEF played a relatively small part in these battles.

16 R.H. Wilson, *Palestine 1917* (Tunbridge Wells: Costello, 1987), 52.

17 Powles, 75.

18 Nicol, 132–3.

19 T. Andrews, *Kiwi Trooper: The Story of Queen Alexandra's Own* (Wanganui: Wanganui Chronicle, 1967), 147.

20 Major A.H. Wilkie, The *Official War History of the Wellington Mounted Rifles Regiment 1914–1919* (Auckland: Whitcombe & Tombs, 1924), 170.

21 Powles, 161.
22 Quoted in Andrews, 160.
23 Nicol, 210.
24 Ibid., 190–4.
25 Lieutenant-General Sir A.P. Wavell, *The Palestine Campaigns* (London: Constable, 1941), 222.
26 Andrews, 198.
27 Only one NZMR horse returned to New Zealand, a mare named Bess.
28 Bellis, 56.
29 *NZH*, 12 Sep 1919.
30 Quoted in ibid., 28 Jan 1926.
31 To be fair, the mounteds had the shortest distances to cover, over ground that at least some of them knew well, having observed and patrolled it for two months. Lastly, they caught the Turks almost completely by surprise, not giving them time to reinforce their weak outposts. Those who followed them enjoyed few of these advantages.
32 H.S. Gullett, *The Official History of Australia in the War of 1914–1918, Volume VII: The Australian Imperial Force in Sinai and Palestine 1914–1918* (Sydney: Angus & Robertson, 1944), 354.
33 Of the 432 members of the Main Body with previous war experience, 37% (160) were in the NZMR Brigade, which made up 26% of the Main Body strength. *New Zealand Expeditionary Force (Europe) 1914 – War Diary*, Appendix 31.
34 General Ian Hamilton, 'Report by the Inspector-General of the Overseas Forces on the Military Forces of New Zealand', 4 Jun 1914, *AJHR*, H-19A, 1914, 22–3.
35 In addition to being a good rider, a horsemaster also knows how to keep horses fit and healthy for prolonged periods. Lieutenant-Colonel A. Bauchop, 'The New Zealand Mounted Rifles', *The Cavalry Journal*, Vol. 9 (1914), 95.
36 In retaliation for the murder of a New Zealander on 9 December 1918, a group of New Zealand, Australian and British troops attacked the village of Surafend and killed up to 40 male Arabs.

Chapter 13: Andrew Macdonald

Thanks must go to Dolores Ho of the Kippenberger Military Archive and Research Library at Waiouru, the always helpful staff at Alexander Turnbull Library and the indefatigable assistants at Archives New Zealand. These collections have made significant contributions to this essay. Thanks, too, must go to my wife Lara, my parents and my late grandmother who have encouraged my interest in the First World War. And, finally, I must also acknowledge historian Glyn Harper, who has willingly given his time to discuss the finer points of the Battle of the Somme, 1916.

1   2 NZ Infantry Brigade, Order No. 20, 14 Sep 1916, War Archives (WA)76/1, ANZ.
2   Lieutenant J.R. Byrne, *New Zealand Artillery in the Field, 1914–1918* (Auckland: Whitcombe & Tombs, 1922), 130.
3   Captain L.M. Inglis, Papers, MS-Papers-0421-48, 31, ATL.
4   Major-General Sir Andrew Russell, diary, 12 Sep 1916, in Gambrill, III.
5   Ibid., 13 Sep 1916.
6   Ibid.
7   Captain G.A. Tuck, letters and diary, MS-Papers-2164-2166, 347, ATL.
8   Sergeant-Major C. Kerse, diary, 9 Sep 1916, Micro-MS-0591, 70, ATL.
9   Private C. Burley, letter, n.d., MS-Papers-7494, 17, ATL.
10 Stewart, *Division*, 70.

11   Lieutenant A.E. Byrne, *Official History of the Otago Regiment NZEF in the Great War 1914–1918* (Dunedin: J. Wilkie & Co., 1921), 118.

12   Tuck, 345.

13   2 Otago Battalion, report on operations 15–17 Sep 1916, 24 Sep 1916, WA76/2.

14   2 NZ Infantry Brigade, report on operations 15–17 Sep 1916, 26 Sep 1916, WA76/1.

15   James Gasson, *Travis V.C.: Man in No Man's Land* (Wellington: A.H. & A.W. Reed, 1966), 59. Travis won the DCM, Rodgers the MM, and Brown the VC.

16   Tuck, 353.

17   Order No. 20.

18   2 Otago Battalion, report on operations 15–17 Sep 1916, 24 Sep 1916, WA76/2.

19   Lieutenant-Colonel W.S. Austin, *The Official History of the New Zealand Rifle Brigade* (Wellington: L.T. Watkins, 1924), 124.

20   Lance-Corporal L.M. Blyth, quoted in Boyack and Tolerton, 59.

21   Inglis, 33.

22   Major J.H. Luxford, *With the Machine Gunners in France and Palestine* (Auckland: Whitcombe & Tombs, 1923), 42.

23   Lieutenant C. Lewis, quoted in Gerald Gliddon, *When the Barrage Lifts* (London: Leo Cooper, 1989), 431–2.

24   Austin, 127; Luxford, 42.

25   Rifleman J.T. Bisman, quoted from an unidentified and undated article by Gail Dowgray in the author's possession.

26   Austin, 127.

27   3 Battalion, report on operations 15 Sep 1916, n.d., WA81/3, box 2, item 7.

28   2 NZ Infantry Brigade, war diary, 15 Sep 1916, WA76/1.

29   Austin, 128, 493–524.

30   Treadwell, 153.

31   3 Battalion signals report on 15 Sep 1916, 19 Sep 1916, WA81/3, item 7.

32   Sergeant A.E. Rhind, diary, 15 Sep 1916, MS-Papers-3772, ATL.

33   Ibid.

34   Russell to Gwen, 15 Sep 1916, in Gambrill, III.

35   Rhind, diary.

36   Inglis, 36, 38.

37   Lieutenant Braunhofer, quoted in Trevor Pigeon, *The Tanks at Flers* (Caobham: Fairmile Books, 1995), 172.

38   Inglis, 42.

39   Stewart, 77–83.

40   Inglis, 43.

41   Ibid.

42   Ibid., 44, 43.

43   Stewart, 81.

44   Inglis, 44.

45   Austin, 131.

46   Burley, 16.

47   Captain H.E. McKinnon, Report on 2 Wellington Battalion operation on 15 Sep 1916, n.d., WA76/4.

48   Inglis, 46.

49   By order of Fourth Army HQ.

50   Austin, 133.

51   McKinnon, Report on 2 Wellington Battalion operation on 15 Sep 1916, n.d., WA76/4.

52   Lance-Corporal R.F. Ellis, *By Wires to Victory* (Auckland: 1st Divisional Signal Company

War History Committee, n.d.), 44–5.

53 Tuck, 356.

54 Burley, 14.

55 2 NZ Infantry Brigade, casualty report for operations 15–17 Sep 1916, n.d., WA76/4.

56 4 Battalion, report on operations 15 Sep 1916, 21 Sep 1916, WA81/3.

57 Second Lieutenant O.E. Burton, *The Auckland Regiment* (Auckland: Whitcombe & Tombs), 108.

58 Austin, 128.

59 Byrne, *Otago*, 121; Lieutenant G.A. Tuck, MC, mentioned in dispatches (mid); Lieutenant V.C. Cooper, Lieutenant C.H.A. Senior, MC, killed in action 29 Mar 1918; Lieutenant F. Stewart, MC; Second Lieutenant W.J.R. Hill, DCM, died of wounds 5 Sep 1918; Lieutenant A.W. Gordon, DCM; Captain S.J.E. Closey, MC; and Captain W.A. Gray, MC; and Sergeant H. Bellamy, DCM.

60 Glyn Harper and Joel Hayward (eds), *Born to Lead? Portraits of New Zealand Commanders* (Auckland: Exisle Publishing, 2003), 68.

61 Austin, 128.

62 Blyth, 59.

63 Inglis, 40.

64 Russell, quoted in Harper and Hayward, 59–60.

65 Godley to Allen, 18, 29 Sep, 15 Oct 1916, WA252/3; Captain P.B. Benham, memoir, n.d., ATL, MS-Papers-1510-4.

66 Harper and Hayward, 36.

67 Malthus, *Armentières*, 96.

68 Tuck, 348.

69 2 NZ Infantry Brigade, report on operations 15–17 Sep 1916, 26 Sep 1916, WA76/1.

70 Major A.D. Carbery, *The New Zealand Medical Services in the Great War 1914–1918: Based on Official Documents* (Auckland: Whitcombe & Tombs, 1924), 193–4.

71 Ibid., 201–2.

72 Ibid., 198.

73 Lance-Corporal R.N. Gray, quoted in Jock Phillips, Nicholas Boyack and E.P. Malone (eds), *The Great Adventure: New Zealand Soldiers Describe the First World War* (Wellington: Allen & Unwin, 1988), 90–1.

74 Carbery, 199, 208.

75 Ibid., 201, 213.

76 Divisional report on Somme operations 1 Sep–4 Oct 1916, WA20/4, box 2, item 6. The figure does not include the number of soldiers reported missing in action.

77 Pugsley, *Te Hokowhitu*, 55; the figure of 603 supplied by the Commonwealth War Graves Commission.

78 Carbery, 204.

79 Tuck, 348–9; Warrant Officer 2 R.W. Hunter, Sergeant J.T. Adams, and Corporal A.C. Peart were killed; Sergeant W.H. Cowan died of wounds; Sergeants D.J.B. Walker, W.A. Lamont, and B.W. Irwin were wounded; *AWN*, 2 Nov 1916; ibid., 12 Oct 1916.

80 Allen to Godley, 19 Dec 1916, WA252/3; ibid., 12 Dec 1916.

81 Ormond Burton, *Spring Fires, A Study in New Zealand Writing* (Auckland: The Book Centre, 1956), 6–7.

82 Austin, 136.

83 Stewart, 89.

84 Godley to Allen, 15 Oct 1916, WA252/3.

85 Christopher Pugsley, *On The Fringe of Hell: New Zealanders and Military Discipline in the First World War* (Auckland: Hodder & Stoughton, 1991), 122.

86   Austin, 136.

87   Inglis, 53.

88   Malthus, 96.

89   Russell, diary, 20 Sep 1916, in Gambrill, III.

90   Burton, *Spring*, 9.

Chapter 14: John Crawford

1   SS Cols to GNZ, 2 Feb 1917, WA230/16.

2   C.E.W. Bean, *Official History of Australia in the War of 1914–18*, Vol. IV, *The A.I.F. in France, 1917* (Sydney: Angus and Robertson, 1933), 14–15; Keith Grieves, *The Politics of Manpower, 1914–18* (Manchester: MUP, 1988), 90–109.

3   Liverpool to Long, tel, 8 Feb 1917, and reply 10 Feb 1917, WA230/16; Allen to Godley, 27 Mar 1917, WA252/4; Kay, 137–8.

4   Robin to Allen, 8 Feb 1917, WA230/16.

5   See draft telegrams responding to the British request, WA230/16.

6   Baker, 45–6, 132.

7   Massey to Allen, tel, 9 Feb 1917, WA 230/16; Long to Massey, 10 Feb 1917, Walter Long Papers, Micro MS 616, Reel 2, AJCPM 1117, ATL; Kay, 183.

8   Allen to Liverpool, 14 Feb 1917, and attached draft reply marked as sent 15 Feb 1917, WA 230/16; Bean, IV, 15–17.

9   Allen to Massey, 17 Feb 1917, Massey to Allen 10 Mar 1917, tels, WA230/16.

10   Long to Liverpool, tel, 6 Mar 1917, G41, Box 26, ANZ; extract from Robin to Godley, 9 Apr 1917, WA230/16.

11   F.W. Perry, *The Commonwealth Armies: Manpower and Organisation in Two World Wars* (Manchester: MUP, 1988), 176–8; Baker, 79–110.

12   Sleeman, 'Reinforcements', in Drew, 1; Chief of the General Staff Branch, *New Zealand Expeditionary Force: Its Provision and Maintenance* (Wellington: Government Printer, 1919), 6–9; Baker, 133; Christopher Pugsley, 'The New Zealand Division at Passchendaele', in Peter H. Liddle (ed.), *Passchendaele in Perspective: The Third Battle of Ypres* (London: Leo Cooper, 1997), 275.

13   Robin to Allen, 8 Feb 1917, WA230/16; Report No. 20 by Brigadier-General Richardson, n.d. but Apr–May 1917, WA231/10.

14   Godley to Allen, 2 Mar 1917, WA252/4; Birdwood to Allen, 23 Mar 1917, Allen 1, Box 9, ANZ; Allen to Massey, draft tel (sent 10 Feb 1917), WA230/16.

15   Russell to Allen, 3 Apr 1917, Allen 1, Box 9; Entry for 28 Feb 1917, typescript copy of Russell diary in Gambrill, III.

16   Godley to Wigram, 10 Mar 1917, WA 252/14, Micro-Z 5083, ANZ; Godley to Allen, 10 Dec 1916, 6 and 27 Jan 1917, Allen 1, M1/15; Herbert Hart, diary, 9 Mar 1917, Micro MS 552, ATL.

17   Godley to Wigram, 30 Mar 1917, WA 252/14, Micro-Z 5083; Russell to Allen, 3 Apr 1917, Allen 1, Box 9.

18   Hart, diary, Mar 1917, Micro MS 552; *Fourthoughts: Being the Journal of the Fourth New Zealand Infantry Brigade Group* (London: Argus Printers Co., 1918), 57, 71, 74.

19   George K.L. Wyatt, NZEF Personal File (PF), ANZ.

20   J.W. Stayte, diary, 30 Mar, 16 Apr 1917, KMARL; Jesse William Stayte, NZEF PF, ANZ.

21   N.M. Ingram, *ANZAC Diary: A Nonentity in Khaki* (Christchurch: Treharne, n.d.), 17 Jun 1917, 32.

22   Peter Howden to Mrs Howden, 21 Sep 1917 (section of letter written on 22 Sep), MS-Papers 1504, folder 4, ATL.

23   3 Otago Battalion, War Diary, Apr 1917, App. I, WA 91/1 (My analysis excludes the

battalion's medical officer and chaplain and is based on information in the appendix and Studholme, *Record*). See also Burton, *Auckland*, 140–1.

24 Luxford, 63.

25 Inglis to fiancée, 29 Apr 1917, MS papers 421, folder 5, ATL; *Fourthoughts*, 69; Luxford, 63–4.

26 Citation for DSO reproduced in Wayne McDonald, *Honours and Awards to the New Zealand Expeditionary Force in the Great War 1914–1918* (Napier: H. McDonald, 2001), 92.

27 Stewart, *Division*, 7–10; Austin, 1–11.

28 Inglis to fiancée, 17 Jun 1917, MS Papers 421, folder 5, ATL; Christopher Pugsley, preface to Frank Glen, *Bowler of Gallipoli: Witness to the ANZAC Legend* (Canberra: Army History Unit and Australian Military History Publications, 2004), xii.

29 Drew, 4–9; Christopher Pugsley, 'The Second New Zealand Division of 1945: A Comparison with its 1918 Predecessor', in John Crawford (ed.), *Kia Kaha: New Zealand in the Second World War* (Auckland: OUP, 2000), 96.

30 Hart, diary, 31 Mar 1917, 9, 12 Apr 1917, Micro MS 552; 4 NZ Infantry Brigade, War Diary, 1–12 Apr 1917, WA87/1.

31 Hart, diary, 9, 19, 23–25 Apr, 9, 14 May 1917, Micro MS 552; Wyatt, diary, 7–10, 22–23 May 1917; Captain F.S. Varnham, diary, 3–19 Apr 1917, MSX 3313, ATL; 3 Otago Battalion, War Diary, Apr 1917, WA91/1.

32 Varnham, diary, 9–16 May 1917, MSX 3313.

33 4 Brigade, War Diary, 19 Apr, 8–9 May 1917, WA87/1; 3 Otago Battalion, War Diary, 21 Apr 1917, WA91/1; *Fourthoughts*, 63.

34 Hart, diary, 13 Mar, 2, 17–19 Apr 1917, Micro MS 552; 4 Brigade, War Diary, 25 Apr, 3 May 1917, WA87/1; Varnham, diary, 7, 25 Apr, MSX 3313; Wyatt, diary, 12 May 1917.

35 4 Brigade, War Diary, 10 May 1917, and App. III, WA87/1; Hart, diary, 11 May 1917, Micro MS 552.

36 Hart, diary, 21–25 May 1917, Micro MS 552; 4 Brigade, War Diary, 21–26 May 1917, WA87/1.

37 Hart, diary, 22–27 May 1917, Micro MS 552; 4 Brigade, War Diary, 27–29 May 1917, WA87/1.

38 Hart, diary, 28 May 1917, Micro MS 552.

39 Report No. 20 by Richardson, WA 231/10; *Fourthoughts*, 76; Carbery, 275–6.

40 *Fourthoughts*, 58. The approach adopted by Hart was similar in many respects to that adopted during the Second World War by Major-General D.N. Wimberley. See Craig French, 'The Fashioning of esprit de corps in The 51st Highland Division from St Valery to El Alamein', *Journal of the Society for Army Historical Research*, Vol. 77, No. 312 (Winter, 1999), 276–92.

41 4 Brigade, War Diary, 1–8 Jun 1917 and App. III, WA 87/1; Hart, diary, 1–8 Jun 1917, Micro MS 552; *Fourthoughts*, 46, 52, 70–2; Godley to Wigram, 13 Jun 1917, WA 252/14.

42 4 Brigade, War Diary, 4, 13 Aug 1917, WA 87/1; Russell, diary, 29 Jul 1917, (copy) QMS-0822; Hart, diary 17–18, 28 Jun, 1, 7, 8, 12, 13, 28 Jul 1917, Micro MS 552; Varnham, diary, 30 Jun, 6, 28 Jul 1917, MSX 3313; Byrne, 248–9; David Ferguson, *The History of the Canterbury Regiment, NZEF, 1914–1919* (Auckland: Whitcombe & Tombs, 1921), 179; *Fourthoughts*, 59, 64.

43 Inglis to fiancée, 17 Jun 1917, MS Papers 421, ATL.

44 Stewart, 246–7; Austin, 227–9.

45 4 Brigade, War Diary, 5 Sep 1917, WA 87/1; Stewart, 248–9; G.C. Wynne, 'The Development of the German Defensive Battle in 1917, and Its Influence on British Defence Tactics, Part I', *Army Quarterly*, Apr 1937, 15–32; Paddy Griffith, 'The Extent of Tactical Reform in the British Army', in Paddy Griffith (ed.), *British Fighting Methods in the*

Great War (London: Frank Cass, 1996), 7, 17–18. Pugsley, 'Passchendaele', 275–8.

46   3 Otago Battalion, War Diary, Sep 1917, App. 22, 23, WA 91/1.

47   See e.g. Varnham, diary, 13, 20, 21, 24 Sep 1917, MSX 3313.

48   Russell, diary, 24 Sep 1917 (copy), Gambrill, III; 4 Brigade, War Diary, 21–24 Sep 1917, WA 87/1; Hart, diary, 21, 24 Sep 1917; W.E.L. Napier, *With the Trench Mortars in France* (Auckland: Alpe Bros, 1923), 46–7.

49   C.H. Weston, *Three Years with the New Zealanders* (London: Skeffington & Son, 1918), 214–15.

50   Austin, 230; John Terraine (ed.), *General Jack's Diary 1914–18: The Trench Diary of Brigadier-General J I Jack, D.S.O.* (London: Cassell, 2000, first published 1964), 306–7.

51   Hart, diary, 19, 24, 25, 28 Sep 1917, Micro MS 552.

52   See e.g. 4 Brigade Order No. 37, 28 Sep 1917, WA20, Box 9, 3/25/168; NZ Division Order No. 111, 1 Oct 1917, WA20, Box 45/35; Hart diary, 30 Sep 1917, Micro MS 552; Varnham, diary, 28–29 Sep, 2 Oct 1917, MSX 3313; Weston, 226.

53   Robin Prior and Trevor Wilson, *Passchendaele: the Untold Story* (New Haven: YUP, 1996), 133–5.

54   Weston, 227–8; Stewart, 254–7; Glyn Harper, *Massacre at Passchendaele: The New Zealand Story* (Auckland: HarperCollins, 2000), 30–3.

55   Burton, *Auckland*, 169.

56   NZ Division Order, No. 111, 1 Oct 1917, and App. A, WA20, Box 45/35; Luxford, 86–9; Byrne, *Artillery*, 186–7; Stewart, 260, 267, 269.

57   Athol Stretton, 'Passchendaele As I Saw It: The Storming of the Abraham Heights. October 4th, 1917', KMARL; *Fourthoughts*, 48; 4 Brigade, War Diary, Oct 1917, App. III; WA 87/1; 3 Canterbury Battalion, War Diary, 1–4 Oct 1917, WA 90/1; Prior and Wilson, 134–5; G.C. Wynne, 'The Development of the German Defensive Battle in 1917 and Its Influence on British Defence Tactics, Part II: The Counter-Attack Divisions', *Army Quarterly*, Jul 1937, 258–9.

58   Ingram, 51.

59   Stewart, 260–7; Hart, diary, 3–6 Oct 1917, Micro MS 552; 4 Brigade, War Diary, Oct 1917, App. III, WA87/1; Burton, *Auckland*, 174–5.

60   Stewart, 271; Hart, diary, 4 Oct 1917, Micro MS 552; 4 Brigade, War Diary, Oct 1917, App. III, WA87/1.

61   Howden to Mrs Howden, 6 Oct 1917, MS Papers 1504, ATL; Russell, diary, 4 Oct 1917, Gambrill, III; Godley to Allen, 7 Oct 1917, WA 252/4; Brigadier-General G.N. Johnston, diary, 4 Oct 1917, 01/12/1, Imperial War Museum, London.

62   Newspaper clippings relating to the operations on 4 October 1917, in Hart, diary, Oct 1917, Micro MS 552; Prior and Wilson, 135–9.

63   Varnham, diary, 5–8 Oct 1917, MSX 3313; Stewart, 273–4; 4 Brigade, War Diary, Oct 1917, App. XIII, WA87/1; Hart diary, 11–14 Oct 1917, Micro MS 552.

64   Inglis to fiancée, 26 Oct 1917, MS Papers 421, folder 5, ATL.

65   Godley to Allen, 2 Nov 1917, WA252/4.

66   Clippings from the *Sun*, 20, 21 Mar 1917, 'Taken to Cabinet' note, 25 Mar 1917, WA230/16; Allen to Godley, 27 Mar 1917, WA252/4.

67   See e.g. Allen to Godley, 27 Mar 1917, WA252/4; clipping from the *NZH*, 30 Jul 1917, Allen 1, D1/6; Allen to Godley, 7 Aug 1917, WA252/4.

68   Ibid., Allen to Godley, 23 Jul 1917; Baker, 86–7, 133–5.

69   Allen to Godley, 23 Jul, 3 Sep 1917, Godley to Allen 13 Sep 1917, WA252/4; Birdwood to Allen, 23 Mar, 24 Jul, 28 Sep 1917, Allen 1, Box 9; Bean, *Official History*, IV, 544.

70   Allen to Birdwood, 24 Sep 1917, Allen 1, Box 9.

71   Robin to Allen, 8, 12 Oct 1917, Allen to Robin, 12 Oct 1917; Richardson to Robin,

telegram (marginalia), 20 Oct 1917, WA230/16; Baker, 136.

72 Baker, 135.

73 Hart, diary, 27–29 Oct 1917, Micro MS 552; Godley to Allen, 2 Nov 1917, WA252/4; Russell to Allen, 7 Nov 1917, Allen 1, Box 9.

74 Godley to Allen, 2 Nov 1917, WA252/14; Russell to Godley, 7 Dec 1917, encl. Godley to Allen, 8 Dec 1917, Godley to Allen, 15, 16 Dec 1917, Allen to Godley, 2 Apr 1918, Allen 1, M1/15.

75 Hart, diary, 27 Oct 1917, 18 Jan 1918; Godley to Allen, 22 Feb 1918, WA252/5; Godley to Montgomery, 16 Jan 1918 (copy), Allen 1, M1/15,

76 Baker, 137.

77 See e.g. Allen to Godley, 11 Oct, 17 Dec 1917, WA252/4; Kay, 9–10.

78 Clive Hughes, 'The New Armies', in Ian F. W. Beckett and Keith Simpson (eds.), *A Nation in Arms: A social study of the British Army in the First World War* (Manchester: MUP, 1985), 100–22.

Chapter 15: Glyn Harper

1 Sheffield, *Victory*, 189.

2 Ibid., 60.

3 John Coates, *An Atlas of Australia's Wars* (Melbourne: OUP, 2001), 72.

4 G.D. Sheffield, 'The Indispensable Factor: The Performance of British Troops in 1918', in Peter Dennis and Jeffrey Grey (eds), *1918, Defining Victory* (Canberra: Army History Unit, 1999), 77.

5 John Terraine, *To Win a War, 1918 The Year of Victory* (London: Cassell & Co., 2000), 37.

6 General Erich Ludendorff, *My War Memories 1914–1918, Volume II* (London: Hutchinson & Co., 1919), 537.

7 Russell 'was not sure that [they] were not in for a catastrophe'. Christopher Pugsley, 'Russell of the New Zealand Division', in *NZ Strategic Management*, Autumn 1995, 48.

8 Corporal G. Beattie, diary, 25 Mar 1918, MS Papers 3908, folder 3, ATL.

9 B. Cottrell to Dad, 10 Apr 1918, Bernard Cottrell Papers, MS Papers 1389, ATL.

10 C. Lawrence, interview, 9 Oct 1989, OH Int 0006/47, ATL.

11 C.E.W. Bean, *Official History of Australia in the War of 1914–1918, Vol. V, The A.I.F. in France: December 1917–May 1918* (Sydney: Angus & Robertson, 1943), 236.

12 H.S. Muschamp, diary, 25 Mar 1918, 91102219 KMARL.

13 C. Jepson, 1918 pocket diary, 26 Mar 1918, Cecil John Jepson Papers, MS Papers 1480, ATL.

14 O.E. Burton, *The Silent Division, New Zealanders at the Front: 1914–1919* (Sydney: Angus and Robertson, 1935), 266.

15 J. McWhirter, Diary of the Great War (written about 1920), MSX 4915 ATL.

16 J.G. Harcourt, diary entry, MS Papers 6293, ATL.

17 W.M. Morris, interview, 4 Jul 1989, OH Int 006/58, ATL.

18 Stewart, 349.

19 Brigadier Sir James E. Edmonds, *History of the Great War. Military Operations France and Belgium. 1918, Volume II* (London: Macmillan & Co., 1937), 35.

20 Bean, *Official History*, V, 129.

21 Burton, *Silent*, 270.

22 Ibid.

23 Burton, *Auckland*, 201.

24 McWhirter, diary.

25 W.M. Morris, interview, 4 Jul 1989.

26 NZ Machine Gun Battalion, War Diary, 27 Mar 1918, WA98/1, ANZ.

27   Luxford, 118.
28   NZ Machine Gun Battalion, War Diary, 27 Mar 1918, WA98/1.
29   Luxford, 118.
30   Capt G.A. Tuck, diary, 27 Mar 1918, MS Papers 2164-2166, ATL.
31   2 Battalion, Auckland Regiment, War Diary, 27 Mar 1918, WA72/1.
32   Edmonds, II, 41.
33   Ibid.
34   Tuck, diary, 1 Apr 1918.
35   Stewart, 367.
36   Bean, *Official History, V*, 141.
37   Edmonds, II, 96.
38   Stewart, 369.
39   4 Battalion, NZ (Rifle) Brigade, War Diary, 5 Apr 1918, WA85/1.
40   Austin, 304.
41   3 NZ (Rifle) Brigade, War Diary, WA81/1.
42   Austin, 305.
43   4 Battalion, NZ (Rifle) Brigade, War Diary, 5 Apr 1918, WA85/1.
44   Quoted in Bean, *Official History*, V, 416.
45   Edmonds, II, 135.
46   Ferguson, 234.
47   Bombardier N. Bailey, diary, 5 Apr 1918, 1999-1010 KMARL.
48   Luxford, 124.
49   GHQ Summary 8-4-18, quoted in NZ Machine Gun Battalion, War Diary, 5 Apr 1918, WA 98/1.
50   Austin, 305.
51   Ludendorff, II, 600.
52   Edmonds, II, 136.
53   See Ian McGibbon (ed.), *The Oxford Companion to New Zealand Military History* (Auckland: OUP, 2000), 606; Stewart, 372; Edmonds, 492.
54   *New Zealand Expeditionary Force, Book XII List of Casualties and a Summary of Casualties in order of Units, Reported from 15th February to 14th May, 1918* (Wellington: Government Printer, 1918).
55   Carbery, 538.
56   Byrne, *Otago*, 288.
57   A copy of this order is on Russell's Personal File, NZDF Personnel Records, NZDF HQ. It also appears in Ferguson, 235–6.
58   Quoted in Pugsley, 'Russell', 49.
59   Godley to Allen, 22 Apr 1918, WA252/5.

Chapter 16: Christopher Pugsley

1   Douglas Haig, diary, 29 Mar 1916, quoted in Justin Wintle (ed.), *The Dictionary of War Quotations* (London: John Curtis and Hodder & Stoughton, 1989), 313.
2   See Jeffery Williams, *Byng of Vimy: General and Governor General* (London: Leo Cooper, 1983).
3   GJDG, 'F.M. Sir Douglas Haig, 1st Earl Haig', in Richard Holmes (ed.), *The Oxford Companion to Military History* (Oxford: OUP, 2001), 393–4. Gerard de Groot, *Douglas Haig, 1861–1928* (London: Unwin Hyman, 1988).
4   Haig Papers, Diary, Volume XIII Jan–Feb 1917, 28 Jan 1917, discussions with Allenby, newly appointed commander 3rd Army, National Library of Scotland (NLS), Edinburgh.
5   A.M.J. Hyatt, *General Sir Arthur Currie: A Military Biography* (Toronto: University of

Toronto Press in association with Canadian War Museum, 1987), 35–43. Bill Rawling, *Surviving Trench Warfare: Technology and the Canadian Corps, 1914–1918* (Toronto: University of Toronto Press, 1992), 29–36. Major A.F. Becke, *History of the Great War, Order of Battle: Part 4, The Army Council, G.H.Qs, Armies, and Corps, 1914–1918* (London: HMSO, 1945), 163.

6   Desmond Morton and J.L. Granatstein, *Marching to Armageddon: Canadians and the Great War 1914–1918* (Toronto: Lester & Orphen Dennys, 1989), 107.

7   Godley to Allen, 20 Jan, 19 Feb, 4 Mar 1916, Allen Papers, ANZ. Haig Papers, Diaries, Vol. IX, Robertson, CIGS, to Haig, 22 Jun 1916, with Haig's penned comment 'No doubt Birdwood is at the bottom of this.' Haig to Robertson, 25 Jun 16, NLS.

8   'Lieutenant-General (James) Gordon Legge', in Dennis *et al.*, 344–5; Rosemary Derham, *The Silence Ruse: Escape from Gallipoli: A Record and Memory of the Life of General Sir Brudenell White KCB, KCMG, KCVO, DSO* (Armadale: Cliffe Books, 1998), 48.

9   G.D. Sheffield, 'The Australians at Pozières: Command and Control on the Somme, 1916', in David French and Brian Holden Reid (eds), *The British General Staff: Reform and Innovation, 1890–1939* (London: Frank Cass, 2002), 112–26. David Horner, *Blamey: The Commander-in-Chief* (St Leonards: Allen & Unwin, 1998), 42–5.

10   Rawling, 86–133.

11   Canadian Corps G530. S109/1 dated 13 May 1917, Battalion Organization (Army and Corps Scheme) RG 9, III, C1, Vol. 3864, folder 99, file 3, NAC.

12   Ibid.

13   Hyatt, 63–7; 'Translation of a Note by the French General Headquarters of the Armies of the East', 11 Nov 1915', RG 9, III, C I, Vol. 3867, folder 107, file 6; 'Notes on Exercise carried out by 4th French Army to demonstrate the New Training of Infantry Units', Canadian Corps G.343 dated 27 Nov 1916, RG 9, III, CI, Vol. 3864, folder 99, file 4; 'Notes on French Attacks, North-East of Verdun in October and December, 1916', Major-General A.W. Currie, 1 Canadian Division, 23 Jan 1917, RG 9, III, C1, 3871, folder 115, file 8; 'Notes on a Visit of a Party of British Officers to Verdun, January 5th–8th, 1917', RG 9, III C1, Vol. 3873, NAC; Shane B. Schreiber, *Shock Army of the British Empire: The Canadian Corps in the Last 100 Days of the Great War* (Westport: Praeger, 1997), 9–14.

14   'Notes on a Visit of a Party of British Officers to Verdun, January 5th–8th, 1917', RG 9, III C1, Vol. 3873, NAC.

15   John A. English and Bruce I. Gudmundsson, *On Infantry* (Westport, CT: Praeger, 1994), 18–31; Bruce I. Gudmundsson, *Storm Troop Tactics: Innovation in the German Army, 1914–1918* (New York: Praeger, 1989).

16   'Notes on French Attacks, North-East of Verdun in October and December, 1916', Major-General A.W. Currie, 1 Canadian Division, 23 Jan 1917, p.5, RG 9, III, C1, 3871, Folder 115, File 8, NAC.

17   David J. Bercuson and J.L. Granatstein, *Dictionary of Canadian Military History* (Toronto: OUP, 1992), 219.

18   2nd Army G.140, 'General Principles on which the Artillery Plan will be Drawn,' included with 2nd Army G.140 to GHQ dated 29 Aug 1917, 2nd Army War Diary, Aug 1917, Vol. XXXII, War Office records (WO) 95/275, UKNA.

19   Haig Diaries, 24 May 1917, WO256/18.

20   A.H. Russell, diary, 24 May 1917, in Gambrill, III.

21   Haig Diaries, 24 May 1917, WO256/18.

22   Ibid.

23   Ibid., 7 Jun 1917, WO256/19.

24   Ibid., 9 Jun 1917.

25 Ibid.

26 Ibid., 22 Sep 1917, WO256/22.

27 Monash letter dated 3 Aug 1917, 3DRL 2316/1/2, AWM.

28 Haig Diaries, 9 Jun 1917, WO256/19.

29 Ibid. Haig would later meet with Brigadier-General John Baird, one of Bainbridge's brigade commanders, who also 'was much down upon the 4th Australian Division for their conduct on the night of the 7th and the morning of the 8th.' Ibid., 11 Jun 1917.

30 Daniel G. Dancocks, *Legacy of Valour: The Canadians at Passchendaele* (Edmonton: Hurtig Publishers, 1986), 90.

31 Haig Diaries, 23 Jul 1917, WO256/20.

32 Hyatt, 76–7.

33 Haig Diaries, 23 Jul 1917, WO256/20.

34 Ibid.

35 Rawling, 142.

36 Haig Diaries, 27 Aug 1917, WO256/21.

37 Ibid., 15–20 Jul 1917, WO256/20.

38 Ibid., 29 Aug 1917, WO256/21.

39 Ibid., 17 Sep 1917, WO256/22.

40 Ibid., 1 Sep 1917.

41 Ibid., 29 Oct 1917, WO256/23.

42 CGS (GHQ) to Plumer (GOC 2nd Army), 3 Sep 1917, WO158/208.

43 Quoted in Hyatt, 79.

44 Dancocks, 100–3.

45 Hyatt, 81–4; Rawling, 147–52.

46 Dean Oliver, 'The Canadians at Passchendaele', in Liddle, 255–71.

47 Dancocks, 223–5.

48 Ibid., 123.

49 Syd Wise, 'The Black Day of the German Army: Australians and Canadians at Amiens, August 1918', and Bill Rawling, 'A Resource not to be Squandered: The Canadian Corps on the 1918 Battlefield', in Dennis and Grey, 1–32, 43–71; Schreiber, 33–69.

50 Hyatt, 98–102.

51 Russell, diary, 24 Jun 1918, in Gambrill, III.

52 General Sir Charles Harington, *Plumer of Messines* (London: John Murray, 1935), 74. Peter Simkins, 'Haig and his Army Commanders', in Brian Bond and Nigel Cave (eds), *Haig: A Reappraisal 70 Years On* (London: Leo Cooper, 1999), 78–106.

Chapter 17: Peter Dennerly

1 Admiralty M13504, 13 May 1914, and NA6/4, 28 Jul 1914, Navy Department records (N)1, 6/4, ANZ.

2 Ibid., Hall-Thompson to SNO NZ, 12 Aug 1914.

3 SS Cols to GNZ, tel 29441/1915, N20, 8, X.

4 NZHC, London, to PM, 3 Apr 1917.

5 SNO NZ, Journal of War, 28 Jul–10 Sep 1914, N20/4; *Philomel*, Cypher Log Aug–Dec 1914, N, Acc W2391, ANZ.

6 DOD to COS, 2 Aug 1914, Admiralty records (ADM)137/4, UKNA.

7 Admiral H. Jackson to COS and First Sea Lord, 8 Aug 1914; also *Correspondence Relating to the Occupation of German Samoa by an Expeditionary Force From New Zealand,* presented to both Houses of Parliament 1915; ADM137/4.

8 Sir Julian S. Corbett, *Official History of the Great War, Naval Operations,* Vol. I (London: Longmans, Green & Co., 1920), 303.

9   These signals are not recorded in *Philomel*'s Cypher Log, N, Acc W2391.

10 Ibid., Aug–Dec 1914.

11 Capt P.H. Hall-Thompson, 'The Work of the "Philomel"', in Drew, 68.

12 Corbett, *Naval Operations*, II (London: Longmans, Green & Co., 1929), 7.

13 *Philomel*, Cypher Log, Dec 1914–Jun 1915, tel, 2 Feb 1915, N, Acc W2391.

14 *Philomel* Discharge Book, N20, 8.VI; Hall-Thompson, 71–3.

15 *Philomel*, Reporting Landing Party in the vicinity of Alexandretta, 17 Feb 1915, N41/1; also Hall-Thompson, 72–3. Hall-Thompson reported three killed and three wounded in his Letter of Proceedings dated 17 February 1915, N41/1. However the extract of the Ship's Log held by the Royal Navy Historical Branch in Britain states that three were killed and two wounded.

16 *Philomel*, Cypher Log, tel, 9 Feb 1915, N, Acc W2391.

17 Reporting Reasons for Landing Armed Party, 10 Feb 1915, N41/1.

18 Hall-Thompson, 73–4.

19 Sailing Orders, *Philomel*, 31 May 1915, N41/1.

20 Hall-Thompson, 76.

21 Ibid.

22 See signals between HMS *Empress of Asia* and *Philomel*, 9–14 Aug 1915, *Philomel*, Cypher Log, Aug to Dec 1915, RNZN Museum, Devonport.

23 See ibid., cables 12, 13, 22 Aug, 18 Sep 1915.

24 *Philomel*, Report of Operations in connection with Military in Aden Hinterland, 29 Sep 1915; also Report by Lieutenant Millar, 28 Sep 1915, N41/1.

25 Ibid., Report by Millar, 28 Sep 1915.

26 SNO Southern Patrol No. 63, Enclosure 1 to East Indies Letter 576/1127, 14 Oct 1915, ADM 137/1148.

27 GOC Aden to SNO Aden, n.d., but with received stamp in *Empress of Asia*, 29 Sep 1915, N41/1.

28 On the Mesopotamian campaign see A.J. Barker, *The Neglected War* (London: Faber and Faber, 1967).

29 Commodore Persian Gulf Memorandum No. 025, 6 Nov 1915, N41/1; and HMS *Philomel*, Cypher Log, message, 2 Nov 1915, timed 2355, RNZN Museum.

30 Hall-Thompson, 78–9. The medical complaints are from E.E. Corner, personal reminiscences, RNZN Museum, DLE 0026.

31 *Philomel*, Cypher Log, cable, 13 Nov 1915, RNZN Museum.

32 *Philomel*, Cypher Log, cable, 4 Jan 1916, N, Acc W2391.

33 *Philomel*, Recommending Member of Crew For Life Saving Medal, 9 Feb 1916, N41/1.

34 Ibid., *Philomel* Letter of Proceedings, 21 Mar 1916.

35 Hall-Thompson, 81–2.

36 *Philomel* No. 16, Reporting State of Affairs at Sharja, 21 Mar 1916; *Philomel*, Letter of Proceedings, 29 Mar 1916, N41/1; see also Hall-Thompson, 81–2.

37 *Philomel*, Letter of Proceedings, 18 Jun 1916, N41/1.

38 Hall-Thompson, in his Letter of Proceedings, reported one death from ptomaine poisoning and two from malaria, which is confirmed in the *Philomel* cypher log. However Form S165 (Return of Ratings Entered or Discharged) states that Adlam and Gaskin died of food poisoning and Dowding of enteric.

39 Photograph of *Philomel* Concert Party, Bombay, 1916, AAC 0063, RNZN Museum. The amount of money remitted is from the Cypher Log, 11 Jun 1916, N, Acc W2391.

40 See various correspondence Aug 1916–Jan 1917 in N1, 6/4/7.

41 HMS *Juno*, Memorandum, 30 Jan 1917, N41/1.

42 *Philomel*, Letter, 20 Apr 1917, N1, 6/4/7.

43 The 4.7-inch guns were fitted to: *Devon*, *Leitrim*, *Pakeha*, *Turakina*, *Rimutaka*, *Paparoa*, *Zealandic* and *Kumara*. See Memorandum to Naval Secretary, Navy Office Melbourne, 5 Apr 1917, N20.7. The seven 3-pounder guns were sent to Malta. See PM to NZHC, London, Aug 1917, N20.7.

44 *Philomel*, Report of Proceedings, 15 Jan 1917, N1, 6/4/7.

45 A 'private ship' is one that does not have a flag officer embarked or a commanding officer who is delegated formal control over other ships.

46 The main references for information on the operations of SMS *Wolf* are: report in ADM137/1430 (essentially compiled from reports of ex-prisoners of war, repatriated when SS *Igotz Mendi* went aground attempting to reach Germany in 1918; and it appears, largely from the reports of T.E. Rees, second mate of the *Wairuna*); Roy Alexander, *The Cruise of the Raider Wolf* (Sydney: Angus & Robertson, 1939). Alexander was the radio officer of the *Wairuna*, captured by *Wolf* in June 1917; Edwin P. Hoyt, *Raider Wolf* (London: Arthur Barker, 1974), which seems to have been, in the main, drawn from Alexander, although he does credit others in his introduction; the track chart of *Wolf* compiled by the Admiralty, 1916–18, ADM137/1445.

47 There was some doubt over the number of mines carried, with the report in ADM137/1430 estimating 500, but the figure of 400 cited by Alexander seems more likely.

48 Hoyt, 11.

49 ADM137/1430.

50 The actual number laid was not ascertained until after the war. N1, 16/21/1, 28 Nov 1918. At the time the figure was thought to be between 45 (Alexander) and 50 (ADM137/1430), New Zealand being advised that 50 mines had been laid (Admiralty cable, 5 Mar 1918, N1, 16/21/1).

51 ADM137/1430.

52 C-in-C China to Admiralty, 15 Jan 1918, ADM137/1430.

53 Nerger did not know that the Royal Navy blockade had been discontinued in December 1917. See Henry Newbolt, *Official History of the Great War, Naval Operations*, Vol. IV (London: Longmans, Green & Co., 1928), 226.

54 CGS to NIO, 22 Feb 1915, AD1, 57/145, ANZ.

55 Hall-Thompson to Def Min, 21 Mar 1917, N1, 16/21/1.

56 *Wairuna* was captured by *Wolf* on 2 June 1917 and *Port Kembla* struck a mine in the Cape Farewell field on 18 September 1917.

57 Hall-Thompson to Def Min, 16 Oct 1917, N1, 16/20.

58 Ibid., *Philomel*, Letter, 15 Oct 1915.

59 Hall-Thompson to Def Min, 29 Nov 1917, N1, 16/21/1.

60 Ibid., Hall-Thompson to Def Min, 7 Dec 1917.

61 Account submitted by NZ Trawling and Fish Supply Company, 1 May 1919, N1, 16/20/1.

62 Ibid., Sailing Orders to Lieutenant Commander C.J. Keily RNR, 9 Feb 1918.

63 HM Trawler *Nora Niven*, Report, 18 Feb 1918, N1, 16/20/2.

64 SNO NZ, cable S/No. 3598, 20 Feb 1918, N1, 16/21/1.

65 C.W.N. Ingram, *New Zealand Shipwrecks 1795–1982* (Wellington: Reed, 1984, 6th edition), 331–32. Routing Instructions SS *Wimmera*, 24 Jun 1918, N1, 20/11.

66 Ibid., C.F. Wilson, 2nd Officer, SS *Wimmera*, Statement to Collector of Customs, Auckland, 1 Jul 1918.

67 NA 18/10 of 7 Feb 1919, N1, 16/20/3.

68 Cable S/No. 5876, 8 Apr 1919, N1, 16/20.

69 Ibid., NA 18/72 dated 3 Oct 1919.

70   Ibid., 'Minesweeping in New Zealand Waters by HMS *Geranium*, *Mallow* and *Marguerite*', Report by Hall-Thompson, 30 Jul 1919.

71   Ibid., *Geranium*, Report, 16 Aug 1919; and 'Minesweeping in New Zealand Waters by HM Ships *Geranium*, *Mallow* and *Marguerite*', Report by Cmdr T.A. Williams, 17 Sep 1919.

72   HMS *Psyche*, Memorandum No. 034, 4 Aug 1914: Copy of Confidential Instructions to NIO of the NZ Division, N1, 13/8/4.

73   PM to GGNZ, 26 Nov 1917, AD1, 23/153; and SS Cols to GGNZ, 10 Dec 1917, G41/31.

74   *Psyche*, Memorandum No. 034, 4 Aug 1914: Copy of Confidential Instructions to NIO of NZ Division, N1, 13/8/4; also various correspondence in G41.

75   NIO to GNZ, 6 Aug 1914, and NIO to GNZ, 17 Oct 1914, G46/1; SNO to GNZ, 4 Aug 1914, G41/1.

76   The actual date of Paymaster Brown assuming the duties of Naval Intelligence Officer is not recorded. However the Governor was advised of his appointment on 19 September 1914 (G46/1). *Torch* paid off on 23 November 1914 and the Naval Intelligence Centre was relocated the next day. See Memorandum for GNZ, 23 Nov 1914, G41/5.

77   Vice-Admiral Sir Arthur Hezlet, *The Electron and Sea Power* (London: Peter Davies, 1975).

78   *Philomel*, Cypher Log, Acc W2931.

79   Commonwealth Naval Board to SNO NZ Division, 28 Sep 1914, G46/1.

80   Ibid., Navy Melbourne to Naval Wellington, 5 Oct 1914, and Melbourne to Naval Wellington, 6 Oct 1914; and Memorandum for Gov NZ, 7 Oct 1914.

81   Ibid., HMS *Sealark* to SNO NZ Division, 21 Sep 1914, and Memorandum for GNZ, 20 Oct 1914.

82   Memorandum for GNZ, 15 Oct 1914, G41/6.

83   *Torch*, 095V, 31 Jul 1916, G41/20.

84   Tel, 17 Feb 1916, G41/16.

85   Letter dated 20 Mar 1916, G41/18.

86   *Torch*, 095V, 31 Jul 1916, G41/20. 'Naval Wellington' was the telegraphic address of the SNO New Zealand.

87   Private Secretary to the GNZ to Actg SNO, 11 Aug 1916, G41/21.

88   Paymaster W.J.A. Brown (*Torch*) to CGS, 2 May 1916, G41/18.

89   *Torch*, 095, 20 May 1916, G41/19.

90   First Assistant Secretary, Post and Telegraph Department, to Paymaster W.J.A. Brown, *Torch*, 24 May 1916, G41/19.

91   PM to GGNZ, 26 Nov 1917, AD1, 23/153.

92   GGNZ to SS Cols, 27 Nov 1917, SS Cols to GGNZ, 10 Dec 1917, G41/31; and Gov Fiji to GGNZ, 7 Jan 1918, G41/32.

93   *Torch*, 095, 7 Jan 1916, and covering memoranda, G41/15.

94   C-in-C China Station to SNO, NZ Division, 12 Oct 1914, annotated with government approval dated 13 Oct 1914, G41/4.

95   R. Bromby, *German Raiders of the South Seas: The naval threat to Australia/New Zealand 1914–17* (Sydney: Doubleday, 1985), 39–40.

96   H.B. Anderson, *The Day's Run* (Christchurch: Caxton Press, 1977). According to the *Navy List*, the officer in 1914 was Engineer Lieutenant H. Mackenzie RN.

97   Anderson, 141–2.

98   SNO to GNZ, 11 Dec 1914, G41/5.

99   *NZOYB*, 1920, 148.

100   SNO, NZD No.028, 4 Jun 1916, G41/19.

101   GNZ to SNO, 21 Aug 1916, G41/21.

102   SNO to GNZ, 22 Nov 1916, G41/23.

103 GNZ to SS Cols, 10 Jan 1917, G41/24.
104 SNO to GNZ, 23 Jan 1917, G41/25.
105 PM to GGNZ, 23 Feb 1918, G41/33.
106 GNZ to SS Cols, 21, 26 Apr 1917, G41/27.
107 GGNZ to SS Cols, 30 Jan 1918, G41/33.
108 Ibid., SS Cols to GGNZ,13 Feb 1918.
109 Ibid., PM to GGNZ, 23 Feb 1918.

Chapter 18: Vincent Orange

1 I gratefully acknowledge the generosity of Errol W. Martyn, my friend and eminent historian of New Zealand aviation, who made available his researches into the careers of Burn and Bannerman.
2 H.A. Jones, *The War in the Air* (Oxford: Clarendon Press, 1937), Vol. V, 251.
3 It first flew in May 1913: Jon Guttman, *Caudron G.3* (Berkhamsted, Herts.: Albatros Productions, Windsock Datafile No. 94, 2002), 3.
4 It first flew in May 1917, but was not ready for squadron service until January 1918: J.M. Bruce, *Sopwith Dolphin* (Berkhamsted, Herts.: Albatros Productions, Windsock Datafile No. 54, 1995), xx, 25.
5 Burn's Service Record, ANZ; *NZ Gazette*, 1916, Vol. 1, 1073; St John's Branch, NZ Genealogical Society's CD-ROM on 'NZ World War 1 Service Personnel & Reserves Index'; *The New Zealander*, 28 Mar 1919, 61.
6 Christopher Draper, *The Mad Major* (London: Air Review, 1962), 35.
7 Annual Report, 25 June 1914–26 June 1915, *AJHR*, H-19, para. 24.
8 Born at Takapau, Hawke's Bay, October 1886, he joined the Indian Army in 1905 and was captured by the Turks on 21 November 1915: the first NZ airman to suffer that fate in the Great War.
9 John F. Hamlin, *Flat Out: The Story of 30 Squadron, Royal Air Force* (Tunbridge Wells: Air-Britain, 2002), 15–17.
10 Norman Dixon, *On the Psychology of Military Incompetence* (London: Futura, 1979), 95–6; Donald Clark, 'Townshend: Surrender, Capture and Disgrace', *History of the First World War*, Vol. 3 (London: Purnell, 1968), 1340–7.
11 Apart from Burn, only Air Mechanic Francis Luke Adams, Australian Flying Corps, born in Christchurch, lost his life: captured at Kut al Amarah, he died of malaria while being marched to Turkey some time between August and November 1916: Errol W. Martyn, *For Your Tomorrow: A Record Of New Zealanders Who Have Died While Serving With The RNZAF And Allied Air Services Since 1915*, Vol. 1, *Fates, 1915–1942* (Christchurch: Volplane Press, 1998), 38.
12 Dixon, 97.
13 CRS A2023, Item A38/7/339, Australian Archives, Canberra.
14 AIR1/140/15/40/306, UKNA; Keith Isaacs, *Military Aircraft of Australia, 1909–1918* (Canberra: AWM, 1971), 46.
15 C.M. Hanson, *By Such Deeds: Honours and Awards in the Royal New Zealand Air Force, 1923–1999* (Christchurch: Volplane Press, 2001), 48; Martyn, 38; Jones, V, 256–7.
16 Letter to Lt-Col E.J.M. Wood, GSO1, Army HQ, India, AIR1/140/15/40/306.
17 Duncan Grinnell-Milne, *Wind in the Wires* (London, 1933: Panther Books, 2nd ed., 1957), 23, 26.
18 *Star,* 12 Aug 1915.
19 *ST*, 15 Oct 1915.
20 As with Burn, so with Bannerman: I owe most of my information to the researches of Errol W. Martyn, who also summarised Bannerman's logbook (in the RNZAF Museum, Wigram) and 79 Squadron's combat and casualty reports (in AIR 1/853/204/5/402 &

406 and AIR 1/1226/204/5/2634/79, UKNA.

21   E.F. Harvie, *George Bolt: Pioneer Aviator, Foundations of a Future* (Wellington: A.H. & A.W. Reed, 1974), 20.

22   Jones, VI, 36.

23   Wayne R. Braby, '"Nothing Can Stop Us": A Short History of 79 Squadron, RFC/RAF', *Cross & Cockade US*, Vol. 5, No. 2 (1964), 168.

24   Oliver Stewart, in Leonard Bridgman, *The Clouds Remember: The Aeroplanes of World War 1* (London, 1936: Arms & Armour Press, 2nd ed., 1972), 64–6.

25   Jones, IV, 271, 272n, 305, 372.

26   Wing Cmdr W.M. Fry, 'In Regard to Major Noel', *Cross & Cockade US*, Vol. 22, No. 2 (1981), 147–51. Fry was responding to criticism of Noel by Lieutenant Edgar A. Coapman, 'Coapman and the C.O.', in Vol. 17, No. 2 (1976), 97–133; see also Brian P. Flanagan, 'Postscript to Coapman and the C.O.', Vol. 19, No. 2 (1978), 184–7. All three contain information about 79 Squadron, including photographs supplied by Bannerman.

27   John Terraine, *To Win A War: 1918, The Year of Victory* (London: Sidgwick & Jackson, 1978), 65.

28   William M. Fry, *Air of Battle* (London: Kimber, 1974), 173–5; Braby, 168–75; David Mulgan, *The Kiwis First Wings* (Wellington: Wingfield Press, 1960), 13, 82.

29   Fry, 174–9.

30   Christopher Shores *et al*, *Above The Trenches: A Complete Record of the Fighter Aces and Units of the British Empire Air Forces, 1915–1920* (London: Grub Street, 1990), 53; see also fn 26.

31   Terraine, 258.

32   Bannerman appeared 14 times, Caldwell 15 times – over a much longer period: Christopher Cole, *Royal Air Force, 1918* (London: Kimber, 1968).

33   Bannerman Papers, RNZAF Museum, Wigram.

34   Peter Gray & Owen Thetford, *German Aircraft of the First World War* (London: Putnam, 1962, 2nd ed., 1970), 79–81.

35   Jones, VI, 531–2.

36   Shores, 62; Hanson, 71.

37   The others were 19, 23 and 87 Squadrons.

38   Gillet, known as 'razor' for obvious reasons, returned to Baltimore after the Armistice and became well known there as a businessman and banker: obituary in *The Sun* (Baltimore), 22 Dec 1969; J.J. Hudson, 'Captain Francis Warrington Gillet: One of America's Top Aces', *Cross & Cockade GB*, Vol. 30, No. 3 (1999), 165–8; Shores, 167–8.

39   *Flight*, 2 Nov 1918, 1247.

40   Ibid., 12 Dec 1918, 1399.

41   *ST*, 5 Aug 1978.

Chapter 20: Ria Keenan

1   Village People, 'Y.M.C.A', sound recording (1978).

2   Barbara McLennan, *YMCA New Zealand: The First 125 Years* (Wellington: National Council of the YMCAs of New Zealand, 1981), 2–3.

3   'Reports and Proceedings', 4th National Convention of the Y.M.C.A. (2–5 Mar 1924), 17.

4   New Zealand YMCA, *"Buckshee", A Pictorial Record of the Work of the N.Z. Y.M.C.A. on Active Service* (London: 1919), 12.

5   Reports and Proceedings (1924) 17. (In 1918 Hay received an OBE for his services with the YMCA. After the war, he established Hay's department store in Christchurch, later to become Haywrights before eventually being merged with Farmers.)

6   Ibid., 24. E.W. Nelson of Hawke's Bay and T. Holden of Te Aroha both funded their own passages overseas in an effort to do anything they could for New Zealand troops. Both

worked as civilian volunteers with the YMCA in France, with Holden also working in Egypt.

7   A.K.Yapp, *Red Triangle Diaries* (n.d.), 1.

8   Reports and Proceedings (1924), 26.

9   Ibid., 22–4.

10 J. Bryant Haigh, *Men of Faith and Courage* (Wellington: New Zealand Army, 1983), 46.

11 Carbery, 312.

12 Burton, *Auckland*, 133–4.

13 'New Zealand Y.M.C.A. in France', n.d., NZYMCA records, ATL.

14 'Reports and Proceedings' (1924), 20.

15 Carbery, 371, states that approximately 3600 men per annum of the NZEF were infected and required treatment; other authors estimate the figure to be higher.

16 Conference of NZ National YMCA Committee and War Auxiliary, Wellington, 25–26 Jul 1917, 2. The NZYMCA got their wish for their field secretaries to become attested members of the NZEF one year later, but they did not receive an honorary rank.

17 *Jewish Chronicle*, 12 Jan 1917.

18 A.K.Yapp, 'The Chief End in View', in *Red Triangle Papers No. 7*, 26 Sep 1916, 2.

19 *Literary Guide*, Feb 1917. This press clipping held in a YMCA scrapbook at the Alexander Turnbull Library describes the reaction of a minister of a 'Free Christian Church in a large northern town' on being asked to sign an agreement to support a number of theological doctrines he found objectionable when applying to serve as a YMCA volunteer in France.

20 *Triangle Trail*, 1919, 9.

21 Anon., *ibid.*, 25 May 1918, 2.

22 Burton, *Silent*, 284.

23 Ernest Crane, *I Can Do No Other: A Biography of Ormond Burton* (Auckland: Hodder & Stoughton, 1986). Burton also married Nell Tizard, one of the organisers of the New Zealand Young Women's Christian Association (NZYWCA), and wrote the Auckland regimental history.

24 John A. Lee, *Soldier* (Wellington: A.H. & A.W. Reed, 1976), 12.

25 Harper, *Letters*, 145.

26 Nicholas Boyack, *Behind the Lines: The Lives of New Zealand Soldiers in the First World War* (Wellington: Allen & Unwin, 1989), 198.

27 Les Cleveland, 'Popular Culture, War in', in McGibbon, *Companion*, 124–8.

28 F.G. Glen, 'New Zealand Army Chaplains at War: 2 NZEF 1939–1945' (PhD thesis, University of Waikato, 1996), Vol 1, 222.

Chapter 21: Bronwyn Dalley

1   Text of the pamphlet reproduced in *The White Ribbon*, Jun 1914. I completed part of the research for this paper while holding the J.D. Stout Fellowship at VUW's Stout Centre during 1997–98. A fuller discussion of the topic of white slavery is Bronwyn Dalley, '"Fresh attractions": white slavery and feminism in New Zealand, 1885–1918', *Women's History Review*, Vol. 9, No. 3 (2000), 585–606.

2   *WR*, Sep 1914.

3   *EP*, 27 May 1916.

4   Better studies of white slavery include Lucy Bland, *Banishing the Beast: sexuality and the early feminists* (New York: The New Press, 1995); Edward Bristow, *Prostitution and Prejudice: the Jewish fight against white slavery 1870–1939* (Oxford: Clarendon Press, 1982); Mark Connelly, *The Response to Prostitution in the Progressive Era* (Chapel Hill: University of North Carolina Press, 1980); Margit Stange, *Personal Property: Wives, White Slaves and the Market in Women* (Baltimore: Johns Hopkins UP, 1998). The full texts of Stead's articles are at www.attackingthedevil.co.uk/pmg/tribute/.

5   See case of Doris Williams: *EP*, 30 Aug 1910, *The Vigilance Record*, Aug 1910. See also
     Superintendent, Wellington to Commissioner of Police, 2 Jun 1915, Police records (P)1,
     1915/1032, ANZ. All archival references are to ANZ unless otherwise stated.

6   *WC*, 6 Mar 1897, 2.

7   *WR*, Oct–Dec 1913, Jan, Mar 1914.

8   Ibid., Apr 1914.

9   *NZPD*, Vol. 153, 1910, 405–9.

10   *WR*, May 1914.

11   Minister of Public Health G.W. Russell suggested conviction, inspection and detention of
     prostitutes if found to be suffering from venereal disease, and of every man convicted of
     consorting with known prostitutes if suffering from venereal disease. See *AJHR*, 1916, H-
     38.

12   The best discussion of venereal disease in New Zealand is Philip Fleming, '"Shadow over
     New Zealand": The response to Venereal Disease in New Zealand 1910–1945' (PhD
     thesis, MU, 1989). An excellent recent discussion of war and venereal disease across the
     British Empire is Philippa Levine, *Prostitution, Race and Politics: Policing Venereal Disease in
     the British Empire* (New York: Routledge, 2003).

13   Godley to Def Min, 4 Jan 1915, AD1, 24/46/6; Jane Tolerton, 'Venereal disease', in
     McGibbon, *Companion*, 554. Boyack, 139ff, and Phillips, *Man's Country?*, 188–9, discuss
     the figures.

14   See Bronwyn Dalley, 'Lolly Shops "of the Red-light Kind" and "Soldiers of the King":
     Suppressing One-woman Brothels in New Zealand, 1908–1916', *NZJH*, Vol. 30, No. 1
     (1996), 3–23.

15   See correspondence between military and Wellington police, 1916–17 in AD1, 24/219.

16   Report of deputation, 10 Aug 1915, AD1, 24/83.

17   Jane Tolerton, *Ettie: A life of Ettie Rout* (Auckland: Penguin, 1992), 162.

18   *WR*, 18 Feb 1918.

19   Ibid., Jun 1918.

20   Geoffrey Wall, 'Flaubert's Oriental Education', *Guardian*, 27 Oct 2001, www.books.
     guardian.co.uk. See also Boyack, 12–31, for a discussion of New Zealanders' views of
     Egypt.

21   Levine, 155.

22   Mrs Archibald Mackirdy and W.N. Willis, *The White Slave Market* (London: Stanley Paul &
     Co, 1912), 44–5.

23   Discussed in Levine, 148ff.

24   Quoted in ibid., 240–1.

25   Yunan Labib Rizk, 'Al-Ahram: A Diwan of Contemporary Life (393)', *Al-Ahram Weekly
     On-line*, 537, 7–13 Jun 2001, www.weekly.ahram.org.eg/2001/537/chrncls.htm.

26   Levine, 79.

27   Tolerton, *Ettie*, 124.

28   Rizk, 'Al-Ahram'.

29   Tolerton, 'Venereal disease', 554, quoted in Boyack, 132.

30   Figures from Phillips, 160–1.

31   Official discussion of the venereal disease rate can be found in AD1, 24/46/1.

32   Ria Keenan, '"In this Sign Conquer": New Zealand military chaplains and their uses in the
     Great War', www.arts/monash/edu.au/history/events/geniddwar/papers/keenan.html.

33   W.H. George to Colonel Anderson 14 Feb 1916, AD1, 26/46.

34   Ibid., Ettie Rout to Colonel Rhodes, 12 Mar 1916.

35   Diary entries, 22 and 29 Jan 1916, MS-Papers-2223/2, ATL; see also Boyack, 131ff.

36   Quoted in Phillips, Boyack and Malone, 26–7.

37 Tolerton, *Ettie*, 124.

38 Fenwick to Def Min, 10 Oct 1915, Allen Papers, D4/65; Godley to Def Min, 4 Jan 1915, AD1, 24/46/6.

39 Levine, 156; Tolerton, *Ettie*, 125.

40 Phillips, 158ff.

41 R. Tate (Adjutant-General) to DMQ, Apr 1917, AD1, 24/46/1.

42 Discussions of this can be found in Boyack, 24–31, and Levine, 155–7.

43 Proceedings of court of enquiry, Cairo, 3 Apr 1915, AD1, 24/86.

44 *WR*, Sep 1915, Apr 1916.

45 Deputation, 10 Aug 1915, AD1, 24/83.

46 *WR*, Jul 1917.

47 [illegible] to Major Gunn, 13 May 1916, AD1, 37/61.

48 *WR*, Nov 1919.

Chapter 22: Ashley Gould

1 *New Zealand Farmer Stock and Station Journal and A. and P. Gazette*, Oct 1919, 1401.

2 Kent Fedorowich, *Unfit for Heroes: Reconstruction and Soldier Settlement in the Empire Between the Wars* (Manchester: MUP, 1995); Paul M. Koroscil, 'Soldiers, Settlement, and Development in British Columbia, 1915–1930', *BC Studies*, Vol. 54 (1982), 63–87; Marilyn Lake, *The Limits of Hope: Soldier Settlement in Victoria 1915–38* (Melbourne: OUP, 1987); Leneman, Leah, 'Land Settlement in Scotland After World War I', *Agricultural History Review*, Vol. 37, No 1 (1989), 52–64. D.G. Marshall, 'Soldier Settlement in the British Empire', *Journal of Land and Public Utility Economics*, 1946, 256–65. Desmond Morton and Glenn Wright, *Winning the Second Battle: Canadian Veterans and the Return to Civilian Life 1915–1930* (Toronto: University of Toronto Press, 1987); J.M. Powell, 'The Debt of Honour: Soldier Settlement in the Dominions, 1915–1940', *Journal of Australian Studies* (Jun 1981), 64–87. J.M. Powell, 'Soldier Settlement in New Zealand 1915–1923', *Australian Geographical Studies*, Vol. 9, No. 2 (1971), 144–60. J.A. Shultz, 'Finding Homes Fit For Heroes: The Great War and Empire Settlement', *Canadian Journal of History*, Vol. 18, No. 1 (1983), 99–110; P.B. Johnson, *Land Fit for Heroes: the planning of British reconstruction 1916–1919* (Chicago: Chicago UP, 1968); W.J. Black, 'Agricultural training for returned soldiers', *Agricultural Gazette of Canada*, V (1918), 1123–7; C.W. Cavers, 'Selecting and training soldiers for agriculture', ibid., VI (1919), 426–8.

3 See T.W.H. Brooking, *Massey: Its Early Years* (Palmerston North: Massey Alumni Assn, 1977), ch. 1; A.B. Thompson, *Adult Education in New Zealand: a critical and historical survey* (Wellington: NZ Council of Educational Research, 1945); Prime Minister Massey asked Alexander Macpherson, while the latter was in the United States for the Panama Pacific International Exposition in San Francisco, to visit agricultural training institutions in the US and Canada which had particular relevance to the agricultural instructional work in New Zealand. His report was supplied to Parliament in 1916 and received high commendation. Macpherson Papers, MS-Papers-1955, ATL. See also Agriculture Department records (AG) 40-1931/11h, ANZ.

4 J.R. Kirk, 'The New Zealand Soldier: His Outlook' (paper read at Royal Colonial Institute, Westminster, 17 Dec 1918), *United Empire*, Vol. 10 (1919), 70.

5 These farms had their genesis under Edward Tregear, who was Secretary for Labour when the first was established at Levin in 1894. Their function was to teach basic manual farming skills to fit the unemployed to earn a living from the land. K.R. Howe, *Singer in a Songless Land: A Life of Edward Tregear 1846–1931* (Auckland: AUP, 1991), 79–80; *Cyclopedia of New Zealand*, Vol. 1 (Wellington: The Cyclopedia Coy, 1897), 1119 [1110].

6 Brodrick to Secretary, Dept of Agriculture, Industries and Commerce, 28 Apr 1916, Lands and Survey Department records (LS)26/1-1, AAMX, W6095, 3430/1, ANZ.

7   *NZ Farmer*, May 1916, 564.

8   Massey to Allen, 13 May 1916, LS26/1-1.

9   *Soldiers' Guide* (Wellington, 1917), 43.

10 *NZPD*, Vol. 179, 525.

11 Ferguson to H.L. Spratt, 24 Nov 1917, NEB records, NEB-Wellington, 2/724, ANZ.

12 Ferguson to Allen, 5 Jun 1918, AD78, 24/140, ANZ.

13 Ferguson to Massey, 10 Dec 1917, National Efficiency Board memoranda book, Vol. 1, qMS, ATL.

14 Ibid., Ferguson to Allen, 26 Mar 1917.

15 In September 1920 a group of soldiers training at Ruakura wrote to Brodrick explaining that they were anxious to get on the land and were interested in a block that they could be employed on to break in and then be given preference for in the subsequent ballot. LS21/149, ANZ.

16 Commandant, NZ Forces, to Under-Secretary for Lands, 7 Aug 1918, LS26/1-4; Report of Defence Expenditure Commission, *AJHR*, H-19j, 1918.

17 *QM*, 25 May 1918, 12.

18 Ibid.

19 Richardson, memo, 27 Sep 1917, WA1/3/10/42, ANZ.

20 Kirk, 68–75.

21 WA1/3/10/42. The blue was a reference to the uniforms worn by the convalescent men.

22 Ibid.

23 Lieutenant-Colonel H. Stewart, 'Education in the New Zealand Forces', *The Empire Review*, 33 (1919), 63–9.

24 George C. Creelman, 'The Khaki University', *Agricultural Gazette of Canada*, V (1918), 1126–7.

25 Kirk, 70.

26 *Triangle Trail*, n.d., clipping on AD65/211, ANZ.

27 AD83/103/50, ANZ. Conferences were held in subsequent years but the New Zealand government did not send delegations. Eventually the inspiration and thrust of the schemes was merged with the educational secretariat of the League of Nations. National Archives of Australia, Canberra.

28 J. Taylor, H.C. Wiltshire and B. Jennings, *1919 Report: The Final and Interim Reports of the Adult Education Committee of the Ministry of Reconstruction, 1918–1919* (Nottingham: University of Nottingham, 1980 reprint).

29 The American YMCA established training courses in agriculture for American soldiers based in France. The US Army took over control of the scheme and established a college of agriculture at Beaune which had 6000 students while another 2600 were at a farm school at Allerey. The US had over two million men in its forces stationed in France and extension courses provided instruction in agriculture to almost every unit in France. Alfred C. True, *A History of Agricultural Education in the United States, 1785–1925* (Washington: GPO, 1969), 299–300.

30 Letter from Sergeant J.B. Condliffe, in *Press*, 5 Oct 1918.

31 Report of the Educational Work of the NZEF for September 1918, WA1/3/4.

32 Kirk, 68–75.

33 Stewart, 'Education'; see also Brigadier-General G.S. Richardson, 'Education in the New Zealand Expeditionary Force', in Drew, 223.

34 NZ Farming Company at Torquay, War Diary, WA148/1, ANZ.

35 See WA148/1, ANZ.

36 Memorandum to the OC, NZEF UK, Aug 1918, AD87, 103/5A, ANZ.

37 WA148/1.

38 AD87, 103/50.

39 E. Griffiths to Minister of Lands, 6 Jun 1918, LS 26/1-4.

40 Briscoe Moore, *From Forest to Farm* (London: Pelham Books, 1969), 32. Mounted Rifles Brigade, daily orders, L & S 26/1–4, AAMX 6095 W3430/1, ANZ.

41 Moore, p.15.

42 Richardson, 'Education', 231.

43 WA40/5/25, ANZ.

44 The Report of the UK Committee for Reconstruction on the subject of re-afforestation was influential in New Zealand. 'Reconstruction Committee's Report and its Applicability to New Zealand', Council of the New Zealand Forestry League, 1919. Pam 1919, NZ For, 4120, ATL.

45 George Ranstead to father, 25 Dec 1918, Ranstead Letters, ATL. Ranstead was an NZEF Main Body man who served throughout the war in Gallipoli and Palestine. He was detained with the NZMR Brigade in Egypt because he was an experienced NCO. While on leave in Britain in mid-1919 he observed the London march past of Allied troops to celebrate the peace. He returned to New Zealand in September 1919. Ranstead Letters, MS Papers 4139, ATL.

46 AD87, 103/50.

47 Stewart left 2 Battalion, Canterbury Regiment, for duty as Director of Education for the NZEF. Ferguson, 287.

48 Kirk, 73.

49 Condliffe, letter, *Press*, 5 Oct 1918.

50 Ibid.

51 War diaries for these camps, WA, ANZ.

52 Byrne, *Otago*, 387.

53 Boyack, *Behind the Lines*, 161–2.

54 Minister of Defence to Opotiki farmer, 24 Nov 1918, AD27/140; Ferguson to Acting PM, 8 Nov 1918, NEB memoranda book, vol. 3, QMS, ATL.

55 *NZ Farmer*, Jan 1920, 125.

56 Kirk, 68–75.

57 AD87, 103/50.

58 W.S. Hill and H.E. Collier, *Land Settlement in New Zealand* (London: NZEF Education Dept, 1919). See Pam 630.93, ATL.

59 Hill and Collier, 9.

60 Ibid.

61 Monthly report of the Director of Education, Apr 1919, in AD87/103/50.

62 Richardson, 'Education', 231.

63 Ibid., 221.

64 Reports of the officers in charge of the education programmes on board various New Zealand bound troopships. AD65/226, ANZ.

65 Pugsley, *Fringe*, 293; Sergeant F J Wootten complained of a lack of information relative to the Discharged Soldiers' Settlement Act provided to the soldiers on board a March 1919 sailing of the troopship *Willochra*. 'Many men wanted to know why an adequate supply of these leaflets were [*sic*] not aboard'. LS26/1-6.

66 AD65/226, ANZ.

67 AD1, 49/70/179, Vol. 1.

68 H.E.L. Mellersh, *Schoolboy into War* (London, 1978), 184.

69 See, e.g., Desmond Morton, 'Kicking and complaining: Demobilization Riots in the Canadian Expeditionary Force, 1918–19', *Canadian Historical Review*, Vol. 61, No. 3 (1980), 334–60; Boyack, esp ch. 6; Pugsley, *Fringe*, ch. 17.

70   Report of the Director of Education for period 28 March to 30 April 1919, AD87, 103/50.

71   Director of Military Hospitals to Director-General of Medical Services, 23 May 1918, AD1, 74/8, ANZ.

72   AD87, 103/5A.

73   Director of Medical Services (sanatoria) to Director, Agricultural Department, 1919, AD49/261/14, ANZ. W.G. Allan, 'The Resettlement of Discharged Soldiers on Crown Land in Canterbury: 1915–1940' (MA thesis in Geography, CU, 1967), 39, 49, discusses the 'rudimentary provision for agricultural training' and then suggests that the Hanmer farm was to cater for all classes of soldier settlers; however, he suggests, 'the facilities were inadequate to provide for everyone'.

74   AD74/32; AAMX W3166, LS-Wellington District 4/65, ANZ.

75   AD74/8, ANZ. A photograph reproduced in at least two general histories purports to show 'soldier settlers' but is in fact a photograph of serving TB infected soldiers in uniform operating machinery at the Tauherenikau property.

76   Montgomery to the District Superintendent, Department of Agriculture, Industries and Commerce, Auckland, 17 Dec 1918, AD87/103/6, ANZ.

77   AD87, 103/6.

78   Defence Forces, Annual Report, *AJHR*, H-19, 1919, 39.

79   AD59/6-14, 2736, ANZ.

80   *EP*, 19 Feb 1916, clipping on LS26/1-4, ANZ.

81   Report of Discharged Soldiers Settlement, *AJHR*, C-9, 1918, 3.

82   Boyack, 202.

83   Internal memo, Army Base Records, 25 Nov 1918, AD27/140.

84   *QM*, 10 Mar 1922, 39.

85   Richardson, 'Education', 231.

Chapter 23: Peter Dennis and Jeffrey Grey

1   These records are available on the Australian War Memorial's website: www.awm.gov.au and click on 'biographical databases'.

2   James Bennett, '"Massey's Sunday School Picnic Party": "The Other Anzacs" or Honorary Australians?', *War & Society*, Vol. 21, No. 2 (2003), 42.

3   Ibid., 54.

Chapter 24: Gavin McLean

1   *Press*, 23 Apr 2003.

2   M.N. Watt, *Index to the N.Z. Section of the Register of All British Ships 1840–1950* (Wellington: NZ Ship & Marine Society, 1962). The Ship Registration Act 1992 replaced earlier provisions in the Shipping and Seamen Act 1952.

3   Anna Green, *British Capital, Antipodean Labour* (Dunedin: University of Otago Press, 2001), 16.

4   Belich, *Paradise*, 66.

5   *NZOYB*, 1915, 468.

6   Ibid., 457.

7   Gavin McLean, *The Southern Octopus: The Rise of a Shipping Empire* (Wellington: Wellington Maritime Museum/NZ Ship & Marine Society, 1990), 194.

8   *NZOYB*, 1916, 466. Some Union Company ships were registered at ports other than Dunedin.

9   Marine Department, Annual Report, 1913–14, *AJHR*, 1914, H-15, 2.

10   McLean, *Octopus*, 182, and *AJHR*, H-15, 1915, 2.

11 *Statistics of New Zealand, 1918, Vol. II: Trade and Shipping*, 1919, 325.

12 *NZOYB*, 1916, 391.

13 Correspondence with Mr George H. Scales, Allen Papers, 4, ANZ.

14 *AJHR*, 1918, H-15, 15.

15 Ibid., 1916, A-1, 2.

16 David Burrell, 'Shipping Economics', in Ambrose Greenway (ed.), *The Golden Age of Shipping: the Classic Merchant Ship 1900–1960* (Greenwich: Conway Maritime Press, 1994), 167.

17 Gordon Boyce, *Information, Mediation and Institutional Development: The Rise of Large-Scale Enterprise in British Shipping 1870–1919* (Manchester: MUP, 1995), 127.

18 McGibbon, *Blue-water*, 29–30.

19 C.W.N. Ingram, *New Zealand Shipwrecks 1795–1975*, 5th ed. (Auckland: A.H. & A.W. Reed, 1977), 331–3.

20 Allan A. Kirk, *Express Steamers of Cook Strait* (Wellington: A.H. & A.W. Reed, 1968), 54–6.

21 McGibbon, *Blue-water*, 20–1.

22 *Union Steam Ship Company of New Zealand 1875 to 1925* (Wellington: Union Steam Ship Company, 1925), 20.

23 *NZOYB*, 1914, 697.

24 Figures taken from Ian Farquhar, *Union Fleet*, 3rd edn. (Wellington: NZ Ship & Marine Society, 2001), 89–105.

25 *NZOYB,* 1918, 455.

26 Peter Plowman, *Passenger Ships of Australia & New Zealand: Volume 1 1876–1912* (Auckland: William Collins, 1981), 166.

27 Neill Atkinson, *Crew Culture: New Zealand Seafarers Under Sail and Steam* (Wellington: Te Papa Press, 2001), 128.

28 Conrad Bollinger, *Against the Wind: the Story of the New Zealand Seamen's Union* (Wellington: NZSU, 1968), 125.

29 Baker, 112, 204, 206.

30 Gordon McLauchlan, *The Line That Dared: A History of the Union Steam Ship Company* (Auckland: Four Star Books, 1987), 61.

31 Gavin McLean, *Rocking the Boat? A History of Scales Corporation* (Christchurch: Hazard Press, 2002), 81–5.

32 Table based on original documents; see Gavin McLean, *Richardsons of Napier* (Wellington: NZ Ship & Marine Society, 1989), 134, Gavin McLean, *Canterbury Coasters* (Wellington: NZ Ship & Marine Society, 1988), 80.

33 The capital was increased from £22,000 to £51,000 in 1914.

34 Boyce, 127.

35 Ibid., 128–9.

36 McLean, *Octopus*, 184–6.

37 Christopher J. Napier, 'Secret Accounting in New Zealand: P&O and the Union Steam Ship Company 1917–1936', in Atsuo Tsuji and Paul Garner (eds), *Studies in Accounting History: Tradition and Innovation for the Twenty-First Century* (Westport: Greenwood Press, 1995), 138.

38 McLauchlan, 67.

39 *Evening Star*, 9 Jun 1917.

40 Russell, Cabinet memo, 13 Jun 1917, Marine Department records (M)1/25/812, ANZ.

41 Ibid., Russell to J. Henderson, 15 Jun 1917.

42 Ibid., Cabinet memo, 19 Jun 1917.

43 Napier, 139.

44 Ibid., 155.

Chapter 25: Peter Cooke

1 General Sir Alexander Godley, *Life of an Irish Soldier* (Dutton: John Murray, 1939), 142, 143
2 Ibid., 146.
3 The 1913 and 1914 exercises (in South Canterbury and the Waikato, respectively) both envisaged an 'Eastern maritime power' landing in New Zealand, but the main scenario was a state of war existing between the British Empire and a leading 'European maritime power'. The manoeuvring therefore could just as easily have been New Zealand forces fighting with a British expeditionary force in France, against an invading German army as was feared. See 'Report on a Staff Tour For Senior Officers, Held under the Direction of the General Officer Commanding, 29 January to 1 February 1913'; 'Headquarters Exercise for Senior Officers', Jan 1914, NZ Military Forces, Wellington (copy in the NZ Defence Force Library, Wellington).
4 Godley, 148.
5 Territorial Force 29,447, Senior Cadets 26,446, General Training Section 2075, Rifle Clubs 8770. See Drew, xiii.
6 Drew, 2.
7 QMG Report to 31 Mar 1915, AD1, 39/19/15.
8 Drew, xiv, 2; Notes on a Deputation to Def Min, 24 Oct 1913, AD1, 54/9.
9 'Mobilisation – Coast Defence Troops, 1914', AD1, 29/30; Peter Cooke, *Defending New Zealand – Ramparts on the Sea 1840–1950s* (Wellington: Defence of NZ Study Group, 2000), 194.
10 'Examination Service', in Cooke, 185.
11 *AJHR*, 1914, H-19A, App. 4, 29; Cooke, 200.
12 'Westport's Special Defences – Armoured Gun Trucks', in Cooke, 183; 'Protection of Shipping', in ibid., 221.
13 Godley to MDs, 16 Aug 1914, AD1, 29/30.
14 Lieutenant-Colonel Courtenay to OC Coast Defences, 6 Aug 1914, AD1 29/27.
15 *AJHR*, 1918, H-19, 4.
16 Ibid., 1917, 4; 1918, 4.
17 War Office to Under-SS Cols, 17 Apr 1912, AD1, 57/5/1.
18 Ibid., Major Johnston, Fort Standford, Plymouth, to GOC, 6 May 1911.
19 Harding Steward to GOC, 9 May 1911, AD1, 57/5/1.
20 Ian V. Hogg, *British Artillery Weapons & Ammunition 1914–18* (London: Ian Allen, 1972), 40.
21 Johnston to QMG, 15 Nov 1911, AD1, 57/5/1; *AJHR*, 1912, H-19, 6.
22 *AJHR*, H-19, 1912, s15, 5; Map PWWDO No.1050, 'Mt Cook Reserve Plan Showing Proposals for Laying Out Reserve, also Suggested Street Improvements', 18 Dec 1914, shows the magazine in use as stables. 'Mt Cook Prison Land', Public Works Department records (PW)1, 25/143/3, ANZ.
23 The statement in *AJHR*, 1912, H-19, 6, s16, that they had been issued to D Battery is incorrect.
24 SS Cols to GNZ, 20 Apr 1912; War Office to Under-SS Cols, 17 Apr 1912, AD1, 57/5/1.
25 Ibid., Johnston to GOC, 29 Apr 1912.
26 Ibid., Steward to NZHC, 2, 7 May 1912.
27 Ibid., Captain R.B. Smythe to HQ NZMF, 8 Jun 1912.
28 Ibid., GOC to Def Min, draft, not sent, May 1912.
29 Ibid., GOC to Def Min, 29 Jul 1912.
30 Ibid.
31 Ibid., Steward to Robin, 24 Sep 1912.
32 Another £6763 was advanced to the War Office for the replacement mountain guns in December 1913, but this was refunded, unspent, in 1916. AD1, 57/5/2.

33 NZHC to PM, 25 Mar 1916, AD1, 57/5/2. T. W. Brown, 'Draft of Broadcast History of the 5th Field Battery', n.d. [1938], ATL.

34 Bean, *ANZAC*, II, 65. Bean did not reveal his source for this tidbit but was at Gallipoli himself as correspondent. He said that, because these guns fired the same shell as those fired by Indian mountain batteries at Gallipoli, 'their cases were sometimes produced by the infantry as evidence of erratic fire of friendly guns'. The Ottoman Empire had gone on a shopping spree to make up losses suffered in the 1912–13 Balkan Wars. Having standardised on the 2.95-inch calibre, it bought not only from Vickers but also from Creusot and Krupp, and took 36 captured guns from Serbia. 'Many new guns arrived in Turkey between August and November 1914 and a certain number were subsequently smuggled in….' In June 1915 the Ottoman Empire fielded an estimated 79 mountain batteries of four guns each, each division nominally having three batteries. *Handbook of the Turkish Army, 1916* (London: War Office, 1916, reprinted 1996).

35 GOC to Def Min, 31 Mar 1914, AD1, 54/9.

36 'Instructions for Rifle Clubs, the Formation of Future Rifle Clubs, the Posting of Recruits to Same, and Their Management', Part II, in *AJHR*, H-19, 1912, 30.

37 Ibid., 1915, H-19, 6, s12.

38 Adjutant-General to Smythe, 30 Mar 1914, AD1, 61/52.

39 Annual Report, *AJHR*, 1912, H-19, 7, s24, 8, s26a.

40 Ibid., 7, s22.

41 This area of catchment reflects, in reverse, the original pre-1910 definition for rifle clubs, which was that they were not to form if within 3 miles of a drill hall (the intention being that a Volunteer Corps embody those men, the rifle club taking those at the greater distance). See Sansum Papers, MS Papers 2172, ATL; *AJHR*, H-19, 1912.

42 *AJHR*, 1912, H-19, Pt II, 30, s1.

43 The 1916 Military Service Act overlaid 21 recruiting districts on the 16 groups.

44 Harry Sansum, Wellington Suburbs Defence Rifle Club, MS Papers 2172, ATL.

45 'Conference – Rifle Clubs, 1912, AD1, 20/2.

46 GOC to Def Min, 31 Mar 1914, AD1, 54/9.

47 This was the NZ Rifle Club Executive, to which clubs affiliated by paying an annual fee of 10s. Godley described expenditure on rifle clubs as a 'waste of public money': 'if the money is to be used for sport, I would far rather see it used for Foot-ball and Cricket matches for the Cadets, in which case it would at least be doing good to their physique, whereas used for the encouragement of antiquated and obsolete methods of rifle shooting, it is doing active harm.' GOC to Def Min, 31 Mar 1914, AD1, 54/9.

48 Wm Hughes Field Papers, ATL.

49 Newspaper cutting, 'Rifle Clubs', n.d. [c.1912], unsourced [*Dominion* or *EP?*], in Wm Hughes Field Papers, 73-128-221, ATL. Wellington and Horowhenua rifle clubs still shoot for the Field Cup.

50 Minutes of Annual Meeting of the NZ Rifle Clubs Executive, 30 Jan 1918, NZ National Rifle Assn Collection, Trentham. At this meeting the executive 'suggested that shooting be ventilated through the Press as much as possible'; it feared 'that rifle shooting is not being brought into prominence sufficiently as far as the public is concerned.' Many thanks to Michael Dobson, Don Whiteman and the NRA.

51 James Franklin, long-time shooter with the Weber Rifle Club, MSX3470 Papers, ATL.

52 *AJHR*, 1913, H-19, 6, s14.

53 Notes on a Deputation to Def Min, 24 Oct 1913, AD1, 54/9. Allen said the RNZA men were also 'much more fully employed than they used to be in looking after defaulters'.

54 GOC to Def Min, 31 Mar 1914, AD1, 54/9.

55 *AJHR*, 1913, H-19, 37, s5.

56 'Rifle Club – Question Whether Members of the Reserve of Officers May Join', AD1, 61/52.

57 *AJHR*, 1914, H-19, 8, s10.

58 R.J. King, in Minutes of Annual Meeting of the NZ Rifle Clubs Executive, 2 Mar 1914, NRA Collection, Trentham.

59 *AJHR*, 1913, H-19, 19, s52.

60 'Reports – Inspector of Rifle Ranges & Rifle Clubs etc. During Year 1916', AD1, 39/53/16; *Army List*, Dec 1918. Colonel Wolfe was appointed in 1913. NZ Rifle Clubs Executive Circular No. 4, 16 May 1913.

61 Godley to Def Min, 29 Aug 1914, AD1, 29/25/1.

62 *Star*, 19 Sep 1919. This refers to the Citizens Defence Corps.

63 CGS to MDs, 31 Oct 1914, AD1, 29/25/1.

64 Major P. Hughes, Wellington MD, to Club Presidents, 5 Aug 1914, AD1, 29/25.

65 Wellington MD, Report by Col Tate to CGS, forwarded 5 Jun 1915, 'Defence Annual Report 1915', AD1, 39/19/15.

66 Ibid., OC Wellington MD to CGS, 5 Jun 1915.

67 *AJHR*, 1915, H-19, 5, s11.

68 'Minutes of Meeting [of NZRC Executive] held in Buckle St Drill Hall', 19 Nov 1914, NRA Collection.

69 Home Defence files, AD1, 10/155.

70 *AJHR*, 1915, H-19, 6, s11.

71 The military had a central role in organising these special mounted constables, known as 'Massey's Cossacks', many of whom were Territorial soldiers. This is covered in John Crawford, 'Overt and Covert Military Involvement in the 1890 Maritime Strike and 1913 Waterfront Strike in New Zealand', *Labour History*, No. 60 (1991).

72 Sherwood Young, 'Happy Campers, A Description of Daily Life in Auckland for the Special Constables during the 1913 Dispute', unpub TUHP Seminar paper, 22 Nov 2003.

73 Lusk to Massey, received 4 Sep 1914, AD1, 10/155/1. In his 80s, Lusk had been Auckland Provincial President of the NZ Farmers' Union.

74 OC Auckland MD to Army HQ, 14 Sep 1914, and GOC, 21 Sep 1914, AD1, 10/155/1.

75 'Defence Annual Reports 1914–15', Lusk to Capt Wright, 5 May 1915, AD1, 39/19/15.

76 *Press*, 28 Oct 1914.

77 Heaton Rhodes to Harper, 2 Nov 1914, Christchurch Citizens Defence Corps, AD1, 61/99.

78 *LT*, 30 Oct 1914.

79 Def Min to PM, 1 Feb 1915, AD1, 61/99; *Star*, 19 Sep 1919. The CDC opened a recruiting office on Hereford Street on 1 May 1915 which 'worked until practically the last day of purely voluntary enlistment', after which it became a welfare, job-finding and hospital-visiting body.

80 OC Otago MD, report for 1915, 'Defence Annual Report 1915', AD1, 39/19/15.

81 *AJHR*, 1916, H-19, 4, s12.

82 Ibid., 1915, 8, s27.

83 BJF and ISR, 'National Rifle Assn,' in A.H. McLintock (ed), *An Encyclopedia of New Zealand* (Wellington: Government Printer, 1966), Vol. 2. Having been formed in 1879, the Dominion Rifle Association was renamed the National Rifle Association in 1922; *AJHR*, 1919, H-19, 5.

84 *AJHR*, 1917, H-19, 6, s11; s10.

85 Wellington MD to GHQ, 21 Aug 1919, AD1, 261/1/2.

86 [Bob Grimwood], *The Petone Rifle Club – Centennial 1989* (Petone: Petone Rifle Club, 1989).

87 *AJHR*, 1915, H-19, 5, s11.

88 NZRC Executive, Meetings, 30 Jan, 6 Feb 1918, NRA Collection.

89 250,000 rounds were issued to each Military District for sale to rifle clubsmen at 15s 8d per 100 rounds, an increase from 5s per 100. Ibid., NZRC Executive, Meeting, 30 Jan 1918.

90 OC Wellington MD to HQ NZMF, 20 Nov 1918, AD1, 261/1/2.

91 Canterbury MD, Report 1914–15, n.d., 'Defence Annual Report 1915', AD1, 39/19/15.

92 Uncredited newspaper clippings dated 4 Dec 1915, NRA Collection. This union of clubs became the Wellington Rifle Association in 1923 but still shot for a Union Shield until well into the 1930s.

93 MD reports for Jun 1915, 'Defence Annual Report 1915', AD1, 39/19/15.

94 NZ Rifle Clubs Executive, Minutes, 9 Jun 1915, and Circular No. 6, 14 Jun 1915, NRA Collection.

95 Ian McGibbon, 'John Robertson 1870–1954', *DNZB* (www.dnzb.govt.nz).

96 NZRC Executive, Meeting, 13 Jan 1916, NRA Collection.

97 *AJHR*, 1916, H-19, 4, s11.

98 Ibid., s10; OC Canterbury MD to HQ NZMF, 3 Sep 1919, AD1, 261/1/2.

99 *AJHR*, 1917, H-19, s11, 6, 1918, s12, 5.

100 NZ Rifle Clubs Executive, Meeting, 6 Feb 1918, NRA Collection.

101 *AJHR*, 1919, H-19, 7, Summary; NZRC Executive, Meeting, 22 Mar 1917, NRA Collection.

102 For example, Levin Defence Rifle Club, *Levin Chronicle*, 6 Oct, 15 Nov 1917, and Old Naval Rifles Club, Wellington, *Dominion*, 28 Sep 1917.

103 'Mobilisation of CD Troops', AD1, 29/24/16.

104 OC RNZA to Commandant, 11 Jan 1918, AD10, 16/16.

105 GOC to Def Min, 31 Mar 1914, AD1, 54/9.

106 Masefield was also won the Ballinger Belt in 1929, 1936, 1939 and 1948.

107 Wallingford to Stewart, 26 Aug 1921, AD1, 54/9.

108 *AJHR*, 1920, H-19, 10, s4.

109 Ibid.; *EP*, 3 Mar 1922. This is not to deny the contribution rifle clubsmen made as members of the NZEF overseas: 188 were killed in action, 287 wounded and many decorated (this from the 57 rifle clubs that returned statistics after the war on their involvement). AD1, 61/53.

110 Newspaper clipping, Mar 1921, AD1, 54/9.

111 Notes relating to page 74 in 'Minutes, 1911/1922, NZ Rifle Clubs Executive', NRA Collection.

112 *NZG*, No. 148, 18 Dec 1919, though the application to disband Te Aroha and Thames clubs was reversed because they were 'carrying on satisfactorily', the OC Auckland MD reported (AD1, 261/1/2). Another seven had been disbanded by 1923.

113 Heard to GOC, 25 Feb 1914, AD1, 61/53.

114 *AJHR*, 1921, H-19, 6, s3.

115 James Franklin, MSX3470, ATL.

116 Harry Sansum, MS Papers 2172, ATL.

Chapter 26: Allan Davidson

This contribution complements the work of Peter Lineham, which looks more broadly at the role and attitudes of churches during the First World War. I am grateful to Peter for supplying me with material from the *War Cry*.

1 Alfred (Alf) C. Young was the author's great-uncle.

2 The wording from the memorial at Messines was copied during a visit by the author, 7 Aug 1999.

3 Mackenzie to Mrs C. J. Young, 2 Aug 1917 (copy in possession of author).

4   Copy of the King's Scroll, held by author.

5   Pierre Berton, *Vimy* (Toronto: Anchor Canada, 1986), 307, cited in Adrian Gregory, *The Silence of Memory: Armistice Day 1919–1946* (Oxford/Providence: Berg, [1994]), 8.

6   Ross Anderson, 'New Zealand Methodism and World War I: Crisis in a Liberal Church' (MA thesis, University of Canterbury, 1983), 126–44. For England, Alan Wilkinson, *The Church of England and the First World War* (London: SPCK, 1978), particularly ch. 8 on 'Death, Bereavement and the Supernatural', 169–96; and Albert Marrin, *The Last Crusade: The Church of England and the First World War* (Durham, North Carolina: Duke UP, 1974). For a Canadian viewpoint see Jonathan Vance, *Death So Noble: Memory, Meaning, And the First World War* (Vancouver: University of British Columbia Press, 1997). For Australian perspectives see, Michael McKernan, *Australian Churches at War: Attitudes and Activities of the Major Churches 1914–1918* (Sydney: Catholic Theological Faculty and AWM, 1980) and K.S. Inglis, *Sacred Places: War Memorials in the Australian Landscape* (Carlton South: Melbourne UP, 1998).

7   Allan K. Davidson and Peter J. Lineham (eds), *Transplanted Christianity. Documents Illustrating Aspects of New Zealand Church History* (Palmerston North: Dept of History, MU, 1995), 241–2.

8   Copy of letter held by author.

9   *Press*, 23 Jun 1917.

10 Copy of sermon held by author.

11 Maclean and Phillips, *Sorrow,* 131.

12 *CG*, 1 Oct 1914, 171.

13 Davidson and Lineham, 292–3.

14 'The European War', *NZ Baptist*, Sep 1914, 172.

15 John Dickie, 'The Empire's Call', *Outlook*, 1 Sep 1914, 14, 26.

16 James Gibb, 'The Church and the World', ibid., 6 Oct 1914, 4.

17 W. Gray Dixon, 'The Church and the World', ibid., 3 Nov 1914, 3.

18 Editor, 'War and Peace', ibid., 9 Feb 1915, 3.

19 'Knox College', ibid., 6 Apr 1915, 8.

20 Hugh Laracy, 'Priests, People and Patriotism: New Zealand Catholics and War, 1914–1918', *Australasian Catholic Record*, Vol. 70, No. 1 (1993), 14.

21 *NZT*, 20 Aug 1914, cited in ibid., 17, 42, 16–18.

22 Nicholas Evan Reid, *The Bishop's Paper: A History of the Catholic Press of the Diocese of Auckland* (Orewa: Catholic Publications Centre, 2000), 27–32. In the first issue Cleary declared its objective as 'to set forth the Catholic viewpoint on current subjects that have a religious or moral aspect'. *Month*, Jul 1918, 3.

23 'To Men and Women of Goodwill in the British Empire', *Outlook*, 26 Jan 1915, 13.

24 Davidson and Lineham, 288.

25 Peter H. Ballis, 'Seventh-day Adventists and New Zealand Politics, 1886–1918', in Peter H. Ballis (ed.), *In and Out of the World: Seventh-day Adventists in New Zealand* (Palmerston North: Dunmore Press, 1985), 68–71.

26 *Harvest Field*, No. 87, 20 Dec 1916, xviii.

27 *White Ribbon*, 18 Nov 1918, 9.

28 J.A. Luxford, 'Our Soldier Boys', *NZMT*, 24 Jul 1915, 10.

29 *White Ribbon*, 18 Dec 1915, 4.

30 Luxford, 10.

31 L.H. Barber, *The Very Rev. James Gibb: Patriot into Pacifist* (Dunedin: Presbyterian Historical Society, 1973), 2.

32 *Church News*, 1 Jul 1915, 1, 2.

33 'Enlist in the King's Army', *NZMT*, 22 Jan 1916.

34   J.S. Ponder, 'Religious Patriotism', *Outlook*, 15 Jun 1915, 21.

35   'St Patrick's Cathedral, An Impressive Service', *NZH*, 26 Apr 1916.

36   *Church News*, 1 Apr 1916, 2.

37   'An Overworked Text', *NZMT*, 18 Sep 1915, 8.

38   'Christmas and War', ibid., 23 Dec 1916, 8.

39   Wilkinson, 175.

40   *Hymns Ancient & Modern* (London: Clowes, 1950), No. 584, 791.

41   'The Cross and War', *NZMT*, 26 Oct 1918, 8.

42   Maclean and Phillips, 103. See also Maureen Sharpe, 'Anzac Day in New Zealand 1916–1939', *NZJH*, Vol. 15, No. 2 (1981), 109.

43   See, e.g., J. Dickson, *Shall Ritualism and Romanism Capture New Zealand? Their Ramifications in Protestant Churches* (Dunedin: Otago Daily Times and Witness, 1912).

44   Dennis McEldowney, review of Allan K. Davidson, *Christianity in Aotearoa: a History of Church and Society in New Zealand* (Wellington: Education for Ministry, 1991), in *Theo Lit*, Jun 1991, 15.

45   *Church News*, 1 Jul 1915, 2.

46   Ibid, 2 Jul 1917, 7.

47   H.L. Blamires, 'Larger Hope of the Life Beyond', *NZMT*, 3 Aug 1918.

48   Wilkinson, 180, 186.

49   *NZH*, 26 Apr 1916.

50   *NZT*, 4 May 1916, 20.

51   *NZH*, 26 Apr 1918.

52   *NZ Baptist*, Oct 1915, 187, 188, 187.

53   *WC*, 19 Jun 1915, 4.

54   *CG*, 1 Jun 1918, 118.

55   *Month*, 15 Aug 1918, 5.

56   *NZ Baptist*, Mar 1916, 50.

57   Guy Thornton, *With the Anzacs in Cairo: The Tale of a Great Fight* (London: Allenson, n.d.), 147–8.

58   *Church News*, 1 Jun 1915, 3.

59   'For the Fallen', ibid., 1 Jul 1915, 11.

60   Ibid., 2 Aug 1915, 13.

61   Ibid., 1 Oct 1915, 5.

62   Ibid., 1 Nov 1915, 11.

63   Ibid., 1 Jun 1918, 4.

64   Sharpe, 101.

65   John Harré, 'To Be or Not to Be? An Anthropologist's View', *Landfall*, Vol. 20, No. 1 (1966), 41.

66   Scott Worthy, 'A Debt of Honour: New Zealanders' First Anzac Days', *NZJH*, Vol. 36, No. 2 (2002), 185–97.

67   'Civil religion' is described as 'a way of thinking which makes sacred a political arrangement or government system and provides a religious image of a political society for many, if not most, of its members.... civil religion is the general faith of a state or nation that focuses on widely held beliefs about the history and destiny of that state or nation.... it is the social glue which binds a given society together by means of well-established ceremonies – rituals, symbols, values – and allegiances which function in the life of the community in such a way as to provide it with an overarching sense of spiritual unity.' Daniel G. Reid, *Dictionary of Christianity in America* (Downers Grove: InterVarsity Press, 1990), 281.

68   *Church News*, 1 Nov 1915, n.p.

69 Ibid., 1 Apr 1916, 4.
70 Ibid., 1 May 1917, 5.
71 *NZT*, 25 Apr 1918, 42.
72 Rory Sweetman, *Spire on the Hill, A History of St Andrew's Church in the Epsom District, 1846–1996* (Auckland: St Andrew's Parish, 1996), 98.
73 Bruce Hamilton, *O Floreat Semper: The History of King's College 1896–1995* (Auckland: King's College, 1995), 80. One hundred and nine old boys and two masters were killed in the war.
74 Burton, *Silent*, 322.
75 Davidson, *Christianity in Aotearoa*, 99.
76 'We are fighting for truth and mercy, for nations cruelly down-trodden, for Christendom, for however we have failed to be true to Christ we still belong to Christendom'. *Church News*, 1 Jan 1916, 1.
77 *CG*, 2 Dec 1918, 235, 236.
78 Presbyterian Church of New Zealand, *Proceedings of the General Assembly*, 1919, 35.
79 Methodist Church of New Zealand, *Minutes of Conference*, 1919, 59.
80 W.E. Leadley, 'The Church and the Returned Soldier', *NZMT*, 18 Jan 1919.
81 Ibid., 1 Feb 1919, 5; 1 Mar 1919, 14–15; 15 Mar 1919, 8; 29 Mar 1919, 1.
82 Ibid., 12 Apr 1919, 13.
83 Jon Davies, 'The Martial Uses of the Mass: War Remembrance as an Elementary Form of Religious Life', in Jon Davies (ed.), *Ritual and Remembrance: Responses to Death in Human Societies* (Sheffield: Sheffield Academic Press, 1994), 163.
84 Barber, *Gibb*; Davidson, *Christianity in Aotearoa*, 100–2, 105–10.

Chapter 27: Peter Lineham

1   *WC*, 5 Aug 1914, 4.
2   *CG*, Nov 1914, 198 (made by a New Plymouth correspondent).
3   J.W. Shaw, 'The War Spirit', *Outlook*, 25 Aug 1914, 4.
4   *NZMT*, 9 Jan 1915, 1, 2.
5   'The War and Missions', *NZMT*, 20 Feb 1915, 1.
6   See General Booth's comments in *WC*, 26 Sep 1914, 5.
7   Editorial, *NZMT*, 15 May 1915, 8; 29 May 1915, 1.
8   *CG*, Dec 1915, 191.
9   Editorial, *NZMT*, 10 Jul 1915, 8.
10 *NZT*, 3 Jun 1915, 25.
11 *CNDC*, Jul 1915, 1–2.
12 *NZT*, 3 Jan 1918, 11.
13 Fr Barra, 'In the Firing Line', ibid., 31 Jan 1918, 13–14.
14 See, e.g., *NZMT*, 9 Jan 1915, 9; 17 Apr 1915, 7.
15 'The Coming Year', *CNDC*, Jan 1916, 2.
16 'A Call to Prayer', *Outlook*, 26 Jan 1915, 4; 'War and Peace', ibid., 9 Feb 1915, 3; Bishop's Letter, *CG*, Feb 1915, 20.
17 For example ibid., Apr 1916, 50.
18 Ibid., May 1916, 85.
19 *NZT*, 4 May 1916, 20.
20 Editorial, *NZMT*, 12 Jun 1915, 8.
21 See the debate in the Methodist Conference, reported in ibid., 20 Mar 1915, 1.
22 Nicholas Hope, *German and Scandinavian Protestantism 1700–1918* (Oxford: Clarendon Press, 1995), 590–1, 593, 596–7.
23 *WC*, 26 Dec 1914, 6; ibid., 9 Jan 1915, 5.

24 *NZMT*, 20 Mar 1915, 5, 8.

25 *WC*, 5 Jun 1915, 4.

26 Ibid., 10 Jul 1915, 3.

27 *NZMT*, 12 Jun 1915, 3.

28 *NZT*, 20 Jan 1916, 29.

29 See e.g. ibid., 6 May 1915, 13, 15.

30 'War and Peace', *Outlook*, 9 Feb 1915, 3; see *CNDC*, May 1915, 18.

31 Citing the Archbishop of York, *CG*, 1914, 216.

32 *NZMT*, 9 Jan 1915, 8.

33 See *Nelson Diocesan Magazine*, Nov 1915, 11–13. On Gibb, see Barber, *Gibb;* Parish News, *CG*, Jan 1916, 6.

34 *NZMT*, 30 Oct 1915, 1.

35 Ibid., 22 Jan 1916, 13.

36 For example *NZT*, 16 Jun 1916, 18.

37 'The Clergy and Military Service', *CNDC*, Mar 1917, 2–3.

38 Stewart A. Brown, '"A Solemn Purification by Fire": Responses to the Great War in the Scottish Presbyterian Churches, 1914–19', *Journal of Ecclesiastical History*, Vol. 45, No. 1 (1994), 82–105.

39 *NZMT*, 2 Jun 1915, 2.

40 Editorial, ibid., 2 Oct 1915, 8; See Editorial: 'Closing the Ranks', ibid., 8 Jul 1916, 8; Our Soldier Boys', ibid., 1 Apr 1916, 14.

41 *WC*, 4 Dec 1915, 4.

42 *CG*, Sep 1914, 154. His full statement was reported in ibid., 162.

43 'The Bible in Schools', *Outlook*, 20 Oct 1914, 5; Supplement to *CG*, Dec 1914.

44 'Our Soldier Boys', *NZMT*, 26 Jun 1915, 9.

45 The Methodist conference in 1915 demanded this; ibid., 20 Mar 1915, 6; and the WCTU, ibid., 3 Apr 1915, 7.

46 Report from Church of England Men's Society, *CG*, Nov 1914, 198; ibid., Nov 1915, 184.

47 Letter from Trentham Camp, cited in ibid., Jul 1915, 101.

48 C.H. Gavin, cited in ibid., Nov 1915, 184.

49 See e.g. Supplement to ibid., Dec 1914, xiii.

50 Julius's address to the Christchurch Synod, Supplement, *CNDC*, Nov 1915, 11.

51 'Near And Far', *NZMT*, 7 Aug 1915, 3.

52 For example ibid., 13 May 1916, 1.

53 'The Day of Intercession – May 8', *CNDC*, May 1918, 3.

54 See e.g. *CG*, Dec 1914, 211.

55 See e.g. *NZMT*, 6 Feb 1915, 6.

56 *NZH*, 3 Sep 1915, 3.

57 *NZT*, 13 Aug 1914, 23.

58 J.W. Shaw, 'Patriotism', *Outlook*, 18 Aug 1914, 3–4.

59 'The Call of the Empire', ibid., 1 Sep 1914, 26.

60 *CG*, Sep 1914, 162.

61 'Perire Fortes', ibid., May 1915, 88.

62 Editorial, *NZMT*, 15 May 1915, 8.

63 'The Higher Patriotism', *Outlook*, 13 Oct 1914, 3–5.

64 'Religious Patriotism', ibid., 15 Jun 1915, 16.

65 Pastoral Letter, *CG*, Aug 1915, 116–17.

66 'God and War', *NZMT*, 27 Nov 1915, 9.

67 'The Church of the Future', *CG*, Jun 1916, 93.

68 Current Topics, *NZT*, 11 May 1916, 17.

69 Albert Marrin, *The Last Crusade: The Church of England in the First World War* (Durham: Duke UP, 1974), 50–118.

70 *CG*, Sep 1914, 164; Apr 1915, 50.

71 'The Higher Patriotism', *Outlook*, 13 Oct 1914, 4.

72 Shaw, 'War', ibid., 4 Aug 1914, 3.

73 'War and Peace', ibid., 6 Apr 1915, 4.

74 J.W. Shaw, 'Patriotism', ibid., 18 Aug 1914, 3.

75 *Methodist Annual Conference*, 1915, 117.

76 *CG*, Sep 1914, 154.

77 Marrin, 125–9.

78 *NZT*, 3 Sep 1914, 34.

79 *Outlook*, 25 Aug 1914, 5.

80 Ibid., 10 Sep 1914, 49.

81 'The Religion of the Battlefield', *Outlook*, 8 Sep 1914, 18.

82 'The War and Service', *CG*, Sep 1914, 164.

83 *NZMT*, 1 May 1915, 1.

84 Editorial: 'Cheer Up', ibid., 8 Jan 1916, 8.

85 'Intercession Day in Wellington', *Outlook*, 24 Aug 1915, 3–4.

86 *CG*, Mar 1915, 37.

87 *Nelson Diocesan Magazine*, Oct 1914, 13.

88 Marrin, 133–4; Wilkinson, 217–18. Cited also in 'The Soul of a Nation', *CNDC*, Jan 1916, 13–14.

89 'A Call to Arms', *CG*, Oct 1914, 183.

90 Supplement to ibid., Dec 1914, i–ii.

91 *CNDC*, 1 Sep 1914, 2.

92 Editorial, *NZ Tablet*, 20 Aug 1914, 33; ibid., 10 Sep 1914, 22.

93 'Welcome War', *Outlook*, 5 Nov 1914, 3.

94 *Methodist Annual Conference*, 1915, 117.

95 *CNDC*, Jun 1915, 2.

96 Ibid., Jan 1918, 2.

97 Editorial, *CG*, Jan 1916, 12–13; 'Women's World', *NZMT*, 1 May 1915, 4.

98 Photograph in *WC*, 5 Feb 1916, 6.

99 Sermon, *NZMT*, 24 Jul 1915, 9.

100 Editorial, *CG*, Feb 1916, 26.

101 Ibid., Oct 1916, 155.

102 *WC*, 10 Jun 1916, 4

103 *CNDC*, Sep 1915, 2; see e.g. ibid., Jul 1915, 1–2.

104 *NZT*, 13 Apr 1916, 30.

105 *NZMT*, 26 Jun 1915, 3.

106 Editorial, *WC*, 19 Jun 1915, 4; Editorial, ibid., 24 Jul 1915, 4.

107 Missions, ibid., 12 Jun 1915, 13.

108 'Not Peace but a Sword', *NZMT*, 19 Aug 1916, 9.

109 J.T. Hardy, 'Militarism, Pacificism and Christianity', *Outlook*, 12 Jan 1915, 3–-5.

110 'With the Chaplain on Gallipoli: the Insensate Folly of War', *WC*, 6 Nov 1915, 3.

111 *CNDC*, 1 Sep 1914, 2.

112 *CG*, Oct 1914, 174.

113 Hope, 590–1, 599, 603–7; John A. Moses, 'Australian Anglican Leaders and the Great War 1914–1918: The Prussian Menace, Conscription, and National Solidarity', *Journal of Religious History*, Vol. 25, No. 3 (2001), 312–14.

114 *The European War: Reply to the Appeal of German Theologians*, 23 Sep 1914.

115 Marrin, 92–118.

116 'War and Peace', *Outlook*, 6 Apr 1915, 4.

117 *NZT*, 20 Aug 1914, 31, 10 Sep 1914, 21.

118 Ibid., 3 Sep 1914, 22.

119 Article by J.T. Pinfold, *NZMT*, 9 Jan 1915, 9; 'Welcome War', *Outlook*, 5 Nov 1914, 4.

120 *NZMT*, 9 Jan 1915, 8.

121 J.W. Shaw, 'The War Spirit', *Outlook*, 25 Aug 1914, 3; 'The Empire's Call', ibid., 1 Sep 1914, 25.

122 'The Religion of the Battlefield', ibid., 8 Sep 1914, 18.

123 Cited by Megan Hutching, 'Turn back this Tide of Barbarism: New Zealand women who were opposed to war 1896–1919' (MA thesis, University of Auckland, 1990), 104.

124 *CNDC*, 1 Nov 1914, 12.

125 *NZT*, 13 May 1915, 31; 'War and Peace', *Outlook*, 9 Feb 1915, 3.

126 Marrin, 103, 133, 139, 175; Wilkinson, 217–18, 251–53. Winnington-Ingram's views were reported in New Zealand, e.g. in *CNDC*, Dec 1915, 12.

127 Moses, 306–23.

128 'A Call to Arms', *CG*, Oct 1914, 182; *CNDC*, Jul 1915, 2; Julius's address to the Christchurch Synod, Supplement, ibid., Nov 1915, 11.

129 Anderson, ch. 3.

130 'The Tightening Grip of War', *NZMT*, 6 Feb 1915, 8.

131 J. Gibson Smith, 'The Spiritual Issues of the Great War', *Outlook*, 19 Jan 1915, 17.

132 Parochial News, ibid., Aug 1915, 122.

133 *NZMT*, 26 Jun 1915, 1.

134 'Knox College', *Outlook*, 6 Apr 1915, 8.

135 'The Modern Hun: A Study of the German Mind', ibid., 26 Oct 1915, 17–22; in a response to a budding short story writer, *NZT*, 29 Apr 1915, 29.

136 Editorial, *NZMT*, 10 Jul 1915, 8.

137 Editorial, *CG*, Sep 1915, 148.

138 Supplement to *CG*, Dec 1915, ix.

139 See e.g. 'The Religious Condition of Germany', *Outlook*, 3 Nov 1914, 12; 'Welcome War', ibid., 4; 'The Religion of the Battlefield', ibid., 8 Sep 1914, 18; 'Modernism in Germany', ibid., 29 Sep 1914, 3.

140 Supplement to *CG*, Dec 1915, xvii.

141 *NZT*, 8 Jul 1915, 36.

142 Letter by W. Edward Lush, *CG*, Apr 1916, 62; 'God and War', *NZMT*, 27 Nov 1915, 9; sermon by Dean Wrey, *NZT*, 13 May 1915, 31, 17 Jun 1915, 22. A Methodist social study endeavoured to overcome uncertainty about exactly what *Kultur* was: Social Service Column, *NZMT*, 12 Oct 1916, 6.

143 *NZMT*, 15 Apr 1916, 1.

144 *CG*, Dec 1918, 236–7.

145 See ibid., 24 Jun 1916, 1; Pinfold, 'The Benefits of War', ibid., 24 Jun 1916, 4.

146 'The Turn of the Tide', *CNDC*, Aug 1916, 2.

147 *NZT*, 7 Mar 1918, 14, quoting a correspondence in the *Dominion*.

148 G.S. King, 'Organising Christian Truth' (PhD thesis, University of Otago, 1998), 167–8; and other sources cited by David Clark in his thesis on Rehbein, 'Our Interests and Christ: The Christian Existentialism of Helmut Rex' (PhD thesis, University of Otago, 2003), 93–5.

149 'The Church and the World', *Outlook*, 6 Oct 1914, 3.

150 Averill, cited in ibid., 13 Oct 1914, 5; 'The Gospel in the Praetorium', ibid., 15 Sep 1914, 3–4; *Nelson Diocesan Yearbook*, 1915, 36–8.

151 Editorial, *NZMT*, 16 Oct 1915, 8; supplement to *CG*, Dec 1915, ix.

152 Editorial: 'Lent and the War', ibid., Mar 1916, 42–3; for one report on the mission see *CNDC*, Jan 1917, 3–4.

153 'Does the World grow Better or Worse?', *Outlook*, 20 Oct 1914, 4.

154 Bishop's letter, *CG*, Jan 1916, 4.

155 *NZMT*, 24 Mar 1916, 2.

156 Republished in the *Outlook*, 21 May 1918, 29.

157 Supplement to *CG*, Dec 1914, xiv.

158 Editorial, ibid., 10 Jul 1915, 8.

159 See *WC*, 20 Mar 1915, 4; and Allen's reply in ibid., 27 Mar 1915, 4.

160 'The National Foe', *Outlook*, 13 Apr 1915, 8.

161 'War and Peace', ibid., 26 Jan 1915, 3–4; 'The Church and the War: An Assembly Forecast', ibid., 23 Nov 1915, 5–6.

162 'The Early Closing Movement', *CNDC*, Jun 1917, 3.

163 Correspondence, *NZMT*, 5 Feb 1916, 12.

164 Averill's sermon to Mothers' Union, cited in *CG*, Jan 1915, 6.

165 See *NZMT*, 1 Apr 1916, 1–2, 12–13; see Editorial, *NZMT*, 13 May 1916, 8; ibid., 5 Aug 1916, 1, and Editorial, 8.

166 Editorial, ibid., 2 Oct 1915, 8; 'The War and Waste', ibid., 19 Feb 1916, 3; Editorial, ibid., 8.

167 Ibid., 21 Aug 1915, 1; see W.H. Fitchett, 'The Red Plague', *NZMT*, 5 Aug 1916, 5; *CG*, Mar 1916, 34.

168 *NZMT*, 29 May 1915, 1.

169 Anderson. See e.g. A.B. Chappell sermon, 'The Bright Side of the War', *NZMT*, 5 Aug 1916, 9; *NZMT*, 5 Aug 1916, 1–2.

170 *NZT*, 27 Aug 1914, 25.

171 Sermon in Wanganui, *NZT*, 24 Jun 1915, 51.

172 *NZT*, 3 Jan 1918, 27–8.

173 Ibid., 10 Jan 1918, 71.

174 Editorial, ibid., 14 Feb 1918, 25–6.

175 *NZT*, 6 May 1915, 34; and the follow-up in ibid., 13 May 1915, 4.

176 Protestant Sentiment, *NZMT*, 4 Sep 1915, 3; editorial, 8.

177 'The Roman Catholic Grip on the Newspapers of New Zealand', ibid., 1 Apr 1916, 13.

178 *NZT*, 24 Jun 1915, 31, 33, 45.

179 Ibid., 6 May 1915, 34.

180 See e.g. ibid., 2 Mar 1916, 17.

181 'The Made in Germany Rebellion', leader, *NZT*, 4 May 1916, 29–31.

182 See *NZMT*, 20 Mar 1915, 3.

183 There are obvious exceptions to this. For discussion of the English minority, see the chapter 'Patriotism is not Enough' in Wilkinson, 197–229.

184 Vesta, Correspondence, *NZMT*, 20 Feb 1915, 5.

185 'Some War Problems', ibid., 10 Jul 1915, 3; Editorial, ibid., 5 Feb 1916, 8; ibid., 18 Mar 1916, 4.

186 See e.g. *NZT*, Editorial, 3 Jan 1918, 25–8; Editorial, ibid., 31 Jan 1918, 26.

187 See Baker, 170.

188 *CG*, Jul 1915, 107–8; correspondence, *NZMT*, 19 Feb 1916, 12; Letter by T.W. Cameron, ibid., 29 Apr 1916, 5.

189 Correspondence, *NZMT*, 8 Jul 1916, 12; C. Murray, letter to editor (on article by Hardy), *Outlook*, 19 Jan 1915, 25; 'To Men and Women of Goodwill... A Message from the Religious Society of Friends', ibid., 26 Jan 1915, 13.

190 See *NZMT*, 24 Jun 1916, 1; and 8 Jul 1916, 1, 22 Jul 1916, 1.

191 *NZT*, 27 Jan 1916, 15.

192 Ibid., 17 Feb 1916, 24.

193 'War and Religion', *CG*, Jul 1916, 110; also 'War and Revelation', *CNDC*, Feb 1916, 15–16; for example Father McMenanin's description in *NZT*, 9 Mar 1916, 19; *NZMT*, 24 Jul 1915, 1.

194 Address to United Churches, *NZMT*, 2 Sep 1916, 9.

195 Ibid., 18 Mar 1916, 5; *WC*, 6 Feb 1915, 4; Reverend. S. Lawry, reporting from his son's letters in *NZMT*, 20 Mar 1915, 14.

196 *NZMT*, 26 Jun 1915, 3.

197 *WC*, 13 Feb 1915, 4.

198 Luxford to S.J. Serpell, *NZMT*, 24 Jul 1915, 10.

199 *NZT*, 15 Jun 1916, 18; 'Fragments of a Diary kept on Gallipoli', *WC*, 30 Oct 1915, 6.

200 'About Men', *NZMT*, 1 Apr 1916, 4.

201 *WC*, 17 Jul 1915, 8.

202 Editorial: 'When the Boys Come Home', *NZMT*, 22 Jul 1916, 8.

203 Views of Chaplain Doyle, *NZT*, 21 Feb 1918, 28; Kelly's response to *ODT*, ibid., 21 Feb 1918, 38–9.

204 *CG*, Feb 1916, 19; Hope, 593–4, 607.

205 *NZMT*, 18 Mar 1916, 4–5; 'Good Friday', *CNDC*, Apr 1916, 2.

206 *NZMT*, 18 Mar 1916, 10.

207 *CNDC*, Jul 1917, 2.

208 'The War, the Church and the Nation', published in the *CG*, republished in *CNDC*, Mar 1918, 12–13.

209 Supplement, *CG*, Dec 1917, xi–xiii.

Chapter 28: *Melanie Nolan*

1 David Mitchell, *Women on the Warpath: the Story of Women of the First World War* (London: Jonathon Cape, 1966); Arthur Marwick, *Women at War, 1914–1918* (London: Fontana paperbacks, 1977); Maurice Greenwald, 'Women Workers and World War: The American Railroad Industry: A Case Study', *Journal of Social History*, Vol. 9, No. 2 (1975), 154–77; Janet McCalman, 'The Impact of the First World War on Female Employment in England', *Labour History*, Vol. 21 (1971) 36–47.

2 Gail Braybon, *Women Workers in the First World War* (London: Routledge, 1981), 13.

3 Gail Braybon and Penny Summerfield, *Out of the Cage: Women's Experience of Two World Wars* (London: Pandora, 1987); Sidney Pollard, *The Development of the British Economy, 1914–1967* (London: Edward Arnold, 1969), 77; Mitchell, 389; J. Stanley Lemons, *The Woman Citizen: social feminism in the 1920s* (Urbana: University of Illinois Press, 1973), 3.

4 Francoise Thebaud, 'The Great War and the Triumph of Sexual Division', in Francoise Thebaud (ed.), *A History of Women, Toward a Cultural Identity in the Twentieth Century* (Cambridge and London: Belknap Press of Harvard UP, 1994), 21.

5 Jan Catherine McLeod, 'Activities of New Zealand Women During World War I' (BA Hons thesis, UO, 1978).

6 Ibid., 1, 106.

7 K.H. Sharp, 'New Zealand Women' (MA thesis, University of New Zealand, 1930); D.M. Carter, 'An Estimate of the Political Development of New Zealand Women' (MA thesis, University of New Zealand, 1947).

8 Braybon, 13.

9 See Ute Daniel, *The War from Within: German Working Class Women in the First World War*, trans Margaret Ries (Oxford: Berg, 1997).

10 McLeod, 'Activities', 1.

11 Thebaud, 75. Deborah Thom, 'Women and Work in Wartime Britain', in Richard Wall and Jay Winter (eds), *The Upheaval of War: Family, Work and Welfare in Europe 1914–1918* (Cambridge: CUP, 1988), 297–325.

12 Others have emphasised consumerism: Belinda Davis, 'Food Scarcity and the Empowerment of the Female Consumer in World War 1 Berlin', in V. de Grazia (ed.), *The Sex of Things: Gender and Consumption in Historical Perspective* (Berkeley: University of California Press, 1996), 287–310.

13 Maureen Molloy, 'Citizenship, Property and Bodies: Discourses on Gender and the Inter-war Labour Government in New Zealand', *Gender and History*, Vol. 4, No. 3 (1989), 293–304.

14 Marie-Louise Simich, 'Women in Employment in New Zealand 1911–1926' (MA research essay, University of Auckland, 1978), 24–6.

15 Alan Everton, 'Government Intervention in the New Zealand Economy 1914–18: Its Aims and Effectiveness' (MA thesis, VUW, 1995), 398–423.

16 Labour Dept, Annual Report, 1914–15, *AJHR*, 1915, H-11, 3.

17 Martin Pugh, *Women and the Women's Movement in Britain, 1914–1959* (London: Macmillan, 1992), 3.

18 Sheila Rowbotham, *A Century of Women, A History of Women in Britain and the United States* (London: Viking, 1997), 76.

19 Public Service Commissioner, Annual Reports, *AJHR*, 1913–19, H-14.

20 'Employment of Women Car Cleaners, pt 1, 1917–19', Railways Department records (R)3 W2476, 17/444, ANZ.

21 *NZOYB*, 1918, 799, 1917, 736.

22 National Efficiency Board, *Woman's War Work* (Wellington: Government Printer, 1917), ATL.

23 McLeod, 85–9.

24 Labour Dept, Annual Report, 1914–15, *AJHR*, 1915, H-11, 10. *Star*, 15 May 1917, 'National Efficiency. Position in Canterbury. Women's Work on the Farms'.

25 Women's National Reserve to the Wellington Women's Society for the Protection of Home and Family, 10 Aug 1917, New Zealand Society for the Protection of Home and Family Wellington Branch, Minute Books, 1916–1919, ATL.

26 Tolerton, *Ettie*, 103.

27 NZ Labour Dept, *Labour Monthly Journal* (Jul 1916), 360; (Jun 1915), 502; (Feb 1916), 113.

28 *EP*, 3 Apr 1916, 8. See also *AJHR*, H-11: 1915, 13; 1916, 2; 1917, 2; 1918, 2.

29 Labour Dept, Annual Reports, 1909–20, *AJHR*, H-11, 1910–21.

30 Labour Dept, Annual Report, 1915–16, *AJHR*, H-11, 1916, 1.

31 Ibid., 1918, 1.

32 Ibid., 1916, 2.

33 Ibid., 1919, 4.

34 McLeod, 119–20.

35 Melanie Nolan, *Breadwinning, New Zealand Women and the State* (Christchurch: CUP, 2000), 15–16, 206.

36 Cecil and Celia Manson, *Doctor Agnes Bennett* (London: Michael Joseph/Whitcombe & Tombs, 1960), 71.

37 Anna Rogers, *While You're Away: New Zealand Nurses at War 1899–1948* (Auckland: AUP, 2003), 45–188; Joan Rattray, *Great Days in New Zealand Nursing* (Wellington: A.H. Reed & A.W. Reed, 1961), 135–6.

38 Tolerton, *Ettie*, 104.

39   *Star*, 12 May 1917, 'The Women's Part. Where they can do more. Mr Russell's suggestion'.

40   *MW*, 2 Feb 1916: Miss A. Robinson, Christchurch Tailoresses and Pressers Union, Miss Rutter, SDP Riccarton and Mrs Jane Donaldson, Wellington Housewives Union.

41   *United Federation for Labor Annual Conference 1918* (Wellington: UFL, 1918), ATL.

42   RSA Provisional Executive Committee Minutes, 4 Jul 1917, NZRSA Headquarters.

43   McLeod, 128.

44   Alan Henderson, *The Quest for Efficiency: the Origins of the State Service Commission* (Wellington: States Services Commission, 1990), App. 11, 397–9.

45   Labour Dept, Annual Report, 1914–15, *AJHR*, H-11, 1915, Graph 2.

46   *NZ Census*, 1911, 1916 and 1921.

47   Deborah Montgomerie, *The Women's War: New Zealand, 1939–45* (Auckland: AUP, 2001).

48   Melling, 56–8.

49   *NZOYB*, 1974, 274–5, 'Strengths of Armed Services in War and Casualties on Active Service'.

50   *NZPD*, Vol. 172, 437 (J.G. Ward); see also 420 (P.C. Webb).

51   RSA Provisional Executive Committee Minutes, 30 Nov 1917, New Zealand Returned Soldiers' Association, Dominion HQ, Wellington; *QM*, 10 Sep 1919, 49 & 81. The government also granted a war services gratuity in 1919. Ibid., 10 Oct 1919, 65; and 1 Dec 1919, 1.

52   For instance PM to SPWC, 10 Aug 1917, New Zealand Society for the Protection of Home and Family Wellington Branch, Minute Books, 1916–1919, ATL.

53   War Pensions Commission, *AJHR*, H-28, 1923 (session II), 3.

54   Baker, 17.

55   'Pay and Allowances Circular, 1,000/5/18-7587', MS AG113, Hocken Library.

56   Pay deducted from dependants 1916, AD78, 47/2, ANZ.

57   Wellington Branch SPWC, Annual Report, 1914–15, 5. NZSPHF Annual Reports 1897–1919, MSx 3292, ATL. See also Wellington Branch SPWC Minute Books, 9 Oct 1914.

58   Director, Base Records, to J.D. Gray, 2 May 1916, AD78, 47/2.

59   Baker, 148–9; *EP,* 30 Apr 1918. Under the 1916 Military Service Act, men eligible for conscription were placed in two Divisions. The first consisted of unmarried men, widowers without children and men who had married after 4 August 1914. As the prospect of conscription in New Zealand grew from January 1917, married men organised themselves into a Second Division League, which demanded three reforms: first, that all married men be told the date of their mobilisation as soon as possible so that they could make domestic and financial arrangements; secondly, that no Second Division man be mobilised ahead of a First Division man; and thirdly, that their pay, pension and separation allowances be increased before they went. Baker, 86–7, 142–52.

60   Defence Forces, Annual Reports, *AJHR,* H-19: 1917, 18; 1918, 20; 1919, 22.

61   *NZ Statutes,* War Pension Amendment Act 1917, s10.

62   NZ Patriotic Fund Board Sick and Wounded Homes, Social Security Department records (SS)7, Acc W2756, 11/2/38, ANZ.

63   *Press*, 3 Aug 1915, 79/82, Newspaper Clippings relating to the Kaiapoi Woollen Mills, Kaiapoi and District Historical Museum.

64   Justin Thomas Strang, 'Welfare in Transition: Reform's Income Support Policy, 1912–28' (MA thesis, VUW, 1992), 194.

65   Pauline Wood, *Kaiapoi, A Search for Identity* (Rangiora: Waimakariri District Council, 1993), 207.

66   Strang, 210

67   Report of Officer in Charge, War Funds Office, upon the War Funds Act coming into force

11 October 1915, SS7, Acc W2756, 11/2/38, ANZ; S.J. Piesse, 'Patriotic Welfare in Otago: A history of the Otago Patriotic and General Welfare Association 1914–1950 and the Otago Provincial Patriotic Council 1939' (MA thesis, UO, 1981); Margaret Anderson, 'The Female Front: The Attitudes of Otago Women towards the Great War, 1914–1918' (BA Hons research essay, UO, 1990); Simon Johnson 'The home front: Aspects of civilian patriotism in New Zealand during the First World War' (MA thesis, MU, 1975).

68 Piesse, 3. See also National Patriotic Fund Board, *Bulletin*, No. 9 (1942), 3, reviewing First World War fundraising: Total Funds raised 1914–18 and balance at 31 March 1919 by provinces.

69 New Zealand Patriotic Society, Wellington Branch, *The Carnival Book: cartoons and sketches of the Queen Carnival* (Wellington: New Zealand Patriotic Society, Wellington Branch 1915), 8.

70 Report on the Conference of Patriotic Societies held in Wellington on 17 and 18 February 1916 (J.P. Luke, Wellington, J.J. Clarke, Otago, C. Williams, Canterbury), 11/2/38, SS7, Acc W2756 11/2/38, Patriotic Societies and War Relief Funds, 1915–68; *Dominion*, 12 Jan 1916.

71 *QM*, 2 Sep 1918, 14. See also discussion of the RSA Annual Report, 2, 14 (Jun 1919), 15–25.

72 Baker, 37.

73 For debate about cost of living rises, see Alan Everton, 'Government Intervention in the New Zealand Economy 1914–18' (MA thesis, VUW, 1995).

74 Wellington Branch SPWC, 22nd Annual Report, 1918–19, 5, NZSPHF Annual Reports 1897–1919, MSx 3292, ATL.

75 Hawke's Bay Patriotic Society records have recently been deposited in ANZ.

76 Yvonne Margaret Robertson, 'A Victorian Lady in an Age of Change: The Life of Mary Downie Stewart 1876–1957' (PGDA thesis, UO, 1990), 51–2.

77 Margaret Tennant, 'Service Organizations', in Anne Else (ed.), *Women Together: A History of Women's Organizations in New Zealand: Nga Roopu Wahine o te Motu* (Wellington: Daphne Brasell/Department of Internal Affairs, 1993), 293.

78 For photographs of the carnivals see *Canterbury Times*, 28 Apr 1915, 37, which provides a detailed account of the crowning of Queen Maude (Nurse Maude), Queen of the Belgium Harvest Festival, and the Christchurch Queen carnival. See 5 May 1915, 30, for Ashburton's Queen; 9 Jun 1915 for Wellington Carnival and so on.

79 Otago Provincial Patriotic Society, MS AG 113, Hocken.

80 No. 311, OSDWC Casebooks, MS 982/138, Hocken.

81 The Otago Benevolent Society investigated the respectability of families on relief much more carefully than the OSDWC. See for instance Otago Benevolent Society's consideration of Mary Lee and her family. By contrast, the OSDWC extended support to Mary Lee during the First World War without investigation. Mary Isabella Lee, *The Not So Poor, An Autobiography*, edited and introduced by Annabel Cooper (Auckland: AUP, 1992), 25–32; No. 1046, OSDWC Casebooks, MS 982/138, Hocken.

82 No. 185, OSDWC Casebooks, MS982/138, Hocken.

83 Ibid., 12 Oct 1918, No. 1194.

84 Ibid., No. 299. See also *Evening Star*, 22 Feb 1916.

85 There are about 11,000 case files on applicants and recipients of the patriotic society's welfare from 1914 to the 1970s. I am interested only in the files on First World War soldiers' 'grass widows', that is women applying and/or receiving welfare while their husbands were serving overseas.

86 OSDWC Acting Secretary to Mrs Breese, 21 Jun 1917, OSDWC Casebooks, MS 982/138, Hocken.

87 This is in keeping with the Return of relationship of dependent applicants for war pension to 31 March 1917, Pension Department report, *AJHR*, H-18, 1917, Vol. 2, 90: 360 wife; 424 widow; 340 father; 1360 mother; 5 guardian; 3 mother-in-law; 1 stepfather; 7 stepmother; 2 grandfather; 2 grandmother; 2 fostered mother; 38 guardian of children; 19 mother of illegitimate child; 1 step daughter; 10 brother; 96 sister; 3 guardian of sister; 2 guardian of brother; 1 guardian of nieces; 2 step-sister; 4 sister-in-law; 9 aunt; 2 uncle; 1 niece; 3 not a relative; total 2698.

88 No. 173, OSDWC Casebooks, MS 982/138, Hocken.

89 Nolan, *Breadwinning*, 71–2.

90 No. 783, OSDWC Casebooks, MS 982/138, Hocken.

91 Melanie Nolan, 'Jane Elizabeth Runciman', *DNZB*, III, 447–9.

92 No. 783, OSDWC Casebooks, MS 982/138, Hocken.

93 Ibid., No. 1355.

94 Ibid., No. 342.

95 Ibid., Mrs C. to Society, 14 Jan 1916, No. 386.

96 Ibid., No. 311.

97 Ibid., No. 784.

98 Ibid., No. 386.

99 Ibid., No. 250.

100 Ibid., No. 6/416.

101 Ibid., No. 1133.

102 Ibid., No. 497.

103 Ibid., No. 215.

104 Ibid., No. 828, No. 386.

105 Ibid., No. 953.

106 Ibid., No. 825.

107 Ibid., No. 965.

108 Ibid., No. 1061.

109 'Address given on the formation of the Otago Women's Reserve', MS 985 44/20, Hocken.

110 The Women's International and Political League (minutes 4 June 1918, qMS NEW, ATL) discussed Eleanor Rathbone's work on British separation allowances.

111 Mary McCarthy, 'Endowment of Motherhood', *MW*, 14 Dec 1921.

112 Wellington SPWC, Annual Report, 1916–17, 4, ATL, New Zealand Society for the Protection of Home and Family, Annual Reports 1897–1919, ATL, MSx 3292.

113 Wellington SPWC, Annual Report, 1917–18, 5, ATL.

114 See similar development in Auckland. Raewyn Dalziel, *Focus on the Family, The Auckland Home and Family Society 1893–1993* (Auckland: Auckland Home and Family Society, 1993), 19.

115 Wellington SPWC, Annual Report, 1917–18, 4, ATL.

116 Ibid., 1919–20, 7; 1920–21, 5; 1921–22, 7–8.

117 Ibid., 1919–20, 7.

118 R.J.F. Aldrich (Secretary Wellington RSA) to the Prime Minister, 5 Jun 1920, Legislative Department records (L)1, Damaged Files Box, 3 1/618, cost of living 1920, RSA and NCW resolutions, ANZ.

119 Ibid., Secretary to the Hon. Secretary to Minister of Labour, 29 Jun 1920.

120 *MW*, 13 Nov 1918, 9, Women's Column 'Wahine'.

121 *NZPD*, Vol. 185, 121–2 (H. Poland), 122 (R. Semple), 122–3 (P. Fraser), 123 (J.P. Luke).

122 For example, Mrs Ruth Day (Corresponding Secretary, Christchurch WCTU) to Minister of Pensions, 8 Oct 1919, SS, Acc W1844, Box 1, A80 Act Amendment 1919 (Pensions Act 1913).

123 *NZPD,* Vol. 161, 1912, 66–7 (Payne).

124 NZ Labour Party 7th Annual Conference, Christchurch, Apr 1923, NZ Labour Party, MS Papers 270, folder 345, ATL. See also *MW,* 29 Mar and 6 Dec 1922.

125 Stephen Garton and Margaret McCallum, 'Workers' Welfare: Labour and the Welfare State in 20th-Century Australia and Canada', in Gregory S. Kealey and Greg Patmore (eds), *Australia and Canada: Labour Compared* special issue, *Labour History,* No. 71 (1996), 133.

126 Francis G. Castles, *The Working Class and Welfare: Reflections on the Political Development of the Welfare State in Australia and New Zealand, 1890–1980* (Wellington: Allen and Unwin, 1985). See Melanie Nolan and Pat Walsh, 'Labour's Leg Iron? Assessing Trade Unions and Arbitration in New Zealand', in Pat Walsh (ed.), *Trade Unions, Work and Politics, The Centenary of the Arbitration System* (Palmerston North: Dunmore Press, 1994), 9–37.

127 Theda Skocpol, *Protecting Soldiers and Mothers, The Political Origins of Social Policy in the United States* (1992; reprint, Cambridge, Mass.: Harvard UP, 1993). See also, Edwin Amenta and Theda Skocpol, 'Taking Exception: Explaining the Distinctiveness of American Public Policies in the Last Century', in Francis G. Castles (ed.), *The Comparative History of Public Policy* (Oxford: Polity Press, 1989), 292–333.

128 Seth Koven and Sonya Michel, 'Womanly Duties: Maternalist Politics and the Origins of Welfare States in France, Germany, Great Britain and the United States 1880–1920', *American Historical Review,* Vol. 95, No. 4 (1990), 1076–114.

Chapter 29: John E. Martin

1 G.R. Searle, *The Quest for National Efficiency* (Oxford: Blackwell, 1971).

2 Baker, 14, 138–40, 225–6.

3 For manpower issues see Baker generally. Also Sir James Allen, 'New Zealand in the world war', in *Cambridge History of the British Empire,* Vol. 7, Pt 2, *New Zealand* (Cambridge: CUP, 1933); Sleeman, in Drew, *War Effort.* Correspondence between Allen and Godley in the Allen Papers, M1/15, ANZ, also offers much insight into these issues.

4 Graph based on figures from Carbery, App. B.

5 Allen to Godley, 4 Jan 1916, Allen Papers, M1/15.

6 Ibid., Allen to Godley, 15 Feb 1916.

7 Barry Gustafston, *Labour's Path to Political Independence: The Origins and Establishment of the New Zealand Labour Party 1900–19* (Auckland: AUP/OUP, 1980), 110–13. Two other Labour MPs who would have voted against the Bill were paired.

8 *NZPD,* Vol. 175, 786.

9 Myers to Cabinet, 18 Dec 1916, National Efficiency Board records (NEB)1, 243, ANZ. Myers supplied a tentative list of essential industries that would be developed by the NEB.

10 Baker, 117, 119.

11 Christchurch *Sun,* 27 Jan 1917.

12 Allen to Robin, 7 Nov 1916, cited in Baker, 138.

13 *AJHR,* 1917, H-43, 3. The files more specifically refer to what industries should be considered 'essential', how women could replace men in the workforce, and the rehabilitation of servicemen. NEB to Allen, 2, 5 Feb 1917, NEB1, 2/1. NEB minute book, Vol. 1, ATL.

14 Allen to Godley, 27 Mar 1917, 25 Aug 1917, Allen Papers, M1/15. See above, ch. 14, John Crawford, 'New Zealand is Being Bled to Death: The Formation, Operations and Disbandment of the Fourth Brigade'.

15 For members of the NEB, see Scholefield and *Who's Who,* 1925. DNZB database, Ministry for Culture and Heritage, Wellington.

16 *DNZB,* III. Henderson, 45. Conrad Bollinger, *Grog's Own Country: The Story of Liquor Licensing in New Zealand* (Auckland: Minerva, 1967, 2nd ed.), 186.

17 *NZ Free Lance*, 16 Mar 1917.
18 *AJHR*, 1917, H-43A. Schedule of recommendations, 11 Jun 1917, NEB1, 581. NEB memoranda, Vol. 1, 1917, report on liquor question, 9 Jul 1917, MS Papers 1525, ATL.
19 NEB1, 243, 696. *NZG*, 31 Jul 1917. *AJHR*, 1917, H-43, H-43B.
20 NEB1, 767.
21 John E. Martin, 'War Economy', in McGibbon, *Companion. Statistics of New Zealand, 1914–1918*. NEB1, 774, 870, 863, 919.
22 Baker, 141. The figure of 35.1 per cent was slightly higher than the percentage of those with rural occupations balloted.
23 *Women's War Work*, 3, copy in NEB1, 77.
24 NEB1, 443. NEB minute book, Vol. 1, letters of 26 Apr, 23 May 1917, MS Papers 1528, ATL.
25 NEB1, 453. *Dominion*, 18 Jun, 2 Jul 1917.
26 NEB minute book, Vol. 1, meeting with Allen, 30 Apr 1917.
27 NEB1, 265.
28 *EP*, 4 Jul 1917. NEB memoranda, Vol. 2, 1917–18, Frostick, NEB deputation to Massey and Ward, 5 Oct 1917, NEB to Allen, 9 Jul 1917. This conference drew in 19 unions and a trades council as well as the Labour Party. Bruce Brown, *The Rise of New Zealand Labour: A History of the New Zealand Labour Party* (Wellington: Price Milburn, 1962), 32.
29 Gustafson, 166.
30 NEB to Allen, 9 Jul 1917, Massey to NEB, 16 Nov 1917, NEB1, 639.
31 Sources cited by Baker, 139.
32 Letter to George Nelson, 1 Aug 1917, NEB1, 688.
33 Ferguson to Allen, 15 Aug 1917, NEB minute book, Vol. 2.
34 Letter to George Nelson, 25 Aug 1917, NEB1, 688. For the resignation and reappointment of NEB members, also see NEB correspondence, 1917, MS Papers 1524, ATL.
35 NEB memoranda, Vol. 2, NEB deputation to Massey and Ward, 5 Oct 1917.
36 Len Richardson, *Coal, Class and Community: The United Mineworkers of New Zealand, 1880–1960* (Auckland: AUP, 1995), ch. 6. John E. Martin, *Holding the Balance: A History of New Zealand's Department of Labour, 1891–1995* (Christchurch: Canterbury UP, 1996), 152–4.
37 Allen to Godley, 11 Oct 1917, Allen Papers, M1/15.
38 Ibid., Allen to Godley, 11 Oct 1917, 27 Nov 1917; Godley to Allen, 16 Oct 1917, 6 Jan 1918.
39 Ibid., Allen to Godley, 26 Apr, 21 May 1918. *NZPD*, Vol. 182, 64–6.
40 NEB minute book, Vol. 2, 10, 11 Jun 1918. *NZG*, Vol. 2, 1918, 2406–8, 24 Jun 1918. National service was defined as employment by the government, road and railway construction, drainage works and in the rural economy – probably shaped more by consideration of public works' kind of employment than by any notion of essential industries.
41 *NZPD*, Vol. 182, 217. See 216–40 for discussion of the section and the antagonism of Labour members towards it if it meant transfer of workers for 'private gain'.
42 Allen to Godley, 6 Sep 1918, Allen Papers, M1/15.
43 *EP*, 9 Feb 1918.
44 NEB minute book, Vol. 2, 14, 17 Jan 1919. NEB memoranda, Vol. 3, NEB to Allen, 15 Jan 1919. Typewritten NEB 1918 annual report of 105 pages, qMS 1523, ATL.
45 NEB, 1918 annual report, 104.
46 Martin, *Balance*, 155–6. NEB1, 784, 987. NEB minute book, Vol. 2, 8 Aug 1918. NEB, 1918 annual report, 20, 24 – memo to government on relations of capital and labour, 24 Jun 1918; NEB to Massey, 10 Aug 1918.

47 Allen to Godley, 21 Feb 1919, Allen Papers, M1/15.

48 NEB interview with Allen, 17 Jan 1919, NEB memoranda, Vol. 2.

49 NEB memoranda, Vol. 3, NEB to Allen, 15 Oct 1918, 'Education Enquiry', 18 Mar 1919. NEB1, 553. NEB minute book, Vol. 2, 4 Oct 1918.

50 Letter to G. Nelson, 10 Mar 1919, NEB1, 688.

51 *NZ Free Lance*, 31 Aug 1917.

52 Roger Openshaw *et al.*, *Challenging the Myths: Rethinking New Zealand's Educational History* (Palmerston North: Dunmore Press, 1993), chs 6–8.

53 Ibid., 121.

54 *AJHR*, 1919, I-12.

55 Ross Galbreath, *DSIR: Making Science Work For New Zealand* (Wellington: Victoria UP, 1998), ch. 1; NEB 1918 annual report, 95 and App. V.

56 A.J. Everton, 'Government intervention in the New Zealand economy, 1914–18 – its aims and effectiveness' (MA thesis, VUW, 1995), 398. Michael Bassett, *The State in New Zealand, 1840–1984: Socialism Without Doctrines?* (Auckland: AUP, 1998), ch. 5.

57 *AJHR*, 1919, H-44A.

58 Martin, *Balance*, 155–9.

Chapter 30: James Watson

1 Avner Offer, *The First World War: An Agrarian Interpretation* (Oxford: Clarendon Press, 1989). See also W.H. Oliver, *The Story of New Zealand* (London: Faber and Faber, 1960), 171, 'Men in the trenches were not New Zealand's sole or even major contribution to the success of Allied arms. A country devoted to the transformation of grass into food and clothing increased in importance when Great Britain's agricultural deficiencies were revealed by threatened sea lanes.'

2 *NZ Farmer*, Sep 1914, 1301.

3 James Belich, *Paradise*, 58; Tom Brooking, 'Economic Transformation', in Geoffrey W. Rice (ed.), *The Oxford History of New Zealand*, 2nd edition (Auckland: OUP, 1992), 230–53; B.L. Evans, *A History of Agricultural Production and Marketing in New Zealand* (Palmerston North: Keeling and Mundy, 1969), 91, 119, 161; Erik Olssen, 'Waging War: The Home Front 1914–1918', in Judith Binney, Judith Bassett, Erik Olssen, *The People and the Land: Te Tangata me Te Whenua* (Wellington: Allen and Unwin, 1990), 302–3.

4 Evans, 107.

5 Baker, 54–5.

6 *NZ Farmer*, Sep 1914, 1389.

7 Ibid., Sep 1915, 1097.

8 *AJHR*, H-19V, 1917, 1.

9 *NZPD*, Vol. 174, 140–1.

10 Baker, 54, 242. See also Belich, *Paradise*, 103.

11 Baker, 55. However, the areas he defined as 'rural military groups' contained two-thirds of the eligible male population and embraced other industries besides farming.

12 The 1916 census, while invaluable in other respects, came after the bulk of volunteers had enlisted and so has no real utility for this exercise.

13 55.6% of the male farm workforce was between 21 and 45, compared with 61.6% of the total male workforce. Figures calculated from *Census, 1911*, Part VIII, 'Occupations of the People', 413, 422.

14 Baker, 244.

15 *NZ Farmer*, Dec 1914, 1799.

16 Ibid., May 1915, 668.

17 Ibid., Jul 1915, 827.

18   Ibid., Aug 1917, 945.
19   Ibid., Feb 1915, 148.
20   Ibid., Aug 1917, 942.
21   Ibid., Oct 1915, 1369.
22   Ibid., Jun 1915, 746.
23   Ibid., Nov 1917, 1249.
24   Ibid., Oct 1915, 1322–3.
25   The reference to 95s to 105s is price per hundredweight (112 lbs).
26   *NZ Farmer*, Oct 1915, 1323.
27   Ibid., Jul 1916, 989.
28   Ibid., Oct 1916, 1425.
29   Ibid., Dec 1915, 1564.
30   Ibid., 1666.
31   Ibid., Apr 1917, 458.
32   Ibid., Aug 1917, 866.
33   Ibid., Apr 1918, 473.
34   Ibid., May 1917, 564.
35   Ibid., Mar 1915, 288–9.
36   David Hamer, 'Buchanan, Walter Clarke', in *DNZB*, II, 63.
37   *NZ Farmer*, Aug 1917, 944.
38   Ibid., Jul 1915, 807; Aug 1915, 1064.
39   Ibid., Aug 1915, 1002.
40   Ibid., Sep 1915, 1097.
41   Ibid., Aug 1916, 1105.
42   Ibid., Jun 1917, 666.
43   Ibid., Feb 1917, 357.
44   Ibid., Aug 1917, 943–4.
45   Ibid., Mar 1918, 258.
46   Ibid., Jun 1917, 948.
47   Baker, 122–3.
48   *NZ Farmer*, Aug 1915, 997.
49   Ibid., Sep 1915, 1095.
50   Ibid., Aug 1917, 948.
51   Ibid., Oct 1917, 1116.
52   '[I]t pays the farmer, on present prices, infinitely better to turn his milk into cheese than butter'. Ibid., Jul 1916, 989.
53   Ibid., Apr 1916, 530.
54   Tom Brooking, 'Use it or Lose it: Unravelling the Land Debate in Late Nineteenth-Century New Zealand', *NZJH*, Vol. 30, No. 2 (1996), 141–62.
55   Olssen, 302–3.
56   *NZ Farmer*, Jul 1915, 924.
57   Ibid., Mar 1915, 288–9.

Chapter 31: Gwen Parsons

I am very grateful to Dr C.N. Connolly, University of Canterbury, for commenting on the draft of this paper.

 1   For example, Baker, 15.
 2   For further discussion regarding New Zealand social stratification see P.J. Gibbons, 'The Climate of Opinion', in W.H. Oliver (ed.), *The Oxford History of New Zealand* (Auckland: OUP, 1981), 266f.

3   Gwen A. Parsons, 'The Christchurch Community at War 1914–1918: Society, Discourse and Power' (MA thesis, UC, 2003), App. 1, 189–92.

4   Oliver, 474, Graph 5: Direction of Exports, 1861–1976.

5   Jim McAloon, 'Colonial Wealth: The Rich in Canterbury and Otago, 1890–1914' (PhD thesis, UO, 1993), 294–9.

6   Oliver, 475, Graph 6: Direction of Imports, 1861–1976.

7   Parsons, App. 2, 193–6.

8   For the directors of the Christchurch Press Company and the Lyttelton Times Company see R.B. O'Neill, *The Press 1861–1961* (Christchurch: Christchurch Press Company Ltd, 1963), App 1, 267; and Guy H. Scholefield, *Newspapers in New Zealand* (Wellington: A.H. & A.W. Reed, 1958), 212–13.

9   John Anderson, 'Military Censorship in World War 1: Its Use and Abuse in New Zealand' (MA thesis, Victoria University College, 1952), 9.

10 Section 4.j of the war regulation gazetted 4 Dec 1916.

11 Baker, 149, 166–7.

12 Parsons, App. 4, 198.

13 Anti-war resolution, *Press*, 3 Jun 1916, 9; protest meetings, *LT*, 22 Mar 1915, 9, *MW*, 28 Mar 1917, 3, *LT*, 19 Mar 1917, 9, *Sun*, 19 Mar 1917, 8; and delegation, *LT*, 24 Mar 1917, 9.

14 Elizabeth Plumridge, 'The Necessary But Not Sufficient Condition: Christchurch Labour and Working Class Culture', *NZJH*, Vol. 19, No. 2 (1985), 131.

15 For comparative circulation figures see Gustafson, *Labour's Path*, 86; and *LT*, 11 Apr 1916, 7.

16 R.L. Weitzel, 'Pacifists and Anti-militarists in New Zealand, 1909–1914', *NZJH*, Vol. 7, No. 2 (1973), 128–47.

17 Irene Willis Cooper, *England's Holy War: A Study of English Liberalism During the Great War* (New York: Alfred A Knopf, 1928), 86–134, J. Bryan Hehir, 'The Just War Ethic and Catholic Theology: Dynamics of Change and Continuity', in Thomas A Shannon (ed.), *War or Peace? The Search for New Answers* (New York: Orbis Books, 1980), 16–18, and Jenny Teichman, *Pacifism and the Just War: a Study in Applied Philosophy* (Oxford: Basil Blackwell, 1986).

18 W.F. Massey, *LT*, 29 Apr 1916, 4; Henry Holland, *LT*, 17 Apr 1917, 4, *Press*, 17 Apr 1917, 7; editorial, *Sun*, 13 Mar 1918, 4; and 'W.S.', ibid., 22 Mar 1918, 4.

19 National chairman of the Victoria League, *Press*, 15 Mar 1918, 2, *LT*, 15 March 1918, 9, 4 Aug 1915, 6, and 'Imperialist', 13 Apr 1916, 9.

20 Sir R. Stout, *Press*, 27 Aug 1915, 5, *Sun*, 27 Aug 1915, 9; All for Empire League meeting, *Press*, 11 Mar 1916, 9; and 'M', ibid., 15 Oct 1918, 2. See also illustration, *Star*, 1 Dec 1914, 4.

21 *Press*, 10 May 1915, 8.

22 Ibid., 9 Mar 1915, 8; Massey, *Press*, 15 May 1915, 8. *LT*, 31 Oct 1914, 10; illustration, *Weekly Press*, 24 Mar 1915, 64; *Press*, 12 Aug 1915, 2; and illustration, *Press*, 26 Oct 1915, 8; 'Horror Struck', *Sun*, 18 May 1915, 6; H. Holland, *Press*, 5 Aug 1916, 7, *LT*, 5 Aug 1916, 11, *Sun*, 4 Aug 1916, 11; *LT*, 27 Mar 1917, 7; and *Press*, 13 Feb 1918, 9.

23 Advertisement, *Sun*, 17 Jun 1916, 14; and advertisement, ibid., 8 Jul 1916, 12.

24 J.A. Frostick, *LT*, 5 Mar 1917, 9, *Press*, 5 Mar 1917, 6; 'Nemo', *Press*, 3 Jun 1918, p.8; and *Press*, 12 Jan 1915, p.7. See also *Star*, 30 Nov 1914, 4.

25 Sir J. Allen, *Press*, 24 Aug 1918, 4.

26 'RMB', *Press*, 4 Aug 1915, 9; and illustration, *Star*, 23 Dec 1914, 4.

27 *LT*, 27 Feb 1917, 7; and 'New Testament', *LT*, 7 Mar 1917, 8.

28 H. Holland, *Press*, 18 May 1915, 8, *LT*, 18 May 1915, 9, *Sun*, 18 May 1915, 8; and editorial, *LT*, 12 May 1915, 6. See also 'Live and Let Live', *LT*, 25 Aug 1914, 10.

29   'Introduction', in Allan Bullock and Maurice Shock (eds), *The Liberal Tradition from Fox to Keynes* (London: Adam & Charles Black, 1956), liv-lv.

30   Massey, *Press*, 4 Aug 1916, 6; and O.T.J. Alpers, *LT*, 5 Aug 1915, 8; *Press*, 24 Feb 1916, 7.

31   H. Holland, *Press* 6 Aug 1918, 8, *LT*, 6 Aug 1918, 5; *Sun*, 5 Aug 1918, 8; *Press*, 13 Nov 1918, 6; and J.T.M. Hornsby, *Press*, 14 Sep 1915, 9.

32   Advertisement, *Sun*, 23 Mar 1918, 8.

33   Massey, *Press*, 4 Aug 1916, 6; and 'Briton', *Sun*, 7 Jul 1915, 6. See also Hornsby, *Press*, 14 Sep 1915, 9; and illustration, *Weekly Press*, 5 Jan 1915, 27.

34   *Press*, 20 Aug 1914, 3.

35   Ibid., 26 Aug 1918, 4; Massey, ibid., 15 May 1915, 8; ibid., 11 May 1915, 8, and 12 May 1915, 7. See also *LT*, 10 May 1915, 6, 25 Oct 1915, 7, and 'Countryman', 26 Oct 1915, 8.

36   Massey, ibid., 29 Apr 1916, 4. See also Rev. Dr Robert Erwin, *Press*, 23 Apr 1917, 5.

37   Dr A.F.J. Mickle, *LT*, 14 Oct 1914, 10; motion of the Christchurch Congregational Union, *LT*, 14 Mar 1918, 4, *Sun*, 14 Mar 1918, 4; J.J. Dougall, *Sun*, 10 May 1915, 9, *Press*, 10 May 1915, 10, *LT*, 10 May 1915, 5. See also *LT*, 26 Aug 1916, 9.

38   W.L. Chrystall, *Press*, 7 Oct 1914, 10.

39   Massey, *LT*, 24 Sep 1915, 9, *Sun*, 24 Sep 1915, 4; and J.A. Frostick, *LT*, 5 Mar 1917, 9, *Press*, 5 Mar 1917, 6.

40   *Press*, 30 Oct 1918, 7.

41   Advertisement, *LT*, 21 Mar 1918, 4; O.T.J. Alpers, ibid., 19 Aug 1916, 9; and advertisement, ibid., 26 Aug 1916, 5.

42   *Press*, 26 May 1915, 8; J. Simpson, *Sun*, 10 May 1915, 6; recruitment poster, *Press*, 11 Feb 1915, 7; 'A practical woman', *Press*, 2 Nov 1915, 4; and illustration, *Weekly Press*, 2 Feb 1916, 62.

43   Dr Levinge, *Press*, 23 Nov 1914, 3; 'Mere Woman', ibid., 22 Jan 1916, 3; and 'Returned Soldier', *LT*, 2 May 1918, 5.

44   Raewyn Dalziel, 'The Colonial Helpmeet: Women's Role and the Vote in Nineteenth-Century New Zealand', in Barbara Brookes, Charlotte Macdonald, and Margaret Tennant (eds), *Women in History: Essays on European Women in New Zealand* (Wellington: Allen & Unwin, 1986), 55–68; advertisement, *Press*, 21 Nov 1914, 6; 'South African War Veteran', *Press*, 23 Nov 1914, 3, and 'Fair Play', *Press*, 13 Oct 1915, 3.

45   Advertisement, *Sun*, 3 Jun 1916, 12, *Press*, 3 Jun 1916, 11; and advertisement, *Sun*, 17 Apr 1915, 11.

46   'S.G.', *LT*, 13 Apr 1915, 8.

47   'South African War Veteran', *Press*, 23 Nov 1914, p.3; and ibid., 3 Feb 1916, 8.

48   Joy Damousi, *The Labour of Loss: Mourning, Memory and Wartime Bereavement in Australia* (Cambridge: CUP, 1999), 30; *Press*, 12 Feb 1916, 10. See also poem, ibid., 27 Jan 1917, 7.

49   O.T.J. Alpers, ibid., 16 Jun 1916, 9, *LT*, 16 Jun 1916, 9; and editorial, *Sun*, 5 May 1915, 6.

50   Advertisement, *Press*, 9 Oct 1916, 6.

51   Christmas message, *MW*, 22 Dec 1915, 10.

52   Fred Cooke, ibid., 5 Aug 1914, p.8; John Roberts, *LT*, 8 Mar 1918, 8, *Press*, 18 Mar 1918, 4; and George Samms, *Press*, 2 Jul 1918, 2.

53   James McCombs analysed the class representation of the Fourth Reinforcements, *LT*, 20 Sep 1915, 8. See also Baker, 54 and 242.

54   *LT*, 18 Jan 1917, p.9, *Press*, 18 Jan 1917, p.3. See also the Anti-Conscription Conference manifesto, *LT*, 28 Jan 1916, 9, 29 Jan 1916, 11, *Press*, 28 Jan 1916, 6.

55   *MW*, 15 Sep 1915, 4, *Press*, 8 Sep 1915, 8, *LT*, 8 Sep 1915, 6, *Sun*, 8 Sep 1915, 9. See also illustration, *MW*, 25 Aug 1915, 1.

56 J.K. Archer, *Covetousness. Presidential Address to the Annual Conference of the Baptist Union of New Zealand* (Christchurch: Frasers Ltd., 1918), 14, quoted in Gustafson, 100. In 1896 Harry Atkinson founded the Christchurch Socialist Church, and early members included J.A. McCullough, and Elizabeth and James McCombs. J.H.G. Chapple became a Unitarian after he was tried for heresy by the Presbyterians; James Thorn, *MW*, 9 Sep 1914, 4.

57 John Robert, *Press*, 18 Mar 1918, 4, *LT*, 18 Mar 1918, 8. See also editorial, *MW*, 19 Jul 1916, 4.

58 'Just a woman', *Sun*, 2 Sep 1915, 6; illustration, *MW*, 2 Sep 1914, 1, 22 Dec 1915, 10. See also illustration, ibid., 23 Dec 1914, 1.

59 Resolution of the Christchurch Presbytery, *LT*, 12 Jul 1916, 10, *Sun*, 11 Jul 1916, 11.

60 Members of the Society of Friends, Christadelphians, and Seventh Day Adventists were exempt from conscription.

61 Illustration, *MW*, 28 Jun 1916, 1.

62 *LT*, 29 Mar 1917, 4. See also Hiram Hunter, *Press*, 20 Jun 1916, 7, *LT*, 20 Jun 1916, 7, *Sun*, 20 Jun 1916, 8.

63 H.E. Holland, *Press*, 22 Dec 1916, 8, *LT*, 22 Dec 1916, 6.

64 H. Worrall, *Press*, 9 Apr 1917, 8; and R. Semple, *Press*, 13 Dec 1916, 3, *LT*, 13 Dec 1916, 5.

65 H. Hunter, *Press*, 20 Jun 1916, 7, *LT*, 20 Jun 1916, 7, *Sun*, 20 Jun 1916, 8.

66 *MW*, 9 May 1917, 1; S. Page, ibid., 26 Apr 1916, 3, *LT*, 29 Apr 1916, 4; motion put to Anti-Conscription meeting, *Sun*, 6 Jun 1916, 12; *Sun*, 1 Jun 1916, 3; and Tim Armstrong, *Press*, 18 Jan 1917, 3, *LT*, 18 Jan 1917, 9. See also advertisement, *MW*, 22 May 1918, 5.

67 L.M. Isitt, *Press*, 1 Jun 1916, 6. See also J. Craigie, *Press*, 1 Jun 1916, 6.

68 Government Statistician, quoted in Alan Everton, 'Government Intervention in the New Zealand Economy 1914–1918: Its Aims and Effectiveness' (MA thesis, VUW, 1995), 412. For comparative figures for the increase in the cost of living in the four main centres see *LT*, 18 Jun 1915, 2, *Canterbury Times*, 11 Aug 1915, 56, and *LT*, 26 Jan 1917, 4.

69 Gustafson, 100.

70 Editorial, *MW*, 9 Jun 1915, 4; ibid., 9 Jun 1915, 4; and Elizabeth McCombs, *Press*, 23 Apr 1917, 7.

71 Illustration, *MW*, 21 Apr 1915, 1; 'The World of Labour' column, *Sun*, 7 Sep 1915, 5; and John Payne, *LT*, 4 Apr 1916, 8, *Press*, 4 Apr 1916, 9. See also illustration, ibid., 23 Jun 1915, 1.

72 Ibid., 23 Dec 1914, 6; and Maurice Gresson, *Press*, 29 Apr 1918, 7, *LT*, 29 Apr 1918, 4. See also S.R. Dickinson, *Press*, 20 Jun 1917, 8.

73 Editorial, *MW*, 26 May 1915, 4; Dr H.T.J. Thacker, *Press*, 29 Apr 1918, 7, *LT*, 29 Apr 1918, 4, *Sun*, 29 Apr 1918, 8; editorial, *MW*, 9 Jun 1915, 4; J. Payne, *LT*, 4 Apr 1916, 8, *Press*, 4 Apr 1916, 9.

74 'Taylor', *LT*, 18 Mar 1915, 3.

75 P.C. Webb, *Sun*, 24 Sep 1915, 4, *LT*, 24 Sep 1915, 9, 6 Jan 1916, 6.

76 Parsons, App 1, 190–2.

77 Elizabeth Plumridge, 'Labour in Christchurch: Community and Consciousness, 1914–1919' (MA thesis, UC, 1979), 106–12.

78 Labour mayoral candidate R.M. Speirs won 35% of the vote in 1914 and 30% of the vote in 1915; James McCombs won 31% of the vote in 1917.

79 H.T.J. Thacker (Port Christchurch League) 5948 (42%), J.J. Dougall (Citizens) 5747 (41%), J. McCombs (Labour) 2306 (16%).

80 Baker, 201.

81 For Christchurch South election results from 1911 to 1919 see *LT*, 18 Dec 1919, p.7.

82 Jim McAloon, 'Hunter, Hiram 1874–1966', *DNZB* (www.dnzb.govt.nz/, updated 4 Apr 2002).

Chapter 32: Graham Hucker
I wish to thank and acknowledge the support and encouragement of my PhD supervisors Basil Poff and Dr James Watson of Massey University.

1 Frederick Voitrekofsky to Florence Journeaux, 10 Dec 1915, Voitrekofsky Letters, MS 199, Taranaki Museum (Puke Ariki), New Plymouth. He was in the NZEF's 6th Reinforcements.
2 Ibid., Voitrekofsky to Journeaux, 15 Sep 1917.
3 Annis Bracken Hamerton to Frances Hamerton, 22 Sep 1914, Hirst Family Letters, MS Papers 5507-12, ATL.
4 *NZ Farmer,* , May 1915, 664–5; *SEP*, 24 Dec 1915, 5.
5 Hamerton to Hamerton, 22 Sep 1914.
6 Pugsley, *Fringe*, 283–95. Boyack, *Lines*, 87, 89, 162.
7 C.N. Barclay, *Armistice 1918* (London: J.M. Dent & Sons Ltd, 1968), xi; H.E. Goemans, *War and Punishment, The Causes of War Termination and the First World War* (Princeton: PUP, 2000), 3.
8 Jay Winter, 'A Taste of Ashes', *History Today*, Vol. 48, No. 11 (1998), 8–13. Lyn Macdonald, *To The Last Man* (London: Penguin Books, 1999); Hugh Cecil and Peter Liddle (eds), *At the Eleventh Hour*, (Barnsley: Leo Cooper, 1998); Adrian Gregory, *The Silence of Memory, Armistice Day, 1919–1946* (Oxford: Berg, 1994); Stanley Weintraub, *A Stillness Heard Round the World: the end of the Great War, November 1918* (London: Allen & Unwin, 1986). For children's literature on the Armistice see Reg Grant, *Armistice 1918* (London: Hodder Headline, 2003).
9 *SEP*, 7 Oct 1918, 3.
10 Ibid., 2 Nov 1914, 4.
11 Graham Hucker, 'Defying Those Who Would Forget – A Hall of Remembrance and its Narrative', *History Now*, Vol. 9, No. 2 (2003), 11, 13; *HNS*, 2 Nov 1818, 8.
12 *TH*, 2 Nov 1918, 7, 1 Nov 1918, 7; *HNS*, 1 Nov 1918, 4.
13 Clifton County Council, Minutes of Meetings, 1 Nov 1918, 432 (New Plymouth District Council); 'Celebrations Peace Day Proposals 1918–19', AD1, 15/183, ANZ.
14 *HNS*, 4 Nov 1918, 4, 2 Nov 1918, 8.
15 Ibid., 4 Nov 1918, 4.
16 Ibid., 5 Nov 1918, 4.
17 *TH*, 4 Nov 1918, 7.
18 Ibid., 2 Nov 1918, 7. See also the notices of Sgt Stanley's homecoming and the proposed Ambury memorial. Lance Corporal Chard is buried at Flesquières Hill (British) Cemetery in France.
19 Ibid., 4 Nov 1918, 7. A fisherman by occupation, Chapman died on 30 September 1918. He has no known grave and is commemorated along with 446 others at the Grévillers (New Zealand) Memorial in France.
20 *SEP*, 15 Oct 1918, 4. A sawmill hand by occupation, Private Rowse is buried at St Sever Cemetery Extension, Rouen, France.
21 Ibid., 11 Oct 1918, 5.
22 Doris Gordon, *Back-Blocks Baby-Doctor* (London: Faber & Faber, 1949), 136.
23 Death Register, D1918, vol. 229A, entry 49, 3468 (Central Registry, Births, Deaths and Marriages, Lower Hutt).
24 Ibid., entry 55. *SEP*, 11 Nov 1918, 5.

25 Gordon, 135–7.

26 Corporal Arthur Burrell (age 25) and Private Donald Smith (25) died on 1 October 1918. Rifleman Charles Potts (35) died on 8 October. Rifleman Louis Bottcher (23) died on 3 November. Sapper Douglas Chamberlain (22), Private Arnold Browning, and Lance-Corporal Allen Walker died on 5 November.

27 *HNS*, 2 Nov 1918, 4.

28 'Diary of 1918', 6, 11 Nov 1918, Voullaire Papers, MS 160, Taranaki Museum.

29 *HNS*, 8 Nov 1918, 8.

30 *TH*, 8 Nov 1918, 7.

31 *SEP*, 8 Nov 1918, 5.

32 *TH*, 8 Nov 1918, 7.

33 *SEP*, 8 Nov 1918, 5.

34 Sergeant John Cleaver (age 21) of the NZ Field Artillery died of wounds on 26 October 1918. He is buried in the Vertigneul Churchyard, Romeries, France. Rifleman Frederick Babbage of the NZ Rifle Brigade died of wounds on 30 October 1918. He is buried in Solesmes Communal Cemetery in France. Sergeant Henry Linn (age 23) of the NZ Rifle Brigade died of disease on 4 November 1918. He is buried in Oxford (Botley) Cemetery, United Kingdom.

35 *HNS*, 8 Nov 1918, 8.

36 *OT*, 8 Nov 1918, 3.

37 *HNS*, 13 Nov 1918, 4, 12 Nov 1918, 4.

38 *SEP*, 12 Nov 1918, 5, 13 Nov 1918, 5.

39 Robert Rutherdale, 'Canada's August Festival: Communitas, Liminality, and Social Memory', *Canadian Historical Review*, Vol. 77, No. 2 (1996), 226; Jeffrey Verhey, *The Spirit of 1914. Militarism, Myths and Mobilization in Germany* (Cambridge: CUP, 2000), 13, 14.

40 Arthur Marwick, *The Deluge* (London: Macmillan, 1973), 260: 'the war seemed to be ending as it had begun; it was like August 1914 all over again'. John Williams, *The Home Fronts 1914–1918* (London: Constable, 1972), 259: 'Once again, as at 11 p.m. on 4th–5th August 1914'.

41 *HNS*, 2 Nov 1918, 8.

42 *OT*, 15 Nov 1918, 2.

43 *TH*, 6 Nov 1918, 4.

44 *SEP*, 13 Nov 1918, 5.

45 *OT*, 15 Nov 1918, 2.

46 *SEP*, 4 Nov 1918, 3.

47 *TH*, 14 Nov 1918, 7.

48 Gordon, 138.

49 Graham Hucker, 'A Time of Sorrow and Misery. Representations of the 1918 Influenza Epidemic in a Rural District of New Zealand' (PGD Arts Research Exercise in History, MU, 1999), 21.

50 *SEP*, 7 Oct 1918, 3; *TH*, 6 Nov 1918, 4.

51 *HNS*, 2 Nov 1918, 8.

52 *OT*, 15 Nov 1918, 2; *SEP*, 4 Nov 1918, 3; *HNS*, 1 Nov 1918, 4, 2 Nov 1918, 8.

53 *SEP*, 13 Nov 1918, 5.

54 *HNS*, 4 Nov 1918, 7. *SEP*, 4 Nov 1918, 3. New Zealand soldiers did serve with the AIF. At least 51 soldiers with next of kin resident in Taranaki volunteered for service with the AIF in 1914–15. Private Herbert B. Watkins who is commemorated in Stratford's Hall of Remembrance, served with the AIF. He was killed in action in France on 12 February 1917, aged 33.

55 *HNS*, 4 Nov 1918, 4.

56   Ibid., 13 Nov 1918, 4. For geographical locations of where soldiers from central and eastern Taranaki are buried or memorialised, see Hucker, 'Defying Those Who Would Forget', 13.

57   *TH*, 1 Nov 1918, 7.

58   *HNS*, 1 Nov 1918, 4, 2 Nov 1918, 8, 4 Nov 1918, 7, 5 Nov 1918, 4.

59   Turuturu-Mokai was a 'small constabulary redoubt' which was attacked by Maori in 1868. James Cowan considered Turuturu-Mokai to be 'the Rorke's Drift of the New Zealand Wars'. Belich, *Wars*, 241; *HNS*, 4 Nov 1918, 4.

60   *HNS*, 1 Nov 1918, 4.

61   Ibid., 12 Nov 1918, 4. See also *TH*, 13 Nov 1918, 2.

62   Gordon, 137–8.

63   Hamerton to Hamerton, 22 Nov 1918, Hirst Family Letters, ATL.

64   *SEP*, 13 Nov 1918, 5.

65   *TH*, 13 Nov 1918, 2; *SEP*, 13 Nov 1918, 5. See also *HNS*, 1 Nov 1918, 4.

66   *HNS*, 1 Nov 1918, 4.

67   *TH*, 14 Nov 1918, 6.

68   *HNS*, 13 Nov 1918, 4.

INDEX

Abbey Road 233, 238
Abraham Heights 260
Aden 312, 314, 320
Adlam, Ab Smn Victor 317
Admiralty, UK 66, 68; and coal 329, 430; controls NZ ship 62; on EF departures 66; and naval intelligence 321, 325; and NZ Naval Forces 309
Afghanistan 55
Africa 33, 41, 52
agricultural training 378–93
Air Board 334
aircraft 44, 47; balloons 341, 349; bombing 120, 349; Caudron G.3, 334, 336–7; and combined arms 307; Curtiss flying-boat 338; DFW 340; Fokker biplane 341; at Gallipoli 203; Maurice Farman 335; at Somme 233; Sopwith Camel 339; Sopwith Dolphin 334, 337–8; in Turkish use 212
Aitken, Mrs J. 92
Albany 185, 312
Albert 274
alcohol 109, 186, 221, 372, 375, 517; in camps 490; and churches 485; prohibition of 471, 521; regulated 521; and RSA 169, 362; and venereal disease 368; and YMCA 357–8
Alexandretta 312, 319

Alexandria 198, 225, 371
Algerian troops 97
aliens 528
Allen, Sir James 64, 179, 380, 485; as Acting PM 125, 250, 411, 423, 525; and Maori conscription 101; and minesweeping 322; Minister of Defence 53, 58, 61, 189, 202, 246, 265, 286, 502, 518, 522, 527, 529, 582; and naval policy 67; and NEB 530; and NZ's war effort 263; and rifle clubs 441; and venereal disease 368
Allenby, Lt-Gen Sir Edmund 222, 226, 290
Allies Day 444
Alsace-Lorraine 82
ambulances 470
American Civil War 52, 394, 515
American Commission to Negotiate Peace 117
American Expeditionary Force 109, 113, 115–17, 120, 267, 527
American Legion 114
Amiens 269–70, 276, 280, 284
Amman, battle for 214, 221
ammunition 41, 45, 153, 202, 270, 443; at Gallipoli 202; NZ-made 495, 522–3; and rifle clubs 443; shortage 198, 200–1, 204
Ancre à la Sambre, Battle of 285
Anderson, Ross 481

Andrews, E.F. 164

Andrews, Eric 131

Anglo-Japanese Alliance 131–2, 139–40

Anglo-Persian Oil Company 335

Anzac Cove 97, 183, 195, 213, 217

Anzac Day 38, 49, 103, 143, 145–6, 149, 156–7, 175–8, 212, 394; Amendment Bill 1921 178; and church service 462, 469, 472; religion 449, 459; war memorials 179

Anzac legend 144–9, 156, 183, 196, 211, 401, 580

Anzac units, 87, 201; Australian & New Zealand Army Corps 206; I Anzac Corps 260, 289, 292–3, 296, 301–2; II Anzac Corps 257, 259–60, 289, 292, 296, 301–3; Anzac Mounted Division 57, 60, 214, 219, 220–2; and Bullecourt, 296; in BEF 291; and Canadian Corps 292; Headquarters 195–6, 200; New Zealand & Australian Division 57, 186, 188, 192, 195

Aotearoa, ss 413, 415

Aparima, ss 415, 418

Apia 63, 65, 310, 325

Apprentices Act 1923 531

Aquitania 207

Arbitration Court 523, 527, 532

Argentina 541–2

Arkwright, John 456

Armenia 77, 580

Armentières 228

Armistice 30, 121, 162, 288, 379, 465, 569–82; Austria-Hungarian 570, 572; celebrations 570; German 138, 570, 575; Russian 267; Turkish 214, 221, 570–1

Armistice Day 124, 178, 580

armoured cars 47, 246, 332

Armstrong, Tim 553, 562, 567

Army Council 263, 433

Army List 397

Arnold, Maj Anthony 340

Arras 295, 339

artillery: 44, 220, 260, 296, anti-aircraft 312, 349; barrage 228; creeping barrage 243, 305; failure of 304; indirect fire 44; mountain guns 426, 432; and NZMR 215; at Passchendaele 261; smooth-bore 317

Ashmead-Bartlett, Ellis 144, 208

Aspinall-Oglander, Brig-Gen Cecil 153

Asquith, Herbert 582

Atkinson, Lily 375, 513

Aubers Ridge 153

Auchonvillers Ridge 272–3

Auckland: City Council 165, 323; Hospital Board 165; naval base 309; RSA 159, 163–4, 167, 176; Waterside Workers Union 440

auctioneers 294, 298

Audoin-Rouzeau, Stephane 157

Auja River, Battle at 214, 221

Australia 32, 39, 42, 55, 58, 61, 64, 87, 143, 147, 401; commemoration 177, 178; conscription 263; grain 539; meat 541; military history 395; nationalism 302, 394; and NZ deserters 417; Peace Conference 125; raises extra division 252, 289; repatriation 172; rifle clubs 437; sea mines 320; war effort 263; welfare 512

Australia, HMAS 64, 310

Australia Squadron 62, 309; Australian Auxiliary Squadron 61

Australian Army 395, 398

Australian Bicentennial 146

Australian Commonwealth Naval Board 326–7, 330–1

Australian Defence Force Academy 395

Australian Freedom League 87

Australian Imperial Force 144 5, 263, 292, 302; Aborigines 399–400; Australian Corps 291, 303, 306; after Bullecourt 301; database 396; departure 66; disbands units 1918, 268; German 1918 offensive 267; and manpower shortage 263; nationalism 306; and NZEF 66–7, 185; New Zealanders 186; NZ Engineers 403; units: *divisions: 1* 185–6, 292–3, 302, *2* 293, 302, *3* 257, 289, 292, 297–8, 302–3, *4* 291, 299, 302, *5* 293, 302, 5 Division Artillery 404; *brigades*: 1 Australian 195, 199, 200, 4 Infantry 186, 188, 274, 281, 1 Australian Light Horse 186, 188, 215–16, 220, 226; *regiments*: 2 Light Horse 192, 10 Light Horse 404, 12 Light Horse 403; *battalions*: *1* 403, 1 Machine Gun 404, *9* 403, *15* 191, *23* 403, *36* 280

Australian War Memorial 144, 147–8, 395, 397–8
Austria-Hungary 34–5, 67, 485; armistice 572; and Bolshevism 575; Bosnian crisis 35; Navy 412, 413; surrenders 570
Avenger, HMS 413
Averill, A.J. 459, 464, 472, 474, 476, 479, 483, 486, 492
Avondale Training Camp 97
Awanui 326–7
Awarua 326–7
Ayrshire, HMT 388
Ayun Kara 214, 220

Babbage, Rfm Frederick 576
Baby 700 188
Bailey, Bdr N. 283
Baker, Newton 109
Baker, Paul 26, 517, 535–6
Baker, Pte Ray 187
Balfour, Arthur 127, 140
Balkan Wars 34–6
Bannerman, Lt R.B. 333, 337, 339, 341–2
Bapaume, Battle of 47, 285
barbed wire 45–6, 232–3, 346
Barclay, C.N. 570
Batten, Claude 160
Bauchop, Lt-Col Arthur 203, 206, 224
Bauchop's Hill 217
Bayley, Lt Charles 574
Bayly, Bessie 574
Bayne, Pte James 185
Beagley, Ab Smn Sidney 319
Bean, C.E.W. 149, 150, 154, 156, 182, 189–90, 192, 196, 205, 280, 395, 404; as correspondent 144; and ethnicity 399; official historian 210, 217, 271, 275, 435
Beattie, Cpl Gerald 270
Beaumont Hamel 272
Becker, Annette 157
Beckham, David 142
Beersheba, Battle of 220
Beeston, Lt-Col Joseph 192
Begg, James 526
Belgium 34, 36–7, 40–1, 43, 56–7, 69–84, 341, 400, 582; refugees 70, 75, 77, 79; Relief Fund 69, 444, 552, 556, 560
Belich, James 55, 59–60, 405, 409
Bell, Francis Dillon 66

Bellamy, Sgt H. 241
Bennett, Agnes 498
Bennett, James 184, 401
Bentinck, Lord Charles 193
Berlin 35–6, 40
Berton, Pierre 447
Bertrancourt 280, 283
Bessell-Browne, Col Alfred 404
Bevan, Thomas 418
Bible in Schools 470–1, 473, 485
Birch, Maj-Gen J.F.N. 297–8
Birdwood, Lady 210
Birdwood, Lt-Gen Sir William 195, 198, 203, 206, 209, 279, 287; and Anzac landing 198; and Australian nationalism 303; and Hill 971 202; and NZMR 216; and prostitution 372; and Quinn's Post 189; visits New Zealand 210
Bisman, Rfm J.T. 233
Bissett Smith, Lt Archibald 418
Black, Jeremy 36
Blackadder 32–3
Blackman, Sgt Arthur 238, 243
Blainey, Geoffrey 39
Blamires, Chap-Capt Henry 458, 491
blockade 33, 43, 320–1
Bluff 414
Blyth, L-Cpl Lawrence 232, 242
Board of Trade: NZ 532, 546; UK 411
Boles, Sgt-Maj G.H. 238, 243
Bolshevism 136, 575
Bombay 316–17, 320
Borden, Sir Robert 124, 127, 131
Bosnian crisis, 1908 35
Botha, Gen Louis 128–9
Boulogne 258
Boulton, S. 538, 548
Bowler, Lt-Col Edmund 21, 194–211
Boxer, Dr Ernest 161, 163, 167, 176–7
Boyce, Gordon 420
Boyle, Alexander 551–2
Braithwaite, Brig-Gen W.G. 243–4
Braund, Lt-Col G.F. 187
Brawley, Sean 131
Braybon, Gail 493
Brest-Litovsk, Treaty of 40
Britain 31–42, 47, 51–4, 60, 63, 76, 143; Anzacs 187; casualties 119; commemoration 178; and NZ 51, 196, 534; NZEF 251–3; Samoa 310;

Territorial Army 195; women 493;
British Army 31, 41, 116, 348; artillery 260; and Chunuk Bair 218; Blackpool depot 257; formations: First Army 300; Second Army 46, 259–60, 296–7, 302–3, 341; Second Army Reserve 269; Third Army 269; Fourth Army 228; Fifth Army 228, 260, 269, 271, 293, 296; Reserve Army 291, 293; IV Corps 270, 274, 280, 291; V Corps 270, 273–4, 291; XIX Corps 301; XV Corps 228, 291; XVIII Corps 260; XXII Corps 291; 14 Divisional Artillery Group 230; General Reserve 269; Imperial Reserve 57; invades Syria 220; manpower shortages 264; New Army 289; new tactics 258; Royal Engineers 197; structure of 291; units: *divisions*: 15 301, 29 187, 41 229, 233–4, 237, 240, 47 229–30, 233–4, 237, 240, 49 348, Guards 44; *brigades*: 20 43, 122 238, 240, *regiments*: 3 Dragoon Guards 44, Foot Guards 44, Royal Horse Guards (The Blues) 43; US divisions with 116
British Empire 32, 39, 45, 50, 52–6, 197, 334; humbled 150; and Maori troops 99; mass citizen armies 289; Mesopotamia 335
British Expeditionary Force 31, 41, 43, 45–7, 57, 227, 256; command of 288; and German 1918 offensive 267, 279–80, 284, 289; in 1918 268
British mounted police 182
British Railways 78
Brodie, Matthew 459, 469
Broodseinde, Battle of 46, 259–60, 262
Brooking, Tom 547
Brotherhood of Men of Goodwill 360
Brown, Col Charles 190
Brown, Paymaster W.J.A. 325, 327
Brown, Sgt Donald 231
Bruce, J.L. 391
Brydon, Capt Robert 242
Buchanan, Sir Walter 419, 543
Buck, Capt Peter 98
Bulgaria 570
Bullecourt 296, 299, 301
Bulls Eye 437
Burke, Dean 490
Burley, Pte Claude 230, 239–40

Burn, John 334
Burn, Lt William 333–6
Burn, Robert 334
Burrell, David 412
Burton, O.E. 247, 260, 272, 275, 357, 464; and YMCA 361
Businessmen's Efficiency League 521
Butler, Gen 298
Byng, Lt-Gen Hon Sir Julian 288, 293
Byrne Lt A.E. 285

Cabinet, Australian 134; Imperial War 126, 252, 268; NZ 173, 251, 264, 422–3, 434, 486, 519, 522, 525, 530, 546, approves NZEF 59, and 4 NZ Bde 252, NZEF departure 66, and Samoa EF 64
Cairo 182, 369; flesh pots 355; newspaper coverage 199; training 186; and venereal disease 371; and YMCA, 372
Caldwell, Lt Keith 340
Caldwell, Sgt R.T. 238
Cambrai 304
Cameron, Col 202
Camp Dodge 115
Campbell, Alex 146
camps 354–5, 469
Canada 32, 39, 41, 178, 429; cheese 540; corps commander 300; grain 539; manpower 250; and naval intelligence 325, 327; Peace Conference 125; war effort 263; women 453
Canadian Expeditionary Force 42, 291, 400; and ANZAC Corps 302; artillery 300, 304; and Arras offensive 295; Canadian Corps 46, 288, 291–4, 300, 304, 306; divisions 291–2; manpower shortages 268; military education 383; tactical innovation 288; training improvements 294
Canal du Nord 45
Çannakale 147
Canterbury University College 386
Canterbury Women's Institute 86–7, 89–90, 94
Cape Farewell 321, 323–4
Cape Horn 53
Cape of Good Hope 53, 325
Caporetto, Battle of 267
Carbery, Lt-Col A.D. 245, 284, 357
Cardiff 82

Carlyon, Les 149, 184
Caroline Is 64
Carr, E.H. 156
Carroll, Sir James 100
Cartwright, Dame Silvia 38, 49, 56
Cashmere TB sanatorium 390
Cassel 269
casualties: Australian 403; British 266; Canadian 296, 301, 305; Gallipoli 97, 517; German 301; Maori 98, 103; naval 314; New Zealand 16, 195, 215, 218, 226, 228, 231–2, 234, 241, 245, 247, 278, 282, 284, 403, 418, 449, 454, 579; Somme 519; South African War 501; US 119
Caterpillar Valley 244
Catholic Women's League 77
cavalry 43–4, 215, 221, 224
Cavell, Nurse Edith 558
Celebes Is 321
censorship: of letters 196; ship movements 411; political 553
Central Flying School: India 335; UK 334
Central Powers 43, 67, 89, 534, 570
Central Repatriation Board 172
Ceylon 400
Chahbar 316
Channel ports 37, 269
Chapelle, Nurse 377
chaplains 116, 359
Chapman, Gertrude 573
Chapman, Pte James 573
Chappell, Rev A.B. 492
Chard, L-Cpl Albert H., 572
Charitable Aid Boards 93
Charmley, John 34, 36
chateau generals 49, 289
Château-Thierry 112, 118
Chatham Is 326, 328
Chauvel, Lt-Gen Sir Harry 188, 223
Chaytor, Maj-Gen Sir E.W.C. 219–20, 223–4, 446
Chief Inspector of Machinery 411
China Station, RN 309
Chinese in AIF 400
Christchurch: Boys' High School 334; City Council 93, 566; Hospital Board 367; RSA 162, 165, 168, 175
Chronicles of the N.Z.E.F. 166
Chunuk Bair 38, 192, 205, 208–9, 213, 217;

Maori and 98; and NZMR 217–18
Church Army 361, 363, 448
Churchill, Winston 53–4, 56, 62, 151, 153–5, 333
Citizens Defence Corps 441–2, 552
Citizen-soldier tradition 430
Clark, Alan 33, 42
Clark, James 463
Cleary, Bishop H.W. 452, 471, 475, 479, 487
Clemenceau, Georges 138, 139
Clifton County Council 571
Clifton, Spr Ernest 187
Clio, HMS 317
Closey, 2Lt S.J.E. 241
clubs, RSA 167, 179
coal 204, 329–31, 411, 522, 532
Coalition government 90, 135, 422, 533
coastal defences 411
Coates, J.G. 166
Cocos Is 67
Coffey, Father Richard 479
Coggins, Ted 406
Colincamps 274, 281
Collins, Col R.J. 446
Collis, Dvr L.J. 345
Cologne 386
Colonial Ammunition Company 522
Colonial Office 124
commandeer 524, 535, 539, 551, 564
Commission on the Responsibility of the Authors of War and Enforcement of Penalties 135
Committee of Imperial Defence 53, 154
Commonwealth & Dominion Line 408
Commonwealth War Graves Commission 215, 457
Companies Empowering Act 1924 532
compulsory military training 58, 85–6, 93, 426, 517; in Australia 87; opposition to 555; and rifle clubs 436–8
concert party 169, 318, 357
Condliffe, J.B. 386
conscientious objectors 92–3, 452, 464, 580; and churches 483, 489; defaulters 536; post-war 559, 567
conscription 41, 93, 101, 251, 382, 428, 442, 451, 455, 518, 520, 559; appeals 92; in Australia 263, 268, 402; and churches 470; eased 527; exemptions

526; of farmers 535–6, 544; industrial
517; introduced 252, 519; and labour
movement 518, 561; of Maori 100, 102;
married men 263, 501; and NEB 531;
legislation 91, 518; opposition to 90–1,
563; and seamen 417; in US 107; of
wealth 565; and women 496
Constantinople 56
Contagious Diseases Act 1869 367
Cooke, F.R. 499
Cooke, Pte Thomas 404
Cooper, Lt Allen 241
Cottrell, Bernard 271
Council of Agriculture 537
Council of Ten 125, 128, 133, 135
Courcelles 281
Courtney's Post 191
Cowan, Sgt William 245
Cowen, Rev Grant 582
Craighill, Lt Edley 116
Crèvecoeur 285
Crimean War 52
Cronin, Father D. 472
Cuddie, D. 540
Cumming, Francis 507
Cunard Line 420–1
Cunliffe Owen, Brig-Gen 202
Currie, Lt-Gen Sir Arthur 288, 290, 300,
304, 306; career 298; and French troops
294; and Haig 306

dairy companies 538, 540 1, 544, 546
Dardanelles Commission 153, 210
Davidson, Gen 298
Davidson, Archbishop Randall 459
Davies, Jon 466
Davies, Rev R.E. 451, 481
Dawson, Maj Tom 183
D-Day landings 155
Decies, Lady Gertrude 207
Defence Act 1903, Australian 399
Defence Act 1909 85, 501, 555
Defence Amendment Act 1912 436
Defence Department 410, 438, 506; and
1913 strike 441; coal 411; rifle clubs
440, 446; female employment 523; NZ
Base Records Section 496
Defence Expenditure Commission 381
Defence Scheme 427
De Groot, Gerard 290

Delville Wood 228
demobilisation 386
departments: Agriculture 380, 390–1, 540;
Discharged Soldiers' Information; 170;
Imperial Government Supplies 539;
Industries & Commerce 532; Labour
497–8, 532; Lands 380–1, 392; Public
Health 506; Railways 437, 496;
Scientific & Industrial Research 531
Deurt Yol 313
Devonport 423
Dickie, Prof John 451, 480, 483
Discharged Soldiers' Settlement Act 1915
170, 379, 393
discipline 108, 225, 301, 358–9, 363, 388,
392, 438; executions 108, 115, 401;
punishment 110
District Agricultural Committee, Food
Production 384
Dix, Lt-Cdr Charles 198
Dixon, Rev W.G. 451, 475, 477, 480
Dominion Executive Committee, NZRSA
164
Dominion Rifle Association 435, 437–8,
442, 445–6
dominions 30, 39, 41–2, 47, 53, 57, 316;
and foreign policy 196; at Peace
Conference 125; and US 129
Doris, HMS 312
Dougall, J.J. 442
Dowding, Hugh 334
drill halls 436, 439, 506
Driver, H.H. 450
drivers 344–53
dry docks 415
Dukes, Rev J. 477
Dunedin RSA 169, 177
Dunkirk 154

East African campaign 41, 287
East Indies Squadron, RN 319
Easter Island 66
Eastern Front 268–9
Eastwood, Maj Thomas 254, 256
Edmonds, Brig-Gen Sir James 153, 280, 396
Edward VII, King 577
Edwin, Capt A.M. 414
Egypt 44, 56–7, 60, 99, 187, 207, 209, 213;
and artillery 433; brothels 369;
cemeteries in 226; leave in 214; and

NZEF 67, 97, 158, 214, 216, 219; revolt in 214, 222, 385; soldiers' education 393

Egyptian Expeditionary Force 219, 220–1, 223–4

Ell, H.G. 567

Elliot, George 526

Elliot, S. 445

Ellis, L-Cpl Roy 240

Emden, SMS 67

Ennis, Lt-Col William 388

Ennor, Harold 28

Entente Cordiale 40, 534

Epsom Camp 216

essential industries 522

Étaples 383, 386

Europe, J.R. 119

Examination Service 411, 430–1

Excess Profits Duty 420

Expeditionary Forces Amendment Bill 567

Factory Corner 238

Fairclough, P.W. 473

Falklands, Battle of the 322, 431

Fanning Island 328

Farmers Union 133, 441, 537

Farrer, J.S. 402

Federal Steam Navigation Company 408, 410

Federation of Labour 525

Fellingham, W.G. 445

Fenwick, Lt-Col Percival 17, 374

Ferguson, Air Mshl Bruce 16

Ferguson, Niall 30, 34, 37, 39

Ferguson, William 380, 520–1, 526, 530

Ffrench, Lt-Col W.R.R. 404

Field, William 437

Fiji 140, 400

Finance Act 1918 528

Findlay, John 367

Findlay, Lt-Col John 216

Finland 400

First Division Mothers League 501

First Division, NZEF Reserve 519, 559

Fischer, Fritz 35

Fisher, Francis 64–6

flamethrowers 266

Flanders 33, 56, 258, 298, 300, 341

Flat Iron Copse 244–5

flax industry 542

Flers 227–8, 231–3, 235–6, 238, 248

Flers-Courcelette, Battle of 228

Folkestone 76

football 142, 169, 178, 345

Förster, Stig 34

forts 239, 430–1

Foster, T.W. 541

Fourteen Points 124, 127, 136

Frame, Tom 32

France 35–8, 40–3, 56–7, 60, 70, 73–4, 99, 116, 202, 350, 400; Australians in 302; and capitalists 33; casualties 119; NZ airmen 339; Paris Peace Conference 126; training in 255; War Ministry 285

Francis, Robert 473

Franco-Prussian War 36

Franz Ferdinand, Archduke 32, 34, 56

Fraser, Malcolm 537

Fraser, Peter 204

'Frazer, Jack' 376

Freemasonry 194

Fremantle 312

French Army 116, 267

French, Fd Mshl Sir John 153, 256, 287

French-Canadians 42

Freyberg, Lt-Col B.C. 62

friendly fire 117

Fromelles 293

Frostick, James 496, 520–1, 524

Fry, Willie 339

Fulton, Brig-Gen H.T. 240, 243, 279

Gair, Sgt Charles 238, 243

Gallipoli 30–2, 38, 49, 56–7, 60, 62, 142, 145–6, 150, 153, 158, 179, 182–4, 187, 195–6, 205, 208, 213, 286, 289, 458, 460, 517, 519, 571; casualties 97, 196, 199–200, 538; commemorated 175, 212; and Crusades 477; described 453, 455; evacuation 195, 214, 219; landing 199; myth of 149, 155–6; national identity 202, 249; New Zealanders 215; NZEF committed to 216; NZMR 213, 215–17, 219, 222; news of 468, 475; official history 153; returning wounded 158, 160; and 2nd Ypres 291; sport, 142; study of 147, 149–51, 184; veterans 161, 178, 396; VC at 403

gambling 357, 486, 517, 521

Gammage, Bill 145, 184

Garland, Canon David 471
Garton Foundation 529
Garton, Stephen 514
gas 114, 119–20, 291, 486
Gatrell, Peter 83
Gavin, Rev G.H. 578–9
Gaza 214, 220, 226
Gaza-Beersheba Line 224
Geo H. Scales Line 408, 416, 419, 424
George V, King 39, 50, 86, 96
George, W.H. 372
Geranium, HMS 324
German Army 31, 37, 40, 43, 138; armies 275, 278; artillery 266, 280; divisions 229, 236, 279, 281; invades Belgium 70; new tactics 258; offensive 267; regiments 282, 301
German Navy 61; destruction of 125; East Asiatic Squadron 64–5, 309, 414, 431, 439; eastern base 331; fleet 38, 54, 63, 320; Samoa 64; U-boat campaign 63, 204, 267, 314, 331–2, 382, 410, 412, 418, 535, 543, 558
German Supreme Command 278, 280
Germany 34–41, 43, 47, 50, 56, 197, 451, 557; and barbarity 555; and Bolshevism 575; and colonies 55, 63, 127, 310; demoralisation 120; occupied 34, 386; offensive 527; Russian armistice 267; and Turkey 67; war's outbreak 35
Gibb, Dr James 454, 470, 473, 483
Gibbon, Lt-Col C.M. 322, 327
Gibson Smith, Rev J. 481
Gillam, Rev W.E. 470, 481
Gillan, Monsignor 455, 468
Gillet, Lt Francis 341
Gisborne RSA 160
Glebe Street 237
Gneisenau, SMS 64–5, 311, 326
Godley, Lt-Gen Sir A.J. 59, 63, 149, 186, 195, 206, 279, 286, 292, 529; alcohol 374; II Anzac Corps 257, 303; and Australians 193; Birdwood 209; criticism of 303; and 4 NZ Bde 253, 262, 264; Haig 297; imperial officers 58, 432; Main Body 67; Maori troops 98; NZ's military reforms 426, 430; Quinn's Post 189, 191; rifle clubs 436–9; and Russell 216; Somme 246, 247; venereal disease 371

Goff, Phil 148
Goldstein, Vida 87
Gordon, Dr Doris 574, 579, 581
Gordon, Sgt T.J. 241
Gore 194–5, 210, 341
Gough, Gen Sir Hubert 291, 293, 295–6
Gould, Charles 551
Gould, George 552
governors-general: Australian 66; NZ 38, 49, 56, 124
Gravenstafel Spur 260
Gray, C.S. 37
Gray, Cpl Norman 245
Gray, 2Lt W.A. 241
grenades 188, 255, 258, 278, 283, 295
Griffiths, Lt-Col G.C. 384
Grinnell-Milne, Duncan 337
Grove Alley 236
Gunson, Sir James 488, 520–1, 526
Guthrie, David 393
Guttery, Rev Arthur 489

Haig, Fd Mshl Sir Douglas 32–3, 46–7, 227–8, 268, 287–9, 297–9; and ANZAC Army 292; and Australian nationalism 303; and Canada 300; diaries of 290; and dominion interference 306; and Lens 300; Messines 297; Monash 298; and NZ Division 298–9; praises NZ 247; Somme 292, 295; and subordinates 290; and tactical revolution 295
Hall, Duncan 131
Hall-Jones, Sir William 433–4
Hall-Thompson, Capt P.H. 308–9, 312, 316, 319, 322
Hamel 270, 274, 280, 306
Hamerton, Annis 569, 581
Hamilton, Gen Sir Ian 149, 151–3, 155, 188, 203, 287, 428; and ammunition 200; and Anzac landing 199, 217; criticism of 196; dismissed 209; and NZMR 216; visits NZ 223, 427, 438
Hananui II, ss 324
Hancock, Maj 198
Hankey, Sir M.P.A. 128
Hanna, Sgt Judson 112
harbour boards 523
Harcourt, Lt John 273
Harding Steward, Gen E. 432–4
Harington, Maj-Gen Tim 296, 298, 307

Harkness, J.G. 541
Harper, Glyn 32
Harper, J.D. 160
Harré, John 462
Hart, Brig-Gen H.E. 27, 46, 254–5, 258–9;
    and 4 NZ Bde 253, 256, 264
Hastings RSA 161
Hawera 179, 540
Hay, James 355
Hay, Rev W. 490
Hazebrouck 269
Heard, Col E.S. 446
Hébuterne 272, 274, 276–7
Hédauville 271–2
Helles 149, 151, 199–200
Herbert, A.P. 151
High Wood 228, 230, 237
Hight, Professor James 386
Hill 60 98, 213, 218
Hill 70 300
Hill 971 202, 205
Hill, Sgt John 241
Hinaki L-Cpl Para 383
Hine, J.B. 166
historiography 17, 25
Hitler, Adolf 37–8
Hobart 185, 312, 407
Hobbs, Col J.T.T. 202
Hogben, George 531
Hokowhitu-a-Tu, Te 96–105
Holdsworth, Charles 407, 421
Holland, Henry 551–2, 557, 566–7
Hollweg, Chancellor Bethmann 35–6
Holmden, Sgt T.N. 373
Holmes, Maj-Gen 299
Home Guard 446
Hong Kong 328
Honorary Soldiers' Pensions & Allowance
    Board 506
Hopkins, F.W.B. 403
Horne, Gen Henry 300
Horner (YMCA Secretary) 362
horses 60; ASC, 344; care of 224; disposal
    222; donated 535; donkeys 31, 32, 33;
    fodder 346; and Gallipoli 216; and
    mounted rifles 215, 219; named 349;
    racing 521; remounts 224; willing 518
hospital boards 165, 494
hospital ships 188, 411
hospitals 218, 245, 573; bills 506; field 112–

13, 348; gas ward, 119; and education
    379, 390; France 244; mental 510; NZ
    in UK 257; and venereal disease 372;
    and YMCA 357, 363
Housewives Union 92
Howard, John 143
Howard, Michael 33
Howard, Rev Ted 554, 567, 571
Howden, 2Lt Peter 254, 262
Howell, E.V. 89
Hughes, Allan 408, 420–1
Hughes, William 124, 129, 131–2, 134, 138,
    303
humour 351
Hundred Days offensive 45, 306
Hunt, Rev G.P. 478
Hunt, W.D. 520–1, 526
Hunter, Capt Joseph 246
Hunter, Cpl Frederick 245
Hunter, D.R. 537
Hunter, Hiram 554, 562, 567
Hunter, Sgt-Maj Robert 245
Hunter-Weston, Gen Sir Aylmer 149

Ibuki, HIJMS 67, 311
ideology 110
Immigration Restriction Amendment Act,
    1920 132
Imperial Conference (1921) 139
Imperial General Staff 57, 435
Imperial Shipping Conference (1907) 410
Imperial War Conference (1917) 520
India 207, 400, 534; and NZ airmen 334; sea
    mines 320; training in 434
Indian Expeditionary Forces 20, 97, 335, 337
Industrial Workers of the World 525
Industries Committee 530–1
inflation 173, 523, 532
influenza pandemic 27, 124, 131, 162, 334,
    514, 574, 576, 578–9, 582; and Samoa
    127
Inglis, Capt L.M. 232, 237, 242–3, 247,
    254, 258, 262
Inglis, Ken 145
Ingram, Pte Neil 254, 261
Inter-Allied Conference for the Study of
    Professional Re-Education 383
Inter-Allied Reparations Commission 136–7
International Committee of Women for
    Permanent Peace 89

International Congress of Women 88
Invercargill 210
Iraq 33, 143, 315, 333
Ireland 79, 387; and AIF 402; Easter
    rebellion 488; home rule 477;
    independence 452, 562; war effort 470,
    487
Irvine, Maj 198–9
Isitt, L.M. 568
Ismalia 371
Israel 213, 219, 226
Italian Army 267
Italy 42, 287, 400, 542

Jacka, Albert 147
James, R. Rhodes 155
Jamieson, Dvr A.J. 345
Jamieson, Jim 352
Japan 35–6, 39, 53–4; and NZ produce 542;
    Pacific naval bases 130; Peace
    Conference 123, 130
Japanese Navy 132, 330
Jeismann, Michael 72
Jellicoe, Adml Sir John 54
Jepson, Pte Cecil 272
Jericho 214, 221
Jerusalem 220
Jewish Agricultural College 385
Jewish War Refugees Committee 77
Joffre, Mshl Joseph 153
Johnson's Jolly 202
Johnston, Brig-Gen F.E. 149
Johnston, Brig-Gen G.N. 432–3
Jonah's Pillar 313
Jones H.A. 338
Jordan 213, 221
Journeaux, Florence 569
Julius, Bishop Churchill 461, 472, 480, 551
Just War theory 555
Jutland, Battle of 478

Kaiapoi 167, 504
Kaikoura 476
Kairanga 345, 353
Karori Rifle Club 437, 440
Katoa, ss 310, 330
Kawakawa RSA 167
Keegan, John 30
Keily, Lt-Cdr Charles 314, 318, 322, 324
Kell, Capt H.J. 323, 413

Kelly, James 452, 487–8, 491
Kemball, Maj-Gen G.V. 337
Kermadec Is 321
Kerse, Sgt-Maj Charles 230
Khaki University 383
King Edward Barracks 441
King George's Sound 67
King, Jonathan 146–7
King, Michael 65
King, Pte John 401
King's College, Auckland 464
Kipling, Rudyard 433
Kirk, Capt J.R. 379, 386–7
Kitchener, Fd Mshl Lord 42, 152, 188, 207,
    210; and Ian Hamilton 200; New Army
    240, 289; Scholarship Fund 387
Kivell, Ab Smn Frank 316
Knowles, Ab Smn William 314
Koromiko, ss 310
Krithia, 2nd Battle of 153
Kyler, Donald 121

La Signy Farm 274, 279, 281–2
Labour Party, NZ 33, 166, 384, 511, 554,
    567; formed 525; 1917 elections 566
land settlement by returned soldiers 163–4,
    170–1, 378, 381
Langley, E.E. 553, 567
Lansing, Robert 135
Laracy, Hugh 452
Latvia 400
law, international 50, 56, 135
Lawrence, Pte Charlie 271
Laws, C.H. 489
Le Quesnoy 47, 285
Leadley, Bill 168, 465
League of Nations 125, 130–1, 139, 465;
    Commission 133; mandated territories
    130; and Massey and 137; NZ and 138
Lee, John A. 166, 361
Legge, Lt-Gen J.G. 293
Legion of Frontiersmen 440
Leipzig, SMS 310
Lemnos Island 213, 219
Lens 300
Levinge, Dr Edward 551
Lewis, Lt Cecil 233
Leys, T.W. 423
Liberal Party 50, 61, 90, 135, 164, 548, 567
Library, Divisional 357

Liddell Hart, Capt Sir Basil 32, 42, 154
Lincoln Agricultural College 385
lions 31–2
Liverpool, Lord 50, 66, 250, 412; and
    armistice 124; hospital ships 414; and
    war's outbreak 19, 85
Lloyd George, David 41, 124–5, 134, 139,
    582; and Peace Conference 126;
    reparations 136
Lloyd, G.W. 175
Local Government Board 78
London 72, 397
Lone Pine 202, 208, 403, 569
Long, Walter 250
Longburn 345
Longueval 16, 228
Louis, W. Roger 127
Ludendorff, Gen Erich 37, 124, 269, 280, 284
Lusitania 558, 580
Lusk, Maj D.H. 441
Luxford, Chap John 453, 491

McCallum, Margaret 514
McCarthy, Mary 511
McCay, Col James 190
McCombs, James 536, 554, 563, 566–7
McCudden, James 340
Macdonald, Rev A. 487
Macdonald, William 380, 528, 546
McEldowney, Dennis 457
McGowan, Capt Henry 384
McIntyre, Ben 344
Mackenzie, Clutha 166
Mackenzie, Sir Thomas 166, 195, 207, 208,
    210, 434, 447
Mackesy, Lt-Col C.E.R. 216
McKinnon, Capt Hugh 239, 242–3
Macky, Lt N.L. 239
McLaurin, Col 198–9
McLeod, Jan 494
McMenamin, Father J.J. 490
McMillan, J.W. 571, 576, 578, 581
McSharry, Capt Terence 190–1
McWhirter, James 272
machine guns 234, 277, 283; aircraft 338;
    captured 221, 279; naval 313; NZMR
    215, 220
Madill, Rev 578
Magdhaba, Battle of 214, 219, 224
Mahan, Adml Alfred 54

Maheno, HS 414, 416–17
Mailly-Maillet 272, 274
Makino, Baron 132
Malcolm, Pte William 362
Maleski, Pte Joseph 112
Mallow, HMS 324
Malone, Lt Col W.G. 21, 185, 187, 206, 571,
    582; and Australians 401; Chunuk Bair
    218; and prostitution 374; Quinn's Post
    189, 191
Malta 204, 309, 312
Malthus, Sgt Cecil 38, 189, 243, 248
Mao Tse-tung 37
Maori 51, 69, 97, 101–3, 203, 581; and
    Anzac legend 197; and armistice 577;
    Cabinet minister 127; conscription 101;
    education 383, 388; franchise 495; haka
    98, 105; land 165; MPs 97; officers 97,
    160; pioneers 98–9; race relations 127;
    returned men 103, 160; ship names
    408; at Somme 234; units 97, 99; see
    also NZEF units: Maori Contingent
Maori, ss 334, 414
Maoriland Worker 89, 92–3, 555, 563
Marama, ss 326, 414, 416
Mararoa, ss 414
Marguerite, HMS 324
Marine Department 411
Marlborough Sounds 309, 440
Marne, Battle of the 339
Marrin, Albert 474
Marriner, H.J. 551–2
Marriott, Lt W.J. 463
Marshall Is 130
Marshall, 2Lt Henry 440, 445
Marshall, Capt J.M. 325
Masefield, John 150
Masefield, William 445
Massey, W.F. 19, 58–9, 66, 85, 90, 129, 163,
    172–3, 178, 208, 380, 422, 441, 513,
    518, 521; and Anzac co-operation 131;
    conscription 92; farmers 534; food
    production 537; manpower 252; on
    NZEF departure 65–6, 68; Peace
    Conference 123; Samoa 64, 125; Sub-
    Commission on Criminal Acts 135
Massey's Cossacks 441
Massey's tourists 401
Matunga, ss 321
Max of Baden, Prince 124

Maxwell, Paul 115
Meadows, Capt T.G. 320–1
meat companies 541, 543, 548, 552
Meaulte 235
medical examinations 436
Mediterranean Expeditionary Force 57
Melbourne, HMAS 310
Meldrum, Lt-Col William 216, 220, 223
Menin Road, Battle of 302
Merz, Lt George 336
Mesopotamia 43, 287, 315, 333, 335
Mesopotamia Flight, RFC 335
Messines, Battle of 46, 256–8, 285, 297–8,
    447, 458, 527; Haig's plan 297; and
    Russell 300
Metz 116
Meuse-Argonne offensive 118, 120
Michael Offensive 118, 124, 267, 279–80,
    284, 339
militarism 56, 79, 91–3, 137, 464; German
    197, 450; opposition to 85, 92, 555;
    Prussian 480, 557, 563
military districts 58, 428, 436, 519;
    Auckland 441; and manpower 264; NEB
    520–1
Military Pensions Act 1866 500
Military Secretary 209
Military Service Act 1916 91–2, 442, 519–
    20, 529, 563; exemptions 330
Military Service Boards 417, 519, 529, 531,
    545
Militia Act 1858 500
Millar, Lt Fitzadam 319
Millen, Julia 344
Mills, Sir James 208, 407, 421, 423
Milner, Lord 130, 133–5, 140, 208
minefields 320, 324
miners 330, 331
Ministry of Munitions 41
Minotaur, HMS 66, 311
Mitchell, George 166
mobilisation 84
Moeraki, ss 414
Moewe, SMS 418
Mombauer, Annika 34
Monash, Lt-Gen Sir John 188, 279, 290,
    292, 297, 404; Australian Corps 288,
    306; and Haig 298–9
Monash Valley 183
Monowai, ss 414

Montcalm 64, 310
Montgomery, W.H. 391
Moore, Briscoe 384–5
Moorehead, Alan 154–5
Moore-Jones, Spr H.M. 161
Moreton, Ab Smn John 309, 313
Morris, Joseph 117
Morris, Pte William 273, 275
Morton, A. 548
Moses, John 480
Moss, Thomas 520–1
mounted troops 43–4, 59, 212–26
Mouquet Farm 291
Moxsom, William 499
Mt Cook Depot 433
Mudros 200, 205, 414
Murdoch, Keith 208, 303
Murray, Charles 490
Murray, Gen Sir Archibald 219–20, 222
Muschamp, Pte Harold 272
music 119, 169, 186, 461
mutiny: 1917 267; executions 109; at
    Gallipoli 209
Myers, Arthur 519
myths 31, 65, 80, 150, 153, 155–6, 466

Napier Boys' High School 402
Napier, Christopher 424
Napoleon 37, 149
National Anthem 519
National Council of Women 93, 513
National Dairy Association 541, 548
National Efficiency Board 517, 528; and
    conscription exemptions 536; disbanded
    530; formed 496, 520; prohibition 522;
    soldier settlement 380
National Fire Union 78
National Peace Council 86
National Registration Act 1915 90, 518–19,
    526
National War Memorial 16, 18
Native Contingent, *see* NZEF units; Maori
    Contingent
Native Contingent Committee 97, 100
native troops 97
Nauru 125, 134; British mandate 134; and
    Peace Conference 126, 133; radio
    station 326
Naval Defence Act 1913 308–9
Naval Intelligence Centre 325, 328

naval preparations 60, 308–32
Navy League 551
Nek, The 154, 199, 217
Nerger, Korv-Kapt Karl 320–2
Netherlands 70, 400; dairy industry 387;
    East Indies 321, 331; and refugees 78
neutrality 50, 56, 62, 78, 82, 89, 311, 475,
    487–8
Nevill, Bishop 473
New Guinea 55, 131, 310, 321
New Hebrides 140
New Zealand, and Birdwood 209; casualties
    16, 41, 195, 202, 205, 215, 218, 221,
    226, 228, 231–2, 234, 241, 245, 247,
    262–3, 278, 282, 284, 403, 418, 449,
    454, 579, 527; Christmas gifts 316;
    churches 448, 466–7; coal 329–30; cost
    of war 137; defeated 214; economy 141,
    424; efficiency 516; farming 535, 537,
    548; home defence 426–46;
    immigration 164; imperial war effort
    264; infantry 45, 60, 62; manpower 41,
    251, 265, 445, 530; military reforms
    435; minefields 323–4, 413; national
    identity 32, 102, 185, 249, 319, 394;
    post-war reconstruction 172, 520; radio
    stations 326–7; and reparations 141;
    reportage 200; return to 214, 222;
    Samoa 310; shipping 308, 325, 330,
    416, 423; strategy 39; threat to 324;
    Turkey 49; welfare 504; women 495,
    508; writing 31, 351
New Zealand Day 176
New Zealand, HMS 23, 62, 330
New Zealand Wars 101, 501, 580
New Zealanders 38, 46, 49, 51–6, 61, 182,
    222, 232, 270, 404; in AIF 400–1;
    airmen 333; and Anzac legend 193;
    behaviour of 185; commemoration 177;
    expatriates 144; fighting quality 226; at
    Gallipoli 98; merchant navy 418; naval
    service 62, 309; Quinn's Post 184, 189;
    at the Somme 247; and US soldiers 116;
    and the war 68
NZ Council of Agriculture 384
NZ Division, RN 309
NZ Employers' Federation 524
NZ Expeditionary Force 16, 157, 250, 255,
    263, 265; advice on 57; Australians in
    186; Base Records 393; at Boulogne,

258; chaplains 361–2, 452; departure of
    66, 212, 213, 427; discipline, 401;
    Divisional Library 357; Divisional
    Provost Marshal 195, 200; education
    378, 385–7; in Egypt, 213; ethnic units
    96, 102; to France, 219; and Godley
    303; Home Service Section 431, 445;
    Main Body 60, 65–6, 517, 311;
    manpower, 268, 431, 442, 518, 536,
    561; National Reserve 436–8, 440–1,
    444, 496; NZEF UK, 210; offered 57,
    213; priority, 439; raised 67;
    reinforcements, 527; repatriated, 167,
    567; Samoa Advance Party 63–5, 265,
    410, 414, 435; and second division 250;
    training camps 428; US units, 116; and
    YMCA 355
NZEF facilities: Avondale Training Camp 97;
    Central School of Agriculture 384;
    Codford Camp 253, 255–7, 351, 389;
    Epsom Camp 216; Étaples Camp 383,
    386; Featherston Camp 391, 428, 471;
    hospitals 382, 390–1; Main Body camps
    355; Mechanical Transport Depot,
    Oatlands Park 382; NZ Base Camp,
    Ismailia 385; NZ Convalescent Hospital,
    Hornchurch 382–3, 386; NZ Hospital
    No. 2, Walton-on-Thames 382; NZ
    Reception Camp, Rouen 386; Rafia
    Camp 384; reinforcement camp, France
    259; Sling Camp 389; Torquay
    Discharge Depot 384, 386, 389;
    Trentham Camp 355, 364, 376, 438,
    442, 469, 472, 477, 490, 503, 510
NZEF units/corps:
    battalions: 1 Auckland 174, 183, 190, 311;
    2 Auckland 229, 231, 241, 245, 274–5,
    278; 3 Auckland 253, 261; 1 Canterbury
    187, 189–90, 243, 253, 271, 273, 282,
    311, 386; 2 Canterbury 229, 241, 253,
    273, 282; 3 Canterbury 253, 257, 261;
    Entrenching 268; NZ Machine Gun
    234, 244, 272, 277, 283; NZ Maori
    (Pioneer) 104, 234, 245, 388; 1 NZRB
    235–8, 272–3; 2 NZRB 233–5, 244,
    274; 3 NZRB 233–6, 240, 244, 274,
    276, 282; 4 NZRB 233, 235, 241, 244,
    281; 1 Otago 199, 208, 224, 270, 311;
    2 Otago 229, 231, 241, 274; 3 Otago
    253–4, 258, 261; 1 Wellington 185,

191, 218, 311; 2 Wellington 229, 239, 241, 272, 274, 276; 3 Wellington 253, 256, 259, 261

battery: 10 Battery, NZA 283

brigades: 252–3, 257–9, 262–5; NZ Composite (1918) 274, 277; 1 NZ Field Artillery 230; 2 NZ Field Artillery 230; NZ Infantry 98, 186, 189, 199, 215, 255, 289; 1 NZ Infantry 258, 262, 274; 2 NZ Infantry 229, 241, 245, 258, 262, 273, 281–2; 4 NZ Infantry 250, 257–8, 264–5, 268, 520, 527; NZ Mounted Rifles 57, 186, 212–26, 265, 384; 3 NZ (Rifle) 46, 229, 232, 240, 245–7, 254, 262, 272, 278, 281

corps: Army Service 344, 347; NZ Engineers 158, 188, 229, 234; NZ Fd Artillery 202; NZ Medical 245; NZ Veterinary 225

division: Broodseinde 262; command 161, 219, 235, 288; Divisional artillery 278–9, 283; Divisional Reinforcement Unit 255; Divisional reserve 268; and Haig 299; and higher formations 57, 291–2, 302–3; Maori Contingent 99; in 1918 267–70, 272, 274, 280, 284–5; official history 238; Passchendaele 260, 262; performance 241, 270; reinforcements 263, 306, 389; Somme 46–7, 227–8, 240, 246–7, 249, 251, 293; strength 268, 519; tactics 47, 258, 295, 297; and US units 116

medical: 1 NZ Field Ambulance 161; 2 NZ Field Ambulance 245; 4 NZ Field Ambulance 257; casualty clearing stations 244

regiments: Auckland Mounted Rifles 212, 216–18, 221; Canterbury Mounted Rifles 212, 334; Otago Mounted Rifles 99; Wellington Mounted Rifles 186, 212, 217–19

reinforcements: 2nd 195, 428, 503; 3rd 428, 503; 4th 355, 536; 5th 218; 20th 253; 47th 572

NZ Flying School 338

NZ Freedom League 86

NZ Institute 529

NZ Merchant Marine 406–7, 424

NZ Methodist 456

NZ Military Forces 251, 265, 427, 435; coast defences 429; defence rifle clubs 428, 431, 435, 440, 442; Director of Military Hospitals 390; Directorate of Military Training 439; Director of Ordnance 432; Director of Recruiting 445; Director of Sanatoria Medical Services 390; General Training Section 436; Inspector of Rifle Clubs, Drill Halls & Rifle Ranges 439, 445; mounted rifle clubs 439, 440; NZ Staff Corps 334; reorganisation of 426; Royal NZ Artillery 438; Royal NZ Engineers 427; Senior Cadets 403, 428–9, 431, 439–40, 443–4; South African War 403; women 498

NZ Naval Forces 62, 308; created 61, 67; intelligence 322, 324, 326; NZ Division, RN 325, 330; volunteers 309

NZ Police 102, 366, 368, 507, 561

NZ Registered Nurses' Association 498

NZ Returned Soldiers' Assn (NZRSA, now Royal NZ Returned & Services' Assn) 158–60, 499, 505; Auxiliary Ladies Committees (Women's Sections) 162; clubs 167, 179; membership 180; and pensions 501; soldier settlement 381; venereal disease 376

NZ Shipping Co 407, 412, 418, 424, 543, 552

NZ Territorial Force 58–9, 195, 255, 345, 426–8, 442; Air Force 342; D Battery NZA 65, 124, 430, 432–3; as first line of defence 436; Garrison Artillery 430, 438; mounted rifles 223, 225; Post & Telegraph Battalion 427; Railways Engineers 427; *regiments*: 3 Auckland 334; 4 Otago 338, 342; 5 Wellington 429; 7 Southland Mounted Rifles 195; 8 Southland 342; 13 Nth Canterbury & Westland 448; rifles for 443; rural 535; unfit men 436

NZ Trawling & Fish Supply Co 323

NZ Volunteer Force 41, 58–9, 203, 216, 252, 426, 435; ex-members 440; units 194, 431

NZ Volunteer Sisterhood 499

newspapers: journalists 148; New Zealand 246, 550, 566; war coverage 199, 553

Newton, Cmdr Robert 325

Ngaruawahia 101

Ngata, Sir Apirana 97, 100, 102, 104; Maori conscription 101; on Maori volunteers 99
Ngati Kahungunu 100
Ngati Maniapoto 101
Ngati Porou 100
Nicholson, Gen Sir William 57
No More War Movement 93
Noel, Maj Maurice 339
non-combatant roles 115
Nora Niven, ss 323
North, J.J. 450, 460, 488
Northcroft, Lt-Col E.H. 387
Norway 400
Noumea 64, 310
nuclear war 37
nurses 162, 377, 392, 498, 510, 558

O'Connor, P.S. 102, 132
O'Neill, Maj E.J. 203
O'Neill, Tpr 221
Ocean Island 133, 328
official histories: Australian 145; British 153–4, 280, 396; New Zealand 210, 257, 279, 284, 357, 395
Old Outpost No. 3 213, 217
Olssen, Erik 547
Orua Downs 353
Otago Patriotic & General Welfare Association 506
Otago Soldiers' & Dependants' Welfare Committee 506
Otaki, ss 418
Ottoman Empire *see* Turkey
Overseas Soldier & Sailor Scholarship Fund, 387
Overton, Maj Percy 217

P&O shipping line 419–23
Pacific colonies, German 43, 123
Pacific Islanders in NZEF 99
Pacific Phosphate Co 134–5
pacifism 86–90, 92–5, 562
Page, Robin 93
Palestine 43, 212, 221, 265, 287, 385
Palmer, Rev 578
Palmerston North 169, 428
Panama Canal 53
Pankhurst, Adela 87
Papacy 487–8
Papakakura, Rev 577

pardons 50
Paris 71, 74, 76, 118, 123–41
Park, Annie 509
Parker, Mrs Harry 207
Parliamentary Elections Postponement Act 563
Party Truce, UK 73
Passchendaele, Battle of (3rd Ypres) 46, 259–60, 264, 269, 285, 301, 304, 346, 527; II ANZAC Corps 303; and Canadians 304; New Zealanders at 215, 249, 264; revenge for 272
Paterson, Capt Hugh 203
Patey, Adml Sir George 310
Patients & Prisoners Aid Society 507
Patriotic: Board 353; committees 503; funds 363, 535, 551–2, 565; societies 505
Paul, J.T. 499
peace celebrations 162, 578, 580–2
Peace Conference, Paris 123–41; British Empire Delegation 126, 128; Japan 130; and mandated territories 128; reparations 136
pensions 171, 500
Pershing, Gen John 109, 111, 115, 120, 267
Persia 316
Persian Gulf 62
Pétain, Gen Henri 267
Philippines 52
Phillips, Jock 344
Philomel, HMS 23, 308, 312, 413; control 61; operations 312, 315–16; returns to NZ 318, 322
pillboxes 46
Pinfold, J.T. 483
Pippin, Horace 113–14
Pitt, Capt William 160
Plugge's Plateau 183
Plumer, Gen Sir Herbert 46, 259–60, 279, 296, 298, 341
Plunket, Lord 207
Poland 37, 400
Polygon Wood 302
Pomare, Dr Maui 127
Ponder, Rev J.S. 455, 473
Pope's Hill 203
Poppy Day Appeal 174, 178–9
Port Chalmers 414
Port Kembla, ss 322–3, 413
Port Line 418

Port Melbourne, HMT 388
Port Said 314, 369; and captured ships 320
Post & Telegraph Dept 124, 326–7, 427
postal service 350
Pozières 279, 291, 293, 404
Presbyterian Church 204, 448, 465, 482–6
Print, Jim 352
Prior, Robin 37
prisoners of war 200, 254, 262, 310
prize ships 416
Progress, ss 416
propaganda 52, 70, 87, 109, 150, 553
prostitution 182, 364–72, 490, 507
Protestant Political Association 165
Prussia 36, 56, 123, 365, 481, 557
Pryor, William 524
Psyche, HMS 64, 309–12
Pugh, Martin 495
Pugsley, Christopher 148, 184, 344, 388
Puisieux 270, 285
Pukeora TB sanatorium 390
Purdy, Capt Robert 240
Pyramus, HMS 64, 309–10, 312, 315–16

Queen Carnival, Dunedin 506
Queen Elizabeth, HMS 151
Queen Mary Military Hospital 390
Quick March 161–2, 174, 180
Quinn, Capt Hugh 189
Quinn's Post 183–4, 188–9

racial issues 102, 110, 131–2, 196, 205, 555;
    in US Army, 109
radio stations 326–7
Rafa, Battle of 214, 219, 220
Rafia Camp 384
railways 437, 496, 522; Baghdad 312; Hejaz,
    221; NZ railguns 430; Sinai 224; troops
    427
Ranstead, G.M. 385
Rathbone, Eleanor 511
rationing 532
Rawling, Bill 293
Rawlinson, Gen Sir Henry 247
Raymond, Ernest 151
Red Cross 551, 355, 498
Red Sea 62, 312
Redwood, Archbishop Francis 470, 482
Reform Party 50, 58, 61, 90, 135, 164, 166,
    485

refugees 69–84, 271
Regnault, Dean Peter 468
Regulation of Trade & Commerce Act 1914
    526
Rehbein, Helmut 483
Reilly, Maj Hugh 335–6
reinforcements 60, 216, 252, 257, 259, 263,
    428, 517, 519, 527–8; Australian 263;
    and conscription 564; Maori 99, 101;
    reduction requested 264; training 255
religion 150, 197, 299, 345, 351, 401, 447,
    571; NZRSA 165; and pacifism 562;
    YMCA 359
remembrance 175
repatriation 171–3, 379, 390–1
returned soldiers: Britain 159; Canada 159;
    NZ 157–81, 378
Returned Soldiers' Associations 157–81, 362
Rhind, Sgt Arthur 235
Rhodes, A.E.G. 551
Rhodes, Lt A.T. 185
Rhodes, Sir R. Heaton 441, 551
Richardson, Maj-Gen Sir G.S. 382–3, 393,
    434
rifle ranges 436–7, 439, 442
Robertson, J. (Labour candidate) 568
Robertson, John 184
Roberston, John (rifleclubsman) 444
Robertson, Fd Mshl Sir William 42, 287
Robin, Maj-Gen Sir A.W. 67, 251, 264, 431,
    444
Robson, Lloyd 396
Rodgers, Cpl Jesse 231
Rogers, C.W. 578
Romani, Battle of 214, 219, 224
Roseneath School 69
Ross, Malcolm 189, 208
Rout, Ettie 368, 373, 377, 499
Rowbotham, Sheila 495
Rowse, Pte Robert 573
Rowson, Pte Charles 574
Royal Air Force 339–41
Royal Australian Air Force 336
Royal Australian Navy 61, 316, 326, 330
Royal Engineers 47
Royal Flying Corps 233, 235, 335, 338–9
Royal Military College, Duntroon 395, 402,
    404
Royal Naval Air Service 332
Royal Naval Division 62, 200

Royal Naval Reserve, New Zealand Section 309

Royal Navy 37, 39, 43, 51, 54, 61–3, 196, 204, 308–9, 328, 413; and armistice 578; Australia Station 61–2, 309, 329; blockade 320; China Station 321, 325, 327–8; Grand Fleet 54, 63; minesweepers in NZ 324; NZ coal 331; NZ subsidises, 61; Pacific battlefleet, 63; *Philomel* 319; Q-ships, 332

Royal NZ Air Force 16, 342

Royal NZ Returned & Services' Association, 158; *see also* NZ Returned Soldiers' Assn

Ruakura state farm 390

Runciman, Jane 499, 509

Rupprecht, Crown Prince of Bavaria 278

Russell, G.W. 90, 422, 499, 567

Russell, Maj-Gen Sir A.H. 47, 222, 259, 269, 272, 274, 288, 292; commands NZMR 216, 223; criticises officers 242; emphasises training 248; French honours 285; Haig 297; 4 NZ Bde 253, 262, 264; NZ Division 219, 228, 285; offered corps command 307; RSA 161, 174; Somme 235

Russell's Top 193

Russia 34-8, 41-2, 86, 332, 400, 430; armed forces 35; and Bolshevism 525; collapses 305; Japanese War 52; offensives, 1917 267; revolution 40

Russians in AIF 401–2

Salonika 42

Salvation Army 355, 361, 366, 469, 507

Samoa 55, 63–5, 310, 326, 430; and peace settlement 125–6, 130

Samoa Expeditionary Force, *see* NZEF: Samoa Advance Party

Sanders, Lt-Cmdr William E. 332

Sargent, J.S. 287, 289, 292

Sari Bair 98, 199, 213, 217

Saunders, Capt H.C. 321

Saunders Page, Sarah 87, 90–1, 93

Saunders, Sgt Wallace 192

Savage, M.J. 141, 499, 525

Sazonov, Sergei 35

Scales, G.H. 411

Scarborough, Pte Fred 183

Scharnhorst, SMS 64–5, 311, 326

Schweitzer, Richard 37

sea routes 53, 61, 63

Seacliff Mental Hospital 510

Seamen's Union 416, 423

Sechault 113

Second Division League 503, 527

Second Division, NZEF Reserve 444, 519, 527

Second World War 38, 175, 265, 363, 416

Seddon, T.E.Y. 166

Self-Denial Week 561

Semple, Robert 166

Senior, Lt C.H.A. 241

Serbia 34–6, 400

Serre 274–5, 282

Seymour, D.J.B. 381

Shadbolt, Maurice 31

Shailer, Ellen 353

Shalders, R.B. 354

Shaw, J.W.C. 403

Shaw, Rev J.W. 474, 481

Shaw Savill & Albion line 407, 412, 418

Sheffield, Gary 32, 140, 267

Shipping Controller 410, 412

shipping industry 522, 542

Shout, 2Lt A.J. 402, 404

Shrapnel Gully 183

Sievwright, Capt A.B. 166

Silvius, F.J. 445

Simich, Louise 495

Simplon, ss 323

Simpson, John 147

Simson, Capt Donald 158–60

Sinai 17, 212, 219, 224

Sinclair, Rev W.A. 484, 582

Singapore 141, 312, 330, 335

six o'clock closing 485, 522, 531

Skocpol, Theda 515

Smith, C.S. 403

Smith, Pte Alfred 183

Smuts, Gen Jan 131–2, 137

Smythe, Capt R.B. 434

social Darwinism 145, 150

Social Democrat Party 91

Society for the Protection of Women and Children 502

Society of Friends 86, 93, 452

Soldiers' Financial Assistance Board 500, 504

Soldiers' Guide, The 380

Soldiers' Wives, Mothers and Dependants'

League 501
Solicitor-General, 423
Somme 45–6, 120, 228, 270; 1916 battle of
47, 227, 251, 258, 285, 292–3, 519;
1918 battle 267, 269–70, 272, 280,
284–6; battlefield memorial 16; Box &
Cox 237–8; coverage in NZ 246;
lessons from 293, 295, 297; and New
Zealanders at 215, 291
South Africa 39, 42, 25, 131–2, 320, 400
South African War 52, 55, 58, 60, 86, 92–3,
99, 152, 158, 160, 186, 216, 224–6,
403–4, 501, 516, 572; armistice 577;
and artillery 433; Boers 55; Maori and
99; NZRSA 159
South America 65, 310
South West Africa 128
Southern Command, UK 255, 256
Spanish American War 52
sport 142–3, 169, 178
Sprott, Capt M.W.C. 460
St George's Day 176
St Mihiel offensive 118
St Quentin 266
Stalin, Joseph 37
Stanley, Peter 148
Stanley, Sgt E.C. 572
Stansfield, Stan 39
Stayte, Pte Jesse 253
Stead, W.T. 365
Stewart, Col Hugh 238, 382–3
Stewart, Lt M.R. 241
Stewart, Mary Downie 509
Stewart, Oliver 338
Stewart, W. Downie 64, 166, 171, 178
Stopford, Lt-Gen Sir Frederick 149, 196,
204, 206
Storkey, Percy 402, 404
Stout, Sir Robert 373
Strachan, Hew 51
Stratford Mounted Rifles 403
stretcher bearers 113, 187, 245, 282, 356
strikes: arbitration 532; drivers 527; *Maheno*
417; miners 526; 1912 Waihi 561; 1913
waterfront 417, 441, 535, 562
Stroud, Rev 580
Studholme, Lt-Col John 210
submarines 267, 314, 321, 331, 411
Suez Canal, 53, 56, 67, 216, 219, 314, 335
Suez Crisis 154

Sugar Factory 276
Sullivan, Chap-Capt J.R.R. 454
Sullivan, Dan 554, 567
Surafend massacre 226, 385
Suva 310, 326, 328
Suvla 204
Sweden 400
Sweeney, Pte J.J. 401
Switch Trench 229–32, 234, 248
Switzerland 70, 82, 194, 400
Sydney, HMAS 67
Syria 213, 219, 220–1, 226

Table Top 217
tactics: artillery 243; fighter 341; machine
gun 254; new 258, 262, 288, 295
Tahiti 65–6, 327
Taieri Plain 428
Taingakawa, Tupu 101
Tainui 101–2
Tait, Lt K.J. 221
Talune, ss 326
tanks 44–5, 239; and combined arms 1918,
307; at the Somme 232–6, 239, 244;
blamed 296; demand for 267; first use
of 228
Taranaki 570; tribe 101
Tauherenikau 390
Taylor, A.J.P. 32
Te Arawa 100
Te Awamutu RSA 167
Te Waikato military hospital, Cambridge 390
Teague, Edith 352
Tel el Saba 220
Temuka RSA 167
Thacker, Dr Henry 568
Thebaud, Françoise 493
Thiepval 279
Thompson, Col Onslow 198–9
Thornton, Chap-Capt G.D. 373
Three Kings Is 321, 323–4
Thuillier, Maj-Gen H.F. 301
Thursday Is 326
Tillman, S.P. 130
Timaru 427
Tinsley, Rev R.B. 579
Todd, Lt-Col T.J. 404
Togoland 65
Tolerton, Jane 497
Tong Way, Rev John 400

Tonga 140, 310
Torch, HMS 309, 325
Toronto 42
Townshend, Maj-Gen Charles 335
trade protection 53, 408
trade unions 440, 499, 525, 553–4
training schools 256, 258
transport 344, 346, 348, 384
Travers, Tim 184
Travis, Pte Dick 231
Treadwell, 2Lt C.A.L. 234
Treasury, The 58
Treaty of Versailles 34, 123, 134, 136, 138, 140
Treaty of Waitangi 100
Treloar, John 185
trench mortars 47, 258, 266, 279, 281, 292
trench warfare 43–4, 103, 150, 286, 346
Trenchard, Sir H.M. 287
Trethewey, William 449
Triangle Trail, The 360
Trigge, Rev Val 469
Triumph, HMS 201
troopships 495; Australian 185; chaplains 4'/1, 481; crewing 411; defensively armed 430; and disease 371; education 379, 387; NZ 185; requisitioning 411; returning drafts 387; shortage 222; venereal disease 371; YMCA 355–6, 361
Trotter, Anne 140
Troy 150
Tsingtao 64
Tsushima, Battle of 54
Tuck, Capt G.A. 230, 240–1, 277, 279
Turkey 38, 49, 56, 67, 142, 147, 335; armistice 214, 221, 570–1; attacks Aden 314; and Baghdad railway 313; cemeteries 226; Gallipoli 184, 188; peace settlement 128; prisoners 200
Turkish Army 152, 201, 221, 226, 435
Turritella, ss 320
Turuturu Mokai 580
Tutanekai, ss 324
Tweedmouth, Maj Lord 43

Union Steam Ship Company 329, 407, 409, 414–15, 420–1, 423
United Federation of Labour 499
United States 39–40, 52, 122, 378, 400; enters war 106, 263, 267; imports from

545; NZ flax 542; and Peace Conference 123; welfare 513; women 493
Unknown Warrior 16–17
US Army 107, 110; *see also* American Expeditionary Force

Vandervelde, Madame 81
Vaughan, Brig-Gen J. 43
venereal disease 358, 364, 367, 374, 486
Verdun 227, 294
vermin 120, 344, 362, 374
veterans, NZ 157–81, 212
Vickers, artillery maker 89, 239–40, 338, 432–5
Victoria College, Wellington 402
Victoria Cross 231, 332, 403–4, 418
Victoria League 551
Victoria, Queen 100
Vienna 34–5
Villers-Brétonneux 280
Vimy Ridge 32, 293, 295, 297
Vincent, Pte Thomas 403
Vivier Mill 228
Voitrekofsky, Pte Frederick 569, 582
von Bismarck, Otto 36, 563
von Clausewitz, Karl 31, 37
von Hindenburg, Fd Mshl Paul 37
von Kluck, Gen Alexander 339
von Moltke, Gen Helmuth 35
von Spee, Adm Graf Maximilian 64–6, 309, 311, 431, 439
Voullaire, Marc 575

Wahine, HMS 414
Waihemo, ss 415
Waikato 101
Waikawa, ss 415
Waimakariri 428
Waimarino, ss 415
Wainwright, Rev Percy 460
Waipouri, ss 310
Waipu 69
Wairuna, ss 321, 322, 413, 415
Waite, Capt Fred 210
Waitemata, ss 415
Waitomo, ss 415
Wake, Cmdre D.St A. 318
Walker, Maj-Gen Harold 293
Walker, Rev William 469, 490
Walker, Sgt 244

Walker's Ridge 187, 193
Wallingford, Capt J.A. 439, 445
war art 114, 161, 287, 449, 463
War College, US 111
war graves 397
War Legislation Act 1917 526
war memorials 175; Bridge of Remembrance
    406; Christchurch Citizens 406; Kaiapoi
    449; living 179; to Maori 103; Menin
    Gate 398; New Zealand 157, 457;
    Scottish National 144; Taranaki 573,
    580; Villers-Brétonneux 404; Vimy 296
War Office, UK 264, 433, 434; and Gallipoli
    152, 202; NZ foodstuffs 540; 4 NZ Bde
    255; reorganises British Army 1918 268
war pensions: Act 1915 170, 501; Act 1923
    173; Appeal Board 160, 173–4;
    Commission 173
War Refugees Committee 75
War Relief Association 506
Ward, Sir Joseph 57, 62, 437, 452; Leader of
    Opposition, 85; NZ Finance Minister
    519, 521, 546; and League of Nations
    125; Peace Conference 123, 135
Washington DC 40
waterfront: 1913 strike 417, 441, 535; and
    national efficiency 526; Wellington 532
Watt, M.N. 407
Waugh, Steve 142
Wavell, Gen A. 221
Wazza (Wazir) 372, 374; prostitutes 370;
    riot 182–3, 226, 375
Wellington Harbour Board 521, 523
Wellington RSA 163, 513
Wells, Ada 87, 89, 93–4
West of Scotland Agricultural College 387
Western Front 30, 38, 40, 42, 44, 49, 59-60,
    62, 116, 151, 155, 202, 227; AEF
    arrives 267; I/II ANZAC Corps 302;
    BEF 301; Canadian Corps 291, 296;
    dominion commanders on 288; Eastern
    Front 269; exhaustion 259, and
    Gallipoli 155; USA 107, 112, 115, 119;
    NZEF destination 67, 216
Western Maori electorate 101
Westmoreland, HMT 388
Westport 167, 329–30, 430
Whangarei RSA 167
White, Gen Cyril B. 299, 303

Whitley Councils 529
Wilhelm II, Kaiser 17, 35–6, 38, 54, 69,
    110, 135, 256, 479, 537, 556, 564
Williams, Pte Ernest 190
Williams, W.J. 456, 467, 470, 478, 484, 486,
    491
Wilson, Fd Mshl Sir Henry 287
Wilson, Trevor 37
Wilson, Woodrow 40, 106, 124–5, 127–8,
    133, 139
Wimmera, ss 323, 413
Winnington-Ingram, Bishop 476, 480
Witty, George 568
Wolf, SMS 23, 320–2, 324, 413, 431
Wolfe, Col G.C.B 439
Woman's Peace Party 87
women: opposition to war 85–95; and duty
    559; war 493; sacrificial mothers 560;
    war work 523
Women's Anti-Conscription League 86, 91
Women's Christian Temperance Union 364,
    375, 452, 480, 514
Women's International League for Peace &
    Freedom 86, 89, 94
Women's National Council of Canada 453
Women's National Reserve 496, 552
Women's Parliamentary Rights Act 1919 494
Women's Peace Army 87
Women's Peace Crusade 87
Women's Sections, RSA 162
Workers Education Association 386
wounded soldiers' funds 318, 538
writing: diaries 205, 218, 344, 353; letters
    196, 211, 225, 350; and YMCA 357
Wyatt, George 253
Wytschaete Ridge 297

Yap Island 326
Young Men's Christian Association 352,
    354–8, 362, 372, 382
Young, Pte A.C. 447
Ypres 258, 260, 269, 340, 350; 1st Battle of
    289; 2nd Battle of 289, 291; 3rd Battle
    of 386, 403, 527; see also Passchendaele
Yugoslavs, Australian 400

Zealandia's Great War conference 18
Zillebeke 43

Echoes of Gallipoli

In the Words of New Zealand's Mounted Riflemen

Terry Kinloch

The Gallipoli campaign of 1915 played an important part in making New Zealand the nation it is today. The heavy sacrifice of life affected the country for generations, and Anzac Day remembrances are still dominated by those battles almost a century ago.

In *Echoes of Gallipoli*, Terry Kinloch brings a fresh approach to these events. He tells the story through the eyes of the men of the New Zealand Mounted Rifles Brigade, which fought at Gallipoli from May to December 1915. He has thoroughly researched their letters and diaries and cleverly weaves their eyewitness comments into his text. Much of this material has not been published before; the result is a book that reads with the immediacy of actually being there. The full story of the brigade is told: the mobilisation of the volunteers and their preparations in New Zealand, the long sea journey with thousands of horses, the frustrations of training in Egypt while the real war went on in Europe, the eventual arrival of the brigade at Gallipoli, the battles and skirmishes that were fought there, the disillusionment as the realities of trench warfare sank in, and finally their remarkable evacuation. The brigade emerged from the campaign battered and depleted, but with its reputation enhanced. More than 700 of the 4000 mounted riflemen who served on Gallipoli did not survive, and another 1200 were wounded.

Heavily illustrated with original photographs, *Echoes of Gallipoli* is the ideal book for anyone wanting to understand what it was like to be a young soldier in 1915, what really happened at Gallipoli and the impact these events had on one of the war's finest fighting formations.

www.exislepublishing.com

Born to Lead?

Portraits of New Zealand Commanders

ed. Glyn Harper and Joel Hayward

New Zealand's military history has been both honourable and distinguished, and the key events of more than 150 years of military involvement have been recorded in a range of official histories and books. But what of the military commanders who led their troops in these conflicts? How do we assess their achievements? And is there a distinctive style of New Zealand command?

Now, for the first time, this book attempts to answer these previously unexplored questions. Glyn Harper and Joel Hayward have assembled an impressive team of New Zealand military historians to profile some of the nation's most important commanders and examine the nature of New Zealand command. Each chapter is written by an expert on the commander concerned, with the subjects drawn from all three armed services: Army, Navy and Air Force. The commanders include both Maori and Pakeha, from the nineteenth century to the recent past: Alexander Godley, Andrew Russell, Edward Chaytor, Keith Park, Bernard Freyberg, Howard Kippenberger, Peter Phipps, Harold Barrowclough, Arthur Coningham, Leonard Thornton, Maori Battalion commanders (including Peta Awatere and James Henare) and commanders of the infantry battalions of the 2nd New Zealand Division. The book concludes with an analysis of the issues that future commanders must address if they are to be successful in their chosen profession.

Born to Lead? is an invaluable resource for students of history and defence studies, while its approachable, easy-to-follow style makes it eminently suitable for a wide range of general readers as well.

www.exislepublishing.com